WINGED VICTORY

WINGED VICTORY

THE ARMY AIR FORCES
IN WORLD WAR II

GEOFFREY PERRET

RANDOM HOUSE
NEW YORK

All photographs: U.S. Air Force Photos

Library of Congress Cataloging-in-Publication Data
Perret, Geoffrey.
Winged victory: the Army Air Forces in World War II / Geoffrey
Perret.
p.   cm.
Includes bibliographical references and index.
ISBN 0-679-40464-3
1. United States. Army Air Forces—History—World War,
1939–1945. 2. World War, 1939–1945—Aerial operations, American.
I. Title.
D790.P43 1993
940.54′4973—dc20   92-56838

Manufactured in the United States of America on acid-free paper
24689753
First Edition

Maps copyright © 1993 by Anita Karl and Jim Kemp

Book Design by Oksana Kushnir

To Dan Mortensen

CONTENTS

1	The Shadow of a Man	3
2	Arnold Phoenix	15
3	Critical Mass	33
4	Spreading Wings	53
5	Zero Hour	74
6	Bombing Range	87
7	Lofty Pursuits	104
8	On Target	121
9	Happenings	133
10	Bloody But Unbowed	145
11	Taking the Scenic Route	160
12	The Lamplighters	175
13	Reversals of Fortune	188
14	Mediterranean Cockpit	199
15	Nearly, Nearly	219
16	The Price of Progress	240
17	Pointblank	262
18	*Jägerschreck*	283
19	Liberation Skies	297
20	Whoosh!	319
21	Bloody Sideshow	334
22	A TAC Attack	350
23	The Country That Was	360
24	Minor Keys	376
25	Disorienting Experiences	391
26	Morale: Mail, Missions, and Medals	408
27	Technical Knockout	419

28	Lucky Numbers	434
29	Superlatives	447
30	Envoi	462
	Acknowledgments	467
	Notes	469
	Index	537

MAPS

WESTERN EUROPE   XII

CHINA-BURMA-INDIA THEATER   XIV

NORTH AFRICA AND SOUTHERN EUROPE   XVI

NORTHERN FRANCE   XVIII

NEW GUINEA, SOLOMONS, AND THE CENTRAL PACIFIC AREA   XX

JAPAN AND THE NORTHERN PACIFIC AREA   XXII

SOUTHWEST PACIFIC AND INDIAN OCEAN AREAS   XXIII

Baltic Seu

Peenemünde

Hamburg

Elbe R.

Neisse R.

POLAND

Aller R.

Hannover

Potsdam ⊚Berlin

GERMANY

Weser R.

Leine R.

Oschersleben

Saale R.

Mulde R.

Torgau

Oder R.

Merseburg

Kassel

Leipzig

Dresden

Chemnitz

Schweinfurt

⊚Prague

Main R.

Bayreuth

CZECHOSLOVAKIA

Pilsen

Nuremberg

Regensburg

Danube R.

tuttgart

Augsberg

Vienna ⊚

Munich

Wiener-
Neustadt

AUSTRIA

Friedrichshafen

Berchtesgaden

Innsbruck

© A·Karl/J·Kemp, 1991

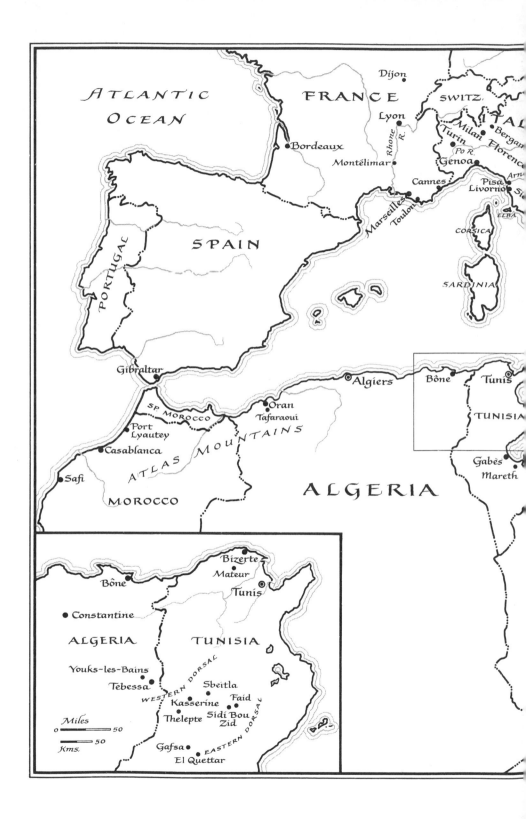

AUSTRIA
HUNGARY
Debrecen•
ROMANIA
•Udine
enice•Trieste
•Ploesti
◉Bucharest
YUGOSLAVIA
Bologna
ber
vitavecchia
◉Rome
Anzio•
•Cassino
Caserta
Foggia
Bari
BULGARIA
ALBANIA
•Naples
Salerno
Gariglian•&
Volturno°
CAPRI•
Gulf of Salerno
GREECE
TURKEY
Marsala
Palermo
Messina
•Reggio Calabria
SICILY •Mt. Etna
Agrigento
Licata
Gela •Syracuse
PANTELLERIA
•MALTA
CRETE
MEDITERRANEAN SEA

◉Tripoli
•Benghazi
Tobruk
Alexandria
El Alamein
◉Cairo

LIBYA
EGYPT

Miles
0 ————————— 300
0 ————————— 300
Kms.

© A·Karl/J·Kemp, 1993

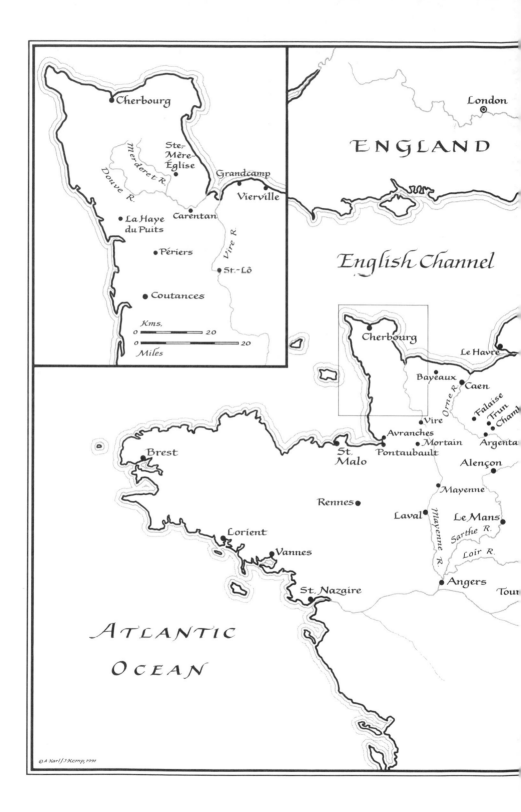

Cherbourg

Ste-
Mère-
Église

Merderet R.

Douve R.

Grandcamp

Vierville

La Haye
du Puits

Carentan

Vire R.

Périers

St.-Lô

Coutances

Kms.
0   20
0   20
Miles

London

ENGLAND

English Channel

Cherbourg

Le Havre

Bayeaux

Orne R.

Caen

Falaise

Trun

Cham

Vire

Avranches

Mortain

Argenta

St.
Malo

Pontaubault

Alençon

Brest

Mayenne

Rennes

Laval

Mayenne R.

Le Mans

Sarthe R.

Loir R.

Lorient

Vannes

St. Nazaire

Angers

Tou

ATLANTIC

OCEAN

© A. Karl / J. Kemp, 1991

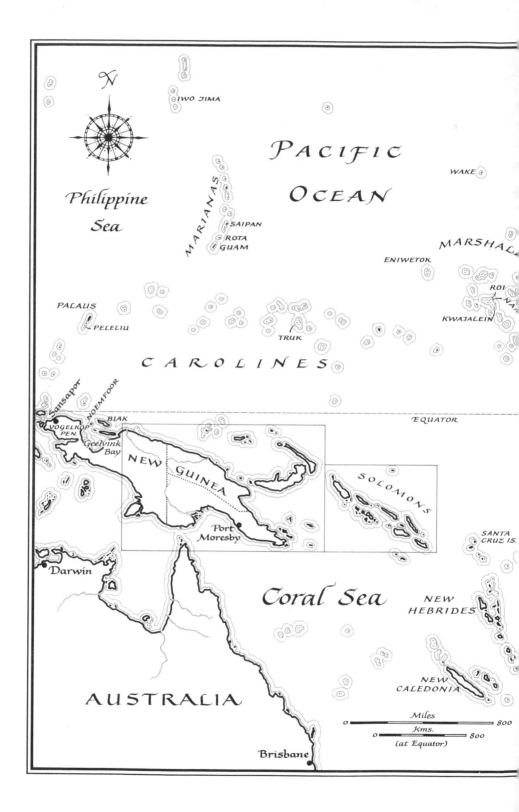

N

IWO JIMA

PACIFIC

OCEAN

WAKE

Philippine
Sea

MARIANAS

SAIPAN
ROTA
GUAM

MARSHALL

ENIWETOK

ROI
NA

PALAUS
PELELIU

KWAJALEIN

TRUK

CAROLINES

EQUATOR

Sansapor
NOEMFOOR
BIAK
VOGELKOP
PEN.
Geelvink
Bay

NEW GUINEA

SOLOMONS

SANTA
CRUZ IS.

Port
Moresby

Darwin

Coral Sea

NEW
HEBRIDES

AUSTRALIA

NEW
CALEDONIA

Miles
0   800
Kms.
0   800
(at Equator)

Brisbane

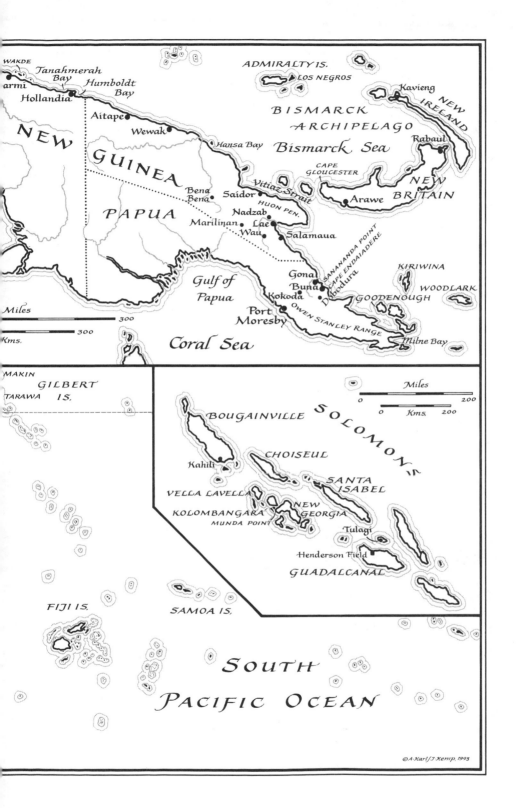

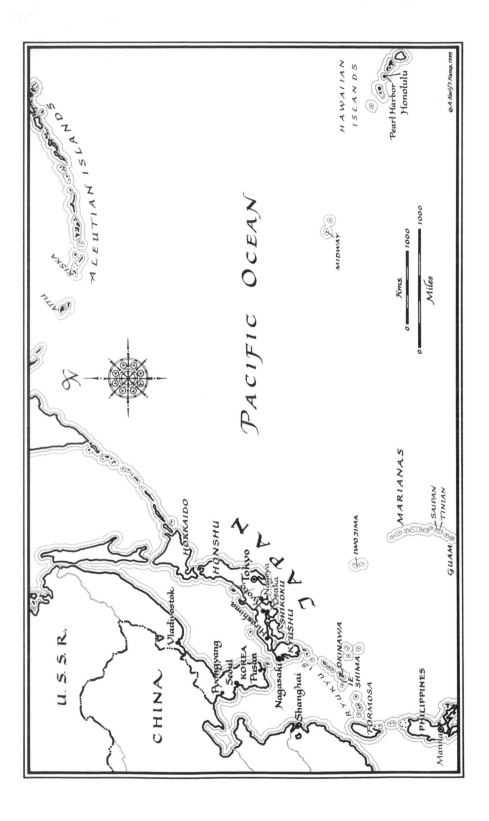

© A. Karl/J. Kemp. 1995

HAWAIIAN ISLANDS

Pearl Harbor
Honolulu

ALEUTIAN ISLANDS

ALASKA

ATTU

PACIFIC OCEAN

MIDWAY

Kms. 1000

Miles 1000

0

0

N

HOKKAIDO

HONSHU

J A P A N

Tokyo
Nagoya
Kyoto
Osaka
Hiroshima
SHIKOKU
KYUSHU
Nagasaki

MARIANAS

IWOJIMA

SAIPAN
TINIAN

GUAM

U.S.S.R.

CHINA

Vladivostok

Pyongyang
Seoul
KOREA
Pusan

Shanghai

OKINAWA
IE SHIMA

R Y U K Y U   I S.

FORMOSA

PHILIPPINES

Manila

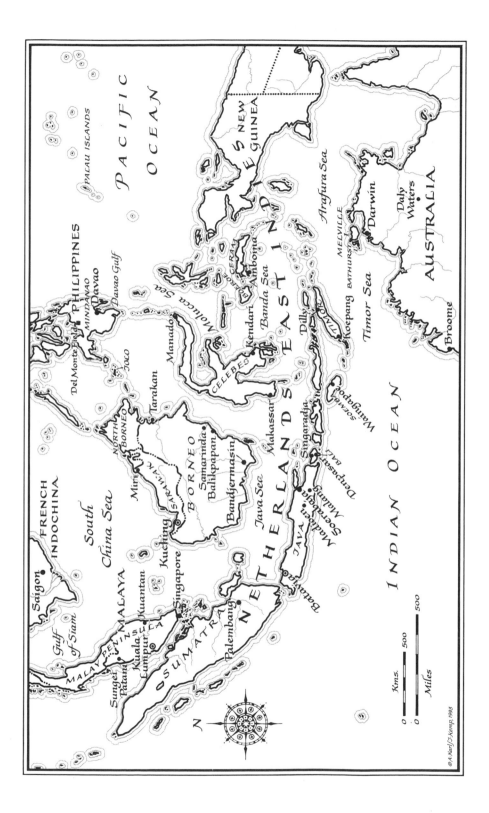

PACIFIC OCEAN

PALAU ISLANDS

PHILIPPINES

MINDANAO

Davao
Davao Gulf

Del Monte Field

JOLO

Manado

CELEBES

Molucca Sea

Kendari

CERAM

Amboina

Banda Sea

NEW GUINEA

Arafura Sea

MELVILLE I.
BATHURST I.

Darwin

Daly Waters

AUSTRALIA

Broome

Timor Sea

Koepang

TIMOR

Dilly

Soemba

Waingapu

NORTH BORNEO

Tarakan

SARAWAK

Miri

Kuching

BORNEO

Samarinda
Balikpapan

Bandjermasin

Java Sea

Makassar

Singaradja

BALI
Denpasar

Malang
Soerabaja
Madoen

JAVA

Batavia

NETHERLANDS EAST INDIES

FRENCH INDOCHINA

Saigon

South China Sea

Gulf of Siam

MALAYA

Sungei Patani
Kuala Lumpur
Kuantan

Singapore

MALAY PENINSULA

SUMATRA

Palembang

INDIAN OCEAN

N

Kms.   500

0

Miles   500

0

© A.Karl/J.Kemp 1983

WINGED VICTORY

1

THE SHADOW
OF A MAN

Near the end of September 1918 General John J. Pershing launched
the American First Army in the operation for which it had been
created, organized and equipped, the Meuse-Argonne offensive. Its
objective was to advance from U.S. bases in northeastern France
and cut the railroad line that provided lateral communications for
the German Army across the Western Front from Belgium to
Switzerland.

The advance of First Army's 600,000 men would be supported by
a combined Franco-American air force of 850 planes, commanded
by Brigadier General Billy Mitchell, one of the most colorful and
controversial soldiers of the war. Mitchell planned to exploit the
inherent flexibility of air power to the full. He would direct his air
arm as needs and opportunities arose: sometimes against the German Air Force, sometimes in direct support of the ground troops,
sometimes against German lines of communications or troop concentrations in the rear. His target depended on the situation each
day.

The feat that brought the most kudos, however, was the search
for the Lost Battalion. Commanded by Major Charles Whittlesey,
this body of 550 men was drawn mainly from 308th Infantry Regiment, 77th Division. Whittlesey's troops advanced into German
territory on October 2, but by nightfall the friendly units on either
flank had fallen far behind. The Lost Battalion found itself isolated
in a ravine in the dense Argonne Forest, and virtually surrounded
by two thousand Germans.[1]

There wasn't anything unusual about American infantrymen getting lost. The U.S. sector of the Western Front covered the Vosges Mountains. Battalions and regiments were constantly losing their bearings in the hilly, heavily timbered landscape. They'd soon run out of pigeons and lose contact.

Mitchell kept a flight of planes that did nothing but look for lost doughboys. Its pilots would fly across the front at treetop level. If the shells coming up exploded in white puffs, they were American seventy-five-millimeter antiaircraft artillery (AAA). When the puffs turned black, the fire was German seventy-seven-millimeter flak.[2] Having established where the front line ran, the searchers then flew even lower and tried to spot a helmet or a uniform. That wasn't as easy as it sounds: sometimes even entire divisions were so frightened by a single airplane they'd duck under ground like rabbits.

The Lost Battalion was virtually besieged but it managed to send its coordinates out by pigeon. These were mistakenly interpreted as indicating an enemy position it wanted attacked. Friendly artillery pounded the battalion.

On October 6, three days after Whittlesey's men were cut off, the mission of finding them was given to the 50th Aero Squadron, an observation unit flying the De Havilland DH-4, an airplane based on a British-designed airframe and an American-made Liberty engine. Each morning Whittlesey's battalion put out its black-and-white recognition panel, hoping the Air Service would drop food, water, bandages and a fresh crate of pigeons.

Twelve of the 50th Squadron's DH-4s flew into the ravine, one at a time. Intense German fire from the ridges above brought down two of them and damaged most of the others. Visibility was poor and the panel wasn't spotted, but supplies were dropped anyway. The German besiegers were bombarded with treats they hadn't enjoyed in a long time, such as chocolate.

Late in the day a final effort was made. A DH-4 piloted by Lieutenant Harold Goettler, with his observer, Lieutenant Erwin Bleckley behind him, flew into the ravine. Bleckley carefully marked on a map where German fire was coming from as the plane flew low and slow, an easy target. A bullet killed Goettler, who managed to turn the plane before dying. It crashed behind French lines. Bleckley died later.[3]

By then, the map had been studied intently. The Lost Battalion's location wasn't marked outright, but it stood to reason that the area ringed by German gun positions had to be it. That night a huge rescue effort, involving three divisions, was set in motion. Twenty-four hours later the survivors had been saved. Two thirds of Whittlesey's men had been killed or wounded.

Finding the Lost Battalion was one of the most renowned feats of the American Expeditionary Forces' pilots. It was fitting, too, that it was achieved by an observation squadron, flying the only American-built combat aircraft to see action during the war. Goettler and Bleckley were posthumously awarded two of the four Medals of Honor* won by American airmen in France.

A month after the rescue of the Lost Battalion the Germans sued for an armistice. The Air Service's contribution to victory was modest: 550 enemy airplanes and balloons brought down (more accurately, claimed to have been brought down), for the certain loss of 340 U.S. aircraft. Nearly 600 American airmen were killed, wounded or missing. Only 138 tons of bombs had been dropped.[4]

These unimpressive numbers told their own tale, yet they were also misleading. What mattered was less the limited experience of war than the effect it had on those who took part. Battle had ignited the spirits and inflamed the imaginations of Mitchell and other ambitious young officers. What they had witnessed in the skies over France was a terrible dream of wars to come, and "in dreams begin responsibilities."

In February 1919 the Cunard liner *Acquitania,* awash with bored and seasick troops, plowed the heavy seas of the stormy Atlantic. Each morning Billy Mitchell strode the *Acquitania*'s decks, pointing and prodding with a gold-headed swagger stick as he conducted a two-hour inspection of the huge liner from first class to steerage. He advanced behind four lustily blowing buglers; at his heels trailed officers in shiny Sam Browne belts. Mitchell himself sported a sharply cut jacket of his own design (bright with silver stars and golden propellers), a British officer's "pink" breeches, and gleaming, high cavalry boots.[5] Here was glamour and glory returning in sartorial triumph to collect its prize—command of the Air Service.

---

*The first Medal of Honor awarded to an Air Service pilot went to Frank Luke, who shot down 14 enemy planes and balloons in only 10 days, during October 1918. The last award went to the American Ace of Aces, Eddie Rickenbacker, who brought down 26 enemy planes and balloons, and survived 134 dogfights. In 1930 one of Rickenbacker's 8 Distinguished Service Crosses was upgraded to a Medal of Honor.

Yet in the brief transit between the shattered Western Front and the pulsating life of New York a new position, director of Air Service, had been established and given to another war hero, Major General Charles T. Menoher, onetime commander of the famous 42nd ("Rainbow") Division in France. He made Mitchell his assistant for training and operations.

A formidable foe of the Germans, Menoher was mismatched against Mitchell. Most pilots either worshipped Billy or, if they were feeling iconoclastic, settled for some less enraptured state, such as admiration. A footslogging director, on the other hand, was never going to claim more than a tepid tolerance from the pilots, who were the backbone of the Air Service.

Not only did Mitchell command strong loyalty among airmen, but he also had a following on Capitol Hill and the press. There was no shortage of politicians or journalists ready to take his appeals for an independent air force far beyond the tight little world of the Air Service.

In 1921 Menoher demanded that Mitchell be dismissed. His demand was rejected by the secretary of war, John Weeks, and the new Chief of Staff, General Pershing. Humiliated, Menoher resigned. Pershing brought in an old friend, Major General Mason Patrick. He seemed the only officer in the Army capable of controlling Billy Mitchell.

Pershing had called on Patrick, a Corps of Engineers expert in forestry, to command the American Expeditionary Forces (AEF) Air Service in France for the last five months of the war. He'd been forced to take this drastic step because of the intense squabbling and jealousy that seemed to follow Mitchell wherever he went.

At first glance Patrick didn't appear the least bit formidable. He wore a toupee and on at least one occasion it was sent flying during an inspection, blown away by propwash. He had loose-fitting false teeth that whistled at every sibilant. Patrick, a solitary drinker, was a loner by nature, and like Pershing he had both imagination and *gravitas*.[6]

All the same, he suffered from a major handicap—no wings. It was like being a one-legged infantryman. Nor, at the age of fifty-nine, did he seem a likely aviation cadet. To bend the Air Service to his will, though, he couldn't remain a kiwi: a nonflying officer. Patrick took flying lessons and managed, after a year of gently paced instruction, to qualify as the world's oldest Junior Military Aviator.[7]

The Air Service created by the 1920 National Defense Act was lean, and getting leaner. Its authorized strength was fifteen hundred officers and sixteen thousand enlisted men, but lack of interest and lack of money saw it fall to half this size by the end of 1922. The great challenge facing officers such as Mitchell and Patrick was to find ways of keeping the service alive.

Although air was now accepted as a combat arm Pershing didn't believe it had made much difference to the outcome of the war. Nor did the Air Service itself make any grand claims. Its own reports stated that air's only major contribution had been in observation.[8]

Mitchell didn't dispute that, but to him, as to his acolytes, the principal lesson of the war was being missed: The first thing that had to be won in any future conflict would be air superiority. *The primary objective had to be the enemy air force.* Once you'd wrecked that, you could observe, bomb, attack, whatever. Without air superiority, though, there'd be no victory.[9]

His order of priorities was reflected in the organization of the Air Service's combat units in the U.S. into three groups: 1st Pursuit Group, 2nd Bombardment Group and 3rd Attack Group. The observation units were assigned to the various armies and corps they serviced.*

One way Patrick controlled his assistant was by keeping him out of Washington for much of the time. And Mitchell, who was curious about everything, interested in everything, didn't mind in the least. He was forever showing up at the new research facility, the Engineering Division, that the Air Service had recently established at McCook Field. Located on the outskirts of Dayton, it wasn't far from that shrine of aviation, the Wright brothers' bicycle shop.

Mitchell would wander around McCook smiling and eager, asking, "What's new? What have you got to show me today?" His mind teemed with visions: helicopters . . . jet engines . . . fleets of four-engine fast bombers. . . .[10]

His favorite outfit, though, was 1st Pursuit Group, at Selfridge Field, north of Detroit. Its commander, Major Carl A. "Tooey" Spaatz, was a superb flyer who'd shot down two German planes and won a DSC. Mitchell dropped in regularly, flying his custom-

---

*In peacetime, observation units provided an aerial taxi service for general officers, congressmen and important businessmen favored by the War Department.

ized DH-4, the *Osprey,* with a long personal pennant of red and blue streaming from its tail.

Mitchell's interest in 2nd Bombardment Group found its strongest expression in McCook's development of the Barling bomber. Air leaders on the Western Front had theorized about what a strategic bombing force might accomplish, but had lacked the planes to do it. Mitchell had high hopes for it, but the Barling proved a lumbering $500,000 dud. Its four Liberty engines were too underpowered even to carry it across the Alleghenies from Dayton to Washington. A vast hangar was built for it, at a cost of $700,000; there it stayed, the crown jewel of dust collectors.[11]

Mitchell took a keen interest, too, in 3rd Attack Group. The Germans had developed attack aviation toward the end of the war. If a pursuit on a strafing run could paralyze an entire division, imagine what a better armed plane, with armor plate to protect it from ground fire, could do against enemy trucks, tanks, railroads and supply dumps.

Ground support of this kind was a further development of aviation as an offensive weapon. It was a prospect that excited even former pursuit pilots such as George Kenney, who'd downed two German aircraft in France. Kenney was an ardent admirer of Billy Mitchell.[12] In the 1920s he became a leading innovator in low-level attack. To him, as to Mitchell, here was the airplane being used properly—offensively. And what a neat idea to call ground support *attack.* That could interest a hot young flyer.

Mitchell's greatest contribution in these years was sustaining morale. One of the ways he achieved it was by going after records. Races and stunts generated public interest and political support; more than that, though, they whipped up excitement and enthusiasm throughout a service that needed to believe in itself.

Mitchell claimed stridently and often that the eastern seaboard was wide open to air attack, but that enemy battleships—the traditional fear—were no threat: airplanes would sink them far out to sea; the Air Service had replaced the Navy as America's first line of defense.

The battleship admirals who ran the Navy protested that Mitchell didn't know what he was talking about and grumbled that the Army was encroaching on the sea. Still, they organized a test to find out just what an airplane might do to a sturdy old battlewagon; namely, the USS *Indiana.*

In October 1920 Navy pilots bombed her, with dummy ordnance, and scored few hits. Out of curiosity, a 900-pound live bomb was exploded on deck. The Navy Secretary, Josephus Daniels, reported gleefully that the old tub had ridden out the dummy bombing splendidly. Then two photographs of what she looked like were leaked to the press: the *Indiana* was a floating hulk, gutted by the single nine hundred–pounder.[13] With its credibility listing and Congress getting interested, the Navy had to give in and put the claims made by Army and Navy flyers to a public test. Besides, there was a fleet just asking to be sunk: the Kaiser's surrendered warships.

In the spring of 1921 Colonel Thomas DeWitt Milling, then commandant of the recently established Tactical School at Langley Field, Virginia, suspended classes and created a new organization, called the 1st Provisional Air Brigade. Mitchell intended to use the brigade's one hundred planes to prove that airplanes could sink battleships. The brigade encompassed many of the best pilots in the Air Service.

A full-scale silhouette of a battleship's upper decks was marked out on nearby marshes. It was bombed without mercy, day after day. Another silhouette, towed by a tug across Chesapeake Bay, was similarly given a royal pounding with bombs loaded with sand. After which the bomber crews went to work with live bombs against the blasted carcass of the *Indiana*.

Alexander de Seversky, a former Russian bomber pilot who'd attacked German shipping in the Baltic, persuaded Mitchell that the place to put the big bombs wasn't on the ship but near it. Above the waterline a modern warship was heavily armored against large-caliber naval shells. Its vulnerable section was well below the waterline. The only way to attack that was with a "water hammer," created by detonating a large amount of high explosive roughly one hundred feet away. A powerful water hammer could pop thousands of rivets and buckle hundreds of plates, opening a ship's bottom like gutting a fish.[14]

The Navy organized the tests and established the ground rules. The attacks began in June with Navy aircraft operating against a German submarine. In mid-July Mitchell's brigade joined Navy air attacks on a German destroyer, using DH-4 light bombers and twin-engine Martin mediums.

The next warship on offer, several days later, was the cruiser *Frankfurt,* a well-designed, well-armored vessel with eye-catching lines. The Navy claimed that bombing would have to be done from at least ten thousand feet to be realistic. Mitchell typically went one better and ordered bombing from eleven thousand. Five Martins dropping six hundred–pound bombs sent the stationary *Frankfurt* to the bottom of the Atlantic in thirty-five minutes.

The last target, the *pièce de résistance,* was the battleship *Ostfriesland.* With her three skins and more than one hundred compartments, she had been designed to withstand mines, torpedoes, and fifteen-inch shells. The *Ostfriesland*'s upper decks were first wrecked by eleven hundred–pound bombs, then she was sent to a watery grave by a salvo of two thousand–pounders, one of which created a perfect water hammer.[15]

The Navy claimed the tests proved nothing; that Mitchell had flouted the rules and used bigger bombs than allowed, the ships weren't maneuvering, there was no antiaircraft fire, the location of the target was known in advance, et cetera. Even so, the Joint Army-Navy Board drew one important conclusion from these tests: the Navy needed aircraft carriers. Navy flyers gained most from Mitchell's attacks on the Kaiser's ships.

In the fall there was an all–Air Service bombing test, against the obsolete battleship USS *Alabama.* This time 1st Provisional Air Brigade made a night attack, using flares for illumination, as well as bombing by day. The *Alabama* was finally sunk by a two thousand–pound bomb.

In 1923 Mitchell got his hands on two more battleships, the old *New Jersey* and the *Virginia.* The Navy pooh-poohed the earlier efforts by Air Service pilots, who'd bombed from three thousand feet. Unrealistic, said the sailors; should be ten thousand at least. The General Staff ordered a high-altitude attack.

It was a struggle to get a Martin bomber carrying a two thousand–pound bomb that high, but most of them managed it. The *Virginia* was sunk quickly and the *New Jersey* turned turtle. The accuracy of the bombing thrilled and surprised some pilots, stirring ambitious thoughts that one day relatively small targets might be bombed in broad daylight precisely.[16]

In April 1924 the Air Service sent four amphibians, called Douglas World Cruisers, on a globe-circling flight that generated reams of favorable publicity. At almost the same time, Congressman Florian Lampert, a Republican from Wisconsin, began holding hearings on every aspect of aviation. It gradually became clear that Lampert was inclined to accept Mitchell's arguments for an independent air force. The cup was being filled at last, only to be dashed from Billy's eager lips.

In March 1925 Mitchell's term as assistant chief of the Air Service would come to a close. Warren G. Harding, a President notoriously tolerant of colorful characters, liked Mitchell. His successor, the strait-laced Calvin Coolidge, emphatically did not.

When his time as assistant chief ran out, Mitchell landed with a bump: reduction to his permanent rank of colonel and banishment to far-off San Antonio. He was now air officer of VIII Corps, occupying an ergonomic slum of an office, with an open latrine against one wall for the clerks.[17]

In his new, painfully diminished domain Mitchell took a strong interest in the only combat unit in the VIII Corps area, the 3rd Attack Group, and forced his overconfident opinions on its pilots. He ridiculed their tactics and training, told them they'd be useless in combat, and reorganized the summer maneuvers they'd planned. When its pilots tried to do things his way four of them were killed, leaving the rest close to mutiny.[18]

Back in Washington, Patrick was urging Congress to create an Air Corps. He said its relation to the Army would be analogous to that which existed between the Navy and the Marines, combining a large measure of independence with an unbreakable bottom line bond.

Mitchell removed was not Billy silenced. He wrote a series of articles, republished as a book, titled *Winged Defense*. While the book was hitting the stores a Navy dirigible, the *Shenandoah,* was making a public relations tour of Midwestern state fairs, at the height of the thunderstorm season. When summer weather fronts closed in on the *Shenandoah,* the dirigible was doomed. It was ripped apart in mid-air, near Akron, Ohio, killing its entire thirty-one-man crew.

The press naturally wanted to know what Mitchell thought of this disaster; it wouldn't have been too hard to guess. Mitchell was afflicted with a Manichean world view in which airmen were the angels; General Staff officers were the devils. He blamed the loss of the dirigible on "the incompetency, criminal negligence and almost treasonable administration of the National Defense."

If he was hoping this hysterical outburst would bring a better pulpit than San Antonio could provide, he got one. In fact, he got two. Coolidge set up a committee, under his Amherst classmate and Wall Street wheeler-dealer friend Dwight Morrow, to look into all aspects of aviation—and get out a report faster than the slow-moving Florian Lampert, who'd been holding hearings for nine months, with no sign yet of concluding. Mitchell would also face a court-martial.

Mitchell was the Morrow Committee's first witness. He offered to read out some of *Winged Defense.* Morrow shrewdly allowed him to do as he wished. Mitchell took up his book and started reading aloud.

This was Mitchell the military Nostradamus, turning out predictions like a man cabled to the future. Shipping an army across the Atlantic again "would be an impossibility." Nor would it ever again be necessary to wage a prolonged land campaign to defeat an enemy. Thanks to the air weapon it would be possible to overleap armies and strike the enemy where it really hurt. The submarine was the new master of the ocean; aircraft carriers would be wiped out by subs. Naval aviation would prove a complete waste of money. Airplanes would soon be able to fly all around the world on one tank of gas. A practical helicopter was at hand. And so forth.

Mitchell seemed to assume that he was offering something akin to hearing Shakespeare read his sonnets aloud. He didn't notice that, as he droned on through *Winged Defense,* even his friends grew bored and increasingly embarrassed.

A better opportunity to shine came a few weeks later, at his court-martial. He was charged under the Old Mother Hubbard Article of War, "conduct prejudicial to good order and discipline." He was tried by an array of generals in a dingy old warehouse. The cramped courtroom held little more than one hundred people, most perching uncomfortably on folding metal chairs. Half the spectators were reporters; the other half seemed to consist of good-looking young women in short skirts, cloche hats and plenty of lipstick. Mitchell was sustained, too, by his second wife, who from time to time put a comforting and proprietorial arm around his shoulders as he confronted nine generals wearing olive-drab uniforms and stern expressions.

Some of the most promising young officers in the Air Service, such as Henry "Hap" Arnold and Carl "Tooey" Spaatz, testified on his behalf. All Mitchell's witnesses said virtually the same thing: the Air Service was in a bad way and it was the War Department's fault. From the first day Mitchell's defense sounded like a broken record, but the last witness was Ace of Aces Eddie Rickenbacker. As a civilian once more, he was free to tear into the General Staff.

It was an opportunity he didn't waste. He damned the "military leaders, in the declining years of their lives" who were so jealous of Mitchell they wanted to destroy him. "It is a crime against posterity. This nation will pay the price of their selfishness."[19] From the perspective of Old Mother Hubbard, however, Mitchell was guilty as charged. Even those who loved Billy, like Hap Arnold, acknowledged the verdict was just.[20]

Duly convicted, he was sentenced to five years suspension from active duty, with forfeiture of all pay and allowances. Coolidge was no fool: he pre-empted possible congressional displeasure by reducing the sentence to a two-and-a-half year suspension. Mitchell, recognizing that he had no future in uniform, resigned his commission.

Morrow's report concluded that, contrary to Mitchell's assertions, the United States was not at risk from the air power of other nations. Nor did the United States need an independent air force. On the other hand, there should be an Air Corps, a more ambitious procurement program and an assistant secretary of war for aviation.

Coolidge accepted Morrow's conclusions, but that wasn't the end of the agitation for an independent air force. The Lampert Committee's report, published just two weeks after Morrow's, favored independence. And Billy's acolytes hadn't changed their minds. They would be heard from again . . . and again . . . and again . . . and

The U.S. Army Air Corps came into existence in July 1926 with better prospects than the former Air Service had ever enjoyed. Coolidge was reputed to have turned down a request a few years earlier to reequip a squadron with new planes, asking, "Why can't they buy just one airplane and let the aviators take turns flying it?" Now, the administration and Congress were alike hoping to see the Air Corps grow in five years from its present level of 1,200 obsolete planes, 900 officers, and 8,500 enlisted men to a force of 1,650 "serviceable" aircraft, 1,500 officers, and 15,000 enlisted men. Mitchell had won even as he lost: He'd lost his fight to stay in the Army, but won his fight to get Coolidge and Congress to take military aviation seriously.

When Patrick retired in December 1927 he was succeeded by his assistant chief, Brigadier General James Fechet, a gregarious former cavalryman who'd begun his military career as a private in the

Spanish-American War and learned to fly in middle age. Fechet was a decisive, clear-headed man with a gift for leadership.[21]

He was effective on the Hill, too. By the time the procurement program drew to a close the Air Corps had received 95 percent of the money originally promised. This was no trifling achievement when dealing with Congress over five years. During Fechet's four-year tenure as chief, the Air Corps would buy two thousand new aircraft.[22]

Fechet was served by an able and ambitious assistant chief, Benny Foulois. In 1931 Foulois found a way to display his talents on a national stage: he organized a provisional air division and led it around the cities of the northeastern United States for two weeks in May. Comprising nearly seven hundred planes (mostly slow, steady observation types), the division formed a twenty-mile long aerial procession as it flew over various cities, concluding with Washington on Memorial Day. It was a sight that thrilled millions for whom aviation was still almost a magical force. There was a beauty and novelty to flight that elevated the spirit as it thrilled the eye. Flight seemed to promise a better future for the entire human race.[23] Foulois's "Big Parade" assured his elevation to chief when, at the end of 1931, Fechet retired.

2

ARNOLD PHOENIX

To Henry Harley Arnold, World War I brought both rapid promotion and daily frustration. In August 1917, at the age of thirty-one, he became the Army's youngest colonel. This seemed a meager consolation for remaining in Washington and trying to pound airplanes into the heads of automobile manufacturers.

Arnold, a 1907 graduate of West Point, was a complex, singular figure—rarely what he seemed to be. His nickname, for instance, was "Hap," and nearly every photograph shows an enigmatic Mona Lisa smile enlivening his slightly cherubic features. Hap stood for "happy," yet the smile he bore through life had nothing to do with happiness: it was a genetically fixed smile, like a dolphin's. Nor was he much inclined to laughter. Arnold had virtually no sense of humor.[1] He was an intensely serious man, with much to be serious about.

Forced by his father to go to West Point in place of his big brother, who'd flatly refused an appointment to the Academy, Arnold developed an ambition to be a cavalry officer. Four days before graduation the West Point equestrian team performed what was traditionally known as "the graduation ride" in front of the assembled faculty and proud parents.

Arnold was an enthusiastic member of the team, but minutes before the show began the senior cavalry instructor rebuked him for having a wad of chewing tobacco in his cheek. He ordered Arnold to spit it out.

Arnold did as he was told, but couldn't resist saying, "Well, I thought all good cavalrymen chewed tobacco." The instructor was incensed at such lip. He gave Cadet Arnold a second chewing out, this time for impertinence.

Arnold spent the four days between the ride and graduation walking punishment tours, but looking forward all the same to being commissioned as a glamorous horse soldier. Graduation came, and he received the worst shock of his life: he'd been commissioned in the infantry. The instructor had disqualified him from the cavalry. It was a long time before that wound healed, if it ever did.[2]

Four years later, in 1911, he applied for a transfer to the Ordnance Corps, hoping to be promoted to first lieutenant; there were no second johns in Ordnance. He was so keen to leave the pedestrian infantry he'd even asked the Signal Corps about learning to fly. Signals beat Ordnance to the punch; a week after making inquiries, Arnold was ordered to head for Dayton, Ohio, and learn flying from the gods—Orville and Wilbur Wright.

He found himself in a class of two. His classmate was a short, slender youth named Thomas DeWitt Milling, West Point '09. Arnold proved to be a natural flyer, but Milling took to flying as if hatched in a nest. Orville Wright taught Milling personally, leaving Arnold to be instructed by the mechanics. It was another slight, one that Arnold neither forgot nor forgave.[3]

The course involved less than four hours in the air. Milling became U.S. Army Aviator Number One. Arnold was Aviator Number Two. The only other Army heavier-than-air flyer at this time was Foulois.

Whether he was being competitive with himself or with Milling, Arnold proceeded to carve out a large and lasting place for himself as a pioneer military aviator. A combat arms officer at heart, he saw the airplane as a weapon, not just as a fancy new addition to Signal Corps communications.

Shortly after finishing the course in Dayton, he and an infantry lieutenant entered a shooting competition against a British team. With Arnold flying the airplane and the lieutenant armed with a rifle, they beat the British by strafing a tin dinner plate and putting six bullets in it.

In 1912, during a maneuver in northern Virginia, he proved the reconnaissance value of the airplane by tracking down a cavalry column half-hidden in leafy country lanes and reporting its position back to headquarters. This feat made him the first recipient of the

Mackay Trophy, awarded annually for the outstanding aviation feat of the past year.

These were not particularly happy days, however. In June 1912 he watched helplessly as the man who'd done most to teach him to fly, Al Welsh, crashed to his death.[4] Shortly after, Arnold himself nearly perished. He was involved in experiments at Fort Riley, Kansas, to adjust artillery fire. He carried an observor who would spot where the shells were falling, scribble the information on orange cards that were weighted with iron nuts, and drop them through a piece of stovepipe to cavalry troopers galloping below.

Suddenly, at about five hundred feet, Arnold's Wright-C airplane stalled and went into a dive. He wrestled furiously with the controls. At barely fifty feet, Arnold managed to recover from the stall and landed safely. Nothing was broken, except his nerve. Arnold grounded himself, never expecting to fly again. He returned to the infantry.

Two years later he met and became friends with an officer on the General Staff, Billy Mitchell, a man who touched the bedrock in people—loving or loathing. Arnold's restless spirit had found its star to steer by.

If leadership is the ability to inspire people to do things they think they don't want to do, Mitchell really had it. In 1916 he convinced a reluctant and still frightened Arnold to fly again. Four years and three weeks after quitting for good, Arnold soloed once more.[5]

Early in 1917, shortly before the United States declared war on Germany, Arnold succeeded Mitchell as executive officer to the commander of the Signal Corps Aviation Section, Brigadier General George O. Squier. It was a good job . . . in peacetime. In wartime, it was a good job . . . for someone else. He wanted to fly, to command, to lead men into danger, not fight the battle of production.

When the United States entered the war, the Aviation Section had 227 airplanes (mainly training types) and 5 balloons. A month after the U.S. declaration of war on Germany, the War Department was still trying to figure out how many airplanes it would need. Then President Woodrow Wilson received a cable from Premier Alexandre Ribot of France requesting an American air arm of forty-five hundred aircraft be made available for the Allied offensives of 1918, with two thousand replacement aircraft each month to cover losses.[6] Ribot's suggested goals were accepted. It was decided, too, that the United States would concentrate on building only one combat aircraft, copying the De Havilland-4, a British airplane, for observation and day bombardment.

The biggest American contribution would be a new engine called the Liberty, for the DH-4. A patriotic myth was cooked up that it was designed by locking two engineering geniuses in a hotel room in Washington and keeping them there for forty-eight hours, until they came up with a piston-driven miracle that would scare the hell out of the Germans. "Oh, Liberty, the crimes that are committed in thy name." In truth, the engine was designed by a dozen engineers over several months and the people the engine would terrify were American pilots.[7]

With a target to aim at and the clock ticking furiously, the race was on to mass-produce airplanes. There was a fond assumption in government and industry that they could be turned out like automobiles. But they couldn't.

This chastening experience left an indelible mark on Arnold. There proved to be a world of difference between the comparatively crude thousand-and-one parts that comprised an automobile and the five or six thousand parts, most of them made to remarkably fine tolerances, that went into a combat airplane. It was a world that no one, including Arnold, knew how to conquer. It was bad enough to be nailed to a desk in Washington during wartime; it was doubly tormenting to spend the only war a soldier had buried up to the eyebrows in a national failure.

Arnold finally succeeded in reaching the front—just as the Germans sued for peace. Inventor Charles Kettering had developed a surface-to-surface missile, a proto-Scud. It had a range of forty miles, carried three hundred pounds of high explosive and was reportedly accurate to one hundred yards. Arnold proposed to field test this futuristic weapon in France.

What he was really hoping for was to get into the action. His diary relates a tale of frustration: "Sat. Nov. 9—Mitchell returned from Souilly and said that firing had stopped. . . . I am sorry that I could not at least ride over the lines when there was firing, but no such luck." "Mon. Nov. 11—Armistice goes into effect 11 A.M. today. I had fixed to go over the lines before hostilities ceased on voluntary patrol. Weather was so thick that we couldn't. . . ."[8]

Colonel Arnold returned from France in low spirits. He was assigned to the Air Service's biggest training center, Rockwell Field, outside San Diego. At the time it held eighty-five hundred officers and men, most of them impatient to get out of the Army. Convinced that there was no future in uniform except for officers who'd seen service in France, Arnold was sorely tempted to quit too.

About the only satisfaction to be derived from his present uninspiring chore was having the help of Major Carl A. Spaatz. The two men had met in Washington in October 1918, when Spaatz returned from the front and Arnold was getting ready to go there. Meeting up again, acquaintance blossomed quickly into a strong, lifelong friendship.[9]

Spaatz had spent most of his wartime service commanding the fighter training center at Issoudun, in east-central France. A brilliant natural flyer and West Point graduate, Spaatz was an obvious choice for the post. All the same, he yearned to get into combat. On receiving orders in July 1918 to return to the United States to make stateside training more realistic, he'd prevailed on Mitchell to assign him to a frontline squadron temporarily. Serving with the defiantly numbered 13th Aero Squadron, Spaatz had shot down three German aircraft in the space of a few weeks. He came home sporting a DSC.

An unprepossessing figure with a dour expression and thin mustache, Spaatz was something of a paradox in the Army's most glamorous combat arm: a whiskey-drinking, cigar-munching, poker-playing soldier—a regular guy who knew how to party yet was softly spoken and taciturn.

Esteemed by his contemporaries as a brilliant pilot, Spaatz was unusually popular too. The secret of his social success was mastery of the guitar. Spaatz could play like a maestro and had a repertoire of comic or risqué songs that kept fellow officers in stitches.[10] "Tooey"* had found a way to socialize successfully without having a lot to say. And when he and Arnold got together to relax, they played chess, a game that does not encourage conversation. Over the years something resembling a blood brotherhood developed between Spaatz and Arnold.

They were both ardent Mitchellians, siding with their hero in

---

*His nickname celebrated his resemblance to a West Point classmate a year ahead of him, Francis J. Toohey, who had bright red hair and a face covered with freckles. Before that, Spaatz was known to fellow cadets as "Count Shoebrushki," a tribute to his appalling haircut.

good times and bad. Like him, they believed in an independent air force. Like him, they felt the Air Service was being hobbled in its development by an uncomprehending Army General Staff that couldn't think of anything better than fighting in the mud.

At the time of Mitchell's court-martial in 1925, Arnold was serving on Mason Patrick's staff. And following Mitchell's conviction Arnold used the printing facilities of Patrick's office to lobby for air independence. An angry Patrick tried to force him to resign. That failed, but Arnold found himself banished to Fort Riley, Kansas, to command an observation squadron equipped with half a dozen obsolescent planes.

Dispirited, he was tempted once again to resign his commission. And what then? Out in California he'd formed a friendship with Donald Douglas. Would Douglas give him a job? I could do that, Douglas replied, but it would be a big mistake: if you stick it out, one day you're going to be Chief of the Air Corps.[11] Fort Riley was a cavalry post. Arnold was treading manure, but Douglas got him looking up at the stars.

Arnold wasn't the bookish kind of officer, but the Army's higher schools played an important part in his career. One thing World War I had taught was that separately or together, American businessmen and politicians couldn't mobilize the economy for war. What they'd produced in 1917–18 wasn't victory but inferior equipment, in small quantities, at high prices, usually behind schedule.

It was an experience the Army had no intention of enduring a second time. In 1924 the War Department created the Army Industrial College: staff and students would devise plans for mobilizing the economy in any future war.

Arnold had been a member of the founding class at the Army Industrial College. He was a logical choice, given his wartime experience in procurement. Given his wartime experience in procurement, he didn't want to go. Ordered to attend, he obeyed, without enthusiasm.

But now, banished to obscure Fort Riley, Arnold saw further education as a potential escape route: a year at the Command and General Staff School, at Fort Leavenworth, only seventy miles east of his present position, was his best hope of getting back into the Air Corps mainstream. His first application to Leavenworth was turned down. He waited for Mason Patrick to retire before applying again. Even so, he was turned down a second time. The commandant at Fort Leavenworth had been a member of the Mitchell court-martial and didn't want Arnold there. He showed up anyway, in 1929, carrying recommendations from Fechet and Davison.[12]

The course offered little that interested him. There was no serious study of air power, although there were Air Corps demonstrations of bombing, strafing and ground support. He couldn't wait for his Leavenworth year to end. He had Mrs. Arnold and the children waiting outside the Riding Hall in a car with the engine running the day he graduated.[13]

He was assigned to command Fairfield Depot outside Dayton. Supply again, but on sacred soil: the depot stood on the former Sims Station. Here, he had learned to fly. Arnold helped push the depot toward its ultimate destination, becoming Wright Patterson Air Force Base. He also seized the chance to expunge Billy's costly error: he burned the Barling bomber.[14]

When Fechet retired in 1931, Spaatz, then working as the Air Corps G-3, persuaded the new chief, Benny Foulois, to give Arnold a command more to his liking. The Air Training Center at Randolph Field would be activated that summer; the primary flight school at March Field, in southern California, would close down. March Field base was scheduled to be transformed into the center of tactical air operations on the West Coast. Foulois assigned Arnold to command it. With the assignment went a promotion, to lieutenant colonel.

Thus began the happiest five years of Arnold's life. March became the base of the 17th Pursuit Group, commanded by Major Frank "Monk" Hunter, a Western Front fighter ace, and the 7th Bombardment Group, under another combat veteran, Major Joseph T. McNarney. An unusually able officer, McNarney had commanded an observation squadron in France. Slightly aloof and forbidding, he looked like a man condemned to a diet of lemons, a total contrast to the dashing bachelor Hunter, who looked like the kind of man who had women lashing themselves to trees and howling.

For Arnold, building March into a major operational base was a thoroughly satisfying assignment. He delighted, too, in going to the Boeing plant in Seattle now and again and ferrying back a new P-12 fighter. Such excursions provided the kind of excitement that made a man want wings in the first place: flying lower than the telephone poles for hundreds of miles over open countryside, hopping over trees, skimming the leaves on duck pods. Arnold loved that kind of flying as much as any pilot in attack or pursuit.[15]

Besides his responsibilities at March, he was heavily committed to making a success of President Franklin D. Roosevelt's job-creation program, the Civilian Conservation Corps. The CCC took young men away from a life of idleness on urban sidewalks and stoops to the clear air of the plains and mountains, to busy days cutting fire trails and clearing streams instead of hanging around pool halls and blind pigs.

The Army created and ran the camps, but it couldn't impose military discipline. It had to rely instead on tapping the leadership abilities of its officers and noncommissioned officers (NCOs). Some resented CCC work, but most eventually came to see it as excellent preparation for the day when they would have to lead young men like these in combat.

Arnold supervised a score of projects throughout California, employing more than fifteen thousand people. Unfortunately, leadership failures at a CCC camp in the Sierras produced a full-blown race riot. He hushed up this scandal for the sake of the CCC and the Air Corps.[16]

Another potential setback was the Long Beach earthquake of March 1933. In the space of a few minutes much of the city was devastated. Arnold couldn't get hold of the officer who was responsible for the emergency supplies the Army maintained for civil disasters. He ordered his men to break down the doors of the warehouses and distribute the supplies.

A formal complaint was lodged against him for exceeding his authority. Arnold was called to account for his actions by the commander of the IX Corps area, Major General Malin Craig. Convinced he'd done the right thing, Arnold had no qualms about flying to the Presidio and putting his case emphatically. He convinced, and charmed, Craig. The two men became friends and golfing partners.

March was fast developing into one of the Air Corps's most important installations. To raise training standards, however, Arnold needed a live fire range for his bombers and fighters. The Pacific was nearby, but the Navy claimed it was already using that for gunnery practice, in a way that suggested it was using the entire ocean.

Arnold decided to try buying up Muroc Dry Lake, which covered much of the Mojave Desert between Barstow and Palmdale. He had a couple of young officers fresh from West Point spend three months making the first survey of the area.[17] Then, just to make sure it would serve his needs, he and Spaatz made a command reconnaissance, telling the curious they were checking road signs for the California Automobile Association. If word got out that the government was interested in buying land, prices would soar.

Muroc Dry Lake was an air commander's theme park. It consisted of a well-baked, superfine clay used in mud packs. Planes landing there rolled as smoothly as on glass. There were no civilians to worry about; a pilot could bomb or strafe his brains out. The facility is known these days as Edwards Air Force Base.

In the winter of 1934 Foulois impetuously committed the Air Corps to carrying the air mail; a venture for which it lacked the right training, the right planes, and the right navigational equipment. In the course of this operation twelve pilots lost their lives, Foulois earned the contempt of the President and the press waxed indignant over blood for mail. The one good thing that came out of this operation was a recognition by Congress that Air Corps's cockpits needed the kind of state-of-the-art navigation instruments that commercial pilots were beginning to take for granted.[18]

By the time the airlines resumed flying the mail in May 1934 the Air Corps was looking for a way of restoring public faith in its flying ability. In this crisis the airmen reached for their interwar security blanket—another record-breaking flight.

The moon-faced, mustachioed assistant chief of the Air Corps, Brigadier General Oscar Westover, decided to lead a mass transit from Washington, D.C., to Alaska and back. Here would be a chance, too, to show off the Army's newest acquisition, the sleek, twin-engined, low wing Martin B-10, the first modern bomber.

Arnold, jaded and disgruntled after running air mail operations west of the Rockies, was leaving on vacation, heading with his wife for Jackson Hole, when Westover decided he didn't want to lead the flight after all. Foulois gave the assignment to Arnold.[19]

There wasn't much for him to do. Westover's assistant, Major Hugh J. Knerr, had already handled the logistical and planning side of the flight. The result was an aerial odyssey of formation flying, but Arnold added a contribution of his own: On the return leg he took the B-10s nearly one thousand miles over open water between Juneau and Seattle.

This diversion incensed the Army Chief of Staff, Major General

Douglas MacArthur. He'd made a pact with the Navy that the Army would claim responsibility for national defense only to the waterline. Anything beyond the shore was a Navy mission. In return, the Navy pledged not to encroach on the land. Flying one thousand miles across the ocean and then boasting that this demonstrated the Air Corps's ability to thwart any attack from the sea made MacArthur appear unable to control his subordinates.

The Air Corps recommended that the Alaska flyers should receive DFCs. All were turned down, but Arnold received the Mackay Trophy for 1934. Two years later, following MacArthur's retirement, he received a DFC for the flight. Knerr and the other Alaska flyers were disgusted, believing that Arnold had used his pull in Washington to make sure he got his reward, while the rest of them might as well have gone fishing.[20]

Certainly the Alaska flight did wonders for Arnold. This was the turning point in his career, where he broke away from his contemporaries and joined the magic circle at the top of the Air Corps. A few months after the flight he jumped two grades, to brigadier general. It was a spectacular rise from the ashes.

Creation of the Air Service in 1920 brought the establishment of a graduate school for its officers, known originally as the Field Officers' School, located at Langley, Virginia, and created by Colonel Milling. In 1922 it was renamed the Air Service Tactical School.

It offered a nine-month course, covering a variety of subjects, such as staff duties, combat orders, and antiaircraft defense. The heart of the matter, though, was the 160 hours of classroom instruction devoted to each of the following: pursuit, bombardment, observation. A further 60 hours were spent on attack. Milling also made an important addition in 1923—nearly 130 hours of flying instruction. This provided an aerial classroom to explore tactical problems.[21]

Graduation from the Tactical School was likely to lead directly to the Command and General Staff School at Fort Leavenworth, the narrow gate that was virtually a prerequisite to higher command. Leavenworth was happy to take them: as many as 15 percent of each class consisted of Air Corps officers and some, such as Lewis Brereton, stayed on as instructors.

All the same, unlike the other combat arms, the Air Corps was of two minds about schools that offered anything beyond technical instruction. This ambivalence extended even to the top: Fechet believed in the Army's higher schools, but Foulois, enormously proud of being a general with only a grade-school education, did not.[22]

Many pilots feared that the schools would take them from cockpits to desks. Some, such as Spaatz, who went to Leavenworth in 1935, were disgruntled even before they arrived. He told his good friend Hap Arnold to make no mistake: "I am going primarily because I have been ordered there."[23]

Leavenworth taught the air power ideas that were promoted by the Air Service, before the creation of the Air Corps. That meant its air element was up to date in 1926–27, but increasingly passé thereafter.[24]

The essential aim of the Leavenworth course was not the promulgation of doctrine, anyway. What the school was really trying to do was to help young officers prepare themselves for high command: to learn how to think on a large scale; to gain an understanding of operations that might involve up to two or three hundred thousand men; and to be ready to act quickly and decisively in commanding major operations.[25]

While some Air Corps officers found the course valuable, many felt they were wasting their time. The biggest map problem at Leavenworth involved an opposed river crossing. The advancing force included fighters and bombers. All the ground students wrote solutions that had the airplanes flying close support for the troops. All the Air Corps officers said to hell with that and turned in solutions that had the airplanes striking deep behind enemy lines at bridges, railheads and supply dumps.[26]

The Tactical School, which moved to Maxwell Field in Montgomery, Alabama, in 1931, was much more to the parochial taste of most pilots. It offered a valuable opportunity for them to reflect on the development of air power. Out in the squadrons the lamp of intellectual inquiry glowed wanly; here, it flared like a wellhead fire.

Life at the Tactical School wasn't stimulating only to the mind; it was highly agreeable in every way. The pace was calm and unhurried. Mornings were spent in class; most afternoons were devoted to flying. Evenings were given over to poker, bridge and barbecues. Weekends were spent swimming, golfing or playing tennis.[27]

The classroom paid no heed to rank. Often, students outranked instructors. The method of instruction copied the Leavenworth system: a lecture, followed by a discussion of possible solutions, followed by a sample problem. The week ended with a four-hour map problem every Friday afternoon.

Milling left the Tactical School at the end of 1925. The curriculum as he'd developed it was broadly based and anticipated a range of air missions. His departure, however, coincided with a shifting view of future air strategy.

After Mitchell resigned his commission, he and a group of friends created the U.S. Air Force Association. Its objective was to promote strategic bombardment. At about the same time the Tactical School ceased teaching that the enemy air force was the first objective. The predominant target became the industrial base on which a modern economy depended.

The leading proponent of this idea was an Italian general, Giulio Douhet. His name was known among American airmen, but there was no complete English-language translation (supervised by Major George Kenney) of Douhet's book, *The Command of the Air,* until 1933.*

That same year, however, the Tactical School curriculum came under the control of Lieutenant Colonel Donald L. Wilson, a man utterly opposed to Douhet. The Italian's strategic thinking reflected his career as an artillery officer: unleash bombs and gas on enemy cities, knowing that amidst the carnage some vital targets are almost sure to be struck. Wilson considered this wanton and ineffective. He sought to identify the vital targets and bomb only them.[28] He strove to prevent Douhet's ideas from seducing Air Corps officers. By the late 1930s the Wilsonian approach to strategic bombing dominated thinking at Maxwell.

Attack aviation was completely overshadowed. During his time as an instructor at the Tactical School, George Kenney had kept interest alive. He preached the creed of fast, low-level attacks and developed fragmentation bombs that descended on parachutes; the slight delay allowed attacking aircraft to avoid being struck by the shrapnel from their own ordnance. After Kenney's departure in 1931 to attend the Army War College, interest in attack waned. Its main function was providing support for ground troops, not an activity that bomber theorists sought to encourage.

Fighters, too, were slighted. The most passionate advocate of

---

*An abridged translation was available in the ACTS library as early as 1923.

their cause was Claire Channault, a man who'd missed out on combat in World War I and felt the loss deeply. On maneuvers in 1931 he created a warning net manned by civilian observers equipped with telephones, binoculars and enthusiasm. They bore out his claim that a properly organized system would give fighters time to rise high and wait in the sun to ambush the incoming bombers.[29]

He still lost the argument. With his deeply lined, crush leather face, eighty smokes a day, perpetual cough and deafness in one ear, he was no debater but the quintessential strong, silent type, a rugged fighter pilot who let his actions do his talking. In 1936 Chennault's chronic bronchitis forced him out of the Air Corps and into Chinese employment.

Bomber instructors such as former Mitchell aides Ken Walker and Robert Olds won the debate fairly. Theirs wasn't the only subject taught at Maxwell. And anyone at the Tactical School was free to make any argument he wanted. Even after Chennault left there were other fighter advocates, such as Earle Partridge and Hoyt Vandenberg, on the faculty. Each side put its case to the students, who were free to decide which, if either, they wanted to believe.[30]

The theorists of strategic bombing nevertheless had an unassailable intellectual ascendancy, powerfully assisted by events beyond the classroom. In 1934 the Air Corps had given Boeing a contract to build a long-range, four-engine bomber. The resulting aircraft, the XB-15, was too underpowered for its seventy thousand pounds.

Downsizing its ambitions, Boeing set its sights on meeting a less demanding Air Corps specification for a new multiengined bomber. The company was hoping for a four-engine plane it could produce in two versions: a heavy bomber and a civil transport.

In August 1935 the resulting airplane, which Boeing called the Model 299 but intended to publicize as "the Flying Fortress," took off for Dayton. There, it would be pitted against Martin's B-12 bomber and Douglas's B-18.

Model 299 covered the twenty-one hundred miles between Seattle and Wright Field flying nonstop, at an average speed of 232 miles per hour. The Martin and Douglas entries were twin-engine aircraft; they offered no great advance over the B-10. Boeing's fast, thirty-five thousand-pound colossus had five gun emplacements and beautiful, flowing lines. It came with a high tingle factor: Just looking at it could prickle a man's scalp.

The plane had the competition as good as won when, still under test at Wright Field, it crashed and burned, killing the pilot and copilot. This setback was pure pilot error: he'd taken off with the new-fangled tail controls locked.[31]

Here was the plane that Mitchell and his followers had talked about, dreamed of, and longed for; yet under pressure from the General Staff, the Air Corps ordered 133 B-18s instead. A development of the DC-2 airliner, it had a gun turret and a small bomb bay. The B-18 lacked range and speed. Bomber pilots looked on it as only a training plane, not a real warbird.

There was a legal loophole that allowed the Air Corps to buy enough examples of any aircraft coming second in a competition to equip a squadron and test them out further. That provided authority to buy thirteen YB-17s.* By the frayed thread of a loophole purchase, the dream machine stayed alive.

Paralleling the development of the B-17, the Navy was working on the Norden bombsight. This revolutionary instrument was capable of remarkable accuracy at altitudes from ten thousand to twenty thousand feet. Ignorance of radar, too, played a part in the rapidly growing creed of bomber invincibility. Little work was done on radar in the United States before 1939, and that little was pushed by the Navy, not the Air Corps.[32]

Antiaircraft artillery (AAA) was dismissed out of hand. "As the bombers approach their objective," Captain Laurence S. Kuter informed students at Maxwell, "antiaircraft gunfire may be annoying but should be ignored."[33]

Technological developments in the mid-1930s conjured up a Mitchellian dream world, where heavy bombers flew unimpeded deep into enemy territory, where endless strings of bombs flashed through the sunlight to shatter small, precise targets at will.

The Tactical School was now the fountainhead of Air Corps doctrine. It was so successful that ambitious young officers no longer felt they had to go on to Leavenworth; Maxwell provided all the graduate schooling they thought they'd ever need.

In the ultimate, the argument for strategic bombing was too

---

*Air Corps designations began with the prefix X for the experimental model of an aircraft. Service test variants had the prefix Y. The first production model began with the letter A. Subsequent models progressed through the alphabet as improvements and modifications were introduced.

seductive to lose out: it gave the Air Corps a claim to a unique, potentially war-winning mission of its own, free from armies on the ground or fleets out at sea. Increasingly, this vision would shape the way the Air Corps trained, organized, equipped and imagined itself.

The Army had a nightmare: If the pilots got their independence, they'd act as the cavalry did in the Civil War—constantly raiding or chasing after wagon trains, leaving the infantry to get on with the real fighting unaided. The General Staff had no intention of letting that happen. MacArthur's solution was to control the Air Corps by employing the old principle of divide-and-rule.

There would be a General Headquarters Air Force, containing all the tactical units. The commander of GHQ Air Force would report directly to the Chief of Staff. What remained—administration, supply, research and development, schools—would be under control of the Chief of the Air Corps. MacArthur imposed this solution on Foulois in 1934 by making it part of a larger restructuring of the Army. The GHQ Air Force began with a staff of two, Brigadier General Frank Andrews, and his aide, Lieutenant Elwood "Pete" Quesada.[34]

Andrews was a former cavalry officer, West Point class of 1908. He'd learned to fly in 1918 but missed the war. He proved to be an enthusiastic flyer, the kind who'd take off when even the birds were grounded. After the Armistice he met and fell under the spell of Billy Mitchell. In time the two men became close friends. In some respects they were alike: handsome, energetic, articulate, and leading other men by making them want to please him. In the charisma stakes, Andrews was Billy's natural successor.[35]

When GHQ Air Force was activated American air power consisted of eighteen hundred planes, scattered all over the United States. Serious training for combat was virtually nonexistent. There was a shortage of ammunition and just four live fire ranges, only two of which were available year-round. Machine guns were kept in Cosmoline as if that were their natural state. Stunts such as the "Big Parade" were relied on to provide experience in navigation. The need for cross-country flying was satisfied by having pilots circle an airfield until they ran low on gas.[36]

The piffling size of the Air Corps made all these training deficiencies worse. In a force consisting of small units scattered over a continent, major exercises weren't possible.

Andrews's first step in tackling the desuetude of his command

was to surround himself with able assistants. His chief of staff was
Major Hugh Knerr, who considered himself "the most integrated
officer in the world."[37] Graduating from Annapolis in 1908, Knerr
tried to get into naval aviation and failed. A year later, to avoid a
court-martial for a breach of Navy regulations, he resigned, after
first applying for a commission in the Coast Artillery. From there
it was but a short hop into the Signal Corps so he could learn to fly.
Once he'd qualified as an aviator, in 1917, Knerr settled down to
being an airman.[38]

For his operations officer Andrews chose George Kenney. GHQ
Air Force's logistics were entrusted to McNarney. Andrews organized his command into three wings, the biggest of which was 1st
Wing, commanded by Arnold and comprising all the tactical units
between the West Coast and the Rockies.* Arnold already commanded these units, but the formation of a wing brought a temporary promotion to brigadier general. And after running 1st Wing
for nine months he was summoned to Washington. General Malin
Craig had recommended him for assistant chief of the Air Corps,
under Foulois's successor, Oscar Westover.

He tried to turn the assignment down. Arnold asked to remain
where he was and be demoted to lieutenant colonel, so he could run
March Field instead of flying a desk in D.C. Happiness meant more
than a star. The Army, though, wasn't in the happiness business.[39]

The principal mission that MacArthur gave GHQ Air Force was
coastal defense. Andrews organized major exercises that shifted
hundreds of aircraft on short notice to coastal areas that were,
theoretically, about to come under attack.

Andrews's efforts got a mighty boost from the increasing size of
the Air Corps. In creating GHQ Air Force, the War Department
accepted the need for more planes. At the same time, the Roosevelt
administration was putting more money into base construction as
an adjunct of the New Deal's public works program. The lean years
under Foulois swiftly gave way to a fatter time under Westover.
Wright Field issued contracts not just for new bombers, but for
pursuit, attack, and observation planes in sizable numbers. As standards rose, so did morale; as resources expanded, so did capabilities.

---

*A wing consisted of three or more groups. Fighter groups might have fifty planes or more;
bomb groups had only thirty to forty.

All might have been rosy except for one thing. The Navy had a nightmare: if the airmen got their way they would assume responsibility for coastal defense so far out to sea there'd be no end to it, because the day was coming when bombers would fly as far as five thousand miles. Who'd need the Navy then?

The Air Corps had its own nightmare: the Navy would come ashore. Patrick had worried about it often, warning his pilots to keep an eye on the sailors. This fearful dread became a kind of sacred trust. And, indeed, Admiral Fletcher Pratt's successor as chief of naval operations (CNO) repudiated the agreement with MacArthur that was supposed to settle the question of coastal defense. The Navy argued that coastal defense began on land, not over water.

Andrews did nothing to reassure them. On the contrary, GHQ Air Force's mission as he saw it was to attack the enemy far out to sea, striking his aircraft carriers or his island bases. The B-17 was sold to the War Department and Congress largely on the grounds that it could defend such vulnerable areas as Alaska, the Philippines and the Panama Canal by sinking hostile fleets far from shore.

All true success flirts with failure; Andrews's promotion of the heavy bomber certainly did. The leading light in the narrow coterie of strategic bombing enthusiasts, he seemed to be shoving the B-17 up the noses of admirals and the General Staff alike. He urged, virtually demanded, that the Air Corps should have only one bomber, the heavy, strategic four-engine kind. He was inflaming the walking nightmares of the Army and Navy Club.

Under pressure from the Navy, Army Chief of Staff Malin Craig gave instructions in 1938 that henceforth the Air Corps couldn't fly more than one hundred miles from shore.[40] At almost the same time, the General Staff ruled that the Air Corps would get no more four-engine bombers. It could have only two-engine B-18s. Plans for a successor to the B-17 were to be shelved.[41]

Arnold played no real part in this dispute. He seemed to be keeping his head down. Besides, he was something of a Malin Craig protégé by now.

On October 21, 1938, Oscar Westover was killed coming in to land at Burbank airport flying an A-17. His plane stalled, then crashed into a house three hundred yards short of the runway.

For eight days Arnold was on tenterhooks. Within the Air Corps there were half a dozen officers who were senior to him. Roosevelt seemed reluctant to appoint Arnold to succeed Westover. His main rival, Frank Andrews, was not only senior but enjoyed the strong backing of the President's military adviser, Major General Edwin "Pa" Watson. There was also a whispering campaign against Arnold, that made him out to be a drunk. In fact, all he drank was sherry; usually a glass or two of Amontillado before his afternoon nap.

The story about Arnold's drinking habits was easily refuted. More importantly, Craig disliked Andrews; for that matter, so did most of the General Staff, because of Andrews's campaign for more B-17s. It was rumored that Craig informed the President he'd resign if Andrews got command of the Air Corps. Whether or not the rumor was true, there was little doubt that Craig pushed hard for Arnold.

Arnold also had the staunch backing of one of the country's leading industrialists, Donald Douglas, a man who sometimes stayed at the White House when he visited Washington. On other occasions, he stayed with the Arnolds. Douglas may have helped turn his prediction of a dozen years earlier into a self-fulfilling prophecy.[42]

One way or another, on October 28, Arnold's waiting ended. It was his Air Corps now, but at a price. Craig ordered him to stop flying airplanes. Arnold would never handle a takeoff or landing again. On the ground, he ran the Air Corps. In the air, aboard his personal DC-3, he couldn't fly as anything but a copilot or passenger.[43]

3

CRITICAL MASS

The year 1938 saw Europe sliding inexorably toward a war between fascism and democracy. Britain and France undertook rearmament programs, mainly in the air. The British could do so openly, but the French government had to be more circumspect. After preaching pacifism for twenty years the French president, Leon Blum, lacked public support for a revitalized military. Early in 1938 the French expressed an interest in buying American planes.

Hitler was counting on the Luftwaffe's growing might to frighten his foes into submission. The shadow of Luftwaffe bombers darkened every sidewalk in the cities of Europe, yet no free nation's air force threatened Berlin. German air power was Hitler's ace and only planes could counter planes.

There was no doubt where Roosevelt stood in the struggle between democracy and fascism, but there were major problems in aiding the French. They wanted to keep the operation secret; they were short of cash; the Neutrality Act made it difficult to sell armaments to foreign powers; and Capitol Hill flew isolationist flags. Even so, Roosevelt was ready to act. In March 1938 he gave permission for a French test pilot to fly the P-36, the newest fighter in the Air Corps inventory. The flight was conducted in total secrecy.[1]

By summer the French were talking of buying more than one thousand U.S. combat aircraft to modernize the *Armée de l'Air*. Then, in October 1938, Hitler conquered prosperous, well-armed Czechoslovakia without firing a shot. Britain and France agreed at

Munich to stand aside. They weren't yet strong enough for a show-down with Hitler. This disgraceful episode gave new urgency to their rearmament, and to Roosevelt's efforts to help them.

On November 14 the President convened a meeting at the White House attended by his closest adviser, Harry Hopkins; Army Chief of Staff Malin Craig; the new Deputy Chief of Staff, George C. Marshall; Assistant Secretary of War Louis Johnson; Arnold; and high-ranking officials from Treasury and Justice.* The President did a little wishful thinking out loud: he'd like to have an air force with twenty thousand combat aircraft and an aviation industry able to turn out two thousand planes a month. Congress wouldn't ac-cept anything like that, so he was aiming instead for a ten thousand-plane air force, and one thousand airplanes a month.[2]

For Arnold here was an embarrassment of glad tidings, spiced with a *soupçon* of bad. At this meeting American air power had received, in his words, "its Magna Carta." On the other hand, the President seemed to think all airplanes were good; yet without a strong foundation of well-trained pilots, modern bases, skilled me-chanics and spare parts, aircraft aren't weapons but toys.[3]

Moreover, when the time came to put his request to Congress, Roosevelt drew back from asking for ten thousand planes. He aimed for a more modest thirty-two hundred. In April 1939 Con-gress went along with the President, raising the Air Corps's autho-rized strength from its present level of twenty-two hundred planes to a limit of fifty-five hundred. It put its money where its word went, providing $180 million to buy new aircraft, plus a further $120 million for training and base development.[4]

Arnold still hoped to build the Air Corps up to Roosevelt's goal of 10,000 planes, a project that he expected to take at least two years. He envisaged a frontline force of 3,750 combat aircraft, a reserve of 3,750, plus 2,500 training planes.[5]

It was a thrilling prospect, but getting there wasn't going to be easy. The British and French seemed to Arnold, Johnson and to Secretary of War Harry Woodring an obstacle to be overcome, even though it was Allied money that was being used to fertilize the

---

*Arnold was adamant that this meeting took place September 28. The official Air Force history accepts his claim, although there is no documentary evidence for it. The record shows, instead, that it was November 17 when Arnold instructed his staff to draw up plans for a major expansion.

anemic U.S. aviation industry into a heavyweight contender. Resistance from the Air Corps and the War Department to providing aircraft for other nations prompted Roosevelt to place the secretary of the Treasury, the youthful and energetic Henry A. Morgenthau, in charge of distributing them between Britain and France, the Air Corps and the Navy. Morgenthau proposed to assign new output evenly between the American services on one side and the Allies on the other. The Navy accepted that; the Air Corps fought it all the way.[6]

No one in the Air Corps seemed to realize just how much might be learned from the British, who possessed an effective radar system, faster planes, better liquid-cooled engines, and aircraft gun turrets. There was a solid basis for mutually beneficial exchanges. But it would be nearly two years before either side acknowledged that.

The Royal Air Force (RAF) had a wish list as long as its arm, everything from trainers to bombers. The French, with less money to spend, concentrated on fighters and a light bomber, the twin-engined DB-7, that Douglas had developed on its own initiative and with its own money. Arnold and Woodring didn't want to let the French anywhere near the plane.

It took an order from Morgenthau, claiming White House backing, to override their objections. Three French officers were permitted to view it from a distance and one, *Capitaine* Paul Chemidlin of the *Armée de l'Air,* was offered a ride in the DB-7 on a brief flight at the Douglas plant's Miner Field. The Douglas pilot disobeyed his instructions, started doing acrobatics at four hundred feet, and shut down one engine. On a sharp bank and turn the DB-7 stalled. It crashed into the North American parking lot, across the street from Douglas. The pilot was killed when his parachute failed to open. Chemidlin, strapped into the copilot's seat, survived with a broken leg and lacerations.[7]

News that a French captain had been riding in one of the most advanced American combat aircraft created a storm in Congress, even though all the secret equipment had been removed before the Frenchmen arrived. Arnold, called to testify before Congress, was in a difficult position. He could take the rap and incur the wrath of Congress. Or he could blame Morgenthau and incur the wrath of Roosevelt. He put all responsibility on Morgenthau. Relations with the White House went steadily downhill from there.

Not even the outbreak of war in Europe at the end of August

1939 weakened Arnold's resistance to sharing American planes with the British and French. Johnson and Woodring, too, remained opposed to anything beyond token sales.[8] The embattled Allies meanwhile got together and created an Anglo-French Purchasing Commission to handle their shopping.

By March 1940 each nation had purchased hundreds of U.S. planes. As much as airframes, though, they wanted the most advanced technologies, such as the turbo superchargers that took American fighters up to forty thousand feet. Arnold absolutely refused to give the necessary permission for the sale of classified matériel.

On March 10, 1940, Arnold gloomily noted, "Was informed this day [by Harry Hopkins] that the President objected very strenuously to the attitude taken by me in connection with aid to Britain. . . . Hopkins expressed himself in no uncertain terms. . . ."[9] Two days later at a White House meeting Roosevelt tore into him. "Oh, boy," Morgenthau gleefully told his staff later, "did General Arnold get it!" The President pointedly remarked that officers who "refused to play ball" were likely to be sent to Guam, a none too subtle way of telling him he'd be retired if he continued blocking the Allied plane program. Arnold had also been leaking freely to the Republican press and courting isolationist Congressmen in an attempt to thwart government policy. The leaks, too, had to stop.[10] Arnold's career was on the line once again, with no chance of a comeback this time.

A month later the Anglo-French Purchasing Commission signed contracts for 2,440 fighters and 2,160 bombers. Nearly a year and a half had passed since Roosevelt launched the post-Munich plane program. And within days this effort was overtaken by events: the Germans overran Denmark and Norway.

In an address to Congress on May 16, Roosevelt raised his sights higher than ever. Now he wanted production raised to fifty thousand airplanes a year. The program launched at the meeting in November 1938 turned out to be merely the prologue to something even more dramatic.

In April 1939 the Lone Eagle, Charles Augustus Lindbergh, reluctantly came home, by sea, moved by a moral certainty that Europe was about to be engulfed by war. Shortly after arriving he and Arnold met incognito at the Hotel Thayer at West Point. There they could talk freely, without interruptions from Arnold's staff or houndings from the press.[11]

The two men had been corresponding for the past year. Now, Lindbergh gave Arnold a tutorial on German air power. He'd met the men who commanded the Luftwaffe, visited the factories, flown German planes. The Germans may have exaggerated their strength, in the hope that through Lindbergh they might convince the United States to leave an invincible Germany with a free hand in Europe. If so, their efforts were in vain. Lindbergh impressed on Arnold the need to match, and eventually surpass, the German achievement.

Several weeks later Arnold established a board to decide which planes and technologies the Air Corps should purchase over the next five years. He appointed Lindbergh and Spaatz to it.

The board's list of priorities began with a better liquid-cooled engine for fighters. It also called for a new heavy bomber, with twice the range of the B-17. Thus was the B-29 begun. The board stressed the need for better research and development, yet made no mention of jet engines or radar.[12]

In September 1939, with Europe at war, Lindbergh gave up his work for the Air Corps so he might lend his famous name and high-pitched voice to the cause of isolationism. He thereby earned the undying scorn of Franklin Roosevelt.[13]

Following the President's call for fifty thousand planes a year, Arnold needed a master plan. The Army Industrial College had been working on plans for mobilizing the economy since the mid-1920s. The air portion was incomplete and passé, reflecting the Air Corps's disdain for the schools and routine staff planning. The airmen would have to improvise.

Arnold made Lieutenant Colonel George Kenney his production troubleshooter, assisted by Major Kenneth B. Wolfe. Out at Wright Field, Kenney, Wolfe and half a dozen officers of the Matériel Command labored over a huge roll of butcher's paper.* On it they wrote out, stage by stage, a blueprint for expansion: so many training planes here . . . so many pilots in flight school there . . . so many fighter groups by this date . . . so many bomb groups by that date.

---

*The new Air Corps command was housed in an imposing new building surmounted with a bas-relief of Rodin's "Thinker." Critics said it couldn't have memorialized the engineers at Wright Field more aptly—chin in hand, deep in thought, never moving.

. . . And so on for the next two years, fitting training schedules to production schedules. All on one piece of paper that was unrolled for how many feet—ten? Fifteen? The exact figure is lost in the mists of memory.[14]

The government provided the manufacturers with much of the equipment that went into Air Corps planes, such as the propellers and engines. Major Orval Cook was told to calculate the total cost of government-furnished equipment for the air fleet emerging on the butcher's paper. When he added it up, he stared at the total in disbelief. He showed it to Kenney. "My God!" said Kenney. Cook had written "$4 billion."[15] That was four times the entire amount spent on Army aviation since 1919. Yet it was, in effect, only a down payment on the entire program.

Cook also calculated there would soon be an aluminum crisis, so the three companies that produced this material were told to start cooperating and work out ways to expand output. Aircraft manufacturers, too, were told to start building new plants. The busy team at Wright Field had no authority to give such orders to civilian companies, nor could they promise contracts would follow. They did it anyway.

Throughout 1940 there were critical shortages in just about everything, not just aluminum. The Depression had ravaged American industry, leaving a dearth of machine tools and a shortage of skilled workers. These were problems that Morgenthau tried to tackle. He created a skilled team of experts to guide the aircraft industry through rapid expansion and overcome such bottlenecks.[16]

A week after calling for fifty thousand planes a year, however, Roosevelt set up a National Defense Advisory Commission, headed by the chairman of General Motors, William Knudsen. Morgenthau's experts were assigned to Knudsen and the secretary of the Treasury gradually faded into the background.

Arnold would later claim that he got along splendidly with the big, jovial Knudsen. The truth was he despised Knudsen, a man whose chief merit in Arnold's eyes was that he wasn't the hated Morgenthau.[17] A Danish immigrant made good, Knudsen was hosannaed in the press as the reigning genius of mass production.

And that was the key to the magic kingdom of the skies.

There was no true mass production of airplanes in the United States. There never had been. General Motors or Ford could mass produce automobiles because around July each year the design of next year's models would be frozen. From September the cars produced for the next twelve months would be identical.

Freezing an airplane design was like trying to freeze a moonbeam. By the time a new plane was delivered to the Air Corps somebody was planning to change it. Engineers at the factory or at Wright Field were forever coming up with refinements. Air Corps pilots, too, were constantly demanding changes.

Even the way airplanes were assembled could clot a Detroit engineer's blood. Consider the B-24 bomber, manufactured by Consolidated Aircraft of San Diego. The wings, the tail and the fuselage were put together inside the factory. These were then hauled out to a huge steel structure, under the hot southern California sun, to be assembled and receive their engines, their hydraulic lines and their wiring. The metal expanded in the sunshine, but unevenly, of course. Countless minor adjustments had to be made to get all the pieces to fit. The nearer the aircraft was to completion the less it could be said to be mass produced. No two B-24s were truly identical.[18]

The sheer complexity of modern planes defied belief. The B-25 medium bomber, half the size of a B-24, contained 165,000 separate items, not counting the 150,000 rivets that held it together. It was little wonder that it took five years, on average, to go from Air Corps specifications to a plane that could meet them.

The aviation industry, however, hadn't been standing still. It got a jump start even before Roosevelt's call for fifty thousand airplanes a year. British and French money had increased capacity and it was now 400 percent bigger than it would have been otherwise. Allied orders almost certainly saved one important engine maker, Pratt & Whitney, from going out of business.[19]

The industry was also being spurred on daily, not only by Arnold but by officers at Wright Field, such as Cook and Kenney and successive chiefs of the Matériel Division, George Brett and Oliver Echols. Everyone the plane makers dealt with was screaming for more planes, bigger planes, more engines, bigger engines, more plants, bigger plants. By the end of 1940 the traditionally impoverished airplane makers had factories rising across the Sunbelt, in out-of-the-way places such as Tulsa and Fort Worth, that a year earlier boasted only an unprepossessing municipal strip as its stake in the Air Age.

In July 1940 Arnold brought one of the most famous figures in the Air Corps Reserve, Major James Doolittle, back to active duty. Arnold made him a troubleshooter and sent him to Detroit to put pressure on Allison (a subsidiary of General Motors) to work the bugs out of its engines.

Doolittle was a pioneer aviator, having learned to fly in 1917 but missing out on the war. In 1921 he'd led a flight of DH-4s in Mitchell's 1st Provisional Air Brigade in the scientific sinking of surrendered German warships. In 1922 Doolittle had won the DFC after flying from Florida to San Diego in less than a day. Thereafter he'd gone on to establish himself as the finest air racing pilot in the United States. Short, stocky, and dynamic, his ironically inapposite name was a byword among American youth.

Doolittle was not only a pilot; he was a thinker. He'd attended MIT in the 1920s and received one of the first Ph.D.s awarded in aeronautical engineering. He was convinced pilots didn't know where they were half the time, and until they got some decent instruments aviation was going to be a fair-weather business.

In 1929 Doolittle made the first ever completely blind flight. Glued to a crude panel of rudimentary instruments that he'd helped develop, he crouched in a cockpit under a black hood, flying blinder than if it were night. A safety pilot, Lieutenant Benjamin S. Kelsey, sat in the cockpit behind him, on the lookout for other planes but with his hands raised ostentatiously above his head throughout the short flight, including the landing.[20]

On this triumphant note Doolittle had left the Air Corps, unable, on a lieutenant's salary, to support a wife, two sons, mother, and widowed mother-in-law. He went to work for Shell Oil Company. During the early 1930s he urged the company's chemists to develop one hundred-octane aviation fuel. Shell had its doubts. All its customers seemed satisfied with the present ninety-one-octane product.

Doolittle persisted with his campaign and by 1934 Shell had a multimillion dollar investment in new equipment that would produce one hundred-octane fuel. The effect on performance was remarkable. The newest fighters got a 7 percent increase in speed and a 40 percent improvement in rate of climb. After 1937 the Air Corps bought nothing but one hundred-octane fuel. The British were supplied with it during 1940 and the 3 percent difference it made to the speed of the RAF's Spitfires offered an edge in dogfighting the technically more advanced Me-109.[21]

When he was recalled to active duty, Doolittle knew next to

nothing about industrial mass production and had been out of the Air Corps for twelve years. Even so, he was still one of the three most famous flyers in the United States (after Rickenbacker and Lindbergh). His high-profile presence showed Allison (and the public) that Arnold was putting the heat on.

Arnold regularly descended on aircraft plants to apply this heat in person, never staying for long, constantly exhorting, forever demanding. He was a smiling Johnny One Note—"Planes! Planes! Planes!"[22] Critical at the outset of Roosevelt's obsession with raw numbers, he'd succumbed to the same virus. If output was god, then he was a devout monotheist.

Arnold's hurricane style did much to energize the drive for production. He stopped buying planes on the basis of competitive bids and prototypes and started buying them on the basis of negotiated contracts and Air Corps specifications. It was risky—especially in the case of the B-29—but it took a year off lead times.

At one point Arnold wanted to cut back on research and development; it was interfering with output. He also told Wright Field to stop buying spare parts; that too was interfering with output. The Matériel Command simply ignored such orders.[23] Echols became increasingly the steady hand on the drive for airplanes, but Echols on his own couldn't curb Arnold's bursts of creative enthusiasm and stressed-out strangeness. Something, or someone, else was needed too.

One of the members of the Yale Flying Unit organized in World War I was the shy, ascetic-looking son of a Western railroad millionaire, a youth named Robert A. Lovett. After the United States entered the war, Lovett became a Navy pilot. He bombed U-boat bases on the Belgian coast and came home with a Navy Cross. In the piping times of peace that followed he became an investment banker, but retained an abiding interest in military aviation.[24]

The spring of 1940 found him in Italy, where he got into conversation with a group of Luftwaffe officers. Nearly everything they told him about the size, strength, and skills of the German Air Force was alarming.

On his return, he visited old friends such as Donald Douglas and Alexander "Sasha" Seversky. The question that gnawed at him was simple: "How does what we have compare with what they have?" The answer was equally simple—it didn't. Not in quality, or in quantity.

While Lovett was conducting his private investigation, Roosevelt was getting rid of the isolationist secretary of war, Harry Woodring, and his bumptious deputy, Louis Johnson. Their places were taken by the septuagenarian former secretary of war Henry Stimson* and an old friend of Lovett's, Robert Patterson. Both men believed the United States would soon be at war.

Patterson, a former federal judge, wore the belt he'd stripped from the still-warm body of a German soldier he'd killed in hand-to-hand combat in World War I. He was responsible now for Army procurement, including airplanes. Lovett talked to Patterson about what he saw as a potentially insurmountable gap between German and American air power. Patterson told him to put it in writing. The report Lovett sent Patterson in November 1940 said the President's aircraft production targets weren't going to be met unless the Air Corps abandoned its traditional emphasis on quality and kept its eye fixed on the real target—quantity.[25]

The Air Corps would also have to overcome its reluctance to rely on the automobile industry, and Detroit would have to stop shying away from aviation. In this crisis the car makers amounted to a pool of subcontractors, able to turn out tail assemblies, wing sections, and engine beds. They were also *the* experts on mass production techniques.

The result of Lovett's report was a call from Stimson, asking him to join his staff. A balding hypochondriac perennially dressed in a blue linen suit and monogrammed shirt, Lovett quit Wall Street next day.

When he arrived in Washington he moved into General Pershing's cramped and gloomy apartment on Connecticut Avenue; Black Jack had taken up permanent residence at Walter Reed.

At the Munitions Building, Lovett found a General Staff that "contained enough dead wood to constitute a fire hazard." As he toiled to breathe a better sense of direction into aircraft procurement, he was at the mercy of hastily recruited, untrained secretaries. The first memo he dictated concerned heavy bombers. Each reference to the B-17 emerged as "the BBBBBBBBBBBBBBBBB."

Arnold wasn't convinced that car makers would ever make good plane makers, yet he knew that Roosevelt's goal of fifty thousand

---

*"Colonel" Stimson (from his service in World War I) had been secretary of war under Taft (1911–14) and secretary of state under Hoover (1929–32).

airplanes a year would never be reached without Detroit. For their part, by late 1940 the auto makers were receiving such a bad press about putting profits before patriotism that most were ready to succumb. The only holdout was Henry Ford.

The RAF, for example, asked in the summer of 1940 for a production line to be opened to turn out nine thousand Rolls-Royce Merlin XX engines for Spitfires. It was incomparably better than any American liquid-cooled engine in production or in prospect. Six thousand units would go to Britain; the remaining three thousand would go to the Air Corps. Henry Ford agreed to make them, but once he discovered that not all the engines were for the Air Corps, he reneged. Knudsen asked Packard Motors to make them instead; Packard even improved on the British design.[26]

Ironically, it was Ford who would run the biggest and most famous airplane plant of all. The old man hated Roosevelt as much as ever, was fiercely pacifistic and isolationist, yet he feared the government would take over his company if he tried to sit out the defense buildup. Ground for a B-24 plant was broken early in 1941, on land Ford owned thirty miles northwest of Detroit, at a place called Willow Run.

Ford's production chief, Charles Sorensen, drew up a plan for a factory that would be one mile long and 440 yards wide—70 acres, all under one roof. While Consolidated Aircraft Corporation aimed to turn out one bomber a day, Sorenson planned to produce one an hour. *That* was mass production. But if the plant was built in a straight line as Sorenson proposed, it would cross over into Wayne County—Democratic, pro-Roosevelt, prolabor. Ford made the Willow Run plant an inefficient L-shape, just to spite Wayne County's unions and politicians.[27]

There were other problems, too. For one thing, Detroit used steel dies to shape metal. Steel, however, scars aluminum, spoiling its aerodynamic properties. Moreover, airplane makers shipped freight cars filled with detailed drawings, which auto engineers couldn't understand; they weren't used to operating to such fine tolerances. All the drawings had to be redone. It was like translating from one language to another.

The airplane manufacturers were contemptuous of their arriviste rivals from Detroit. "You cannot expect blacksmiths to learn how to make watches overnight," scoffed the president of North American Aviation, James H. "Dutch" Kindleberger.[28] Nevertheless the contempt had an edgy tone. Suppose by some miracle the blacksmiths turned out to be competent plane makers? They might be tempted to stay in the aircraft business long after the defense crisis had passed.

Besides pushing for a major effort by the automobile makers, Lovett devoted much of his time to nursing the production of machine tools and getting more powerful engines developed. The design of airframes was racing ahead. This was one area in which the United States rapidly caught up with the Europeans.

What use, though, was a better-designed airframe if an under-powered motor made it an inferior weapon? The Allison liquid-cooled V-1710, for example, was currently rated at eleven hundred horsepower. German and British engines exceeded sixteen hundred horsepower.

As he wrestled with specific tasks like these, Lovett never lost sight of the broad challenge. At the beginning of 1941 he guess-timated that U.S. production capacity was presently about 33 percent of Germany's. He put British capacity roughly on a par with that of the United States. For the Allies to draw level, American capacity would have to double (always assuming the Germans stayed where they were). And for Allied strength to reach the 2:1 ratio it needed to assure air superiority, American capacity would have to increase 500 percent over its present level. To achieve that, production at most aircraft plants would have to go on a seven-day, twenty-four-hour footing, indefinitely.

Lovett gave much thought to the fundamentals of air power: what it was, how you got it, what to do with it. He believed that air power didn't consist of the planes presently in operation but the number that would be produced next year, and the year after that. After a few months in Washington he believed, too, that he'd discovered the true aviation potential of American industry. He told Stimson that the production goal for 1942, of three thousand planes a month, was too low. It should be possible to reach five thousand a month.[29]

Lovett's relationship with Arnold got off to a shaky start, but he won Arnold's respect by being right on three issues Arnold cared about deeply. One was strategic bombing. By 1941 Arnold, who'd played almost no part in the struggle to establish strategic bombing as the supreme task of the Air Corps, had become an ardent advocate.

In the spring of 1941 Lovett sold the case for the four-engine bomber, first to Stimson, then to Marshall, finally to Hopkins, and through these three to Roosevelt. Building a large force of heavy bombers was a potential threat to Roosevelt's cherished fifty thousand planes a year: For the price of a B-17 you could get four fighters or three light bombers. Lovett's missionary efforts paid off when, in May 1941, Roosevelt agreed to a target of five hundred heavy bombers a month.

The second point in Lovett's favor was his belief in an independent air force. Here, too, Arnold had been muted or silent as he made his way to the top. Even after he got there, his precarious standing with the White House kept the gag in place. Whenever he and Spaatz got together socially, however, "We talked mostly about having the Army around our necks."[30]

The third, and for now most compelling reason, for Arnold to trust and respect Lovett was that Lovett was fighting hard to save the Air Corps from the RAF.

By the end of 1940 the British were just about broke. They'd nearly exhausted their gold and dollar reserves. To keep the flow of American arms crossing the Atlantic, Roosevelt proposed what he termed "Lend-Lease." He made it sound like lending the British what they needed to keep fighting Hitler; most people knew that more than 90 percent would be given without any illusions about getting it back. The legislation was written by Morgenthau and the Treasury Department.

Shortly after the law was enacted, in March 1941, the White House decided that all production from new aircraft plants would go to the British so long as the United States was not at war. Arnold protested strongly that this would cripple the Air Corps.

For one thing, by mid-1941 the British would have taken delivery of nearly two thousand American airplanes since the war in Europe began. In the same period the Air Corps would receive roughly one thousand. It lacked planes even to train itself for war.

For another thing, the British wanted American planes to be modified so they suited RAF operations, such as area bombing and night bombing. American planes were ruggedly built and heavily armed. The British wanted more speed, less armament and lighter construction. Gearing the U.S. aviation industry mainly to producing planes to RAF specifications would jeopardize Air Corps tactics and training.[31]

These were anxious days for Arnold. He felt duty-bound to fight for more aircraft so the Air Corps could meet its own expansion goals. At the same time, he needed to avoid an open clash with the Lend-Lease Administrator, Harry Hopkins, who had the clout to get him fired. For much of 1941 Arnold worried constantly (and rightly) about keeping his job.[32]

Relations between the Air Corps and the RAF were close but tense. In May 1940 Arnold sent Spaatz, Kenney and Frank "Monk" Hunter, the World War I ace, to Europe to provide first-hand accounts of the air war. Other experts were sent to investigate British bombsights and aircraft gun turrets.

For their part, the British were reluctant initially to share their most important technologies. Americans had a poor reputation for keeping secrets.

By the fall of 1940 the British had put their doubts to one side. Spaatz particularly had won their esteem. When he arrived there his feelings were neutral. He soon swung over to the British side. Moreover, when the Battle of Britain was at its height many Americans (Arnold included) assumed the British would lose the battle and, with it, the war. Spaatz reported that the Germans were handling their air power so poorly that they could not achieve air superiority against Fighter Command's defenses, which were based on an effective radar net and a system of ground controllers who directed fighter squadrons to the enemy formations.[33]

By thwarting the Luftwaffe, the RAF had won the respect of the Air Corps. Yet disagreement over airplane allocations remained. Lovett, who had been and still was in favor of aiding Britain, added his protests to Arnold's. American air power was being strangled in the cradle by an excess of presidential generosity. The British, he argued in early 1941, have too many planes and not enough pilots, while we have more pilots than planes.[34] And, indeed, the British, not knowing how long this good thing would last, were forever trying to build up huge reserves of (free) aircraft.

With feelings rising on both sides of the Atlantic, Arnold decided to journey to England in April 1941. Hopkins prepared the way, writing to Prime Minister Winston Churchill in advance. He described Arnold as an able officer, but one who saw only the needs of his own service. The case wasn't hopeless, however. If the British took the trouble to win Arnold over, there was a good chance his views might be modified. Maybe, Hopkins suggested, Arnold might be invited to meet the King?[35]

Arnold arrived in England April 12 to be fêted like a visiting potentate. He was invited to spend a weekend with Churchill. Lord

Beaverbrook, the minister of aircraft production, spent a day with him. The recently installed forty-seven-year-old commander of the RAF, Sir Charles Portal, talked to him for hours, leaving Arnold convinced that here was "a brilliant man who does things, is capable and knows his job."[36]

He lunched with air pioneer Tom Sopwith who'd flown against him in 1911 in the competition to shoot a dinner plate from an airplane. The British showed him the most secret thing they had, the jet airplane. And he got an open-ended, man-to-man audience with the King that ran on so long that Arnold finally called the conversation to a halt. British reserve? He hardly got a glimpse of the critter.

Maybe they'd won him over. Maybe they hadn't. Maybe he was merely trying to keep from being fired by doing what he knew Roosevelt and Hopkins wanted. For whatever reason, Arnold repaid this sedulous wooing. He astounded the RAF by offering one-third of all Air Corps training facilities for British use. Over the next two years, nearly ten thousand British aviation cadets would come to the United States, and half would return to Britain with pilots' wings. Most of the rest became navigators or bombardiers.

He tackled head on the issue of getting planes to Britain. Churchill had complained to Hopkins that hundreds of RAF combat flyers were being diverted from action to do nothing but ferry planes from North America to England.

Arnold had already tried to ease the problem by hiring civilian pilots, recruited through TWA and Pan Am, and paying them large tax-free bonuses for each plane delivered. It was a hazardous task in the long nights and short days of winter. Planes and pilots disappeared over the Atlantic, never to be heard from again. As word spread of how dangerous ferrying was, the flow of recruits dried up. Nor did sending disassembled planes over in crates offer a real solution. By the spring of 1941 hundreds of planes destined for Britain were stacked up in U.S. ports for want of shipping.

His solution was to assume complete responsibility for getting planes to the RAF: Air Corps pilots would fly them over. Shortly after Arnold's return he created the Ferrying Command, entrusting it to the charismatic, dynamic commander of 2nd Bomb Group, Colonel Robert Olds.[37]

One way or another, Arnold seems to have tempered his view of the RAF as a parasite that was killing the growth of his Air Corps. He chaired the joint aircraft committee that monitored the distribution of American aircraft in a way that drew praise from the British, and staunchly defended the committee's decisions before a skeptical U.S. Congress.[38]

The British were presently clamoring for B-17s. The RAF had preached the creed of strategic bombardment since World War I, yet had done almost nothing to develop four-engine bombers. There were few B-17s to go around, but Arnold sent them twenty. When the RAF tried using them against well-defended targets, the Luftwaffe cut the aircraft to ribbons. As Arnold ruefully acknowledged, two hundred might have accomplished something; twenty was a mistake. The RAF, naturally, wrote off the B-17 as a "duff" airplane, unable to do what the Americans claimed—make hard-hitting attacks in broad daylight.

The British were a lot happier with the P-40. Arnold sent them hundreds, mainly for service in North Africa. He also sent them two of his most promising fighter pilots, captains John Alison and Hubert Zemke, to show them how to fly the plane and how to maintain it.[39] The P-40 wasn't as advanced as the Spitfire or the Me-109, but it was robust and well armed and gave a good account of itself out in the desert as a fighter-bomber.

Two months after Arnold returned from Britain the Germans invaded the Soviet Union. Henceforth, the Soviets too were going to receive American planes, many thousands of them, under Lend-Lease. The Kuomintang government of China was also clamoring for aircraft to resist the advance of the Japanese, with whom they'd been at war since 1937. Even after he'd come to terms with British demands, Arnold had plenty of reason to go on feeling frustrated. At times he may have wondered whether the Air Corps would ever become more than an elaborate paper fantasy of the future, like an astrologer's charts.

When Congress increased the authorized size of the Air Corps to fifty-five hundred planes, the Air Staff drew up a plan for the air defense of the United States. It was based on fleets of B-18s patrolling five hundred miles out to sea, well beyond the range of carrier-based aircraft.[40]

In July 1940, a month after the fall of France, a new plan was drawn up. It envisaged a force of fifty-four groups, comprising four thousand combat aircraft (plus thousands of noncombat planes) and two hundred thousand men. The fifty-four groups were to be operational by April 1, 1942. Marshall demanded that the new plan include hundreds of dive bombers. He was deeply impressed by what German Stukas had achieved in supporting ground troops, first in Poland, then in France. The Air Staff did as he wished, knowing in their hearts it was a big mistake. If you didn't own the sky or if there was a lot of low-level AAA, the dive-bomber was a suicide weapon.[41]

The German attack on the Soviet Union on June 22, 1941, got off to a stunning start. The Wehrmacht looked just about unbeatable. Suppose the United States entered the war, could it win? On July 9 Roosevelt asked Stimson and secretary of the navy Frank Knox to provide an estimate of what it would take to defeat Germany, Italy, and Japan.

The War Plans Division (WPD) of the General Staff was responsible for providing the Army's estimate. By good luck, Arnold had just created an Air War Plans Division of his own. It was raw and untried, but the head of the new AWPD, Colonel Harold George, saw danger here, and an opportunity.

If the WPD drew up a large-scale plan for defeating the Axis, the Air Corps would find itself limited to close air support, parachute drops, reconnaissance, and the like. Marshall was heartily in favor of a bigger Air Corps but, as his belief in dive-bombers showed, when the chips were down he was an infantryman and airplanes became flying artillery. If the WPD of the General Staff determined air strategy in the document that went to the President, the Air Corps would have no independent role, no chance to show what strategic bombardment could do.

Hal George was one of the high priests of strategic bombing. He'd flown bombers in Mitchell's Day Bombardment Group in France, flown in Mitchell's First Air Brigade and bombed the *Ostfriesland,* taught bombing theory at Maxwell, commanded 2nd Bomb Group, and recruited some of the most outstanding young officers away from fighter cockpits and into bombers. George decided to try short-circuiting the usual procedures. He made an offer to Brigadier General Leonard Gerow, the head of WPD: let us, the AWPD, write the air part of the plan, instead of assigning Air Corps officers to you and sending over our data.[42] Possibly because the WPD contained only seven officers, yet its workload was growing exponentially, Gerow accepted his offer.

The AWPD itself was going to be stretched to produce a plan. George claimed the services of Laurence Kuter, who was presently assigned to the War Department's G-3 Division. Kuter had been both a student and an instructor at Maxwell. He was rakishly good-looking—resembling a thin John Gilbert, articulate, bright, ambitious and much favored by Marshall.

A 1927 graduate of West Point, he hadn't joined the Air Corps out of a burning desire to fly. A year after receiving his commission, Kuter was a carefree lieutenant in the field artillery, happily rearranging the landscape around Camp Ord, California. The only thing that seemed to spoil his efforts was the hapless contribution made by Air Corps pilots who tried to adjust his battery's fire by sending him bewildering or incomplete instructions. Kuter was certain that if they couldn't do it, he could. He applied for flight school, "so I could become a better artilleryman." He intended to return to his guns, but flying got him hooked.[43]

George roped in Haywood S. Hansell, from Air Intelligence. Hansell was another former instructor at Maxwell. He'd just returned from England, where he'd been given access to the RAF's data on such German targets as aircraft and engine plants, railroads and Luftwaffe bases. The British handed over nearly a ton of target folders, which were flown back in time to provide data for the new plan.[44]

The fourth member of George's team was Colonel Ken Walker. Tall, pale, bespectacled, Walker looked like a college professor, an image reinforced by the many hours he'd spent at Maxwell happily chained to a typewriter, pounding out bombing theories at a desk covered with black scars from the cigarettes he'd allowed to burn out while the creative juices flowed. Walker taught that bombers were the basic arm of the Air Corps, much as infantry was the basic arm of the Army.[45]

The AWPD team assumed it would take a couple of years after the United States went to war for the Army to raise, train, and deploy the millions of men needed to invade the continent of Europe. They planned to mount a strategic bombing campaign that would reach its peak during the six months preceding the invasion, an event they guessed would take place in spring 1944.

Back at Maxwell they'd taught that it wasn't necessary to destroy an entire country to shatter its ability to wage war. A modern nation's economy revolved around a fairly limited number of key facilities. The intellectual challenge was to identify them. Which were the specific marshalling yards, the electricity substations, the oil refineries, the machine tool plants, on which German industrial output was absolutely dependent?

Many of the most modern German plants had been built between 1925 and 1937 with American loans. There were detailed plans in bank vaults in New York. These were retrieved and studied closely—how thick were the walls? the roof? what part of the plant housed the really vital equipment? Using this information and the thousands of target folders contributed by the RAF, the planners identified 154 targets and worked out aiming points.

George, Kuter, Hansell and Walker believed to a man that daylight precision bombing was feasible. Yet there was a crucial unresolved problem, a worm nibbling the heart of their design. Even with the best modern bombsight, bombing was still in the Middle Ages. The chance that one plane dropping a bomb from more than three miles up would strike a target one hundred feet square (which was the basis of their calculations) was around 5 percent.

Increasing the number of planes making an attack would, of course, improve the odds. The planners didn't seek perfection: they aimed for a 90 percent probability of destruction. Using the RAF's experience attacking the battleship *Scharnhorst,* George's team figured that 220 bomber sorties would be needed to destroy a small, well-defended target in mediocre weather. That translates to one bomber flying 220 times, 220 bombers flying once, or some combination in between.

Walker was the Air Corps's expert on bombing probabilities. He'd compiled the Air Corps's bombing tables. He was a conscientious and honest man, yet the depressing truth was that the tables were profoundly misleading. If the 220 bombers flew in close formation, as everyone assumed they would, then every aircraft would have to drop its bombs on a single sighting from the lead airplane. Yet if that one sighting was wrong—and the chance was around 95 percent that any single sighting would be wrong—none of the bombs would hit a target only one hundred feet square.[46] Most would not even hit within a mile of it. This fundamental flaw was ignored, like something too painful to think about.

The force structure that George, et al., devised added up to 98 bomb groups, each comprising 70 aircraft, for a total of 6,860 bombers. To this figure had to be added bombers to protect the United States, to defend positions in the Pacific, and to attack Axis targets outside Germany. Worldwide, the total came to 13,000 heavy bombers, plus nearly 9,000 fighters, whose main responsibility would be defending bomber bases.

Where, though, were all these bases going to be? Only 39 were available in England, but more than 150 would be needed. The solution was to plan on having 3,000 very long-range bombers, the projected B-36, flying from New England to Germany; to have thousands of B-29s flying from Egypt and Northern Ireland; and to cut the number of fighters to 1,600.[47]

Besides these aircraft, the Air Corps would need many others—trainers, reconnaissance, light bombers, dive-bombers, and transports. In all, the plan projected an Air Corps of 251 groups, with 63,500 operational aircraft, not counting large numbers of replacements. It was assumed that aircraft losses in the strategic bombing campaign against Germany would run at 20 percent a month, and personnel losses at 15 percent. At the end of the six-month campaign, the original attacking force would have been wiped out and completely replaced.

Kuter was assigned to calculate the manpower requirements of the plan, known as AWPD-1. On his figures, the Air Corps would have to grow to 2,160,000 men. This was a force as large as the entire American Expeditionary Forces that Pershing commanded in World War I.

Completed, AWPD-1 covered five major tasks: the defense of the Western Hemisphere, a strategic bombing offensive to pave the way for an invasion of the Continent, air support for a strategic defensive in the Pacific, close air support of the armies landing in Europe, and a strategic air offensive against Japan once Germany had been defeated. Its ambitious architecture encompassed the Air Corps's longing for strategic bombing, the Army's demand for tactical air, and the tentative agreement reached with the British for a strategy of Germany First.

Kuter explained the plan to Marshall in a four-hour oral presentation.[48] Marshall was impressed and had him repeat the performance for the General Staff. Some staff officers were vehemently critical, but Marshall ended the discussion, saying, "The plan has merit." He ordered Hal George and his team to present it to Stimson, thereby circumventing the Joint Board, where the Navy might tear it to pieces.[49] Stimson accepted it more or less as it stood.

AWPD-1 was incorporated into the War Department's Victory Program, the master design for what to do just in case the United States was pushed, pulled, drawn—or chose to jump—into what was fast becoming a truly world war.

4

SPREADING
WINGS

Shortly after he became Chief of the Air Corps, Arnold presented Malin Craig with a chart. It showed the Chief of the Air Corps dealing with forty-two government agencies.[1] At the same time, he was denied complete control of the Air Corps: GHQ Air Force reported not to him but to the Army Chief of Staff. Craig simplified things. When Frank Andrews's four-year tour commanding GHQ Air Force expired in March 1939, Craig put it under Arnold's direct control. This gave a major boost to Arnold's status within the Army and within the Air Corps.

In his four years commanding GHQ Air Force, Andrews had made it into a pulpit for pushing the case for Air Corps independence. He was equally outspoken about B-17s, arguing that they should constitute all the Air Corps's bombers. The General Staff was dead set against heavy bombers. In August 1938 it had flatly ruled out any more B-17s and anything bigger than B-17s, on the grounds that they were obviously weapons of aggression, not defense.[2]

Before Andrews's tour came to an end, the General Staff had even ended his right to choose his own staff. Some of his closest colleagues were punished for espousing his views. His G-3, George Kenney, was sent to Fort Benning to teach machine gun tactics to infantry officers. His turbulent chief of staff, Colonel Hugh J. Knerr, was banished to Kelly Field, as air officer to VIII Corps. Knerr would occupy the office Billy Mitchell had been sent to in 1925.

Knerr arrived and was given Mitchell's old desk, with Mitchell's photograph on one wall, and a latrine against another wall for the benefit of the office clerks. Despite this treatment, Knerr refused to shut up, so he was pressured into applying for retirement.

Seeing fresh possibilities in civilian life to agitate for heavy bombers and air independence, Kneer agreed to make the application. A retirement board duly met. To Knerr's horror, the board's psychiatrist ruled in favor of retirement on the grounds that Knerr showed signs of mental illness resulting from a traumatic obsession with the B-17.[3]

In March 1939, a month after Knerr left the Air Corps, Andrews's command of GHQ Air Force expired. He was demoted to colonel and sent to Kelly Field as VIII Corps's air officer—same recently vacated desk, same photo of Billy, same latrine. Arnold seemed to have gotten rid of his great rival, while Craig had slapped down a man he'd never liked.

They had overlooked George Marshall. When Marshall had joined the General Staff in July 1938 as chief of War Plans, Andrews had prevailed on him to take a nine-day tour of Air Corps installations and aircraft factories. By the end of the nine days the two men were friends.[4]

Andrews was one of the most engaging senior officers of his time—good-looking, straight-forward, intelligent and decisive. He was the kind of bold and imaginative problem-solver Marshall was always drawn to. Shortly after Andrews was exiled to Texas by Arnold and Craig, Marshall was named Army Chief of Staff. One of his first actions was to bring Andrews back to Washington, with a star on his shoulder.

Andrews became assistant Chief of Staff, G-3. He was now responsible for Army operations and training. This was by far the highest position any airman had ever held. What's more, the G-3 Division had been the bedrock of anti-Air Corps sentiment on the General Staff. The revolution had come and in 1940 Andrews got a second star.

Marshall acknowledged the transformation in the Air Corps's standing in the fall of 1940 when he made Arnold one of three deputy Chiefs of Staff of the Army. Yet Arnold's exalted position as deputy Chief of Staff (Air) was anomalous. He was allowed to sit in on some Joint Board meetings with the Navy, but not on others. He was responsible for air defenses in the Pacific, yet was denied access to the Army's most highly classified material, decrypts of Japanese codes. He was on the inside and the outside at the same time.

Meanwhile the organization of the Air Corps was being tested to the limits of the envelope. Lovett had nothing but scorn for the way the Air Corps was still divided. Arnold handled logistics and administration, but GHQ Air Force ran the tactical units. This division only encouraged the Army to treat air as an auxiliary of the ground troops. Until the entire Air Corps was organized rationally and the autonomous character of air warfare was accepted by the Army, the advantage of operating even the best airplanes was sure to be wasted.[5]

Lovett demanded a major reorganization. The time wasn't right for outright independence. For one thing, the General Staff wouldn't grant it. For another, even if offered, independence now would amount to a poisoned pill.[6]

A free-standing air force would have to create its own supply organization and be ready from day one to compete with the Army and Navy for scarce industrial resources at a time when these resources were all but sewn up. It would be out in the cold. The Army and Navy would laugh themselves giddy as the uppity Air Corps fell flat on its face and hollered for help.

Lovett revived Mason Patrick's idea of autonomy along the lines of the Marine Corps's relationship with the Navy. Stimson and Marshall accepted that idea. The outcome, in June 1941, was the creation of the U.S. Army Air Forces, with Arnold as commanding general.

The new HQ AAF was a fairly small operation that determined policy and coordinated activities. It contained a new agency, the Air Staff, headed by Spaatz. HQ AAF had clear powers of command over all branches of the AAF.

Creation of the Army Air Forces provided a lot of autonomy, but it still wasn't run in an orderly way. Lovett remained baffled by the way everything of consequence seemed to be done on the basis of personal relationships and telephone calls.[7]

Nor did the new structure do anything to repair Arnold's shaky standing with the White House. On the face of it, Arnold's new command more than justified a promotion, yet he simply couldn't get a third star.

In September 1940 Arnold, under pressure from the White House, had commissioned the President's second son, Elliott Roosevelt, as a captain in the Air Corps.[8] Elliott was near-sighted, so he couldn't become a pilot. Nor had he any experience or training that justified a commission. All Arnold got for his pains was a nation's scorn. A million lapel badges sprouted that fall declaring "Papa, I Want to Be a Captain Too." There was even a mocking popular song.

Elliott was put into procurement and sent to Wright Field. Then, when the press uproar broke, he was hastily moved a long way from journalistic haunts and sent on long flights to even more remote regions. Meanwhile, the President was making his controversial bid for a third term. Roosevelt was embarrassed, even if Elliott's commission was his own idea. He seemed to blame Arnold for going ahead with it.

Making his displeasure clear, a month after Elliott was commissioned Roosevelt created the first ever three-star general in aviation—Delos C. Emmons, an officer two years behind Arnold at West Point and still, ostensibly, subordinate to him. Emmons was running the Air Force Combat Command, the successor to GHQ Air Force.

Not even falling into line over planes for the British in April 1941 altered Arnold's lowly standing at court. As if to rub it in, Frank Andrews got a third star in July and went off to Panama. Marshall had created the Caribbean Defense Command, assigned it to him and got him promoted to lieutenant general. Yet Arnold, the commanding general of 240,000 men, still had the same rank he'd held when the Air Corps numbered 20,000. By promoting his subordinates over him, Roosevelt was putting pressure on Arnold to retire.[9]

Nor did establishing the Army Air Forces do much to stabilize relations with the rest of the Army. The AAF was seen by some General Staff officers as nothing more than a stalking horse for outright independence. And Spaatz was soon claiming the AAF had a right to plan air operations independently of the WPD.[10]

It was no secret that William Bradford Huie's *The Fight for Air Power* would soon be published, or that his coauthor was Hugh Knerr. The book would damn the Navy and the General Staff in roughly equal parts for blocking an independent air force. Wendell Willkie, running for the White House in 1940, had campaigned for an independent air force. Legislation had been introduced in both the House and Senate to create one, with sub rosa assistance from Arnold's staff.[11]

Lovett was equivocal on independence. He was in favor of it, he told Stimson, but "not at this time." Throughout the summer and fall of 1941, Marshall worried that one fine morning Lovett was going to send him a memo demanding a divorce. Stimson told him not to worry about that. The issue wasn't put to rest until November, when the secretary of war compiled his annual report. He explicitly ruled out any break between the Army and the AAF so long as the present war lasted. He showed the draft to Lovett. The secretary's annual report was considered almost a sacred document; to demand major changes would precipitate a crisis that could end in somebody having to resign. Lovett left Stimson's draft much as he found it. Stimson was jubilant. He'd stopped the independence movement in its tracks. Reflecting on a lifetime of high-level politics, he considered this one of his greatest coups.[12]

In 1938 the Air Corps had trained three hundred pilots. Roosevelt's post-Munich plane program was obviously going to demand thousands of pilots each year. In December 1938 Arnold raised the 1939 pilot-training goal to twelve hundred; the figure for 1940 was increased to forty-five hundred.

Arnold was sure he could find enough young men able to fly every plane the country could produce. He guessed there were about one million young men (out of a total population of 120 million) who could meet the Air Corps's physical and educational requirements for pilot training. Of these, maybe 50 percent could learn to fly up to Air Corps standards. That gave him a potential pool of five hundred thousand military pilots.[13] But he couldn't count on them coming to the Air Corps; the Air Corps would have to go to them first.

Arnold was a master of public relations; the Elliot Roosevelt gaffe was a rare misstep. And ever since World War I airmen had counted on a flattering press to keep them in business, however miserly the appropriation from Congress, however hostile the General Staff. And now, with glamorous airplanes and dashing pilots to parade, they had a mother lode of photogenic assets to mine for a press that was rabid for stories on national defense as the Depression became yesterday's news.

The zeitgeist provided a tail wind. Throughout 1940 and 1941 the press was filled with articles that hailed the new air age and made being "air minded" almost the same as being American. The emphasis was on educating the young to understand that their world, a world of airplanes and air distances, was different from all that had gone before—the world of feet, the world of horses and wagons, the world of sail, the world of steam, the world of automobiles.[14]

Young people were encouraged to identify with the Army Air Forces. High school students made recognition models that the AAF used to train Civilian Air Patrol observors. John Steinbeck, at the height of his popularity after publishing *The Grapes of Wrath,* was persuaded to write a nonfiction account of AAF training programs, called *Bombs Away!* It made even the most mundane training routine seem thrilling and was calculated to appeal to just about every healthy teenage boy in the country.

In magazines and books, on the radio and in films, the AAF was promoted as being the quintessentially American military service, born of the progressive, dynamic, inventive genius of the American people; the national character that had tamed a rugged continent now looked to mastery of the skies. The AAF was promoted as being a democratic elite; aviators were a natural aristocracy. Aviation cadets, wrote Steinbeck, "are drawn from a cross-section of America, but they are the top part of the cross-section. They are the best we have."[15]

Passage of the Selective Service Act in August 1940 brought a flood of recruits, but this wasn't going to suffice. An intense recruiting campaign was launched, targeted at college students. Reserve officers were called to active duty to beat the bushes.

One enterprising extempore recruiter, Major Reed E. Davis, sat in an office in Omaha shipping out bundles of letters and stacks of franked envelopes to American Legion posts and Elks Clubs all over the great plains states. Legionnaires and Elks Club members were asked to send a letter to every male college student whose address they could get hold of.

At the top of the letter that Major Davis had written was a drawing of pilot's wings. There followed five hundred words of patriotic prose: "This appeal is sent to you, a red-blooded, keen-spirited young American who is looking forward to early enlistment in some active branch of your country's service. . . . The Air Corps is proving the most attractive and rapidly expanding section of the Army. . . . Thousands of our finest young men are in training as Aviation Cadets. . . . Graduates, newly commissioned, are at the controls of fast-flying airplanes. . . . This appeal is written to you in the belief that you, in common with many of the best men in the land, share in this admiration of the Air Corps. America needs superb pilots. . . . In joining the U.S. Army Air Corps you will find yourself among the cream of American youth, doing the most glorious and thrilling of all defense work. . . ."[16]

There were advertising campaigns, too, in big-city newspapers. Half-page ads urged young men to choose before they were chosen.

Most effective of all were visits. Arnold had recently qualified pilots, straight out of flying school and still glowing, descend on college campuses. These recruiting teams headed straight for the ROTC students. With the youthful recruiters went a doctor, to give preliminary physicals there and then, while interest was at its peak.[17]

When the fifty-four group program was adopted in July 1940, the figure for pilot training was raised to twelve thousand a year. In December, when Lovett arrived in Washington, the figure was raised even higher, to thirty thousand a year.

To step up pilot output, Arnold had taken over nine civilian flying schools in 1939. There, cadets would get their three months of primary instruction. Then they went on to three months of basic training from AAF instructors, after which came three months of advanced trianing at an AAF airfield. In effect, the course to a pair of wings had been cut from a year-long jog to a nine-month sprint. The contents hadn't been changed, though, and all the civilian instructors had to go to Randolph and pass a flying exam before they could instruct aviation cadets in primary. Moreover, several Air Corps officers were assigned to every civilian flying school. They were likely to find themselves sitting on orange crates in a broom closet in a corner of the hangar. Their duty was to maintain standards.[18]

Lovett, however, felt that standards had turned into a fetish. He believed that with pilots, as with planes, air superiority was a function of big numbers. He had managed to get the projected number of pilots trained in 1941 raised to thirty thousand, but Arnold was still insisting on two years of college for aspiring pilots, at a time when less than 10 percent of the population had any college at all.

Arnold's refusal to commission anyone who lacked two years of college was one issue where even the press was critical. As the New York *Daily News* editorialized, "Rickenbacker Didn't Go to College."

It wasn't only this requirement that was a barrier but the AAF's qualifying examination. It was claimed most college graduates probably couldn't pass it. Curious to see what it was like, Lovett asked for two copies; one for himself, one for the president of MIT. Both of them flunked.

The president of MIT then had a large group of his upperclassmen take the qualifying exam. The highest score was recorded by a young woman from Brooklyn—someone the AAF wouldn't even consider for pilot training.[19] Maybe, Lovett told Arnold, the present system doesn't identify the people you need. A modern aptitude test would be likely to provide a better guide to native intelligence than two years of college or the present qualifying exam.

Spaatz agreed with Lovett, calling the traditional entrance requirements "archaic." Arnold was unimpressed. "It will be an unfortunate day for the safety of our country," he insisted, "if we ever permit the pilot standard to be lowered."[20] Congress nonetheless passed Public Law 99, which created a small force of enlisted pilots from men who had only a high school education.[21] Enlisted pilots eventually provided the foundation of two fighter groups that would be among the AAF's most successful, the 79th and the 82nd. Others went on to be excellent bomber and transport pilots. Arnold could live with a handful of enlisted pilots; otherwise he was still hanging tough on requirements as 1941 drew to a close.

New Deal meant new barracks. In the struggle to end the Depression, spending on public works didn't draw the line at the military. Army posts across the country got new buildings. Some places got more than that. Big new airfields were built at Randolph Field, Texas; Maxwell Field, Alabama; Hamilton Field, California; and Hickam Field, Hawaii. Older airfields were brought up to date. It was timely construction: the faster, bigger aircraft developed in the late 1930s needed longer, stronger runways.

Even so, the post-Munich expansion called for an increase in facilities that would dwarf everything built since 1918. Back in the 1920s an airfield needed about two hundred acres. These days, it would need at least two thousand; some broke the four thousand-acre mark.[22] The AAF found itself caught up in a land rush, along with the Army and Navy. Eventually it would end up with as much land as if it owned New Hampshire, Vermont, Connecticut, and Massachusetts combined.[23]

Congress made it clear that it expected the new, mainly conscripted, military to be well housed and well cared for. The bases that were built in 1940–42 were spacious and, as such places went, comfortable.

The initial outbreak of constructive energies meant that by the end of 1941 the AAF would find itself supervising 45 civilian flying schools and operating 114 airfields in the continental U.S. Most of the major installations had a swimming pool for the officers, a bowling alley for the enlisted men. It was a country club life compared to what the hard-bitten interwar professional Army had known.

Three of the original nine flying schools Arnold had taken over were in Lincoln, Nebraska; Chicago; and St. Louis. They proved poor choices. The weather prevented them from producing their quota of students. One class from Nebraska had to fly through the 1940 Christmas vacation in order to make the deadline for starting basic at Randolph in January 1941. Flight training made no sense in the North.

There had already been a shift toward the Southwest during the interwar years, with the result that there were probably more Air Corps pilots from Texas than any other state. A major expansion into the good-weather areas was logical, but logic always has its limits. It seemed that every county or parish, every city and town below the 37th parallel (running roughly from Norfolk, Virginia, to Monterey, California) was demanding an airfield. Political pressure to share the wealth and put a large proportion of the new facilities in the (then) solidly Democratic South was intense.[24]

One way or another, the new flying schools and major airfields were spread across what one AAF officer, Colonel David Schlatter, termed "the sunshine belt."[25] Technical training facilities were distributed more evenly across the continent.

As the AAF moved into the Sunbelt, so did the plane makers. The shift was partly symbiotic, but land for new plants was cheap in the South and Southwest, even if there were sometimes problems finding labor. Federal money and advanced industrial skills were pouring into what had long been considered backward regions. The old western-oriented frontier was over. In its place was emerging a new, south-looking frontier destined to reshape American life.

The wars that raged in Europe and the Far East in the late 1930s were of little interest to the Air Corps. The Spanish Civil War and the undeclared Japanese war in China and Manchuria rang up the curtain on modern aerial combat, yet Arnold and other senior Air

Corps officers assumed there was nothing much to be learned in the world beyond Maxwell Field or Langley, Virginia. Foreign wars were fought by people who didn't know how to use air power properly—people who believed that bombers needed to be escorted, that fighters needed warning nets, that low-level attacks could be effective. Instead of studying foreign wars, the Air Corps ignored them.

Some airmen got involved nonetheless. Usually they were people who'd retired from the Air Corps, or washed out in training, or been denied regular commissions. One of the first was Claire Lee Chennault, who'd spent five years teaching fighter tactics at Maxwell.[26] After poor health forced his retirement in 1937, Chennault went to China to advise the Kuomintang government of Chiang Kai-shek on how to build and run an air force.

What he found was a heterogeneous "International Squadron" that was being pushed back steadily as the Japanese advanced along China's east coast. Chennault revised its tactics, created a warning net, and improved its training, but there wasn't much he could do to halt the relentless drive of the Japanese Army as it overran Chinese airfields.

He returned to the United States in 1940, hoping to be recalled to active duty, but Arnold wouldn't offer him anything beyond a chance to instruct observation pilots on how to tow targets for the coast artillery to shoot at.[27] Chennault preferred to stay with the Chinese and command fighter pilots in combat.

Not that he had an effective air unit yet, but he was working on that. There was considerable goodwill toward China; then as now, many Americans felt a special interest in that country, without knowing much about it. Such sentiments were epitomized by Franklin Roosevelt, who felt that with modern American help China would emerge as a great, and potentially democratic, power. In 1941 the Chinese were given access to the Aladdin's cave of Lend-Lease.

Chennault meanwhile was claiming that with 350 fighters and 150 bombers he could wreak such havoc on Japanese lines of communication that the war in China would be turned around.

There were no fighter planes to spare, but Chennault got the British to agree to surrender their claim to one hundred P-40Bs in exchange for a promise from the manufacturer, Curtiss-Wright, to provide a much better model for them later. By the time Curtiss got around to producing these one hundred planes, a much improved leakproof gas tank was available and the resulting aircraft was designated the P-40C.

Chennault's P-40Cs were underpowered, lacked radios, gunsights and any fitting for a belly tank. What they had was good armament (four .30-caliber machine guns, two .50s) and a bad reputation for killing pilots. Chennault got a diminutive fighter pilot, John Alison (a man who carried a four-inch leather cushion around) to put on a demonstration of the P-40's maneuverability at Bolling Field for the benefit of Chinese officials. Before 1940 the Air Corps had discouraged acrobatics: too dangerous. Alison mastered them all the same. He'd practised extensively—at night. In just five minutes Alison left the Chinese, and Chennault, awestruck. They accepted the plane.[28]

All Chennault needed now was personnel. This venture had an undeniably mercenary side to it. Pilots would be paid $600–$750 a month; mechanics would get $250. Any pilot who scored a confirmed kill on a Japanese plane qualified for a $500 bonus. Fighting the Japanese might provide valuable experience for American pilots before the United States entered the war, yet as he tried to recruit them in the early months of 1941, Chennault ran into a brick wall (Arnold) and bounced off that into the barbed wire (Marshall). They didn't share Roosevelt's sentimental attitude toward the Chinese. They saw instead a dismal swamp sure to swallow up scarce combat resources.

Nevertheless, Chennault had the firm backing of the White House. Another supporter was Navy Secretary Frank Knox, a onetime Rough Rider under Teddy Roosevelt. Chennault was allowed to scour U.S. military installations and make his pitch. He soon found the one hundred pilots he needed to get his operation underway, but Arnold absolutely refused to let him have even one staff officer. He also hired a couple of hundred ground personnel and a Chinese-speaking Lutheran missionary, Paul Frillman, to serve as his chaplain and welfare officer.

The pilots were a mixed bag. More than half were Navy flyers. Many had lied about their experience, claiming to have flown fighters when they had never even sat in one. A few, such as Alex "Ajax" Baumler, had combat experience. Baumler, after washing out of advanced fighter training at Kelly Field, had flown for the Spanish Loyalists against the German Kondor Legion and came home claiming seven kills. The Air Corps let him return to Kelly Field, finish the course, and receive his commission.[29]

Some of Chennault's recruits were undeniable misfits, such as Marine pilot Gregory "Pappy" Boyington, who drank too much and gambled too readily. He was so deep in debt he was ordered to sign up so he could start paying off what he owed.[30]

Assured they wouldn't lose their American citizenship if they fought for a foreign country, Chennault's volunteers applied for passports. Many claimed to be school teachers.[31] Chennault's passport described him as a "farmer." In the summer of 1941 they set sail for Rangoon, aboard a variety of vessels, pretending, unconvincingly, to be tourists.

For Frillman, traveling with a large group of Chennault's non-flying personnel was an education in itself. Chennault had recruited some of the sharpest, most adaptable people Frillman had ever encountered. They were quick witted, opportunistic and energetic. They constantly surprised him. There was, for example, the case of the Singapore starlets.

His ship stopped in Singapore for two weeks. The day after it arrived, Frillman noticed a full-page ad in the *Straits Times* announcing that two talent scouts from Hollywood were looking for young women who'd be interested in competing for a one-year contract with a major studio. Frillman was only mildly interested, until he noticed the names of the talent scouts—the group's finance officer and the official photographer. By the time the ship left port these two had copulated with some of the sexiest and most beautiful women in Singapore, if not the whole of Asia.[32]

Chennault persuaded the British to allow him to assemble his command at an unmanned RAF airstrip at Toungoo, in southern Burma. The four thousand-foot asphalt runway was surrounded by mountains and had no lights, no radar and no homing beacons, but it was a place to begin. And as the P-40s started to trickle in that fall, Chennault commenced instruction. There were seventy-two hours of ground school and sixty hours of flying the P-40, with exhilarating mock dogfights under Chennault's beady eye.

The P-40 was a pig of a plane to land on a hot runway in the jungle. Steam heat rippled from the asphalt in waves. A dozen planes were wrecked; pilots were killed or crippled. The primitive conditions under which the men had to live and train came as a shock to many volunteers after life at modern airfields back home. But gradually a fighting unit started to emerge, albeit one with a false, anodyne identity. Chennault's volunteers were ostensibly civilian employees of an aviation company known as CAMCO, whose business was to buy and maintain transport aircraft for the Chinese government.

Then, on November 15, a pilot named Charles Bond, Jr., was leafing through the magazine section of a British newspaper. It showed an Australian P-40 somewhere in the Western Desert. An amateur artist had painted a snarling tiger shark's mouth in red, white and green around the lower nose section, and added a pair of black, red-rimmed eyes. "Gee!" thought Bond, "I'm going to paint my P-40 that way!"[33] By December 7, there were snarling tiger shark mouths flashing pointed white teeth all over dank Toungoo.

On September 4, 1939—the day after Britain and France declared war on Germany—the renowned Canadian flyer of World War I "Billy" Bishop, a man with sixty aerial victories, phoned magazine illustrator and old friend, Clayton Knight, in Akron, Ohio. Bishop, now Air Vice-Marshal William Bishop, Royal Canadian Air Force, asked Knight, an American who'd served with the Royal Flying Corps on the Western Front, if he'd be willing to recruit Americans to serve with the RCAF. Knight said he'd do it gladly and returned to his dinner guest, the attorney general of Ohio. When Knight started to tell his guest about Bishop's call, the attorney general covered his ears. "What you're talking about is illegal. I can't listen to this!"[34]

Legal or not, Knight refused to be dissuaded and formed a partnership with a tall, burly Canadian businessman named Homer Smith. They set up headquarters at the Waldorf-Astoria. Handwritten slips of paper started to appear mysteriously on municipal airfield bulletin boards, mainly in California, which had the largest concentration of unemployed aviators in the United States. Pilots with extensive flying experience were invited to phone such-and-such a number to inquire about potential employment. Those who did so were then invited to a hotel room somewhere and asked how they felt about the war. Other recruits were former aviation cadets, such as Chesley Peterson, who'd washed out of basic at Randolph for "lack of flying ability."

The prospective RCAF pilots would be given money and tickets by the Knight Committee to take a Canadian "vacation." Some, though, such as Peterson, were turned back at the Canadian border by the Federal Bureau of Investigation.[35] J. Edgar Hoover was closely watching the Knight Committee. He didn't like the way it was flouting the neutrality laws.

Following the fall of France, however, the committee moved from darkness into light. U.S. authorities suddenly became cooperative, provided the committee didn't draw undue attention to itself. A refresher course for Canada-bound pilots was set up at the Spartan School of Aeronautics in Tulsa, one of the civilian flying schools Arnold had taken over. The Knight Committee was allowed to set up a recruiting booth at Maxwell Field to attract Air Corps washouts.[36] It didn't simply receive applications; it was deluged. By the fall of 1941 nearly 50,000 people had applied to the committee and 6,700 had been accepted. Not all were pilots. Many were aviation technicians.

The Knight Committee did not toil uniquely. An American millionaire who lived in Britain, Charles Sweeny, had his son, brother, and nephew recruiting American pilots in London. Sweeny had originally hoped to form something like the old Lafayette Escadrille and send it to fight with the Finns against the Soviets in the Winter War.* After the Finns sued for peace, he offered his handful of pilots to the French *Armée de l'Air*. Following the fall of France, five of them made their way to Britain, hoping to be accepted by the RAF. Sweeny continued his recruiting efforts, but the Knight Committee screened the people Sweeny found.

Others found their own way of hammering at the RAF's door. One of the earliest of these enterprising individuals was William Dunn. He'd served in the U.S. Army in the late 1930s hoping to get into the Air Corps, but was rejected for flight training because he hadn't been to college. Dunn left the Army, paid for flying lessons and had 160 hours when he set off for Canada in the winter of 1939. He enlisted in the Seaforth Highlanders, hoping that would take him to Britain and maybe once he got there, he'd be able to join the RAF. When the time came, he wrote his 160 hours in a way that looked like 560. Soon thereafter Dunn found himself in advanced fighter training, before going on to fly a Hurricane.[37]

More typical of the individual effort was the course followed by John T. Godfrey. He was only one of thousands of young Ameri-

---

*The Eagle Squadrons are widely assumed to have been much like the Lafayette Escadrille. They weren't at all alike. Escadrille pilots were upper class and college educated. Most Eagles came from blue-collar backgrounds and few had more than a high school education. Escadrille pilots tended to be politically motivated and loathed German imperialism. Eagle pilots tended to be in love with flying and indifferent to political issues and foreign affairs.

cans burning to fly fighters but lacking two years of college and unable to pass the Air Corps's qualifying exam. Godfrey's solution was to take a train to Canada in August 1941 and enlist in the RCAF. He promptly applied for pilot training and weeks later was on a ship to Britain.[38]

By the summer of 1940 there were dozens of American pilots flying with the RAF. It was inevitable that there'd be demands to form an American squadron. Yet the Air Ministry was not, as the British say, "best pleased" about putting Americans together in their own unit. It might prove too unruly; Americans were notoriously indifferent to what the British considered good discipline. Churchill, however, saw the proganda windfall, the reams of favorable publicity in the U.S. press, that even one American squadron would generate. The Air Ministry was overruled.

In September 1940 71st Fighter Squadron was formed, the first Eagle Squadron, commanded by Squadron Leader William E. G. Taylor, a former U.S. Navy pilot. By the summer of 1941 it had been joined by two more Eagle squadrons, numbers 121 and 133. At first, the Air Ministry's doubts seemed vindicated. The 71st Squadron got off to such a poor start that when Arnold visited England in April 1941 the head of Fighter Command, Air Vice Marshal Sholto Douglas, told him frankly its pilots were no good; not warriors but "prima donnas."[39]

After the lash, redemption. The competitive spirit of the 71st's young Americans was roused. More training and experience helped, too. In October 1941, and again in November, 71st Squadron led the entire RAF in downing German aircraft. By then, Chesley Peterson had become the squadron commander, having finally made it to Canada and into the RAF. The squadron could also boast the first American ace of the war, Bill Dunn.

There were thirty observation squadrons serving with the Army in 1941. They adjusted artillery fire, performed battlefield reconnaissance and flew ground-force generals around.

Apart from these squadrons, a gulf of mutual incomprehension divided the AAF from the Army Ground Forces. There was almost as much rivalry between airmen and footsloggers as between the Air Corps and the Navy. Marshall and Andrews tried to promote a common outlook by having an entire class of newly qualified pilots, 40A, spend six weeks with the infantry at Fort Benning in 1940. The only planes they saw were from terra firma.[40]

Although there had been a score of joint maneuvers in the 1930s, they never amounted to much. The airmen would rough it for a week or so, living in the field and feeling rugged, but they had no illusions about playing a major role in the mock battles taking place around them.[41]

More than any previous Chief of Staff, Marshall believed in maneuvers. He counted on them to lay bare shortcomings in training, flaws in doctrine and the abilities of individual commanders. Nearly every month of 1941 brought a major maneuver as he stepped up the pressure on the Army, always watching, it seemed, an invisible clock whose hands were spinning so fast they were starting to blur.

Arnold readily committed the AAF to these maneuvers. Although few airmen were going to be as enthusiastic as the ground soldiers, the maneuvers were valuable all the same. They offered a chance for able colonels to get in line for stars in the event of U.S. entry into the war. Ira Eaker was recalled from a mission to England in the summer of 1941 just to take part in the Carolina maneuvers. "I want you to have your opportunity," Arnold told Eaker, and made him commander of the Red Force's fighters.[42] His opponent, commanding the Blue fighters, would be another promising young officer, Lieutenant Colonel William E. Kepner.

Arnold provided nearly five hundred airplanes for the biggest maneuver of the year, in Louisiana in September. The airmen played a vital part in the opening stages for the Blue Force commander, Major General Walter Krueger, and his chief of staff, Colonel Dwight D. Eisenhower.

The first day opened under dripping skies. The Red Force's mission was to cross the Red River and attack Blue, but Red's pilots didn't take off. They were waiting for the overcast to lift. Blue's fighters risked it, quickly found Red's armored spearheads racing toward the river, and slowed them down with mock strafing runs. This gave Eisenhower time to rush truckloads of infantry to the river and pin the crossing Red forces into a shallow bridgehead.[43] This was the high point of air operations in Louisiana.

Some ground generals, such as George Patton, were air atheists: they totally disbelieved there was any such thing as air power. When a flight of aircraft simulated bombing a temporary bridge that his 2nd Armored Division engineers were erecting, an umpire ruled the bridge destroyed. Patton was incredulous. "Destroyed? The Air Force can't destroy anything. To hell with that." All he'd concede was minimal damage and had his engineers stop work for thirty minutes. Marshall sent word down that night that any commander who ignored an umpire's ruling would be relieved of command.[44]

The only unit that really believed in close air support was the 3rd Attack Group, based at Barksdale Field, Louisiana. It might have hoped to play a large role in these maneuvers, but it made little impression. Its A-20s were occupied mainly with laying smoke screens and simulating strafing runs.[45] As Arnold informed Spaatz, "There was little or no cooperation between the ground and the air."[46]

As the maneuver season ran its course, Army Air Forces units were increasingly heading overseas. Ready or not, the AAF was edging closer to the war. In June 1941 a B-18 squadron deployed to Gander, Newfoundland, to fly antisubmarine patrols. If a U-boat was spotted, its position was reported to the RCAF and the Canadian Navy.

In August, 33rd Fighter Squadron arrived in Iceland, flying thirty P-40s off the carrier *Wasp*. The 5th Infantry Division was about to occupy Iceland, thereby relieving a division of British troops for service in the Western Desert. The Germans had bombed Iceland a few months earlier.

Week by week tension was rising as Roosevelt tried to maneuver the United States into war with Germany. To counter any surprise attack by the Luftwaffe or the Germany Navy, fighter groups were shifted into the Northeast, which had the country's biggest concentration of major ports. Bombers were moved out. New England didn't have enough airfields to accommodate all the fighter squadrons that moved in. P-40s were parked in cow pastures; airmen lived in dairy barns.[47]

Tension was also rising sharply in the Pacific. There, the focus of AAF concern was the Philippines, and in April 1941 Arnold sent Brigadier General Henry B. "Sue" Clagett to oversee the buildup of airpower in the archipelago. Clagett was a tall, thin alcoholic. His chief of staff, fighter pilot Colonel Harold H. George (not to be confused with bomber pilot Harold L. George), was his complete antithesis—short, stocky, aggressive, energetic. An ace in World War I, he'd won a DSC. Since then he'd graduated from Maxwell and Leavenworth.

Almost from the moment he arrived in the Philippines, George began pushing for a strong force of heavy bombers as the archipelago's best defense. Clagett's views were more or less irrelevant. For one thing, Arnold despised him (and in 1942 would throw him out of the AAF). For another, Clagett spent much of his time on inspection trips or in hospitals, drying out.[48]

George determined air strategy in the Philippines. He had little trouble selling his ideas to both Arnold and Field Marshal Douglas MacArthur, military adviser to the Commonwealth of the Philippines and de facto commander of its armed forces.

The General Staff had concluded in 1939 that the Philippines couldn't be defended against a determined Japanese attack. The only thing to do was hold out as long as possible. MacArthur was completely opposed to this idea. He believed the islands could and should be held. The loudly touted ability of the B-17 to shatter invasion fleets at long distance emboldened his conviction and gave him an ace to play in his debates with the War Department over strategy.[49]

In July 1941, after the government of Vichy France yielded French bases in Vietnam to the Japanese Navy, the United States ended oil sales to Japan. This raised tension in the Pacific almost palpably and MacArthur, who'd retired from the Army in 1937, was recalled to active duty. Roosevelt made him commander of a new entity, U.S. Army Forces in the Far East; best known by its acronym, USAFFE.

MacArthur had few doubts that the Japanese were preparing to attack the Philippines. He even thought he knew when the blow would fall—in April 1942. By his calculations, the Japanese couldn't be ready before then.[50]

Meanwhile Spaatz and the Air Staff were planning to get B-17s to the Philippines in such numbers they might act as a deterrent or, more likely, would ensure that any invasion would cost the Japanese dearly. They intended to have 163 B-17s in the Philippines by March 1942.[51]

In September 1941 Arnold made a down payment: 14th Bomb Squadron, with nine B-17Cs commanded by Emmett "Rosie" O'Donnell, set off from Hawaii for Clark Field, seventy miles north of Manila. It was followed a month later by a mass flight of twenty-six B-17s of 19th Bomb Group. These flights were supposedly secret, but the Japanese knew they were coming: for much of the way there was nothing on the radio but aural torture—plinkety! plink! samisen music—swamping every frequency that the AAF used.[52]

Other units were shipped by sea. A reinforcement convoy

brought the ground echelons and pilots of two pursuit squadrons and the 27th Bomb Group (Light) to Manila on November 20. Their planes, P-40s and A-24 dive-bombers (an AAF variant of the Navy's Douglas SBD), were in San Francisco.

That fall, Arnold ended the embarrassment of having Clagett represent the AAF at MacArthur's headquarters. Clagett had gone on a trip to China and spent most of it getting drunk with his aide, Lester Maitland. To him fell the unhappy distinction of being busted out of a star twice.[53]

Philippine and U.S. air units were organized under a new head-quarters, Far Eastern Air Force (FEAF). Its commander would be Major General Lewis Brereton, a bespectacled, cocky, articulate officer who'd begun his military career at Annapolis. Unable to overcome seasickness, Brereton had resigned from the Navy three days after graduation. He'd switched to the Army Signal Corps, learned to fly, served on Mitchell's staff in World War I and commanded 13th Aero Squadron in combat on the Western Front.

One of the AAF's most prominent officers, Brereton was commanding 3rd Air Force when he was ordered to the Philippines. One of his first actions was to seek extra base sites in Australia.

Arnold took a close personal interest in the reinforcement of the Philippines. The evening of December 6 he arrived at Hamilton Field, forty miles north of San Francisco. He bid farewell to the crews of two squadrons of B-17s about to set off on a flight staging through Hawaii to Clark. Their guns were still in cosmoline: no one expected to use them.[54]

As the big bombers lumbered into the air, however, Harold George was assembling most of his pursuit pilots in the movie theater at Nichols Field, the principal fighter base near Manila. He told his pilots, "Men, you are not a suicide squadron yet, but you are damned close to it. There will be war with Japan in a few days. It may come in a matter of hours."[55]

The commander of the Hawaiian Air Force, Major General Frederick L. Martin, was a worried man, and it showed. He was a famous flyer, having commanded the round-the-world flight in 1924. Martin had spent thousands of hours in the air since and the strain had left him with a chronic ulcer. He looked a decade older than his fifty-eight years.

When he took command of the Hawaiian Air Force in the fall of 1940, Martin's most pressing problem was getting hold of some modern aircraft. He'd inherited a force of P-26 fighters and B-18 bombers. Arnold did what he could to update Martin's command, sending him scores of P-40s and a dozen B-17s, but the need to reinforce the Philippines had priority. Luzon seemed an incomparably more likely target of a Japanese air attack than Hawaii.

Almost no one in the islands, including Martin, believed the Japanese could move so far without detection and strike a surprise blow. When his operations officer, Lieutenant Colonel Albert Hegenberger, told him in July 1941 that the Japanese could make a sneak attack with six carriers, he railed, "I will not have an officer on my staff who thinks like that!"[56] Hegenberger was fired and sent to command the 11th Bomb Group.

The subject of a Japanese attack was nevertheless discussed, studied, even practiced. About once a month, a Navy squadron or two would mount a sneak attack from one of the Pacific Fleet's carriers against the sleepy denizens of Wheeler Field around seven-thirty on a Sunday morning, coming over the field at low altitude and running up the prop pitch to make a goddawful din. Wheeler was the home of the 14th Pursuit Wing. P-40s would scramble off its runways to engage the Navy's Grumman F4Fs in mock dog-fights over Honolulu and thrilling nose-to-tail chases around the mountain peaks.[57]

This was good training for pilots, but it played no serious part in the preparations Martin and Lieutenant General Walter G. Short were making to defend Hawaii. They believed the threat to the islands came from within, not without; from sabotage, not enemy aircraft. The islands had a large Japanese population. As if to underline their fears, they only had to drive to Wheeler Field. One of Honolulu's busiest roads skirted the perimeter fence.

Short was a ground soldier with an impressive reputation as a trainer of troops. He loved manuevers and organized several in 1941. He also insisted on retraining half the personnel of the Hawaiian Air Force to fight as infantry. Maintenance suffered as a result, cutting into the already small number of operational aircraft.[58]

The belief that the Japanese couldn't pull off a sneak air attack was nourished daily, by decryptions of Japanese codes. The military codes hadn't been broken, but Japan's diplomatic communications were almost an open book. As the Japanese prepared to go to war, the United States knew it. On November 27 the War Department sent a message to Hawaii and the Philippines saying war might begin at any time.

In the Philippines, Brereton dispersed FEAF's aircraft, sending nearly half the thirty-five B-17s in his command from Clark down to Mindanao, four hundred miles to the south, and stepped up air patrols. MacArthur refused to let him send recon flights as far as Formosa, however, where Japanese air strength was being concentrated. In Panama, Andrews dispersed his planes and camouflaged them at a variety of auxiliary airstrips.[59]

The Hawaiian Air Force (HAF) had practiced two kinds of alert. One was known as the combat alert, in which some fighter squadrons were dispersed to outlying airstrips, while those remaining at Wheeler were placed in covered and camouflaged revetments, gassed up, fully armed, ready to fly, with pilots sleeping next to their planes. The other alert, "antisabotage," involved putting the planes together in front of the hangars, emptying them of fuel and removing their ammunition boxes. Armed guards then watched over the aircraft.[60]

When the war warning came from Washington, seven of the eight fighter squadrons of the HAF were on combat alert. Taking counsel of their fears, Short and Martin decided to switch over to antisabotage. Arnold seemed to endorse this action by sending a message on November 28 that addressed the danger of sabotage, with not a mention of any other kind of attack.[61]

Only at outlying Haleiwa airstrip, near the northwest shore of Oahu, was there a fighter squadron left ready to fly. The 47th Pursuit Squadron was engaged in gunnery training, against targets towed by obsolete B-10s. The squadron would take off around seven-thirty each morning and head out over the sea. When the squadron finished training on Saturday December 6 the 47th's commander, Captain Gordon H. Austin, asked his operations officer "Do you think we ought to fly on Sunday?"

As Austin later recalled, "We kind of wanted to fly but I figured the men had been working pretty hard and maybe they needed a day off. We could not decide [so] we got out a new fifty-cent piece and flipped it to see if we would fly on 7 December or not. It came down 'No, give the boys a day off.' We stood the squadron down."[62]

5

ZERO HOUR

On five Hawaiian peaks SCR-270 mobile radars mounted on truck bodies looked out to sea and probed the sky. They were linked to a drab, two-story building at Fort Shafter that housed the Aircraft Warning Service control center. On the ground floor, in the center of the building, plotters slid aircraft markers across a huge map of the islands and the surrounding Pacific. Looking down from a balcony above were the controllers, equipped with telephones, monitoring the flow of information from the radar sites.[1] There was no information from the Navy. It held aloof, disdainful of other people presuming to do anything over water.

The Aircraft Warning Service was run by the Signal Corps, not the Army Air Forces. Signal Corps personnel assigned to it were few in number and virtually untrained. The mobility of the radars was an advance, but in other respects they were outmoded. Although new, they couldn't give the height of incoming aircraft. Nor could they tell friend from foe.

Identification friend or foe (IFF) was a proven technology. The British had developed IFF and used it effectively in the Battle of Britain. RAF aircraft carried a transponder that was activated by British radar signals and sent back a pulse that showed up in radar stations as a green light. All other radar returns triggered red lights. The green lights were filtered out of the data that went to the plotting board: the only aircraft that appeared on it were enemy planes. RAF aircraft were then vectored by the ground controllers to intercept them.

The British had offered their IFF know-how as far back as August 1940, but the Signal Corps was too proud to take gifts from foreigners. Arnold and Lovett were helpless, but not speechless, in the face of Signal's obduracy. The mobile radar system it was so proud of was virtually useless in case of an attack.[2]

There would be three chief signal officers in as many years as Marshall struggled to whip the organization into a sense of urgency. Even so, the Signal Corps retained a choke-hold on the development of AAF radios and radar.

The most reliable of the five SCR-270 sets in Hawaii was the one located at Opana Point. At 0715 on Sunday, December 7, PFC Joseph L. Lockard picked up incoming aircraft on his radar screen.

He reported this to the Aircraft Warning Service, but there was no controller on duty. The only officer available was an AAF fighter pilot temporarily assigned to the AWS for "observation and training," who was on his second visit to the center. And without the British IFF device on the radar, all he could do was make a guess. He surmised that what Lockard had picked up was the B-17s that had set off from Hamilton Field the previous night. Or maybe they were from the two Navy carriers returning from delivering planes to reinforce Midway and Wake island. The Navy invariably sent its aircraft to Hawaiian airfields before the carriers docked. That way they could continue flying while the ships were tied up.[3]

The pip on Lockard's radar screen was growing rapidly. He'd picked up the first wave of Japanese aircraft (nearly 200 fighters and bombers) which had just taken off from carriers 150 miles northwest of Hawaii.

The principal targets were the Navy's big ships at Pearl Harbor, the Marine airfield at Ewa, and the two big AAF bases—Wheeler, home of the 14th Pursuit Wing, and Hickam, base of 18th Bombardment Wing and the Hawaiian Air Depot.

The Japanese opened their attack on the AAF by bombing the Hawaiian Air Depot at 0800. Then they switched their attention to the bombers, gathered in front of the hangars like the fighters over at Wheeler Field.

Hickam was a big new base, built in recent years and boasting six long runways that formed an isosceles triangle. It had huge, modern barracks, and as the bombs fell hundreds of men poured out in their pajamas or underwear. Some, crouching behind trees or sprawled flat on the ground, noticed amid the falling bombs, the exploding aircraft, the eruptions of flame and smoke from the blazing depot, that one Japanese pilot brought his plane down and landed, for a second or two, on runway 6. Then he took off from American soil.[4]

A few pursuit pilots were in the officers' club at Wheeler drinking cold beer, trying to shake off hangovers after a late-night poker party. When the Japanese roared over the field, they assumed it was the Navy again, pulling the old sneak-attack-on-a-Sunday-morning prank. Then came the sound of explosions.[5]

Most of the HAF's pursuit pilots found they were out of the battle before it began. They could only watch helplessly as Zeros flew low, wing guns winking red, strafing the rows of unfueled, disarmed fighters huddled on the concrete aprons in front of the hangars.

Only the 47th Squadron's P-40s at Hailewah were ready to fly and fight. Two of the 47th's pilots, second lieutenants George Welch (heir to the Welch grape-juice fortune) and Kenneth Taylor, were awakened as they slept at Wheeler Field's bachelor officers quarters by the scream of descending dive-bombers. Dressing on the run, they jumped into a jeep and burned up the eight miles of road to Hailewah. Around 0825 they took off from the airstrip: fifteen hundred feet of pierced steel planking, with a stretch of leveled earth in front.

Climbing and turning, they bored into Japanese aircraft making the final phase of the first wave attack. Over Wheeler Field, Welch plunged into an enemy formation and shot down two bombers. He couldn't help admiring the precision of the Japanese as they methodically attacked. There was a perfection to their formation flying he'd never seen American pilots match.[6]

The first wave of Japanese flew back out to sea, bombs and bullets gone, and returned to the six carriers steaming northwest of Oahu. There was a twenty-minute lull. Welch and Taylor landed to refuel and rearm. At Hickam, three B-17s and four A-20s were still in flyable condition. They were refueled and crews rounded up for them. At Wheeler, six obsolescent P-36s and several P-40s were refueled and rearmed amid falling bombs, choking smoke and exploding boxes of machine gun ammunition. Five pilots from the 45th Squadron, including a Polish-American lieutenant named Francis Gabreski, managed to get airborne.[7]

The twelve B-17s incoming from the mainland and running short of gas started putting down wherever they could. Some had been shot up in fleeting encounters with Zeros. Two came down on the

Hailewah strip. One landed on a golf course. The rest landed on pockmarked runways at various fields.

Just before 0900 the Japanese second wave—another 160 aircraft—began its attack. Wheeler and Hickam were pounded once more, but the heaviest blows were being struck at the Navy. By a great stroke of luck, though, none of the ships that really counted, the carriers, was in port. So the Japanese concentrated their bombs on battleship row. They ignored the huge oil tanks holding two million gallons of fuel oil, without which the Navy would have had to retreat to San Diego. Ignored, too, were the machine shops that eventually were able to save nearly all the sunk and damaged ships.

Welch and Taylor hurled themselves into the battle again. They were joined by four more planes of 47th Pursuit and the five planes that managed to get airborne from Wheeler. Welch splashed two more Japanese aircraft, including one on Taylor's tail.

The only real aerial opposition the Japanese faced came from the 15th Pursuit Group's pilots. Eleven managed to get into the air the morning of December 7, and flew a total of fourteen sorties. All told, they had ten confirmed kills. On the other hand, the bombing of Wheeler Field had killed twenty-three of the group's pilots.[8]

By 1000 the attack was over. The Japanese returned to their carriers and their commander, Admiral Chuichi Nagumo, rejected strong pleas from his pilots to make another attack next day. Instead, the Japanese fleet withdrew the way it had arrived, northwesterly.

Hickam still had its three intact B-17s. Bombed up, two of them took off to search for the Japanese fleet; the third plane careered of the runway. Three of the A-20s got airborne to join in. Martin ordered a search south of Oahu. When that drew a blank, he switched it to the northeast.[9]

At dusk, the bombers returned with tired crews and empty fuel tanks. Shortly after dark six Navy fighters from the carrier *Enterprise,* returning from Wake, approached Pearl Harbor. Jumpy AAA gunners shot five of them down. General Martin was meanwhile suffering a nervous collapse.[10] On this depressing note, the day of infamy drew to its bitter close.

One thing was certain: if war came, Japan would have to strike the first blow. That was national policy and common sense. Even those who, like Roosevelt, thought the United States should go to war wanted to fight Hitler, not Tojo.

MacArthur, the American commander closest to the enemy, took the policy farther than anyone else. He was bending over backward to avoid provoking the Japanese.[11]

From December 2, Japanese planes made reconnaissance flights over Luzon every night. FEAF paid no return visits: Brereton was ordered firmly by MacArthur not to send any U.S. plane more than two-thirds of the way to Formosa.*

Brereton's command numbered 316 planes, but his only modern combat aircraft were 35 B-17s and 90 P-40s. Nor would all of these fly. One P-40 in three was so new its engine still had to be broken in and its guns were still in Cosmoline. Even had they all been able to fly, a shortage of oxygen meant that most would be limited to about fifteen thousand feet—far below the Japanese bombers.

Brereton's B-17s were based at Clark. The field was wide open, lacked revetments, adequate drainage, and effective antiaircraft artillery. It was not a base that inspired confidence. The personnel dressed in beards and shorts. The entire facility had an easygoing air that clashed with the ethos of the newly arrived 19th Bomb Group, which considered itself a military elite. The men of the 19th had been virtually handpicked and specially trained. Operations at Clark did not impress them, at least, not favorably.[12]

Clark had no radar, a remarkable decision given the fact that the Philippines were always considered a more likely target than Hawaii. There was a Filipino-manned warning net, but it was short of training, telephones, and leadership.

The poor drainage meant that although Clark covered roughly fifty square miles, the heavy bombers couldn't be dispersed around it. They had to huddle together in the small area that didn't turn into a quagmire when it rained.

It was possible to disperse B-17s from Clark to the Del Monte plantation, on the southern island of Mindanao. But this airstrip had no servicing facilities; it was merely a scratch on a meadow between mountains that towered four thousand feet above it. The big bombers landed and took off over the sea at the end of the

---

*The Navy appears to have ignored this instruction. Its PBYs conducted reconnaissance flights over southern Formosa daily in the two weeks prior to December 7.

meadow. Coming into Del Monte in poor light or bad weather provided even experienced Fortress pilots with white-knuckle time.[13]

Del Monte probably had enough room to fit 35 B-17s, but 7th Bomb Group was expected to start arriving in the Philippines any day. So Brereton split up 19th Bomb Group, sending only two of its squadrons down to Del Monte and leaving room for the 7th. As for the two squadrons remaining at Clark, he could only spread them about a bit more, and hope.

News of the Pearl Harbor attack reached the Philippines in the early hours of December 8. The other shoe was surely about to fall. What was discussed and decided between MacArthur, his chief of staff, Major General Richard K. Sutherland, and Brereton, while they waited for its descent has never been settled. They probably talked of sending a reconnaissance mission to Formosa, then mounting an attack with the B-17s. But just who said what or did what is a mystery. No two accounts by those involved agree.[14]

Formosa was fogged over on the morning of December 8. When the fog cleared, it gave way to a south-moving intertropical front. Roughly 150 Japanese bombers and nearly 100 Zeros took off from Formosan airfields and hid in the weather all the way to Luzon. The clouds broke over the mountains. At 1240 fifty-four Japanese bombers appeared over Clark in two perfect V-formations. There wasn't an American fighter in the sky. Four P-40s were hurriedly scrambled, but stood no chance of reaching the bombers.

The Japanese devastated nearly every building Clark possessed. The communications center was destroyed in the first salvo. The Japanese bombed at their ease for thirty minutes, leaving dozens of fires raging and hundreds of people killed or injured. As the bombers droned back over the mountains, flights of Zeros flashed through the passes like shoals of ivory fish, strafing the field exultantly, dipping to ten feet, in a stunning display of flying skill and unleashed destructive power.

Nearly every B-17 was destroyed where it stood. The few that weren't were badly shot up. A choking column of black smoke rose from Clark, rooted in tongues of flame and intermittent detonations. Fortunately, during Lester Maitland's brief tenure as base commander he had ordered slit trenches dug. On December 8 these saved many lives.

The Japanese also bombed and strafed the main fighter base

outside Manila, Nichols Field. They did so much damage it had to be abandoned.[15] MacArthur's air power, the one threat the Japanese feared, had been eviscerated.

Next day a P-40 pilot, Lieutenant Grant Mahoney, flew a night recon mission that located a Japanese convoy heading for northeastern Luzon and the airstrips at Aparri and Vigan. FEAF organized an antishipping strike for the morning of December 10. Five B-17s from Del Monte, escorted by two fighter squadrons from the Manila area, attacked the convoy at dawn, put down at Clark hoping to get bombed up, but had to pull out in a hurry because of an air-raid warning.

After this attack the world was informed that a B-17 flown by Captain Colin Kelly had sunk a Japanese battleship, probably the *Haruna.* This cheering news thrilled the nation. In all likelihood, Kelly sank nothing. As for the *Haruna,* it was nowhere near the Philippines.[16]

On the afternoon of December 10 the Japanese made a major air attack, but this time the objective wasn't Clark; it was the four fighter fields still guarding Manila. They were left in a shambles. The Philippine Air Depot was wrecked. A dozen P-40s were shot down in furious dogfights over the city's rooftops.

On December 12 the Japanese landed three thousand men on the south coast of Luzon, at Legaspi. An air attack was launched against the invasion fleet two days later, with a force of five B-17s and two squadrons of fighters. Two B-17s were lost and no serious damage inflicted on the invaders.

After this disappointment the eleven remaining flyable Fortresses were flown out to Australia. Their new base would be desolate Batchelor Field, forty miles from Darwin. Batchelor was a bleak, depressing place in the middle of nowhere.[17]

On December 22 the main Japanese invasion fleet started putting forty-three thousand men ashore in Lingayen Gulf. Hours later nine of Batchelor's B-17s attacked Japanese ships off Davao, in the southern Philippines, then flew on to Del Monte. Next day four of them flew up to Luzon and struck at the invasion fleet in Lingayen Gulf.

Nearly twenty thousand American troops were in the Philippines in December 1941. Of these, some fifty-six hundred were Army Air Forces personnel. Life overseas had come as a shock to many of them. The lack of running water, revetments, hangars, gun emplacements, hard-surface runways, spare parts, clean quarters and the like bore almost no relation to the camps where they'd trained and worked back home.

Yet there was hope. Roosevelt and MacArthur assured them help was coming. The number of flyable planes fell sharply from day to day, but Brereton's airmen toiled eagerly to welcome the promised reinforcements. Dressed like Filipino laborers, wielding basic tools and relying on carabao carts, they carved out several fields, including a secret base north of Manila at Lubao.

This was a masterpiece of camouflage. Hacked out of a cane sugar plantation it was disguised as a . . . sugar plantation, half harvested, half being planted. Japanese aircraft flew over it every day and never spotted the Lubao airfield.[18]

Meanwhile, a small army of Filipino laborers, aided by AAF personnel, was carving out four new fighter strips and a five thousand-foot runway for B-17s on the peninsula of Bataan. The B-17 facility had hardstands and ample stocks of bombs and fuel. All it needed was aircraft.[19]

MacArthur's dream of crushing the invaders on the beaches or fighting them to a standstill on the central plain of Luzon simply fell apart. The Philippine Army had little of the training and equipment his plans had called for. Although they had the invaders outnumbered better than two to one, most Filipino troops were unable to stop even green Japanese infantry, who had at least learned the rudiments of soldiering and carried modern weapons. The Philippine Army, with its American officers, advisers and sole U.S. infantry regiment, was soon retreating toward Bataan, in two large formations.[20]

Bataan's rugged terrain made it a natural fortress. And just south of Bataan, in Manila Bay, was the tadpole-shaped island of Corregidor, where MacArthur had moved his headquarters, to a huge tunnel cut deep into the rock.

The American ground force commander on Luzon, Major General Jonathan Wainwright, fought a brilliant delaying action that allowed his two widely separated forces to slip into Bataan intact. Nothing, though, could save Manila. It was proclaimed an open city to spare it from the devastation of a battle.

On December 24 Brereton left for Australia and dumped everything onto Hal George. FEAF simply shut down, like a business that's gone belly up without any warning to its creditors.

While Brereton was being rowed out to a PBY on Laguna del Bay, twenty miles southeast of the city, thousands of Army Air

Forces personnel were streaming into Bataan. The flyable aircraft George inherited consisted of sixteen scarred, battle-worn P-40s hidden at Lubao, and four obsolescent little P-35s with worn out engines. He could also hope to receive four more P-40s from the Philippine Air Depot.

The depot had shifted most of its operations to Quezon City after the December 10 attack on Nielson Field. It continued to provide repair and maintenance services to the tactical units. Increasingly, though, the focus of its work became the large dance floor of the Santa Anna Cabaret. There, depot personnel were trying to conjure four new P-40s out of eight wrecks. When everybody else headed for Bataan, they refused to move. The aeronautical saga of welding and wiring at the Santa Anna continued.[21]

Over the next week four born-again P-40s were pushed out as they were completed, one at a time, onto broad throughfares skirting the cabaret. At first light, they'd roar down the street, take off and skim across Manila Bay to Bataan. The last P-40 took flight New Year's Day as the Japanese entered Manila from the south.

The retreat into Bataan, from which few could hope to escape, was one of the most somber episodes in American military history. In those dark days of December 1941, the only cheering news seemed to be provided by a handful of American pilots fighting against overwhelming odds. People knew who they were. These were individual fighting men with recognized names and faces: Colin Kelly, "Buzz" Wagner, Grant Mahoney, William E. Dyess, Jr. . . .

Nevertheless, without taking anything away from the resourceful and courageous airmen of FEAF, the picture that was given to the country wasn't the one that was given to Arnold. The painful truth was, the AAF had just started ascending the war's learning curve. Right now, it looked almost vertical.

According to Brereton's chief of staff, Colonel Francis M. Brady, the excellence of many pilots ended the moment they touched the ground. Out of the cockpit, they failed to measure up as officers. The desperate scene in the Philippines was one of frenzied effort that lacked direction. There was abundance of courage and a shortage of leadership. Some pilots assumed the moment they'd finished flying their work was done. Under the wretched circumstances prevailing in the Philippines, it had only just begun. Aircraft machine guns, for example, didn't get cleaned, because no one would accept responsibility for making sure they were taken care of. In this and other ways too many superb pilots failed as officers.[22]

By New Year's Day the airmen on Bataan were learning to fight like infantry, starve like infantry. Rations were cut in half, then cut again. Carabao were slaughtered and jaw-breaking efforts expended to consume the meat.* Yet even now hope was strong. MacArthur continued to claim reinforcements were coming. Until they arrived, Hal George's little Bataan Air Force intended to keep 'em flying.

Arnold was shooting quail in California with Donald Douglas when the Japanese attacked Pearl Harbor. Back in Washington, Lovett and senior AAF officers gathered in Spaatz's office, sitting on the floor with their backs to the wall, as they discussed what to do. Tactical units were rushed to the West Coast and planes loaded for shipment to Britain from East coast ports were reclaimed. Those already aboard ship were put back on the dock.[23]

The only combat-ready unit waiting to deploy overseas when war began was the 22nd Bomb Group, a new B-26 outfit at Langley. On the night of December 7 it received orders to go west. Next morning its planes took off crammed with tents, cooking equipment and emergency rations. The 22nd landed at Muroc Dry Lake and its crews lived in the desert. The B-26s flew antisubmarine patrols off southern California for three weeks, before being loaded aboard ship and sent to Hawaii.

In the first few weeks after Pearl Harbor the fear of air attacks gripped the West Coast. On the night of December 8 the Army reported thirty Japanese aircraft flying over San Francisco. Several nights later AAA batteries fired blindly for half an hour against phantom bombers over Los Angeles, as searchlights stirred the stygian sky with long white wands.

Someone in Washington ordered that all the West Coast aircraft plants be camouflaged. Armies of men, wielding four-inch paint brushes (the Painters Union banned spray guns) got to work. The camouflage campaign wasn't much appreciated by AAF pilots in

---

*There was a simple recipe for carabao stew: "Put a rock in a pot of water. Add your vegetables and a hunk of carabao. Bring to a roiling boil. When the rock melts, your carabao is ready."

the months that followed as they tried to land at a Douglas plant or a Lockheed facility whose runway had been made to look like a lumber yard or a suburban housing tract.[24]

The P-38s of 1st Pursuit Group were deployed from Langley, Virginia, to San Diego. The group's mission was to defend southern Californian air space against Japanese intruders. In the meantime, a P-39 squadron was ordered from Fort Wayne, Indiana, to Bellingham, Washington, to tackle any Japanese submarine attack on new warships leaving the shipyards. Just how a P-39 might be expected to fight a submarine was a mystery to the squadron commander.[25]

When 1942 arrived, anxiety subsided on the West Coast, only to grip the Eastern seaboard. Two days after Congress declared war on Japan, Hitler vented his contempt for American military prowess and expressed solidarity with the Japanese. He declared war on the United States.

Fortunately, Hitler had not yet built up a powerful U-boat force. Only a dozen boats were available to fight a campaign in the western Atlantic, and it took a month to get them into position from Cape Cod to the Caribbean.

While they were making the transit, the Navy and the AAF were getting jumpy about the Vichy French fleet, which included the aircraft carrier *Béarn*. Suppose Pétain's sailors made a sudden, secret descent on New York? They might shell the Brooklyn Navy Yard and do to Mitchel Field what the Japanese had done to Wheeler and Hickam. The 20th Bomb Squadron, equipped with new B-25s, was ordered to Mitchel Field immediately to patrol the sea lanes off Long Island.[26]

Even after the alarm over the Vichy Fleet passed, the 20th scoured the wintry Atlantic from dawn to dusk looking for U-boats. The East Coast provided German submariners with rich pickings. In January 1942 an average of one merchant ship a day was sunk in American waters. In February the figure rose to nearly two a day.

The war against the U-boats was run by the Navy's Eastern Sea Frontier headquarters in New York. No one, not even the Navy's warmest admirers, ever claimed it was run well in 1942.[27] The Navy had not developed a strong coastal patrol arm. The ESF had 103 aircraft available for antisubmarine warfare; most were trainers or transports. Admiral Ernest J. King, the chief of naval operations, demanded hundreds of B-24s under construction for the AAF be assigned to the Navy so it could carry long range antisubmarine patrols deep into the Atlantic. Arnold resisted this demand and committed I Bomber Command of First Air Force to shoulder the burden. The bomber command began searching with an initial commitmment of 9 B-17s, 6 B-18s and 31 B-25s.

Admiral King was unwilling to admit the Navy's unreadiness to cope with the U-boat threat. When civilians offered to help by operating patrols of light aircraft over coastal waters and under military direction, Spaatz endorsed the idea. King rejected it. In March 1942, however, the situation grew serious enough to make King relent.

By May, sinkings were exceeding new construction. The Battle of the Atlantic hung in the balance. The AAF was drawn increasingly into the U-boat war. Its ability to build up effective bomber forces in Europe and the Pacific was compromised, even though the bulk of its contribution to the antisubmarine campaign was being borne by obsolescent B-18s. Nearly every operational B-18 in the United States was flown to Savannah, Georgia, to join the search. The B-18 wasn't much of a bomber, cruising at a sedate 130 miles per hour, but it did have a big fuel tank. It could stay aloft for as long as seventeen hours.[28]

Even so, it was an effort that went largely unnoticed. Week by week, almost day by day, people along the East Coast grew impatient with the Army Air Forces. Few saw I Bomber Command's planes flying out to sea at first light or returning at dusk. Instead, what they noticed was AAF planes flying overhead in broad daylight while ten miles offshore ships were being blown up by enemy submarines. From some coastal towns as many as four tankers could be seen blazing at night. And pilots flying U-boat patrols over the Gulf stared in disbelief at the coastline of Florida: the sunshine state was bordered black with oil.[29]

The chances of an aircraft spotting a U-boat were remote. The planes could fly only in daylight, when the U-boats were submerged. They surfaced usually at night to recharge their batteries and give the crew some fresh air.[30]

What was needed was a radar small enough to fit into an airplane and generating a short radar wave that would give a good return from something as small as a submarine periscope. The British had been working on the problem since 1939 and in 1941 developed a small but abundant power source for radar, called the cavity magnetron, around which an airborne set might be built. The British asked the United States to perfect and produce cavity magnetrons for sub-hunting radar. The Navy, however, dismissed the whole idea of hunting submarines with radar and the project made haste slowly.[31]

Not until the spring of 1942 did these efforts pay off in the production of a reliable airborne radar that generated a ten-centimeter radar wave; an electronic scalpel compared to the one-and-a-half meter radar that preceded it.

RAF Coastal Command's Wellington bombers started taking a heavy toll on the Germans in the Bay of Biscay, swooping down through the clouds at night on a radar sighting and switching on a dazzling searchlight that blinded astonished *Unterseeboot* crews relaxing on deck. Riding the light came a hail of explosives.

In April, and again in May, B-18s made radar-assisted attacks on U-boats off the East Coast. On July 7, off Cape Hatteras, a B-18 scored the AAF's first confirmed radar kill of the war.[32] The Navy was simultaneously putting pressure on enemy submarines by organizing coastal convoys that were so well shepherded by destroyers and aircraft they were suicide targets for any lone submarine to attack.

The pressure on the U-boats forced them to pull back into the mid-Atlantic. Yet the curve of Allied shipping losses continued to rise. Long-range replenishment submarines, or "milch cows," brought the U-boats more fuel, more torpedoes, fresh rations, allowing them to remain on patrol for months. They began operating in wolf packs of as many as twenty boats, able to tear even the biggest convoy to pieces with well-coordinated attacks.

A crooked shadow had fallen across the Victory Program and the strategy of Germany First: if the U-boats controlled the sea lanes, how was an army of five million men to be shipped across for the liberation of Europe? Industrialist Henry J. Kaiser and aviation pioneer Howard Hughes proposed to build fleets of enormous wooden flying boats to carry the troops across, but neither Arnold nor the Air Staff believed for a moment that planes carrying as many as three hundred troops were practical. Hughes beavered on, just to prove them wrong, and gave wing to an icon that flew only once, the *Spruce Goose*, leaving a legend behind it.[33]

6

BOMBING RANGE

To the true believer, the heavy bomber was the ultimate arm of twentieth-century conflict. It was the only weapon with the potential to win a war on its own. There was no denying its versatility. It reached its apogee when used offensively, yet it could be employed defensively, to destroy hostile fleets threatening the United States. It was so dominant in the skies it didn't need protection. With its speed it could outrun most of its pursuers. With its guns it would shoot down the rest.[1]

The heavy bomber would reshape the theory and practice of war. Karl von Clausewitz had taught that to defeat an enemy you must bring his forces to battle, amass overwhelming strength at the crucial point, then destroy them. After which you could impose your will on the enemy. The theory of strategic bombing did away with all that. You didn't have to fight your enemy's ground troops or sink his fleet. You didn't even have to destroy his air force. You went straight for the jugular and bombed his industrial economy to bits, shattering his ability to wage war. As Ken Walker had taught it at Maxwell, "A well-organized, well-planned, and well-flown air force attack will constitute an offensive that cannot be stopped."

The vast majority of military flyers wanted to be fighter pilots. Bombers were a staid second best. Yet, as strategic bombing theory evolved, some able and ambitious officers who were in fighters, such as Tooey Spaatz and Laurence Kuter, moved over to bombers. Others, such as Lauris Norstad and Ira Eaker, found themselves transferred out of fighter cockpits and into bombers by senior officers who believed that talent belongs to the future.[2]

The fight for the heavy bomber also had a romantic side. It became a cause to officers like Hugh Knerr. The fierce resistance of the General Staff made it seem like a struggle between the short-sighted middle-aged on one side and visionary thirtysomethings on the other.

The only rival to the heavy bomber was a guided missile, a revised version of Charles Kettering's World War I "bug," which Arnold had taken to France in October 1918. In 1940 Kettering got development money from the Air Corps and encouragement from his old General Motors colleague, William Knudsen, to produce an updated bug. After eighteen months of unremitting effort, he had a missile that was accurate to within one hundred yards and carried a five hundred-pound warhead.

Tens thousand bugs could do as much damage as a whole fleet of B-17s, while sparing the lives and limbs of countless airmen. Arnold was tempted by Kettering's missiles, but they had one ir-reedemable flaw: short range. They flew two hundred miles. Launched from southern and eastern England, they could strike the Benelux countries and France north of the Loire, but most of Germany would be out of reach. In December 1941 Arnold, Kettering, and Knudsen agreed to drop the bug. Bombers it would have to be. The visionaries would get their chance.[3]

The lowest rung on the bombing ladder was attack, and the men who flew attack in the 1930s simply loved it. They weren't allowed to do dangerous flying: they were expected to do it. The 3rd Attack Group, under the command of Lieutenant Colonel Horace Hickam, may have had the highest ésprit de corps of any unit in the Air Corps.

Attack pilots reveled in being the lowest of the low. One of the 3rd's pilots, Archie J. Old, went home to north Texas one weekend in the early 1930s, buzzed the town and made the horses rear. A citizen complained and the group adjutant, First Lieutenant Nathan Twining, held an inquiry.

Old admitted that most of what the complainant said was true and confessed to having done some acrobatics too. Asked how high he was flying during these acrobatics, he said around two hundred feet. Twining sprang to his feet and banged his fist on the desk.

"Goddamit, Archie, if I ever hear of you being up at two hundred feet again, I'm going to court-martial you!"[4]

Attack pilots routinely flew at seventy-five feet. They had to climb to land. A new pilot joining 3rd Attack would be asked to show his low-altitude skills. He'd skim the trees, land with twigs in his undercarriage and be mocked. "You call *that* low?" The newcomer wouldn't be accepted until he'd flown under some power lines.

Hickam delighted in their daring. One young pilot cracked up an airplane and gave a statement to the investigation board that offered no excuses: "As I was making a climbing right turn, my wingtip struck a telephone pole." Hickam was as tickled as a proud parent. He told the story throughout the Air Corps.[5]

The group experimented with low-altitude formation attacks, using pistol-target silhouettes to represent ground troops. Its pilots worked out low-level bombing tactics using twenty-five-pound bombs that filled the air with small metal fragments and peppered the tails of the their own aircraft. Time fuses helped solve that problem, but bigger bombs provided a different challenge: they tended to bury themselves in the dirt. George Kenney solved that by giving each one a small parachute, which slowed the descent, prevented premature burial and gave the attacking aircraft time to fly out of harm's way. During a trial run at Langley in 1932, however, a bomb whose parachute failed took the tail off a plane Kenney was flying, nearly killing him.[6]

He survived to teach low-level attack at Maxwell, but in 1935 he left to serve under Andrews at GHQ Air Force. In 1936 Hickam was killed trying to land a Northrop A-17, the newest attack plane. Two years later Westover also perished in an A-17.

By this time the intellectual tide was flowing strongly in the direction of the heavy bomber. Moreover, attack was considered by many Air Corps officers to be no more than a fancy name for ground support, a mission that tied the beautiful airplane to the ugly infantry. The skills and spirit of the 3rd Attack Group seemed doomed to fade away, like those of the horse cavalry.

Nevertheless, some designers believed the attack airplane would have a future if it went to two engines. Douglas proposed to build an attack aircraft around two of the new Pratt & Whitney R-1830 engines, rated at eleven-hundred horsepower. It would have a three-man crew: a pilot, a navigator-bombardier in the nose and an aerial gunner manning a twin thirty-caliber machine gun mount midway between cockpit and tail. The prototype, designated the Douglas 7B, made its maiden flight in October 1938.[7]

This was a plane the French *Armée de l'Air* was eager to buy. The scandal over the crash in January 1939 with *Capitaine* Chemidlin aboard soon died down, and the French placed orders for 380 examples of an improved version, known as the DB-7.

Until July 1939 this aircraft was a private venture undertaken by Douglas. The Air Corps hadn't spent a dime on it or shown much interest in it. It was only the French contract that made it possible to move into production. In July the Air Corps relented, and placed an order for sixty-three planes, which were given the designation A-20. These planes would be equipped with Wright Cyclone engines rated at 1,600 horsepower. They would fly at 390 miles per hour, the speed of a fighter. The Havoc, as it was known, was a hot plane, yet astonishingly easy to fly.[8] However, subsequent models of the A-20 involved extensive design changes, increased weight and lower speeds.

The plane made its combat debut, in the DB-7 configuration, with the French. About seventy sorties were flown against the Germans before France capitulated. Most of the DB-7 order was collected by the RAF. British pilots restrained their excitement at flying planes whose instruments were in metric and whose manuals were in French.

Arnold and the Air Staff remained skeptical of the need for the A-20. The RAF, too, had its doubts, even though it had contracted to buy 150. Arnold was told in April 1941 that the RAF couldn't see a place for light bombers. "Nothing that the LB can do that a Medium or Heavy cannot do better," he reported in his diary.[9]

The best role the Air Staff could see for the A-20 was as a reconnaissance aircraft for the ground forces. The AAF had inherited the long-standing Army requirement for observation squadrons that would be under ground-force control. A split developed, however, between what ground commanders wanted to have and what air generals wanted to provide. Armor and artillery were demanding light planes, "puddle jumpers," to regulate artillery fire and provide column control. Arnold and General Leslie McNair were both convinced that small, light planes wouldn't survive above the battlefield; only fast, armed and armored planes would do.[10] Some of the early A-20s were converted to see how well the plane might fill the reconnaissance mission.

Thinking light bombardment might satisfy the ground force's insistence on close air support—that is, on attack—the Air Corps ordered two thousand A-20s in 1941. Like their predecessors, these were glass-nosed models designed to drop a twenty-six-hundred-pound bomb load from altitudes of five thousand to ten thousand feet. While not attack, this was level bombing, as opposed to dive bombing, which air generals like Spaatz considered would prove fatal if attempted against German flak.[11]

In 1942 the A-20 was pushed into the hunt for U-boats. Armed with fifty-pound bombs, Havoc squadrons patrolled one hundred miles off the East Coast, where they handed over to the B-18s and B-25s.[12] The Soviets meanwhile had fallen in love with the plane. Given a batch under Lend-Lease, they clamored for thousands more. Using it in an attack mode, they'd found it highly effective against German armor.

Reluctantly following suit, the AAF ordered 2,850 examples of a new, ground-attack version, the A-20G. This aircraft had a metal nose that bristled with four twenty-millimeter cannon and two fifty-caliber machine guns. It also had armor plate protecting the crew and wing racks for small bombs.

When the RAF took delivery in 1941 of the 150 A-20s it had ordered a year earlier it tried, but failed, to employ some of them as night-fighters.[13] It had more success using them to make high-speed, low level raids on targets in France and the Low Countries. In May 1942 the Army Air Forces dipped a toe into the European air war by sending the 15th Bomb Squadron to train with an RAF A-20 unit.

On July 4 six U.S. crews and six RAF crews flew a mission against four airfields in Holland. They ran straight into a wall of low-altitude flak. Two of the six American-crewed Havocs were lost. A third was downed but bounced back into the air, suppressed the flak tower that had just shot out one of its engines, and flew back to England on the other. The British lost one plane. Only two of the American crews dropped their bombs on target.[14]

By this time, 3rd Attack Group no longer existed. The AAF had dropped "Attack" from its vocabulary, replacing it with "Light Bombardment." And in a concession to the Army's infatuation with the Stuka the AAF had equipped the 3rd with Navy SBD-4 Dauntless dive-bombers (given a new designation, the A-24, and deprived of their carrier-landing gear). The unit found itself in the

South Pacific in 1942 as the 3rd Light Bombardment (Dive) Group, its proud name and traditions only a memory.[15]

North American Aviation was founded in 1928 by an editor on *The Wall Street Journal*. It was a holding company, specializing in aviation stocks and shares. In 1934 it became an aircraft manufacturer and its ambition was to make nothing but planes for the Air Corps.[16]

NAA's president, James "Dutch" Kindleberger, had qualified as a junior military aviator shortly before the Armistice, then left the Air Service to work for aviation pioneer Glenn Martin. He'd moved on to become chief engineer at Douglas, where he was a major figure in development of the DC-2 which, given a bombardier's "greenhouse" and a nose gun turret, was turned into the B-18. Bomber pilots despised the B-18, but Douglas had a follow-on model, the B-23—and competition: NAA offered the XB-21 "Dragon." Neither plane was much of an advance on the mediocre B-18, but had it not been for the Munich crisis and the sudden salvation of the B-17 one of them would probably have been adopted and put into mass production.

With the Dragon slain, Kindleberger and his chief designer, J. Leland Atwood, turned their thoughts to a light bomber that would compete with Douglas's DB-7. They produced a design that offered crisp, clean lines, shoulder wings and tricycle landing gear. The day of the tail-dragger was coming to an end. Tricycle gear, which put a wheel directly under an airplane's nose, brought a revolution in visibility and ground handling. European manufacturers looked on tricycle landing gear as another American gimmick, but it was going to enable wartime pilots, trained to a lower standard than their prewar predecessors, to handle the new generation of fast, powerful warplanes.[17]

North American's light bomber, designated the NA-40-1, looked deadly, yet was beautiful with it: wing span sixty-six feet, length forty-eight feet three inches, powered by a pair of Pratt & Whitney R-1830 engines rated at 1,100 horsepower. To get even more speed, these were soon replaced by Wright Cyclones, rated at 1,350 horsepower. The fuselage was slender and graceful and the engines were housed in streamlined nacelles. The plane had twin tails that rose directly in the prop wash. With a top speed of 285 miles per hour and a crew of three, the NA-40-2 would carry twelve hundred pounds of bombs. In March 1939 the plane was flown to Wright

Field, to compete against the DB-7. Two weeks later it was destroyed in a crash. The Air Corps bought the A-20 instead.[18]

The Air Corps was interested, however, in acquiring a fast medium bomber and the Matériel Division's engineers had liked the look of the North American plane. Maybe it could be developed further? Attwood did a redesign, giving it a new number, the NA-62. He widened the fuselage so the bomb load would be doubled and the copilot would sit side-by-side with the pilot. The crew rose from three to five. An extra fifty-caliber gun was added, in the tail. The wing was brought down from the shoulder to mid-fuselage and two Wright Cyclones rated at seventeen hundred horsepower would be installed.

It was a hot design, but it came second to a real scorcher from Martin, the Model 179. Only because production capacity at Martin's Baltimore plant limited its ability to produce the 179 in large numbers did North American get a a contract for medium bombers. In September 1939 NAA agreed to produce 184 NA-62s.[19]

When the first plane was rolled out, in August 1940, it had acquired a new designation, the B-25, and a name, the Mitchell, in honor of Billy Mitchell. He'd died in semi-obscurity in 1937 but his reputation was now going straight up. In 1942 Congress voted him a posthumous Congressional Gold Medal.

The B-25 proved to have stability problems, which were cured by giving it a gull-wing. In 1941 the AAF ordered sixteen hundred B-25Cs. That summer the first Mitchell unit, 17th Bomb Group, became operational, at McChord Field, Washington. On December 24 one of 17th Group's B-25s claimed the AAF's first submarine kill of the war, against a Japanese boat off Puget Sound.

In April 1942 a force of sixteen B-25s commanded by Jimmy Doolittle scored a stunning coup by taking off from the carrier *Enterprise* and bombing Tokyo (see Chapter 10). Doolittle's crews were drawn from 17th Bomb Group.

In 1942 the AAF placed another big order, purchasing twenty-three hundred B-25Ds. Throughout that year there was a steady trickle of B-25 squadrons to the South Pacific. They were modified in the field until the nose of a Mitchell sprouted up to eight fifty-caliber machine guns.[20]

As with all combat aircraft, there was always a tendency to make the plane heavier. There'd be factory additions— self-sealing tanks, extra guns, more armor, powered gun turrets—from one model to the next. The B-25D came with external wing racks that doubled its bomb load to 5,200 pounds. And in the fall of 1942 the Air Corps bought 405 examples of a version designed for ground attack, the B-25G—it would carry a seventy-five-millimeter gun in its nose. This really was flying artillery.[21]

The Model 179 was a breakthrough in aircraft design. Martin had a long record of success with combat aircraft. His MB-2 bombers were used by Mitchell's First Air Brigade to sink the *Ostfriesland* and other German warships. He'd also provided the Navy with its first successful torpedo bombers. His B-10 bombers had created a stir when they appeared in the early 1930s.

When the Air Corps announced a design competition for a fast medium bomber capable of three hundred miles per hour, Martin's able design team came up with a barn-burner of a plane. They proposed to build a sleek craft with small wings and two huge engines. Martin's design promised not only high speed but a big bomb load. It easily outscored the competition. North American's design for what became the B-25 came second, but it wasn't a close second.

However, the Air Corps wanted 385 fast medium bombers. Martin's Baltimore plant was already busy turning out planes for the French. He could produce only 201 medium bombers for the Air Corps. That was why NAA got a contract for 184 B-25s, despite losing the design competition.[22]

The Martin B-26 was one of the most modern planes of its era. It was loaded with electrical systems. It incorporated plastics and its rounded fuselage was formed mainly of large cast aluminum panels held in place by a modest number of rivets, unlike the B-25 which contained thousands of small plates held in place by tens of thousands of rivets. This added to the smoothness of the B-26's skin, which was refined even further with a special "baking" treatment that removed wrinkles. Here was the Rolls-Royce of combat airplanes. To make a B-26 involved nearly forty thousand man-hours. You could build a B-17 and a P-40 in the same amount of time.[23]

With two Pratt & Whitney R-2800 engines rated at 1,850 horsepower, huge three-bladed propellers that nearly touched the ground, and a sleek cigar shape, the B-26 could reach 315 miles per hour. Its sixty-five-foot wing span, however, made it a handful to land. With a stalling speed around ninety miles per hour it had to be landed at around 105 miles per hour—the same as a modern jet fighter.[24]

If it came in like a jet, the B-26 took off like a heavily loaded World War II heavy bomber. The small wings meant a pilot needed a twenty-five-hundred-foot takeoff run to get airborne. The completely circular fuselage provided a huge bomb bay, able to carry 5,600 pounds of bombs, and a large fuel supply. Although half the weight of a B-17, the B-26 had nearly as much range and bomb carrying capacity.[25]

The first B-26 flew in November 1940, and reached 323 miles per hour. Three months later the first B-26 unit, 22nd Bomb Group, at Langley, started taking deliveries and a further 139 planes were ordered.

There were problems from the first. The plane was plowing into the ground on landing. Among the dead pilots was the Air Corps representative at the Martin plant, Lieutenant Colonel Elmer D. Perrin. Air Corps pilots would go to Baltimore, learn to fly the plane, then take off for Langley. At the plant, though, one thousand pounds of lead weights and engineering tools had been placed in the tail to simulate the tail gun turret the plane would eventually receive. Before the plane left for Langley, the weights and tools were removed, making the plane nose heavy. No one thought to tell the pilots the plane's center of gravity had been altered. Landing, they flew it into the ground.[26]

Even after this problem was solved, there were others. MacDill Field, in Florida, opened the first transition training school for the B-26. The propellers got so much power from the huge engines they tended to overspeed on takeoff. When that happened, the pitch of the propellers altered, but if it happened on only one engine, the effect was to spin the airplane around and throw it into the ground, or the water offshore.[27] "One a day in Tampa Bay" became famous throughout the AAF. The real figure was more like one a week, but the whole B-26 program was placed in doubt.

Called "The Marauder" by Martin's publicity department, it was called "The Murderer" by frightened pilots. There were instructors as well as students who refused to fly it. Arnold didn't know what to do with it. He asked Doolittle to fly it and tell him what he thought. Doolittle thought it was a great plane.[28]

Arnold also got the country's leading aviatrix, the glamorous and fearless Jacqueline Cochrane, to fly it. She too thought it a terrific airplane, and called those who were afraid of it "sissies."[29]

A special board chaired by Spaatz decided the Air Corps should stick with the plane, provided an extra six feet was added to the wingspan. By the end of 1941 a further thirty-one hundred B-26s had been ordered. Most would have the longer wings; they'd also be fitted with two thousand horsepower Pratt & Whitney Wasps.

To underline how safe the plane was, Cochran's Women's Air Service Pilots delivered B-26s to various flying fields throughout the United States, making the jaws of male pilots who'd heard the plane was impossible to fly fall open.[30]

Even so, a cloud hung over the Marauder. It was simply too hot for the average pilot fresh from advanced training, where he wouldn't have flown anything more demanding than an AT-6 Texan trainer. It was also a hard plane to maintain. The engineers at Wright Field continued to have doubts about it.

The B-26 nevertheless went to war. In April 1942 the 22nd Bomb Group started operations in New Guinea, flying against the Japanese from rivet-popping dirt strips in the jungle. The airplane, the 22nd's pilots reported back, was not just a brilliant flying machine—it was a superb weapon.

In October 1942 the Air Corps had yet another committee trying to decide whether to cancel Marauder production and put the entire medium burden on the B-25. Thanks to the enthusiasm of B-26 pilots in the Pacific and their dedicated ground crews, the Marauder would stay in the war.[31]

Following the October 1935 crash of Boeing's Model 299A at Wright Field, the Air Corps was allowed to make a purchase of thirteen service test models, called Y1B-17s. These came with more powerful engines, four Wright Cyclones rated at 930 horsepower. One was sent to Wright Field for static tests; the remaining twelve went to 2nd Bomb Group at Langley, where each was treated as if it were made of pure gold, with platinum seats and diamond-encrusted instruments.

Prudence paid. The 2nd Bomb Group didn't lose a plane, or even suffer a serious mishap, despite numerous long range flights, including trips to South America, where maintenance wasn't easy. Early Fortress pilots were drawn from the cream of the Air Corps. They were expected to be able to do it all—fly, navigate it, use the bombsight, handle the guns, operate the radios, and fix the engines if they had to. A pilot needed a minimum of two thousand flying hours before he was allowed to take one up.[32]

The Y1B-17 was a great success, but the War Department would allow only one additional purchase, for an extra test model, the Y1B-17A, which would have more powerful engines, Wright Cyclones rated at one thousand horsepower, and was used for developing turbosuperchargers that would take the big bomber up to thirty thousand feet.[33]

Despite the breakthrough in performance that the B-17 represented, the General Staff's opposition to heavy bombers seemed to have brought the program to a close in August 1938. The Munich crisis rescued it. The Air Corps was allowed to order thirty-nine examples of a fully developed operational version, the B-17B, but it would be more than a year before any more purchases were made, despite the outbreak of war in Europe.

In early 1940 thirty-eight B-17Cs were ordered. These would mount Wright Cyclones rated at 1,200 horsepower, giving a top speed of 323 miles per hour. Major General George Brett, commanding at Wright Field but no procurement expert, objected to the contract. With support from the isolationist secretary of war, Harry H. Woodring, he demanded that the cost be reduced from the $205,000 per airplane agreed with Boeing, to $198,000. The amount of money involved, $266,000, was small change in a procurement budget of $180 million. Still, Brett was prepared to jeopardize the entire Model 299 program to get his way. Boeing was barely breaking even on the plane. The Air Corps was demanding that it take a loss. Boeing decided to drop the program rather than risk bankruptcy.[34]

At the last minute, Spaatz proposed a solution: reduce the amount of standard equipment, such as the external bomb racks, on the next order. This brought the price down about $3000, while reducing the plane's effectiveness as a weapon. Still, it was a compromise Boeing and the Air Corps could live with. The company was rewarded with a contract for forty-two B-17Ds.

Following Roosevelt's call in May 1940 for fifty thousand planes, Brett's interest in penny-pinching was overtaken by events. Congress voted billions for aircraft. The B-17D got more equipment than any previous Fortress, including self-sealing fuel tanks, and an extra gunner, bringing the size of the crew to ten men.

In 1941, responding to British demands for some heavy bombers, Arnold let the RAF have twenty B-17Cs. These were really training aircraft. They had a combat radius of only seven hundred miles when carrying a modest bomb load of twenty-four hundred pounds. Their biggest drawback though was lack of armament (five thirty-caliber machine guns) and no protection against head-on attacks or attacks directly from the rear.

The RAF gave them green crews and proceeded to use the planes, in twos and threes, against well-defended German targets. The B-17Cs were savagely mauled by the Luftwaffe.[35] The B-17Cs and Ds operating in the Pacific in the first few months after Pearl Harbor were similarly vulnerable from the front and rear. They too were used in small numbers. They too got mauled.

The British dismissed the plane as "the Flying Target." American belief in daylight precision bombing provoked as much scorn as if Arnold had declared he'd joined the Flat Earth Society. In vain did he try to tell the British they'd misused his bombers.

It was clear that some improvements were needed to turn the Fortress into a truly effective weapon. A huge, sweeping dorsal fin was designed, to give greater stability at high altitude. Extra fuel capacity extended the combat radius to one thousand miles, with a bomb load of eight thousand pounds. The biggest advance was in armament. The number of guns was increased to fourteen; thirteen were fifty-caliber. There was a tail turret and a machine gun in the nose.

In September 1941 the AAF started taking delivery of the 512 B-17Es it had on order. After Pearl Harbor it was obvious that many more Fortresses would be needed, far more than Boeing could produce on its own. Oliver Echols's solution was to force other manufacturers to make some. Lockheed's Vega division, which built light bombers for the British, was ordered to participate; so was Douglas. A secret body known as the BVD Committee drew up plans to pool information and standardize production methods.* In 1942 orders were placed for twelve thousand Fortresses, in a number of variants.

In July 1942 the first B-17Es arrived in England, assigned to the 97th Bombardment Group. On August 17 the group opened the AAF's strategic bombing campaign when twelve of its planes made a daylight raid on the marshaling yards of Rouen. The target was hit, no planes were lost. German fighters, however, seemed to be

---

*When the committee's existence became known, it received a threat of legal action for breach of copyright from the underwear manufacturer BVD.[37]

hanging back, sizing up the new combatant in the air war over Europe.[36]

David R. Davis had been involved in aviation from the time he financed Donald Douglas's first airplane, but in 1938 he was virtually broke. His one hope was to sell an idea for a new kind of wing, an airfoil whose cross-section would be shaped like a falling teardrop. Davis was convinced it would provide more lift than anything in existence. He managed to persuade Reuben Fleet, president of Consolidated Aircraft, to pay for a model and get Cal Tech's professors to try it out in their wind tunnel. The professors tested the model three times simply because they couldn't believe the result: 102 percent efficiency.[38]

There was probably something wrong with the wind tunnel, but Fleet was so impressed he built a new flying boat, the Model 31, around Davis's wing, which was unusually long and narrow. The Model 31 was the projected successor to the Catalina flying boats that Consolidated was building for the Navy.

In January 1939, as the Model 31 neared completion, Arnold asked Consolidated to design a heavy bomber that would outperform the B-17, especially in range, bomb load and ceiling: three thousand miles with a twenty-five-hundred-pound bomb load and an altitude of thirty-five thousand feet. Fleet, a World War I Air Service pilot, decided to use the data already developed from the Davis wing to make a submission. Consolidated's design would be based on the 110-foot Davis wing, a twin tail and four Pratt & Whitney Twin Wasps, generating 1,200 horsepower.

Consolidated was given a contract in March to produce a prototype, the XB-24, before the end of the year. On December 29, 1939, the XB-24 made its maiden flight. It was a plane loaded with innovations, including a "wet wing." All bombers carried fuel in their wings, but in heavy, self-sealing tanks that took up a lot of space. In the B-24 the long tapering Davis wing was liberally coated on the inside with Duprene sealer and pumped full of fuel, saving the space and weight of self-sealing tanks.[39] These savings gave the B-24 greater range and a bigger bomb load than the B-17.

Fleet was proud of his aircraft, but he was troubled aesthetically. The big, slab-sided plane had an ugly snub nose. He decided to add an extra three feet, just to make it look prettier.[40]

Seven service test aircraft, the YB-24/B-24A were ordered while the prototype was still under construction, such was the Air Corps's eagerness to get a heavy bomber with longer range into production. The B-17 was a six-year-old design in 1940; the B-24 offered to bring a more modern weapon into the armory. In 1940 the Air Corps placed orders for 2,434 Liberators; most would be B-24Ds, for delivery in 1942.

To boost output of the Pratt & Whitney 1830 engine that powered the B-24, Colonel Clarence Irvine of the Matériel Command got a race going. The two most competitive divisions of General Motors were Chevrolet and Buick. Irvine signed up both divisions to produce RB-1830s. The Chevrolet-Buick rivalry generated a huge output of engines, at dramatically reduced prices.[41]

The British and French, too, wanted the new plane. They placed sizable orders, but France fell before any of these aircraft were built. The British, however, started taking delivery of their aircraft, along with those originally ordered by the French, in early 1941. They also received six of the seven service test aircraft. They liked the B-24 from the first, but insisted the Duprene sealer be replaced by self-sealing fuel tanks. These added an additional three thousand pounds to the Liberator's weight, reducing its range, but making it more combat worthy.

In the fall of 1941 two specially equipped Liberators were being fitted out for spy flights over Japanese positions in the Pacific. Pearl Harbor was attacked before they could fly even one mission. One of these aircraft was destroyed on the ground at Hickam on December 7.[42]

The Liberator II also appeared that fall, under contract to the British. It incorporated the extra three feet Fleet wanted on the nose. It was also equipped with two British-manufactured, power-operated gun turrets. In all, the plane was armed with fourteen .303 machine guns. Following the attack on Pearl Harbor, the seventy-five Liberator IIs awaiting delivery to the British were requisitioned by the AAF. Fifteen were sent to Australia in January 1942 to reequip 19th Bomb Group, which had fallen back from the Philippines and was down to a handful of battered B-17s.

Others were deployed to Java, to reinforce 7th Bomb Group, which was also taking a beating. The spring of 1942 saw Liberators attacking enemy shipping as the AAF tried to stem the Japanese advance toward Australia.

A force of twenty-three B-24Ds commanded by Colonel Harry Halverson was deployed to China, by way of the Middle East, in

May 1942 to bomb Japan. The force was detained en route and on June 11, flying from RAF airfields in Egypt, a dozen Liberators bombed the Romanian oil complex at Ploesti. The Halverson Detachment never made it to China: it remained in the Middle East, as the seedcorn of 9th Air Force, commanded by Major General Lewis Brereton.

Meanwhile AAF bomb groups at home were taking delivery of B-24Ds, with self-sealing tanks, three power-driven gun turrets, turbo charged Pratt & Whitney engines and a speed of 303 miles per hour. To get more Liberators, Wright Field had already twisted the arm of Ford, which agreed to make subassemblies to be built into finished aircraft by Douglas, Convair and Consolidated. Before 1942 ended, Ford's huge Willow Run plant, too, started producing entire B-24s.

Not even this would suffice. In the twelve months following Pearl Harbor more than ten thousand Liberators were ordered. North American was ordered to open a B-24 assembly line. Before the war ended more Liberators would be produced than any other U.S. combat aircraft. It was going to be a great, if undervalued, success.

In August 1938 the General Staff appeared to have fought the B-17 to a standstill, but what really worried the ground generals was the Air Corps's demand for aircraft even bigger than the B-17. There seemed no limit to the behemoths the airmen wanted to spawn—not in number, not in size.

Bomber enthusiasts were demanding planes with vastly greater range, and range was a function of an airplane's size: the bigger the plane, the farther it could fly. You could put bigger engines, even more engines, on it and carry more fuel. The ranges that the airmen talked about infuriated some officers on the General Staff. They couldn't see how a bomber with a ten thousand-mile range had anything to do with supporting the Army or defending America's shores. You didn't need the brains to buy a plane ticket to see that such a bomber was an offensive weapon.[43]

The B-17 came about only after an attempt to design an even bigger airplane, the XB-15, looked like failing. The B-15's engines, four Pratt & Whitney Twin Wasps, generated a modest 850 horsepower each, nowhere near enough to make the plane successful.[44] Even so, in November 1937 Douglas received a contract for an even bigger plane, the XB-19, with a projected range of ten thousand miles.

After nine months of design work, Douglas begged off, saying this plane, too, wasn't worth pursuing. The Matériel Division disagreed and insisted it build at least one. Even if the plane never went into production its flight tests might yield valuable data. In July 1941 the XB-19 finally flew. It was an awesome object: wing span 212 feet, length 132 feet. It was twice the size of a B-17 and even with four Wright Cyclone engines rated at two thousand horsepower it was struggling. Yet the Matériel Division felt the experiment was worth the effort, for there could be no turning back now from the drive to build very long range bombers.

In November 1939, acting on the Kilner Board's recommendations, Arnold had asked the aviation industry for a heavy bomber that would have a two-thousand-mile radius of action and be "in all respects superior" to the B-17. The radius of action is nearly half a plane's range; that is, the farthest distance it can fly to reach a target and return to its starting point. As a rule of thumb, combat radius is two-fifths of an aircraft's range. The board was asking for a plane that could fly five thousand miles without stopping.

The B-17A had a combat radius of only eight hundred miles (or a range of two thousand), carrying a ton of bombs. This would rise to a radius of eleven hundred miles in later models; an improvement, but no leap in magnitude.

Four companies were invited to compete for the new heavy bomber. Boeing submitted what Wright Field judged the best design. In September 1940 the company was awarded a contract to produce two prototypes, designated the XB-29. Just in case the Boeing design didn't pan out, Consolidated was asked to build a comparable aircraft, the XB-32.[45]

The B-29 would have a wing span of 142 feet and a length of 99 feet; roughly the size of the failed XB-15, but at 120,000 pounds it would weigh twice as much. Arnold was betting that Wright could develop engines powerful enough to carry this colossus successfully.

Hardly had detailed design of the B-29 and B-32 begun than the prospect of a German conquest of Europe, including Great Britain, brought an extra twist to the story. In the spring of 1941 specifications were written for a heavy bomber with a range of ten thousand miles, with a maximum speed of three hundred miles per hour and an operating ceiling of thirty-five thousand feet. The contract was awarded to Consolidated, which submitted a six-engine design, with a wing span of 230 feet and a gross weight of 278,000 pounds.

Two prototypes were ordered. This plane was designated the XB-36.[46]

It took Boeing two years to build the first B-29 prototype. Its four Wright R-3350 engines generated 2,200 horsepower and gave it a top speed of 350 mph. Heavily armed with fifty-caliber machine guns and twenty-millimeter cannon, the plane had a range of forty-one hundred miles and a bomb load of twenty thousand pounds. It wasn't clear, though, that it could be brought into production: its overburdened engines kept bursting into flame as they struggled to generate enough power.

The plane was a gamble, involving more money than was spent on the atomic bomb. What Arnold was really gambling, however, had no price. He was betting the future independence of American air power.

7

LOFTY PURSUITS

The great leap forward of aviation technology in the mid-1930s affected fighters as much as bombers, although this wasn't fully appreciated in the United States. In European countries, the primary air mission was securing air superiority, either for home defense, in the case of the British, or to enable ground forces to advance, in the case of the Germans. A lot of effort, therefore, went into the development of modern fighters.

The bulk of European fighters were interceptors; their main function was the destruction of enemy bombers. The interceptor was usually a weapon of point defense, protecting a city or an air base, an industrial complex or a railroad system. It needed a high rate of climb and a ceiling greater than the aircraft it was defending against. It didn't need to carry much fuel. It would go up, fight for thirty minutes or so, then land, be rearmed, refueled and made ready to go up again within an hour or two.

In trying to shoot down enemy bombers, the interceptor might first have to dive through a defensive belt of escort fighters. The escort fighter would probably carry two engines and a crew of two or three. Roughly the size of a light bomber, the escort's role would be to keep the interceptors away from the bombers. Ideally, it would fly as fast as the interceptors, yet have the range of the bombers it escorted; in reality, no one plane had achieved this.

Despite the drive for heavy bombers by some of the Maxwell Field theorists, the Air Corps showed almost no interest in escorts. What fighter interest survived was focused on interceptors and, in

1935, the Air Corps organized a pursuit competition to develop a new generation, capable of three hundred miles an hour.

Curtiss-Wright of Buffalo confidently put forward its P-36, powered by a 775 horsepower Wright radial. To everyone's surprise, the saturnine and tempermental Alexander Seversky entered a plane that looked similar to the Curtiss entry, but was powered by an 850 horsepower Wright Cyclone, a radial heretofore used only in bombers.

The competition ran for months, ending in the spring of 1936. Seversky's P-35 hit a top speed of 289 miles per hour and won, over screams of "Foul!" from the Curtiss team. Seversky was rewarded with a contract to produce seventy-seven P-35s. Curtiss was asked only to build three more P-36s, for further testing.[1]

The company hit back by coming up with a new design, the XP-37, the first fighter with an Allison liquid-cooled engine. The plane was so streamlined it looked more like a racing plane than a fighter. The XP-37 could reach 340 miles per hour at twenty thousand feet. Curtiss also challenged Seversky to a rematch at Wright Field in 1937, pitting the P-36 against the P-35 again, but with a more powerful Wright engine that generated 1,050 horsepower. This time Curtiss won, and received an order for 210 planes. In 1938 the Air Corps started taking delivery of production model P-36As, which could reach thirty-three thousand feet and fly at three hundred miles per hour. It was a fun airplane and a mediocre weapon: no armor, only two thirty-caliber machine guns, no self-sealing fuel tanks.[2]

Meanwhile, the Air Corps was having trouble with its P-35s. It was a difficult plane to fly. Only the best, and luckiest, pilots could land it safely every time. The P-35 and P-36 were the first U.S. fighters to have retractable landing gear. On the P-35 there was no way for the pilot to tell whether it was down and locked in place. It wasn't long before a score of P-35s were wrecked attempting to land.[3]

Besides buying these interceptors, the Air Corps was also experimenting with a long-range escort fighter, the Airacuda. This was an aerial curiosity, manufactured by one of the newest aircraft companies, Bell. Designated the XFM-1 (for experimental fighter, multiplace), it made its first flight in September 1937. A five-man aircraft propelled by two Allison liquid-cooled engines, it was armed with four fifty-calibers, two thirty-calibers, two thirty-seven-millimeter cannons and offered a range greater than a B-17.[4]

The Air Corps ordered nine service test models, the YFM-1. These turned out to have a top speed of 270 miles per hour—40 miles an hour slower than the B-17A. They also lacked maneuverability. The Airacuda was a lot like Germany's three-man escort fighter, the twin-engine Me-110, which RAF fighter pilots ate raw in the Battle of Britain.

The other way escort might have developed was by extending the range of the single-seat interceptor. This had been precluded. Shortly after becoming chief of the Air Corps, Arnold banned external bomb racks on fighters. He didn't believe in attack and wouldn't allow fighters to be used as attack aircraft. He also ruled out external fuel tanks. Mountings for tanks might be used to accommodate bombs.

Fighter pilots like Major William E. Kepner, commander of 8th Pursuit Group, protested these decisions. Kepner had organized a range-extension experiment with the help of the Navy, which was developing external fuel tanks. He was specifically ordered not to put an extra tank on his planes. He was told they'd compromise a fighter's maneuverability.[5]

The engineers at Wright Field decided to do some good by stealth. They considered Arnold's arbitrary decisions on tanks and external bombs foolish. The Matériel Division wrote specifications for future fighter airframes that gave extra strength in places where bomb racks or fuel tanks might have to be placed, on that happy, if distant, day when the chief changed his mind.[6]

The views of the bomber enthusiasts remained fixed in the reinforced concrete of received wisdom: no escort would be needed or possible. Still, when Colonel Millard Harmon became assistant commandant at Maxwell in 1939 he, as an old fighter pilot, questioned the doctrine of "bomber invincibility" and demanded more attention be paid to pursuit. The number of hours given to fighters increased and the need for long-range escort was studied. Harmon stood little chance of success, though, while the Department of Air Tactics and Strategy remained in bombardment hands.[7]

Moreover, the fighter versus bomber argument had already been thrashed out *in extenso* between Chennault and his most splenetic antagonist at Maxwell, Clayton Bissell. Chennault believed an adequate warning net would give interceptors such an advantage over unescorted bombers they'd make a prolonged bombing campaign too expensive for any air force to bear. Bissell ridiculed his warning net, and history seemed on Bissell's side: in 1940 Bissell was a lieutenant colonel on the War Department General Staff and Chennault was a civilian on Chiang Kai-shek's payroll.

In 1939 the Air Corps placed orders for a total of eight hundred new fighter aircraft, a modest number given the huge increase in appropriations and the near doubling of its authorized strength. Moreover, these were planes which lacked bulletproof tanks, armor and firepower. The British and French, purchasing much the same planes, insisted that these deficiencies be corrected on the models they purchased. It was Allied money that financed the modernization of U.S. fighters.

Until 1943 fighter aircraft continued to have a low priority. First came heavy bombers, then medium/light bombers, then reconnaissance aircraft, then transports, and finally, in fifth place, came fighters.[8]

The placement of the first air-defense ground-control interception station, too, told its own story. It was placed, almost whimsically, it seems, in Seattle.[9]

Generally speaking, the future for fighters in the Air Corps looked bleak. The ethos in which doctrine was formulated and airplanes purchased was guided by such people as Harold L. George, who confidently pronounced, "The spectacle of huge air forces meeting in the air is a figment of the imagination of the uninitiated."[10]

Little wonder that AWPD-1 was based on an assumption of bomber invincibility. All the fighters it envisaged were interceptors, to defend bomber airfields in Britain: not a single escort fighter among them.

In 1937 the Air Corps asked five manufacturers to enter a design competition for a twin-engine interceptor able to climb to twenty thousand feet in six minutes and reach a level speed of four hundred miles per hour. Lockheed's design team offered the Model 22.

What they were proposing was a fighter shaped in large part by the need to accommodate two long engines and two turbo superchargers. The engines would be Allison V-1710s rated at 950 horsepower. The turbo superchargers (hereafter "turbochargers") represented an American approach to a universal problem.

The problem was that as an aircraft rises into ever thinner air, internal combustion engines suffer a gradual loss of power. Depending on the plane and the engine, maximum efficiency is somewhere between ten and twenty thousand feet. Higher than that, and a point comes where a plane flies slower and slower because there is too little oxygen to burn the plane's fuel easily. For a fully loaded B-17 this height might be only ten thousand feet. For an interceptor it might be fifteen thousand.

The way to maintain an engine's power is to install an air compressor that compresses huge amounts of air and feeds it back to the carburetor. Compressing air, however, heats it up, so the air must go through an intercooler before entering the carburetor. This technique might take a World War II fighter as high as forty-four thousand feet, where the air is so rarified it can't be cooled.

In most aircraft, the power to drive the compressor came directly from the engine, through two sets of gears. This was the method the British preferred. Pratt & Whitney developed a similar gear-driven supercharger for the Navy.[11]

Wright Field preferred turbocharging. This used some of the exhaust gases from the engine to drive a small turbine. The turbine, with potential speeds exceeding fifteen thousand revolutions per minute, was a powerful air compressor. The first U.S. combat aircraft to receive turbo-charging was the Y1B-17A that was originally bought for static tests at Wright Field. In collaboration with General Electric, a turbocharger was developed that enabled its Wright Cyclone engines to take the bomber up to twenty-five thousand feet.[12]

The first fighter to get a turbo-charged engine was the Curtiss XP-37. There was a widespread feeling, though, that turbochargers were simply too heavy and tricky for single-seat fighters. A pilot could spend a fair amount of time just regulating the thing, not something he was likely to benefit from while engaged in a dogfight.

Lockheed was offering to push back the technological frontiers with the Model 22. The company proposed putting turbochargers in twin booms that led back from the two engines to twin tails. The company also offered three other important innovations: the first tricycle landing gear in an American combat aircraft, counter-rotating propellers, and the first high-lift maneuvering flaps to go into a fighter. Putting a wheel in the nose would enable the plane, which had a stalling speed of 105 miles per hour, to be landed safely at high speed. And having the two engines counter-rotate would virtually eliminate torque, producing a new level of stability.[13]

Lockheed won the design competition and in January 1939 rolled out the Model 22 (XP-38). With a wing span of fifty-two feet and a length of nearly thirty-eight feet, it was 50 percent bigger than the average single-seat fighter. No one had more faith in it than the Air Corps project officer assigned to the plane, Lieutenant Benjamin S. Kelsey.

The XP-38 certainly had a fighter's speed. Shortly after it was rolled out, Kelsey set off from California, heading for Wright Field. Waiting to greet him was Arnold, who urged him to fly on to Mitchel Field and break the cross-country flight record currently held by Howard Hughes. More than that, Arnold wanted to announce that the United States had a four-hundred miles per hour fighter, something the Germans claimed to possess.[14]

As Kelsey approached Mitchel Field he lost power in both engines, probably due to carburetor icing. Unable to extend his glide, Kelsey came down on a golf course adjoining the field. He survived the crash landing without serious injury, but the plane was wrecked. No matter. His time of seven hours and two minutes gave an average cross-country flying speed of 350 miles per hour, and at 20,000 feet it had hit 399 miles per hour. That was good enough for Arnold. He rounded it up to 400.

Even before the XP-38 flew, the Air Corps had contracted for thirteen service test YP-38s. It was September 1940 before the first Y-38s were delivered.[15]

One major problem had been anticipated, but no one knew the answer to it; at least, not in the United States. Back in 1937 one of the Lockheed design team, Clarence "Kelly" Johnson, had warned that once an aircraft exceeeded four hundred miles per hour it might become impossible to control. The problem was known as "compressibility." If the airflow over the wings of the plane came close to the speed of sound it would generate such pressure on the ailerons the pilot wouldn't be able to control the plane. Johnson's fears were confirmed: when the YP-38s were put into a dive and passed 425 miles per hour they simply refused to respond, flying faster and faster until they plowed into the ground.

German airplane designers had already solved the problem, and in the mid-1930s even published articles on the subject. No one in the Air Corps or the U.S. airplane industry appears to have bothered reading German aviation literature. The answer was swept-back wings.[16]

A fierce debate broke out after several pilots were killed flying YP-38s. Kelsey nearly joined them, in a dive that took the tail off his plane. He bailed out and survived with a broken leg.

The majority faction blamed the tail and it was raised thirty inches. The minority, including Kelsey and Johnson, blamed the wings. High-speed wind-tunnel tests proved them right, but Lockheed never found a real solution to it. The best Lockheed could do was add a new kind of flap, to slow its dive.

By the time the YP-38s were delivered, the Air Corps had already ordered 673 P-38s, P-38As and P-38Ds. There were no B or D models because Arnold, trying to make up for lost time, demanded that Wright Field and Lockheed guess what improvements might be incorporated in a B and a C, and put them all into the P-38D, untested.[17]

The French had ordered 417 P-38s; the British took 667. The British had also given the plane the name by which it would be renowned, "Lightning," although when they received the first batch they didn't like them much—no turbochargers, no high performance. They canceled the rest of their order.

The Air Corps took the planes, because even if they were no use for combat, they could be used for training. Serious doubts, however, were setting in about the value of the P-38. Arnold was tempted to cancel the plane.[18]

The first true combat variant was the P-38E, which went into production in November 1941. A fighter version, armed with four fifty-caliber guns and a twenty-millimeter cannon, accounted for 201 of the P-38Es; a further 99 were equipped with cameras and became the F-4 photo-recon aircraft.

By mid-1942 P-38 squadrons were deployed to Iceland, the Aleutians and New Guinea, where their unusually long range made them valuable and their limited acceleration and maneuverability were not great handicaps. The threat of cancellation lifted.

In August 1942 Lieutenant Elza K. Shahan, flying from Iceland, shot down a German FW-200 patrol bomber over the North Atlantic, scoring the first victory by an American aircraft in the European Theater of Operations. Shahan received the Silver Star and the Lightning won a paean of praise.[19]

Shortly after Lockheed had won the competition for a twin-engine interceptor, Wright Field issued another challenge. The objective this time was to design a single-engine interceptor that could meet similar criteria of speed, altitude, rate of climb, and carry a twenty-three-millimeter cannon.

The winning entry this time came from Bell Aircraft Company of Buffalo. In 1935 Consolidated had moved from Buffalo to San

Diego. One of Consolidated's vice-presidents, Lawrence D. Bell, and its chief engineer, Robert Woods, chose to stay on in Buffalo and form a new company. Two years later Bell was an aviation subcontractor living a hand-to-mouth existence producing wing panels for Consolidated's PBYs. Its hopes of making whole airplanes were pinned on the doomed Airacuda.

Woods was Bell's chief designer and he had been impressed by a recent demonstration of a thirty-seven-millimeter cannon manufactured by Oldsmobile. What would it take to put a weapon like that in the air? he wondered. Woods built a mock-up of a sleek airframe that placed a thirty-seven-millimeter cannon on the centerline, firing it through the propeller hub. It may have been the first time a fighter was tailor-made for a specific weapon.[20]

Wood's first design placed the cockpit behind the engine and behind the gun; it was so far back that the pilot would have a tough time seeing anything forward. So a second mock-up was constructed. This put the engine behind the pilot. Visibility would be excellent and by placing the engine behind the plane's center of gravity, instead of in front of it, the aircraft would have marginal stability, making it an edgy, acrobatic, dogfighting machine.

Bell submitted a pile of drawings, and a thirty-minute movie of the two mock-ups undergoing wind-tunnel tests. He won the design competition with the second mock-up. The other competitors trailed far behind. In October 1937 Bell received a contract to build a prototype. Seven months later, on Air Force Day (April 6, 1938) the Bell XP-39 made its debut at Wright Field.

The plane was a small sensation: wing span thirty-six feet, length twenty-eight feet eight inches, and weighing only fifty-five hundred pounds gross. It had tricycle landing gear and a cockpit that was entered through an automobile type door with a rolldown window. Its turbocharged Allison V-1710 produced 1,150 horsepower, allowing it to climb to twenty thousand feet in five minutes. With a top speed of 390 miles per hour, it was as fast as any fighter in the world.

The Wright Field engineers went to work on it. They altered the XP-39 so radically it became the XP-39B (there was no A). It gained a foot in length, and lost nearly two feet in wingspan. It also got a less powerful Allison engine and no turbocharger. These modifications resulted in an airplane that flew slower and lower.

By offering a fast airplane armed with a thirty-seven-millimeter cannon at a time when attack was in transition, Bell Aircraft had fallen into a black hole from which its plane would never climb out. Having asked for an interceptor, the Air Corps was suddenly mesmerized by a vision of something different. That huge cannon started people thinking maybe this was a ground-support machine in an interceptor's clothing. They thrust changes on it that ended its potential to develop into a first-class agile fighter.

No one battled to maintain the integrity of the design. Larry Bell was too short of money to argue with Wright Field. Having cut down the wings and the power, Air Corps engineers proceeded to add six machine guns and armor plate. By the time the thirteen YP-39 service test models were delivered in 1940 the airplane had been compromised beyond redemption. It was neither a real fighter nor a true attack aircraft. It went into a flat spin if the pilot scratched himself and tumbled if he coughed.[21]

Yet this deeply flawed work, the P-39, saved Bell from bankruptcy. The Airacuda was a colossal failure. It had put the firm deeply in the red, and Brett's blinkered defense of the tax dollar had brought the ax down not only on Boeing but on Bell. When Larry Bell realized in April 1940 that Brett was going to make him finance the YP-39's flight tests, he knew he couldn't do it. The company was about to go bust. In desperation Bell headed for New York and sold the plane to the equally desperate French, sight unseen but promises dazzling. He emerged with an advance payment of $2 million and an order worth $9 million.[22]

Later that year he convinced Knudsen that Bell Aircraft, which in all its history had built only fifteen airplanes, could produce five a day. Shortly afterward, he got contracts for nearly one thousand P-39s, mainly P-39Ds with self-sealing tanks, a thirty-seven-millimeter cannon, four fifty-caliber machine guns, two thirty-calibers, a shackle that would take either a seventy-five gallon fuel tank or a five-hundred-pound bomb, but still no supercharger. Without one, the P-39 was no fighter plane. It took forever to reach twenty thousand feet and was a sluggard when it got there.

Turbochargers relied heavily on tungsten alloys, and there was a severe tungsten shortage. Even before Pearl Harbor priority for turbochargers went to four-engine bombers. What was left over went to high-altitude P-38s and P-47s, not to bastardized P-39s.[23]

What's more, the P-39, which the British named the "Airacobra," was locked in to the Allison liquid-cooled engine, a decidedly mediocre power plant before 1943. Had Allison or Wright Field put a serious effort into developing advanced gear-driven superchargers in the late 1930s, the engine might have been on a par with its European counterparts. As it was, the P-39 was at its (unimpressive) best below twelve thousand feet. This pushed it even deeper into the support role, for which it wasn't well suited.

The plane was too hard to maintain, too difficult to fly, too small and too fragile to make a good attack airplane. Ironically, it wasn't even well-armed. The thirty-seven-millimeter cannon invariably jammed after firing one or two rounds. And much of the time it couldn't carry a bomb, because it had to carry extra fuel instead; when self-sealing tanks were put into its tiny wings the plane had lost one-third of its fuel capacity. Arnold's strictures against hanging external fuel tanks or bomb racks on fighters had to be ignored.

Only the Red Air Force liked the P-39, and took half of all production. The Soviets would gladly trade a free plane and a half-trained pilot for two German tanks and a truck.

Rushed to the South and Southwest Pacific in 1942, the P-39 soon demonstrated that it couldn't catch a Zero, couldn't dogfight on even terms, couldn't knock down enemy bombers. What it was unsurpassed at was falling out of the sky. In April 1942 the 8th Fighter Group arrived in northern Australia. It soon deployed to New Guinea, 250 miles away. Of the forty-one P-39s that took off for Port Moresby, fifteen crashed en route.[24]

That summer, the Guadalcanal campaign began. Soon, the senior Army officer in the South Pacific theater, former fighter pilot Lieutenant General Millard Harmon, was complaining caustically about the P-39. He asked Arnold not to send him any more. The P-39, said Harmon, was demoralizing to the pilots who had to fly it and was harming the reputation of the Army Air Forces with the Navy, the Marines and the Allies.[25]

Development of the P-40 followed a circuitous route, starting in 1937 with the design of the Curtiss XP-37. The plane was breathtakingly sleek and came with a turbo-charged Allison engine. In 1938 Curtiss got a contract for thirteen service test YP-37s, but the turbocharger was bug infested. The plane never amounted to much.

All was not lost. Curtiss used the experience derived from the XP-37 to build a new fighter prototype, the Model H-81 (XP-40). This consisted of the old Curtiss P-36 airframe mated to a new Allison liquid-cooled engine, without turbo-charging.[26]

The XP-40 made its debut at a great time for a less-than-great airplane. Its maiden flight was in October 1938, just as the President started talking about wanting a ten thousand-plane air force, just as the British and French started waving their gold and dollar reserves under the starved aviation industry's pleading eyes.

Opinion in the Matériel Division was against the plane: it was another Curtiss flop. The Allison engine had a published rating of 1,160 horsepower. That may have been true at a test bench in Detroit, but in an XP-40 at ten thousand feet it produced considerably less, around 700 horsepower.[27]

Still, Curtiss was the only manufacturer able to start large scale production of a new fighter. The chief engineer at Wright Field, Colonel Oliver Echols, overrode his subordinate's criticisms and ordered 524 P-40s. The engine may be no good now, he told them, but there's plenty of potential there for improvement. The less picky French ordered close to 1,200; the British wanted 250.

Meanwhile Arnold continued hoping someone would present him with a small, lightweight interceptor. Curtiss came up with yet another plane, the XP-46. It was really an advanced version of the P-40, but Curtiss said it would fly at 410 miles an hour.

While Curtiss got to work building two prototypes, the Matériel Division urged Arnold to stop production of the P-40. A six-month halt of the Curtiss production line for retooling would cost the Air Corps two hundred obsolescent fighters, in place of which it would get thousands of modern combat aircraft. Arnold said No. Nothing, but nothing, could be allowed to interfere with production. It would be better, he argued, to take the P-46's engine, if that turns out all right, and put it into future P-40s.[28]

In the end, Arnold was right. When the stripped down XP-46 prototype made its maiden flight in February 1941 it hit four hundred miles an hour. Its sister ship, however, was a combat-ready aircraft, with self-sealing fuel tanks, armor plate for the pilot, and ten machine guns. It flew at 355 miles per hour, not much faster than the current P-40B.[29]

The P-40C was about to go into production and couldn't be modified without a major interruption. The next 2,342 planes, however, P-40Ds and P-40Es, would get the engine from the XP-46, an Allison that generated a true 1,150 horsepower. Too bad it lacked a turbocharger, or even a modern two-stage, two speed gear-driven supercharger.

The nearest thing to a solution was to equip the 1,311 P-40Fs ordered in late 1941 with Packard-built Merlin engines. These came equipped with an integral two-stage supercharger that brought some improvement above fifteen thousand feet, but not enough to make it a high altitude interceptor.

All P-40s, in fact, would be at their best at low altitudes. Between five and ten thousand feet, the P-40Es and Fs were as good as Spitfires.[30] Over fifteen thousand feet they were ordinary. They were well-armed, carrying six fifty-caliber machine guns in the wings, arranged to converge in a small circle at 250 yards. They also had huge slabs of armor plate protecting the pilot. A P-40's weight allowed it to dive out of trouble. This wasn't a plane made for dogfighting. It was made for bushwhacking—one killing, diving pass, then head for the deck and home.

The British deployed hundreds of P-40Bs, Cs and Ds to the Western Desert in 1941–42, where they played an important role in keeping the Luftwaffe from turning occasional air superiority into a permanent state of affairs.[31] January 1942 found Chennault's American Volunteer Group defying the Japanese by flying obsolescent P-40Bs with unlooked for success over Burma. Chennault devised tactics that allowed his outnumbered pilots to exploit all the P-40's hidden strengths and overcome its obvious defects.

Then and later, this rugged, reliable aircraft was overshadowed by more glamorous foreign rivals, but many who flew the P-40 loved and trusted the aircraft. One, Robert Lee Scott, hoped to raise a monument in its honor on the immortal sands of Kitty Hawk.[32]

The P-39 and P-40 were expected to provide low-altitude pursuit. It would have been folly, though, to leave the entire high-altitude interception burden on the complex P-38. A simpler, single engine airplane was needed too.

In the spring of 1939, shortly after the YP-38 was ordered, the Air Corps held yet another interceptor design competition. It was won by Sasha Seversky, with a turbo-charged entry called the AP-4. The plane he offered would be powered by a Pratt & Whitney Wasp, a radial that generated eleven hundred horsepower. Seversky's company got a contract to build thirteen service test aircraft, called YP-43s. There wouldn't be an X prototype; time was too short.

Seversky was no business executive. Seversky Airplane Company was run haphazardly, according to its founder's whims and idiosyncracies. Wright Field doubted its ability to mass produce planes without a change of management. He'd also earned the antagonism of Arnold. Seversky kept telling him he was going to have to build thousands of long-range escorts. Arnold didn't want to believe it, didn't want to hear it.[33] In October 1939 Seversky Airplane Company, under pressure from Arnold, ousted dynamic, colorful Sasha and was reorganized as Republic Aviation.

Work continued on building the service test YP-43s, and Republic had yet another design to offer, for a plane to be designated the P-44. This would be powered by a radial that generated fourteen hundred horsepower and flew at four hundred miles per hour. The Air Corps ordered eighty P-44s.

There was a groping quality to the search for modern fighters. Many people, including Arnold, thought the most important element was a fighter's armament. Others emphasized maneuverability or the airframe. The most important part, however, was the engine.

No fighter was better than its power plant, and some were worse. A mediocre engine would cripple the most brilliant design. A powerful reliable engine was the bedrock on which a true weapon could be built. By putting their trust in radials Seversky and his chief designer, Alexander Kartveli, defied the general view that radials were too bulky and too wind resistant for fighters.

They had failed, though, with the P-35; they failed again with the design for the P-44. Not one plane was built.

Fourth place in the 1939 high-altitude interceptor design competition had gone to a Seversky entry known as the AP-10, a small fighter with an Allison engine. Seversky had covered both sides of the coin, well aware of the Matériel Division's preference for slender, liquid-cooled engines in fighters. When the P-44 project ran into the sands, Kartveli went back to the AP-10 and reworked it, offering it to the Air Corps as the XP-47. Wright Field gave Republic a contract to produce two Allison-powered prototypes: the XP-47, which would be a light, nimble fighter carrying two fifty-caliber machine guns, and the XP-47A, an ever lighter plane, with a projected gross weight of only sixty-four hundred pounds.[34]

As Kartveli completed the design for the XP-47, Arnold came to see him. Take out that Allison, said Arnold, and put in a radial. Arnold wasn't going to bet the farm on liquid-cooled engines.[35] There were three fighters under development: the P-38, P-39, and P-40. All were powered by Allison, yet the engine was failing to generate the amount of power the company promised.

Kartveli started redesigning the XP-47, to take an eye-popping two-thousand-horsepower, turbo-charged Pratt & Whitney radial and eight machine guns. He was putting a heavyweight's fist into a middleweight's glove. In September 1940, Republic got an order for 773 planes, just on the basis of the new design.

The prototype, the XP-47B, was rolled out in May 1941. It was huge. It had a wing span of forty feet nine inches, and length of thirty-five feet exactly—reasonable for a fighter. But the weight! Without guns or armor plate it tipped the scales at twelve thousand pounds, gross. It was nearly as heavy as the much bigger P-38, twice as heavy as the P-39, and 50 percent heavier than the P-40.

The huge reliable radial made light work of its avoirdupois. The XP-47B hit 412 miles per hour at 28,000 feet. Its great weight made it roll faster than anything in the air, and when it went into a dive it touched 550 miles per hour.[36] Some of the early P-47s shredded their tails and lost their radio masts in high speed dives.[37]

The plane inevitably ran into compressibility. Kartveli thought it might kill his design but, like Lockheed, he found a solution in dive flaps. Pilots were also told to take their hand off the stick when the controls froze: the plane would slow down and the stick unfreeze of its own accord. Compressibility ceased to be a problem.

The XP-47B and early production models had a disappointing rate of climb for an interceptor. They lacked acceleration in flight. They also needed a long takeoff run to get all that weight into the air. Yet there was no denying the tremendous potential of this airplane. It was fast, rugged, maneuverable, and with its turbocharger, it could reach forty-two thousand feet.

When it first saw the XP-47B, the Matériel Command wanted to turn the plane down. Kartveli planned to fill its thin wings with heavy machine guns and two thousand rounds of ammunition. The wings, said Wright Field, will flutter. No, they won't, said Kartveli, sticking . . . to his guns.[38]

Mass production began in July 1942, with the P-47B. By this time it had become known as the Thunderbolt; its engine had been uprated and the plane now flew at 430 miles per hour. The first outfit to receive it, and serve more or less as amateur test pilots and exuberant guinea pigs, was 56th Fighter Group, at Mitchel Field, Long Island, a few miles from the Republic plant at Farmingdale. The 56th's commander, Lieutenant Colonel Hubert Zemke, spent a lot of time working on improvements with Kartveli.[39] In the fall, 56th Group prepared to deploy to the Eighth Air Force, and take the Thunderbolt to war.

. . .

One day in April 1940 "Dutch" Kindleberger, the president of
North American Aviation, went to see the head of the aviation
division of the British Purchasing Commission, Sir Henry Self, at
his office on Wall Street. Would the British like to buy the B-25? he
inquired. The answer was No.[40]

What Self was interested in these days was fighters. Before the
year was out, the Luftwaffe was likely to be seeking air superiority
over the beaches of England. The British were already buying
P-40s, but Curtiss had a new plane under development, the XP-46.
Essentially it was a sleek, streamlined P-40 with a more powerful
engine and ten machine guns. Curtiss was so swamped with orders
for the P-40, however, that it couldn't go into production with a
new type. Would North American be interested in taking over the
Curtiss design? asked Self.[41]

Kindleberger went to Buffalo and returned to see Self next day.
Some of Curtiss's ideas must have been worth adopting, because
NAA paid $56,000 for use of its designs. All the same, North
American had no intention of building someone else's airplane. If
the British would place an order, Kindleberger would guarantee to
have an advanced fighter in production in twelve months. North
American had never built a fighter, but Self was willing to take a
chance. Without drawings or specifications, he placed an order for
400 planes, at $40,000 each. All 400 were to be delivered by the end
of September 1941.

Kindleberger and his chief designer, Edgar Schmued, were dying
to build a fighter. Both men had already given considerable thought
to what the ideal interceptor would be like: a plane armed with four
twenty-millimeter cannon, designed around a man 5 feet 10 inches
tall and weighing 140 pounds, and flying faster than any combat
aircraft in the world.[42]

In September 1940, NAA rolled out a prototype, the NA-73, but
without an engine. In October, it was ready to fly, powered by an
Allison generating eleven hundred horsepower. The NA-73 contained a number of features that derived from the XP-46. Wing area
and weight were virtually identical.

The two biggest differences were the placement of the radiator
and the design of the wing. The radiator was positioned below the
fuselage, to reduce drag, and the air from the radiator expanded in
proximity to the engine. When the heated air was expelled it

boosted the plane's speed by an extra fifteen to twenty-five miles an hour.[43]

The second major design improvement was in the wing, which was a laminar flow airfoil, which shifted the thickest point of the wing from near the leading edge to roughly the middle of the wing. The effect was to make the air that flowed over it do so in laminations, numerous even layers, one on top of another. Air passed over the laminar-flow, square-cut wing so smoothly that even when the Mustang flew at 450 miles per hour there were no compressibility effects because at no point did the airflow approach the speed of sound.[44] In other fighters the airflow was so disrupted that when the plane reached Mach 0.7 the air passing over the wings was close to Mach 1, putting unmanageable pressure on the ailerons.

The superb high-speed performance designed into the P-51s wasn't appreciated for more than two years. The Allison engine lacked the power to bring out the potential in the airframe.

The AAF demanded two copies of the first production models. Designated XP-51, the first of these was delivered to Wright Field in August 1941, but was too flawed to be tested extensively. The Matériel Command turned its efforts instead to perfecting the P-38 and the P-47.

The RAF wasn't too excited either when, shortly before Pearl Harbor, it started receiving its (delayed) Mustangs. The plane had a top speed of 380 miles an hour, and without a supercharger wasn't much good above 12,000 feet. It was a low-altitude fighter. The British sent it to the Western Desert where, in July 1942, it made its combat debut, as a ground attack airplane, employing its eight thirty-caliber machine guns for strafing Italian and German vehicles.

The British use of the Mustang in an attack role was mirrored by the AAF. In early 1942, as Mustang production hit its stride, almost the only person at Wright Field who believed in the plane was Ben Kelsey. To get it into mass production for the AAF he sold it not as a fighter but as a dive-bomber. Under pressure from the Army to organize eighteen dive-bomber groups, the Matériel Command ordered five hundred with dive brakes and bomb racks; it was designated the A-36A.

Meanwhile a British test pilot employed by Rolls-Royce flew one of the RAF's Mustangs and wondered what might happen if a Merlin engine was substituted for the Allison. He managed to overcome the Air Ministry's doubts and five Mustangs were modified accordingly. The first flew in England in October 1942 and fully vindicated his faith: it flew at 420 miles per hour and could reach 20,000 feet in less than six minutes.

In the United States Packard-built Merlins were already being installed in two Mustangs straight from the NAA plant at Inglewood, California. Designated XP-51s, they too performed brilliantly. With the integral two-speed, two-stage gear-driven supercharger of the Merlin engine, they could hit 441 miles per hour at 30,000 feet.[45] The performance of these aircraft soon led to orders for nearly 2,000 P51-Bs.

There were still many shortcomings to be overcome. The P-51 embodied so much state-of-the-art technology it posed one headache after another. All would be resolved, but it would take time.

In retrospect, the effort to make the P-51 into a dive-bomber or attack aircraft seems misguided and costly. The American air attaché in London was Major Tommy Hitchcock, a one-time pilot with the Lafayette Escadrille. Between the wars he'd become famous as one of the world's finest polo players. Blond, boyish and a daredevil flyer even in middle age, Hitchcock conducted dive-bombing experiments with Mustangs sent to Britain.

Hitchcock continued to practice dive-bombing techniques, curious to see if this plane really could be made into an attack aircraft. In a high-speed dive over England one day in the fall of 1942 his Mustang disintegrated.[46] Coincidentally or not, interest in the plane's dive-bombing potential, never high, more or less ended right there.

By the end of 1942 the Army Air Forces had the five fighters on which it would have to depend for winning the war in the air. Whether they flew as interceptors, escorts or fighter-bombers, the range was complete.

8

ON TARGET

To turn an airplane into a weapon it needed guns, bombs, bomb-sights, and armor. Otherwise, ran a flyer's joke, all you could hit an enemy with was a dirty look.

Shooting in the air had always been a mystery, an arcane practice cultivated by a chosen few, surrounded by rituals that suggested control, but depending largely on luck. As many a pilot discovered, learning to shoot in motion at a moving target was as hard as learning to fly.

There were two kinds of shooting: the fixed-gun variety, which required maneuvering the entire plane in order to aim the gun—this was the province of the fighter pilot; and what was termed "flexible" gunnery, which required aiming a gun on a mount in almost any direction—this was the domain of the aerial gunner aboard a bomber.

For most of World War I, the fixed gun had been dominant. In World War II flexible gunnery would become so important that when great fleets of bombers took to the sky roughly half the men in the air were gunners. Flexible gunnery grew, though, from humble, unpromising beginnings.

Back in the 1920s the pioneering 3rd Attack Group had tried to push research into gun turrets, foreseeing the day when aerial gunners would need to be protected not only from freezing to death as planes climbed above ten thousand feet, but from return fire. Nothing came of its efforts. In 1938, when the Air Corps research-and-development budget stood at $2.5 million, the portion devoted to armament—which covered machine guns, cannon and turrets—was $25,000, exactly 1 percent of the total. About the same amount was spent on research into balloons.[1] Before World War II the armament officer of every Air Corps squadron was a pilot. Fighter pilots were concerned about fixed gunnery, not the flexible kind. Surprisingly, not even bomber pilots paid much attention to flexible gunnery. Despite the Air Corps's creed of the self-defending heavy bomber, little was done to realize it. The Air Corps's specifications for the B-17 called for three thirty-caliber machine guns: one in the nose, one atop the fuselage, one in the floor. Some fortress. It was Boeing that decided to add two more guns, in blisters on either side of the fuselage.

The Air Corps had doubts about putting a gun in the nose. In 1939 tests were held at Wright Field in which a P-36 attacked a B-10. The conclusion drawn was that head-on attacks were no threat. By the time the P-36 pilot got close enough to identify the bomber, he had to break away sharply to avoid a collision. So who needed a nose gun? There were also doubts about a tail gun. Wright Field's engineers concluded a tail gun probably wasn't feasible—modern combat aircraft accelerated so rapidly that the human body couldn't endure the strain of riding in the tail.[2]

The impetus behind the development of turrets in the United States came therefore, not from the Air Corps, but from the airplane manufacturers. The first Air Corps bomber with an enclosed turret was the Martin B-10, which had a turret in the nose and two ring mounts (one on the upper fuselage, one in the floor). The Air Corps tolerated the turret because it weighed only eighty pounds and didn't take the plane over its specifications; otherwise it would probably have been rejected.

In 1937, when the Matériel Division learned the Navy was getting Curtiss to develop manually operated turrets for a thirty-caliber machine gun, it requested that some be installed in the B-18. A streamlined, power-operated version of the Curtiss turret was perched on the B-18's nose. Bomb groups continued to regard it as suitable only for training.

The British and French were absolutely convinced that modern bombers needed gun turrets, and plenty of them. In the procurement pandemonium following the Munich crisis they urged the Air Corps to think turrets, but there was no stirring of interest.[3] The British offered to provide turret designs; these were easily ignored, because they were designed to accommodate thirty-caliber machine guns. The Air Corps was moving toward fifty-calibers. The fifty-calibers had a slower rate of fire than the thirty-calibers, but its higher muzzle velocity gave a flatter trajectory, making it more accurate and providing considerably greater range.

The heavy machine gun made a power-operated turret imperative. Few people could hand crank a turret that mounted a pair of fifty-calibers. The specifications for the XB-19 called for two thirty-seven millimeter cannon, four thirty-caliber machine guns, and four fifty-calibers. It was the first aircraft for which the Air Corps ever demanded a power-driven turret, but the turret was no more of a success than the plane.[4]

The kindest word for the Air Corps's approach to aerial gunnery is casual. A bomber board had estimated that 80 percent of all fighter attacks on bombers would come from the region of the tail.[5] Yet B-17 models A, B, C and D lacked tail guns.

Consolidated, meanwhile, was building the B-24 for the French, who demanded a tail turret. The Air Corps hadn't asked for one. What this contract required was "complete protection," provided by seven gun installations—to be manned by three members of the crew. The trouble with the Consolidated turret was that you had to be about four feet eight inches tall and weigh roughly one hundred pounds to get into it. The vibration of the gun was so tremendous it was almost impossible to get it on a target and hold it there. Even so, by 1942 the demand for a nose turret in combat meant that this torture chamber was reproduced on the nose, where it had appalling drag effects and made the Liberator wallow.

By and large, the story of U.S. gun turrets from 1939 to 1943 is a tale of woe. A futile attempt was made to come up with a joint Army-Navy-British powered gun turret acceptable to all three parties. There were also projects to devise a central control that would mass all the guns aboard a bomber against particular targets. This proved too complicated.

By the time of Pearl Harbor the AAF had half a dozen manufacturers scrambling to produce turrets. The engineers who designed the turrets knew next to nothing about gunnery. They were airplane designers, not ordnance experts. Few ever went shooting. They also approached the problem backward. In a gun turret, which comes first, the sight or the turret? The correct answer is to get a good sight and design the turret around it. Nearly every American designer concentrated on the turret, and let somebody else worry about the sight to put into it.

Bottom turrets were probably the worst. The one installed underneath the B-25 was more than a challenge. The gunner had to ride on his knees, sight through a periscope, bring the guns to bear and rotate the turret as he did so. "A man could learn to play the violin good enough for Carnegie Hall," grumbled Jimmy Doolittle, "before he could learn to fire this thing."[6] The lower turret on the B-17 wasn't much better. Its placement ensured it got coated with oil on takeoff, leaving the gunner in a fog.

The only successful turret the AAF acquired before 1943 came from Martin. When the B-26 was designed one of the design team, Peyton Marshall Magruder, a young Annapolis graduate, decided to add a turret. In three weeks he masterminded the design, construction, and testing of a power turret for a pair of fifty-calibers. Magruder, who would go on to become a successful novelist and playwright, had a hit on his hands. Some fifty-six thousand Martin dorsal turrets would eventually be produced and fitted into nearly thirty different types of U.S. and Allied aircraft.[7]

Apart from this solitary success, aerial gunnery was in trouble. At the time of Pearl Harbor, the AAF had not trained one aerial gunner. Anyone aboard a bomber who wasn't otherwise occupied when it came under attack was expected to man a gun. The job was treated as nonessential.

Three gunnery schools had been opened, but so far they'd trained only a handful of instructors. Shortly after Pearl Harbor four more gunnery schools were established.[8] The schools offered a six-week course. The first half was mainly ground school: theory of ballistics, machine gun maintenance, ammunition handling, and so on. Trainees moved from BB guns to twenty-two-calibers, to shotguns, to machine guns. They spent hours shooting clay pigeons, so they'd learn how to lead a target. They fired at moving targets from moving trucks. In the second three weeks they spent much of their time in the air, firing at towed targets.[9]

At first, all aerial gunnery students were volunteers. But the numbers needed turned out to be so great (nearly three hundred thousand) and the losses in aerial combat so high that the volunteer program ended. Men were assigned to be aerial gunners. At least one reluctant gunner was reported to have escaped from the program, and into the stockade, by carefully riddling the plane that was towing his targets.

Hitting a fighter closing on you at four hundred miles an hour was hard to do, even with a pair of heavy machine guns and good eyesight. The lack of skilled, highly trained aerial gunners, equipped with state-of-the-art powered turrets was one of the most serious shortcomings the AAF suffered in the first two years of the war. Bomber crews would pay the price of casualness.

The first bomb ever dropped from an airplane fell to earth in January 1911 at the Presidio of San Francisco, from a Wright C piloted by Lieutenant Philip O. Parmalee. The bomb dropper was Lieutenant M. S. Crissy. From this simple beginning followed a tortuous relationship between aircraft and explosives.

Before the creation of the AAF, the Air Corps depended as much on the service branches of the Army as did the infantry or the artillery. Army weapons came from the Ordnance Corps. All the radio equipment came from the Signal Corps. Construction was handled by the Corps of Engineers. It was never a happy arrangement as far as the Air Corps was concerned.

The Army Ordnance Corps in particular posed problems. For example, it persistently tried to force Wright Field to arm fighters with .30-caliber machine guns. Kenney, as head of the Production Division at Wright Field, resisted until Ordnance finally backed down and let him have .50s. Kenney also demanded .50s that had a higher rate of fire than the present 575 rounds a minute. He got it increased to 800 rounds per minute.[10]

During his command of GHQ Air Force, Frank Andrews had managed to get an Aviation Ordnance section established at Aberdeen Proving Ground. There, the Ordnance School ran a three-month course for Air Corps armorers. It was useful and necessary, and tolerated by Ordnance because such a venture was no threat to its dominance.[11]

Trying to take advantage of the post-Munich mood, Arnold attempted to have all research and development of aviation armament assigned to the Air Corps. Ordnance absolutely refused to accept any change, and continued to control the development of bombs, bombsights, aircraft guns and aircraft armor, even though it currently had more work than it could manage efficiently.[12]

In World War I bombs had tended to be tear-shaped, with long fins to provide stability. Allied bombs had an arming mechanism, consisting of a vane in the nose. While the bomb was being carried in the aircraft a wire through the nose of the bomb kept the vane from turning. When the bomb was dropped, the wire was pulled out and the vane began to rotate. After some preset number of turns, the fuse was armed and would explode the bomb on impact. If the bomb had to be dropped over friendly territory, the arming wire was left in the nose of the bomb.[13]

Between wars bombs became cylindrical and fuses were improved. Short, squared-off fins were developed that improved stability. A tail fuse was developed, in case the nose fuse failed. By 1940 Ordnance was providing a range of bombs, from twenty-pound fragmentation bombs, which were really recycled shells rejected by the field or coast artillery, to sixteen-hundred-pound demolition bombs. The filling for these bombs should have been more than 95 percent TNT, but there was a TNT shortage that would last for years. In the meantime Ordnance used a less powerful mixture consisting of TNT and ammonium nitrate.

There was a substitute called cyclonite, or RDX, which was more powerful than TNT. The British used RDX. Another possibility was to boost the explosive power of demolition bombs by adding aluminum oxide, as the Germans did.

The RAF pushed for large-scale production of cyclonite in the United States. The Navy, too, liked cyclonite. Arnold and the AAF liked cyclonite. Ordnance didn't like cyclonite, so cyclonite production for the AAF was delayed while Aberdeen experimented with something *it* liked, an Ordnance-developed explosive called "ednatol." Only after wasting years on ednatol and failing to get it into large-scale production did the Ordnance Corps put RDX into the AAF's bombs, and then in a weaker formulation than the British used. As for adding aluminum powder, the war was almost over before it went into American bombs.[14]

Bomb specifications were drawn up by a committee that comprised Army Ordnance experts, Navy Ordnance experts, and Air Corps experts. The Air Corps could, and sometimes did, find itself equipped with bombs it knew were second-best, but which a majority on the committee preferred.

For much of the war there was an unresolved dispute among experts as to which was the more effective: blast or fragmentation? In 1940, on the basis of British reports, Ordnance opted for fragmentation. It reduced the amount of explosive in American bombs to 30 percent and provided a thicker casing to produce more and bigger fragments. Six months later opinion shifted again, casings were made thinner and the explosive content increased to 50 percent. Then the British started dropping four-thousand-pound bombs on Germany and the Germans replied with four thousand-pound bombs dropped on London, with awesome blast effects. Arnold saw the devastation wreaked by a single one of these bombs and concluded, "We must have some at once."[15] By August an American equivalent was available, crammed with thirty-two hundred pounds of high explosive. It would be some time, though, before Fortresses and Liberators were ready to carry four thousand pounders, and then they'd have to be attached to the wings. Blast would prove to be best against structures, fragmentation against personnel. Most bombs over one hundred pounds were "general purpose"—they tried to combine both blast and fragmentation.

Ordnance never seemed to recognize that when it refused to allow the Air Corps to develop its own bombs it took on a special responsibility to ensure the airmen's needs were met. On the contrary, it failed repeatedly to meet its obligations. In December 1941 the AAF found itself pitched into war short of bombs. The dearth was so acute that the Air Staff wanted to know if there were any plants available to turn out fins and lugs for large-caliber artillery shells. Maybe these could be used to overcome the bomb shortfall.[16]

The AAF's dealings with Ordnance featured the basic elements that people soon learn to recognize when they're dependent on a monopoly supplier: arrogance, inferior products, inexplicable delays, and failures of supply.[17]

Early in 1932, Benny Foulois heard that Navy planes were going to be equipped with a new bombsight, manufactured by C. L. Norden and Company of New York. Foulois asked the Navy to buy twenty-five of these sights on behalf of the Air Corps. When they were delivered in April 1933 Foulois and every Air Corps officer who examined them was deeply impressed. All agreed that this gizmo was a huge improvement over the crude instruments in use since World War I. Those now looked like black magic; the Norden sight was science.

When GHQ Air Force was organized in 1935, the 19th Bomb Group, at Rockwell Field, California, did the Air Corps's first bombing with this sight. With a little practice, it enabled a bombardier at 15,000 feet to put bombs regularly within 164 feet of a target that Arnold said was "no bigger than a woodshed."[18]

Andrews, commanding GHQ Air Force, was skeptical about the claims for the Norden sight until Major Barney Giles, operations officer of 2nd Bomb Group at Langley, got him to see it in action. A circle two hundred feet in diameter was painted on the bombing range at Plum Island. On the first pass over the target at fifteen thousand feet a two thousand-pound live bomb was dropped, and hit inside the circle. On the next pass a second two thousand-pounder was dropped. It exploded twenty feet from the circle's center.[19]

Demonstrations such as this made the case for daylight precision bombing so powerful; they clothed the skeleton of theory with the muscle of things seen. Given the right plane and the right sight, it seemed possible to destroy anything from the air.

Foulois ordered more and more sights, until the total asked for came to two hundred. By early 1936 only half had been delivered, however, and the remaining half were in doubt. The Navy was claiming the right to take all of current production, which was running at a mere twelve sights a month.[20] Wright Field seemed unable to do much to bridge the gap. It was working on a sight invented by Seversky, a complicated device that was ahead of the technology available. A precursor of the modern computing bombsight, it really needed a microprocessor to become practical.[21]

Frank Andrews, commanding GHQ Air Force, urged Oscar Westover, Foulois's successor, to find some new source of modern bombsights. The best possibility was Sperry Gyroscope Company, which was working on a simpler device than Norden's. Sperry may have been motivated to get into a bombsight competition if only because Carl L. Norden was a former employee.

Nothing, however, came of Andrews's demand for an alternative source. The Matériel Division was hoping the Seversky sight might work or that Norden would come its way. It was 1940 before the Air Corps gave Sperry a contract to build bombsights that would duplicate Norden's success.

The secret of the Norden sight was that it linked two mechanisms. One was the M-1 bombsight, which put the plane over the target. The other was the C-1 automatic pilot, which made the airplane a stable weapons platform so the bombs would strike the target.

When the bombardier put his eye to the rubber-rimmed eyepiece on the sight, his busy fingers went to work on the controls, feeding information into it. The sight included a small mechanical calculator that absorbed the bombardier's data on the airplane's altitude, speed and drift. The calculator computed the exact flight path needed to put the aircraft in optimum position for the dropping angle of the plane's bomb load. It would direct the automatic pilot accordingly.

As the plane neared the target, the bombardier remained glued to the sight. The mechanism was stabilized by a gyroscope, so that the movements of the plane didn't make the sight waltz all around the target. When the cross hairs on the sight covered the target, the bombs werewere released. There was scope, though, for talent. Most men, under the pressure of combat, would fail to keep the cross-hairs on the target for the second or two that the bombsight needed. They'd become too excited, or too afraid, maybe even both. Only a few bombardiers had the nerves and coordination to get maximum performance out of the sight.

In the last couple of minutes of the bomb run, the bombardier effectively flew the airplane, through the automatic pilot. All the human pilot had to do was keep a close watch on the position direction indicator. The PDI needle had to remain centered on the dial. In high winds or the concussion of heavy flak the automatic pilot sometimes wasn't delicate or responsive enough to achieve perfection unaided; the pilot might have to make tiny adjustments on the controls, but that was all he could do. If the PDI needle was centered the bomber was exactly where the sight said it should be.

The Sperry S-1 bombsight and the A-5 automatic pilot worked on the same principles as the Norden and the C-1, but Sperry was trying to achieve the same results without infringing Norden's patents. Flight tests of the S-1 began in May 1941. The first production type was installed in a B-24 in February 1942 and made its first flight a month later.

The S-1 had serious defects from the start, the worst being "optical jitters"—the bombsight vibrated too much to maintain a fix on the target. Moreover, it lacked the ability to make calculations as rapidly as the Norden sight, so a sixty-second approach was required in straight and level flight to the target; the Norden sight required only thirty seconds. This made the bomber itself an easier target for enemy flak and fighters.[22]

Despite these shortcomings thousands of S-1 bombsights were installed in airplanes destined for Britain and the Soviet Union. The AAF was so desperate for bombsights it installed S-1s and A-5 automatic pilots in many of its own aircraft, mainly Liberators. The limited supply of Nordens went into B-17s.

Just acquiring these sights was infuriating and humiliating. Navy officers had to be present at any meeting the airmen had with the Norden staff. All purchases had to go through the Navy's procurement system. In July 1941 Arnold got former Navy man Robert Lovett to try to negotiate a pact for sharing Norden sights, but the Navy wouldn't oblige. It had financed the research-and-development costs of the sight. It had put up the money for the company's expansion. Why should it share the wealth now?

In January 1942 Kenney, as head of the Production Division, tried seizing the Pearl Harbor moment. He demanded that the AAF be allowed to finance new plants that would make the bombsight under license from Norden and supervision by the AAF. This time the Navy uttered an even more emphatic "No." Any new plants should be considered Norden subsidiaries, under its control. Arnold had no choice but to go along. The new plants would be financed by the AAF, would make bombsights for the AAF, but would be run by the Navy. It would be mid-1943 before they started producing anything.

The Norden sight became a quasi-mythical instrument of war, written and spoken of with awe, as if it contained a secret power that verged on the magical. It was treated by the Navy and the AAF alike with a solemnity that was almost religious in its intensity.

Trainee bombardiers took a twelve-week course, during which they dropped scores of one hundred-pound blue practice bombs filled with sand. The heart of their training, though, was the three-week section devoted to the Norden sight. When it wasn't in the aircraft, it was in a safe. Between the safe and the airplane it was under armed guard. Trainees weren't allowed to take notes; everything they were told about the sight had to be memorized.[23] Much thought, too, was devoted—in vain—to devising ways of destroying the sight if the aircraft carrying it was brought down over enemy territory.

The Germans had had the secrets of the Norden sight since 1937. A German-born American citizen named Hermann Lang who worked for Norden had provided German intelligence with blueprints of the device. In 1938 Lang even took a German vacation so he could answer various technical questions that the Luftwaffe's bombsight experts wanted to put to him. Copies of the Norden bombsight went into German Air Force bombers.[24] There was, in truth, nothing secret about it by the time the AAF went to war.

The sights put in fighter planes seemed fairly straightforward by comparison with the Norden and Sperry bombsights; only they weren't. Things had moved on since the iron ring-and-bead sights of World War I. Reflector gunsights had been developed that provided an illuminated cherry-red ring. The Matériel Command and Ordnance came up with a seventy-millimeter gunsight. They declined to copy the one-hundred-millimeter sight used by the RAF.

Here's an example of how it worked. The deflection needed was expressed in terms of the radius of the sight. An American fighter pilot closing on an enemy aircraft flying at 370 miles an hour on a course that would cross in front of him had to divide 370 by 70 to figure out the deflection. In this case, the answer was 5.3 radii. While he was working this out he might easily lose the chance to shoot down the enemy plane. An RAF pilot had only to divide 370 by 100 to come up with 3.7 radii on his reflector gunsight. He'd get his guns shooting while his American ally was still busy with math.[25]

The other shortcoming of American gunsights was the Matériel Division's implicit assumption that all fighter pilots were the same height. Fighter gunsights were fixed, absolutely immovable. For the five-foot-four-inch pilot, that meant rising from his seat in a half-crouch to take aim. The six-foot-one-inch pilot had to double up to look through the same sight. Why the sights weren't made adjustable by a few inches was a mystery known only to the engineers at Wright Field, none of whom was likely to fly a fighter in combat.

Nobody wanted armor plate in airplanes except the people who had to fly in them. The resistance from aeronautical engineers was strong. As weight went up performance went down. High-ranking staff officers, too, opposed armor plate, even for slow-flying transport planes like the C-47. They weren't unique in this. The head of the RAF's Bomber Command, Air Marshal Sir Arthur Harris was resolutely opposed to armor plate in aircraft: "The gun has it over armor."[26]

And no matter how tough the armor, someone will always come up with a gun to punch a hole in it. A truly armored airplane would be a groundling, not a weapon. Still, large numbers of combat injuries are due to small pieces of metal which, by hitting a vital spot, may kill or simply make a man unable to perform his duty. World War II infantrymen wore helmets not so much to stop bullets as to absorb the impact of shrapnel, rocks and falling debris. Helmets made soldiers more effective by keeping them fit to fight, over and above whatever loss of performance was involved in wearing a heavy steel pot that made the neck ache.

The aircraft in which American air crew went to war had almost no armor.[27] In 1942, however, armor spread through airplanes like crabgrass in suburban lawns. Men went to war sitting on old stove lids. Scrap-metal plates were hauled into bombers and placed around seats to offer protection against bullets coming through the side. Bomber pilots flew missions wearing infantry helmets jammed uncomfortably over their earphones. Fighter pilots removed the radio that was installed behind their seats and replaced them with steel plates.

No one had thought to armor the floors or noses of bombers—a strange oversight, considering that flak usually came from below. So did a lot of fighter attacks. Crew members, such as aerial gunners, would clamber aboard carrying large pieces of metal, which they would stand on throughout a flight.

The Matériel Command relented and in the later models of AAF bombers, light armor plate crept into specifications. Flak curtains were produced. Looking like lumpy blankets, they contained hundreds of small pieces of high-grade steel several inches square. They could be hung up near crew positions. Flexible plate was developed, too, which could be shaped according to where the crew wanted to place it.

It was obviously impossible, though, to turn a Flying Fortress into a real one. Something else would have to be done. The solution the AAF would hit on would be to armor the man, not the airplane. But that is getting ahead of our story. . . .

9

HAPPENINGS

Pearl Harbor brought Arnold a third star. Whatever doubts Roosevelt may have had about him, there could be no question now of a change in command, nor could running the AAF remain a two-star assignment. In December 1941 Arnold commanded thirty-three groups and a force numbering nearly three hundred thousand men. There were ten thousand aircraft, but of these a mere eleven hundred were modern combat types.

His knowledge of the aviation industry, his close personal ties to the men who ran it, and his awareness of the scale of output required to win the air war were unmatched in the senior ranks of the AAF.[1] He was also a master of public relations.

Early in 1942 the press was filled with alarming stories about the brilliant performance of Me-109s and Zeros. American planes were derided as inferior machines, virtual death traps for brave American boys. Such stories provoked anguish in the homes of young flyers, disquiet on Capitol Hill, and demoralization in the airplane factories.

Arnold had a chart prepared consisting of performance curves that indicated the abilities of the world's leading fighter aircraft, showing how they performed at various altitudes. Nothing on the chart revealed which curve belonged to which airplane. Then he asked one of the country's most outspoken aviation writers to examine the chart and tell him which aircraft the AAF ought to buy. The writer's first choice turned out to be the P-47; second was the P-38; third was the P-51. His newspaper, the *New York Herald-*

Tribune, went overnight from being one of the AAF's fiercest critics to being one of its most reliable friends. When Arnold pulled the chart trick on another hostile aviation writer, the man was so thoroughly converted he gave up his job and joined the AAF.[2]

Arnold was a driving and driven man. He made a hundred decisions a day and some were simply inspired. For example, the AAF would be unlike the Air Corps, where virtually every officer was a pilot. The AAF would have to find more than one hundred thousand officers who were ground-pounders.

They'd have to be trained at officer candidate schools, but building schools would take time Arnold didn't have. His solution was to take over more than five hundred war-vacated hotels in Miami Beach. He saved the taxpayers a fortune and swiftly trained the large force of gravel-crunching second lieutenants the AAF was going to need all over the world.

The AAF was also going to need hundreds of thousands of mechanics. Arnold made heavy-bomber manufacturers train five AAF mechanics on the factory floor for every airplane they delivered. In overcrowded Seattle this meant lodging the trainees in church basements and local jails, but it would eventually achieve what the wartime AAF motto demanded— "Keep 'Em Flying!"[3]

Arnold's conception of what the post–Pearl Harbor crisis demanded brought conflicts with senior Army officers, such as Lieutenant General Hugh Drum, commander of First Army, with headquarters in New York. Although the AAF had various air-defense centers in operation in 1942, the most Arnold thought the Germans might manage would be a lightweight, sneak raid against an East Coast city.* Drum, on the other hand, wanted air units tied to a defensive role. Arnold saw the air defense mission as an opportunity for training—training, that is, for offensive missions. When Drum refused to stop interfering with air matters, Arnold got him retired.[4]

Friction between air and ground was commonplace in the febrile post–Pearl Harbor atmosphere. Arnold's former aide, Colonel Elwood "Pete" Quesada, was commanding the air defenses of the Philadelphia area. Ground officers, however, controlled the AAA

---

*At the Arcadia Conference in December 1941 Portal bet him £5 that not one German bomb would fall on U.S. soil. At the end of the war, Arnold gladly paid up and Portal framed the £5.

and searchlights. One night in January 1942 they turned on the searchlights as a P-40 came in to land, blinding the pilot and making him crash. Quesada ordered the searchlights to remain turned off in future when aircraft were landing. The local ground commander, a major general, protested and tried to get Quesada fired. The issue went up to Marshall, who backed Quesada. Arnold's reaction was to make Quesada a brigadier general, for winning a small victory over the groundlings.[5]

In the summer of 1940, shortly after creation of the Air Staff, Arnold and Spaatz had proposed reorganizing the War Department. The present system was inefficient and inexcusable.

This wasn't news to Marshall. The sprawling, sclerotic structure he had to work with defied belief. Scores of people had a right, at least in theory, to see him. The real death-grip on the Army, though, was exercised by the chiefs of the various combat arms and service branches. Many had cultivated powerful friends in Congress. They had a strong investment in maintaining the status quo and none in promoting reform.[6]

In July 1940 Marshall could only resort to an interim measure. He established General Headquarters, under Leslie J. McNair, to oversee the Army's most important current operation—training. By December 1941 GHQ had become a bloated monstrosity. To keep other duties, such as overseas deployments, away from the chiefs, these responsibilities were dumped on GHQ. McNair urged Marshall to get rid of GHQ. So did Arnold. He didn't want McNair making decisions on the deployment overseas of air units.

Pearl Harbor provided the psychological and political moment the reformers needed. Marshall entrusted the task of reorganization to an AAF officer, Brigadier General Joseph T. McNarney. Aided by Major Kuter and two ground officers, McNarney proposed a three-way split of the War Department on functional lines—air forces, ground forces, and supply. The power of the chiefs would be broken, the War Department's structure would be simplified, and Marshall could take real control of the Army at last.

McNarney confronted the chiefs and told them bluntly the game was up. "This is what the reorganization is going to be. It is not to be debated. You are not being asked whether you like it or not. We start implementing the changes today."[7]

Meanwhile Marshall went to Congress and sold the new organization to the politicians. Most of the chiefs were forced into retirement. Bitterness and resentment were strong among those who remained, but in March 1942 the new system went into effect. McNair became chief of Army Ground Forces and Lieutenant General Brehon B. Somervell, an outstanding Corps of Engineers officer, established Army Service Forces. For airmen, this was a moment to savor. The Army Air Forces, under Arnold, had achieved ostensible parity with the ground. Air was now more than half way to independence.

No one who worked with him ever claimed Arnold was a deep thinker or long-range planner. He was pragmatic, decisive and, in the words of one of his aides, Lauris Norstad, "the original quick study in this world."[8] Illuminating his character from within, like the glowing filament in a light bulb, was a burning impatience that threatened to consume him. "Stress" doesn't come close to describing Arnold's normal state. And his fiery temperament was often at odds with the large, fast-growing organization he commanded.

He would arrive for work around seven-thirty each morning and tackle the stack of cables that had come in overnight. There would be as many as one thousand messages from around the world. All would have been reviewed; the most important forty to fifty were on his desk. There would be a pile of plans, studies and reports to read, but Arnold insisted that the contents of each be reduced to a half-page summary. He'd read the summary. Occasionally he'd ask for the original document. The hundreds of letters that arrived each day were reduced to a list of one-sentence summaries. He'd scan the list and decide which letters he wanted to read in full. Reading alone would keep Arnold occupied for much of the day.[9]

When he had finished with the cables and correspondence, the briefers would come in and offer a thirty- to forty-five-minute rundown on operations in theaters of war throughout the world during the past twenty-four hours. They'd offer a statistical breakdown on what the AAF had done and its state of readiness. They'd also provide him with the latest top-secret information from spies or code-breaking that affected the air war.

The rest of the day was spent mainly talking to people, in person or on the phone. Arnold was blessed, moreover, with an ability to read an official document while holding a conversation. That enabled him to continue reading as documents flowed unstoppably across his desk.

Major General Mason Patrick, the Chief of Air Service, learned to fly at the age of sixty. He is being greeted here by his second-in-command, Brigadier General "Billy" Mitchell, at Bolling Field in 1923.

Lieutenant General Henry H. "Hap" Arnold visiting Ninth Air Force units in North Africa after attending the Casablanca Conference in February 1943.

Above: Brigadier General Ira C. Eaker
briefs the press after the August 1942
bombing of a French marshalling
yard that opened the Air Force's
strategic bombing offensive.

Left: Spaatz and Arnold toured the
Normandy beachhead shortly after
D-Day. They are shown here at a
Ninth Air Force airstrip that had been
built under fire and was operational by
the morning of June 9.

Generals Carl A. Spaatz, George Patton, Jimmy Doolittle, Hoyt Vandenberg, and "Opie" Weyland meet up at the end of the liberation of France in September 1944.

Above: Benjamin O. Davis, destined to become the first black general of the Air Force, led the all-black 99th Fighter Squadron into combat in 1943.

Above left: Hubert Zemke, commander of the 56th Fighter Group, shortly before he was shot down and captured.

Left: Major General Elwood "Pete" Quesada, commander of IX Tactical Air Command, was one of the most effective air leaders of the war.

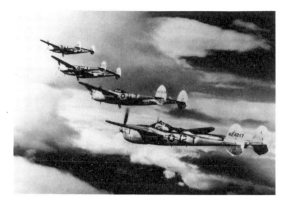

The twin-boom, twin-engine P-38 initially bore much of the escort burden. Four Lightnings are shown here on an escort mission with the Italian-based Fifteenth Air Force.

P-47 Thunderbolts with "invasion stripes" wait on an emergency airstrip in southern England. The runway was made of steel mesh "Marston Mat," which could be unrolled and placed on almost any surface.

A B-25 of Ninth Air Force flies across the North African desert in 1943. The shadows on the sand are cast by a preceding B-25 formation.

The long-range escort problem was eventually solved by the P-51, which carried enough fuel to fly as far as a B-17. These Mustangs of XV Fighter Command are flying over Italy.

A B-17 group in England in 1944 moves along a perimeter track prior to takeoff.

B-24s flew the first Ploesti missions at low level to improve the accuracy of their bombing, but the cost was high.

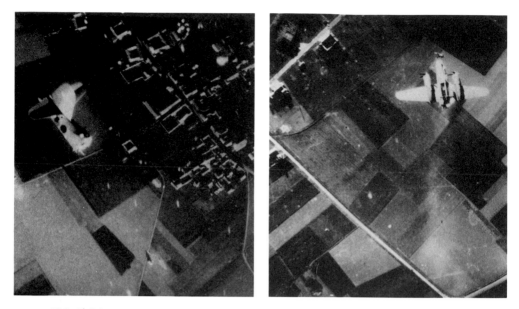

This B-26 on a mission to attack German V-1 sites in France has been cut in half by flak.

Flak was a major threat to bombers until the end of the war in Europe.

Two B-17s, returning from a mission over Germany in the winter of 1944, have collided in the fog that has descended on their airfield in England. There were no survivors of the spectacular collision.

The tail gunner of this B-17 stands next to the damage done by the cannon fire of a German fighter on a mission in July 1943. Meanwhile the aircraft of another bomb group come in to land.

Another XIX TAC P-51 is caught in this gun camera photograph as it flies through the debris of a German fighter, which a Mustang pilot has just shot out of the sky.

In the first few months after Pearl Harbor he went to his office every Sunday morning. Dwight Eisenhower, the head of the War Department Operations Division, joined him. For two or three hours they'd pore over maps, trying to memorize the geography of the entire world in excruciating detail. There were scores of remote peninsulas, obscure mountains and far-flung islands that were to become militarily important in the years ahead. They intended to know them almost as well as if they'd walked over them.[10]

One thing Arnold wouldn't do was hold regular staff meetings. He abhorred staffs, committees, paperwork, routine. Instead, if he wanted a group discussion on a subject he'd bring down both hands on his telecom box and hit all the levers. Lights would flash and bells would ring in a dozen offices. Within minutes there'd be a score of AAF officers standing in front of Arnold's desk. Who knew about this? What was happening with that? Those who had something to say on the matter were told to stick around. The rest were dismissed.[11] When he wanted something done, he didn't issue a directive. He simply scrawled a brief sentence or two on a yellow pad, tore off the sheet and sent it to the officer responsible for implementing his order.[12]

Even staff members who found his aversion to bureaucratic routine a strain were impressed by Arnold's acute intelligence. He enjoyed a rare ability to ask penetrating questions on issues he seemed to know little about. Without ever studying a complex subject closely he could nonetheless go straight to the essentials and leave his staff floundering. His personal approach to problems, his habit of talking directly to the man rather than sending a memo to the man's office, probably seemed to Arnold to be a way of simplifying life. Yet this aversion to standard operating procedures extended even to his own Air Staff, which found itself trying to draw up plans for air operations in an intellectual vacuum.

For the first few months of 1942, Spaatz's friendship with Arnold provided a bridge between the Air Staff and the chief. After Spaatz departed for England in May to run Eighth Air Force, the bridge collapsed. Dealing with the chief came to resemble consulting the Oracle of Delphi: it was hard to reach the Oracle and when you got there you didn't learn much. What the Air Staff needed was regular staff meetings with the chief. It never had even one.

Fortunately, by the time of Spaatz's departure, Arnold had established a small group, the Advisory Council, to engage in long-term policy-making. The Council became the conduit through which the Air Staff learned what the chief was thinking, hoping, intending.[13]

To many at the time, and later, Arnold *was* the Army Air Forces. He threw himself into his work in a way that was both impressive and deplorable. He didn't pace himself. It was all or nothing at all. Arnold simply couldn't delegate anything, unlike Marshall, who freely delegated to mere majors and lieutenant colonels powers that few generals would ever possess. Every day Arnold got involved in decisions large and small, like a man suffering from perspective deprivation.

Instead of having deputies with real authority he had five aides, with fancy titles, but they were little more than messenger boys.[14] Marshall, by way of contrast, chose strong, able and decisive staff officers, such as McNarney, whom he made deputy chief of staff. Like Marshall, they believed in the power of well-run organizations to get desired results and he trusted them to make decisions in his name, often without even telling him what they'd done. Arnold couldn't bring himself to do that.

The pivot of Arnold's management style was his legendary impulsiveness. He would stop people walking past his door and tell them to drop whatever they were doing and go across the country, or overseas, and tackle some problem that had just landed on his desk. On one famous occasion he ordered the chief air surgeon to head for Wright Field and work the bugs out of a troublesome engine.[15] He'd noticed the brigadier general's stars, but not the Medical Corps insignia. The impulsiveness was a form of stress management: A problem was stress, and by dumping it into someone else's lap he'd gotten rid of it for now.

Arnold's impatience was nothing new. When the French pilot was injured in the DB-7 crash at the Douglas plant in January 1939 the AAF project officer at the scene, Major Kenneth B. Wolfe, sent a coded message to Washington describing what had happened. Arnold couldn't wait for the message to be decoded. He phoned Wolfe and had him repeat the message, in plain English, over the phone. The chief signal officer was incensed. It would cost the Signal Corps $50,000 to devise a new code to replace the one Arnold had compromised.[16]

He was also casual in his demeanor to a degree that many Army officers considered shocking. A young flyer returning from China in the summer of 1942 was ushered in to see him. "General Arnold was sitting with his blouse unbuttoned and with one foot in the lower drawer of his desk."[17]

Despite the combination of impulsiveness and military bohemianism, Arnold was completely at home in those rarified purlieus where the military blends with the political. That had been his domain since 1917. Even Hugh Knerr, devoted as he was to Andrews, conceded that although Andrews was the more intelligent, Arnold was the more skillful operator.[18] In wartime Washington that kind of knowingness may have counted for more than knowledge.

Shortly after going to work as Stimson's assistant, Robert Lovett had written a memorandum that criticized the poor work and shortsightedness of Spaatz and the Air Staff. The memorandum was forwarded to Marshall without Arnold even seeing it.[19]

No one who was familiar with the AAF in 1941 could fail to notice its erratic way of doing business. There was an abundance of talent and initiative, but no management whatever. Arnold would suddenly take off for California or England and there was no one who could decide anything in his absence. Lovett's first task was to bring a sense of continuity to what the Air Corps was doing and to squelch crazy ideas that people tried to push through while Arnold was out of town.[20]

By 1942 the Arnold-Lovett relationship had become one of mutual respect. As Arnold put it in his memoirs, "Bob Lovett possessed the qualities in which I was weakest. When I became impatient, intolerant, and would rant around, Bob Lovett would know exactly how to handle me."[21]

Arnold's leadership owed a lot to his ability to solve complex problems with simple solutions. Some of his ideas were brilliant; others were simply impossible. It fell to Lovett to put his arm around Arnold's shoulder from time to time and tell him, "Hap, you're wonderful, and this is an interesting idea, but how are we going to convince the Navy? the President? the War Production Board? Will it help us get an independent air force?"[22]

Lovett was a methodical thinker. Before 1941 the Air Corps didn't collect a lot of statistics. Neither did the aviation industry. As an investment banker, Lovett believed in the power of figures as poets believe in the majesty of words.

He got hold of an Army captain who was a statistical wizard, Charles B. Thornton, and had him create a reporting system that gave Lovett an air-power bank statement each morning—so many planes were available, so many pilots, so many bombs, so many ground crews, so many spare parts. . . . After Pearl Harbor he set up a program, run by four Harvard Business School instructors, to produce even more sophisticated statistics to help the AAF conduct the business of war with optimum efficiency.[23]*

In April 1942 Roosevelt elevated Lovett, making him assistant secretary of war for air. His work didn't change one bit, but he'd gained a title that proclaimed its importance.

Following Pearl Harbor, Roosevelt and Arnold had a rush of planes to the brain. Arnold raised the production goal for 1942 from 36,000 planes to 50,000. The President went one better and demanded 60,000 in 1942, and 125,000 in 1943. Arnold gladly backed him up.

Lovett didn't believe any of these figures could be achieved. Even if they were possible, it would have to be at the cost of essentials, such as airplane spare parts. The present policy was to produce spares equivalent to twenty-five completed aircraft for every one hundred airplanes delivered. That statistic wasn't included in overall production figures, and if too much pressure was placed on plane makers to step up output they'd simply scrap the spares. If that happened, combat groups all over the world would soon be grounded or reduced to flying a handful of planes a few days each month.[24]

The great "Feasibility Dispute" of 1942 produced a head-on collision between Somervell, whose Army Service Forces handled Army procurement, and the War Production Board. Arnold continued to support the target of 125,000 planes in 1943, but Lovett convinced Stimson, Marshall and the Navy to demand a downward revision to 107,000.[25]

The WPB was reluctant to accept it, believing as Lovett did that even this would prove impossible. In the end, American industry produced 47,800 aircraft in 1942 and 86,000 in 1943. Forty percent of all the planes produced were trainers. The rest were combat aircraft and transports.

Lovett took a close interest not only in the aviation industry's output, but in the efficiency of its management. He was disgusted,

*After the war, Thornton created Litton Industries. One of the Harvard instructors was Robert S. McNamara.

for example, with the way the highly eccentric Glenn Martin ran his company. The weak management structure of Martin Aviation led to delays in improving the B-26 to reflect combat experience. Lovett got Glenn Martin eased out as president of the company and a new management team installed. In the course of the war Lovett brought about a shake-up in half a dozen aircraft companies and got Curtiss-Wright, a major manufacturer of bomber engines, completely revamped.

It was Lovett rather than Arnold who tied production to strategy. Every day, including Sundays, he briefed Marshall on the air war. Through these sessions with the Chief of Staff, Lovett was able to influence Allied strategy so it reflected the AAF's ideas, capabilities, and interests.

There were times, as we'll see, when Arnold worried about Lovett's expanding role. There was room, as he saw it, for exactly one commanding general of the Army Air Forces. Despite occasional pinpricks of jealousy, however, Arnold came to trust and like the assistant secretary of war for air. For Lovett's birthday in September 1942 Arnold had something special made for the assistant secretary—a pair of silver AAF command pilot's wings, with an armchair replacing the shield in the middle.[26]

A week after Pearl Harbor Winston Churchill crossed the Atlantic to spend Christmas at the White House. He arrived with a retinue of top brass to thrash out strategy among the tinsel and trimmings. The ensuing discussions with the War and Navy Departments ran on for three weeks and were termed the Arcadia Conference, after a region in ancient Greece fabled for the happiness of its inhabitants.

If the War and Navy Departments were to talk to the British on a one-to-one basis, they had to do so through a structure similar to the Imperial General Staff (IGS), which consisted of the heads of the three British military services. The result was the Joint Chiefs of Staff (JCS). Arnold had to be on it, so there'd be someone to deal face-to-face with the RAF's Chief of Air Staff Sir Charles ("Call me Peter") Portal. The Chief of Naval Operations, Admiral Ernest King, however, resisted this idea. Having Arnold on the JCS was as good as giving Marshall two votes. To mollify the Navy, Marshall proposed to bring in a retired admiral, William D. Leahy, as chairman of the JCS, giving the Navy equal rights. King grudgingly accepted this compromise.

The JCS came into operation at the end of Arcadia. Henceforth, the JCS and the IGS formed the Combined Chiefs of Staff (CCS), whose chairman was Marshall and whose headquarters was in Washington.

The principal decision of Arcadia was the strategy tentatively agreed upon six months earlier, that if the United States entered the war the Allies would seek the defeat of Germany first. They would assume the strategic defensive in the Pacific.

In reality, this was going to prove impossible. Public opinion, congressional pressure and the breathtaking offensives the Japanese mounted in 1942 all demanded an aggressive response. For the first two years after Pearl Harbor the Pacific absorbed as much of America's military might as did the war against Germany.

From Arnold's point of view, Arcadia offered a chance to cut back on Roosevelt's excessive generosity in giving away American airplanes. The AAF was taking delivery of one plane of every three the U.S. produced. The British, Soviets, and others got the other two, yet lacked pilots to fly so many planes. It took five months of argument with the RAF and the White House, but by mid-1942 Arnold had firmly established a new policy: the AAF would get two planes out of three.

The meetings of the JCS and CCS placed demands on Arnold for ideas on strategy and policy that were, as he openly acknowledged, beyond his creative powers. There was a streak of modesty and simplicity to Arnold that even the operator in him never muddied or confused. And, convinced as he was that no one over forty-five was truly creative, he turned to Major Lauris Norstad, a thirty-four-year-old West Point graduate, and to an even more youthful West Pointer, Major Fred M. Dean, a stripling of twenty-six. They were given the imposing title of the Air Staff Advisory Council.[27]

Their job consisted of reading the position papers produced by the Army, the Navy and the British, then figuring out what was really behind them and what the implications might be for the AAF. Thanks to them, when Arnold went to a JCS or CCS meeting he didn't walk in naked.[28] The Advisory Council also read the overnight cables and produced the half-page summaries for him. Increasingly, he treated it as an alternative to the Air Staff, which grew steadily during the war. The bigger it grew, the less Arnold wanted to deal with it—paperwork! . . . bureaucracy! . . . meetings!

The Air Staff also embarrassed him at times. In July 1942 Marshall returned from England and wanted to know why the airmen at remote ferrying stations between Canada and Scotland had no athletic or recreational equipment. The Air Staff had ignored the morale and fitness needs of these men.[29]

The Air Staff, on the other hand, was frustrated. It needed to know what Arnold was doing. The commanding general was forever starting new projects, without telling his own staff what he'd done. There was, for example, his decision to put all AAF photographic activities under a new headquarters. The Air Staff knew nothing about it until it received a nice letter on the new outfit's stationery.[30]

In the course of the war the AAF Advisory Council's membership changed from time to time. Arnold, recalling with some bitterness how he'd been forced to miss out on combat in World War I, rewarded his protégés with six-month combat commands. Afterward, they returned to Washington, more experienced and more valuable than ever. Every one went on to become a general.*

Arnold's place on the JCS brought him closer than ever to Marshall. The two men had known each other since 1912, when they were stationed in the Philippines. After Pearl Harbor, Marshall had Arnold move to Fort Myer and they would often ride to work together. It was believed among senior AAF officers that in 1940–41, when Roosevelt had wanted to fire Arnold, it was Marshall who'd talked him out of it.[31]

After the AAF was created, Marshall assured Arnold of real autonomy: the AAF's budget went directly to Arnold's headquarters—it wasn't filtered through the General Staff. Arnold, moreover, was one of the few people allowed to call the Chief of Staff "George." Not even the President did that, at least not to his face; he did it only when writing Marshall a note or sending a birthday greeting.

Much as Admiral King feared, Arnold became Marshall's trump in the JCS. Leahy got so hooked on being close to Roosevelt he skipped most JCS meetings, preferring to hang around the White House or Hyde Park instead. Before JCS meetings Marshall would tell Arnold what he wanted and how he wanted to get it. Then they'd go and whipsaw King.[32]

Something similar worked in the CCS, where the British would

---

*Norstad did best of all. In 1952 he became the youngest four-star general in U.S. history, at the age of forty-five.

find themselves arguing furiously with Arnold. As necks got redder and redder and tempers frayed, Marshall would sit back, in the posture of a judge listening to squabbling attorneys. At the right artistic moment he'd intervene, offering what looked like a compromise, but which was what he'd wanted from the beginning.[33]

Arnold was energetic, optimistic, and shrewd; quick witted rather than clever; generous to the young but suspicious of his contemporaries; happily subordinate to Marshall yet never at ease with Roosevelt; receptive to new ideas but constrained by old habits. He seems to have been too busy, too hurried, and too deeply involved in too many problems to be at ease with himself. If he ever did relax enough for his nickname to fit, it appears to have been when, on long trips overseas or across the United States, he sat in the copilot's seat and flew all alone in the cockpit for an hour or two in mid-passage, feeling this was the real man—Hap Arnold, aviator.[34]

10

BLOODY BUT UNBOWED

Feisty little Colonel Hal George could hardly believe the hand he'd been dealt on Christmas Eve 1941 when General Brereton departed hurriedly for Australia. He'd finally realized every officer's dream, a major command. "But what a command!" he said dejectedly into his newly-grown beard. "Twenty airplanes, a lot of trucks and five thousand kids without a leader."[1]

On Christmas Day, George began moving what remained of American air power in the northern Philippines into the rugged Bataan peninsula. By early January he was a brigadier general, but with only fifteen P-40s still in operation—nine were at Bataan Field and an additional half-dozen five hundred miles to the south, at Del Monte, on Mindanao. Most of the missions the Bataan Field's pilots flew were reconnaissance for the hard-pressed ground troops on the peninsula, roughly seventy thousand Filipinos and eight thousand Americans. Half the Americans were airmen hurriedly undergoing on-the-job training as infantry. A further eleven thousand people (mainly Americans) were crowded into the tiny island of Corregidor, where MacArthur had his headquarters, off the southern tip of Bataan.

Signals intelligence and various recon missions monitored a buildup of Japanese aircraft at Nielson and Nichols fields, outside Manila. It was a safe bet this concentration was in preparation for a renewed Japanese offensive against Bataan. George intended to strike first, when the moon was right and the night skies clear.

As darkness fell on January 26, seven P-40s prepared to take off

from Bataan Field. One ran off the runway and three of the fragmentation bombs slung under its right wing exploded. The other six
fighters got airborne and swung out over Manila Bay. They flew
low across the airfields, bombing neat rows of Japanese planes
conveniently parked wingtip to wingtip, then coming back to strafe
them. It was a gratifying but unrepeatable experience.[2]

Hunger was undermining everyone on Bataan, but pilots were a
special case. Without extra rations they lacked the physical strength
to continue flying. They were given more food. And if that isn't
enough, said the ground crews, you can have a share of our (meager) rations, too.

On March 2 the Bataan Field Flying Detachment got in another
blow. Four P-40s heavily laden with five-hundred-pound bombs
and led by Captain William E. Dyess, Jr., took off to attack enemy
shipping in Subic Bay. They sank one tanker and ran another
aground, but one P-40 was shot down. The remaining three crashed
coming in to land.[3]

By this time MacArthur had been ordered to leave. His personal
preference was to die in Malinta Tunnel on Corregidor with a gun
in his hand, his face to the foe. Marshall and Roosevelt may have
had no serious objections to that prospect, had it been guaranteed.
What couldn't be countenanced, though, was for MacArthur to
become a prisoner of the Japanese. He was ordered several times to
escape and finally, reluctantly, obeyed.[4]

On the night of March 12 four PT boats collected MacArthur, his
wife, his son, his son's Chinese nurse, and seventeen members of
MacArthur's staff, including Hal George, who left under protest.
George begged MacArthur not to take him out.[5] After a hazardous
voyage, the Navy delivered all its passengers safely to Del Monte
field forty-eight hours later.

Three B-17s were dispatched from Australia to collect MacArthur's party. One plane had to turn back when an engine failed. The
second crashed into the sea. The third reached Mindanao in poor
mechanical condition. Incensed, MacArthur refused to fly in it. He
sent a cable to Marshall demanding "the best three planes in the
United States or Hawaii."[6]

What he got was three more war-scarred B-17s from Australia,
one of which he boarded hesitantly. Flown to Darwin, Australia,
and then on to Alice Springs, he refused to trust his person to the
AAF any longer. An ancient, rickety train took him on to Mel-

bourne. Word quickly spread that "Dugout Doug" had a fear of flying.[7]

On April 8 the ground troops on Bataan were forced to surrender. Starvation had left even the most defiant spirits too weak physically to resist Japanese attacks. Corregidor continued to hold out, but its fate was sealed now that the Japanese could bombard it at leisure from southern Bataan.

One final air strike was mounted—from Australia. Three B-17s and ten B-25s flew the fifteen hundred miles from Darwin to Del Monte. There, they were refueled and bombed up. For two days they raided enemy shipping and airfields all the way up to Manila. One B-17 was lost, on the ground. Three enemy planes were shot down.[8]

Shortly before Hal George's departure, submarines had started taking out key personnel, such as B-17 first pilots. In the closing weeks of the doomed Philippines campaign planes arriving at Del Monte brought AAF officers with lists of people who were to be flown out to Australia, such as mechanics with enough skill and experience to change an engine. Navigators and fighter pilots, on the other hand, were likely to find themselves left behind.[9]

On May 6 the Japanese landed three light tanks on Corregidor. The prospect of them firing into Malinta Tunnel, which was crammed with thousands of sick and wounded, was enough to force the commander of all remaining U.S. forces in the Philippines, Lieutenant General Jonathan Wainwright, to surrender. As many as sixty thousand Filipinos were taken prisoner. So were nearly fifteen thousand Americans, of whom one in three was an airman. Filipino and American alike trudged into an agonizing captivity that many would not survive.

Japan, whose sole resource was the abilities of its people, had gone to war largely to seize the oil and mineral wealth of Southeast Asia. Without these, the Japanese military believed, Japan could never be secure. An Allied headquarters was hastily put together shortly after Pearl Harbor, combining Americans, British, Dutch, and Australians. Known as ABDA, its commander was a British field marshal, Sir Archibald Wavell. He had the hopeless task of stopping the Japanese descent on Southeast Asia with an array of ill-assorted, half-trained and at times mutually incomprehensible Allied air, ground, and naval forces.

The ABDA command's strategy was to hold the Malay Barrier, which stretched nearly two thousand miles from Singapore to northern Australia. Singapore was assumed to be able to defend itself: The great fortress city was crammed with eighty thousand troops and hundreds of guns. Defense of the Malay Barrier depended on retaining island airfields in the Dutch East Indies, so that as many as a dozen fighter squadrons could stage up to them from Australia.

The Japanese wasted little time neutralizing Dutch airfields on Borneo with a relentless bombing campaign, before landing troops on January 10. The soldiers pushed inland aggressively and overran the airfields. Borneo foreshadowed what strategically placed Java could expect.

In Australia the 24th Pursuit Group, which had been wiped out in the Philippines, was re-created, with five provisional squadrons formed from P-40s and pilots straight off the boat from the U.S. In late January one of these squadrons, the 17th Pursuit Squadron (Provisional), was rushed up to Java. Its pilots were fresh from flying school—well, not exactly fresh . . . they hadn't flown for two months. Few had ever flown a modern fighter anyway. A civilian aviator named Paul "Pappy" Gunn showed them the way across more than five hundred miles of open sea to eastern Java, flying ahead of them in a beat-up old Beechcraft.[10]

On February 3 the Japanese opened their bombing campaign against Java. The obsolescent planes flown by the Dutch were no match for the Japanese. The 17th Pursuit Squadron fared better, without faring well. It had good leadership but sorely lacked training. The most important mission the fighter squadrons had was to defend the vital Dutch naval base at Soerabaja from enemy air attacks. It was a pretty vain hope. The P-40s couldn't climb high enough or quickly enough to intercept Japanese bombers. On the few occasions when contact was made, Japanese escort fighters kept the Americans at bay.

Attempts to provide major reinforcements failed. Some 142 P-40s were sent toward Java, by air and by sea, after the 17th Pursuit Squadron. Only 39 made it. The rest were sunk, shot down, lost in accidents, or destroyed to prevent capture by the Japanese.[11]

Meanwhile the 19th Bomb Group redeployed from Del Monte to Australia. In late January ten of its B-17s were flown up to Java. From there they opened an antishipping campaign. They were soon joined by six B-17s and four LB-30s (an export version of the B-24) of the 7th Bomb Group.

A typical operation for the 19th Bomb Group would be to take off from an airfield in Java after lunch, attack Japanese shipping between Australia and the Philippines, land at Del Monte after dark, gas up, bomb up, collect as many pilots and mechanics as there was room for, take off before dawn, and attack more shipping on the way south.[12]

There were large stocks of bombs and aviation fuel at Del Monte. It also helped that the Dutch had bought B-10s a decade earlier from the United States. They had a stockpile of bombs on Java that would fit the American bomb shackles. Unfortunately, nearly all the ordnance expended between Del Monte and Java was being dropped in vain. Heavy bomber crews had never practiced hitting moving targets with bombs before they had to try it against Japanese ships.[13]

A squadron of A-24 dive-bombers from 27th Bomb Group deployed to Java in early February. When the Japanese invaded Bali the dive-bombers struck the Japanese landing barges hard, but like all dive-bombers the A-24 needed fighter escort. The squadron suffered heavily without it.[14]

With Bali in their hands the Japanese could mount regular fighter attacks against the heavy bomber fields on Java. The end was nigh. The bomb groups got ready to pull out.[15]

As they did so, the Malay Barrier was outflanked by the fall of Singapore on February 15.

This was a devastating blow to Allied morale. It came at a time when the air units defending Java were physically exhausted and emotionally drained. The severe shortage of ground personnel meant that aircrews were having to maintain and service their own planes between flying missions. The bomb groups were especially demoralized. They were barely the size of squadrons. Replacement B-17s arrived—some mysteriously carrying $250,000 in cash*—but there were never enough planes to bring the 7th and 19th up to

---

*Where did the money come from? Probably from the $10 million in cash and gold that Eisenhower was given by the War Department to find ships and crews to run the Japanese blockade around the Philippines. What happened to it? Most, possibly all, appears to have gone up in flames when the Japanese caught these planes on the ground.

anything resembling full strength.[16] Their puny size made them ineffective. Bomber crews had no illusions about it.

Three days after the fall of Singapore, the Japanese attacked the only good port in northern Australia, Darwin. They struck with more than one hundred carrier-based planes. The 33rd Pursuit Squadron rose to defend the town. Of the twelve P-40s that got into the air, eleven were shot down by Zeros.[17]

The next day, February 19, Japanese ground troops landed on Java. American units started flying out their planes. Ground crews were evacuated by ship, through shark-infested waters that were dominated by Japanese aircraft. Luck was on their side this time: they reached Australia safely. The curtain rang down anticlimactically on the doomed attempt to hold the Malay Barrier against the victorious Japanese.

At Christmas 1941, when the British chiefs were in Washington for the Arcadia Conference, the RAF's Chief of Air Staff, Sir Charles Portal, remarked to Arnold that the United States could repay the Japanese attack on Pearl Harbor in kind. It seemed to Portal that a carrier-launched air strike against Tokyo was feasible.[18]

It was an idea that appealed strongly to Roosevelt, Arnold and Marshall. But was it really possible to get close enough to the heart of the Japanese Empire to attack it with short-range carrier-borne aircraft? The Navy didn't think so.

Then, in early January, a Navy captain named Francis S. Low went to Norfolk, Virginia, where the brand-new carrier *Hornet* was getting ready to go to sea. Pilots assigned to the carrier were practicing short takeoffs at a nearby airfield where a one-to-one outline of the *Hornet*'s flight deck had been painted on the ground. Twin-engine AAF medium bombers were also joining in the fun by using the outline to practice anticarrier air attacks.[19]

Watching the bombers making their runs set Low to wondering. Could a twin-engine bomber actually take off from a carrier flight deck? He went to see Admiral King.

When the Navy put the question to the AAF the answer was that the B-26 was out: those little wings demanded a long take-off run. A B-25, however, could do it. A fast carrier such as the *Hornet* had a top speed of thirty knots. With the aid of a light wind of fifteen to twenty miles per hour passing over the deck, combined with the ship's speed, a B-25 should be able to get airborne in less than five hundred feet. On the other hand, it couldn't return to the carrier: its tail was too high, and too weak, to take an arrester hook.

Arnold gave a lot of thought to finding someone to command this mission. He settled on Jimmy Doolittle, whose daring was never in doubt, whose flying ability was second to none.

Doolittle sought volunteers from the 17th Bomb Group and 89th Reconnaissance Squadron, based at Pendleton, Oregon. These units had been flying B-25 antisubmarine patrols off the Pacific Northwest coast. The Navy assigned one of its best flyers, Lieutenant Henry L. Miller, to teach Doolittle's volunteers the short take-off techniques used aboard carriers. It was a heart-stopping experience to take off steeply in a bomber, knowing the plane's tail was within inches of striking the ground.

The sixteen planes the Doolittle Raiders would use had to be modified so they could carry a ton of bombs and fly as far as twenty-four-hundred miles. Their B-25s got extra gas tanks inside the fuselage, new bomb shackles, specially adjusted engines, and broomsticks painted black to simulate fifty-caliber tail guns. Their Norden bombsights were removed—no use at low altitude. The Raiders' armament officer, Captain Ross Greening, devised a twenty-cent gizmo out of two pieces of aluminum and it worked just fine at fifteen hundred feet.

The bottom gun turret on the B-25 was almost impossible to master.[20] Doolittle had it removed; an extra gas tank took its place.

He went to see an old friend from St. Louis, Major Richard Hughes, one of the Air Staff's targeting experts, for target data. Not a lot was known about Japanese industry and military bases, but there was enough for Doolittle's purposes. Besides, Hughes and everyone else involved in the project accepted this mission for what it was—a morale-boosting operation. It wasn't going to do any real damage to Japan's ability or will to fight.[21]

On April 1 the sixteen B-25s were loaded aboard the *Hornet* in San Francisco Bay. Ten days later, north of Midway, the *Hornet* rendezvoused with the carrier *Enterprise*. Surrounded by escorting destroyers and cruisers, the two carriers steamed toward Japan.

This Navy task force, commanded by Vice Admiral William F. Halsey, was on the kind of high-risk mission that Halsey's combative temperament was made for. There was a real danger that if the Japanese detected the task force, they could attack with superior naval and land-based air power. The loss of the *Hornet* and the

Enterprise at this stage of the war would have crippled the Navy for a year.

Doolittle hoped to get to within 450 miles of Japan before launching his strike. The intention was to fly on, across the Sea of Japan, and land at airfields in China. Days before the *Hornet* left San Francisco, Arnold informed Chiang Kai-shek of the impending raid. Chiang was appalled.[22] The only outcome he could see for the Chinese was an orgy of revengé by the Japanese army in China.

Japanese signals intelligence picked up Halsey's task force heading west. The Japanese guessed that a carrier strike was going to be made against Tokyo. They assumed, too, that it would have to be launched at a maximum range of three hundred miles—the range, that is, of U.S. Navy attack aircraft. They expected its location would be pinpointed in ample time for them to launch a devastating preemptive attack before the intruders got airborne.[23]

The morning of April 18, the task force was spotted 650 miles off the Japanese coast by one of the many small trawler pickets screening the sea approaches to Japan. The trawler, in turn, was detected by the task force.[24]

Doolittle and Halsey agreed: The B-25s had to be launched at once, twelve hours ahead of schedule and two hundred miles farther out than planned. Doolittle flew the first plane from the *Hornet,* taking off in just 467 feet. All remaining fifteen bombers took off safely. Each B-25 carried three five hundred-pound high explosive bombs plus a five hundred-pound incendiary.

Although 650 miles off the coast, the carrier task force was nearly one degree of longitude north of the Japanese capital, which stands, moreover, 50 miles inland. The flight to Tokyo would cover 800 miles. This was considerably farther than anyone had expected to fly. The Raiders arrived over the city at midday, just as a practice air-raid drill ended. They hit factories, barracks, and the oil-storage tanks. Targets were also bombed and strafed in Kobe, Yokohama, and Nagoya.

The original plan had called for a night attack and reaching the Chinese coast at dawn. Instead, the Raiders found themselves flying across the Sea of Japan as the sun went down. As darkness fell, the weather grew stormy and the B-25s started running out of fuel. Doolittle's pilots began wondering why they couldn't pick up the homing beacons they expected to bring them in to friendly airfields.

Claire Chennault had established an air-warning net in eastern China that could have led the Raiders to friendly airfields. Although Chennault had not been informed of the raid in advance, Halsey was supposed to flash a signal to him when the Raiders took off, asking him to alert the warning net that friendly planes were on their way into Chinese airspace. Once the net's spotters picked up the Raiders' aircraft, the homing beacons could be turned on.

Unfortunately, no message was sent to Chennault. Maybe Halsey didn't want to push his luck.[25] Therefore, fifteen B-25s crash-landed blind into China. One, blown far off course, came down in Vladivostok. The crew was interned by the Russians. Stalin wasn't going to give the Japanese any excuse to declare war on the Soviet Union while his country was battling the Germans.

Doolittle, like nearly all the Raiders, survived. He was bitterly depressed. He'd inflicted minimal damage on the enemy while his force had lost every plane.

The Japanese captured some of the Raiders. Others were handed over by the Chinese. All told, eight found themselves in enemy hands. Three were executed. The other five were sentenced to life imprisonment.

The real focus of Japanese reprisals, however, was the people of Shekiang province, where most of the B-25s came down. Thousands of Chinese peasants were massacred. Those Chinese who had helped, or even made fleeting contact with the American flyers were tortured to death. The city of Chuchow, toward which the B-25s were heading, was razed to the ground.

To Americans, the raid was a brilliant and heartening feat of arms, a swift kick in the teeth for the Emperor at the very peak of Japan's seemingly unstoppable advance. Doolittle returned to a nation's acclaim and, to his embarrassment, the Medal of Honor. He protested feelingly that he didn't deserve "the big medal"; he may well have been the one person in the United States who believed that.

Days after the Japanese attack on Pearl Harbor, Claire Chennault redeployed the American Volunteer Group and its sixty combat ready planes to parry the inevitable Japanese thrust into Southeast Asia. The strategic objective he had to defend was Chiang Kai-shek's Lend-Lease lifeline. Most of what the Chinese received from Uncle Sam was shipped to the Burmese capital, Rangoon. From there, it was moved by rail to Lashio, in northern Burma. Then began a tortuous nine-hundred-mile journey along the Burma

Road, through jungle-clad mountains, to Chiang Kai-shek's capital, Chungking.

Chennault organized the AVG into three squadrons. The 1st and 2nd squadrons moved from Toungoo, in Burma, to Kunming in the far southwest of China. At Kunming the Chinese had built an impressive air base in a picturesque setting; it fringed a pretty lake, against a backdrop of mountains. The AVG moved into the Kunming University campus, which offered many of the comforts of home, including hot showers.[26] From their new base the AVG's pilots could defend the northern end of the Burma Road.

Chennault's 3rd Squadron was redeployed to an RAF base at Mingaladon, twelve miles east of Rangoon. There it would join the RAF in the fight to keep the city's docks operating.

It was the AVG pilots at Kunming who got into combat first. On December 20, 1941, some twenty P-40s intercepted a Japanese bombing force over the city. Six enemy planes were reported shot down. None of the P-40s was lost.[27]

Three days later, the 3rd Squadron intercepted a force of fifty-four Japanese bombers escorted by twenty fighters that had just bombed Rangoon. The Americans claimed six enemy planes downed, while losing two of their own.

On Christmas Day the Japanese returned to Rangoon with nearly one hundred aircraft. The 3rd Squadron rose to defend the city and claimed nineteen enemy aircraft brought down; the RAF claimed seven.

Shortly after Christmas, Chennault rotated the 3rd Squadron back to Kunming, and sent his 2nd Squadron down to Mingaladon. It arrived in time to meet a five-day onslaught. From January 3 through January 7, 1943, the Japanese attacked day and night. The 2nd Squadron reported thirty kills and a further thirty probables.

There was air action over southern Burma nearly every day. The pilots at Kunming grew restive as reports flowed in of the 2nd Squadron's successes. Chennault organized a mission for January 22 to be flown from Kunming—an attack on Japanese positions near Hanoi.

The mission was to be flown by eighteen elderly Soviet medium bombers of the Chinese Air Force, escorted by AVG P-40s from Kunming. The bombers failed to rendezvous with the fighters; the mission was aborted. A second attempt was made two days later. This time the targets were obscured by low cloud. Bombs were dropped into the soup. If any damage was done nobody in the AVG ever heard of it.[28]

Throughout February the Japanese advanced steadily into Burma from Thailand. The AVG's 2nd Squadron flew strafing missions over Thailand all month long, trying to slow the enemy's march. Toward the end of the month there was a renewed aerial onslaught against Rangoon. On February 26 and 27 the Japanese mounted major attacks, employing more than one hundred aircraft each time.

Over these two days the 2nd Squadron claimed forty-three enemy planes, without a single loss, but wear and tear and a shaky maintenance system reduced the squadron to six flyable aircraft. With the enemy knocking at the gates of Rangoon the squadron was ordered to pull out.

The RAF, too, abandoned Mingaladon. It concentrated most of its remaining thirty flyable combat aircraft at Magwe, an airstrip in central Burma roughly two hundred miles north of Rangoon. Magwe was also being used from time to time by the 3rd Squadron as it raided Japanese airstrips.

Days after Rangoon fell the Imperial Japanese Army Air Force (IJAAF) began operating out of Mingaladon. On March 20, though, the RAF made a surprise return visit to its old base. A dozen Japanese planes were destroyed on the ground. Incensed, the IJAAF struck back, attacking Magwe with 266 planes on March 22. It attacked in force again the following day. The RAF in Burma was virtually wiped out. The AVG's 3rd Squadron was reduced to four flyable P-40s.[29]

Chennault's riposte was to send ten planes to shoot up the biggest Japanese air base in northern Thailand, Chiang Mai. Two pilots were lost, but the eight who returned claimed they'd destroyed at least thirty Japanese planes on the ground.

The Japanese continued moving steadily through Burma, heading toward Lashio. Attempts by British and Chinese troops to stop them were hopeless against a determined enemy who skillfully used the jungle to outflank blocking positions on the few available roads.

The end was in sight, but by this time the men of the AVG had become quasimythical figures. They had been enrolled with the most heralded fighting brotherhoods of modern times. The twentieth century fighter pilot was the embodiment of an ideal of the individual warrior that had been in flower at least since the days of Achilles. And here, in an outlandish setting, was a ragtag bunch of

American individualists, colorful, incredibly brave, carefree, and casual, simply blasting the Japanese out of the skies.

In six weeks fighting over Rangoon, for example, the AVG claimed to have shot down 217 Japanese planes, with 43 probables, for a loss of 7 pilots and 12 P-40s.[30] It was simply incredible, but people believed it.

Similarly, the Chiang Mai raid was reported in U.S. newspapers to have cost the Japanese forty planes; in fact, all they lost was three.[31] Still, at a time when the Japanese seemed unstoppable everywhere else, it was heartening—maybe necessary—to think that in one place, however remote, they were hurting, too.

Henry Luce, the publisher of *Time,* was the son of American missionaries in China. The Luce publishing empire was always interested in Chinese stories. It played this one to the hilt. Clare Boothe Luce herself wrote effusive articles on Chennault's pilots. And it was *Time* that spread their fame to the world, and beyond that to posterity, as "the Flying Tigers."[32] It was a creation of the Walt Disney studios. The pilots didn't use this moniker among themselves and it was wildly incongruous with their shark-mouthed airplanes. Yet, paradoxically, it seemed to fit. A tiger with wings is a mythical beast indeed.

Even as their fame was carried cheeringly into every American home, the Tigers were becoming embittered. Pushed back into northern Burma and southern China, they were being ordered to fly strafing and low-level reconnaissance missions. The aim was to boost the morale of British and Chinese troops who were being routinely thrashed by the advancing Japanese.

Strafing in a P-40 was a hair-raising experience and incomparably more dangerous than aerial combat. The P-40C was unmaneuverable and slow below five thousand feet, an inviting target for ground fire. In that kind of combat a rifleman was on an equal footing with the best fighter pilot alive. Chennault thought these low-level missions were stupid, but felt he had little choice. Chiang insisted on them, to improve the morale of his troops. Soldiers the world over love to see friendly planes striking enemy positions.

Almost since the time the AVG fired its first shot in anger there had been attempts to bring it under the Army Air Forces' control. In January 1942 Chennault offered a solution: "The best possible arrangement would be to have me appointed a General Officer in the U.S. Air Corps and Air Officer Commanding in China. In this position I could control both the AVG and any regular Air Corps units sent to China in the future."[33]

His present position was anomalous. His military rank was honorary colonel in the Chinese Air Force. It wasn't until April 1942 that he was brought back to active duty.

This put him under the control of the recently appointed commander of the China-Burma-India (CBI) theater, Lieutenant General Joseph W. Stilwell. An old China hand, Stilwell assumed direction of the one hundred thousand Chinese troops in Burma. And, like Chiang, he demanded low-level missions from Chennault's pilots.

Chennault soon came to despise Stilwell, and he had little but contempt for Stilwell's air officer, Colonel Clayton L. Bissell, who was an old acquaintance. Chennault, with his craggy face and piercing eyes, looked like a combat-scarred ace, but was never in a dogfight in his life. It was Bissell, whom Arnold had clearly sent to control Chennault, who was the ace. Back in 1918 he'd shot down five German aircraft.

Nobody would have suspected it. Bissell was pale and frail. He dressed like a gin-sipping British colonial administrator, in pith helmet and brown baggy shorts. He was also, as Arnold acknowledged in his diary, "an old woman."[34]

Given his ace status and closeness to Billy Mitchell, Bissell never felt he had much to learn from Chennault. The two men had clashed fiercely over fighter tactics when they'd served as instructors at Maxwell in the 1930s. And now here was Bissell, sent halfway around the world to torment Chennault some more.

On April 18 Chennault was ordered to send his 2nd and 3rd Squadrons to escort a half dozen obsolescent RAF Blenheim bombers to raid Chiang Mai. The last visit to Chiang Mai had cost the AVG two pilots. The Blenheim was a low, slow, flying cream puff. This mission wasn't going to hurt the enemy. Simmering resentments boiled over.

Chennault had a pilots' revolt on his hands. A petition was circulated among the two squadrons and twenty-eight out of thirty-four pilots signed it. They refused to fly the Chiang Mai mission. We came to fight the Japanese Air Force, the pilots protested. We didn't come here to make futile sacrifices just so demoralized ground troops will feel a bit better.

After a stormy confrontation, Chennault relented. You're right, he told his recalcitrant pilots. These missions don't make sense. From now on all our operations will have one objective—clobbering the Japanese. The Tigers roared.[35]

During the pilot's revolt Chennault was promoted to brigadier general. So was Bissell, with date of rank one day ahead of Chennault. That gave him seniority.

The Japanese marched into Lashio a week after the pilots' revolt, shutting down the Burma Road. On May 8 they took Myitkina, and its airfield, in northwestern Burma. Fighters based at Myitkina could cut direct flights between India and Kunming. The Japanese now controlled both ends of Chiang's lifeline. A new one would have to be created—by air.

The British troops were pulled back to the borders of India. Stilwell, offered a chance to fly out of Burma to safety, chose instead to hike two hundred miles and added to the personal legend he was rapidly creating for himself.

The AAF had been planning for months to induct the Flying Tigers into a new outfit, the 23rd Fighter Group, which started arriving in the CBI theater that spring. As the lost battle for Burma drew to a close, Bissell addressed the men of the AVG. He was supposed to recruit them into the 23rd Fighter Group. Instead, he thoroughly antagonized them. He made veiled threats that those who refused to stay and join the AAF would be drafted into the Army. They could count on spending the rest of the war as infantrymen. He told them to forget any idea they might have of getting jobs with civilian airlines back home. The airlines didn't want them.

By this time, fewer than half of Chennault's original AVG pilots and ground crew were still in China. Some were dead; others were recovering from wounds or sickness. Most of the survivors longed to return to the United States, to see their families and sweethearts. They would then decide what to do. Certainly for the many former Navy personnel in the AVG, the idea of joining the Army Air Forces was not a thrilling prospect. Only five AVG pilots and fifteen ground crew signed up for the 23rd Fighter Group. Despite that, it was going to be a top-notch outfit. What remained of the American Volunteer Group was inducted into the AAF on July 4, 1942. It passed into history.

Its claim of 299 confirmed aerial victories, a further 153 probables, and some 200 enemy aircraft destroyed on the ground was staggering. These successes were said to have been won, moreover, in the teeth of appalling odds. Its own combat losses were put at 13

American pilots and 73 planes. The Flying Tiger legend, based on these figures, was an evergreen, passed from generation to generation.

The truth was less awesome, and more interesting, than the legend. Up to March 1942 the AVG faced an enemy that had it outnumbered by less than two to one. It was not up against the best flyers the Japanese had, who were in the naval air arm. Nor did it have to contend with more than a handful of Zeros, which was essentially a Navy fighter. The fighter the Japanese army flew was the Nakajima "Nate," a plane that wasn't as good as the Zero.

Chennault taught his pilots to avoid dogfights. The P-40 lacked maneuverability, especially above twelve thousand feet. The Flying Tigers were trained to attack only when they had a height advantage, to make one firing pass, then dive away. These were much the same tactics as the RAF had used to win the Battle of Britain. They were especially effective when a pilot could use the P-40's weight (happily enhanced by two slabs of armor plate behind the pilot) to head for the deck at a speed no lightweight Japanese fighter could match.

In March 1942 the AVG started receiving the P-40E, a vast improvement over the P-40C. Almost at that moment, however, the number of serviceable AVG and RAF planes fell to about fifty— just as the Japanese received major reinforcements, taking their inventory to more than two hundred aircraft. Up against odds of better than four to one, the good days were over.

As for the AVG's record of aerial victories, the only well-researched estimate of Japanese losses puts the number at 110 to 120.[36] This gives Chennault's command a victory margin of just under two to one, which puts it on a par with the RAF's successes in the Battle of Britain.

Considering the handicaps under which Chennault's pilots had to fight, this was a tremendous achievement. It needs neither exaggeration nor embellishment. It is a free-standing testimonial to what a handful of courageous, well-trained men can do under someone like Chennault, an officer abundantly blessed with the greatest gift any soldier can have—the ability to inspire other men to fight.

11

TAKING THE
SCENIC ROUTE

As it pushed into the South Pacific, the Imperial Japanese Navy took Rabaul, at the junction of the Bismarck Archipelago and the Solomon Islands, in January 1942. Brooded over by six smoldering, purple volcanoes and fringed by picture-postcard tropical scenery, Rabaul has one of the world's finest natural harbors. A short distance inland are excellent airfield sites.

To secure this strategic prize, the Japanese decided to extend southeastward and take the whole of the Solomon Islands, and southwestward to take Papua New Guinea. They landed at Lae and Salamaua, on the northern shore of Papua New Guinea, in early March, to seize the airstrips there. Papua held nothing that the Japanese wanted or needed, but they intended to prevent the AAF from using it as a base from which to attack Rabaul.

To tighten their grip on Papua still more, they intended to capture Port Moresby, on the southern shore of New Guinea. Located two hundred miles over the Owen Stanley Mountains from Lae and Salamaua, Port Moresby was the only town of any size in Papua and its sole developed harbor. Coming after the loss of Java, the swift Japanese advance into Papua New Guinea sent fear of invasion throughout Australia, just as the rickety ABDA Command collapsed.

Ten days after the Japanese invaded New Guinea, MacArthur escaped from the Philippines. Allied forces were reorganized under a new command, the Southwest Pacific Area, or SWPA. This would be MacArthur's theater. The other Pacific theaters would be commanded by Admiral Chester Nimitz. The Allied Air Forces of SWPA would be commanded by Lieutenant General George Brett, a former acting Chief of the Air Corps* and Wavell's deputy at ABDA Command.

The Japanese were planning to control Papua mainly by air power. Arnold had already funneled what were, for the time, major air reinforcements toward Australia. In the three months following Pearl Harbor nearly six hundred combat aircraft had been sent from the United States.[1] Roughly 130 planes had been lost in defending Java, however. More than 100 had been lost in accidents. By mid-March 1942 the AAF had only about 180 flyable fighters in Australia. The Royal Australian Air Force was even more poorly equipped, flying 110 obsolescent, mainly British, aircraft.

The bomber picture was depressing. There were fewer than thirty heavy bombers in Australia in March 1942, and keeping more than a dozen in commission proved hopeless. A B-17 needed to be cleaned regularly. Those sent to war in 1942 also needed repainting, with lightweight paint. A B-17 that was dirty and coated with heavy paint was noticeably slower and less responsive than a clean one in lightweight paint. Bomber engines were powerful, state-of-the-art machines that needed frequent overhauls to keep operating. Yet in the whole of Australia there wasn't one depot that could provide cleaning, repainting and engine overhauls for heavy bombers.[2] Modern depots would have to be built. In the meantime, there was a war to fight.

Once the Japanese had established themselves at Lae and Salamaua, they raided Darwin regularly. Brett deployed the 49th Pursuit Group in mid-March to join the RAAF in defending the town.

The 49th was commanded by Lieutenant Colonel Paul "Squeeze" Wurtsmith, one of the most experienced pursuit pilots in the AAF. Wurtsmith had forty-eight hundred hours in fighters.[3] He also had one of the greenest outfits ever pitched into an air battle: 90 percent of the 49th's pilots had no fighter time before joining the group. Darwin provided pursuit OJT.

Even so, the 49th Fighter Group was well led. Wurtsmith taught

*Under Arnold, who created the position after becoming one of three deputy chiefs of staff to Marshall in October 1940.

his pilots the same modern fighter tactics that Chennault had picked up from the RAF: Fly in two-plane elements, don't dogfight, make one pass from above, then get out of there.

The 49th was flying the P-40E, which was a major advance over earlier models. It carried six point fifties in its wings, providing devastating firepower against the lightly armed Japanese fighters, whose twenty-three-caliber bullets and badly fused twenty-millimeter cannon shells did little structural damage to the sturdily-built P-40 and couldn't penetrate armor plate.

The 49th's biggest advantage in the defense of Darwin, however, was Wurtsmith's intelligence operations: he was monitoring the radio transmissions that directed the Japanese squadrons flying out of Timor. These intercepts, combined with the radar set at Darwin (which the Japanese never attacked) gave the 49th Fighter Group an hour or so to take off, assemble and gain maximum altitude in time to ambush the incoming Japanese.[4]

Timely warning and simple shoot-and-run tactics gave the 49th the edge they needed not just to survive, but to win. During a four-month struggle in the skies over Darwin, punctuated by long lulls between major attacks, the 49th claimed to have shot down sixty-six enemy planes. Its own combat losses came to sixteen planes, with only seven pilot fatalities.[5]

Japanese air operations in SWPA from March to July were leading up to a planned amphibious assault to take Port Moresby in the summer. This dusty, unprepossessing backwater became the focus of a bitter struggle for control of Papua.

Americans and Australians were hacking airfields out of the surrounding bush wherever there was a well-drained, level area. Each field was named for its distance from the town. There was a Three Mile Field, a Seven Mile Field, and so on. The Japanese raided the airfields early every morning and late every afternoon. They also sent a couple of bombers after dark, to make sure nobody on the ground got too refreshed by having a good night's sleep.

Brett deployed two squadrons of the 8th Fighter Group to Port Moresby in late April. Of the forty-one P-39s that set out to cross the Coral Sea to Papua, fifteen crashed before reaching Seven Mile Field.[6]

The pilots of the 8th Fighter Group raided Lae and Salamaua several times and suffered serious losses. Attempts to intercept high-flying Japanese planes over Port Moresby were even more disappointing. After a month in combat the group was withdrawn.

It optimistically claimed forty-five enemy planes downed, for a loss of twenty-six P-39s.

The 8th handed the defense of Port Moresby over to the 35th and 39th Fighter Groups. These were equipped with the P-400, an export version of the P-39. The P-400 carried a twenty-millimeter cannon, instead of the P-39's thirty-seven-millimeter gun. The gun jammed after a few shots. Many pilots preferred the P-400, with its more reliable cannon. The big drawback was the lack of oxygen equipment, limiting the P-400 to operations below fifteen thousand feet.

Sometimes there was a warning of an impending raid on Port Moresby, but successful interceptions were rare. The Japanese could bomb Port Moresby and its airfields whenever they felt like it, at dime store prices.

When not defending Port Moresby, fighter squadrons were often called on for volunteers to escort the 22nd Bomb Group, a pioneer B-26 outfit that was taking the war to the Japanese from crude jungle airstrips. When the call came on June 8 to provide escort withdrawal for B-26s that were attacking enemy shipping at Lae, eight pilots of the 35th Fighter Group got into their P-39s and P-400s and took off.

One of the eight was Lieutenant Jack Jones, leading the second flight of four. "As we were crossing the mountains we could hear the bombers calling for Charlie, our call sign. . . . Luckily I spotted a glint in the general direction I expected the bombers to be coming from. . . . As I got down closer I could see a lot of Zeros—between eight and twelve. . . . I picked one of the Zeros as my target. . . .

"We came in gently to the right in trail formation, one of us right behind the other. As we pulled around I heard my number-4 man, John Price, say 'Is that you behind me Bartlett?'—referring to my number-3 man. Bartlett came back in the negative, and Price said 'Uh oh!'

"I looked back . . . there were *five* of us in our flight. I made an extremely tight right-hand 180-degree turn and went back down the string to engage the Zero that was stalking Price back there. . . .

"The Zero started up in that typical vertical-climb business—hanging on his prop, up and up, expecting me to stall out. If I had stalled, he would have come right back and shot me to pieces. . . . I began firing all my guns in real short bursts. . . . I was sure I saw just one of my 20mm shells explode just forward of the front end of his cockpit. The Zero flattened out and I saw movement. . . . Sure enough, it was the pilot. He was climbing out. . . .

"I passed the Zero in a tight turn. . . . I looked at the pilot and he looked at me. He was looking at me like I was the last man he was going to see alive. . . ."[7] Japanese fighter pilots never used parachutes. This pilot, Warrant Officer Satoshi Yoshino of the Imperial Japanese Navy, went to his death a triple ace.

By this time the Japanese offensive in Papua was bogging down. On May 5 the Fourth Fleet's Carrier Striking Force had sailed from Rabaul, heading for the Coral Sea. Its mission was to secure the sea lanes for a fleet of troop transports carrying ten thousand naval infantry who would make an amphibious assault on Port Moresby. U.S. Naval Intelligence was by this time reading much of the Japanese navy's main fleet code. On May 7 the carriers *Lexington* and *Yorktown* made a spoiling attack.

The *Lexington* was sunk, as was a small Japanese carrier. The Japanese had won a tactical victory and Port Moresby was wide open. Many of its defenders had fled to the surrounding hills. Had the Japanese attacked, the town would almost certainly have fallen to them. Instead, the Battle of the Coral Sea shook their nerve. They canceled the amphibious assault and the victorious Japanese fleet sailed back to Rabaul.

The Japanese army came up with a new plan. It would seize the grass airstrip at Buna, a missionary outpost on the northern coast, and build an airfield at Milne Bay, near the southeastern tip of New Guinea. This would provide the air cover needed to send ground troops over the Owen Stanley Mountains to seize Port Moresby from behind.

Brett and MacArthur were also interested in Buna and Milne Bay. An AAF officer and an Army engineer officer were taken to Milne Bay by Catalina and native canoe in early June to survey it for airfield sites. A month later several thousand Australian troops and two U.S. Army engineer battalions were busily carving out an airfield for RAAF P-40s.[8]

The AAF's 8th Photo Reconnaissance Squadron, flying a specially modified version of the P-38, was meanwhile taking pictures of the area around Buna. Six American and Australian officers flew into the mission's small grass airstrip and made a more detailed examination on foot to locate a site for something more ambitious. MacArthur decided to take Buna, sometime, and build an airfield there. His mind was on taking Rabaul, rather than fighting for Papua, which he didn't believe the Japanese could capture.

On July 22 the Japanese seized Buna from a handful of missionaries and Australian civil servants. They prepared to send some seven thousand infantrymen to cross the Owen Stanleys, whose highest peaks rise to nearly fifteen thousand feet.

From Buna, Port Moresby was 130 miles away, down the narrow, treacherous Kokoda Trail. Much of the way the trail was little wider than a thin man's shoulders. There were vertiginous gorges to be crossed by means of bridges consisting of ropes and wire. The jungle was slimy, dark, and frightening. Yet the Japanese were in good heart, confident they could beat the mountains and take the town. If they did, the first victim would probably be MacArthur, whose career was on the line.

In June 1942 a party of fact-finders appeared unannounced, unbidden and unwanted at SWPA headquarters. The group consisted of an AAF colonel assigned to the Operations Division (OPD), Samuel Anderson; an Army colonel, Francis Stevens, also from the OPD; and a lieutenant commander in the Naval Reserve, Texas Congressman Lyndon B. Johnson.

Anderson and Stevens had been sent to check out the situation on behalf of the War Department. Johnson was there as the personal representative of his mentor and idol, Franklin D. Roosevelt.

MacArthur concentrated his considerable charm on the egotistical and ill-informed Johnson, who needed at least one wartime "mission" if he was going to secure his political base back in Texas against ambitious returning war heroes. Johnson's report to the White House could be critical to MacArthur's future. The President had privately called the general's defense of the Philippines "criminal."[9] One more major setback and MacArthur was likely to conclude an illustrious military career hurriedly and in disgrace.

The fact-finders were allowed to ride on a B-26 mission flown by 22nd Bomb Group from Seven Mile Field against Japanese shipping off Lae on June 8. The plane Stevens was riding in was shot down and Stevens was killed. Anderson and Johnson got back safely, thanks mainly to the skills and courage of the B-26 crews, and to the fighter cover provided (as described on page 163) by eight volunteers from the 35th Fighter Group.

MacArthur awarded Stevens a posthumous DSC. He gave Anderson and Johnson the Silver Star. The flight crews of the planes they'd ridden to Lae, including the airmen who'd perished with Stevens, got nothing, excepting the dead—they got Purple Hearts.[10]

Returning to Washington, Anderson reported to Marshall, who had one question to put to him: "Should I relieve General Brett?" There were rumors, stories and whispers, that much of the problem with air operations in SWPA was due to conflict between MacArthur and Brett. They lived in the same hotel, yet weeks would pass without their exchanging a word.

Brett was not cut out to be a combat commander. After the fall of Java he considered northern Australia as good as lost and moved his headquarters to Melbourne, on the southeast coast.[11]

Before MacArthur's departure from Corregidor, Brett was the senior American officer in Australia. He resented MacArthur's arrival, but, like many people in Australia, concluded that the general's days were numbered anyway. Australian politicians who despised MacArthur encouraged Brett to see himself as the future SWPA commander. Those political friendships killed him at MacArthur's court.[12]

Anderson's answer to Marshall's question was, "Yes, sir. As long as General MacArthur and General Brett are the commanders in the Southwest Pacific, there is going to be no cooperation between the ground and the air, and I don't think you are going to relieve General MacArthur."[13]

Arnold told MacArthur that Andrews could take Brett's place, without informing Andrews first. When he learned of it, Andrews was incensed. In 1935 MacArthur, as Chief of Staff, had given Andrews a written reprimand for extolling the B-17 before a congressional committee.[14]

Arnold then offered MacArthur Doolittle, but MacArthur had been infuriated by the Doolittle Raid. He'd been told that air and naval reinforcements weren't possible for the Philippines, yet the AAF and the Navy could attack Tokyo! MacArthur turned down Doolittle. "Wisely," Doolittle later remarked.[15]

At this point Kuter had an idea. Major General George Kenney was on his way to Washington from San Francisco. Kenney was heading for Cairo to organize the Middle East Air Force which would aid the British Eighth Army in the Western Desert. Why not offer Kenney to MacArthur, suggested Kuter. He was able, aggressive, and a combat veteran. He was also outspoken and tactless.

There were doubts that MacArthur would take anyone like that. To everyone's surprise, though—including Kenney's—he did.

Like Arnold and Andrews, Kenney had been rescued from the trash heap. Exiled to Fort Benning in 1937 as punishment for pushing the independent air force idea too hard, Kenney had spent eighteen months teaching machine gun drill and other infantrivia. He then made a personal plea to Malin Craig to be put back on Air Corps duties. Craig relented and Kenney was given command of an observation squadron at Mitchel Field—a job for a lieutenant, not a lieutenant colonel, but Kenney was glad to get it.

It was the Munich Crisis plane program that really got his career going again. Kenney became Arnold's troubleshooter on various projects: scouting future airbase sites in the Caribbean, testing self-sealing gas tanks, getting better oxygen equipment into production. In January 1940 he went to France and returned six months later with a long list of recommendations and an electrically heated flying suit taken from a German pilot downed near the Swiss border. It was far ahead of the heated flying suits produced in the United States. Don't try to improve on it, he told Wright Field. Just copy it.

In January 1941 Arnold made Kenney the assistant chief of the Matériel Division. Kenney's restless, combative temperament was unleashed on the plane producers. Even so, Kenney had no desire to spend the war in production. "When do I get a command?" he asked Arnold. "When output hits 4,000 planes a month," Arnold replied.[16]

In March 1942 it reached 4,020 airplanes. Kenney reminded Arnold of his promise. Kenney was given command of 4th Air Force, defending the West Coast.

The 4th had performed unimpressively in the 1941 maneuver season. It also had an abysmal accident record: pilots bailing out of P-38s and hitting the tail, B-24s crashing and killing entire crews, A-29s ground looping all over the Golden State. Kenney was sent to raise standards of training, discipline and morale. He succeeded so well that only four months later he got a combat command in a critical theater of war, the Middle East.

Then came the assignment to SWPA. Kenney intended to make a clean sweep when he got there. He told Arnold and Marshall that once he became MacArthur's air commander he was going to fire nearly every AAF general in the theater and send him home.[17] He proved as good as his word. Kenney knew Brett's top staff officers and considered them mediocre. They were an unwanted legacy. Before the year was out he would relieve four generals and dozens of senior colonels.

Before leaving for Australia, Kenney got Arnold to give him fifty P-38s, a plane that Arnold didn't care for. He also demanded fifty pursuit pilots from 4th Air Force, by name. At the top of Kenney's list was Lieutenant Richard I. Bong, a young pilot he'd had to discipline for buzzing a house near Hamilton Field. Bong reminded him of himself when young—the daring Lieutenant Kenney who'd been reprimanded for flying under the Brooklyn Bridge the day he'd gotten his wings in 1917.[18]

When he reached Brisbane, he checked into Lennon's Hotel, where MacArthur was living. Kenney was treated to an hour-long lecture on the shortcomings of the AAF and the disloyalty of General Brett. Loyalty, that was the main thing. MacArthur was obsessed with the subject. When MacArthur paused dramatically at the end of his oration, Kenney told MacArthur as plainly as he could that loyalty wasn't going to be an issue between them. If he ever felt he couldn't give MacArthur total loyalty then he, George Kenney, would ask to be relieved. MacArthur embraced him and pronounced they were going to get along all right.[19]

Brett returned to the United States, evidently thinking he was still in line for a top job—such as taking Arnold's place. He left behind a kind of testament for Kenney to study. MacArthur, he'd written, "detests the Air Corps, through his own inability to understand it. . . ." Nor did he understand what conditions were like in New Guinea, or even northern Australia, because neither he nor his staff ever went there. They had no understanding of the logistical problems in the combat zone. Morale was low and promotions or decorations were almost unheard of, especially among junior officers. MacArthur's chief of staff, Major General Richard K. Sutherland, was "a bully," whose lack of ability posed no handicap to his career since he had MacArthur's complete backing.[20]

As Kenney almost immediately discovered, Sutherland was a major obstacle. With five hundred hours in light, mostly civilian, planes to his credit, Sutherland considered himself an authority on aerial warfare. He was writing operational orders for AAF units, picking the targets, and prescribing bombs, altitudes, units. During his brief visit Anderson had concluded that the main source of the trouble between Brett and MacArthur was Sutherland.[21]

Such conflicts meant that command and control in SWPA was bizarre. Bomber units in New Guinea received a constant flow of mutually irreconcilable orders from various headquarters. Nor did MacArthur realize the folly of trying to run the air war in New Guinea from Brisbane, one thousand miles away.[22]

On August 4 Kenney took command of Allied Air Forces. Brett, he found, had carried the ideal of Allied unity to a ludicrous extreme. He had mixed Americans and Australians aboard the same aircraft despite different training methods, different leadership styles and different technical vocabularies. He had also reorganized USAAF units so they were like the RAF. The resulting setup bewildered many American officers, including Kenney.

He informed Arnold that he wanted an American air force created, and asked for the number five—one of his two lucky numbers.[23] (The other was thirteen, and he occupied Flat 13 at Lennon's.) American air units were reorganized again, along American lines. Kenney would remain Allied Air Forces commander, while running Fifth Air Force directly.

During his initial meeting with MacArthur he'd learned the 1st Marine Division would go ashore on Guadalcanal, in the southern Solomons, on August 7. The Japanese were building an airfield there, to secure their position at Rabaul, some 450 miles to the north. Although Arnold had his doubts about the Marines' ability to endure a prolonged major battle, King and Marshall had no intention of letting the Japanese get this airfield into operation.

Kenney went to see what conditions were like at Port Moresby and was appalled. The 35th Fighter Group was "chaotic . . . lackadaisical."[24] There was no warning system worth talking about. Heavy bomber missions, staging up from Australia to fly on to attack targets such as Rabaul, usually began with six planes. Of these, two or three would abort with engine trouble within thirty minutes of take off. At the first sign of enemy fighters, the remaining planes would dump their bombs and head for home.

Brett had ruled out building a depot in New Guinea, because it might get bombed. We'll put a depot here, said Kenney. Even if it gets bombed we'll be better off than we are now, sending planes back to Australia all the time.

Living conditions in New Guinea were squalid. The food was execrable. There was no mosquito control, so malaria was rife. Dysentery flourished. Morale was rock bottom. And the Japanese had the initiative.

Kenney's airmen weren't going to be able to do much until they'd won air superiority over Papua. He installed Brigadier General Ennis C. Whitehead, one of the most admired fighter commanders in the AAF, to run an Advanced Headquarters in New Guinea. He sent Wurtsmith to Port Moresby to control fighter operations, promising him a star if he succeeded, an ignominious return home if he didn't.

Kenney ordered his medium bomb groups, flying B-25s and B-26s, to attack the Japanese airstrips at Lae, Salamaua, and Buna without letup, and assured them they'd get fighter escort. He grounded all the A-24 dive-bombers. It was a useless craft and an impediment to job one: winning air superiority over Papua.

When Kenney returned to Australia he got a blank check from MacArthur to fire anyone he wanted. There was one person he couldn't fire, though—Sutherland. So he offered MacArthur's chief of staff a showdown in MacArthur's office to find out which of them was in charge of SWPA's air power. Sutherland backed down and stopped writing air mission orders. And, to MacArthur's delight, thirteen B-17s attacked Rabaul's main airfield, Vunakanau, on August 7, as the Marines landed, unopposed, on Guadalcanal. The B-17 crews claimed seventy-five Japanese planes destroyed on the ground.

This mission convinced MacArthur that Kenney, unlike the hapless Brett, could deliver. Kenney had asked MacArthur why, given his background as a maverick, MacArthur had been willing to take him. "Because you gave me so much trouble over air independence when I was Chief of Staff," said MacArthur. "In time of war you need a rebel."[25]

The thousands of Japanese troops and mules winding their way over the Owen Stanleys in August 1942 kept on coming. An Australian infantry brigade was sent to stop them before they reached the village of Kokoda, roughly halfway between Buna and Port Moresby. Several hundred reinforcements were flown in by air from Port Moresby. C-47s dropped supplies to the Australians, while B-25s and A-20s tried, with little success, to strike the advancing Japanese.

The enemy infiltrated around the Australians, attacked from the flank and rear and cut the brigade to ribbons. A second brigade was sent to hold Kokoda. The Japanese defeated that brigade, too, inflicting heavy losses.[26]

At Milne Bay, however, the Australians pulled off a major victory. Intelligence pointed to a Japanese assault at Milne Bay on August 25 or 26. The afternoon of the 25th seven planes from 35th Fighter Group raided Buna, just as ten Japanese fighters were taxiing for takeoff. The Australians shot down three enemy planes, and destroyed the remaining seven on the ground.

The Japanese landed twelve hundred troops at Milne Bay that night, unaware that fifteen miles away an airbase was under construction. One pierced steel-plank fighter strip was already operating; two more were close to completion. There were two RAAF P-40 squadrons at Milne Bay, along with eighty-five hundred troops, mainly Australian militia, but with a stiffening of U.S. Army engineers and Australian veterans from the Western Desert.

On the 26th eight B-17s of 19th Bomb Group attacked the invasion fleet. One Fortress was shot down, another was destroyed on landing and the remaining six suffered serious damage. That same day the 22nd Bomb Group bombed the Buna airstrip, hindering Japanese fighters from using it to provide air cover over the Milne Bay invasion force.[27]

At Milne Bay, reinforced with two light tanks and another six hundred troops and supported by fire from destroyers just offshore, the Japanese pushed deep inland, but remained heavily outnumbered. After a shaky start, the ground defenses steadied and RAAF P-40s "strafed until their gun barrels were lopsided."[28] The Japanese fought a hopeless battle for ten days, taking more than 50 percent casualties, before pulling out. It was the first Allied land victory in the Pacific.

By mid-September, though, there were five thousand hungry and tired Japanese soldiers only thirty miles from Port Moresby. They were confident, all the same, that they would soon take the town.

MacArthur had never wanted to fight for New Guinea. He didn't believe it would take him where he wanted to go, namely back to the Philippines. Not as long as the Japanese held Rabaul. He believed in destroying the center of enemy strength. Do that, and the rest would fall like ripe fruit. In SWPA, the center of Japanese strength was Rabaul. The alternative to taking Rabaul was a long, slow crawl up the two thousand mile northern shore of New Guinea. That didn't appeal to him for a moment, but he had to stop the Japanese from taking Port Moresby.

MacArthur decided to deploy one of the two U.S. divisions in Australia, the 32nd, to New Guinea. The division commander,

Major General Edwin Forrest Harding, was a Marshall protégé but his unit, a National Guard outfit from Wisconsin, was only half-trained before being hurriedly deployed to Australia.

Harding's staff, and Sutherland's, started drawing up plans to send the troops by sea. Kenney offered to get them there quicker—by air. MacArthur was intrigued. Could it really be done?* Kenney flew 230 men of the 126th Infantry Regiment across the Coral Sea on September 15, and asked for more. The rest of the 126th, however, was already aboard ships. "All right," said Kenney, "give me the next regiment to go, the 128th, and I'll have them in Port Moresby ahead of this gang that goes by boat."[30]

Using Kenney's sixteen C-47s and twelve civil airliners wangled from the Australian Air Ministry, Fifth Air Force delivered the entire regiment as promised. The division headquarters, too, was flown to New Guinea. All told, Fifth Air Force carried forty-five hundred soldiers across the Coral Sea.

On September 20 the Japanese advancing on Port Moresby received orders from Imperial Army Headquarters to pull back and secure the area around Buna. The battle on Guadalcanal and the defeat at Milne Bay had been a shock. Time to consolidate. The Japanese turned around, angry and dismayed, and ascended the Owen Stanleys once more.

The Australian 7th Division, a veteran outfit recalled from North Africa, prepared to go after them. The 32nd Division, too, would be heading north, but mainly by air.

A month or so earlier, Kenney had made a command reconnaissance along the Papuan coast from Milne Bay to Buna, scouting potential airfield sites at an altitude of one hundred feet. Roughly halfway between these two points was Wanigela Mission, where the tough, razor-sharp kunai grass grew to a height of three or four feet. In other parts of New Guinea it grew to nearly ten feet. The flat land around Wanigela, Kenney concluded, was probably dry and hard—airfield material. And an airfield at Wanigela would enable the 32nd Division to fly over the Owen Stanleys and strike at Buna from there. He proposed to make an airborne drop at

---

*Troop airlift had already been proven in war. In 1936 Francisco Franco had airlifted 20,000 troops from Morocco to Spain in a week to bolster his coup against the Republican government. The success of the airlift was the first major victory for the Nationalists in the Spanish Civil War.[29]

Wanigela to seize the site, then develop it into an airfield that would take large numbers of transports. Then he would fly Harding's division in. At first doubtful, MacArthur finally accepted Kenney's plan.

On October 4, a C-47 dropped basic hand tools at Wanigela to native laborers. They started cutting away enough of the kunai grass so that transports could land Australian troops who would have earth-moving equipment.

Ten days later the airlift of the 32nd Division to Wanigela got under way. Bad weather delayed the operation. Once it was under way, Japanese fighters began lurking near the mountain passes that Kenney's heavily laden, low-flowing transports had to fly through to cross the Owen Stanleys. A dozen C-47s were shot down or wrecked in crash landings.[31] It was mid-November before two-thirds of Harding's troops had been flown to Wanigela, along with thousands of tons of supplies.

North of Wanigela were large swamps and it was still fifty miles to Buna. Kenney had already picked out yet another airfield site, at Dobodura. This was roughly fourteen miles south of Buna. The methods used to get Wanigela into operation were employed once more and on November 8 the airlift of 32nd Division troops from Wanigela to Dobodura began. On November 19 Harding began his attack to capture Buna.

He had only two-thirds of his division and none of his artillery, but at first he mistakenly believed there were fewer than one thousand Japanese at Buna, weakened by hunger and disease. Instead, there were four thousand Japanese, well dug-in, well-armed and ready to fight. The terrain gave the defenders every advantage. The few land approaches to Buna consisted of narrow paths winding between huge swamps. From superbly camouflaged bunkers, the Japanese could bring machine gun and mortar fire to bear on the few trails.

The ideal tool for breaking open the bunkers was the plunging fire of the 105mm howitzer. A standard infantry division had forty-eight of these pieces. Harding, however, wasn't allowed to take his howitzers with him. Sutherland felt that keeping them supplied with ammunition was going to be too difficult. Besides, Kenney rashly boasted, "The artillery in this theater flies."[32]

In the event, close air support was minimal and ineffective. Air-ground cooperation at Buna was poor and each side blamed the other for it. A greater obstacle was the jungle.

If it was hard for an infantryman to spot a bunker from more than fifteen feet away, what hope had a pilot? Photo reconnaissance could do only so much. The cameras in use in 1942–43 showed only what the human eye could see. Attempts to mark targets with colored panels or even bed sheets weren't much help, either. Nor was radio the answer. The humidity of the jungle played havoc with portable radio equipment.

Struggling to strike the small targets that ground troops identified, A-20s flew as low as sixty feet, and medium bombers came down to one hundred. Friendly troops were so close to Japanese positions that it was fifty–fifty as to which side took the casualties. Even Kenney grew discouraged.[33]

Army officers persuaded him to fly in four 105mm howitzers, broken down, aboard B-17s and C-47s, but with little ammunition to fire they weren't able to accomplish much. Eight artillery pieces were flown in for the Australians besieging Gona.

Fifth Air Force carried out these operations with virtually no interference. The Japanese decision to concentrate on the fight for Guadalcanal handed air superiority in Papua to Kenney's pilots.

Nevertheless, Buna proved a grinding, bloody struggle, a ground battle fought for a few yards a day. Malaria, too, caused large numbers of noncombat casualties. Fifth Air Force began a medical evacuation service from Dobodura, using ten DC-3s and ten C-60s which eventually brought out thirty-five hundred sick or wounded soldiers.[34]

The decisive element in the fight to take Buna was logistics. So long as logistics was bad, the fight for Buna got nowhere. After the logistical picture improved, around Christmas 1942, the end came fairly swiftly. A fresh regiment was flown from Port Moresby, building the ground force at Buna up to full-division strength, the ammunition supply improved, tanks were shipped from Milne Bay. By then, though, Harding had been made a scapegoat and fired.

One reason for the rapid logistical improvement was that after flying in the troops Kenney's planes were able to concentrate on bringing in supplies. At about the same time, more shipping became available to bring forward supplies from Milne Bay. By the time the Buna campaign ended the Fifth Air Force had brought in roughly twenty-four hundred tons of supplies, including vehicles; about one-third the amount brought in by sea.[35]

On January 22 the Buna campaign ended, concluding the first successful Allied offensive of the war in the Pacific.

12

THE
LAMPLIGHTERS

In the spring of 1942 the British held the crucial Libyan port of Tobruk, but Rommel was closing in on it. If Tobruk fell, Egypt and the entire Allied position in the Middle East would be in peril. The Germans might be able to cut the overland aid route to the Soviet Union. At this critical juncture, Arnold sent Major General Lewis Brereton, to Egypt from India, where Brereton had just established the Tenth Air Force.

Brereton's mission was to organize the Middle East Air Force. MEAF would join the RAF in the fight for air superiority and provide close support to the British Eighth Army on the ground.

When General Brett had toured the Middle East back in the fall of 1941, he had been highly critical of British air operations. Everything seemed hasty and improvised. But as the RAF's Middle Eastern commander-in-chief, Air Marshal Sir Arthur Tedder, pointed out, in a real war you improvise all the time and nothing really works the way you thought it would back in peacetime.[1]

Tedder was an exceptionally able air officer, one of the best the war produced. He'd spent much of the 1930s in procurement and production, giving him a reputation as a nuts-and-bolts man, not a combat commander. Churchill had been reluctant to give Tedder this crucial assignment, but Portal insisted on it and Portal proved to be right.

The desert was aircraft hell. Sand destroyed engines. The heat felled ground crews. Metal became too hot to touch. Tedder's first task was to reorganize the RAF's maintenance and repair operations in the Middle East. No matter how many planes he had, he would never win air superiority without winning the maintenance battle first. That nuts-and-bolts background was about to pay off.[2]

At first, Tedder was simply outnumbered by the Germans and Italians. Then, when he managed to accumulate a superior number of single-engine fighters, he faced a quality gap—the Germans had better planes.

Simply preventing the German Air Force from winning was a kind of victory and, in September 1941, Tedder managed to get the prime minister to make what the RAF saw as a critical ruling. "Never more," Churchill informed the British army, "must ground troops expect, as a matter of course, to be protected against the air by aircraft." And when decisions were made on which targets aircraft would attack, air commanders would have an equal say with ground commanders.[3]

With this clear-cut declaration to rely on, Tedder devised an air plan that fell into three phases: first, the RAF would attack Rommel's jugular—his supply lines, at sea, on land and in the air; second, it would attack Luftwaffe bases and try to force the Luftwaffe into the air, where its planes could be shot down and its pilots killed; finally, it would provide close support to the ground troops as they advanced.

Aided by Ultra intelligence, which often allowed the British to read German Army and Air Force codes with ease, the Royal Navy and the RAF were destroying Rommel's supplies and the ships that carried them. By mid-1942 the British enjoyed air superiority most of the time; air supremacy, which is uncontested air superiority, wasn't yet possible.

As the air battle swung against them, the Germans wouldn't oblige the British by coming up and mixing it against superior numbers. Instead, German pilots used their advantage in speed and rate of climb to get high in the sun and wait for RAF stragglers. Or they'd make a single pass at a plane on the outer limits of a formation.

Nonetheless the RAF's Desert Air Force, commanded by a New Zealander, Air Vice-Marshal Sir Arthur Coningham, had the upper hand. Most of the time it controlled the skies over the battlefield. Despite this, the Eighth Army was in deep trouble. Tobruk was besieged and would soon fall. Such was the situation Brereton confronted when, at the end of June, he activated the Middle East Air Force.

Short, slender and bespectacled, Brereton looked like central casting's idea of a college English professor. He had, in fact, enjoyed a highly successful military career. He'd graduated from Annapolis in 1911, but he knew the Navy wasn't for him—he got seasick too easily.[4]

He transferred to the Army and in 1913 became one of its first aviators. In World War I he had commanded 12th Aero Squadron and an observation wing in France and finished the war with a DSC. He was close to Mitchell and served on Mitchell's defense team during the 1925 court-martial.[5]

Brereton was cocky, amusing and highly intelligent. He was also lazy, liked rich living, attractive women and partying till dawn.[6] Between the wars Brereton had held some of the top slots in the Air Corps and when expansion came so did his first star, in October 1940. After leaving the Philippines at Christmas 1941 he'd spent a couple of months in Australia before moving on to India to create 10th Air Force. Then came the assignment to Egypt.

At first, Brereton's command consisted of a B-17 unit he'd brought with him from India, the 9th Bomb Squadron, and a force of twenty-three B-24s that had set off from the United States for China under Colonel Harry "Hurry Up" Halverson. They were on a mission to bomb Tokyo from China. Just as they reached the Middle East, however, came news that the Japanese had driven deep into Chekiang province in response to the Doolittle raid and overran the airfields the B-24s were expected to use.

Arnold came up with another mission for them: bomb the huge oil complex at Ploesti, Romania. Some thirteen planes took off on this twenty-four-hundred-mile mission. Twelve reached Romania, but couldn't see Ploesti when they got there, so they dropped their bombs into the overcast and headed for Iraq. The RAF had two major air bases in Iraq, but one was then besieged by thousands of anti-British Iraqi rebels. Four planes short of fuel landed in Turkey, where their crews were interned.[7]

By the time Tobruk fell, on July 20, Arnold had three groups on their way to Brereton: the 57th Fighter Group, flying P-40s; the 98th Bomb Group, flying B-24s; and a B-25 group, 12th Medium Bomb. Brereton would retain direct control of his heavy bombers. His mediums and fighters were under American command, but their targets were often chosen by Coningham.

The P-40s seemed unlikely to survive against German Me-109s. The British turned many of them into fighter-bombers. The prewar

Air Corps had rejected the fighter-bomber idea, but the RAF had proven their value and hung small bombs even on Spitfires. It was using fighter-bombers effectively against enemy airfields, supply dumps and troop concentrations. And the ruggedly built, heavily armed P-40 made a better fighter-bomber than the Spitfire ever would, even though it was not as maneuverable as the British fighters at low altitude. The P-40 pilots, though, had to be retrained.

So did Brereton's bomber crews. The RAF had learned the importance of fighter cover for bombers, but the Air Corps had explicitly and repeatedly rejected the need for fighter escorts. American bombers were supposed to be so heavily armed they could defend themselves. Brereton's bomber crews didn't know how to work with fighter escorts. The retraining of American pilots would take time.[8]

While they were learning from RAF instructors, the Eighth Army was retreating eastward from Tobruk. Its losses were staggering: five thousand combat casualties, forty thousand men taken prisoner, hundreds of tanks destroyed or abandoned, thousands of trucks and hundreds of artillery pieces lost.

Rommel pursued the British four hundred miles and crossed the border into Egypt, where he ran into well-prepared defenses. His supply system was on the verge of breakdown, but he wouldn't pull back now.

A month after the fall of Tobruk the Eighth Army got a new commander, General Sir Bernard Law Montgomery. Above him would be a new theater commander for all British forces in the Middle East, General Sir Harold Alexander. Both Montgomery and Alexander accepted Tedder's air strategy. They asked only one thing in return—air supremacy. Once it was established, the rebuilt Eighth Army would launch a new offensive to drive the Germans out of Egypt.[9]

By October 1942 MEAF had become a major player. There were four thousand American airmen in the Middle East and more were on their way. The advance elements of the 376th Bomb Group and the 79th Fighter Group had arrived and the 316th Troop Carrier Group would soon reach the theater. The 98th Bomb Group and 9th Bomb Squadron were regularly attacking Axis shipping and docks. The 12th Medium Bomb Group was attacking Axis airfields. And the 57th Fighter Group had become experienced enough to fight Me-109s successfully.

On October 21 Montgomery launched his major offensive against Rommel at El Alamein. The German Air Force was exhausted and Tedder had a three-to-one superiority in serviceable aircraft.[10]

After a week of resolute attacks Montgomery's troops broke through the German defenses. During the battle Brereton's B-24s had continued their attacks on shipping. His B-25s had provided close support. And 57th Fighter Group claimed to have shot down twenty-three German planes in the course of the battle. Ten days after Montgomery's offensive began, Rommel began retreating westward.

Tedder had a practice of categorizing his pilots. The A pilots drew the toughest tasks, on the basis of proven competence. His B pilots got the less demanding operations. The 57th Fighter Group accounted for 12 percent of Tedder's fighter pilots, but from them came 40 percent of all those classified A. Between El Alamein and Tripoli (the last major Axis-held port in Libya) the group would claim a total of seventy-four enemy aircraft, while losing only five of its own. And by the time Tripoli was reached, the entire 57th consisted of A-rated pilots.[11]

During this long drive westward there were three major developments: Frank Andrews arrived in Cairo, to become the U.S. Middle Eastern Theater Commander; MEAF became the Ninth Air Force; and, on November 8, American and British forces landed in Morocco and Algeria, deep in Rommel's rear.

When Churchill spent Christmas 1941 at the White House he had tried to get Marshall and Stimson to consider an American landing in North Africa. They had flatly rejected it. The Army believed heart and soul in landing in France, marching into Germany and killing the Nazi beast in its lair. Arnold and Spaatz, too, wanted to go straight for Germany and bomb it hard, preferably into submission.

The War Department's Operations Division, headed by Brigadier General Dwight D. Eisenhower, spent the spring of 1942 planning to launch an invasion of France in the spring of 1943. This time it was the British who refused to agree.[12]

As the strategic arguments dragged on into the summer, Roosevelt was assuring the Soviets that a Second Front would be opened somewhere in the West before 1942 ended. And Field Marshal Sir Alan Brooke cooked up a plausible excuse for Churchill's pet project: clearing the Axis from North Africa would free a million tons of Allied shipping that presently had to travel all the way around the Cape of Good Hope to reach the Middle East.

It was a ludicrous idea, rejected by both Allied navies. A large ground force in the Mediterranean would need more than a million tons of shipping to keep it supplied. Besides which, the British were so wasteful of shipping that even a million-ton windfall was likely to be frittered away.[13]

Churchill used Brooke's arguments to revive the debate. And Roosevelt was growing restive to see American troops fighting the Germans. Besides, a North African operation could be presented to the Soviets as a kind of Second Front, something that had been specifically promised Stalin's foreign minister, Vyacheslav Molotov, in May. On July 24 the President ordered the North African venture be launched. He did so against the unanimous advice of Arnold, Marshall and King.

The resulting plan was complicated and fraught with danger. The first objective was to get the Vichy French forces in Morocco, Algeria and Tunisia to defect to the Allies, with as little fighting as possible. Once the Allies had secure ports and airfields in northwest Africa, Rommel would be caught in a gigantic pincers movement as U.S. and British invasion forces moved east along the southern Mediterranean shore and Montgomery's Eighth Army advanced west from Egypt.

The operation, code-named Torch, called for three task forces to make half a dozen landings over 360 miles of North African coastline, east and west of the Straits of Gibraltar. The Western Task Force, to be commanded by Major General George S. Patton, Jr., would be the principal U.S. contribution. Patton's thirty-four thousand ground troops would go ashore at three widely separated points in Morocco. They would take Cazes airfield, outside Casablanca; capture a minor port one hundred miles to the south where tanks could be unloaded; and capture the vital air base at Port Lyautey, seventy-five miles north of Casablanca. Port Lyautey possessed one of the few concrete runways in French North Africa.

Center Task Force, consisting of seventeen thousand ground troops, most of them American, would seize the Algerian port of Oran and the airfield at La Senia on the outskirts of the town. Fifteen miles south of Oran was Tafaraoui air base, equipped with concrete, all-weather runways. Because of its distance from Oran this objective was earmarked for capture by a battalion of para-troopers.

Eastern Task Force was assigned to capture Algiers and its air-field, Maison Blanche. This force consisted mainly of British ground troops, but with a sizable American representation. Once Algiers and Maison Blanche were secured the troops of Eastern Task Force were to head east, toward Tunisia. With its two excellent ports and four all-weather air bases, Tunisia was *the* strategic prize in North Africa.

Operation Torch was made as American as possible, in the hope that that would make it easier for the French to change sides. The Vichy French had no love of the British, who had attacked the French fleet at anchor in Oran in July 1940, killing twenty-four hundred French sailors. Mainly for that reason Eisenhower was named supreme commander of the Allied forces involved in Torch.

Shortly after Roosevelt's final decision to mount this operation, Arnold sent for Doolittle, who was about to leave for England to command 4th Bomb Wing, the medium bomber arm of Eighth Air Force. He told Doolittle about Torch and the need to create a new, numbered air force for it, the Twelfth. Would Doolittle like this command instead? Doolittle talked it over first with Patton, who was reputedly hell on airmen. The two men hit it off. Doolittle told Arnold he'd be delighted to have Twelfth Air Force.[14]

As a result, Doolittle was imposed on Eisenhower more or less as a *fait accompli.* Eisenhower thought Doolittle was brash, reckless, and out of his depth. He didn't want this racing pilot and reserve officer, who'd never commanded more than sixteen airplanes, running an air force in an operation as complex as Torch. He accepted Doolittle only under pressure from Arnold and Marshall and didn't hide his distaste.

Arnold chose Doolittle's top staff officers, giving him Colonel Hoyt S. Vandenberg as his chief of staff and Colonel Lauris Norstad as his chief of operations. Norstad had proven his worth on the Advisory Council. Vandenberg, the nephew of a powerful Republican politician, Senator Arthur Vandenberg of Michigan, had been Spaatz's principal assistant on the Air Staff at a remarkably young age.[15]

Ruggedly handsome, never seen without one of the innumerable cigarettes that would lead him to an early grave, Vandenberg had been distinguished at West Point for the number of punishment tours he'd walked.[16] He was bright but lazy. After qualifying as a fighter pilot he became a flying instructor, then moved on to Maxwell. Sent to Leavenworth, he barely scraped through, but in 1938 he attended the War College.

Soft-spoken and perpetually calm, he possessed a languid manner that concealed considerable ambition. He was on the inside track. Vandenberg and Norstad's first task on Doolittle's staff was to write the air plan for Torch.

Nearly half of Twelfth Air Force was created by stripping the Eighth. Doolittle got the 1st and 14th Fighter Groups, flying P-38s; the Spitfire-equipped 31st and 52nd Fighter Groups; the veteran 15th Bomb Squadron, equipped with A-20s; and two B-17 groups, the 97th and 301st, from England. From the United States would come the 68th Observation Group and the 81st and 350th Fighter Groups, equipped with P-39s; the 33rd Fighter Group, flying the P-40; two new B-25 groups (310th and 321st), three B-26 groups (17th, 319th, 320th), and 47th Bomb Group (Light).[17]

It would be some time before Doolittle would get even half his groups into action. There was a shortage of shipping and a dearth of air bases to be overcome. There was also the reaction of the Germans to consider.

The key question was what they would do about Tunisia. Not a single German soldier was there in early fall of 1942, but Allied intelligence calculated that there were enough transport planes in the Mediterranean to carry more than ten thousand lightly armed infantry from France to Tunisia in two weeks.[18]

The British urged parachute drops on the air bases at Tunis and Bizerta to seize them on the first day of Torch, but the American planners rejected this. They wanted to be sure of seizing Tafaraoui first, just in case the Germans managed to threaten the long and vulnerable American line of communications across northwest Africa by attacking from Spain or Spanish Morocco. Torch called for a steady advance into Tunisia and its conquest by Christmas Day 1942.

The German Air Force was monitoring the Torch buildup, flying a daily reconnaissance mission over the major ports of southern England every day in October. The ports were crowded with ships deep in the water. There was a flight every day, too, over Gibraltar. There, more than three hundred planes (mainly Spitfires) gathered. Fighters' wings overlapped, like planes on an aircraft carrier.[19]

While German intelligence made wrong guesses about what the

buildup meant, the senior German officer in the Mediterranean, Field Marshal Albert Kesselring, was certain there'd be an invasion of French North Africa. Kesselring, a Luftwaffe officer, managed to build up air strength on Sicily and Sardinia to four hundred fighters and bombers.[20]

The AAF's role on D-Day would be modest. The air cover mission fell to the two navies involved, which could put up only 166 aircraft. Once Port Lyautey was in Allied hands, however, the 33rd Fighter Group would fly its seventy-seven P-40s off a converted tanker, the USS *Chenango.** When La Senia and Tafaraoui were secured, Spitfires from 31st Fighter Group would fly in from Gibraltar.

The biggest AAF mission on D-Day would be the attempt by 60th Troop Carrier Group (TCG) to make a twelve hundred-mile night flight in thirty-nine C-47s from England across the Bay of Biscay, across Spain, across the Mediterranean and drop five hundred American paratroopers on the airfield at Tafaraoui. A secret agent known as "Bantam" was to turn a homing beacon on that would guide the C-47s to the airfield. It was hoped, too, that the Vichy French would allow the planes to land, sparing the paratroopers a combat jump; in which case they'd be able to fly on and make a jump farther east, at an airfield in or close to Tunisia.[21]

Blown off course by storms over the Pyrenees, their navigation hampered by ground fog, thirty-two of the 60th TCG's pilots arrived over Algeria at dawn carrying the 2nd Battalion, 503rd Parachute Infantry Regiment, commanded by Lieutenant Colonel Edison D. Raff. There was no beacon from Bantam. A few C-47s managed to find Tafaraoui, but were greeted with AAA fire. Low on fuel, most C-47s headed for a dry lake twenty-five miles northwest of Tafaraoui.

The paratroopers disembarked and started walking toward the airfield. By the time they reached it, American tank crews were already in possession of the field.[22]

The battle for La Senia, closer to Oran, swung back and forth throughout the morning. The airfield was taken quickly, but the

---

*The 33rd was a typical fighter group deployed overseas at full strength. It consisted of three squadrons, each with twenty-five planes. This would allow each squadron to operate sixteen planes per mission, leaving nine for out-of-commission aircraft. The remaining two planes were assigned to group HQ.

French counterattacked and recaptured it. In the early afternoon, American troops captured it again and two squadrons of 31st Group Spitfires started arriving from Gibraltar. One was shot down by a French fighter while coming in to land. Three French planes were shot down in reply.

Other Spitfires were ordered to strafe an advancing French Foreign Legion armored column. One pilot came back weeping and retching: a truck filled with French troops had blown up, filling the air through which the Spitfires flew with severed arms and legs.[23] The column was stopped short of La Senia. The Spitfires also suppressed a battery of French 75s that were shelling the field. By evening La Senia was secure.

At Algiers, the ground troops had pressed inland quickly at dawn to overrun the Maison Blanche airfield. Doolittle's pilots were landing on the runways by mid-afternoon.

The biggest battle of Torch was the fight for the Port Lyautey airfield in Morocco. It took three days of determined attacks by the Navy and nine thousand troops commanded by Major General Lucian K. Truscott to seize it. By the time it fell the runways were so damaged by Navy bombs and shells that the first squadron of P-40s of 33rd Fighter Group that tried to land on it after being launched from the *Chenango* wrecked most of its planes. The group commander, Lieutenant Colonel William W. Momyer, ordered the other two squadrons to fly south to Casablanca's Cazes airfield, which had fallen to U.S. troops the previous day.[24]

By November 12 the Vichy French had stopped fighting and most had defected to the Allied side. The landings had been a great success from Doolittle's point of view.[25]

Looking to the future, though, the situation was ominous. On the evening of November 9 the French colonel commanding El Aouina airfield in Tunisia had flown into Algiers. He claimed forty Stuka dive-bombers had landed that afternoon at El Aouina. Two days later came reports of a large buildup of German transports at Trapani airfield in Sicily. On November 12, a photo reconnaissance flight showed 120 Axis planes parked at Tunisian airfields.[26] There'd be no race for Tunisia: the Allies would have to fight for it.

Eisenhower was eager to make a grab for it all the same. His main instruments for doing so were paratroopers and the 51st Troop Carrier Wing, commanded by Colonel Paul L. Williams. By November 12 all three of the 51st's groups—the 60th, the 62nd, and the 64th—had reached North Africa.

On November 12 the 64th Group carried 300 British paratroopers to capture the airfield at Bône, 275 miles east of Algiers and only 50 miles from the Tunisian border. The Germans bombed the airfield, but next day more C-47s escorted by P-38s brought in AAA guns and enough fuel for the P-38s to operate from the field against the bombers.[27]

On November 15th 60th Troop Carrier Group dropped Edson Raff's parachute battalion at Youks-les-Bains, a French bomber field near the Tunisian border. The following day, the 64th Group dropped four hundred British paratroopers on the airfield at Souk-el-Arba, one hundred miles southeast of Bône. These advanced airfields provided support for British and American ground units and secured their left flank as they moved eastward into Tunisia, under the command of British Lieutenant General Kenneth Anderson. By November 26 his troops had reached Tebourba, sixteen miles west of Tunis.

Two days later the 62nd Troop Carrier Group carried 530 British paratroopers to seize the airfield at Depienne, twenty-five miles south of Tunis. Colonel Williams piloted the leading C-47.[28] The airfield was seized quickly and next day the paratroopers moved fifteen miles north, to Oudna airfield. Tunis was now only ten miles away.

More than twenty-five thousand German and Italian troops were in Tunisia by November 26; most had arrived by air. A sea ferry system brought in their tanks, trucks, ammunition and fuel. What they lacked was artillery, but Stukas and ground-strafing Me-109s took up the slack. Starting November 28 the enemy mounted punishing counterattacks against Anderson's units advancing from Tebourba. Over the next five days German planes and armor drove the leading U.S. and British ground units back more than twenty miles. The paratroopers at Oudna had little choice but to withdraw too.

Even as they were falling back, Eisenhower was writing a long, gloomy letter to Marshall explaining why the grab for Tunisia had failed. There was no shortage of reasons—everything from poor logistics to bad tactics—but above all he blamed the lack of air support for ground troops.[29]

The situation was far worse than that. Air-ground coordination *was* poor. Even had it been good it wouldn't have altered one fundamental fact: there were swastikas all over the sky. The Germans had 270 bombers operating from excellent modern runways in Sicily and Sardinia. It took as many as six squadrons of fighters to escort a single small convoy from Algiers to Bône. For a time the German Air Force bombed Algiers every night, and on November 20 struck Maison Blanche hard with a raid by thirty Ju-88 bombers. This attack wiped out the only RAF photo reconnaissance unit in Northwest Africa, a critical loss to both ground and air.[30]

GAF fighters, including the new FW-190, were flying from paved runways in Tunis and Bizerte. The FW-190 was a fast, well-armed, thrillingly responsive single-engine fighter with a powerful radial engine. No Allied fighter of 1942 could match it. Fortunately there were few FW-190s in operation.

When the North African winter rains fell—something they did in depressing abundance—American and British fighters at the advanced airfields near the Tunisian border sank into the mud, but the Germans could still fly from paved and well-drained airfields. The few hard runways the Allies possessed were far to the rear, out of fighter range, and the lack of hard stands at captured airfields meant there were hundreds of planes too deep in the mud to be pulled onto the runways.

Doolittle had to move half his bombers far inland, away from the soggy coastal plain. In early December, Army engineers found well-drained land on the Algerian plateau and created a new medium bomber airfield at Telergma. And at Biskra, on the northern edge of the Sahara Desert, they created a new B-17 base, with a steel plank runway wide enough for B-17s to take off three abreast.[31] Although a small, rickety railroad line reached Biskra from the coast, building this base and keeping it going was made possible only by the exertions of 51st Troop Carrier Wing, which flew in the engineers, construction equipment, stocks of aviation fuel, rations, bombs, spare parts and everything else needed to mount heavy bomber operations.

Closer to the front, however, there was no alternative to using crude, unimproved airfields and living in squalor. Early in December the 14th Fighter Group moved its P-38s into Tebessa, an Algerian town close to the Tunisian border. Tebessa stood on a wide plain. Army quartermasters saw it as an excellent site for supply dumps. The 14th's commander was less impressed. The formerly French airfield, he reported, was "comparable to an abandoned latrine."[32]

The Twelfth Air Force's most advanced airfield was even worse. Pilots from Youks-les-Bains had reported making emergency landings on a small but well-drained level stretch of terrain at Thelepte, forty-five miles southeast of Tebessa. In mid-December, two squadrons from 33rd Fighter Group were deployed to Thelepte. There was nothing there, just wet alpha grass covering five or six square miles. Pilots and ground personnel alike dug holes in the ground and moved into them, like gophers.[33]

Farther north, the Germans continued to push U.S. and British troops away from Tunis and the port city of Bizerta. Christmas Eve, Anderson made an attempt to pierce the Germans' defensive perimeter and failed. Eisenhower called off all major operations in Tunisia until the weather improved, and so did his air power.

13

REVERSALS OF FORTUNE

As the drive into Tunisia bogged down Spaatz, to his dismay, was removed from commanding Eighth Air Force in England and sent to Algiers to become Ike's acting deputy commander for air. At the New Year Eisenhower temporarily established the Allied Air Forces, entrusting this command to Spaatz. Whatever arrangements were made, they would achieve little so long as Spaatz lacked planes up front. On January 1, 1943, there were nearly 700 Axis aircraft in or within range of Tunisia, to the Allies' 480.[1]

The other thing Spaatz lacked was less easy to fix. There was a kind of artistry to running the air war in which experience was the pearl beyond price. "The balance between fighter-bomber and bomber action in direct support of the land battle, fighter and bomber action against the enemy air forces and action against enemy seaborne and airborne supplies, was a delicate one," wrote Tedder after the war, *changing daily.*"[2] (Italics added)

What Spaatz offered was a steadiness that was sorely needed. Doolittle's relations with the British were bad. Discipline in Twelfth Air Force was poor, and was not aided by Doolittle's determination to be one of the guys, flying combat missions and carousing with his pilots afterward.[3] When he allowed *Life* photographer Margaret Bourke-White to fly with 97th Bomb Group on a mission to bomb El Aouina, Eisenhower wanted to fire him. Burke-White, though, was no ordinary war correspondent; she was sleeping with the group commander, Colonel J. Hamp Atkinson.[4]

Spaatz pleaded for Doolittle to be given a second chance. This brush with disgrace had a sobering effect on Doolittle. Spaatz also toned down the anti-British feelings that Doolittle had encouraged, making it easier for Eisenhower to achieve Allied unity in the face of the enemy.

In mid-January 1943 Roosevelt and Churchill traveled to Casablanca to meet with their top commanders and determine strategy for the coming year. Marshall was astonished to find Eisenhower "almost in tears" over the logistical chaos that was undermining operations in Tunisia.[5] General Somervell happened to be in Casablanca and arranged an emergency shipment of seven thousand trucks.

Eisenhower's other immediately pressing problem was defeating the German Air Force. Air operations were reorganized yet again. A Mediterranean Air Command was created, to be run by Tedder. He would control everything, from Gibraltar to Palestine. Spaatz would take command of a new headquarters, Northwest African Air Forces. NAAF would have a strategic air force commanded by Doolittle, a tactical air force commanded by Air Vice-Marshal Sir Arthur Coningham, a coastal command under Air Vice-Marshal Hugh Pugh-Lloyd, a training command under an American, Brigadier General John K. Cannon, an air service command, and a photographic reconnaissance wing, to be commanded by Lieutenant Colonel Elliott Roosevelt.

The British had been pushing for a combined command covering the entire Mediterranean, made up of alternating layers—American, British, American, British, and so on—from Eisenhower's headquarters in Algiers down to a fairly low level of operations. This meant putting the units of one country under the command of a superior headquarters run by an officer of the other country, with Americans and British "interleaved." And now they had it. The new organization would go into effect when Montgomery's Eighth Army crossed the border from Libya into Tunisia.

The Axis army in Tunisia continued to grow. It would eventually number one hundred fifty thousand men, under the command of a hard-bitten veteran of the Eastern Front, Jürgen von Arnim. Eisenhower's strategy was to wait for the rainy season to end, then push the U.S. II Corps across central Tunisia to the east coast. This would prevent Rommel and the seventy-five thousand Axis troops retreating across Libya from linking up with von Arnim's army. If Ike's strategy succeeded, it would be possible to defeat the two Axis armies in detail.[6]

The key to his plan for a renewed offensive was the forward airfield at Thelepte. Planes operating from Thelepte would help American and French troops hold on to the passes in the hills of central Tunisia through the winter and support the projected advance when the weather broke.

Eisenhower was an optimist by nature, a realist by experience. He knew that his ambitious plans rested on precarious foundations. The II Corps commander, Major General Lloyd Fredendall, had only eighty thousand green troops holding a front that was seventy-five miles long and more than fifty miles deep.

The front line for Fredendall's troops in January 1943 was a long succession of high, treeless hills known as the Eastern Dorsal. At the northern end of the Eastern Dorsal was a French corps of twenty-five thousand lightly armed troops defending Faid Pass. North of the French was the British First Army.

Fredendall's rear defenses, some twenty to forty miles back, were based on another line of high hills, known as the Western Dorsal. The southern gateway through the Western Dorsal was Kasserine Pass. Less than ten miles from Kasserine Pass stood the alpha grass landing grounds of Thelepte.

The Twelfth Air Force had established XII Air Support Command to aid II Corps, but many airmen were irked by the fact that under current doctrine, expressed in Field Manual 31–35, Fredendall had the final decision over which targets would be struck. To independence-minded AAF officers this was a blow to their self-esteem and an impediment to effective operations. The manual, however, had been produced not by Army Ground Forces, but by the AAF.

Besides, Fredendall rarely interfered in target selection. He left 90 percent of air decisions to the XII ASC commander, Colonel Paul L. Williams.[7] A former commander of the 51st Troop Carrier Wing, Williams was unlike many AAF officers: he believed wholeheartedly in ground support.

Air support was an uphill struggle in Tunisia, not because of interference from the ground, but because of interference from the German Air Force. Spaatz hadn't grasped early enough that air superiority would have to be fought for. He'd concentrated instead on keeping Doolittle's B-17s under American control and carving out a major mission for them, telling Eisenhower in mid-December 1942 that only thirty-six B-17 sorties a day would be needed to cut off Axis supplies to Tunisia.[8]

Air and ground alike also suffered from a lack of training and equipment. Ground troops had been pushed into North Africa with few of the light, mobile antiaircraft weapons, such as quad-50s, which they needed to defend themselves from attacks by Stukas and strafers. Aircrews, like the ground soldiers, had been sent to England on the assumption that they'd finish their training there, but were shipped off to participate in Torch instead. Doolittle estimated 75 percent of his airmen were only partially trained.[9]

There was virtually no warning against German air attacks, because the early radar sets were almost useless in the mountainous terrain of northern and central Tunisia. XII ASC thus found itself under intense pressure to provide air umbrellas over ground units.

Williams was also asked to take responsibility for photo reconnaissance for II Corps. The RAF's PR unit, which was assigned to serve the field commands, had seen nearly all its equipment destroyed in a German raid. Elliott Roosevelt's Third Photo Group was ordered to help II Corps, but Roosevelt lacked equipment, experience and trained photo interpreters. He was also short of trained pilots. In his first five weeks in North Africa his group lost ninety-two of its original ninety-five pilots. Also, as he frankly admitted, he had no understanding of aerial tactical reconnaissance. The II Corps fought its battles without Tac R.[10]

Major Philip Cochran had arrived at Thelepte in late December with a batch of replacement pilots and P-40s for the two squadrons of 33rd Fighter Group that had deployed there a couple of weeks earlier. Everywhere, including inside the airplanes, were signs of dysentery, the result of living in holes amid mud and squalor.

Operations were haphazard. The Germans would fly over at first light and keep the Americans nailed to the ground for most of the morning. On one occasion they dropped a taunting note that read, "We are the Moelders Geschwader—the ones with the yellow wingtips. We have moved into your area and we want you to know it." It was like a scene out of the film *Wings*.[11]

Cochran was a handsome, hotshot fighter pilot who cut a wide swathe through chorus girls and hat-check personnel back home. A cartoon-strip character, Flip Corkin of "Terry and the Pirates," was based on him and his impressive chin. As the ranking officer on the scene, he took over at Thelepte.

A former instructor, Cochran taught P-40 pilots how to stay alive against the Me-109G by using their one advantage—they could easily outturn a Messerschmitt. When the weather permitted and the sole steel-plank runway at Youks-les-Bains wasn't completely lost in the mud, he got 14th Fighter Group P-38s to come up and chase the Germans' dawn patrol away and let his pilots fly.

Cochran's main mission was helping the French to hold on to Faid Pass. Doolittle funneled planes to Thelepte to keep him in business. Cochran's losses were daunting. During one four-day period he went from having twenty-eight operational aircraft to just four. Despite the appalling conditions, he and his men were so willing to fight that they'd fly whatever they had, but Cochran soon learned that if he put up eight planes he'd probably lose four or five. If he waited until he could put up eighteen, he might lose only one.[12] It was a lesson that fighter unit commanders learned the hard way.

Around the middle of January the 33rd's commander, "Spike" Momyer, arrived. Cochran left Thelepte, to pass on what he'd learned to units freshly arriving in the theater, such as the 325th Fighter Group and the black 99th Fighter Squadron.

On January 31 von Arnim hit the French at Faid Pass. After two days the French were forced to retreat. Fredendall's front line was in danger of unraveling. As he struggled to shore it up on the ground, XII Air Support Command flew itself to exhaustion in the air. Williams's pilots were trying to do it all—fly umbrellas, strafe advancing enemy troops, knock out enemy tanks, attack locomotives, defend their own airfields—and do it without air superiority. XII Fighter Command units did what they could to help, but they too were hurting. Momyer's 33rd Fighter Group was so worn out its survivors had to be flown to Morocco aboard C-47s so they could recover. The 33rd handed Thelepte over to the 31st Fighter Group.

In mid-February Rommel and fifteen thousand veterans of the old Afrika Korps detached themselves from the combined German-Italian army that was retreating sedately in front of Montgomery. Rommel hurried toward the Eastern Dorsal, intending to strike II Corps a crippling blow before the Americans learned how to fight.

Skirting the southern end of the Eastern Dorsal, he hit 1st Armored and 1st Infantry Division troops in the flank near a town called Sidi-bou-Zid. More than three thousand Americans were killed, captured or taken prisoner. The survivors retreated toward the Western Dorsal, pursued by the victorious Germans.[13]

Rommel was heading for Kasserine Pass, one of the few openings in the Western Dorsal. Thelepte stood barely seven miles from the pass and on the line of the German advance. The 31st Fighter Group took off, abandoning the field, as German tanks rolled over the nearby hills, which were dotted with thousands of fifty-five-gallon drums of aviation fuel.[14] The drums were so widely dispersed the Germans didn't have time to pick up more than a fraction; the red-dyed one-hundred-octane stuff was too powerful for them to use anyway.

On February 20, the Germans brushed aside the small force defending the road that ran through Kasserine Pass. They inflicted about six hundred U.S. casualties. From the reports in the American press people could be forgiven for thinking their soldiers had suffered a defeat on the scale of the British disaster at Tobruk or Rommel's trouncing at El Alamein.[15]

The Germans had failed to seize the heights from American troops, who'd managed to scale them with mortars, howitzers and heavy machine guns. Rommel advanced down the road, but without the heights he risked seeing it cut behind him. Two days later he was stopped, by British infantry and U.S. artillery. He retreated back through Kasserine Pass. XII ASC joined in the pursuit, but bad weather prevented it from striking much of a blow.[16]

While these events were taking place, Montgomery had crossed the Libyan-Tunisian border and the combined command agreed upon at Casablanca became operational. With the activation of Northwest African Tactical Air Forces (NATAF) Coningham took command of the RAF's 242 Group,* supporting First Army; the Desert Air Force, supporting Montgomery; and XII Air Support Command, supporting II Corps.

Coningham was a New Zealander of the rugby-playing All Black variety: six feet tall, hairy knees, strong chin, pugnacious attitude and broken nose. Like all the best military commanders he was an opportunist, not a dogmatist.

He introduced practices that were by this time common in the Desert Air Force. For example, he overrode USAAF doctrine, which banned putting bombs on fighters and thereby compromising their maneuverability. Coningham ordered that bombs be hung

---

*An RAF group (normally six squadrons) was roughly equivalent to a USAAF wing, while an RAF wing of three squadrons was equivalent to an American group.

on P-40s, turning them into fighter-bombers. Coningham also abolished aerial umbrellas over ground troops. Above all, and to the delight of American airmen, he promoted the principle that air commanders must have equality with their ground counterparts.[17]

To achieve air superiority, he assigned the RAF's 242 Group and XII Air Support Command to unrelenting attacks on Axis airfields in Tunisia. These were struck repeatedly, day and night, forcing most enemy air units back to Sicily, southern Italy and Sardinia. Doolittle's Strategic Air Force B-17s and B-26s then reached out and hit the Sicilian airfields. The B-17s caught the enemy off guard by flying even farther and hitting the airfields on Sardinia. Axis losses soon exceeded all hope of replacements.

To build up his air power in Tunisia, Hitler had stripped the German Air Force's schools of planes and instructors. He'd pulled entire bomb groups out of the Soviet Union, even though the battle of Stalingrad was reaching its climax. By March 1943 there was nothing left to strip.

Coningham was prepared to provide intensive close support, if the opportunity was right. When Ultra revealed that Rommel was planning a major attack on Eighth Army's lines in early March, XII ASC and 242 Group were primed to hit the Axis troops hard when they launched their assault. The resulting aerial onslaught combined with the fire of Montgomery's antitank guns to kill and wound nearly seven hundred Germans and destroy nearly fifty tanks. A week later Rommel left Africa forever.

Starting on March 26 Montgomery sought to break through the German defenses along the Libyan-Tunisian frontier. Coningham gave him lavish air support, which compensated for Monty's weakness in artillery. Both AAF and RAF doctrine held it was a misuse of combat aircraft to have them strike targets within range of friendly artillery. Coningham, however, didn't let that stand in his way.[18]

Despite operations such as these, there were limits to what Coningham would provide. He refused to sanction direct communications between troops on the ground and the planes providing support, for example. One consequence of this was more losses from friendly fire than there should have been.

Friendly fire had long been a sore point among ground troops in North Africa. The issue came to a head on April 1.

This was the fifth day of a II Corps offensive to advance eastward. There was little hope of its troops breaking through to the east coast, as Eisenhower had hoped. Its role now was to strike German defenses in eastern Tunisia in the flank, helping Montgomery's frontal attack to succeed. XII ASC flew more than three hundred sorties that day in support, but one of Williams's planes killed Patton's favorite aide, Captain Richard Jenson. Overwrought and grieving, Patton, who'd replaced Fredendall as commander of II Corps after the battle at Kasserine Pass, sent out a situation report that fiercely criticized the airmen for failing to protect the ground troops.

Coningham's equally robust response was to put out a signal that suggested that at best American soldiers were incompetent and maybe even cowardly. Eisenhower, in despair at failing to keep his subordinates under control, prepared to resign. Tedder saved the situation by ordering Coningham to retract his signal and apologize in person to Patton.[19]

Far from failing the ground troops, only two days later XII ASC got rid of the scourge they feared most. On April 3 its fighter pilots shot down fourteen Stukas, for the loss of one Spitfire. The Stuka was rarely seen again by American troops for the rest of the war.

The withdrawal of the Stukas was as clear a sign as could be that air superiority had swung to the Allied airmen. As the rains tapered off and the ground dried out Army engineers carved out new airstrips in central and southern Tunisia, covering them with rattling pierced-steel-plank (PSP). Replacement aircraft and pilots were pouring in. Air supremacy was in sight.

The ground offensive was by now in its closing stages, as the Germans and Italians were squeezed into a shrinking bridgehead around Tunis and Bizerta. They were running out of everything an army needs, except fighting spirit. As supplies of fuel, food and ammunition began to dry up, they prepared to see the struggle through to its bitter end.

Tedder established a list of priority targets for the combat units under Mediterranean Air Command. Enemy shipping stood first on the list. Ports came second.

Shipping was the lifeline of Axis forces in North Africa. Hitler and Mussolini had made a gigantic mistake when they got cold feet and backed away from attempting to invade Malta. Without Malta they couldn't control the sea and air between southern Italy and

North Africa. The British, by holding on to Malta, could track and attack the ships and planes on which Rommel and von Arnim depended.

Doolittle's Strategic Air Force carried the brunt of the war against Axis shipping. The SAF consisted of XII Bomber Command, with a token British presence in the form of two squadrons of obsolescent twin-engine Wellington bombers. Even before Tedder arrived Doolittle had forged a potent weapon. Bomber crews had taken serious losses on unescorted missions against well-defended targets early in the campaign. Doolittle used P-38s, with a range of twelve hundred miles, to escort his heavies. The need for escort in the face of potent GAF defenses was such that even the fast B-26 and B-25 mediums needed escort, from P-40s, to survive.[20]

Following the practice of the Desert Air Force, Doolittle made his fighter escort squadrons share the base of the bombers they escorted. This eliminated rendezvous problems, but it infuriated fighter pilots who felt they'd been downgraded from warriors to nursemaids.[21]

The medium bomb groups assigned to the Coastal Air Force also joined the war on Axis shipping. Mediums had endured a miserable life in the first three months of the campaign. The primary mission of the mediums was counterair—attacking enemy airfields, that is; covering them with twenty-three-pound parafrag bombs that wrecked planes and disabled personnel.

There were endless problems with weather, with the shortage of paved runways, with logistics and so on, but worse still were GAF airfield defenses. The flak was so thick below six thousand feet that when the mediums flew into it they got slaughtered. Yet if they bombed from above ten thousand feet, they lost so much accuracy (they didn't yet have Norden bomb sights) they accomplished little.

The antishipping campaign gave medium groups a new *raison d'être*. They could come in low and fast, as they'd been trained to do, against Axis ships. The B-26 groups learned skip bombing. Some B-25s got a seventy-five millimeter gun in the nose for low-level attacks.[22] The mediums of Coastal Air Force became the main antishipping weapon. Heavies could rarely hit ships, unless they happened to be in port. Allied aircraft accounted for two-thirds of all Axis ships sunk.[23]

Attacks on the ports were devastating in their own right. They wrecked cranes, making it take several days to unload a ship—days in which the ship could be attacked from the air. They also killed or demoralized dock workers. The Germans had to bring in five thousand battle-hardened longshoremen from Hamburg to replace Italians and Arabs who had quit.[24]

A spectacular B-17 raid against Palermo by 301st Bomb Group on March 22 did so much damage it effectively shut down the port. Thereafter, Axis shipping had to stage down from Naples. This was a major setback.

Hitler and Kesselring had read all the wrong lessons from the size of the Italian merchant fleet, which contained as much as a million tons of shipping. With that, plus nearly half a million tons seized from Vichy France, they'd assumed there would be plenty of shipping to support a campaign in Tunisia. Besides, the Strait of Sicily was so narrow that a ship could cross it overnight, under cover of darkness.

Poor maintenance meant only half the shipping could actually be used. And within the half that was seaworthy there was a shortage of the small, fast ships needed to make a speedy crossing. Instead of one and a half million tons of shipping, Axis forces were depending on a mere three to four hundred thousand tons.[25]

Moreover, British signals intelligence had cracked the Italian fleet codes. The Allies knew when ships were about to sail. The shortage of photo reconnaissance to disguise the source of their information, however, put some limitation on the use of this intelligence, allowing many ships a safe passage they hadn't earned.

The Italian Navy tried to create safe channels through the Strait of Sicily by covering it with minefields. The British then laid mines within the minefields, making the channels so narrow that ships could hardly maneuver, depriving them of their best defense against air attack.[26]

The Germans created a new kind of ferry, the Siebel, which was a large motorized raft with two to four eighty-eight millimeter flak guns bolted on. Low-level attacks against Siebel ferries could be hair raising, but they were too small to make much of a contribution to German logistics. In February 80 percent of all the supplies sent by sea got through to North Africa. In March the figure fell to 50 percent.[27]

Axis shipping was being supplemented by a major airlift. The GAF had committed nearly five hundred Junkers Ju-52 trimotor transports and thirty of the giant six-engine Me-323 transports to the Mediterranean. Until April 1943 airlift losses were comparatively light.

This airlift, however, was an open book to Allied intelligence. The problem was how to shoot the transports down in large numbers without compromising Ultra. Flights from Sicily were so short that any ambush would almost certainly look like the result of an intelligence coup.

American and British pilots were itching to wade into the GAF's airlift, but Tedder bided his time. Ships and ports remained firmly at the top of the list. By April, with air superiority finally achieved, he gave the go-ahead. The GAF's fighters were in no position to protect German transports. German defenses on the ground were crumbling. At sea, shipping had fallen off dramatically. The risk of the Germans figuring out what had gone wrong with the airlift, when everything else was going wrong for them, seemed slight. In the space of two weeks more than two hundred German transports were shot down, for the loss of ten Allied aircraft.[28]

By late April the plight of German and Italian troops was desperate. The two British armies were converging on Tunis. The II Corps, commanded now by Major General Omar Bradley, was closing on Bizerta. The Germans fought on, but shortages of fuel and ammunition meant they couldn't make strong counterattacks. In effect, all they could do was resist until Allied troops came in and got them.

On May 7, Tunis and Bizerta fell. Some 238,000 enemy troops surrendered; two-thirds were German. It was a bigger haul of prisoners than the Red Army had captured three months earlier at Stalingrad.

For the AAF it was a gratifying end to its first major campaign. Its own losses were modest: five hundred planes, seventeen hundred combat casualties.[29] The lessons learned in North Africa would shape AAF operations around the world for the rest of the war.

14

MEDITERRANEAN COCKPIT

During the Casablanca Conference the Allies agreed that once North Africa was cleared of Axis forces the next major objective would be Sicily. An invasion, code-named Husky, was tentatively scheduled for July.

Marshall suggested that before Husky was launched, the small island of Pantelleria, located roughly midway between Tunisia and Sicily, should be captured to provide extra fighter cover over the invasion fleet. Eisenhower had his doubts about Pantelleria, but came around to Marshall's view. It would be a useful experiment, he reasoned, for studying the effects of bombing on coastal defenses.[1]

Spaatz, too, saw Pantelleria as a case study. He intended to bomb the garrison into submission, as a demonstration of what air power could do.[2] Pantelleria, called "the Italian Gibraltar," was defended by eleven thousand Italian troops and eighty modern coastal guns. In the center of the island was Marghana airfield, a large, modern facility with a huge underground hangar.

Professor Solly Zuckerman, one of the RAF's top operations analysts, moved in to a villa with Norstad, Spaatz's chief of operations, to monitor the campaign. It opened May 19 with an attack by Doolittle's Strategic Air Force. Naval vessels moved in to start a blockade.

The brunt of the aerial onslaught would be borne by Doolittle's bombers, with additional strikes coming from Coningham's Tactical Air Force. Spaatz could attack with eleven hundred operational aircraft, including four groups of B-17s. The GAF and Italian Air Forces had approximately eight hundred combat aircraft within range of Pantelleria, plus one hundred at Marghana. By the end of May the island was completely isolated from reinforcement.

Zuckerman meanwhile was concentrating the bombing campaign against the sixteen coastal batteries. He advised that the bombers be loaded with five hundred-pound and one thousand-pound bombs armed with instantaneous fuses. Zuckerman asked the airmen to place up to as many as sixty bombs within one hundred yards of each coastal gun. If the number of effective guns was reduced by 33 to 50 percent, he said, the invasion would succeed.[3]

Marghana airfield, the island's small port and the town of Pantelleria, were also pounded. When the underground hangar's roof proved to be bombproof, P-38s tried skip-bombing five hundred-pound bombs into the hangar's doors, in vain.[4]

On June 8 Doolittle's B-26s and B-17s made a massive attack, dropping a torrent of bombs on four gun batteries. As the dust cleared Coningham's fighter-bombers flew over, bombing, strafing and dropping surrender leaflets.

Two days later the battleships and cruisers offshore moved in to lay down an awesome naval bombardment. The bombers returned, flying eleven hundred sorties that hit the island harder than ever. When the bombing and shelling stopped, thousands more surrender leaflets fluttered into the dust.

An amphibious assault by the British 1st Infantry Division was set for June 11. The division commander and Field Marshal Alexander thought it would end in disaster.[5]

Shortly after dawn on June 11 Doolittle's Strategic Air Force appeared overhead once more. When the SAF had finished, around ten that morning, Coningham's planes began an hour-long attack. At noon, waves of landing craft approached the island.

The feared coastal guns were silent. Most gun crews had run away. Nearly half the coastal artillery had been damaged or destroyed. Italian casualties were nonetheless light—fewer than two hundred people killed, around two hundred wounded. The town of Pantelleria was in ruins, but its people had fled to the hills or taken refuge in the vast Marghana hangar.

Pantelleria's military governor had ignored all previous calls to surrender, but supplies of fresh water were now exhausted. Thirst will bring any army to its knees.[6] British troops moved warily ashore but there was a large, freshly painted white cross adorning Marghana's main runway. The governor surrendered without a fight. The sole Allied casualty was a British soldier bitten by a jackass.[7]

Reducing Pantelleria from the air required fifty-three hundred sorties and sixty-two hundred tons of bombs. Allied losses came to eighteen bombers and fifty-seven fighters.[8]

The experiment was a success, yet it showed beyond a doubt that even from twelve thousand feet, heavy bombers were not as accurate as airmen claimed. And their most devastating effect was on morale, not fixed defenses. Even so, Doolittle was jubilant. His Strategic Air Force had dropped 80 percent of the high explosive that rocked Pantelleria, compared to 18 percent for Coningham's planes. The Navy's shells accounted for the remaining 2 percent.

Doolittle boasted to the press that Pantelleria proved strategic bombing could win the war, implying there wasn't much left for the Army or Navy to contribute. Eisenhower forced him to retract his statement. But . . . "He that complies against his will/ Is of his own opinion still."[9]

The invasion of Sicily would involve four major airborne operations. Two would be American and two British, but the AAF would provide virtually all of the airlift.

Troop carrier wasn't a responsibility that Arnold or the Air Staff had anticipated. Throughout 1941 they had been deaf to people like Donald Douglas and Eddie Rickenbacker who'd urged them to buy transport planes. Arnold and the Air Staff were interested almost entirely in combat aircraft. Under Secretary of War Robert Patterson, who oversaw procurement, even threatened to shut down plants that produced transport planes. Far from being afraid of having too few transports, the AAF seemed afraid of having too many. Only two thousand of the fifty thousand planes produced in 1942 would be transport types.[10]

After Pearl Harbor the light finally dawned. With a global war to fight, tens of thousands of transports would be needed. Lieutenant General Oliver Echols, the head of the Matériel Command, was prepared to shut down P-38 production if that would give him another two thousand transports in 1942.[11]

The one officer on Arnold's staff who appears to have anticipated future transport needs was Lieutenant Colonel Ray Dunn, an Arnold protégé. Dunn had been with him on the flight to Alaska and was presently serving as his executive officer. The Army was creating the world's first true airborne division, the 82nd. The AAF would have to carry it into battle, yet Arnold was reluctant to create a command that would be exclusively tied to ground soldiers.

While Arnold was away from Washington on an extended trip, Dunn used his authority as Arnold's exec to change the Air Transport Command into the Troop Carrier Command.[12] Arnold returned and was indignant, but he couldn't abolish Dunn's creation now without looking stupid and without provoking a fight with the Army. The friendship between Arnold and Dunn, however, was over.

The primary mission of I Troop Carrier Command was carrying the airborne. It set up shop at Stout Field, Indiana, equipped mainly with DC-3s surrendered by the commercial airlines. Numerous modifications were made to the DC-3, resulting in the C-47. Whatever changes were made, the C-47 was less than ideal for Troop Carrier work. For one thing, it carried only 16 paratroopers.

The ideal plane would have been the four-engine C-54, based on the DC-4, but resistance from Arnold and Patterson had lost eighteen months' development of the C-54.[13] The earliest date now for C-54 mass production was fall 1944, after the invasion of France.

For the first year of its existence I Troop Carrier Command was grateful for any plane it could get. There was a tremendous shortage of aircraft for training throughout the AAF. The lack of troop carrier planes forced the Airborne Command to limit the 82nd and 101st Airborne divisions to two regiments of paratroopers each. The remaining regiment in each division would crash land into battle, in gliders.

The glider chosen was the Waco CG-4A, a fairly sturdy craft (as gliders go) built around a light but strong frame of tubular steel. Needless to say, though, until 1944 there was also a shortage of gliders.

There was no shortage of potential glider pilots. There were tens of thousands of eager young men desperate to fly just about anything. Washouts from pilot training saw gliders as their second chance. Those who couldn't pass the AAF flight physical saw it as their only chance.

The engine pilots of the AAF refused to accept glider pilots as their equals. A new grade, "flying officer," was created, equivalent to an Army warrant officer. Glider pilots got wings, with a large "G" in the middle. They boasted it stood for "Guts" and pointedly rcfused to take their parachutes when they flew combat missions.[14]

Troop carrier pilots trained to go in low and slow: 110 miles an hour and around 450 feet when carrying paratroopers, 120 miles an hour and about 2,000 feet when towing gliders. They could expect to fly into a wall of ground fire, yet the AAF rated them as "noncombat personnel."[15] Given the fact that they were flying close to the ground in planes that lacked armor and self-sealing gas tanks, they probably faced a higher risk of perishing in flames than the average fighter or bomber pilot.

Dunn tried to get some light armor and self-sealing tanks for Troop Carrier's C-47s. The Matériel Command modified seventy-five planes, but Arnold's deputy, Major General Barney Giles, put a halt to the program. He felt the extra weight reduced the plane's range too much.[16]

By this time, Dunn was a colonel in North Africa. He'd gone to England in the fall of 1942 and trained the troop carrier groups that played a major part in making Torch a success. Following the February 1942 creation of Northwest African Air Forces he was given the task of organizing the NAAF Troop Carrier Command.

When the Tunisian campaign ended Spaatz gave the royal order of the boot to Brigadier General Paul L. Williams. As commander of XII Air Support Command, Williams had shown what to some airmen seemed deference to ground commanders. Spaatz got him out of combat and into "noncombat": Williams was given NAAF's Troop Carrier Command. Dunn stepped down to command 51st Troop Carrier Wing, but as he was *the* expert on troop carrier Williams followed his advice. In June 1943 Eisenhower made Dunn a brigadier general.[17]

NAAF Troop Carrier Command contained two wings, the 51st and 52nd. The 51st was in Algeria, training with the British 1st Airborne Division. The 52nd was training in Morocco with the 82nd Airborne Division. Troop carrier would spearhead Husky, taking the British in by glider and the Americans would jump.

The Husky operation envisaged by the Joint Planning Staff called for the British Eighth Army to land near Catania, on Sicily's east coast, while Patton and the U.S. Seventh Army landed one hundred miles away, near Palermo, on the northwest coast. Most of the Sicilian airfields were close to Catania and Palermo, and both towns were substantial ports. With secure logistics and ample air cover, the two armies would then converge on Messina, in northeastern Sicily, which is the key to holding the island. Although this plan involved an initial dispersal of forces, converging attacks would deprive the defender of the advantage of fighting on interior lines; he would be unable to concentrate his strength against a single axis of advance. Finally, this plan would give each invading army its own port, thereby securing its logistical base.

Montgomery rejected the plan. He insisted, over strong objections from the AAF, the RAF and the Royal Navy, on substituting a design that reduced the Seventh Army to a mere flank guard for the Eighth Army. He was depriving American troops of a port, secure supplies and an independent role. He made no provision for taking the airfields that Tedder insisted were crucial to success.

Montgomery would not be dissuaded. His star was in the ascendant these days and he insisted on a new plan, one that would allow him to advance on Messina in unrivaled glory, adding to the personal legend.[18]

The revised Husky plan treated the AAF and the RAF as mere adjuncts of the Eighth Army. Ironically, Montgomery had written an influential pamphlet on how to achieve effective cooperation between ground and air, but it was produced just as his relationship with Coningham ended in mutual bitterness and sulking. The NAAF Tactical Air Force commander resented the glorification of Montgomery in the British press and was contemptuous of Monty's ponderous, inflexible way of making war.[19]

Montgomery's Husky plan came at a critical stage in the struggle for American air independence. Following Tunisia there was a movement within the AAF to produce a new field manual on air operations. General McNair of Army Ground Forces flatly opposed any revision of doctrine that gave the AAF more latitude in providing close air support. Marshall, however, supported Arnold and on June 9, 1943, he authorized the new manual, FM 100-20.[20]

It opened melodramatically: "LAND POWER AND AIR POWER ARE CO-EQUAL AND INTERDEPENDENT FORCES; NEITHER IS AN AUXILIARY OF THE OTHER." Priorities for tactical air were clearly spelled out: first, air superiority; second, interdiction; third, close air support. The air plan for Husky was produced before FM 100-20 was published, but the thinking behind the plan was virtually identical with the thinking that went into the manual. To the indignation of ground commanders the Husky air plan avoided offering them what they wanted most—air umbrellas and flying artillery.[21]

No one denied that gaining air superiority was crucial to Allied success. Ultra intelligence had indicated that as many as eight hundred Axis aircraft—mainly German—would be able to strike the invasion fleet. Eisenhower's naval deputy, Admiral Sir Andrew Cunningham, feared he might lose three hundred ships and landing craft to enemy air attacks in the first few days.[22] The Navy wanted, but didn't get, an assurance of air cover.

The air plan spoke of three phases to the air campaign. First came the battle for air superiority. Second came interdiction, which aimed at isolating the battlefield. There was what might be termed "shallow interdiction," against targets near the battlefield, such as bridges, or against enemy forces heading toward it, such as truck convoys. And there was "deep interdiction" against key elements in the enemy's logistical system. Last of all came close air support.

When the Tunisian campaign ended the Strategic Air Force started pounding German and Italian bomber fields in Sicily and Sardinia. By early June Axis bombers had been withdrawn to northern Italy and southern France. From such distances their poorly trained crews had a hard time even finding invasion ports and bases in North Africa to bomb them.[23]

The new Allied counterair offensive was a clear signal that a major invasion was coming. The Germans built up strength in the Mediterranean accordingly, yet dispersed it widely. Fresh divisions that might have gone to the Eastern Front were funneled into Sardinia and Greece. The German Air Force's strength in the Mediterranean was raised to nearly thirteen hundred planes, mainly by diverting hundreds of single-engine fighters from the defense of Germany. The GAF based seven hundred planes in Sicily and southern Italy; the same area held nearly one hundred Italian Air Force planes.

Following the fall of Pantelleria, the counterair campaign picked up tempo. With the bombers forced back, the goal now was to drive the GAF and IAF fighters out of the airfields in western and central Sicily.

Doolittle's bomb groups, with P-38 escorts, operated from Tunis, Bizerta and Tripoli. Lightnings escorted heavy bombers all the way to the Strait of Messina and on the way back added to the counterair effort by strafing airfields.

The burden of airfield attacks, however, was borne mainly by the mediums. The B-26 was ideal for this work. Marauder squadrons skimmed the waves at high speed, flying below enemy radar, appearing over Sicilian airfields without warning and covering them with hundreds of twenty-three-pound parafrag bombs. Then B-25s would make follow-up attacks, dropping one hundred-pound bombs to "post-hole" the runways. German and Italian pilots never mounted an effective defense to this campaign against their airfields.

Axis pilots were equally helpless against the B-17s, which were bombing Sicilian ports. Although the enemy soon learned to manage without docks, operating over the beaches instead, German fighter pilots couldn't simply ignore the Fortresses. Many were understandably reluctant to plunge into the massed machine gun fire of tight formations of B-17s. When Goering learned of this he ordered that one fighter pilot from every group in Sicily be chosen at random and court-martialed for cowardice.[24]

The counterair campaign forced the GAF out of every airfield in western and central Sicily. By early July its pilots were reduced to just two fully serviceable airfields, near Catania.

The fight for air superiority succeeded because, besides shutting down airfields, Allied airmen destroyed enemy planes faster than they could be replaced. The GAF and the IAF always had some fighters available, but they'd lost the critical mass needed to be an effective fighting force.

Spaatz and Tedder, on the other hand, were getting stronger and stronger. They had nearly 5,000 planes, of which roughly 3,000 were fighters and bombers. Axis air forces had been reduced to 415 planes within range of Sicily; of these, only 50 planes were still based there.[25]

Allied airmen knew they had achieved the first part of the air plan. They had won a superiority that verged on air supremacy for the invasion. Montgomery, however, refused to believe it and continued to criticize them.

The assault would take place on eight beaches along a one hundred-mile stretch of Sicilian coastline. Monty's Eighth Army would land in the southeastern corner of the island. Three U.S. infantry divisions (the 1st, 3rd and 45th) would land on the south coast and protect the Eighth Army's left flank.

When night fell on July 9 a gale lashed the central Mediterranean. With a fleet of nearly three thousand ships and landing craft already in motion, Eisenhower let the invasion proceed. Troop carrier C-47s took off from Tunisia, heading east, toward Malta. They were to skirt the island before turning north for Sicily.

The 52nd Troop Carrier Wing had 226 planes in the air, carrying 3,400 paratroopers of the 82nd Airborne Division. The paratrooper's mission was to seize high ground and a road junction north of the small fishing port of Gela. That would enable the U.S. 1st Infantry Division to advance inland from the invasion beach.

Strong winds broke up the C-47 formations. Many pilots didn't even see Malta. They made their north turn by guesswork. The 52nd Wing's planes were scattered all over central Sicilian airspace. They dropped the 82nd's paratroopers (plus hundreds of dummies) from one end of the island to the other in the early hours of July 10.[26]

Meanwhile, the 51st Troop Carrier Wing was towing 109 Wacos toward a vital bridge near Syracuse, the primary objective of Eighth Army. RAF planes joined them, towing thirty-five Wacos and eight British-built Horsa gliders. All the gliders had British pilots. They'd had little time to train with the tow pilots in the C-47s and had no experience of landing gliders at night. Despite the lack of training the gliders were to be released at 3,000 feet a mile from shore.

The wind scattered the 51st Wing's planes, and as the leading aircraft approached the Sicilian coast enemy flak opened up and blinding searchlights flooded C-47 cockpits. Many pilots veered off course and never got their bearings again. They had been ordered not to bring gliders or paratroopers back, whatever happened. This policy had been imposed to eliminate aborts for anything but mechanical failure. Pilots released tow ropes even though it was impossible to judge height or the distance to the shore.

These releases were disastrous. About seventy gliders came down in the water, drowning hundreds of British soldiers. The rest were scattered all over eastern Sicily, except for sixty-five men who landed near the bridge, and took it.[27]

By dawn, as the invasion fleet appeared offshore to start landing 150,000 seasick troops, reports that 20,000 to 30,000 paratroopers had landed were flooding into the headquarters of the officer responsible for Sicily's defenses, General Emilio Guzzoni. He began to organize a counterattack against the invaders, but at breakfast time an American bomb scored a direct hit on his headquarters. Guzzoni's communications were knocked out for twelve hours.[28]

In both the American and British sectors the invaders got ashore with little difficulty. And they knew exactly where they were: every rifle company commander reached the sand carrying photo maps of his section of the beach, provided by the NAAF Photographic Wing.[29] When night fell American patrols were ten miles inland.

Spaatz had the 31st Fighter Group on Malta, the 79th Fighter Group on the adjacent island of Gozo, and the 33rd Fighter Group on Pantelleria available to provide air cover over the American invasion beaches and the fleet offshore. On D-Day AAF pilots flew eleven hundred sorties in support of the invasion. That didn't prevent the Navy from complaining bitterly about lack of air cover. Yet it was impossible to provide large numbers of planes on patrol over the ships from dawn to dusk. Most fighter pilots flew three sorties, but could spend only about thirty minutes over the fleet or the beaches on each one. It was inevitable that some German planes would get through, and FM 100-20 referred to "the impracticability of gaining complete control of the air."

The Germans were helped, moreover, by the Navy's practice of firing on every plane that came within range of its ships. It was a practice followed in all theaters and persisted throughout the war. As a result, NAAF fighters covering Husky were forced to fly as high as fourteen thousand feet to avoid the Navy's fire.[30] This provided GAF pilots with a gap to exploit. Still, it wasn't much of one: instead of losing three hundred vessels to enemy air attacks, the invasion fleet lost just twelve vessels before it withdrew on D + 5.

Late at night on July 10 Guzzoni's communications were restored. A counterattack was organized for the morning of July 11. Three panzer battalions from the Herman Goering Parachute Panzer Division would advance on Gela, while the Livorno Division, one of the best units in the Italian army, attempted to storm the town.

In one of the fiercest ground battles seen in the Mediterranean, Gela was held by the 1st Infantry Division, the 82nd Airborne, the Rangers, and the U.S. Navy, which risked its ships on the sandbars that lie off the Sicilian coast and took on enemy tanks and troop concentrations at what amounted to point-blank range for naval guns. By nightfall the Livorno Division had been wrecked and the three panzer battalions were virtually wiped out.

The air forces played no part in this struggle, even though the GAF and IAF managed to fly four hundred sorties in support of the Gela counterattack. Close air support for ground units came last on Coningham's list of priorities. Instead, tactical air was devoted to maintaining air superiority, which meant attacking airfields; and isolating the battlefield, by shooting up truck convoys moving toward the beaches. Doolittle's Strategic Air Force was taking the interdiction campaign farther afield, bombing marshalling yards in southern Italy through which supplies for Sicily were routed.[31]

Ground commanders had insisted on having another airborne operation, set for that night: two thousand paratroopers of the 82nd Airborne Division would make a reinforcement drop near Gela. The commander of the 82nd, Major General Matthew B. Ridgway, had informed the Navy three days earlier of the route the 144 planes of 52nd Troop Carrier Wing would follow. He secured the Navy's agreement to hold its fire provided the planes remained within the agreed corridor.

As the C-47s left Tunisia, the wind was picking up. They flew east, then north, as before. Approaching Gela they missed the agreed landfall by six miles. After a three-hundred-mile night flight at an altitude of three hundred feet in a twenty-five mile per hour wind, a six-mile miss was excellent flying, but it put them outside the agreed corridor.[32] Someone on a ship, or possibly some 1st Division AAA gunner, started firing. In minutes the night sky lit up like the Fourth of July.

C-47s weaved crazily to evade the streams of red tracer fire. Most pilots hurriedly dropped their paratroopers, scattering them across southeastern Sicily. Some 23 C-47s went down in flames; another 37 took hits. Nearly 100 paratroopers were killed by friendly fire and 132 were wounded. As many as 60 AAF personnel were killed.[33]

There was a secret casualty—Ray Dunn, who'd planned the operation, although he didn't think there was any need for it. Drew Pearson learned that Dunn had demanded self-sealing fuel tanks for troop carrier planes and been turned down by General Giles. Self-sealing tanks might have saved many lives the night of July 11.

Arnold and Giles believed, wrongly, that Pearson had acquired his information from Dunn. They attempted to force him to leave the AAF. When that failed, Dunn lost his star and was reduced to lieutenant colonel. The creator of Troop Carrier Command was banished to an Army general's staff in Hawaii and, in effect, was out of the AAF for the rest of the war.[34]

Despite the disastrous mission the night of July 11, the fourth and final airborne operation went ahead twenty-four hours later. The 51st Troop Carrier Wing would provide 124 C-47s to make a combined parachute drop and glider assault by British airborne troops to seize a bridge north of Syracuse. A safe corridor had been agreed by the Royal Navy for the planes to fly through as they passed over the British fleet.

Almost as soon as the troop carrier aircraft appeared, British ships opened fire. Two C-47s were shot down. The rest, taking evasive action, were widely scattered by the time they made landfall. They ran into a wall of flak from the alerted German AAA batteries. Nine more C-47s went down. A further 34 were hit and one collided with a barrage balloon. A score of pilots turned back. Only 250 British glidermen and paratroopers reached the objective, yet they took it and held on to it.[35]

Even with secure beachheads, the fight for air superiority had to continue, if it was to be maintained. Then, a week after the invasion, the GAF and IAF found the strain intolerable. They started pulling out their last remaining squadrons, withdrawing to the vast complex of airfields around Foggia, on the Italian east coast, two hundred miles northeast of Sicily.

Meanwhile, Zuckerman was masterminding the deep interdiction campaign. He had Tedder turn the Strategic Air Force against six major marshalling yards from Rome to the Strait of Messina. By disrupting rail traffic he intended to devastate the logistics of the 50,000 Germans and 230,000 Italians who were defending Sicily.

On July 19 Doolittle unleashed the heaviest Allied air attack so far in World War II. He would strike the two main marshalling yards of Rome. Considerable care was taken to avoid hitting outstanding religious sites and Catholics were exempted from flying the mission. Two days before the attack leaflets were dropped warning the people around the railroad tracks to leave. At midday on the 19th, 270 heavy bombers struck the marshalling yards, while 250 mediums attacked the airfields around the city. Despite the advance warning, the GAF and IAF put up almost no resistance. Only two bombers were lost.[36]

This attack broke Mussolini's will. Six days later he was overthrown. The Italian government asked the Vatican to open negotiations for Italy's surrender.

Northwest African Air Forces was joined in this and other raids by Brereton's Ninth Air Force, which had made the trek from El Alamein to Tunis with the Eighth Army. Monty's pursuit of Rommel had been made possible largely by the "flying pipeline" provided by 316th Troop Carrier Group, which flew gasoline to his tanks and trucks. Now, the Ninth's bombers were adding their weight to the Sicilian campaign. In a daring low-level attack, Brereton's B-24s shattered the huge ferroconcrete sheds at Messina that sheltered enemy supply trains. In another low-level raid, they destroyed a major Italian ammunition plant at Crotone.[37]

From the airmen's point of view, the first two weeks in Sicily were a success, but Patton and his generals were dissatisfied. What they wanted was instant and massive close air support. They weren't going to get it. The biggest weakness in close air support was the poor communications between troops on the ground and the air units providing the support.

The British had developed good air-ground cooperation in the Western Desert. That system still prevailed between Eighth Army and the Desert Air Force, which was providing support to Monty's troops on Sicily. Air liaison officers in jeeps operated up front with the infantry and relayed their needs to a command post where air and ground officers together decided which targets would get air support. The air liaison officer then directed tactical aircraft to the target. In late July the Seventh Army got a similar system, called Rover Joe. It didn't give ground commanders what they really wanted, which was a swarm of planes overhead all day which they could call down on a few minutes' notice, but it was a major improvement all the same.[38]

Coningham stuck unwaveringly to the priorities of the air plan and put isolating the battlefield ahead of close air support. His tactic for shallow interdiction was to flatten Sicilian villages and towns and fill the few decent roads in Sicily with mountains of rubble. Unfortunately, the systematic destruction of villages and towns had no evident effect on enemy movement. The Germans and Italians simply detoured around the rubble heaps. All Coningham achieved was to add to the misery of the peasants, who lost their homes.

Sicily also saw a dismayingly large number of friendly fire incidents. Ground troops grew so aggrieved at Allied air attacks they disobeyed orders and frequently fired on friendly planes.

Despite the complaints over close air support airmen made some valuable contributions directly to the ground battle. For example, air power was crucial to 1st Infantry Division's monumental struggle to take the fortified hill town Troina. The attackers moved down a road through enemy lines that was unmarked on any map but was found by Elliott Roosevelt's photo recon pilots. Seventy-two A-36 fighter-bombers breached the town's defenses before the final assault was made.[39]

Montgomery spent three weeks trying to fight his way through strong defenses across the eastern slopes of Mount Etna. He was a flat-earth commander: all his successes in World War II came on level terrain. While he battered and bludgeoned his way forward, Patton was making a 250-mile drive, going to the west coast, then along the north coast, heading for Messina. By the end of July the Germans and Italians were falling back inexorably toward the Strait of Messina, which separates Sicily from the mainland by a mere four and a half miles.

Patton hoped to cut off the retreating enemy with a combined airborne and amphibious assault in their rear, but there were no suitable drop zones. Ideally, it would have been possible to make an amphibious landing in Calabria, on the Italian side of the Strait, cutting off all the Germans and Italians fighting in Sicily. That wasn't to be. Nearly all the ships and landing craft needed had been withdrawn to prepare for the Salerno invasion. The Combined Chiefs of Staff weren't going to cancel Salerno to achieve a neat finish in Sicily.

Moreover, Admiral Cunningham had been a young naval officer during the disastrous attempt by the Royal Navy to force a passage through the Dardenelles in 1915. Cunningham was unwilling to pit his ships against shore-based defenses. He had no intention of sending them into the heavily defended Strait of Messina. This left it to air power to block movement between Sicily and Italy.

Throughout the first week of August, Monty's intelligence officers and the commander of the Desert Air Force, Air Vice Marshal Harry Broadhurst, warned that an evacuation might begin at any time. Coningham, however, was no more inclined than Cunningham to push his forces into the Strait of Messina. It was defended by five hundred flak guns, the biggest concentration of AAA in the world.

His fears about the flak were understandable, but exaggerated. In the first two weeks of August twenty-five hundred sorties were flown (mainly by fighter-bombers of the Desert Air Force) against targets in the Strait of Messina. The loss rate was 1.23 percent. These flak defenses also suffered from a major weakness: they contained no guns that would reach higher than twenty-four thousand feet.

A redesigned eighty-eight millimeter gun, the Flak 41, had been developed to shoot down B-17s flying at 29,000 feet, but Hitler had sent the entire first production run to Tunisia. There, they fell into Allied hands. Without the Flak 41 the Strait of Messina's defenders were helpless against the B-17.[40]

What's more, Coningham had been given first call on the services of Doolittle's fortresses if he needed them. On August 11, he decided he didn't, and released them for other missions. Coningham made two assumptions: any major evacuation would take place at night, and his Wellington squadrons, which specialized in night attacks, could break it up by bombing assembly points.[41]

By chance the evacuation, code-named Lehrgang, got rolling that very night. And the Wellingtons got in some effective strikes, throwing the Germans well behind schedule. But the paucity of strong air attacks during daylight allowed them to shift to round-the-clock operations. It was August 14 before senior Allied commanders realized what was happening. The air campaign against the evacuation began August 15, just as Lehrgang was drawing to its scheduled close.

Axis losses in this operation amounted to twenty ships destroyed and five damaged. Forty thousand Germans lived to fight another day, along with sixty thousand Italians. They took with them roughly ten thousand vehicles and twenty thousand tons of supplies.[42]

The air effort against the evacuation was too little, too late. Coningham's release of the B-17s was a mistake. B-17s bombing from thirty thousand feet were so inaccurate it's unlikely they would have done much damage, but who knows what a few lucky hits might have achieved? The attempt should have been made.

NAAF Tactical Air Force should also have made a greater effort against the single paved road that ran to the evacuation beaches in Sicily and the single paved road away from the evacuation beaches in Calabria. Coningham doesn't seem to have realized the importance of these two roads to Lehrgang.

The whole campaign frustrated Spaatz. Eisenhower wanted him to act like Tedder's deputy, but Tedder simply ignored him. Nor did he have any power over Coningham. On the contrary, Coningham was inclined to communicate directly with Tedder to control the operations of AAF units. During the first week of the campaign Spaatz struck back by creating an all-American communications system, the Redline, which restored much of his power over AAF operations.[43]

Even before the Sicilian campaign ended, Allied airmen were preparing the way for the next invasion. Doolittle's Strategic Air Force attacked the Rome marshalling yards again, on August 13. And a new counterair struggle began, this time against the Foggia airfields.

Air superiority had made a successful amphibious assault of Sicily possible. The interdiction campaign had pushed Italy more than halfway out of the war. The third great contribution of the AAF in Sicily was felt elsewhere, in the European theater of operations. In July 1943 the Eighth Air Force finally began its strategic bombing campaign against Germany. By November the Eighth stood on the brink of defeat. Yet without the heavy fighter losses inflicted on the GAF in Sicily in June, July and August 1943 the Mighty Eighth might have been crushed.[44] In a global war all skies are one.

In June 1942 Arnold sent Norstad to England and replaced him on the Advisory Council with another bright young colonel, Jacob E. Smart, who'd just celebrated his thirty-third birthday. From being a flying instructor, Smart had gone on to play a major role in the pre-Pearl Harbor training explosion.

In early 1943, after returning from the Casablanca conference, Smart watched some A-20 pilots in training hit moving targets, such as tanks, while flying low and fast. With that kind of accuracy, it should be possible to knock out anything . . . even Ploesti.[45]

There was no more tempting strategic target than the huge complex of Romanian refineries that provided Hitler with 35 percent of his oil. Apart from the ineffective Halverson raid in June 1942 and two nuisance raids mounted by the Red Air Force, the lynchpin of Hitler's oil supplies had passed through three and a half years of war intact. Smart thought he could change that, with a massive attack that would slip under German air defenses and strike with nine groups of B-24s at altitudes as low as fifty feet.

He sold his idea to Arnold, the JCS and the Combined Chiefs. Arnold backed him all the way. Air planners had assumed it would take numerous high-level attacks by large numbers of heavy bombers to knock out Ploesti. Roosevelt was fascinated by the drama of

Smart's proposal. Churchill too was intrigued. He tried to get Smart to let RAF navigators lead the mission to Ploesti.

Not everyone was sold on Smart's idea. Ira Eaker, commanding Eighth Air Force, was vehemently opposed, because he would have to provide three of the groups, undermining his attempts to bomb Germany from England. The AAF's leading expert on targeting, Colonel Richard Hughes, protested that the AAF lacked the skills, the experience and the numbers to pull off an attack as complex as this one.

Probably the strongest opposition came from the AAF's chief authority on air defense, Brigadier General Gordon P. Saville, currently serving on Spaatz's staff. The plan called for a twenty-seven-hundred-mile mission, with perfect navigation, to put up to three hundred bombers over seven refineries and do it all with flawless timing. "This goddamned thing," said Saville fervently, "is ridiculous and suicidal."[46]

Brereton, however, took to it completely. His Ninth Air Force would provide the bases and two of the groups. The mission would be flown by IX Bomber Command. Brereton's aviation engineers created a full-scale outline of the Ploesti complex in the Libyan desert, using whitewash and oil drums. The RAF provided a detailed scale model for pilots and bombardiers to study. A forty-five minute movie was produced for briefing the crews. It opened with a lingering shot of an attractive, naked young woman and an encouraging (if untrue) statement: "Ploesti is a virgin target."[47]

Because of the Sicilian interdiction campaign the operation was limited to five bomb groups. And the demands of Husky, plus the bombing of Rome, drew on the services of all five (the 44th, 93rd, 98th, 376th, and 389th Bomb Groups). Only after the Rome mission on July 19 could they settle down to doing nothing but training for Ploesti.

As August 1, the mission date, drew near, the five group commanders and the head of IX Bomber Command, Major General Uzal Ent, signed a letter to Brereton asking to be allowed to go in at high altitude.[48] Ike and Tedder urged Brereton to cancel the mission. He insisted it had to go ahead.

The morning of August 1, 176 B-24s assembled; 11 aborted. The leading group was the 376th, commanded by Colonel Keith K. Compton. Flying with Compton was General Ent. The 376th's lead navigator was in another plane, which ditched in the Mediterranean several hours into the mission. Compton mistook the initial point* and led his group toward Bucharest, the capital of Romania, thirty miles south of Ploesti. Three of the five groups were already behind schedule and having trouble keeping to the right course. Compton's error was all it took to undo the entire plan.

The attack on Ploesti by the 164 planes that reached it was almost unbelievably ragged, confused, courageous and spectacular, as B-24s roared among the refineries lower than the towers of the cracking plants and flew through sheets of flame that, as oil tanks exploded, reached 300 feet high.

Ent's pilots were threading their way through the second strongest concentration of AAA in the world: nearly three hundred flak guns, plus hundreds of machine guns. There was a deadly flak train that panted along the network of railroad tracks, almost keeping pace with the low-flying bombers and giving flak gunners more time to hit their targets.[49] Aerial gunners aboard the B-24s engaged in fierce duels with flak gunners on the train, in water towers, in fake hay stacks, in church steeples and in the refineries. Besides the intense flak, Ploesti was also defended by 120 GAF fighters and 200 fighters flown by the Romanian Air Force.

The 98th Bomb Group of Colonel John R. "Killer" Kane was the only one to fly its assigned course and arrive on time. Kane flew the lead aircraft, navigated by Lieutenant Norman M. Whalen. As Ploesti loomed into view, Kane dropped to the deck. The plane's machine guns erupted in a point-blank duel with the flak batteries.

"In the deafening roar," wrote Whalen later, "I recognized the Astra Romana refinery, now belching fire and huge clouds of black smoke. . . . We seemed to be dead on course, heading precisely as planned. . . . I stepped back so the bombardier could operate his bombsight unhindered. . . .

"In a panoramic view I could see several balloons poised above Ploesti and found myself hoping their cables would not shear off our wings. As we neared the refineries, Colonel Kane pulled up to 250 feet to clear the smokestacks, themselves 210 feet high. Passing over the Phoenix Orion refinery, which lay between us and the Astra Romano, a storage tank exploded and the lid of the tank, almost 100 feet in diameter, rose into the air, its framework outlined

---

*The IP was a distinctive feature on the ground, such as a river or a railroad line, about ten miles from the target.

like the spokes of a wheel. In a second we were racing through the flames that funneled up from the burning tank, enveloping momentarily half of our left wing. Why engines one and two did not ignite I shall never know."[50] For his courageous leadership this day, Kane won the Medal of Honor.

The determination of the air crews attacking Ploesti almost defies belief. It was epitomized by Lieutenant Lloyd D. Hughes, of the 389th Bomb Group. His squadron, commanded by Captain Philip Ardrey, would be the last to drop its bombs on Ploesti.

The 389th plunged into a cauldron of greasy black smoke and pillars of flame. "We were on our run in," Ardrey recalled nearly forty years later. "There, in the center of the target, was the big boiler house. . . . Already the flames were leaping higher than the level of our approach and there were intermittent explosions lighting up the black pall . . . a gauntlet of tracers and cannon fire of all types made me despair of ever covering those last few hundred yards. . . . From the target grew a column of flames, smoke, and explosions and we were headed right into it. . . .

"I looked to the right for a moment and saw a sheet of raw gasoline trailing Peter Hughes's left wing. . . . He must have known he was hard hit because the gas was coming out in such a volume that it blinded the waist gunners in his ship from our view. Poor Pete! Fine religious, conscientious boy with a young wife waiting for him back in Texas. . . .

"I didn't think I could possibly come out alive, and I knew Pete couldn't. Bombs were away. Everything was black for a moment. We must have cleared the chimneys by inches—and as we passed over the boiler house another explosion kicked our tail high and our nose down. . . . Pete was on fire, all around the left wing where it joined the fuselage. I could feel tears come into my eyes and my throat clog up. His bombs were laid squarely on target along with ours. . . ."[51]

Once off the target, Hughes turned toward a river several miles away, but had to ascend to clear a bridge. As he came down again, his right wing caught the slope of the river bank. The B-24 spun in, burning fiercely. Two of his crew survived. Ardrey wrote a citation that brought Hughes a posthumous Medal of Honor.

Ent had expected to lose 50 percent of his planes and crews. He was almost right. Seventy-three B-24s were lost. Another fifty-five suffered major damage.[52] Nearly five hundred air crew were killed or wounded. More than one hundred became prisoners of war. Besides Hughes and Kane, three other airmen were awarded the Medal of Honor—the most for a single engagement in World War II.

Brereton claimed the attack on Ploesti had destroyed up to 60 percent of its output. In fact, it made no appreciable difference. Ploesti had a production capacity of 9.5 million tons of oil a year, but was actually producing only 4.75 million, because it lacked the transportation to ship more. What was knocked out in the raid was replaced by bringing unused or underused plant into production.[53] Ploesti still stood, a smoking magnet that would continue to attract American planes for more than a year.

15

NEARLY, NEARLY

The British, with their longstanding military and political interests in the Mediterranean, could think of a dozen reasons for invading Italy. American planners were hard-pressed to think of one. In the end, the British view prevailed, because no one expected an Italian campaign to last long or cost much. At the least, it would knock Italy out of the war and, for the Army Air Forces, it promised to bring many strategic targets in southeastern Germany, Eastern Europe, and the Balkans within range of its heavy bombers.[1]

The ideal place to invade would have been the Gulf of Gaeta, close to Rome, but that was beyond the range of fighters operating from Sicily. The invasion would have to be made in the Gulf of Salerno, close to Naples. Even this called for setting a precedent. Until now no one had tried providing air cover more than 90 miles from fighter bases. The invasion beaches at Salerno were 180 miles from Messina. Only a few fighter squadrons would be on patrol over the beaches and the fleet at any time.

The assault, code-named Avalanche, would be made by the Fifth Army, commanded by Lieutenant General Mark C. Clark. The invasion beaches were divided by the Sele River. He would land the British 10 Corps north of the Sele. The U.S. VI Corps would land south of the Sele and ten miles from the nearest British unit. If the Germans moved fast enough toward the beachhead, they could defeat Clark in detail. He counted on air power to stop them moving that quickly.

This time Tedder provided an elaborate air plan, one that offered plenty of detail, but it spelled out the priorities clearly: air superiority, interdiction, close air support.[2]

The new counterair campaign began August 16, the day before the fighting on Sicily ended, with an attack by eighty-nine B-24s of Ninth Air Force against the airfields at Foggia, on the eastern side of Italy and only seventy miles from Salerno.

On August 25 Doolittle sent 130 B-17s and 140 P-38s to Foggia. Attacks by heavy bombers made huge craters, but weren't as effective as low-level attacks by mediums that spread destruction over a large area with twenty-three-pound frag bombs. Foggia had fifteen airfields and plenty of dispersal room. And the GAF was fighting back. It was attacking Avalanche shipping in North African ports with raids by as many as ninety bombers.

While hitting German airfields, the Strategic Air Force was also striking hard at the railroads of central Italy. This interdiction campaign aimed to isolate the battlefield by impeding the movement of German troops toward Salerno once the landing was made. Zuckerman had convinced Tedder that the key point was the marshalling yards. He wasn't trying to demolish railroad track, which was easily replaced, but to destroy crucial elements within the yards, such as signaling equipment, which was not.[3] There were seven first-class German divisions and various independent brigades in northern Italy, under command of Rommel. If Zuckerman's tactics worked, they would have a hard time moving south.

On September 3 Montgomery and the Eighth Army crossed the Strait of Messina and advanced along the eastern side of Italy. Avalanche was scheduled to take place the night of September 9.

Two days before the troops landed the Allies made shallow interdiction strikes against bridges on roads leading toward Salerno. A lack of fighter-bombers, however, meant these attacks were carried out by mediums that weren't really suitable for this kind of work. And the shortage of Norden bombsights forced the AAF to use an obsolescent British bombsight that wasn't accurate enough for attacks on small, fixed targets. What was needed was a large force of fighter-bombers, which could hit fleeting targets and strafe enemy road and rail transportation. Despite a total force of four thousand planes, Tedder lacked enough fighters for that.

Rich in the air compared to the enemy, Allied airmen undertook Avalanche on what felt like a shoestring. The B-24 groups lent to Ninth Air Force by Eaker had to return to England and the air losses suffered in the invasion of Sicily hadn't been made good.[4]

As the invasion fleet sailed into the Gulf of Salerno at sundown on September 8 the news came that Italy had quit. The assault troops rejoiced, thinking they were going to walk ashore, where they'd be embraced by happily surrendering Italians. When they landed in the early hours of September 9 they found themselves up against angry and indignant Germans who were more than willing to fight. The German 10th Army had only one German division at Salerno but three more began moving toward it, all highly-rated veteran outfits.

On D-Day Allied airmen flew more than a thousand sorties over the Gulf of Salerno. The B-17s of 97th and 99th Bomb Groups attacked road bridges. The B-24s of Ninth Air Force struck Foggia. The air superiority campaign had been successful: the GAF presented no opposition to the landing.

Air cover, however, was worryingly patchy, despite the presence offshore of Royal Navy carriers with 110 Seafires (the naval version of the Spitfire). Montecorvino airfield fell to British troops on D-Day, but it was within range of German artillery and couldn't be used. In the U.S. sector a battalion of aviation engineers was carving out a pierced steel plank airstrip at Paestum, though it too was under German fire.

There were soft spots and holes all over the fleet and the beaches for the GAF to penetrate. When cover was briefly reduced the morning of September 11, German planes darted in. Within minutes they scored hits on three cruisers.[5]

After an attempt to link up the British and U.S. beachheads failed, the British, the Germans started advancing into the gap between the allied forces. A regiment of the U.S. 45th Division was landed to renew the drive inland, but it too was forced back. And the arrival of elements of the 29th Panzer Grenadier Division from the south on September 12 enabled the commander of the German 10th Army, Heinrich von Vietinghoff, to organize a major counterattack for the 13th. The only good news was that the Germans were mismanaging their fuel supplies. One result was that the 29th Panzer Grenadiers had arrived piecemeal and late.[6]

Despite this, when they counterattacked on September 13th the landing was plunged into dire jeopardy. The GAF flew 250 sorties in support on the 13th, but lost a score of pilots and dozens of planes it could not replace. Clark's troops held on, in the toughest fight they could ever have imagined. And two more German divisions were arriving.

Clark had to get more troops into the beachhead. That night, 51st and 52nd Troop Carrier Wings flew toward Salerno, navigating by the flames of the volcano Stromboli. They dropped thirteen hundred of Ridgway's paratroopers onto the sand.[7]

In the morning, Strategic Air Force sent its heavies and mediums to make tactical air strikes against the advancing Germans. SAF flew two thousand sorties September 14th in direct defense of the beachhead. Clark's American troops were driven to the water's edge and he had his staff start planning an evacuation. They were saved this humiliation by the fighting spirit of their troops and by the Navy's bombardment of German armor. The guns of the cruiser *Philadelphia* were accurately directed by P-51 Mustangs, acting as spotter aircraft.[8]

That night 51st and 52nd Troop Carrier Wing C-47s returned, to drop another twenty-one hundred paratroopers onto the beach. And because in this crisis no one had thought to cancel it, 51st TC Wing also made a scheduled drop of six hundred paratroopers thirty miles inland, on the hill town of Avellino.

On September 15, the third day of the counterattack, SAF flew fourteen hundred missions to support the beachhead. As night fell, the counterattack petered out. Von Vietinghoff claimed victory, then retreated, falling back toward Naples.

Pulling the 29th Panzergrenadiers out of southern Italy had speeded the advance of the Eighth Army along the east coast. On September 17, with the British heading toward it, the GAF started pulling out of Foggia. By this day VI Corps had linked up with British 10 Corps. The beachhead was expanding. The Paestum airstrip was in operation, with A-36 dive-bombers taking off regularly to attack targets only a few miles away.[9]

On October 1 American troops advanced into Naples and British troops overran Foggia. The Allies now had three good ports—Naples, Taranto, and Bari—and plenty of airfields. Avalanche had achieved all its objectives.

Even so, the Navy had complained bitterly about the inadequacies of air cover. Clark had protested what he considered a woeful lack of close air support. As in Sicily, the emphasis had gone on air superiority and interdiction. While the air superiority campaign had been an undoubted success, the interdiction campaign had mixed results.

There weren't enough fighter-bombers available to knock out bridges and strafe vehicular traffic moving toward Salerno. Medium and light bombers were used instead, so the fighters could provide air cover over the fleet and the beaches. As it turned out, medium and light bombers weren't effective against small targets, and when they turned houses into piles of rubble that filled village roads, the Germans simply detoured around the ruins.

Interdiction hadn't isolated the battlefield. This failure allowed the Germans to make a counterattack that nearly defeated the invasion of Italy.

Hitler didn't intend to fight south of Rome. He planned to fight in northern Italy, along the deep, wide Po River. Kesselring convinced him it would be possible and worthwhile to fight in the mountains of central Italy. It could be done, he insisted, despite Allied air superiority. Kesselring was both a Luftwaffe general and an experienced ground commander and was one of the few senior commanders whose opinions Hitler was inclined to take seriously.

In the fall of 1943, while Clark's Fifth Army advanced along the western side of the Italian peninsula and Montgomery's Eighth Army moved up the eastern side, Kesselring had an army of Italian laborers at work creating awesome defenses in the mountains with dynamite, concrete and steel. Hitler used the troops being held in the north to create another army, the 14th, under Eberhardt von Mackensen. The German 14th Army would join Vietinghoff's 10th Army in one of the bitterest defensive struggles of the war, one that would cost all the participants a total of one million casualties.

This was a development that Clark hadn't expected. He had been persuaded that Allied air power would make it impossible for the Germans to sustain large forces in the Appennines.

As fall rains lashed the slopes and at night turned to flurries, both Doolittle and Coningham unleashed a fierce campaign against engineering features, such as bridges, tunnels and viaducts. This mission fell mainly on medium bombers, but it took hundreds of medium bombers to knock out a bridge, for want of a decent bombsight. Tactical's P-40 fighter-bombers, which might have done better, were occupied with close support. Its A-36 dive-bombers were both too few in number and too vulnerable to ground fire to accomplish anything.

American and British troops died of hypothermia on the slopes of the mountains, while the Germans were snug inside designer defenses. The Allied advance came to a halt. Positional warfare took over. As it did so, there came major changes in command.

Coningham and Doolittle left for England. Coningham's successor in command of the Tactical Air Force was his deputy, Major General John K. "Uncle Joe" Cannon, one of the most popular figures in the AAF.

Cannon's command had three components: XII Air Support Command, supporting Fifth Army; the Desert Air Force, supporting Montgomery; and the Tactical Bomber Force, comprising 42nd and 57th Medium Bomb Wings, under Cannon's direct control.

There were major changes higher up, too. Tedder, like Coningham and Doolittle, went to England with Eisenhower, taking his bombing guru, Solly Zuckerman, with him. Eaker moved to Bari, to command a new organization, the Mediterranean Allied Air Forces, the successor to Tedder's Mediterranean Air Command.

Shortly after Cannon took the Tactical Air Force, there was another change: XII ASC was assigned to the fiery and outspoken Brigadier General Gordon P. Saville. Cannon believed in close air support more than Coningham and would strive to improve it. So would Saville. His first action was to locate his headquarters with Clark and tell him frankly, "I'm a separate air force guy. You and I are not going to fight about it one bit. But when I get through here, you are going to be one of the greatest proponents for a separate air force the world ever saw, and the reason is that you are going to know I know my stuff, and you and your staff don't."[10]

The biggest weakness in close air support was the lack of communications between the ground unit that needed it and the air unit that supplied it. During that long, dreary winter, improvements were worked out. Joint air-ground teams in the rear decided which requests would be accepted. Air controllers working in the front lines were provided with AAF-type FM radios so they could communicate directly with pilots and put them right on the target.

In time, Italy would bring another refinement known as Horsefly: an L-5 spotter plane with an air controller aboard would direct flights of fighter-bombers already in the air to hit targets requested by ground troops. Elapsed time between request and delivery fell to fifteen minutes, sometimes less, and strikes were more accurate.

Even with improved communications there were friendly fire losses, but the British Bombing Survey Unit concluded that flying five hundred close support sorties cost the lives of three pilots and the loss of four and a half aircraft, yet saved between 250 and 300 ground troops from death or wounds.[11]

A lot of interdiction was still being flown. There were numerous attacks on bridges, tunnels and viaducts in an attempt to cripple the Italian railroad system. MAAF headquarters continually claimed the effects were devastating, but bomb damage assessment wasn't much more effective than the old Roman practice of looking at sheeps' entrails for signs of divine will. Elliott Roosevelt's photo recon pilots were struggling with inadequate planes and cameras. Whether interdiction was accomplishing anything was unclear.[12]

Lieutenant Bill Colgan arrived in Italy in September and was assigned to 79th Fighter Group, one of the first AAF units that had deployed to a North Africa. It had become a pioneer fighter-bomber outfit and adopted RAF tactics. Replacements like Colgan had to be retrained before they were ready for combat. His first mission was in support of Clark's hard-pressed troops at Salerno.

"I was scheduled as Red Two, on the leader's wing, where most pilots fly their first mission. This was an eight-ship effort, each P-40 loaded with a five-hundred-pound general purpose or high explosive bomb, and twenty-pound fragmentation bombs on the wings. . . . In the air, it was an extremely hazy day, with poor visibility. Between that and the natural tendency of a first-timer to fly too close to his leader, I had to fight myself quite a bit to stay out where I should be. . . .

"My first view of flak came before reaching the target area . . . bright red-orange fireballs and black, greasy-looking smoke . . . around the beachhead, up came more 88s, this time much closer. . . . The leader did an excellent job of swinging wide over some prominent coastal checkpoints and then finding and confirming the target. . . . The bomb release was fine . . . but on pullout I lost the leader in the haze and smoke. . . . Luckily, I found him again right away. The same thing happened after the next pass of releasing the other ordnance and strafing the target area. . . . We went home in pairs. . . . I had one rather firm feeling: *Seventy-nine more of these was going to be a lot.*"[13] It had been a typical mission, a typical day for the 79th Fighter Group's pilots.

This strike, like most that fighter-bombers flew, consisted of two flights of four planes each. One would fly cover while the other attacked; then they would reverse roles—only the flight now flying cover would probably have used up all its ammunition strafing ground targets.

To Colgan and other fighter pilots strafing was a heated subject. It was just about the most death-defying thing they were ordered to do. The Germans had an abundance of automatic light flak guns.

German troops were trained to put up a wall of small-arms fire as their best defense against enemy aircraft. Medium and heavy bomber pilots faced skies melodramatically black and flashing orange tongues of flame from heavy AAA bursts, but the most dangerous stuff of all may have been down near the ground.

Strafing a ground target meant flying as low as fifty feet. As you closed on the truck or the tank or the train in your sights you'd be flying at about four miles a minute. To strike it with maximum firepower you had to close to 750 feet, where the fire from the wing-mounted .50s converged. As you came off the target, you'd be around 200 feet from it—less than half a second from a fatal collision. And if it turned out you'd strafed an ammo truck, it would almost surely bring you down when it exploded.

Strafing took strong nerves, superb coordination and more luck than most humans are blessed with to get away with for long. Yet however much they hated it, fighter-bomber pilots had to do it day after day.

About the only thing that surpassed strafing for stress was tossing one-thousand-pound bombs with delayed-action fuses into railroad tunnels. An Italian tunnel was usually frowned down on by several thousand feet of mountain—a small, threatening mouth set deep in a granite face. Tunnel missions called for flying one hundred feet or less above the railroad tracks, getting close enough to toss the bomb into the tunnel, then pulling away hard before you smacked into the granite. A bad throw and the bomb could ricochet off the mountain and back at your airplane as you flew upward.

The 79th Fighter Group moved to Foggia in October and Colgan flew a score of missions in Coningham's bridge-tunnel-viaduct campaign. The group was ordered to knock down a large bridge over the river Sangro. It was crucial to the German defenders who were blocking Monty's advance.

In North Africa, veteran 79th Fighter Group pilots told Colgan, they could attack a bridge a dozen times and think they had wrecked it. Then when the ground troops got there, it'd turn out the pilots had barely scratched the girders and the troops would just drive across. This time, though, the 79th busted the bridge in a day. Even so, the occasional success was not going to redeem Coningham's interdiction campaign.

To break the winter stalemate in the mountains, Churchill demanded a second invasion, outflanking the strong belt of defenses, known as the Gustav Line, that stretched across Italy from the

Adriatic to the Tyrrhenian Sea. The landing would be made at Anzio, a beach resort forty miles south of Rome and sixty miles north of the Gustav Line. Code-named Shingle, it was scheduled for January 22, 1944.

The air plan for Shingle followed the well-established pattern of priorities: superiority, interdiction, close air support. The GAF at this time had only 575 aircraft in the entire Mediterranean, of which roughly two-thirds were within reach of targets in central Italy. The Germans maintained twenty long-range reconnaissance aircraft at Perugia. The first blow of the new counterair campaign was struck on January 7, when Cannon's B-25s attacked Perugia airfield. The next day counterair attacks were unleashed against GAF airfields across central Italy. The Germans pulled their planes back to airfields in the shadows of the Alps.

Meanwhile, the tempo of the interdiction campaign picked up. The focus of deep interdiction was on seven key railroad bridges and eleven marshalling yards (from approximately one hundred M/Ys the Italians still had in operation). There were numerous shallow interdiction strikes against road and rail traffic in the Anzio area. The interdiction strikes to isolate the battlefield were concealed within a wide pattern of air attacks, so it didn't become obvious that Anzio was about to be invaded.

A follow-up attack on Perugia by B-24s on January 19 shut down the airfield for four days. The invasion fleet approached Anzio undetected. The troops of VI Corps, commanded by Major General John P. Lucas, walked ashore, facing nothing but scattered small arms and mortar fire.

On D-Day, seven hundred sorties were flown in support, but once again an invasion was being mounted at the outer limits of air cover. There was a gut-churning shortage of fighter fields within range of the invasion beaches.

Colgan was by now a flight leader, taking four P-40s over the beaches. A force of roughly twenty Focke Wolfe 190s and Messerschmitt 109s tried to penetrate the fighter screen. Some got through and dive-bombed the beaches. As they turned north, 79th Group pilots tried to head the raiders off. A running fight ensued, with P-40s and RAF Spitfires chasing the raiders all the way back to Rome. Half a dozen Germans were downed, as was one of the 79th's P-40s. On the way back to Foggia the fighter-bombers strafed German truck traffic along the Appian Way.[14]

In the days that followed Colgan and fighter-bomber pilots got used to flying three-in-one missions to Anzio: carrying bombs to drop on German positions, followed by half an hour of patroling, with a strafing attack on German troops and vehicles on the return to base. After the first week of the new landing, the GAF operated mainly at night, with ineffective attempts to hit shipping by means of radio-controlled bombs dropped by fast, medium bombers.

Lucas expanded his bridgehead cautiously despite the lack of strong opposition. The landing had been mounted with too little assault shipping and too few troops for him to do anything ambitious his first week ashore, such as take Rome.

By nightfall of D-Day Kesselring was moving troops from northern Italy, southern France and the Balkans. He even pulled men out of the Gustav Line. By mid-February one hundred thousand Germans were containing the Anzio beachhead and preparing to attack. Hitler insisted the beachhead must be wiped out: the loss of seventy thousand Allied troops in a single battle might cancel the expected invasion of France.

Moreover, the Germans held the high ground overlooking Anzio. They could see almost anything that moved, and pound it with their artillery. To bolster the coming attack, another one hundred GAF planes were sent to Italy. Day by day the fighting at Anzio intensified, as German troops arrived and German artillery tried to prepare the battlefield for an armor-led infantry assault.

Clark had agreed to Shingle in the belief that it would force the Germans to weaken their defenses along the Gustav Line, allowing his troops to break through and head north for Anzio and Rome. To do that, he had to crack the German position at Cassino, the lynchpin of the Gustav Line.

On a rocky pinnacle forty-five hundred feet high stood the world-famous monastery of Monte Cassino; half a mile below it stood Cassino town. A New Zealand division would attack the town, while an Indian division would try to fight its way past the monastery. The Indian division commander, convinced the Germans were in the monastery, asked for it to be bombed. His corps commander disagreed, and requested a close-support mission instead, for February 16, against German troops dug in close to the monastery.

Instead of being handled like a normal close air request, this one went to Eaker, to Clark, and ultimately to Field Marshal Alexander, whose army group headquarters coordinated the operations of Fifth and Eighth armies. Eaker flew over the monastery in an L-5 and returned claiming the Germans were inside. Saville, who'd made his own investigation, vehemently disagreed.[15]

The involvement of the top brass turned a routine request for close air support into one something else. Once the decision had been made, the request got filed at the top of the chain of command, instead of the bottom. It wasn't handled normally. The result was one of the heaviest bombing attacks of the war. It was also brought forward twenty-four hours, ostensibly because of weather, but no one gave advance warning to the troops, whose plan of attack anticipated close support on the 16th.

On February 15 more than 100 B-17s of Fifteenth Air Force and 112 mediums from Twelfth Air Force dropped 572 bombs, razing the monastery to its medieval foundations. The ruins provided the Germans with instant defenses, which they rapidly moved into. Their position was stronger than ever. Flying the mission a day early had preempted the ground attack, which couldn't be brought forward twenty-four hours. So the ground troops gained no military advantage.

Events at Cassino were swiftly overshadowed by a crisis at Anzio, where the German counterattack erupted on February 16. The next few days saw a reply of the desperate struggle on the beaches of Salerno. The patchy air cover allowed GAF fighters to fly close support missions that drew praise from Kesselring. Naval gunfire and American artillery backed up Allied troops, but the German infantry kept on coming, despite fearsome losses. Lucas's front was dented and a gap was opening up between the American and British sectors.

The next day eight hundred Allied aircraft dumped one thousand tons of bombs on German frontline positions. It was the biggest close support operation that had been flown anywhere.[16] The Navy performed prodigiously once more, but the ultimate accolade belonged to the ground troops, who refused to be beaten.

The German counterattack continued on the 18th, driving the defenders back to their last defensive line, only one mile from the sea. By nightfall, though, the Germans were played out, and it showed.[17]

Throughout this epic struggle, and to the indignation of ground commanders such as Major General Lucian Truscott, the interdiction campaign continued against road and rail movement.[18] To them, the fighting at Anzio was an emergency that justified putting everything into close air support. What use would a successful interdiction campaign be if the four divisions on the beach were wiped out and the survivors taken prisoner?

Nevertheless, the interdiction campaign was having a cumulative effect that no Allied soldier could see but every German could sense. Kesselring's troops moved by road, traveling at night. That absorbed all his limited truck resources, forcing him to rely on the Italian railroads to move their supplies. The railroads found it increasingly difficult, though, to handle artillery ammunition.

By weight, ammunition was the biggest item a modern army had to deal with. And despite the many logistical triumphs of the U.S. Army in World War II the one problem it never solved was keeping the supply of artillery ammo flowing smoothly so there was always a regular and adequate supply at the front. In many battles American troops attacked with inadequate artillery support for want of ammo.

For the Germans, the problem became infinitely worse, as the air attacks on marshalling yards and railroad bridges in central Italy continued remorselessly. The Germans had hurriedly developed a 170mm artillery piece that outranged American 155s. The shells were huge. Shipping them to Anzio to wipe out the American artillery must have absorbed much of the transportation that got through. Fortunately, the 170mm shells proved to be 90 percent duds, so the effort to move them at the cost of other calibers was completely wasted.[19] The Germans also had some wildly inaccurate but huge 280mm railroad guns which fired shells weighing a ton. What was true of bombs was equally true of artillery: a large number of explosions in a confined space does a lot more damage than a few big explosions in a wider pattern. Seemingly unaware of this, the Germans persisted in shipping hundreds of 280mm shells to Italy, instead of replacing them with thousands of rounds of 100mm ammunition to keep its basic artillery piece in operation. Hobbled by such mistakes, German artillery was reduced to firing fifteen hundred rounds a day. Allied artillery fired an average of twenty-five thousand a day in reply.

On February 19, the VI Corps counterattacked. In less than twelve hours all German gains were wiped out. The initiative swung back to the Allies. It would remain with them despite a second German counterattack ten days later, in response to incessant orders from the Führer.

Hitler wanted to mount a third counterattack. Kesselring sent his chief of staff, Brigadier General Siegfried Westphal, to explain why it couldn't be done. There was, Westphal reported, a severe shortage of artillery ammunition. Hitler was astonished; artillery ammunition production was rising spectacularly in 1944. Westphal replied that more could be shipped but, "It is impossible to bring it to the front owing to the daily severance of rail communications in Italy by bombing attacks."[20] For once, Hitler didn't have a response. And although Anzio remained under siege, fresh Allied divisions were pouring into the beachhead.

Before the first Allied soldier set foot on the Italian mainland Spaatz had plans for Foggia. He wanted to create a new air force, base it at Foggia and use it to attack dozens of strategic targets that were beyond the range of Eighth Air Force, such as Ploesti.[21] Striking from the south would stretch German air defenses, which presently faced west, and make them easier to penetrate. Besides, the weather was better in Italy than in England.

Eaker was emphatically opposed to Spaatz's proposal, and the RAF supported Eaker. The new air force could be created only by slowing the buildup of the Eighth. Eaker argued that Foggia was cut off by mountains from decent ports and the southern Italian railroads had been wrecked by Doolittle's bombers. Supply and maintenance problems would be endless. And what mattered wasn't the weather over the base but the weather over the target.[22]

Eaker sent his chief of staff, Brigadier General Idwal Edwards, to Washington to argue this case. Edwards, however, didn't present it with much enthusiasm—he thought putting a strategic air force at Foggia was a great idea.[23] The issue was finally settled when Somervell visited Italy and said the logistical problems were as bad as Eaker claimed, but Army Service Forces could handle them.

The new air force, the Fifteenth, was activated November 1, 1943, under the command of Jimmy Doolittle. It was created by taking the Twelfth Air Force's six groups of heavy bombers, mainly B-17s, and its three groups of P-38s. The Fifteenth was promised fifteen more bomb groups, mainly B-24s, that had been originally slated to go to England. The Twelfth became a tactical air force. It would support the prolonged ground campaign in Italy.

Foggia was in no shape yet to handle heavies. It was okay for fighters and some medium bombers, but for all practical purposes it would have to be rebuilt. During the first couple of months of its existence the Fifteenth flew from North Africa. It opened its account by flying a mission from Tunis to bomb the Messerschmitt plant at Wiener-Neustadt, in southern Austria, on November 2.

At year's end, the Fifteenth moved into Foggia. It also got a new commander, Major General Nathan Twining, former commander of the Thirteenth Air Force in the South Pacific. He'd returned to Washington in late December to check himself into Walter Reed. Twining was suffering from malaria and various other tropical diseases. While he was on his way back to the United States, there had been a major shake-up of command arrangements in Europe: Doolittle was going to replace Eaker in command of the Mighty Eighth. Who should get the Fifteenth?

Arnold sent for Twining, who protested he was too sick to take on a new assignment. Tough. He was allowed to spend Christmas in a Walter Reed hospital bed, but by New Year's Eve he was shivering in Italy.[24]

Living conditions at Foggia that winter were miserable. Officers and men lived under canvas on muddy hillsides overlooking bleak airfields covered with acres of curling pierced-steel-plank. There was little hot food, no hot water. It was the tents that etched themselves into the memory of a young B-17 pilot, Lieutenant John Muirhead. "Like houses in a village, they varied in style and elegance. Some were models of good labor . . . with wood floors made from bomb crates and crude furniture made from the same material. A few even had flowerpots hung from the doorframes. . . . There were other tents beyond redemption, erected in contempt of any acknowledgement of permanence. Their poles were awry; their lines slack and poorly pegged. They shuddered, flapping in the cold February winds like the tattered pennants of desperate men."[25]

The Fifteenth Air Force didn't have an appreciable effect on thinning out German air defense and, ironically, it suffered more from bad weather than did the Eighth. One thing it did do was make the Germans stop producing armaments in northern Italy.[26]

Twining's biggest target was Ploesti. He would send the Fifteenth to attack it on average every three weeks until the end of the war. He wryly called it "Number One on the Hit Parade." The Fifteenth's second biggest target was the synthetic oil plants the Germans had located near the Polish border, to keep them safe from Allied bombers.

The Italian stalemate had Arnold deeply worried. Suppose the Army blamed the AAF for letting it down? The wide latitude granted by FM 100-20 might be jeopardized. He urged Eaker to consider using every heavy and medium bomber in the theater and blast a path through at Cassino, with six thousand tons of high explosive a day.[27] Eaker replied that a carpet bombing mission was being planned, to obliterate the town of Cassino, allowing the New Zealand Corps to break through.

Gordon Saville's XII ASC would provide many of the planes involved in the operation, but when Saville looked over the plan he doubted it would work. To find out, he had some of his fighter-bombers make a small, experimental attack. The buildings of Cassino were made of a kind of adobe. After a few explosions the air was so full of plaster dust no one could see anything. Large friendly-fire casualties were inevitable, and were likely to paralyze the assaulting troops. Moreover, few Germans were in the town. Most were dug in behind granite boulders above it. Finally, many of Cassino's houses had cellars. Destroying the houses would open up the cellars, creating hundreds of tank traps.

Eaker rejected Saville's criticisms. He was under such pressure from Arnold he probably couldn't do anything else. Saville asked to be relieved of his command; he refused to be associated with a plan that was so mind-bogglingly stupid. Instead, he was sent on leave to Algiers, while his XII ASC pilots prepared to fly their part of the mission.[28]

Weather delayed it for nearly three weeks, but on March 15 it went ahead. Strategic contributed three hundred heavy bombers; Tactical chipped in with two hundred mediums. In the space of a few hours they dropped more than one thousand tons of bombs—and accomplished nothing. Much of the bombing was wildly inaccurate. There were nearly two hundred friendly-fire casualties. The entire town was flattened. The stunned New Zealand Corps advanced slowly, to flounder in craters and cellars.[29]

Eaker had assured Arnold there was another plan being developed, on which he pinned much greater hopes of breaking the stalemate. It was a plan that emerged from renewed debate over interdiction; a debate revived in part by the departure of Tedder and Zuckerman and in part by the clear failure to isolate the Anzio battlefield from a nearly fatal counterattack.

The issue revolved around which was the real weak point in enemy logistics: bridges or marshalling yards? An Italian general who'd continued working with the Germans after his country's surrender defected to the Allies in early 1944 and claimed the attacks on bridges in fall 1943 had nearly forced the Germans to abandon Rome, because they couldn't keep the city fed. Recent research in the German records casts considerable doubt on the defector's claim, but to the bridge believers it was manna from heaven.[30]

They had other factors in their favor, too. There simply weren't enough bombers in MAAF to keep dozens of marshalling yards blocked. Repairs would be made at night and in weather that kept planes grounded. Moreover, the Germans had learned to cope with marshalling yard attacks by making up trains in Austria and running them into Italy at night. They were also drawing on the tens of thousands of locomotives and one million plus freight cars available in the occupied countries of Western Europe.

Zuckerman's argument against bridges was that it could take as many as one thousand sorties to knock out a single structure, which could then be repaired in a week or so. A well-wrecked marshalling yard, on the other hand, spread friction throughout the whole system, putting an increasingly intolerable strain on it. Zuckerman was an anatomist by profession and he was trying to create a kind of fatal virus that, once introduced, would spread through the rail net. The body would eventually die, even though most parts of it seemed to function right up to the end.[31]

MAAF's Bombing Policy Committee produced a new plan, called Operation Strangle, which would try to break the stalemate by driving the German railheads back one hundred miles from Anzio and Cassino. Allied intelligence estimated there were fourteen German divisions south of a line from Pisa to Rimini. It calculated that these divisions required four to five thousand tons of supplies a day to survive. About five hundred tons moved each day by sea, aboard small ships that hugged the coast and moved only at night. The rest went mainly by rail.

If the Germans were forced to unload their trains one hundred miles from the front they would have to keep the fourteen divisions supplied by road. But with fighters and fighter-bombers strafing anything that moved in the daylight, road movement would prove so difficult the supply system would collapse. The Germans would be forced to retreat.[32]

Strategic would continue to attack the biggest marshalling yards in northern Italy, but the big difference in Strangle was the changed role of Tactical. In earlier interdiction campaigns its mediums focused on marshalling yards. This time the bombers would concentrate on bridges, tunnels and viaducts. XII Air Support Command's fighter-bombers would also be unleashed on such targets and would attack crews attempting to repair the tracks.

Attacks by medium bombers on the railroad net in the fall of 1943 had been disappointing. The difference now was the supply of Norden bombsights for B-26 groups. The Marauders were at last able to bomb small, fixed targets with a high degree of precision. The B-26 groups had done the only truly accurate bombing at Cassino.[33]

What they couldn't do was dive-bomb, and Italy's mountainous terrain called for a lot of dive-bombing. The A-36 was a poor dive-bomber; the P-40 was mediocre; and both had highly vulnerable liquid-cooled engines. Fortunately, large numbers of P-47Ds were arriving at Italian airfields in early 1944.

The P-47D was just what fighter-bomber pilots like Bill Colgan were praying for, and especially now that their stint was being upped to one hundred missions.[34] Its four tons gave the Thunderbolt the diving characteristics of a falling anvil; its huge radial engine protected the pilot like a wall of steel; and it could drop twenty-five hundred pounds of bombs. It could fight on equal terms with the FW-190 yet was also the war's supreme bridge buster.

Strangle began days after the failed bombing at Cassino. It was hampered from the start by rainy weather, which kept the mediums grounded three or four days each week. Even so, by early April the Germans stopped trying to run trains to the front and unloaded them one hundred miles back onto trucks. The trucks tried to push through during daylight, but so many were bombed and strafed that on April 15, Kesselring ordered a halt to all daylight movement.

The first part of Strangle had succeeded brilliantly, but the rest was flawed by false calculations. The fourteen German divisions in the front lines needed only twenty-eight tons of supplies a day to survive. And that was about all they got. There wasn't enough trucking to rebuild their artillery ammunition stocks. There was a shortage of fuel. There was also a shortage of fodder. This was a serious blow, because German quartermasters relied heavily on horse-drawn carts to haul supplies in the mountains.[35]

Vietinghoff's 10th Army along the Gustav Line and Mackensen's 14th Army containing Cassino hadn't been forced to retreat. Instead, Strangle robbed them of all tactical mobility. They could fight only where they stood, but they couldn't maneuver and couldn't counterattack. It is one of the oldest maxims of war that whoever fights only on the defensive is defeated.

Disappointed Allied commanders felt that Strangle had failed. For that, the airmen had themselves to blame—they had promised too much. In doing so, they obscured what Strangle had achieved. By immobilizing the Germans, air power had ensured the security of Anzio. At the same time, it enabled Allied forces to continue probing and testing German positions with impunity along the Gustav Line.

Beyond that, the airmen had created a situation in which the breakout offensive could be mounted with no possibility of a German counterattack to exploit Allied weaknesses or mistakes. In a war between modern states that was something almost unknown, but Allied ground commanders were starting to take it for granted.

Italy in the spring of 1944 represented in microcosm the war that the Air Staff and officers in the War Plans Division had foreseen before Pearl Harbor. Here were 450,000 Allied troops about to take the offensive against an enemy who was equal in numbers, holding the high ground and benefiting from well-prepared defenses. There was no hope of achieving the three-to-one superiority in manpower that staff colleges taught an attacker needed to be sure of success. Clark had to rely instead on superior firepower and mobility to make up for the missing divisions. In Italy, as in nearly every theater of war, the AAF provided much of the firepower and mobility advantage the Army needed.

The breakout attempt, code-named Diadem, was scheduled for May 12. A new air plan was developed, by "Uncle Joe" Cannon, to succeed Strangle. There would be a preparatory phase, from April 25 to May 11, in which the emphasis would be on transportation attacks but with a renewed counterair offensive to assure air superiority was maintained. There would also be attacks on German supply dumps to reduce present stocks of fuel and ammunition.[36]

The assault phase would start on D-Day and attempt to smash German command and control. Ultra had revealed the locations of more than a dozen German headquarters and command posts. The Strategic Air Force would join the Tactical Air Force in hard-hitting attacks designed to take them out. Counterair would continue, as would interdiction.

The idea behind Diadem was to make yet another attack on Monte Cassino. Putting even a slight crack in the German position would make it possible to reach the Liri Valley. The Germans would be forced to pull back. As they did so, Allied troops would be able to break into the valley.

Air power having successfully driven the railheads back one hundred miles from the front, Cannon's goal for Diadem was to drive them back another forty miles. And hoping to make good some of the flaws revealed by Strangle, Cannon planned on flying interdiction missions at night, using his A-20 light bombers.

Shortly before midnight on May 11, Diadem opened with the roar of two thousand artillery pieces. Over the next few days the German defenders at Cassino fought off a spirited attack by Polish troops.

Tactical's fighter-bombers flew hundreds of close support missions each day in support of the ground troops. The 42nd and 57th Medium Bomb Wings, meanwhile, were bombing towns and filling the streets with rubble to slow the movement of German reserves to the front.[37] Mediums also went to work on the railroads, while Strategic's heavies hit the major marshalling yards.

After a week of hard fighting, the Poles were stopped tantalizingly short of their objective. Twenty thousand French mountain troops from North Africa began infiltrating the unbelievably rugged and overgrown razorback ridges southwest of the monastery. They were able to threaten the German rear. Kesselring committed the last of his reserves to try shoring up 10th Army's position, but it was too little, too late. By May 22 Vietinghoff's 10th Army was pulling out.[38]

At dawn on May 23 every gun in the Anzio beachhead opened up and the second breakout began. If VI Corps, now commanded by Truscott, could drive inland to Valmontone it had a chance of cutting off 10th Army as it retreated up the Liri Valley. The German 14th Army would try to keep VI Corps away from Valmontone long enough to allow the 10th to escape.

Strategic was ordered to attack Valmontone. Unleashing the heavies against it would flatten the town, block the roads and, with luck, destroy 14th Army headquarters. "It was a rush call, and there were no photographs available, just maps," recalled Leroy Newby, a navigator with the 460th Bomb Group, flying B-24s.

"When we got to the target area there was a 10/10ths undercast. . . . Suddenly, the extra navigator who was riding in the nose turret said, 'There's a break in the cloud, and I think I see the target!' . . . What a break! *Look out German Command Post, here we come!* There it was, a peanut-shaped city among all the mountains. A novice could spot Valmontone from where I sat . . . we saturated the center of the town."

The group returned to Foggia, jubilant. Several hours later photo recon brought back pictures of the bombing. The photographs were captioned "Unidentified Target." The 460th "Black Panthers" later discovered they had demolished the peanut-shaped town of Velletri, twelve miles from Valmontone.[39]

Cannon's interdiction campaign against the railroads succeeded in pushing the railheads back, forcing an even greater dependence on road transportation. Yet the loss of trucks was becoming unbearable. The 10th Army was getting about thirty-five Italian-built replacement trucks each day—and losing as many as one hundred. The sole bright spot for the Germans was the narrowness of the fronts they had to defend at Anzio and on the Gustav Line. This enabled them to concentrate what trucks they had to keep the troops on those narrow fronts provided with enough matériel to fight a rearguard action. They lacked the fuel and ammunition reserves to counterattack, but they could avoid being overrun.

As 10th Army fell back in the Liri Valley it moved mainly by night. Allied air attacks to demolish buildings hadn't been much use in Sicily, where it was possible to detour around the rubble or have tanks clear paths through them. Now, the skies were so full of fighter-bombers that daylight detours off the roads were suicidal and no tank could hope to survive in the open for long.

Some trucks made a run for it by day, taking a hair-raising risk, but even the night was no longer completely safe. A-20s caught several convoys negotiating mountain passes by dropping flares. Unfortunately, only a few squadrons were capable of tactical operations at night.[40] Interdiction at night was really beyond the available technology. Despite Allied aircraft the retreating enemy received just enough ammo, just enough fuel, and just enough darkness to get out as an army, orderly in retreat, not as a horde of individuals scrambling away in panic for safety.

The German 10th Army might still have been reduced to that, but for a monumental error of judgment by Mark Clark. As American troops battled their way into a position to cut off the retreating 10th Army as it withdrew through Valmontone, Clark directed six of Truscott's seven divisions to turn northwest and head for Rome.[41] The 10th and 14th Armies withdrew into the broken, hilly terrain of northern Italy, more followed than pursued.

16

THE PRICE
OF PROGRESS

Shortly after Pearl Harbor the Air Force Combat Command became the Eighth Air Force. The Air Staff drew up plans to send it to the Middle East to support the British Eighth Army. British reverses in Libya and the lack of shipping forced a rethink. The embryonic Eighth found itself slated to go to the United Kingdom instead.

Its commander would be Major General Carl Spaatz, chief of the Air Staff and Arnold's closest friend. Even before setting off for England, Spaatz set a clear goal for the Eighth: destroy twenty GAF combat aircraft a day, whether in the factories or in the skies, and that will break the back of the Luftwaffe.[1]

Spaatz and Arnold chose their mutual friend, Brigadier General Ira Eaker, to run VIII Bomber Command. When Arnold told him of his new assignment, Eaker was dumbfounded. "But I've been in fighters all my life!" "I know," said Arnold. "We want the fighter spirit in bombardment aviation."[2] The VIII Fighter Command* was assigned to another old friend of both Arnold and Spaatz, Brigadier General Frank O'D. Hunter, the highly decorated World War I ace.

In June 1942 the first units of the Eighth started arriving in Britain: the 1st and 31st fighter groups, the 97th Bomb Group, and

---

*Most numbered air forces comprised a fighter command, a bomber command, an air support command, and an air service command, which took care of logistics.

the 60th Troop Carrier Group. British construction companies were at work carving out dozens of new airfields for the AAF along England's east coast. They wouldn't be built to the same high standard as airfields in the United States. There would be no sewers, for example, and their runways would be five thousand feet, instead of six thousand feet.[3] Creature comforts would be basic. All the same, the men of the Eighth were envied mightily by hundreds of thousands of American airmen posted to jungles, mountains, deserts and remote islands.

Spaatz established his headquarters at Bushy Park, a suburb on the southwest side of London. Eaker located VIII Bomber Command thirty miles away, northwest of London, at High Wycombe Girl's School, close to the headquarters of the RAF's Bomber Command. Hunter similarly placed himself near RAF Fighter Command's headquarters at Bentley Priory.

There was already a symbiotic relationship between the AAF and the RAF. Combat only drew the services closer. From start to finish there was a much happier partnership between Allied airmen than Allied ground soldiers ever achieved. It was typical that Eaker spent his first three months in England as the house guest of Air Marshal Sir Arthur Harris, the outspoken and single-minded commander of RAF Bomber Command.

Among Americans, Air Marshal Sir Charles Portal, the RAF Chief of Air Staff, was the most highly esteemed member of the Combined Chiefs after George Marshall. Portal had emerged from World War I with more than four hundred hours of combat flying in observation and bombardment. He'd shot down at least one German plane. After the war he became the RAF's chief flying instructor. By the mid-1920s he was clearly "Boom" Trenchard's protégé.

The 1920s were an anxious time for the RAF. The British army and navy tried to get it disbanded. The RAF saved itself by creating a new, peacetime role—"air policing." The British had to contend with rebellious nationalists from Iraq to Afghanistan. What the British government sought was control without occupation. The RAF offered to provide that by bombing recalcitrant Iraqis, Afghans, Persians, Pakistanis and Indians into submission. Towns and villages where nationalist leaders lived were bombed, making their people homeless. As they ran for safety they were strafed from the air. Both Portal and Harris advanced their careers through air policing, Portal in Aden, Harris in Afghanistan.[4]

When Britain declared war on Germany in 1939, however, the RAF had a firm policy of not bombing civilians—at least, not white, European civilians. For nearly a year the RAF dropped only leaflets on German cities. The night of August 24, 1940, however, the GAF accidentally bombed London. Churchill ordered reprisal raids on Berlin.

Although the gloves were now off, the RAF was not equipped to destroy cities. It had no four-engine bombers and attempts to attack Germany in daylight with mediums led to horrendous losses. The RAF tried night bombing, but its navigation was abysmal. Aircrews had trouble finding anything but the largest towns and cities. In 1941 RAF Bomber Command's standard of accuracy was such that any bomb landing within five miles of the aiming point was deemed to be on target.[5]

The British increasingly came around to the idea of making area attacks by night; not attacking targets in towns and cities, but bombing the towns and cities themselves. It was the only means they had of hurting the Germans from the air. In the fall of 1941 Portal, then head of Bomber Command, asked for four thousand bombers and began planning such a campaign.

Shortly after this he became Chief of Air Staff, handing Bomber Command over to Harris. As such, Portal's role was inter-service and inter-Allied planning. His deputy and probably closest friend, Air Marshal Wilfred Freeman, ran the RAF. Neither Freeman nor Portal, however, had much real control over Harris, who came to his new assignment with a simple idea and a powerful supporter. Harris, with his moon face, thick glasses, short sighted squint and bristling mustache, looked like an elderly clerk, but was as hard as a chrome-vanadium icepick. He believed with all the fervor of a religious fanatic that he could defeat Germany by burning it to the ground on moonless nights. And he had Churchill convinced it was at least worth trying.

Harris ridiculed those who had different ideas on strategic bombing as "panacea merchants, wanting to send a bomber to pull the plug out of Hitler's bath so he would die of pneumonia."[6] On May 30, 1942, Harris launched the first thousand-bomber raid, against Cologne.

The entry of the Eighth Air Force on the scene just as Harris got his bombing campaign revved up simply intensified the debate over how best to bomb Germany into defeat. Freeman and a handful of Air Ministry officials believed the AAF could bomb in daylight, precisely and effectively, once it could deploy a large number of heavy bombers. Portal had his doubts, mainly because he didn't believe the B-17 would be able to defend itself against German fighters.

The only use RAF Fighter Command could envisage for the B-17 was as a flying magnet.[7] It was almost impossible after 1940 to get the German Air Force to come up and fight in Western Europe. The GAF saved its strength for North Africa and the Eastern Front. Fighter Command, under Air Marshal Sir Sholto Douglas, regularly launched huge fighter sweeps over France and the Low Countries, accomplishing nothing beyond losing three or four planes (mainly to ground fire) for every GAF aircraft destroyed.[8] The B-17, on the other hand, might draw German planes into the air, where Fighter Command could shoot them down.

The best use RAF Bomber Command could envisage for the B-17 was to join its night bombing campaign. Harris and Portal pressed Churchill to convince Franklin Roosevelt of this. The President should simply order Arnold to have the Eighth fly with Bomber Command under the cloak of night. By January 1943, when Roosevelt headed for Casablanca, he was more than halfway persuaded. The Eighth's daylight precision bombing campaign looked DOA—dead on arrival.

In the summer of 1942 Arnold was struggling to turn the AAF into an effective fighting force against depressing odds. Marshall simply ordered that fifteen groups of medium and heavy bombers scheduled for the Eighth be diverted to defend Australia and to aid the Marine invasion of Guadalcanal. A week after this decision, Roosevelt ordered that Torch be mounted. To create an air force for Torch the Eighth was stripped of most of its present unimpressive strength.

In the late fall of 1942 the Eighth started over again, virtually from scratch. And in December it lost Spaatz, who became Ike's deputy for air in North Africa. Eaker took command of the Eighth.

One evening in January 1943 he received a telegram from Arnold telling him to be in Casablanca in the morning. When Eaker arrived in Morocco, Arnold told him that Churchill had convinced Roosevelt to order the Eighth to join Harris's night bombing campaign.[9] It was up to Eaker to change Churchill's mind.

Eaker held a journalism degree and loved to write long missives to Arnold. Now, though, he astutely reduced his arguments to less than a single page before he went to meet with Churchill. The Prime Minister arrived dressed as an RAF air commodore. (When meeting sailors, he dressed as a rear admiral; with generals, he appeared as a British brigadier.) Eaker handed Churchill the single sheet of paper and watched intently as Churchill, lips moving, read: the Eighth was equipped and trained to fly by day . . . time would be lost retraining and reequipping . . . there wasn't enough air space over eastern Britain for two big bomber forces to assemble safely at night . . . finally, "If the RAF continues night bombing and we bomb by day, we shall bomb them round the clock and the devil shall get no rest." Churchill savored that last sentence. He reconsidered the matter with Roosevelt. The Eighth should be given more time to show what daylight bombing could do.

Besides resolving the protracted debate over night versus day bombing the Casablanca Conference had other important consequences for the air war. With Eisenhower now assigned to the Mediterranean, a replacement was needed to command the U.S. Army (including Army Air Forces) in the European Theater of Operations. The post went to Frank Andrews, almost certainly on Marshall's insistence.[10]

The other important development was the approval by the Combined Chiefs of the Casablanca Directive. This directive was an ambiguous statement that tried to reconcile various interests. Harris interpreted it as sanctioning his morale bombing campaign. Eaker could read it as endorsing the Eighth's eventual strategic bombing offensive against German industry. Ground commanders saw it as a binding pledge that air would make a successful invasion of France possible.[11]

It fell to Eaker, Possum Hansell and two RAF officers to turn this loosely worded directive from on high into a strategic plan, known as the Combined Bomber Offensive. The CBO's premier target was the German aircraft industry. Second (at the urging of Robert Lovett) came ball bearings.[12] Third came oil. There followed a list of fourteen other targets, all carefully ranked.

At the Trident Conference held in Washington in May 1943 Roosevelt and Churchill approved the Combined Bomber Offensive. The airmen were jubilant. They had finally convinced their political masters that air's primary objective had to be the enemy air force.[13] The stage had been set for a fight to the death between the Eighth and the Luftwaffe.

· · ·

Neither Spaatz nor Eaker was in any hurry to push VIII Bomber Command into action. They wanted to build it up into a powerful force before unleashing it on Western Europe. Arnold, on the other hand, was champing at the bit. The British press, moreover, was denigrating the B-17. On August 15, 1942, Arnold held a press conference to defend the plane, but the most effective thing anyone could do to show the AAF really did believe in the Flying Fortress was to send it into action. Two days later, eighteen B-17s of the 97th Bomb Group set off for France—six on a diversion route, the remaining twelve to bomb a marshalling yard outside Rouen.

The pilot of the leading aircraft heading for Rouen was Major Paul W. Tibbets, Jr., one of the best and most fearless flyers the AAF possessed. Tibbets had dropped out of medical school in 1937 to join the Air Corps. He'd graduated first in his class at Randolph and, to his instructors' bemusement, asked for observation. A really hot pilot headed for pursuit, or at least bombardment. But *observation* . . . ? Tibbets reasoned that he'd simply fly more that way. And he was right. He got in about one thousand hours a year, twice as much flying as most pilots enjoyed.[14]

Still, the AAF wasn't going to leave one of its best talents in a happy backwater. Tibbets was transferred to 3rd Attack Group in 1940, and to the 97th Bomb Group in 1941. Like Doolittle, he could fly anything others could build.

In June 1942 the half-trained, under strength 97th deployed to Polebrook and Grafton Underwood, in southeastern England. What little discipline it possessed fell apart. The group commander and his deputy were taken up by the Rothschilds, who had an estate nearby. The group desperately needed training, but didn't get it. Only a handful of zealots like Tibbets took their assignments seriously. The wayward beginnings of the 97th, and its eventual redemption under an able, hard driving commander, were turned into the best novel and the best movie about the wartime air force, *Twelve O'Clock High.*[15]

The new group commander was Eaker's executive officer, Colonel Frank A. Armstrong, Jr. As the 12 B-17s headed toward Rouen, Armstrong sat in the copilot's seat next to Tibbets.* A cool, tough, no-nonsense North Carolinian, Armstrong ran the 97th with a firm grip. This first target, Rouen, was nonetheless picked because it

---

*General Eaker also flew on this mission as an "observer."

should be fairly easy, few French civilians would be endangered and it was well within range of fighter escort: the 12 Fortresses were shepherded by 108 Spitfires.

Spaatz and Eaker didn't see this lavish escort as the shape of things to come. On the contrary, they were convinced that once they could mount raids with large numbers of B-17s the bombers would have such massed firepower they would be able to defend themselves on the deepest raids into the Third Reich. Indeed, Spaatz believed that with only fifteen hundred heavies and mediums, plus eight hundred fighters (to defend his airfields), he would have "complete aerial supremacy over Germany within a year." He dismissed the effectiveness of GAF fighters and flak, reporting to Arnold that "Bombing accuracy does not diminish under fire, but rather increases."[16]

The Rouen raid did little damage, but nothing more was expected. What mattered was to make it a public relations success. In that respect, it achieved total victory.

With American bombs now falling on the enemy, Spaatz picked up Harris's habit of carrying bomb-damage photographs in his pockets. These were flaunted, like pictures of the wife and kids, to impress other people, such as the Prime Minister or the President. Arnold in turn copied Spaatz, and found the results so gratifying that a photo magazine called *Impact* was launched. It was classified "Confidential," which give it a certain cachet, yet it circulated freely not only within the AAF but throughout the government. It was a venture in public relations and morale building.[17]

As for the pioneering 97th Bomb Group, two days after the Rouen mission it bombed a large German fighter field in support of the British-Canadian raid on Dieppe. On his third mission a few days later, against a railhead at Le Trait on the Franco-Belgian frontier, Tibbets had a passenger, Brigadier General Newton Longfellow, commander of 2nd Bomb Wing.

Tall, sallow and somber, Longfellow was flying what was known as "combat orientation" and standing between the pilot's and copilot's seats. Longfellow had been chosen for his present assignment by Eaker, his close friend since they'd served together in the Philippines in 1919.

As it came off the target, the formation was jumped by Me-109s. One, making an overhead pass, put a twenty-millimeter cannon shell into the cockpit. It shattered the instrument panel, ripped off most of the copilot's left hand, and wounded Tibbets. "Newt panicked. He started grabbing for the throttles and we had a critical situation at altitude with the B-17, which had hand controlled turbos. If you got them to surging, you were in a hell of a fix. And he started grabbing throttle and turbo controls. I told him to quit. He didn't even hear me," Tibbets recalled. "The only thing I could do was hit him with my right elbow. I was able to catch him under the chin, while he was leaning over, and I knocked him flat on his fanny. . . . He calmed down then, and when he got back on his feet he got his first aid kit and started bandaging people up, and I was able to bring the airplane back under control and come on back."[18]

By October four more heavy groups were operational: the 44th, the 92nd, the 301st and the 306th. The 305th Group, commanded by Colonel Curtis LeMay, was about to deploy to England. But just as VIII Bomber Command began to gain some weight, it was stripped. In order to create the Twelfth Air Force for Torch, the Eighth had to give up 1,250 planes and nearly 30,000 personnel. Its few experienced units, such as the 97th, departed, never to return.

The principal target of VIII Bomber Command that fall was the German U-boat pens at Lorient and St. Nazaire. Two great but hard-pressed navies were demanding action. Eaker's bombers would attack sub pens in France by day, while Harris's bombers attacked U-boat construction yards in Germany by night. The Battle of the Atlantic remained delicately poised. In some months the U-boats were sinking Allied shipping faster than it could be replaced.

To Laurence Kuter, commanding Eaker's 1st Bomb Wing that fall, the attack on the sub pens was a misuse of heavy bombers. Arnold had sent Kuter overseas for six months to get some combat experience, but he never flew a mission. The five hundred-pound bombs his B-17s dropped simply bounced off the twenty-foot concrete roofs that covered the pens. And even if they'd penetrated, said Kuter, "We might have destroyed two submarines."[19]

Eaker, on the other hand, considered these missions an excellent training exercise.[20] His bomber crews were less convinced. They felt it was the Germans who were getting the training. Both GAF fighters and AAA units were honing their skills against B-17s taking predictable routes to and from their targets.

Flying over the Brittany peninsula, pilots could see "German fighters boiling up from various airfields along the way," then circling in force, ready to pounce when the escorting fighters turned back.[21] On the ground, the Germans seemed to mass their flak guns as if they knew what target VIII Bomber Command would hit today. And when the flak fired in barrages it filled the air with such concussion the control wheels seemed about to be ripped from pilots' hands. It was a terrifying, even if educational, experience.

Aircrew sought what protection they could. Many pilots flew in steel Army helmets. Aerial gunners would lug sheets of steel aboard to stand or sit on. A hundred pounds of extra weight in the tail could seriously affect the fuel consumption of a B-17. The gunners were told to get rid of their boilerplate, but protested feelingly, "I've got to protect the family jewels!" A more elegant solution was found by Lieutenant Carl Shutting, a navigator with the 381st Bomb Group. He persuaded an armorer to make an armor-plated jock strap for him; he never flew without it.[22]

In its first six months of operations VIII Bomber Command faced a myriad of problems. As Kuter found, his wing consisted of "Four groups, poorly trained, all very under strength, living in the mud . . . the housekeeping was unbelievable."[23] Eddie Rickenbacker made an inspection tour on behalf of Stimson and sent back a long, detailed report on equipment failures. The oxygen system consisted of rubber masks that froze against the skin at twenty thousand feet; compasses were lousy; there were too many controls for pilots to operate in combat; the most vulnerable spot on a fighter had always been the rear, but not one American fighter had been designed with a rearview mirror . . . and so on.[24] He identified more than fifty defects in American aircraft. Every one could be fixed, but it was going to take time.

Not surprisingly, those initial six months of operations consisted largely of scattering bombs over the West European landscape. The first eleven hundred sorties were flown in good weather, against light opposition, yet the bombing was dismal. Once they'd reached the initial point (usually some easily recognized ground feature ten to fifteen miles from the target) pilots would start the bomb run. All took evasive action to avoid flak on the way to the aiming point. They turned every fifteen seconds or so, while maintaining altitude. Constant turning made the Norden bombsight useless.

When in December 1942 Spaatz handed the Eighth over to Eaker, Eaker in turn gave VIII Bomber Command to Newton Longfellow. Perpetually overwrought, Longfellow struggled to overcome its difficulties by shouting himself hoarse.

Eaker, meanwhile, was fighting off British demands to convert American industry to production of Lancasters and to commit VIII

Bomber Command to night attacks. In defending his command, Eaker appears to have oversold it, even to himself.

When Spaatz traveled to Casablanca he took a long walk on the beach with Arnold and assured him the Eighth would realize the promise of strategic bombing once it had fighter escort for long range missions.[25] Eaker arrived and assured Arnold that he didn't need long range escort. With three hundred heavies on a mission, said Eaker, I will be able to strike anywhere, with a low rate of loss.

His confidence reflected the claims of his aerial gunners. Ever since the first shallow penetrations into French airspace the Eighth's gunners had been putting in astounding claims for enemy fighters downed. On a mission to Lille on October 9, 1942, for example, the gunners claimed to have destroyed 102 GAF planes in the air. The true figure was one.[26] The British ridiculed American claims (although their own could be just as absurd) but Eaker loyally supported his men. At Casablanca he informed Arnold's deputy, Barney Giles, that his bombers had a kill ratio of six to one against enemy fighters. Give me more heavies, he urged Giles, and I will win complete air superiority over Germany.[27]

Eaker's optimism was based not only on these figures but on reports that the Germans had created a coastal fighter belt from Hamburg to Brittany. Once the bombers had punched their way through the fighter belt, they'd be in clear air space the rest of the way to and from the target. Long range escort wouldn't be necessary.[28]

Such beliefs made it possible to ignore the fact that on escorted missions VIII Bomber Command had a loss rate of 2 percent. On unescorted missions it was losing nearly 7 percent. That meant the average bomber crew could expect to survive fourteen or fifteen unescorted missions.[29] The standard tour at this time was twenty-five missions. If more than half turned out to be unescorted the chances of surviving an entire tour were slim.

The GAF, meanwhile, was doing everything it could to make the odds even worse. Instead of a coastal fighter belt, the Germans were creating five defense zones, each roughly twenty-five miles deep, providing fighter coverage more than one hundred miles inland from the coast.

GAF tactics were becoming more menacing, too. Like fighter pilots all over the world, the Germans had been taught to attack bombers from the rear. The twin fifty-calibers in the tail of a B-17 came as an unpleasant surprise. The only spot not covered by defensive fire was the nose. In November 1942 an incredibly bold German pilot, Hauptman Egon Mayer, started making head-on attacks, at closing speeds of five hundred miles per hour, firing a one-second burst into the bomber's cockpit before diving sharply away a hair-raising instant before collision. Not every pilot had Mayer's nerve or timing, but where one man will lead, other men will follow. There were some spectacular head on crashes, but the nose attack was the most effective way to bring down a B-17. The B-24 was easier: it had no belly turret. The B-24s got mauled from below during their first six months in Europe.[30]

The GAF had trained to attack in squadrons. In January 1943 it started attacking in groups. Heavy bomber crews got used to seeing twenty or thirty fighters form up on a parallel course out of the range of fifty-caliber fire, then forge three or four miles ahead, turn into the path of the bombers, and come straight at them, guns brightly winking hot lead and twenty-millimeter cannon shells. Such methods were so effective that at a conference of top Luftwaffe officers in February 1943 the chief of fighters, General Adolf Galland, reported to Goering that his pilots had solved whatever problem the American heavy bombers might have represented.[31]

In the early months of 1943, however, the Eighth felt it was making headway. Brigadier General "Possum" Hansell took command of 1st Bomb Wing. Kuter went to North Africa to rejoin Spaatz. On January 3 Hansell led sixty-eight bombers to attack St. Nazaire in the heaviest attack yet on the sub pens.* There was no attempt at precision bombing. The planes flew a close formation and dropped when bombs fell from the plane carrying the lead bombardier. The AAF oxymoronically hailed this as "formation precision bombing." It was, in truth, pattern bombing—neither more, nor less. Seven planes were lost and forty-seven damaged.[32]

The frustrating campaign against the sub pens gave way to unescorted daylight raids into Germany. The first was against the naval dockyards at Wilhelmshaven on January 27. Ninety-one bombers took off; fifty-three found the target. Only two B-24s and one B-17 were lost. The mission was a gratifying success.[33]

---

*In flying this mission, Hansell showed tremendous grit. On his combat orientation flight, with Tibbets, he'd been paralyzed with fear and huddled on the floor of the radio operator's compartment, unable to move.[34]

Miserable weather and lousy maintenance kept the Eighth grounded for most of February. Then, on March 18, ninety-seven heavy bombers attacked the submarine construction yard at Vegesack. Only two B-24s and a B-17 were lost. Aerial gunners claimed fifty-two GAF fighters downed for certain, with another twenty probables. Photo reconnaissance showed the bombing had been remarkably accurate. Vegesack seemed to vindicate Eaker's faith.[35]

A month later, however, 106 heavies attacked the Focke Wulf factory at Bremen. This was a target the GAF willingly rose to defend: 15 Allied bombers were shot down; another was lost to flak; 46 were damaged.[36]

That spring VIII Bomber Command stood on the verge of becoming a mighty force. It had never been able to mount a raid in three-figure strength. On May 13 four more heavy groups (94th, 95th, 96th and 351st) became operational. Delighted, Eaker celebrated by sending 210 bombers to Kiel, Antwerp, Courtrai and Ijmuiden on May 14.

Twelve of these bombers were B-26s of the 322nd Bomb Group, making the Marauders' combat debut in the Eastern Theater of Operations. The AAF considered counterair the best role for mediums, and VIII Bomber Command wanted to use them against German airfields. The RAF begged to differ. It pressed for American mediums to be used against railheads and power stations—the kind of daytime targets, that is, that the RAF attacked with its Lend-Lease B-25s.

The target for May 14 was the power station at Ijmuiden on the Dutch coast. The twelve Marauders skimmed across the North Sea, screaming over Ijmuiden at low altitude and dropping British bombs with thirty-minute delayed action fuses. All planes returned safely to base.[37]

Photo recon showed that most of the bombs had failed to go off. Longfellow ordered another attack be mounted May 17. The group commander, Colonel Robert Stillman, protested to his wing commander, Brigadier General Francis Brady, that the Germans would be alerted and waiting for a return visit. "You know that's stupid." Brady didn't deny it, "But we're all soldiers. We've got to do what we're ordered to do." Stillman chose to lead the attack. He had no intention of allowing his pilots to fly what he considered a suicide mission without him.

The Marauders crossed the North Sea at an altitude of twenty-five feet. They spotted a convoy that Stillman assumed was British, but with radio silence he couldn't tell it not to shoot. So he turned his formation south to avoid its likely antiaircraft fire.

Shortly after this, one of the B-26s aborted. Stillman wasn't aware of it, but when the plane pulled out of formation, the pilot took it up to one thousand feet. It's almost certain that it appeared on German radar.

"Just as we were about to hit the coast," said Stillman, "we ran into small-arms fire. . . . Evidently there were a lot of machine guns dug into the beach and camouflaged to look like humps of sand. . . . I saw tracer fire coming from three different points in front of me, within an arc that I could cover with my guns. . . . It was easy to aim the guns by using the rudder and elevator controls. The tracers stopped coming from two emplacements after I had given each of them a long burst. Then that third gun started firing at me. . . . The lights went out. . . . When I came to the ship was out of control. . . . I remember thinking to myself, 'Well, the Air Forces are losing a damned good man.' . . . the plane must have gone in at better than two hundred miles an hour and upside down." Stillman survived and was taken prisoner.[38]

Because the group missed its intended landfall, it had to travel half the length of Holland to reach Ijmuiden. This prolonged transit over a well-defended country took a staggering toll: every one of the eleven Marauders was brought down. Appalled, Eaker shifted all B-26s from the bomber command over to VIII Air Support Command.

Galland's assurance to Goering that his pilots had overcome the challenge posed by VIII Bomber Command reflected the rise in GAF single-engine fighter strength in the West, combined with better armament. By mid-1943 there would be almost eight hundred aircraft, more than double the mid-1942 figure, and it would go on rising.[39] Additional aircraft made it possible to deepen the air defense zone. By the summer of 1943 the GAF would have a fighter network that was 450 miles deep, boasting dozens of auxiliary airfields, each well stocked with fuel and bombs. It would be possible for GAF fighters to fly two, three, even four sorties against a B-17 mission.

When Longfellow attacked Wilhelmshaven with 123 planes on May 21 his pilots encountered German twin-engine fighters firing rockets into their formations. The rockets were wildly inaccurate, but worrying. On subsequent raids something even more ominous appeared, FW-190s equipped with thirty-millimeter long-range cannon. This weapon easily outranged the fifty-calibers carried by the Eighth's aircraft and its exploding shells had a lethal radius of one hundred yards. The FW-190s would lob cannon shells into American bomber formations to break them up, while Me-109s circled like hungry wolves to fall on bombers that were damaged or isolated. Fortunately the thirty-millimeter cannon never reached its full potential. Despite having the world's best optical industry, the Germans never devised a good sight for it.[40]

All the same, VIII Bomber Command was taking heavy losses. On June 13, the 4th Bomb Wing attacked Kiel and Bremen with 102 bombers; 26 were shot down. Setbacks such as this revived British criticisms of the B-17 and the daylight bombing campaign. Eaker had a morale time bomb on his hands: the Eighth's aircrews depended on British newspapers and the BBC for much of their information.

The shrill chorus of disdain was led by Britain's leading aviation writer, Peter Masefield, nephew of the noted poet John Masefield. Eaker sent for Archie Old, commander of the 96th Bomb Group, and ordered him to convince Masefield he was wrong about daylight bombing.

The 96th was one of the best trained, best led groups in VIII Bomber Command. Old was a country boy from Texas who'd served in the 3rd Attack Group with Frank Armstrong and Nathan Twining. He was fearless, shrewd and combative. Old flew missions regularly.

A group commander's job wasn't to pilot the plane but to sit in the copilot's seat or stand in the top turret and watch what his other pilots were doing. From time to time Old was ordered not to go on particular missions. He got hold of a Mosquito and would zoom around his group, closing it up, so it hit the Continent in immaculate condition. The 96th believed no one could fly a more compact formation than it did. Its morale was high, its discipline excellent.

Old's regime paid dividends. When in May 1943 the crew of the *Memphis Belle* of the 91st Group completed the first twenty-five-mission tour of any plane in the Eighth, they were immortalized in American folklore for miraculously overcoming impossible odds. In Old's 96th Bomb Group, twenty-six of his original thirty-five aircrews survived their twenty-five-mission tour, including some of the toughest assignments of the war.[41]

Old's answer to the Masefield problem was to ask Masefield to visit the group, to get to know the men and the planes. Tall, lanky and exquisitely cultivated, Masefield became a familiar sight around the 96th. The question that really gnawed at Masefield was: Just what is it like up there? Old provided the answer. When the 96th bombed Le Bourget airfield outside Paris on Bastille Day, July 14, it was an outward and visible sign to Parisians of eventual liberation. GAF fighters were all over the sky, and Masefield was blazing away at them, manning a waist gun aboard one of Old's B-17s. It was the thrill of his life. He arrived back in England a convert to daylight bombardment.[42]

The Eighth needed all the friends it could get. Eaker's poor choice of subordinates, such as Longfellow, was becoming embarrassingly obvious, inspiring a stream of sarcastic letters from Arnold. Longfellow's nonstop ranting had earned him the nickname "Screaming Eagle." At the end of June he was sent home, a burned-out wreck.

His replacement was the commander of 4th Bomb Wing, thirty-seven-year-old Brigadier General Frederick L. Anderson, a 1928 graduate of West Point. Tall, well built, and ruggedly good-looking in the strong-jawed John Wayne style, he had women swooning.[43]

The greatest strength of the AAF in 1943 was probably not to be found in its top level leadership but in the excellence of its group and wing commanders; not with the senior generals or Arnold favorites, but with the colonels and one-stars such as Old and Anderson, who'd risen rapidly and entirely on merit since 1939.

Sent overseas, they were up against challenges that no service school could have foreseen, no training program could have specifically addressed. They had to improvise instant solutions to unimaginable problems. Entirely pragmatic, they cared little about doctrinal struggles, who'd said what at Maxwell, or high military politics.

First of all the groups had to be reorganized. They were arriving in England with thirty-five planes, divided into three bombing squadrons and a recon squadron. The GAF would eat a lightly armed recon squadron alive. The recon squadrons became bombing squadrons.

In the spring of 1943 Armstrong took command of the 306th Bomb Group. He teamed up with LeMay and the 305th to experiment with new formations. In the spring of 1943 they devised what became known as the combat box, to be flown by a three-group combat wing. The idea was that each group assigned to a mission would put up twenty-one planes; the remaining fourteen would be undergoing maintenance or repair. Three twenty-one-plane groups would fill a combat box. The top group would fly above and slightly to the right of the middle group; the bottom group would fly below it and slightly to the left. The middle group would fly slightly ahead of the other two.[44] Viewed from the side, each group resembled a flying wedge, like so: <. Yet if viewed from above or below, it was clear the aircraft were staggered so that no plane was directly above or below another.

The combat box uncovered every plane's guns. They could fire in just about any direction with minimal risk of striking a friendly aircraft. There were obvious drawbacks. Formation integrity meant there could be no more evasive action. Twenty planes in every group would be bombing on a signal from the lead bombardier. The bombsight was removed from nearly every B-17 and replaced with a nose gun. Their bombardiers would simply toggle their bomb loads when the leading aircraft dropped its bombs. High-level precision bombing was as good as dead. The Eighth (and the Fifteenth) would earn its money by pattern bombing.

From the initial point each group would make its own bomb run to the target. Beyond the target they would reassemble at a designated rally point and reform the combat box for the return to base.

LeMay toured the groups, carrying half a dozen model airplanes to teach the new formation.[45] Training had long been a passion with LeMay, although the depth of his emotions never appeared on his face. He suffered from Bell's palsy, a paralysis of the seventh, or facial, nerve, which makes the muscles of the face droop. He propped them up as best he could by clenching a cigar between his teeth. This only added to the impression of grim determination. He couldn't smile even if he wanted to. He was also going deaf, the common fate of former open-cockpit flyers.[46]

LeMay was soft-spoken, tightly controlled. He had physical and moral courage. Pilots didn't love LeMay. He was too demanding and seemed to lack human warmth. Yet virtually every airman admired him, because he knew more about the planes they flew than they did, could fly them better than they did and could navigate better than they ever would. He debriefed squadron and group commanders so closely he seemed to end up knowing more about the mission they'd flown than they did.[47] LeMay was a leader among leaders, one of the most effective commanders of the war.

The combat box forced group commanders to beat down resistance from the aircrews, who resented giving up evasive action. Lead pilots were even more indignant at having to turn over control of their aircraft from the initial point to the aiming point to bombardiers, who flew the B-17 by linking the Norden bombsight to the automatic pilot.[48]

Two combat wings were formed to field test the combat box idea. Armstrong commanded one, the 101st; LeMay commanded the other, the 102nd. In mid-July 1943, with VIII Bomber Command under new management and heavy bomber availability reaching Eaker's magic figure of three hundred, the moment of truth was at hand. All the Eighth needed now was a break in the weather.

Brigadier General Frank "Monk" Hunter was a logical choice to lead VIII Fighter Command. In the early 1930s he had commanded 1st Pursuit Group in Arnold's 1st Bomb Wing. When the 23rd Demonstration and Test Group was created to try out the Tactical School's ideas, Hunter led it. Arnold had sent him to Britain as an observer in 1940 and he'd stood on the white cliffs of Dover with Spaatz to watch the Battle of Britain swirling over their heads. With his big, British-style military mustache, his British swagger stick and a chestful of medals from the Western Front, Hunter clearly admired the RAF.

Air Marshal Sir Charles Portal was not keen, though, to see an American fighter command established. He hoped to integrate American fighter groups into RAF Fighter Command. Arnold refused to consider it. Even so, VIII Fighter Command operated so closely with the RAF the point was pretty academic.[49]

The British sought to remedy the training shortcomings of the newcomers. American pilots, they found, could fly well, but couldn't shoot a gun in the air with much hope of hitting anything. The Americans also lacked another essential—airplanes. The first group deployed to England was 31st Fighter Group. It had trained on P-39s, but arrived without them. The RAF reequipped it with one hundred Spitfires.

After some intense transition training, six 31st Group pilots went into combat July 26, 1942, in a combined AAF-RAF fighter sweep over northern France. The group was a nursery of talent; four of these six pioneers went on to become generals.[50] On August 19 the 31st flew 123 sorties in support of the raid on Dieppe, against fierce GAF opposition. One justification for the Dieppe operation was to get the GAF to fight. That part of the plan worked.

The 31st loved the Spitfire. Unlike the P-39, it was a plane that promised to keep a pilot alive, provided he remained alert. It lacked range and by American standards it lacked firepower. It was so light that trying to dive in one was like trying to dive a leaf. At the same time, the Spit was so maneuverable and so responsive that if you saw the other guy first, he'd never get you. And if you saw him first, you made one pass, and kept on going.

Compared to World War I, American fighter pilots were going to do little dogfighting this time around. Planes were so fast by 1942 and so well armed that usually one good pass was all it took.[51] And if it didn't? You lived to try again.

The AAF had trained its fighter pilots to fly in three-plane V formations. The British flew in flights of four; each flight consisting of two elements; each element consisting of a leader and his wingman. In most situations the leader would do the shooting while the wingman protected his tail. Hunter's pilots were retrained to fly the RAF way.

On patrol, the RAF flew in line abreast. Entire squadrons (12 aircraft in the RAF, 16 in the AAF) would fly in line abreast, presenting the massed firepower of 96 (in a P-47 squadron, 128) machine guns to anything in front. It took some getting used to, but American pilots in the ETO and the Mediterranean learned how to fly line abreast too.

These tactics were nothing new, of course, to the pilots of the three Eagle Squadrons. They were scheduled to be incorporated into the AAF in late September 1942, as the 4th Fighter Group. The Eagles were bringing a wealth of experience, evidenced by their seventy-three and a half aerial victories. The 71st Squadron, commanded by Chesley Peterson, was one of the top-scoring units in the RAF. Besides the sweet taste of success, they knew the price of defeat, too. Only days before the 4th Group was activated twelve Eagles took off to escort a B-17 mission to Morlaix. Only one pilot returned.

By October Hunter's force had grown to four groups, then three left for North Africa, leaving him with only the 4th. In December the 78th Group arrived, with P-38s, but all its planes and nearly all its pilots moved on to Tunisia, as replacements for other groups. In January 1943 the AAF's first P-47 outfit arrived, the 56th Fighter Group, commanded by Hubert Zemke. He'd already had an interesting war, spending nearly a year in the Soviet Union teaching Red

Air Force pilots how to fly P-40s. The Soviets taught him something in return: he came home an expert chess player.[52]

The P-47 still had serious problems. Zemke was given the task of sorting a lot of them out, while commanding the 56th. The plane was so rugged that it saved many a careless pilot's life when it crashed, but so hard to handle that it crashed a lot. Eighteen pilots in Zemke's group died in accidents before the 56th deployed overseas.

RAF pilots looked over the Thunderbolt, shuddered and politely but emphatically informed Zemke's men that they were about to die. The P-47 was too big, too slow, too unresponsive to live in the same sky as nimble 109s and the awesome 190s.[53] Zemke had to convince his men the experts were wrong, that they could fight in a P-47 and survive.

The 4th Fighter Group was transitioning into the Thunderbolt; twice as big as a Spitfire and nowhere near as lovely. They simply hated it. The 78th was being rebuilt, as a P-47 outfit, and its pilots, too, disliked the plane.

For all the help RAF Fighter Command provided, it was not the ideal role model for Hunter's pilots. It had been created, trained and equipped for the air defense of the British Isles. Once Britain's survival was assured, by the German invasion of the Soviet Union, RAF Fighter Command began launching huge fighter sweeps over the Continent, with a few mediums as bait to get the GAF to rise and fight. These sweeps bled RAF squadrons without even scratching the Germans.

The role of AAF fighters in Britain, as Spaatz and Eaker envisaged it, was to defend U.S. bases and to provide limited escort on shallow penetrations until VIII Bomber Command was big enough to manage deep penetrations on its own. The threat to air bases was real enough. About three times a month in 1942–43 the GAF made night raids, but they usually struck RAF airfields or British cities.

Hunter studied the escort problem by flying on several B-17 missions. In the first few months he had his fighters fly RAF-style escort, which consisted of an umbrella several thousand feet above the heavies. Once the GAF started making nose attacks the bomber crews demanded escort that was only seventy-five feet off the wingtip—and a few hundred feet in front of the nose. Hunter ordered closer formations, but aerial gunners were so jumpy and so poor at aircraft identification they frequently shot up their own escort as it came in to take up position.[54]

The 125-mile combat radius of the Spitfire and the 225-mile combat radius of the P-47D didn't provide a whole lot of escort possibilities on missions to Germany. During raids against such places as Kiel, Vegesack and Wilhemshaven there was escort halfway there and halfway back, but during the crucial three or four hours of flying in between the bombers had no coverage at all. Nor would Hunter fly his P-47s to the limit of their range. He wanted his pilots to have enough fuel to be able to fight their way out of trouble if they were jumped on the way home.

Hunter simply didn't believe escort missions were the best use of his fighters, anyway. He much preferred using sweeps, like the RAF. What he longed for was big, World War I–type air battles, with huge numbers of fighters dogfighting from the trees to the cloud tops. Give him those, and he would make the air safe for Eaker's bombers to fly through. During VIII Fighter Command's first year of operations two thirds of its missions were sweeps; only one third were escort.[55]

The demand for escort wasn't going to disappear, however. In response to urging from Rickenbacker, Portal and others, Wright Field modified twelve B-17s to serve as long range escorts, or "convoy defenders." They carried three more machine guns and twice as much ammunition as the B-17E.

These aircraft, YB-40s, made their combat debut in May 1943 in raids against the sub pens, and flopped comprehensively. The Matériel Command had gone overboard and added more than a ton of armor plate to each plane. This made the YB-40s so heavy and slow that on the return they couldn't keep up with the B-17s which, after dropping their bombs, were traveling light.[56]

Hunter's fighter pilots weren't performing brilliantly either. The 4th Fighter Group went into combat for the first time on March 10, in a sweep over northern France that achieved nothing. On April 15, Don Blakeslee got the first ever P-47 kill, downing an Me-109 during yet another sweep. Blakeslee was an aggressive, skilled pilot, who took a perverse pride in being considered one of the worst shots among the Eagles, yet he had two confirmed aerial victories before joining the AAF.

Zemke's 56th Fighter Group flew its first mission, a sweep, on April 8, and never saw an enemy plane. It was probably as well. The

56th had no experience and not much luck. What it did possess was a lot of potential. Zemke's three squadron commanders all eventually got their own groups. He'd also picked up Francis Gabreski, a Notre Dame dropout and one of the handful of 15th Group pilots who'd risen to challenge the Japanese over Pearl Harbor.

Eager to get into action again as soon as possible, Gabreski had asked for, and gotten, temporary assignment to one of the eight Polish fighter squadrons in the RAF. Gabreski honed basic lifesaving skills with the Poles, but didn't shoot anyone down.[57] After the creation of the 4th Fighter Group he sought to transfer to it. The 4th refused to take him, so he was offered to Zemke, who gladly took Gabreski into the 56th.

It was a unit that could use his knowledge. The fledgling 56th had appallingly bad flight discipline, with many pilots trying to fight the war on their own. Not surprisingly, the first two planes the 56th claimed were Spitfires. It was two months before it got its first enemy kill, by Walter Cook, on June 11.

In mid-June 1943 VIII Fighter Command as a whole didn't have much to brag about. It had downed fifteen German planes, and lost seventeen in action. That was depressing. Worse was the fact that Hunter had completely misread what was needed. The challenge before him was the dull business of range extension, not preparing for huge dogfights that were never going to happen unless he could fly deep into Germany.

VIII Fighter Command needed a revolution in fuel tanks, of which there were three basic kinds: internal tanks, wing tanks, and belly tanks. The Air Corps had flown with belly tanks between the wars, but they were a major safety hazard. There were wing tanks, too, but they reduced maneuverability. In 1938 Arnold had abolished wing tanks on fighters. The commander of 8th Fighter Group, Lieutenant Colonel William E. Kepner, thought this was foolish and had tried to acquire some Navy wing tanks to put on his P-36s. Eaker sent for Kepner, and in Arnold's presence sternly rebuked him and told him to stop.

Hunter was still opposed to wing tanks five years later. The only immediately available tank was a huge and unwieldy two-hundred-gallon ferry tank made out of layers of paper and glue, but it leaked and lacked pressurization, which made it of little use above twenty-two thousand feet, which was where the P-47 performed best.

The British were developing a 108-gallon belly tank that was faired to fit snugly beneath a Hurricane, but neither Eaker nor

Hunter showed much interest in these tanks. In response to pleas from the fighter groups, however, the head of the Eighth's Technical Service Section, Colonel Cass Hough, was going flat out to produce a drop tank. In civilian life Hough was the millionaire president of the Daisy Air Rifle company, whose products gladdened many an adolescence. He was developing droppable, pressurized tanks that would give the P-47 an extra one hundred miles range.

The turning point in the drive for range extension came with the visit of Robert Lovett to England in mid-June. A week after Lovett's return to the Pentagon, Arnold gave Giles six months to solve the long-range escort problem.[58]

Arnold sent for Kepner, currently a brigadier general on the West Coast, and told him to come up with a solution to the fuel tank problem. Kepner was not an engineer, though. He'd served in the 3rd Infantry Division in World War I, as a private. He'd been shot in the ear, shot in the jaw and had a bayonet driven through his left hand in one-on-one combat. He'd won the DSC. Between wars he'd become a record-setting balloonist, before moving on to be a fighter pilot. Kepner had also played a crucial role in getting the Air Corps to put heavy machine guns into pursuit planes.

The challenge now, Arnold told him, is to get more range for our fighters. Kepner couldn't resist saying, "Well, general, I think I'll hang some gas on the outside of those airplanes." Down came the Arnold fist, bang! on the desk. "I don't give a damn how you do it! We're going to Berlin!"[59] Kepner headed for California first, to pressure the plane makers into creating extra tankage.

Shortly after this Arnold sent a cable to Eaker, bitterly criticizing Hunter's handling of VIII Fighter Command.[60] It was a signal that Hunter would soon be replaced, but the life-or-death struggle of the Eighth was already underway. The weather had suddenly broken.

17

POINTBLANK

The growing strength of the German fighter arm cast a shadow over Allied hopes of ultimate victory. When Hitler declared war on the United States, German fighter production was running at 360 planes a month. By June 1943 the German air minister, Erhard Milch, had raised output to 1,000 fighters a month, despite resistance from Goering and the Luftwaffe chief of staff, Hans Jeschonnek.[1] Yet unless the Allies won air superiority, they could not successfully invade France in 1944 and could not mount a strategic bombing campaign.

On June 10, 1943, the Combined Chiefs of Staff issued a directive known as Pointblank. It put German fighter strength at the top of the target list, in a category all its own.[2] This directive, in effect, ordered the Eighth Air Force to destroy the German aviation industry and secure air superiority over the Continent.

No order could have been more welcome to Eaker and Fred Anderson, but in Europe the weather was more of an obstacle than the enemy. When the weather finally broke, in late July, Anderson unleashed a series of attacks known as Blitz Week.

On July 24 the Eighth struck targets in Norway. The 1st Bomb Wing, commanded by Brigadier General Robert Williams, destroyed a nitrates factory. Williams was one of the most colorful figures in the Eighth. Despite having lost an eye in the London blitz, he continued flying B-17s. The 4th Bomb Wing, commanded by Curtis LeMay, attacked U-boat facilities in Norway. The only loss was a 1st Bomb Wing plane that made a forced landing in Sweden.[3]

On July 25 the 1st Bomb Wing attacked Kiel and Hamburg. Harris's Lancasters had ignited Hamburg the previous night. The smoke was so thick next day that American bombardiers couldn't see much. Despite the devastation, German defenses seemed unaffected: nineteen B-17s were shot down. Meanwhile, the 4th Bomb Wing was attacking an FW-190 assembly line at Warnemunde, but without much success.

On July 26 VIII Bomber Command sent more than three hundred planes to attack a variety of targets in northwestern Germany. Only three YB-40s were available to escort all the way to the targets and back. The price paid was twenty-four downed B-17s.

Weather foreclosed operations next day, but on July 28 Anderson put 302 planes into the air. The targets were a fighter components plant in Kassel and an FW-190 plant in Oschersleben. Only 39 planes flew the entire Oschersleben mission, the longest penetration of the war so far; 15 were shot down. Total losses for the day were 22 aircraft, even though the bombers had more escorts than ever.

This was the first mission flown by P-47s with droppable tanks; huge unpressurized two hundred-gallon belly tanks originally designed for ferrying. Thunderbolts from 4th Fighter Group assigned to provide escort withdrawal used belly tanks to catch the GAF by surprise. Instead of turning back as the Germans expected, the 4th flew all the way to the Belgian-German border and tore into enemy fighters that were attacking stragglers. The 4th claimed nine victories.[4]

On July 29 the 4th Bomb Wing returned to Warnemunde to attack the Focke-Wulf assembly line again, while the 1st bombed Kiel's U-boat yards and dropped 770,000 propaganda leaflets.

Blitz Week concluded July 30 with 1st and 4th Bomb wings returning to Kassel. Of the 134 planes that reached the target 12 were shot down. The 4th and 56th fighter groups provided escort almost all the way across Holland. They lost 7 planes, but claimed 25 enemy aircraft.[5]

A week of intensive operations had reduced Anderson's force from a daily availability of 300 + bombers to roughly 175 and done little to attrit the German fighter arm.

The attacks on aircraft plants in Blitz Week only nibbled at the challenge of German fighter strength. Output in July exceeded twelve hundred planes. Something bigger, something dramatic and swift, was called for.

The man who had to think of something bigger was Colonel Richard D'Oyly Hughes, the Eighth's chief target picker. Hughes was a singular figure. Born in Salt Lake City to English parents, he'd left the United States before he could speak, been educated at Wellington and Sandhurst, spent nearly twenty years in the British Army, served with distinction in World War I, but moved back to the United States in 1929 when he married a woman from St. Louis. In 1941, with a new war under way and American participation likely, he applied for a commission in the AAF. Wearing an AAF uniform covered with British Army decorations, he'd worked on AWPD-1, and more or less by chance became a targeting expert.

It occurred to Hughes, as he studied his maps of Germany, that it might be possible to cripple German fighter production with a three-pronged attack from England and the Mediterranean that would swamp the GAF's defenses. Half of Germany's fighters were produced in just two places: Regensburg, in southeastern Germany, and Wiener-Neustadt, south of Vienna. And more than half of ball-bearing production was in Schweinfurt, also in southeastern Germany.[6] B-17 groups in England could reach southeastern Germany; B-24 groups in North Africa could reach Wiener-Neustadt.

Anderson warmly endorsed Hughes's idea, but the first ten days of August brought rain and dense clouds over Germany. The three-pronged, one-day strike idea was dropped. On August 13, five B-24 groups (including three on loan to Ninth Air Force) took off from North Africa, heading for the huge Messerschmitt plant at Wiener-Neustadt, twelve hundred miles away. All five groups were under-strength after their heavy losses over Ploesti, and overhaul facilities for heavies in North Africa were poor going on nonexistent. Some sixty-five B-24s reached the target. The Luftwaffe had few fighters in Austria. The bombing was mediocre, but only one plane was shot down. Another crash-landed in Switzerland.[7]

The attacks on Regensburg and Schweinfurt were still scheduled to go ahead. The plan was for LeMay's 4th Bomb Wing to fly to Regensburg, bomb the Messerschmitt plant, then take a course which would carry it across northern Italy and the Med, to land in North Africa. LeMay's groups had been reequipped with the new B-17F. In the F model extra fuel cells had been added to the internal wing tanks. These increased fuel capacity from eighteen hundred to twenty-six hundred gallons, making it possible, crews joked, to fly to Tokyo and back.

The Germans would no doubt expect the 4th Bomb Wing to

return to England the way it had come. Hughes and Anderson calculated the Luftwaffe would put up strong resistance to the 4th Wing's penetration so deep into German air space. The 4th would have to fight a hard battle all the way to the target. Then the German fighters would land and refuel so they could attack LeMay's bombers on their way back. The clever part of the plan, however, was to have the 1st Wing follow only fifteen minutes behind the 4th Wing, taking the same route to southeastern Germany, before turning away to bomb the ball-bearing plants at Schweinfurt. By the time the Germans had figured out that the 4th Wing wasn't returning and the 1st Wing was heading for Schweinfurt, their fighters would be on the ground, short of fuel and ammunition, giving the 1st Wing an easy ride to the target.

To soften up the opposition in advance, the Eighth unleashed nearly five hundred planes against airfields in France and the Low Countries on August 15. Next day the 1st Bomb Wing struck Le Bourget with 169 B-17s, escorted all the way there and back by P-47s. The 4th Fighter Group returned claiming 18 victories, to the envious dismay of Hub Zemke's pilots, who'd flown the same mission and returned empty-handed.[8]

August 17 dawned mistily over the British Isles, but there was bright sunshine over south central Germany. By coincidence, it was exactly one year since VIII Bomber Command had flown its first mission, when twelve B-17s attacked the marshalling yard outside Rouen.

LeMay had trained his pilots in instrument takeoffs. They didn't like them, but they could do them if necessary, praying hard at the same time not to collide with one another. Collisions during group assemblies over the cloudy, foggy British Isles were commonplace.[9] LeMay's rigorous training might just allow the 4th Bomb Wing to take off into heavy mist and complete cloud cover. Anderson gave the go-ahead, and Archie Old boarded the leading aircraft: the 96th was going to lead this historic mission. At the last moment a jeep pulled up alongside, LeMay got out, and calmly bumped an indignant Colonel Old from the copilot's seat. Old ran to another B-17 and clambered aboard.[10]

The 4th Wing was ninety minutes behind schedule. Had it been delayed any longer it wouldn't have been able to reach North Africa by nightfall. With LeMay in the lead, 139 B-17s crossed the Dutch coast, in a column fifteen miles long.

Escort was provided by the 353rd Fighter Group, flying its first combat mission. The neophyte 353rd was hard-pressed to defend the bombers. Six B-17s went down over Belgium before the fighters turned back at Eupen, on the German border.

The Germans were concentrating on the rear groups of 4th Wing. Squadrons in the rear and in the low position of a combat wing were the most vulnerable to attack. They didn't enjoy the same mutual support as planes higher in the formation, which benefited from the defensive fire of other aircraft. The low position was known as "coffin corner."

The Regensburg-Schweinfurt plan called for the biggest aerial diversion so far attempted. The 3rd Wing's three Marauder groups, plus two RAF B-25 squadrons, were scheduled to raid coastal airfields, escorted by 150 Spitfires. When the 4th Bomb Wing took off, however, Anderson postponed the diversion operation. It would be mounted later, solely for the benefit of the 1st Wing, which was going to need all the help it could get on the way to Schweinfurt.

The 4th Bomb Wing meanwhile was being mauled across southern Germany. Another eight planes went down between Belgium and Regensburg. By the time the 96th Group's lead bombardier, Captain John L. Latham, took over at the initial point, the 4th was down to 122 planes able to bomb the Messerschmitt factory. They would attack from less than twenty thousand feet—a concession to the importance of the target. The result was some spectacularly accurate bombing.

As the 4th left Regensburg, the 1st Bomb Wing was assembling over the North Sea. It had taken off five hours behind schedule, thereby effectively vitiating the basic plan. Some 222 planes crossed the Dutch coast, escorted by RAF Spitfires. A German attack was beaten off. The Spitfires shot down five enemy planes and only one B-17 was lost. After the Spitfires turned back, 78th Fighter Group P-47s arrived, eight minutes late. The 4th Fighter Group was scheduled to provide escort too, but missed the rendezvous.

The Germans assumed the 4th Bomb Wing would be flying back from Regensburg and were massing their fighters as never before, bringing groups down from Denmark and northern Germany. They even threw in night-fighters. In all, three hundred fighters were available to attack the 1st Bomb Wing. At Eupen, on the Belgian-German border, the 78th turned for home. Minutes later the German fighters, knowing exactly how far the escort would stretch, attacked.

They concentrated their attention on the three leading groups. The 1st Bomb Wing's twelve groups flew in four Armstrong and LeMay-style combat wings of three groups each. A three-group combat wing was about all that one man could control directly under fire. And this day, the 101st Combat Wing (the 91st, the 381st, and a composite group of squadrons drawn from various groups) was leading the way to Schweinfurt. The GAF fighters attacked the 101st Combat Wing unmercifully.

Twin-engine fighters fired a few rockets and tried air-to-air bombing, but these attacks were experiments. The hammer used to break up B-17 groups was the nose attack. To John Comer, a flight engineer with a grandstand seat in the top turret of a 381st Group B-17, "At times it looked like the entire Luftwaffe was lined up at twelve o'clock high."[11]

By mid-1943 many German fighter pilots had mastered the nose attack. The B-17Es and Fs that flew on August 17 had been equipped with one thirty-caliber nose gun and two thirty-caliber cheek guns, manned by the navigator and bombardier. And to Lieutenant Edwin Frost, a 381st Group navigator in the nose of a B-17, firing a cheek gun, "It was just pandemonium. It seemed that every gun in the ship was firing at once and the noise was terrific. . . . Most [German fighters] were coming straight through, tearassing right through us. . . . I remember one which seemed to be coming straight at us. Our bombardier accused me of throwing myself down behind him for cover. It was an instinctive reaction. I'd never seen them that close."[12]

By the time the 101st Combat Wing reached the Schweinfurt IP, it had lost 17 planes: nearly one third of its strength. In the 1st Bomb Wing as a whole, 24 B-17s had gone down. All told, 196 planes reached the IP able to bomb the target, but this wasn't the IP for which crews had been briefed. Originally the attack was to have been made from the east, so pilots wouldn't be flying into the rising sun. The five-hour delay had changed that: the attack would now be made from the west, so pilots wouldn't be squinting into a setting sun.

The four ball-bearing plants at Schweinfurt were half-hidden and widely spaced. Finding them from an unexpected approach would be tough on a good day, but as the 101st Combat Wing approached, the Germans turned on artificial fog generators. A gray haze spread over the town.[13] The 101st scattered its bombs over the outskirts of Schweinfurt. The nine groups following dumped their loads everywhere, hitting fields, the town, the factories.

While Schweinfurt was being attacked the GAF's fighters were refueling and rearming. Thirteen groups had been massed to oppose the expected return of the 4th Bomb Wing, but it was the 1st that would get their attention. As the 101st Combat Wing passed north of Frankfurt it was attacked ferociously. Getting out was proving as hard as getting in.

Probably the most prestigious fighter group to take the air for the GAF in this battle was II/JG 26, led by Major "Wutz" Galland, brother of Adolf Galland, the chief of fighters, and credited with fifty-five aerial victories. When the leading planes of 101st Combat Wing approached the Belgian frontier, he led his pilots into a frontal attack. Two B-17s went down. Galland's pilots re-formed, to line up for an attack on the next combat wing to come through.

Hub Zemke's 56th Fighter Group had flown escort on the outward journey for the 1st Bomb Wing, returned to England, taken a three-hour break while its planes were refueled, then set off to provide withdrawal escort. This time Zemke's pilots took a gamble: they held onto their cumbersome ferrying tanks for an extra ten minutes. If they had been jumped by 109s or 190s then, they would have been massacred. The gamble paid off. The 56th Group flew fifteen miles beyond Eupen and arrived to catch eight Me-110 twin-engine fighters deploying to attack an oncoming B-17 group. Zemke led his pilots down, guns blazing.[14]

The Thunderbolt wasn't much of a fighter below twenty-two thousand feet. It had a slow rate of climb and poor acceleration. Its huge weight and bulk made it sluggish and it turned ponderously. Above twenty-two thousand feet, with the turbocharger whirring at high rpms, it got better and better the higher it flew. From thirty thousand feet up the ugly duckling turned into a deadly swan. In thin air, it became maneuverable, responsive and faster than any German fighter. Its seven tons enabled it to outdive and outroll 109s and 190s. Pulling out of a dive, it could outzoom anything the Germans possessed.

Zemke had trained his pilots to stay high, dive quickly on enemy aircraft, and use the zoom to recover altitude. German pilots had grown used to heading for the deck when they wanted to break off an attack or get out of trouble. They were about to make a terrible discovery: nothing could outrun a diving Thunderbolt.

As two of Zemke's squadrons piled into the Me-110s, the third

jumped Galland's II/JG 26. B-17 crews watched, thrilled and enraptured, as the 56th shot down eleven German fighters in the space
of a few minutes.[15] Among those who fell was Galland, killed, in all
probability by Walker "Bud" Mahurin, who would finish the war
with twenty-one victories. The 1st Bomb Wing lost only one plane
as it withdrew over Belgium. The price to 56th Fighter Group was
three dead pilots.

As the sun went down, LeMay's 4th Wing was crossing the coast
of North Africa. Many of his planes were virtually out of fuel.
Fifteen twin-engine fighters had pursued the 4th Wing across southern Germany and shot down three B-17s. Two planes crash-landed
in Switzerland. There was little GAF opposition on the other side
of the Alps.

VIII Bomber Command had 60 B-17s shot down. In return,
aerial gunners claimed to have downed no fewer than 288 German
fighters, but German losses actually amounted to 48 planes: 36 shot
down (mainly by fighters) and 12 written off.[16]

LeMay had been assured that when he reached North Africa
facilities would be available to repair battle damage and get his
planes into the air again. What he found was poorly stocked fuel
and bomb dumps. His crews hand pumped gas into their undam-
aged planes and got ready for a return mission.[17] Eaker had rejected
Hughes's suggestion of a bombing mission on the return, until
Arnold told Eaker to do it. Hughes picked an airfield outside Bordeaux for LeMay to bomb. Abandoning nearly sixty damaged
bombers in North Africa, 4th Bomb Wing returned to England by
way of Bordeaux, losing three more planes to German fighters.

In planes lost, written off, or abandoned the Schweinfurt-
Regensburg mission had cost VIII Bomber Command 147 B-17s:
40 percent of the force dispatched.[18] Arnold grieved, but the operation was presented to the public as a great success.[19]

No doubt Regensburg was hit hard. In terms of lost production,
this attack cost the Luftwaffe around one thousand Me-109s, or
three weeks of total fighter production. The attack on Schweinfurt
achieved no substantial results. Three of the five factories were
severely damaged, but comparatively few of the machine tools that
produced ball bearings were destroyed. The bombs provided by the
Ordnance Corps simply weren't big enough or powerful enough.

What loss in production occurred was made good by getting the
German Army to dip into its huge reserve stock of ball bearings and
by purchasing more from Sweden. Arnold tried to bribe the Swedes

into not selling ball bearings to Hitler by offering the Swedish Air Force P-51s and C-47s.[20] The production loss didn't amount to anything much, anyway: finished German ball bearing output may even have been higher in September 1943 than in August.[21]

Originally, the 1st Bomb Wing was to have dropped incendiaries on Schweinfurt, to light the way for an RAF night attack. Harris, however, had been ordered to strike the German V-1 production and testing site at Peenemünde. The best night for this attack happened to fall on August 17. The RAF destroyed Peenemünde, but lost forty Lancasters.[22]

The Schweinfurt-Regensburg operation initially scared Hitler and his armaments minister, Albert Speer. For Hans Jeschonnek, the young Luftwaffe chief of staff, it was the last straw. He couldn't handle Goering, and Milch's dire prophecies of what would happen if the day fighter arm wasn't built up to a level where it could stop the American bombers were coming true. Overwrought and in despair, on August 18 Jeschonnek blew his brains out.[23]

Kepner had spent much of July tormenting the plane makers. He visited Lockheed, and demanded the company put sixty gallons in the wings of the P-38. Lockheed's engineers told him it was impossible: the plane would become too unstable to fly. Kepner visited North American, and told the company to put fuel into the wings of the P-51. North American's engineers told him it couldn't be done. The phone lines sizzled between California and Wright Field. Did the Matériel Command know there was a crazy fighter pilot running wild and trying to ruin two wonderful airplanes? The Matériel Command threatened to prefer charges against Kepner for tampering with aircraft specifications.[24]

Giles, however, backed Kepner's ideas. When they worked out, he claimed them for himself. Rank, as Army officers of the time used to say, has its privileges. All talk of preferring charges was dropped. With tanks going into the wings of P-38s and P-51s Kepner headed for England in mid-July to replace Hunter. He spent more than a month familiarizing himself with VIII Fighter Command before taking over. The unit that impressed him most was the 56th Fighter Group.[25] Hunter returned to the United States to take command of the First Air Force.

Kepner moved into Hunter's vacated office. There was a sign on the wall declaring, "The primary job of VIII Fighter Command is to bring the bombers back alive." Arnold had visited Kepner's pilots and told them emphatically, "The bombers are going to bomb Berlin, and by God, you are going to protect them all the way. Then bring them back."[26] Kepner left the sign where it was, although he had doubts. He considered a fighter an offensive weapon, at its best when going after enemy aircraft and destroying them. Using fighters defensively was not his policy but Eaker's.

The VIII Fighter Command was growing rapidly. Two more P-47 groups (352nd, 355th) became operational in mid-September, giving Kepner a total of six, with two more about to arrive. The increasing number of fighters in the air posed new challenges. In the August 16 attack on Le Bourget, Hunter had chosen Blakeslee to fly around on the perimeter of the air battle and try to choreograph the operations of the P-47s as they mixed it up with 109s and 190s. Not even Blakeslee, though, could control such a melee.

On a typical 56th Group mission, Zemke's pilots would fly into the Continent at thirty-one thousand feet; three squadrons of P-47s flying in line abreast; forty-eight Thunderbolts flying one hundred yards apart. The bombers would be five to ten thousand feet below.[27]

This kind of umbrella escort had been learned from the RAF, and the P-47 could do it better than any plane had ever done. The tremendous diving ability of the Thunderbolt let it fly high above the bombers and fall like a brick on anything that tried to attack them from the side or below.

That was how, for example, Francis Gabreski got his first kill. By August 1943 Gabreski, recently promoted to command the 60th squadron in 56th Fighter Group, was beginning to wonder if he'd ever shoot down an enemy plane. On August 24 he was on an escort mission to cover the withdrawal of B-17s which had bombed an airfield at Evreux. "My ears were filled with the shrill wail that let us know the Germans were trying to jam our radios. It was very annoying, but we were still able to hear each other. . . . After a few minutes on station I spotted seven FW-190s at ten thousand feet below us trying to get into position for a head-on attack at the bombers. This was it! I was in perfect position for the bounce. I glanced quickly at my wingman, and then pushed over into a dive. My speed built up rapidly as the big P-47 dropped out of the sky. . . .

"I opened fire on the leader of a flight of four and could see immediately that I was hitting him. Pieces started flying off his fuselage and wing, and a puff of smoke burst from his fuselage. . . .

"I broke off to avoid running into the 190. He dropped a wing and then nosed over and dived into the ground. I saw no parachute, so I assume the pilot was killed, probably by my gunfire. I was still moving at well over four hundred miles per hour, so I used my speed to [zoom] back up toward the bombers. . . ."[28] The remaining German fighters scattered, pursued by other pilots in Gabreski's squadron.

On occasions like this the umbrella escort system worked, but it was frustrating. It gave the Germans too much of the initiative and wasted the fighter's offensive potential. With experience and a steadily rising tally of confirmed kills Zemke's pilots were increasingly eager to move away from the bombers and start hunting down Germans. As summer drew to a close the 56th was interpreting "escort" broadly, with two squadrons remaining near the bombers, while the third ranged far ahead at high altitude looking for trouble.[29]

The problem of range remained. The British were working on a 108-gallon tank that was so promising Eaker decided to tell Wright Field to drop its own belly tank project. Back in March the British Ministry of Aircraft Production had agreed to produce metal tanks for the Eighth, but Eaker had given them a low priority and declined to place a large order, so development lagged. After visiting Britain, Arnold pushed hard to speed it up.[30]

By chance, it was during that visit that the 56th Fighter Group started getting the benefit of Cass Hough's labors. At the end of August the Technical Services Section delivered pressurized, metal 75-gallon belly tanks (which actually held about 85 gallons), extending the combat radius of the P-47 to 340 miles. In September VIII Fighter Command lost only fourteen planes, but claimed forty-one enemy aircraft, as Kepner's pilots flew steadily deeper into Germany.

On September 6, the day before Arnold's visit to the Eighth ended, Anderson mounted a major mission against a roller-bearing factory in Stuttgart. While 69 B-24s flew a diversionary mission, 338 B-17s headed for the primary target. Stuttgart was completely clouded over. Many planes overflew the city or crisscrossed it, hoping for a break in the clouds. The net result of wandering around was to loosen up formations, which offered rich pickings to enemy fighters. Thirty-three planes were shot down; another twelve ditched in the

Channel, out of fuel.[31] Any hopes Eaker entertained of impressing Arnold that day ended in gloom and ashes.

After Schweinfurt-Regensburg, the whole future of daylight bombing was open to doubt again. Following the Stuttgart fiasco Anderson had the 422nd Bomb Squadron of 305th Bomb Group fly eight missions with RAF Bomber Command, learning the techniques of night bombing. Anderson himself went on two night bombing raids with the RAF.[32] It was still possible that the Eighth would take refuge in the night.

Apart from the Stuttgart fiasco and participation in an unconvincing deception operation to make the Germans think an invasion of France was imminent, September was a fairly quiet month for Anderson's bomber crews. VIII Bomber Command was building up its strength for another sustained offensive.* On September 27 it mounted an experimental mission to Emden.

Thunderbolts equipped with seventy-five-gallon belly tanks were able for the first time to fly all the way to and from a mission into Germany. Second, the bombers were led to the target by several B-17s equipped with radar. Eaker had created the 482nd Group (Pathfinder) to overcome bad weather. Its two B-17 and one B-24 squadrons were equipped with British H2S radar.†

One of these squadrons guided the mission to Emden. The H2S radar gave a reasonably good picture of terrain that featured a coastline, a lake, or a large river. RAF Bomber Command blithely ignored warnings that H2S emissions would eventually provide German fighters with a beacon to home in on.[33] But it was still fairly new and only seven B-17s, from a force of nearly 250, were lost on this mission. On October 2, Anderson launched a return visit to Emden. This proved to be a milk run: two bombers were lost out of 349 dispatched. The escort shot down five German fighters; one of these victories made Zemke an ace.

Two days later nearly three hundred B-17s bombed industrial targets in Frankfurt. For once, Luftwaffe defenses were poorly

---

*Having reached twenty-one groups, VIII Bomber Command was reorganized once more: 1st Bomb Wing became 1st Bomb Division; 2nd Bomb Wing, consisting of B-24s, became 2nd Air Division; LeMay's 4th Bomb Wing became 3rd Air Division.
†H2S stood for Home Sweet Home. A later, U.S. version was H2X, known to aircrews as "Mickey," for Mickey Mouse.

directed, but twelve B-17s flying to Frankfurt and four B-24s on a diversion flight failed to return. The German performance infuriated Goering. After surveying the abundance of airfields that American bombers had to fly over to reach cities in central Germany, he ordered that henceforth every fighter pilot would be expected to fly three sorties during the five hours B-17s were over Germany during deep penetrations.[34]

The Frankfurt mission featured the introduction into combat of the B-17G. The YB-40 had been a disappointment, but some good came from it. Bendix had developed a nose turret for the YB-40 that mounted two fifty-calibers. Installed under the nose of a B-17 as a "chin" turret it eventually proved a deterrent to head-on attacks, but only a few groups would get B-17Gs before the end of 1943.

The target on October 8 was a familiar one: the submarine yards at Bremen and Vegesack. Familiar, but awesome. Bremen was defended now by 250 AAA guns, and more than 100 fighters could be expected to oppose any attack. Some 399 bombers flew this mission, escorted most of the way in and out by 274 Thunderbolts. Thirty bombers went down.[35]

All the same, the Luftwaffe's losses of experienced pilots was starting to show. Flight engineer John Comer of the 381st Bomb Group watched in disbelief as four FW-190s dove on the tail of his B-17 so close together they looked like one airplane. "The greenest German pilot should have known better, but they kept on coming. . . . Almost all top turrets, some balls and all tails poured a heavy barrage at those four unfortunate fighters. The enormous mass of fifty-caliber slugs was so devastating that there were four puffs of black smoke and a sky filled with debris. . . ."[36]

On the 9th, 1st and 3rd Air Divisions attacked aircraft factories at Anklam and Marienbad, while the 2nd Air Division's B-24s struck shipyards on Germany's Baltic coast. The Marienbad bombing was done from thirteen thousand feet and was stunningly accurate. Hitler ordered construction of bombproof fighter factories after this raid. The Eighth lost twenty-eight Fortresses shot down; eight more were beyond repair.

In one week Anderson had lost more than one hundred heavy bombers, shot down, crashed or written off. His determination to hit the Germans hard acquired a new focus. The target for Sunday, October 10, would be Munster, a town of no evident military importance. The aiming point would be the cathedral steps at noon, just as the congregation was leaving after the eleven o'clock Mass.[37]

When the target was briefed, some men cheered. Grieving for dead friends, they craved revenge. Second thoughts, however, brought a change in the time of the attack, to three that afternoon. The cathedral steps remained the aiming point.

The 2nd Air Division would fly a diversion mission, while the 1st and 3rd assembled sixteen groups to attack Munster. Leading the way would be the defiantly numbered 13th Combat Wing, with the 95th Group in the lead, the 100th Group in low position, and the 390th in high position. To make combat wings more manageable, the number of planes a group sent into action had been reduced to 18, giving a combat wing at full strength 54 aircraft.* In all, 260 bombers set off for Munster 300 miles away.

The 13th Wing expected escort nearly all the way there, but one group assigned to provide penetration escort, the 355th, was fogged in and never took off. The 4th Fighter Group missed the rendezvous and only caught up with the bombers as they approached Munster. By then, the fighters were low on fuel and had to turn back. The 13th Wing was being savaged.

The Germans started with the Bloody Hundredth, in the low position, and virtually wiped it out before it reached Munster. Then they concentrated on the 390th over the target. Finally, they swarmed around the 95th as it battled its way out. This would soon become a commonplace tactic—trying to destroy one group at a time.

There was a legend, though, that the 100th was the object of a German vendetta; that one of its planes had once taken a hit that lowered its undercarriage, which was the recognized signal for an aircraft trying to surrender. Several GAF fighters that closed in to escort it to a German airfield were shot down by the plane's gunners, who were unaware the undercarriage was showing. An alternative, more likely, explanation is that the 100th Bomb Group deployed to England filled with instructor pilots. They refused to believe anyone could teach them anything. Long on individualism, short on firm leadership, they flew ragged formations, and when they drew the low spot they paid the price.[38]

---

*A group comprised three or four squadrons and was a permanent organization. A wing, on the other hand, was merely a headquarters that controlled the activities of two or more groups. An air division was a headquarter that controlled two or more wings.

The Luftwaffe's rockets were finally beginning to be effective. Scores were fired at B-17s flying toward Munster, bringing several Forts down. During the withdrawal thirty-five Me-110s formed up behind the 390th Bomb Group, just out of range of tail-gun fire, and let loose a barrage of as many as seventy rockets. These projectiles were twenty-one centimeters (about eight inches) inches in diameter, seven feet long, and weighed five hundred pounds. Two B-17s took direct hits; a third fell out of the sky after colliding with the debris.

The main weapon of the German Air Force, however, remained twenty-millimeter cannon fire. Its effects could be just as awesome. Lieutenant Paul Perceful, a copilot with the 95th Bomb Group, saw a B-17 "simply cut in two by the concentrated cannon fire of a German fighter. . . . It appeared to happen in slow motion. The Fortress was struck and slowly came apart at the radio room. From the front half of the fuselage, wings, still functioning engines, and the cockpit, seemed to slowly rise upwards, completely separate from the rear fuselage and tail unit. Then both halves twisted and tumbled down and away."[39]

Zemke had received the first consignment of British 108-gallon belly tanks a week before this mission. His P-47s now had a combat radius of 375 miles. Assigned to provide escort withdrawal, the 56th Group's pilots appeared over the target to bring their charges home. It was the last thing the Germans had expected. Zemke's pilots cashed in, shooting down ten German fighters, without loss.[40] Attacking Munster was nonetheless expensive. Thirty Fortresses went down, and half a dozen more were written off.

This mission proved merely a warm-up, however, for something worse: a return to Schweinfurt, on October 14. When the mission was a briefed to the officers there was a storm of boos and groans that flight engineers and gunners waiting outside listened to with dismay.

Probably the only man who was glad to hear the news was Colonel Archie Old. The plane he'd boarded on August 17 had aborted. Since then he'd moved up to command the 45th Bomb Wing. He wasn't going to miss out on the return to Schweinfurt. He would fly in the copilot's seat of the same 96th Group aircraft that LeMay had bumped him from on August 17.

Sixty B-24s of the 2nd Air Division would fly a diversion toward northwestern Germany. Some 291 B-17s crossed the Dutch coast, heading for Schweinfurt. The 96th would lead the 3rd Air Division to the target, as it had done two months before.

Thirty minutes ahead of the 3rd was the 1st Air Division. LeMay's old command, the 305th Group, was eight minutes late for the assembly. It had to move into the only available slot, in the low position of the 4th Combat Wing of 1st Air Division. It was to suffer for its tardiness.

The 353rd Group was flying penetration escort for the 1st Air Division. GAF fighters bounced the 353rd over Belgium and stripped most of it away from the bombers, which then became prey for more than one hundred twin-engine, rocket-armed fighters and a squadron of Stuka dive-bombers. They concentrated against the 305th. The Stukas attempted air-to-air bombing, unsuccessfully. The real threat came from the rockets.

From a distance of one hundred yards or more the twin-engine fighters launched them into the tightly organized combat boxes, scoring a few direct hits and making bomber pilots duck and weave to avoid them. This loosened up the formations, creating opportunities for single-engine fighters to bore in at high speed with cannon fire.

A well-organized 109 or 190 squadron would hit a bomber with three or four planes at a time, striking from various angles, thus dividing the Fortress's defensive fire. And one of these thrusts was likely to be right on the nose, chin turrets notwithstanding.

While the 305th took a pasting—it lost twelve planes on the way to Schweinfurt—the 91st Group, leading the 1st Air Division, got off relatively lightly. It flew over the IP right on the money. And this time the fog generators hadn't been switched on. The lead bombardier, Lieutenant Samuel Slayton, put his group's bombs on target. The 1st Air Division dumped most of its bombs on, into and around the ball-bearing factories.

The 3rd Air Division's penetration escort was provided by the 56th Fighter Group. It stayed with the bombers as far as Aachen and shot down three GAF fighters before having to turn back.

The 3rd Air Division lost several bombers before it reached Schweinfurt, and when it got there smoke and dust covered the town. Worse, Old's plane took a flak hit in the nose as it approached the aiming point. The lead bombardier was wounded. He missed the target. So did the rest of the group. In fact, most of the

3rd Air Division seems to have bombed the smoke, unable to see anything else.

The 13th Combat Wing's three groups—390th in the lead, 95th in high position, 100th in low—brought up the rear. As they reached the IP, the lead aircraft of the 95th took a flak hit and fell through the 100th. Lieutenant Robert L. Hughes, piloting *Nine Yanks and a Little Jerk,* put his plane in a dive to avoid the falling bomber. As he leveled out, his bombardier called out "Skipper, target dead ahead!"

Hughes and his crew found themselves flying completely alone. Having broken formation, Hughes felt he hadn't the right to commit his crew to what might be a suicidal attack. "This will have to be 100 percent volunteer," he told his copilot. The crew was asked to vote, starting with the lowest-ranking man. Everybody wanted to attack.

"We had the element of surprise on our side," said Hughes later, "and we could maintain the appearance of a crippled aircraft by not opening our doors until just before 'Bombs away!' We also doubted the flak guns would fire upon the one ship, but would allow us to leave the area and become fighter bait. It was our best guess that they did not want to draw attention to the steam-plant and its allied ball-bearing shops by firing on one ship. If we couldn't find it, they weren't going to disclose it.

"Dick Elliott opened the doors just long enough to release the bombs. . . . He set the selector switch to Salvo. . . . All fell in the MPI.* The roar on the intercom was PICKLE BARREL!"[41]

As the 3rd Air Division came off the target, refueled and rearmed GAF fighters that had mauled the 1st Air Division on the way in were swarming up like furious hornets to pursue the 3rd on the way out. The 96th, which had put up thirty-six planes for this mission (some groups now had more than fifty planes; the 96th flew as groups 96A and 96B to Schweinfurt) took the brunt of the new onslaught. Worse, fog over England had nailed the escort withdrawal groups to the ground. The 3rd Air Division had to sit and take it. Most of its gunners were by now out of, or nearly out of, ammunition. The B-17 carried only seven thousand rounds, enough

---

*Mean Point of Impact: the point from which all bombs dropped in a raid were measured for accuracy.

for about seven minutes of shooting; not exactly riches on a deep penetration mission.

As for Lieutenant Hughes, who'd done the most accurate bombing all day, he returned safely. LeMay ordered him to attend the critique; something that few pilots experienced. Hughes told his story, and LeMay confirmed it, with strike photos. "That's right gentlemen—ten bombs MPI. The lieutenant should have a commendation."

The losses for the second Schweinfurt attack were worse than those the first time around: sixty planes shot down, another ditched in the Channel, six wiped out in crash landings, and seven more written off.[42] In two weeks VIII Bomber Command had lost or written off more than two hundred heavy bombers. Nor was there anything to show for it.

Hitler and Speer were alarmed by the second attack on Schweinfurt. The damage done to the ball-bearing factories and their machine tools was more severe this time, but it soon became evident that German forces weren't going to be hurt by it. The Luftwaffe turned out to have its own hidden stocks, which covered much of the loss in production. "Not a tank, plane, or other piece of weaponry failed to be produced because of a lack of ball bearings," said Speer.[43] German weapons output continued to grow strongly for the next eleven months.

At Anderson's headquarters, the mood was grim. No one believed that VIII BC could continue losing more than one hundred heavies a week. At this moment, the Germans were winning the strategic air war. The second attack on Schweinfurt had finally crushed the idea of the big, self-defending bomber formation.

The real bomber success story in the second half of 1943 was being written by the B-26 groups. The Marauder crews had trained for low-level attacks, mainly against enemy airfields. Their engines had been designed for maximum performance below six thousand feet. The Germans had learned from American counterair operations in Tunisia and Sicily how effective the B-26 could be flying at high speed and low level. They covered European airfields within Marauder range with forty-millimeter automatic light flak guns, and after the Ijmuidin disaster all B-26s in the ETO were grounded.

Arnold sent two troubleshooting colonels, Samuel E. Anderson and Clarence Irvine, to tackle the problem. Anderson figured out that light flak wasn't effective above seventy-five hundred feet, and medium flak wasn't quick enough to track fast aircraft flying below thirteen thousand feet. Irvine made field modifications to the engines and Norden sights were installed.[44]

The four B-26 groups flying from England in the summer of 1943 (322nd, 323rd, 386th, 387th) were retrained to bomb in eighteen-ship formations from ten to twelve thousand feet. Escorted by RAF Spitfires, these groups repeatedly attacked German airfields from northern Holland to the Brittany peninsula. They also struck marshalling yards, chemical plants, power stations and communications centers, but the emphasis was on counterair.

In mid-October the Marauder groups were transferred from the Eighth to the Ninth Air Force. They had flown four thousand sorties and posted the lowest loss rate of any AAF bombardment groups of the war. The 3rd Bomb Wing lost just one B-26 per 335 sorties flown. They had also achieved the most accurate bombing in the ETO.[45]

From the time he'd activated VIII Bomber Command, Eaker had been more cautious than Arnold about how the Eighth's heavy bombers should be used. He intended to build up the scale of operations gradually. Arnold was always in favor of putting every plane you could into action every day the weather allowed.[46] Arnold didn't think much of Eaker's staff and criticized them bitterly to Frank Andrews, the ETO commander, shortly before Andrews's death.[47]

In May 1943 Andrews was flying back to the United States aboard a B-24. The plane crashed into a mountain on Iceland. It was widely assumed among those who knew him that Andrews, who was in the copilot's seat, was flying the plane.[48] No one knows for sure. He was succeeded as ETO commander by Lieutenant General Jacob Devers.

Arnold regularly sent scathing messages to High Wycombe, criticizing the number of aborts in the Eighth or the level of maintenance; he couldn't understand why Eaker didn't demand more airfields; he wanted to know why major missions weren't flown more often; and so on. Eaker had an emphatic response to Arnold's nagging letters. He threw them in the waste basket, which he called "the nut file."[49]

During his late-summer visit Arnold had his personal pilot and a master sergeant conduct a two-man roving investigation of the Eighth. They reported back that Eaker and his staff were remote figures who almost never visited the groups to find out what the problems were and offer encouragement or advice.[50]

If this was bad, worse was to come. Twelve days after second attack on Schweinfurt, Kuter produced a report on the Eighth's operations since April. He asserted that the Eighth Air Force had failed to hit Pointblank primary targets with its full weight. Most of the Eighth's efforts had been expended against other, easier and less important targets.[51]

As group commanders in the Eighth, like Medal of Honor winner Leon Johnson of 44th Bomb Group recognized, Eaker's strategy was to fly a lot of sorties toward the end of each month against milk-run targets, where losses were almost sure to be low. In the monthly summary of operations that made the totals for sorties flown, tonnage dropped and loss rates look reasonable, maybe even excellent, but it was a gimmick to try to keep Arnold off Eaker's back, and the GAF was getting a break it didn't deserve.[52]

Even allowing for Eaker's attempts to manipulate the statistical summaries, the Eighth was clearly hurting. From July to November the loss rate was 3.8 percent per mission. That meant that out of every one hundred aircrew in July, by December sixty-four would be dead, seriously wounded, or prisoners of war.[53]

A defeat like the second Schweinfurt attack brought an inevitable pause in operations. Everyone now recognized that the air superiority challenge had to be overcome if strategic bombing was to have any chance of success, and that long-range escort was the key. Meanwhile, Arnold ordered all the P-38 and P-51 groups deploying overseas to be sent to Britain.[54]

It would be spring 1944 before this decision could be expected to have much effect. Winter weather was closing in. Securing air superiority before the invasion of France, scheduled for May 1, was going to go right down to the wire. In the meantime, the bombers still had to fly.

Eaker sent them against comparatively easy targets, such as Paris, Wilhelmshaven and Norway. There were no deep penetration missions for three months after second Schweinfurt, even though there was escort up to 450 miles available in the form of the newly operational 55th Fighter Group, flying P-38s. Another P-38 group, the 20th, would become operational in December.

The GAF was rarely seen, and when it did appear the P-38 had trouble handling the highly maneuverable Me-109G or the heavily armed (and armored) FW-190A/6, which had been developed to shoot down B-17s. The Lightning's engines and turbocharger performed badly in the intense cold and high humidity of winter in northwest Europe.

The biggest hazard to VIII Bomber Command's operations now wasn't the GAF, but the weather. Throughout November 1943 thick clouds covered Western Europe nearly every day. Anderson's command, grown to twenty-two groups, could put more than five hundred heavy bombers in the air, but they had to try bombing with the aid of radar. Not only was this kind of bombing depressingly inaccurate, but the weather was so bad on some missions half the force aborted.[55]

Arnold's impatience with Eaker was reaching a furious pitch. When he traveled to Cairo for the Combined Chiefs conference the first week in December he was in a wrathful mood. The CCS agreed to Eaker's relief.[56]

Arnold proposed to create a new headquarters, the U.S. Strategic Air Forces in Europe (USSTAFE), under Spaatz. This arrangement would ensure that control of the heavy bombers in the Eighth and the Fifteenth remained in American hands. Besides that, however, it might augment the status of Tooey Spaatz and of the AAF.[57]

Eaker would go to Italy, to command a new headquarters, Mediterranean Allied Air Forces (MAAF). He would take the place of Tedder as overall air commander in that theater.

Being fired was, as Eaker wrote to his former mentor General Fechet, "a severe shock which is heartbreaking."[58] At the time and later it was stressed that Eaker hadn't been demoted. All the same, he didn't get a fourth star, which would have given him rank equal to Tedder's. He remained a three-star commander until his retirement in 1947.

The new commander of Eighth Air Force would be Jimmy Doolittle. Two days after Christmas, Arnold sent a message to Doolittle and Nathan Twining, the commander of the newly activated Fifteenth Air Force. Arnold's message concluded, "This is a *MUST* . . . *Destroy the Enemy Air Force wherever you find them, in the air, on the ground, and in the factories.*"[59]

Several days later, Doolittle visited Kepner's VIII Fighter Command headquarters. As he entered Kepner's office, he noticed the sign on the wall. Doolittle pointed at it. "Take that thing down."[60]

18

JÄGERSCHRECK

During the Cairo Conference in December 1943, Eisenhower was chosen to be Supreme Commander for the invasion of France.[1] There was already a large transfer of leadership, troops and assault shipping in progress from the Mediterranean to England. Major General Lewis Brereton moved his Ninth Air Force headquarters from Cairo to Sunninghill, one of England's most beautiful stately homes. The Ninth's aircraft were absorbed by the Twelfth.[2]

The Ninth would become a tactical air force, supporting Omar Bradley's First Army in the invasion of France. The nucleus around which it was formed was the former 3rd Bomb Wing's four Marauder groups, under the command of Brigadier General Samuel Anderson. These became IX Bomber Command, which was destined to grow into a force of eleven hundred light and medium bombers. There would also be a IX Fighter Command, under Pete Quesada, another arrival from the Mediterranean.

The British were doing something similar, creating the RAF's Second Tactical Air Force, commanded by Arthur Coningham, to support Montgomery's troops. Over Brereton and Coningham would be Air Marshal Sir Trafford Leigh-Mallory, commanding the Allied Expeditionary Air Forces.

Leigh-Mallory was pompous, arrogant, and open to doubt. He'd been totally wrongheaded in the Battle of Britain and barely loyal to the brilliant head of RAF Fighter Command, Hugh Dowding. Leigh-Mallory had insisted on assembling huge fighter forces in the air before attacking the German intruders. The Luftwaffe came, bombed and went home before his "big wing" had assembled. As commander of RAF 11 Group, Leigh-Mallory had run the calamitously expensive fighter sweeps over France in 1941–42.

He and Dowding's successor at Fighter Command, the outspokenly anti-American Sir Sholto Douglas, were nonetheless close friends. Besides, although the British would not countenance an Allied strategic air force, because the Americans were sure to demand it be put under Spaatz, the Air Ministry was all in favor of creating a tactical air force headquarters and putting it under an RAF officer. Leigh-Mallory's deputy would be Vandenberg.[3]

As various commanders arrived from the Med, Eaker was packing for Italy. On January 5, 1944, VIII Bomber Command flew its last missions under Eaker, striking Kiel once more and various airfields in France; twenty-five bombers were shot down.

The next day, Spaatz's U.S. Strategic Air Forces was activated, in London. Frederick Anderson became deputy commanding general for operations. Doolittle assumed command of the Eighth and had tactical control of the bombers. Kepner, however, continued at VIII Fighter Command.

Doolittle's first mission was to dispatch 420 heavies to Ludwigshaven, on the German-Swiss border, on January 7. The target was the I. G. Farben petrochemicals complex. Only twelve planes were shot down.

Bomber crews nevertheless protested fiercely against Doolittle's decision to free the fighters from close escort. Losses were already so high that only one B-17 crew member in four could expect to survive twenty-five missions. Overtly freeing the escort came as a shock. Under Eaker they had enjoyed close escort, which forced the fighters to weave constantly, burning up fuel, reducing their combat radius and putting them at a tactical disadvantage if attacked.

The new system of escort in relays provided areas for the bombers to fly through. RAF Spitfires were responsible for areas over the Channel and the North Sea, to a distance of about 100 miles. Thunderbolts then took over, providing area cover for the next 150 to 200 miles. Then P-38s took responsibility for another 100 to 150 miles.[4]

This phased escort system would provide fighter cover to about 450 miles. With the arrival of the first Mustang P-51Bs in England in the late fall of 1943 and the rapid development of 75-gallon wing tanks, it would soon be possible to stretch escort cover to 600 miles; more than enough to reach Berlin.[5]

The first Mustang group in the ETO was the 354th, assigned to the Ninth Air Force, which planned to use it for strafing. Neither Eaker nor Hunter had shown much interest in the P-51. Kepner, however, knew as well as any man alive what potential the P-51 had for long range escort. In mid-January 1944 he argued vehemently to get the P-51 groups transferred to VIII Fighter Command. In the end, Kepner got Spaatz to assign most P-51 groups to him and the 354th, although still assigned to the Ninth, was placed under Kepner's control.[6]

On January 11 Doolittle dispatched his three air divisions to attack aircraft plants in central Germany. German radar monitored the assembly over the North Sea and from the track of the bomber stream air defense controllers decided the Eighth was probably heading for Berlin. The GAF put up five hundred fighters.

The weather deteriorated rapidly almost as soon as the 1st Air Division entered German air space. The 2nd and 3rd Air Divisions were recalled, but one wing of the 3rd pressed on. Meanwhile, nearly two hundred B-17s of the 1st Air Division were closing on Oschersleben, which had a large Focke Wulf assembly line, and the Junkers plant at nearby Halberstadt.[7]

When most of the bombers were recalled, much of the escort was recalled, too. The 303rd Group, leading the 1st Air Division, took a beating: ten of its planes went down before the group reached the target. The 354th Group rendezvoused as planned, but outnumbered four to one, the P-51s were nearly overwhelmed trying to defend the bombers attacking Oschersleben and Halberstadt.

After shooting down an Me-110, Mustang pilot James Howard, a former Flying Tiger, got separated from his squadron. He flew along with the 351st Bomb Group, in the vulnerable low position. More than thirty enemy aircraft formed up to hit the 351st. Howard plunged into them. For half an hour he broke up numerous attempts by the Germans to deploy into attacking formations. He shot down three enemy planes and, even after running out of ammunition, made diving passes to distract German pilots trying to attack the B-17s. Howard would receive the Medal of Honor.[8] And for the Luftwaffe, the presence of American fighters so deep into Germany came as a shock.

All the same, January 11 proved a costly day for the bombers. Sixty were shot down, a dozen more were written off. It was like Schweinfurt all over again, but by this time there were so many replacement aircraft and crews flowing into Britain that the Eighth took it in stride.

Doolittle intended to hammer Pointblank targets unrelentingly. At this moment, however, a new threat arose, one that couldn't be ignored. Hitler's scientists and engineers were sprinting down the road that Kettering had shown Arnold back in 1941. The Germans were on the verge of producing unguided missiles that threatened to lay waste England's cities.

Despite the RAF's massive attack on the missile research site at Peenemunde on August 17, 1943, by winter scores of launch sites for the V-1 were nearing construction on the Channel coast of France and Belgium. An offensive, known as Crossbow, was organized to bomb V-weapon facilities.

As the new Ninth took shape it found itself devoted, along with Coningham's Second TAF, to attacking Crossbow sites. The Eighth, too, was brought into the struggle. On Christmas Eve 1943 it made its biggest attack under Eaker's leadership when it sent seven hundred bombers and six hundred fighters to attack V-1 ramps in the Pas de Calais.[9]

On January 13 the Ninth sent 200 B-26s and A-20s to attack these sites. Next day, the Eighth hit them with the weight of 527 heavies. Harris's Bomber Command was also making repeated attacks, yet it lacked the tools and the experience for this kind of bombing. To the frustration of Doolittle and Brereton, the Eighth and the Ninth would be drawn ever deeper into the Crossbow offensive. Only their bomber crews had been trained and equipped to make daylight precision attacks on small, fixed targets. The Pointblank offensive would continue, parallel to Crossbow, but in early 1944 nearly half the Eighth's missions and more than half the Ninth's were against V-1 launch ramps.

On February 10 the Eighth nevertheless managed to attack aircraft plants at Brunswick, in central Germany. Only 138 bombers reached the target area; 29 were shot down.[10]

Next day the Eighth started receiving its own Mustang groups and by the end of the month the 4th, now under command of Don Blakeslee, would have transitioned into P-51s. The P-38 groups, too, would soon turn in their Lightnings for Mustangs.

Under the new arrangements Quesada's IX Fighter Command was going to be composed of Thunderbolts, except for two groups of P-51s. The P-47, meanwhile, was getting much improved performance, thanks to paddle propellers that dramatically allowed it to outclimb the FW-190; water injection that boosted speed by thirty miles an hour for short periods; and a new gyro-stabilized gunsight. Until Pointblank ended the brunt of fighter-versus-fighter combat would continue to be borne by Thunderbolt groups.[11]

Crossbow attacks and bad weather had delayed a plan which had been on ice since November. That plan proposed to hit the German aircraft industry with coordinated strikes by the Eighth, the Fifteenth and RAF Bomber Command. Colonel Hughes had remained in England as the Eighth's target picker. He had drawn up a list of targets for once the weather improved. It included some familiar names—Schweinfurt, Regensburg—and some new ones. It was likely to prove expensive, because the point was to hit them all in less than a week.

On February 19 the weather forecasters prophesied clear skies over Germany within twenty-four hours. Hughes took his plan to Anderson, who approved it. They took it to Spaatz, who wondered about the potential for disaster. Suppose every target turned out to be a second Schweinfurt . . . or worse? The GAF had around fifteen hundred fighters available to defend the Reich.

Spaatz gave the go-ahead, but for only the first day.[12] February 20 dawned over an England that was covered with thick clouds, and a dusting of snow. The Eighth dispatched more than one thousand planes to attack twelve targets, all involving aircraft production, in central Germany. The GAF's defenses had trouble covering the spread of targets and the strong escort discouraged attacks. Only twenty-one bombers were lost. That night Spaatz okayed Hughes's entire list.

On February 21 Doolittle dispatched 767 heavies to attack Brunswick again, plus various airfields. Brunswick was hit hard, and this time only three aircraft were lost.

The weather over Germany was expected to be cloudy on February 22, but the Eighth put up 250 bombers. More than half would attack Regensburg; an hour later it would be bombed by 84 Liberators from Twining's Fifteenth Air Force. After the August attack the Messerschmitt factory there had been repaired; production was higher than it had ever been. This one-two attack virtually wiped out Regensburg, but 35 B-17s were shot down (as were 13 Liberators). The Eighth's losses for the day came to 41 bombers destroyed and at least half a dozen written off.[13]

Doolittle's men were exhausted. He pleaded with Anderson to give them a rest.[14] Many bomber crewmen were living on chemistry.

Bill Rose of the 92nd Group was probably typical. "The squadron surgeon palled around with us. He knew what shape we were in, how many combat missions we'd flown and what the crew situation was. In February 1944 I was on pills to put me to sleep and on the morning of a mission I was on pills to wake me up and keep me going. Sleeping at night became so bad we started taking pills from our escape kits."[15] Anderson rejected Doolittle's plea, but the next day the weather was terrible; the troops got a break anyway.

The next big target on the list was Schweinfurt. On February 24 the Eighth dispatched nearly 500 heavies: 231 B-17s would strike Schweinfurt, while 236 Liberators from 2nd Air Division attacked the Me-110 plant at Gotha. Eleven Fortresses and 37 Liberators were shot down.

Anderson ordered the Eighth to fly again next day. It was going to attack Regensburg once more, the Messerchmitt plant at Augsburg, and the ball-bearing factories at Stuttgart. This day thirty-one bombers were lost.

The weather turned abysmal again, but everything on Hughes's target list had been hit at least once by day. Many had been torched at night by the RAF. These operations, known as Big Week, had cost the Eighth three hundred planes (mainly bombers) lost or written off. More than twenty-five hundred airmen had been killed, wounded, or fallen into enemy hands. Nearly ten thousand tons of bombs were dropped on the German aircraft industry and ball-bearing plants—a greater tonnage than the Eighth had dropped on all targets in 1943. As many as one thousand complete or nearly complete GAF aircraft had been destroyed.[16]

On the face of it, the Luftwaffe had been dealt a crippling blow. Milch, however, responded by shrewdly making the damaged factories at Brunswick and Oschersleben appear as if they were still in operation. This would give the American bombers something to attack while the program for constructing underground factories was speeded up. Whatever couldn't be hidden would be widely dispersed. Two of the new factories would be devoted to building the Me-262 jet fighter. Hitler was counting on it to clear the skies over the Reich of American bombers.[17]

Air Intelligence analysts figured Big Week had reduced German plane production to about 650 planes a month. This was a wildly optimistic judgment. In the spring of 1944 output was around 1,500 a month, and Luftwaffe acceptances of single-engine fighters were higher in March than they'd been in January. All that had been achieved was to slow the rate at which German output continued to rise.[18]

The most important effect of Big Week was that it had brought German fighters up where the Thunderbolts could get at them. The two Mustang groups involved had only a few successes. The P-51B had a problem with its ammunition feed; in a tight turn the ammo feed chute got jammed and the guns dried up. Pilots returned to England boiling over with frustration at the kills they'd missed out on, or the friends they'd lost needlessly. Jim Howard's heroic feat had seen him down to one operable gun before his ammo ran out.

The P-47s got the kills. The 56th Fighter Group led the way in February, shooting down seventy-two German fighters for the loss of two Thunderbolts.[19] The top American groups were simply draining the pool of experienced German fighter pilots. That month the GAF lost 33 percent of its single-engine fighters and 20 percent of its fighter pilots, including several credited with more than one hundred victories.[20] Their replacements would be downy-cheeked youths thrust into combat with less than half as much training as the greenest American at the controls of a P-47.

After taking command of the Eighth, Doolittle intended to lead the first mission to Berlin personally. He'd already initiated American bombing of two Axis capitals, Tokyo and Rome. He was eager to see the first American bombs explode on the target that appeared on briefing room maps as "Big B." The trouble was, he now knew too much about Ultra and about the coming invasion. He was banned from flying over enemy territory.[21]

The first big mission in March came on the 2nd, when Doolittle sent nearly 250 bombers to attack the marshalling yards at Frankfurt. There was 10/10 cloud over the target, so it had to be bombed by radar. The GAF put up only moderate opposition, and some unknown Thunderbolt pilot flying escort shot down and killed Egon Mayer, a man credited with 103 victories and originator of the dreaded nose attack.[22]

The weather forecast for March 4 seemed just about good enough to allow a big attack on Berlin. The 1st and 3rd Air Divisions dispatched five hundred B-17s, but high cloud over Germany built up so rapidly the bombers were recalled. Everyone turned back, except for a combat box consisting of two squadrons from the 95th Bomb Group and one squadron from the 100th. Lieutenant William Charles, a 95th Group navigator, watched in amazement as, "Formations all around us began making 180 degree turns. Within minutes, they were all gone, disappeared to the west. . . . Our 29 Forts droned deeper into Germany . . . the tense radio silence was broken by a nervous pilot in the low squadron. 'The other formations have turned back, colonel.' "

After a momentary pause, the officer commanding the combat box, Lieutenant Colonel Harry C. Mumford, replied, "We will continue to the assigned target." Charles was stunned. "It was suicide! I swore softly. Had the colonel gone mad?"[23] The box radio operators had not received the correct recall code; the morse message they picked up appeared to be a false German transmission. It was a common trick in the air war. Mumford was gambling that by pressing on alone his planes would be returning from Berlin after the GAF fighters now taking off had landed.

The Fortresses were nonetheless in for a rough time: They had to run the gauntlet of Berlin's flak defenses. Pilots and gunners watched in awe as vivid red flashes erupted far below. Seconds later the eighty-eight-millimeter flak shells would appear, startlingly clear against the snow-covered landscape below, rising rapidly, before exploding all around and, sometimes, scoring direct hits on their planes.

Sergeant Philip Kanarkowski, a top-turret gunner, recalled reaching the outskirts of Berlin when "A flak shell bored a six-inch hole in the bottom of the fuselage of our Fortress and blew a hole three feet across in the top as it burst. The explosion knocked our right waist gunner, James Kollmeyer, against the ball-turret gears six feet away without a shell splinter hitting him, but it blasted the left waist gunner, John Hurley, full in the face and chest and out of the plane."[24] Despite the huge hole in the fuselage, the B-17 flew on and bombed its target in a suburb southwest of Berlin.

These twenty-nine planes would have been massacred had not three P-51 groups been allowed to stay with them when VIII Bomber Command realized that one combat box hadn't turned back. Virtually no damage was done to the target. Five B-17s and four Mustangs were shot down.[25]

Two days later Doolittle put up just about everything that could fly: 730 heavies and nearly 800 fighters. The 1st Air Division would lead the way, with 3rd Air Division behind it and 2nd Air Division bringing up the rear. The bomber stream was 60 miles long.

The Germans realized very quickly that a force this size could have only one target—Berlin. They put up nearly five hundred fighters to attack it. While many concentrated on the leading combat wings of the 1st Air Division, others intercepted the escort responsible for covering the 3rd Air Division before it could rendezvous with the bombers. The middle of the bomber stream was exposed for the best part of an hour to relentless attacks.

These fell hardest on the 13th Combat Wing, composed of the 95th, 100th and 390th Bomb Groups. The entire high squadron of the 100th Group was shot down within minutes. By the time the mission ended the Bloody Hundredth would lose fifteen out of the twenty-one planes it had dispatched.

The primary targets on March 6 were a ball-bearing plant, an electrical equipment plant and an engine factory in the southeastern suburbs of Berlin. The weather was reasonably clear, but not even one of the primary targets was hit.[26]

GAF fighters, rearmed and refueled, pursued the heavies across the Reich. According to Allan R. Willis, copilot of *Flakstop,* a B-17 in the 452nd Bomb Group, "The German fighters came like the proverbial swarm of bees. Six 109s and FW-190s took the 452nd as their quarry and the fun really began. Virtually all passes were made from ten to twelve o'clock high. Our intercom was kaput and I could make no attempt at fire control. The second pass raked the fuselage from nose to tail. The third did the crucial damage. It must have hit the starboard side oil, electrical and fuel lines because both starboard engines began to splutter . . . I hit the feathering switches but nothing happened. The props simply windmilled. The wide variations in rpms started *Flakstop* vibrating and we fell out of formation. . . . There was no panic yet. We could see the Zuider Zee on the horizon. We didn't want to bale out over Germany. . . .

"I saw one of our gas caps fly off. The only explanation I could think of was that intense vibration . . . the entire starboard wing was, in a flash, a sheet of orange flame! In that single moment *Flakstop* gave up her role as a mighty Flying Fortress and became a flying coffin. . . . As I hit the bale-out bell I glanced at the altimeter: fourteen hundred feet over Holland."[27] The Dutch underground hid Willis for six months. He eventually returned to the 452nd.

The escorting fighters had a phenomenal day, claiming eighty-two German planes shot down for eleven aircraft lost and three written off.[28] Blakeslee's 4th Fighter Group accounted for fifteen victories, while the recently activated 357th, also flying Mustangs, accounted for twenty. The cost of bombing Big B was 10 percent of the force dispatched. Seventy-five Fortresses were shot down, crashed on landing, or weren't worth repairing.[29] Two days later the Eighth was on its way back to Berlin with nearly six hundred heavies.

On March 8 the GAF was still reeling from the battle two days before, and the size of the escorting force was even greater this time: nearly nine hundred fighter pilots were credited with flying the mission. Thirty-seven bombers and seventeen fighters were shot down. The escort claimed eighty-seven German fighters; the 56th Fighter Group accounted for twenty-seven of these, mainly by shooting down enemy planes landing to refuel.[30]

On March 9 the Eighth went back, but was forced to bomb through 10/10 cloud. By the end of the month all three air divisions would include a specially trained Pathfinder squadron equipped with H2X radar. Some days, though, the weather was so bad even the Pathfinders couldn't take off. And despite being an electronic wonder, H2X bombing was at best only half as accurate as visual bombing. It was really area bombing by another name. Nearly three hundred B-17s attacked Berlin that day; AAA brought down nine of them. Not one German fighter was scrambled.[31]

On March 15, 330 heavies bombed Brunswick. This time, the escorting fighter groups roamed far and wide, hunting down the Germans before they could reach the bombers. Zemke's Wolf Pack had been doing this kind of thing in a modest way for several months. On this day it shot down twenty-four of the thirty-five enemy fighters claimed by American pilots. One bomber was lost to German fighters.

Next day the Eighth struck the aircraft plants at Augsburg and Friedrichshafen with six hundred bombers. The Germans partially hid Friedrichshafen, sending out smoke floats on Lake Constance. Twenty-three bombers were shot down; a further sixteen crash-landed in Switzerland.

March 22 brought yet another mission to the war industries of Berlin. The Eighth attacked with 650 bombers; only 12 were shot down—all by AAA.

A shaken German Air Force was rethinking its tactics. In recent weeks the Luftwaffe had started redeploying much of its fighter strength, pulling it back from the coast and concentrating in central Germany to defend the heart of the Reich. In part this was due to the frequent attacks on GAF airfields near the North Sea coast by the Ninth Air Force. In part it was a reflection of the shock spread through the Luftwaffe by Big Week. The attacks on Berlin were the final straw.

Tactics were changing, too. The GAF had created a force of "battle observation aircraft." These were twin-engine planes such as the Me-110 and the Ju-88, which would fly ahead of the single-engine fighters, report on the weather, seek weak spots in the American bomber formations, and coordinate the fighter attacks. The Mustangs started wiping out these Luftwaffe shadowing aircraft.[32]

Bomber crews soon noticed the change. GAF fighters stopped flying along with the bombers for as much as an hour, trying to peck the formations to death by diving in repeatedly when they saw a loose or weakened group. Instead, they would assemble in large numbers well inland, make one furious diving pass into the bomber stream, and fly away.[33]

The redeployment of fighters to the heartland of the Reich brought nothing but frustration to Thunderbolt pilots. The prize they sought was maddeningly on the horizon, just beyond their reach—but not beyond a Mustang's. In the second half of March the P-47s shot down comparatively few enemy planes, while the Mustang groups were getting rich.

Frustrated beyond words at the lack of fighter action on the March 22 mission, Zemke's pilots flew out of Germany on the deck, shooting up locomotives and shipping.

The commander of the 353rd Fighter Group, Glenn Duncan, suggested to Kepner that he be allowed to form a volunteer unit that would develop strafing tactics for the P-47. Kepner agreed. Duncan's "Buzz Boys" were made up of one flight each from the 353rd, 355th, 359th and 361st groups. They began hitting German airfields. On March 29 they strafed Bransche, but no enemy aircraft were in sight. Duncan led them on to Vechta. Paydirt!

"I passed across the front of the hanger line," Duncan reported, "and saw many twin-engine and single-engine aircraft. I lined up two of the twin-engines and let go. The first one lit up quite well, but never did blow up or catch fire while I was coming on it. The second one caught fire. There were five or six single-engines dispersed in a line across the field. . . . I was able to get a few hits on each." By now, forty-millimeter flak was erupting all around. One of Duncan's pilots strafed a flak gun that seemed to be picking on him and destroyed it.

The Buzz Boys flew on to a third airfield, Twenthe-Enschede. On the approach Duncan spotted a staff car driving near some parked aircraft. "I called for the flight to go down and, believe me, the boys were really flying good this day. They stayed together very well. We came across the 'drome in good four-ship line abreast, each individual picking a likely target. The staff car caught quite a lot of .50 caliber. . . ."[34]

Missions like this, carried out at four hundred miles an hour with Thunderbolts that sometimes came back with scratches and dents on the bottom fuselage where they'd scraped bushes and treetops, became an increasing feature of P-47 operations. To encourage them, Kepner gave credit for enemy planes destroyed by strafing. And as every pilot knew, it was more dangerous to get one on the ground than in the air. Five times more Eighth Air Force pilots would be shot down while strafing than in aerial combat.[35]

The last week of March had its own frustrations for the bomber crews. They were briefed for missions that were scrubbed because of weather, or they attacked Crossbow sites. The few missions that were flown produced mass aborts. Even so, it had been an expensive month for VIII Bomber Command: 345 heavies shot down or written off.[36] On March 31 Pointblank came to an end; at least, formally.

As of April 1 Spaatz's USSTAF headquarters and Leigh-Mallory's AEAF would come under the direction of Eisenhower's Supreme Headquarters, Allied Expeditionary Force (SHAEF). The Eighth's efforts from this point on could be expected to shift sharply away from targets in Germany toward isolating the invasion beaches in France. However, Eisenhower informally allowed the Pointblank offensive to run on until April 14. The Eighth continued to hammer the GAF and the factories on which it depended.

On April 8 all three air divisions participated in attacks on Brunswick and major airfields in northwest Germany. Of the 639 bombers dispatched, 34 were shot down. Next day the Eighth sent nearly 400 heavies to airfields and aircraft factories in eastern Germany and Poland. Mustangs could not yet fly as far as Poland, although the day was coming when they would do it. No diversionary raid was mounted to dilute GAF defenses. Enemy fighters were able to concentrate on several unescorted combat bombardment wings. Thirty-two B-17s and B-24s were shot down.[37]

April 10 brought a breather—attacks on aircraft plants in France and Belgium. With GAF fighters concentrated in central Germany, this was a milk run. Next day was completely different. The Eighth sent more than eight hundred bombers to attack Oschersleben and other aircraft plants as far as the Polish border. The 3rd Air Division had to fly as far as Poznan without escort, which enabled the Luftwaffe to mass its twin-engined fighters against it. The 3rd lost thirty-three aircraft. The mission as a whole was costly: sixty-four bombers, nearly 10 percent of those which entered German airspace, were shot down. Six more had to be scrapped.[38]

On April 12 a major mission to industrial targets in Germany was recalled due to high clouds. GAF fighters pursued the withdrawing bomber stream and shot down six Liberators.[39] On the 13th Doolittle sent nearly 400 heavies to attack Schweinfurt and the Messerschmitt plant at Augsburg, while another 180 bombers hit GAF airfields. A total of 38 bombers were downed by enemy fighters and flak. In less than a week the Eighth had lost more than 200 heavies in action or to battle damage.[40]

By April 14 Pointblank was history. It had achieved its principal objective, securing air superiority, but Tedder was prepared to throw this victory away. He ordered that Crossbow targets be given priority, overriding even the destruction of the GAF. Spaatz protested vigorously. Eisenhower upheld Spaatz.[41]

Pointblank had succeeded, but not in the way intended or expected. The heavy bombers hadn't smashed the GAF into the ground. Nor had they halted the remorseless increase in German combat aircraft. Instead, by striking at the aircraft factories and by bombing targets in Berlin they had forced GAF fighters into the air—and to their doom.

Veteran groups such as the 4th and the 56th, the 78th and the 353rd, were bursting at the seams with aces. Some pilots, like the 4th's Don Gentile and his wingman John Godfrey, were as famous as movie stars, with looks to match. Others, such as Gabreski, were well on their way to lasting renown. Goering, on the other hand, was accusing his fighter pilots of *Jägerschreck*—"fear of fighters."[42]

Kepner's pilots claimed 825 GAF planes in April 1944. Of these, nearly 500 were destroyed on the ground.[43] Even so, the GAF was reeling from personnel losses. In the first four months of 1944 it had lost 1,684 fighter pilots.[44] Losses on this scale were almost impossible to make good. Ultra was monitoring Luftwaffe messages which bemoaned the growing shortage of pilots.[45]

Training was shortened to get bodies into cockpits, but these replacements were noticeably more interested in avoiding American fighters than they were in attacking American bombers. They lacked the numbers, the spirit and the training needed to challenge the bombing of their homes, the strafing of their airfields and the destruction of their factories. The first task in any air war—winning command of the skies—had been won by the AAF.

19

LIBERATION
SKIES

The projected date for the Normandy invasion, code-named Overlord, was pushed back to early June to allow more time for the
construction of assault shipping. This delay gave airmen an extra
month to secure command of the sky.

Overlord would have the usual three-phase air plan for a combined arms offensive: air superiority–interdiction–close air support.
With hopes pinned firmly on Pointblank to produce air superiority
in time for the invasion, the next question was how best to isolate
the battlefield.

Air Marshal Sir Arthur Tedder, Eisenhower's deputy for air, had
brought Solly Zuckerman with him from the Mediterranean. The
professor produced a target list of 101 rail centers in northern
France and the Low Countries. He recommended 45,000 tons of
bombs be dropped on them by D-Day.[1] The aim of these attacks
was to channel rail movements in northern France so that when
German divisions headed toward the beaches to attack the invasion
forces, they would be limited to narrow corridors, which the
fighter-bombers would dominate.

Zuckerman's proposal, known as the Transportation Plan,
sparked one of the most furious debates of the air war. Dropping
45,000 tons could be accomplished only by having Eighth Air Force
and RAF Bomber Command unload most of this ordnance.
Spaatz, Doolittle and Harris were completely opposed to what they
saw as a diversion of heavy bombers to a tactical air operation of

dubious value. Besides, if the pressure of the Pointblank offensive slackened, the GAF could make a comeback.[2]

Meanwhile, fighting fire with fire, Colonel Richard Hughes had gotten a couple of young American professors installed at the U.S. Embassy in London, in an office called the Economic Objectives Unit. Hughes loathed Zuckerman and looked to the EOU to provide better advice than Tedder was getting. His professors recommended oil. The EOU claimed that just four synthetic oil plants and thirteen refineries provided Hitler with half his oil. Knock out these seventeen targets and the Wehrmacht would clank to a halt. Spaatz enthusiastically advanced the Oil Plan as an alternative to the Transportation Plan. The Luftwaffe wasn't going to defend marshalling yards in France, but it was inconceivable that the Luftwaffe would let the Eighth wipe out its fuel supplies without a fight. Oil attacks would advance the fight for air superiority.[3]

Harris was equally opposed to seeing his Lancasters used on yet another "panacea target." He claimed attacks on marshalling yards, nearly all of which were in densely populated areas, would kill and cripple as many as 160,000 French and Belgian civilians.[4]

Eisenhower gave everybody something. The bulk of the interdiction effort would go to Transportation Plan attacks. When the weather was bad over France but clear over Germany, Spaatz could attack oil targets. Churchill, however, held back from endorsing the Transportation Plan. He feared high French casualties. The Allies were supposed to be liberating the people of occupied Europe, not slaughtering them. The plan was put on ice while Churchill sought Roosevelt's opinion.

The President felt the risk of high civilian casualties had to be borne if the invasion was going to succeed.[5] As a result of this protracted debate, it was early May before the Transportation Plan really got going.

By this time American airmen and the EOU were insisting on attacks against bridges. To them, it was obvious that bridge-busting was a better way of isolating the battlefield than wrecking rolling stock and locomotive repair shops. Zuckerman, on the other hand, claimed it would take nearly seven hundred sorties to knock out each bridge.[6]

One man who believed fervently that the P-47 could drop bridges quickly and cheaply was Leigh-Mallory's chief of operations, Brigadier General Frederick H. Smith, a fighter pilot who'd recently arrived in the ETO from New Guinea. Smith had been offered to

Eisenhower by Kenney as an expert in the use of air power to support an amphibious assault. He drew up a list of twenty-two bridges crossing the lower Seine that he thought should be dropped before D-Day. Supported by Frederick Anderson, he was allowed to set up an experiment.

There was a large railroad bridge that crossed the Seine at Vernon, thirty-five miles downstream from Paris. On May 7, sixteen Thunderbolts of the 365th Fighter Group headed for the bridge, with a squadron of Mustangs flying top cover. Each P-47 carried an eleven hundred-pound bomb. The first two to dive on the bridge were shot down by light flak. The third plane released its bomb perfectly. The Germans had mined the Vernon bridge with about half a ton of explosives. When the American bomb went off, it triggered a sympathetic detonation. The two explosions tore the huge structure to shreds and filled the river with twisted metal.[7] One bomb, one bridge, and one impressed German eyewitness—Erwin Rommel, who happened to be visiting Vernon that day.[8]

The Thunderbolt pilots had made their point. Bridge busting would go into the air plan, but it wouldn't begin until two weeks before D-Day. There was no point in giving the Germans time to repair downed bridges.

On May 21, Allied Expeditionary Air Forces fighter squadrons made their own contribution to the Transportation Plan, in Operation Chattanooga Choo-Choo. Nearly eight hundred fighters swept across northern France attacking the railroads, while five hundred long range fighters from the Eighth Air Force did the same over southern Germany. They strafed locomotives, repair sheds and signal boxes. They used their auxiliary fuel tanks as incendiaries and set trains alight. These attacks put an end to daytime railroad operations in France.[9]

On May 25, Eighth and Ninth Air Forces continued Chattanooga missions over northern France and the Low Countries. And on the 29th the Eighth carried them into eastern Germany and along the Polish border with nearly six hundred Mustangs and Lightnings.[10]

By this time the bridge-busting campaign was well under way, aiming to drop every one of the twenty-two bridges crossing the Seine below Paris before June 5, the scheduled D-Day. Dozens of bridges were also being attacked in the Pas de Calais, to keep the Germans guessing.

May 1944 saw the Eighth rapidly approaching its maximum

strength, of forty heavy groups, plus fifteen groups of fighters. All the same, it was fully stretched. It was committed to attacking German aviation plants, GAF airfields, marshalling yards, Crossbow sites and the Reich's oil industry.

Germany's V-weapons program made steady progress, despite intensive bombing. The V-1 was a crude air-breathing missile usually launched from a narrow ramp about 180 feet long. It lacked a guidance system and when it ran out of fuel dropped from the sky, carrying a five-hundred-pound high-explosive warhead with an instantaneous fuse. Given a target the size of London, the V-1 was almost certain to wreck buildings and kill people wherever it struck. In May Allied air forces flew forty-six hundred sorties against V-weapon sites and dropped forty-six hundred tons of bombs on them. By June activity at the launch sites in the Pas de Calais had fallen off so sharply the threat seemed to have been lifted from London.[11]

Losses incurred attacking the V-weapon sites were low, and enemy fighters were rarely seen. Here as elsewhere the GAF hunkered down. After April 1944 most bombers that were lost would be victims of AAA, but when the Eighth made its first big strike against the synthetic oil plants on May 12, it was like pushing a stick into a hornets' nest. The GAF put up 300 fighters. The plants were well defended, too, by AAA. Of the 935 bombers sent on this mission, 46 were lost to flak and fighters; a further nine were written off. The escort lost 7 fighters, but the GAF lost 65.[12]

Repeat attacks on May 28 and May 29 brought similar responses, similar losses for both sides. For the Luftwaffe, the sudden drop in synthetic oil production was crippling. The German Army would get fuel priority; the GAF's allocation plummeted.[13]

The Ninth's counterair campaign against the GAF began May 9. The aim was to drive it out of airfields within 130 miles of Caen, the biggest city in Normandy and Montgomery's D-Day objective. Dozens of airfields were hit, repeatedly, by Anderson's B-26s and A-20s dropping parafrag bombs and by Quesada's P-47s dive-bombing with five-hundred-pounders and strafing everything in sight.

Kepner converted one of his Lightning groups, the 55th, for bombing. The armament (four fifty-calibers and one twenty-millimeter cannon) was removed from the nose of several P-38s. This created just enough space to install a bombsight and wedge in a bombardier. If the plane was hit, the bombardier had no way of getting out. This modification created a strange bulge, hence the modified Lightning's nickname, the Droopsnoot. The idea was for a Droopsnoot to lead a squadron of P-38s to the target and when the bombardier dropped his bombs, the rest of the squadron would do the same. The P-38 could carry four thousand pounds of bombs, almost as much as the B-26.

The first mission flown wasn't encouraging. Operating in a strange new way, the Lightnings couldn't find the primary. They attacked another airfield, but to this day no one's sure which one it was.[14] Nor was the P-38 much of a dive-bomber. Major Edward Giller commanded a 55th Group squadron. "I remember dive-bombing a French bridge," Giller later recalled, "which resulted in a one thousand-pound bomb going into an enormous greenhouse and probably set back brussels sprout production for a whole year. Another one thousand-pounder went into a huge haystack and as a result there was hay in the air at two thousand feet. I am not sure anybody hit the bridge."[15]

In the first few days of June the essential task for both the Eighth and the Ninth was to soften up coastal defenses in Normandy, but those in the Pas de Calais were hit even harder. Zuckerman's Transportation Plan targets had been clobbered with seventy-one thousand tons of bombs, far more than he'd asked for.[16] The GAF had not one operable airfield in Normandy and was desperately short of fuel. Air superiority was so certain that when Eisenhower went to address American troops preparing to board assault ships he promised them, "If you see airplanes overhead, they will be ours."[17]

Although Allied commanders relied heavily on Ultra to monitor German positions and movement, the largest single source of air intelligence was aerial reconnaissance. The story of aerial photography in the AAF centers around George Goddard, one of nature's born enthusiasts and a man whose colleagues considered him both "a genius" and "a pest."[18]

Goddard's passionate belief in aerial photography brought development of the gun camera. In the 1920s he'd devised cameras and flash bombs that produced the first night photography from aircraft. He had also developed the strip camera, which took photographs through an aperture nearly as fine as a human hair. The result was something almost like a movie film, but showing more detail. Looking ahead, Goddard argued the case for fast reconnaissance aircraft and better cameras as essential tools of war.

Always a controversial figure, Goddard clashed with a young officer whom Arnold greatly liked, Minton Kaye, who had ambitions to take over AAF photography. In 1943 Colonel Goddard was relieved of his position in aerial photography by Arnold and sent to the 2nd Air Force, commanded by Major General St. Clair Street. Arnold told Street flatly, "For God's sake, don't let him get anywhere near a camera. Give him something else to do."[19] The AAF's greatest authority on aerial photography thus found himself tackling the exacting assignment of VD officer at Morris Field, in Charlotte, North Carolina, which boasted the highest VD rate in the AAF.

Meanwhile, photo recon was in serious trouble. Goddard's warning years earlier that fast, high-flying photo recon planes were essential had been slighted.[20] As a result, the AAF went to war with unarmed, camera-laden Lightnings, known as F-4s, which were neither fast enough nor able to fly high enough to cope with German fighters, and with B-17s, which needed fighter escort. The lack of a good plane for strategic reconnaissance hundreds of miles behind enemy lines would dog the AAF throughout the war.[21] Fortunately this was an area in which the RAF excelled and the AAF could draw on British experience.

After a few months as VD officer, Goddard managed to get himself attached to the Navy, which was interested in his strip camera. The camera offered excellent prospects for studying beach defenses on islands the Marines would have to assault.

Arnold would no longer listen to him, being under the influence of Kaye, whose wife was a close friend of Mrs. Arnold. Vandenberg, on the other hand, took Goddard to see Lovett, who was appalled to learn that only the Navy was getting the benefit of something the AAF had developed and needed to play its part fully in the invasion of France. Lovett ordered two hundred strip cameras and sent Goddard to England to see if he could get an AAF assignment.[22]

There, he met up with Elliott Roosevelt. Four years earlier when Roosevelt was stuck in procurement, Goddard had shown him a colored aerial photograph he'd taken of Hyde Park and, in the usual Goddardian way, given him an enthusiastic talk on the marvels of taking pictures from airplanes. That had inspired Roosevelt to ask for a transfer out of procurement and into photo reconnaissance. And now he asked for Goddard to be assigned to his new command, the 325th Photo Recon Wing of the Eighth Air Force.

For strategic recon there was a modified P-38, known as the F-6, which, with drop tanks, could fly from England to Poland and back, taking excellent photographs. But even now this plane lacked the altitude and speed to escape the fastest German fighters. It had to be escorted by P-51s. The AAF never had a strategic photographic aircraft like the RAF's plywood Mosquito, able to run away from trouble. Losses in Roosevelt's command averaged 25 percent per month.[23]

The Eighth's photographic concerns were mainly to make bomb damage assessments (BDAs), to survey German airfields, and to locate flak concentrations. Its photo experts also produced drawings, based on photographs, to show radar operators what targets such as synthetic fuel plants or marshalling yards would look like on H2X.[24]

The photography work of the Ninth was conducted by the 67th Tactical Reconnaissance Group and the 10th Photographic Reconnaissance Group. In the months leading up to Overlord they mapped much of the Continent, performed BDA flights, kept an eye on GAF airfields; above all, they surveyed the beach defenses of Normandy.

In the spring of 1944 they began flying "dicing" missions, which meant flying 50 feet above French beaches at low tide at speeds of 375 miles per hour, taking pictures with strip cameras. A few pilots also flew ultra-low altitude missions—the same thing, but at 25 feet.[25] To keep the Germans guessing, they flew even more missions over the beaches of the Pas de Calais as part of the deception plan, called Fortitude, which helped mislead Hitler into thinking the Normandy invasion was merely a feint.

The pilots in the photo groups were an elite; not only were they fighter trained, but they were recon trained too, with flying skills that few men ever acquired. Both the 10th and the 67th received Presidential Unit Citations for their work over the beaches of northern France.

The weather forecast for June 5 was so bad Eisenhower had to postpone D-Day until June 6. The first D-Day mission flown was by the 155th Night Photo Squadron of the 10th Group, which brought back pictures of Normandy's roads at midnight—no sign of unusual activity. Fifteen minutes after midnight, twenty C-47s flew over the coastline of the Cotentin peninsula on the Normandy coast carrying 260 Pathfinders for the 82nd and 101st Airborne

Divisions, which would spearhead the invasion. The Pathfinders carried recognition beacons to guide the troop carrier pilots who would bring in the jumpers and glidermen.

The Overlord assault would hit five beaches along fifty miles of coastline. The two most westerly were Omaha and Utah. The U.S. airborne troops were to seize various causeways that led inland from Utah, making it possible for the 4th Infantry Division to move off the beach.

Unexpected low clouds over the Cotentin forced the troop-carrier pilots to climb above them before dropping the Pathfinders, who found themselves scattered far and wide. An hour later nearly five hundred C-47s of 50th and 53rd Troop Carrier Wings flew over the Cotentin, carrying seven thousand paratroopers, four hundred glidermen and thousands of dummy parachutists about three feet tall and festooned with firecrackers. The Pathfinders were still trying to figure out where they were. Few turned on their beacons. All but a handful of paratroopers missed their assigned drop zones.

Before the day was over, IX Troop Carrier Command would bring in another six thousand parachutists and four thousand glidermen. The widespread dispersion of airborne troops and their simulacra would add to the panic that seized the Germans, who reported they were fighting ninety thousand paratroopers.[26]

First light on D-Day revealed scattered clouds around two thousand feet, thickening until, at twelve thousand feet, cloud cover was solid. A month earlier Frederick Smith had gone to each division commander, British and American, and asked what effect each wanted from bombing on his assigned beach—personnel casualties among the defenders? disrupted enemy communications? suppression of coastal guns? What? Bomb loads were made up accordingly.[27]

The thick cloud now undermined Smith's efforts. It forced the Eighth's heavies to bomb by (inaccurate) radar. Also, the fact that underwater demolition teams were emerging onto the beaches to clear lanes through the beach obstacles led bombardiers flying over Omaha to delay a few seconds before dropping. The defenses at Omaha were formidable and unscathed by bombing. American ordnance slaughtered herds of dairy cows grazing half a mile inland.

Sam Anderson had anticipated bad weather. He'd taken the old low-level sights out of the warehouse, removed the Nordens from his B-26s, and briefed his pilots to go in low. The mediums of IX

Bomber Command, attacking defenses at Utah, would do the most effective bombing of D-Day.[28]

For men such as Lieutenant Carl H. Moore, a B-26 bombardier in the 344th Bomb Group, it was the high point of the war. As his aircraft descended through the dense cloud layer that covered the Bay of the Seine, Moore looked out on the scene coming into view and, "I could hardly believe what I saw. Ships of all sizes from huge battleships to fragile landing craft literally blackened the surface of the English Channel . . . you could almost walk from England to France. . . .

"Our twenty 250-pound bombs had to be dropped before the ground troops landed. The bombs were to blow enough holes in the beach to give some protection for the troops—predug foxholes, so to speak. . . . Over the beach at exactly 6:20 A.M. and 'bombs away.' What a sight! . . . As we passed over the beach the first wave of troops was poised to jump off. . . . It was almost too exciting to be scared. . . ."[29]

The mediums flew a second mission in the afternoon, hitting beach defenses. Most heavy bombers flew a second mission, demolishing twelve towns, to create roadblocks. Some flew a third mission, adding to the rubble on the roads.

To hold down friendly-fire casualties, Allied aircraft in the invasion had broad white strips painted around their wings and fuselages. And to encourage the trigger-happy Navy to hold its fire, Kepner put his Lightning groups over the fleet. The Germans had nothing that looked remotely like a P-38. It worked almost perfectly: the Navy shot down only two American planes, both P-51s on recon flights.[30]

Kepner had the rest of his fighters flying around in huge defensive circles from the shore to fifty miles inland.[31] With VIII Fighter Command providing the air cover, IX Fighter Command roamed over Normandy on armed reconnaissance.

The Allied advantage in the air was overwhelming. The two strategic air forces had 3,500 heavy bombers; the tactical air forces operated 1,500 mediums and nearly 5,500 fighters. The GAF had only 319 aircraft in the whole of France. There were plans to send hundreds of planes to France within hours of the invasion, but Hitler refused to allow it in case the Normandy landings proved to be a feint.[32] The GAF's response was too little, too late.

Shortly after dawn the first aerial victory of D-Day was scored by Lieutenant Joe Conklin, flying a Mustang of the 15th Tactical

Reconnaissance Squadron, part of the 10th Photo Group. He shot down an FW-190 over Dreux. Most Allied pilots, however, didn't see a GAF aircraft all day. There was no sizable response until late afternoon, when 70 GAF fighters got into the air.

Zemke's 56th Group pilots were flying their seventh and last mission of the day when, about seven o'clock in the evening, they got their first glimpse of enemy opposition. Approaching Dreux in company with the Mustangs of 352nd Fighter Group, Zemke spotted an FW-190 "trying to sneak up on one of our lower elements. Turning right and down to attack him, he saw me coming, changed his mind and fled to the west. I rapidly overtook him in the dive. The Focke-Wulf pilot then broke right to engage me and as I came in behind him he tightened his turn, suddenly losing control and spinning down into the ground. I never fired a shot." Minutes later as Zemke closed on another 190 "a P-51 came slicing out of the blue to fire on the enemy at close range. The Focke-Wulf immediately burst into flames and the pilot baled out. I could see his clothes were afire and flames were licking around his head. Fixing the descending pilot in my sight I opened fire to end his pain and misery."[33]

D-Day cost the Eighth and the Ninth 71 aircraft, mainly fighters. Nearly all the planes lost were downed by ground fire.[34] The GAF lost 28 fighters. That night the GAF launched 175 bomber sorties against invasion shipping, losing half a dozen aircraft and sinking nothing.

Despite the establishment of air supremacy on D-Day there was a calamitous interdiction failure: the Germans were able to launch an armored counterattack that stopped the British from advancing seven miles inland as planned and taking Caen. Three panzer divisions were near the invasion beaches—21st Panzer, 12th SS Panzer and Panzer Lehr. The 21st Panzer was deployed near Caen. In midafternoon it advanced to counterattack the British troops who had taken Sword Beach.[35] The German's ability to maneuver armor in daylight when the AEAF was flying more than ten thousand sorties is hard to understand. It may possibly have reflected the fact that Montgomery and Coningham by this time simply loathed each other and tried to have as little direct contact as possible.[36] In any event, the 2nd TAF failed to stop the 21st Panzer. The consequence of not taking Caen on D-Day was that access to the Falaise Plain and the open terrain that led to Paris was blocked. Allied armies found themselves hemmed in. They would be forced to fight a long and bloody ground battle in the hedgerows.

With the invasion site no longer a secret, it was possible to start attacking the bridges over the Loire. The intention was to force the Germans to move through a forty-mile gap between Paris and Orléans. The fighter-bombers would make movement through the gap so perilous by day that German troops would be forced to detrain one hundred miles away and move toward the beachhead on foot, at night, at a time of the year when there were at most four hours of darkness.

Until D-Day the German Seventh Army, which occupied Normandy, had received enough fuel and ammunition to survive but not enough to accumulate stockpiles. With close combat thrust upon it and rail and road movement disrupted, this army soon starting running out of supplies. The key road junction of Carentan, for example, was a vital objective for Omar Bradley's First Army. It had to take Carentan to link up the forces at Omaha and Utah. The Germans quit the town on June 12 after running out of ammunition.[37]

The five invasion beaches gradually coalesced into a strong, if shallow, beachhead, aided by the fact that Hitler continued to believe the real blow would fall on the Pas de Calais—that Normandy was only a feint. When the truth dawned, it was too late for the Germans. The Allies were ashore to stay.

With air supremacy secured, Allied artillery could fire without fear of giving its location away. Guns, like trucks and tanks, moved in broad daylight without interference. Ninth Air Force and 2nd TAF set up shop on whatever ground suited them. Group commanders didn't have to camouflage their airfields or even disperse their planes.

All the same, the Ninth Air Force got off to a bad start with the First Army. Bradley detested Brereton (a sentiment some AAF officers shared) for his lazy, self-indulgent ways. There had been virtually no air-ground training in England between Ninth Air Force and First Army, despite Bradley's pleas.[38]

The Ninth nevertheless contained commanders who believed strongly in supporting the ground troops, notably Elwood O. "Pete" Quesada and Otto P. "Opie" Weyland. With Allied armies ashore in France, Quesada's IX Fighter Command was split into two tactical air commands: IX TAC, under Quesada, which would support First Army, and XIX TAC, under Weyland, to support Patton's Third Army once it was activated. In the meantime XIX

TAC's groups would operate under Quesada's general supervision in support of Bradley.

The GAF's reaction to the invasion was to send another 300 fighters and 135 bombers to France by June 10, but the airfields were such a mess after repeated Allied attacks that planes couldn't be dispersed properly. The railroads were so damaged they couldn't bring in the bombs and fuel needed for anything but small-scale operations. The GAF could fly no more than 350 fighter sorties a day and 50 bomber sorties a night.[39] Allied air superiority went unchallenged thoughout June and July.

Nevertheless, much of Allied air power was diverted from the battlefield. On June 15 the long-dreaded V-weapon offensive began. In the space of twenty-four hours the Pas de Calais sites launched three hundred rockets at London. British civilians suffered four thousand casualties from this onslaught. On June 18 Eisenhower made V-weapon sites the number-one priority for all four air forces. Only emergencies in the beachhead would take precedence over Crossbow missions from now on.

The Germans got a lot of help, too, from the weather: for most of June and July it was wretched, grounding the heavy bombers most days, but posing no obstacle to rocket launches. The ramps were small and many were hidden in innocuous-looking farm buildings. And those that were in the open were camouflaged and almost impossible to pick up in a bombsight.[40] Despite the renewed bombing, which was more intense than anything before in Crossbow, the V-1 attacks continued unabated.

Even though VIII Bomber Command was grounded much of the time, Kepner's VIII Fighter Command pilots were kept busy flying sweeps; they rarely had a chance to engage enemy planes. Increasingly the Mustang groups exited France low and strafing. On a typical departure, for example, a P-51 pilot flying over Normandy fired a burst of incendiaries into a hay wagon driven by what appeared to be a farmer's wife in a Mother Hubbard. What made him suspicious was the way all the farm vehicles on the road were spaced evenly, like a military convoy. As the hay burned off, it revealed a German artillery piece lashed to the wagon. After that the whole column got strafed.[41]

In planning Overlord staff officers had projected a strong German counterattack would be launched by D + 14. It never materialized. Interdiction made it impossible for the enemy to move troops quickly into Normandy or to mass them once they arrived. Many

German tanks and trucks heading for Normandy contributed unwittingly to their own destruction: they carried five-gallon jerry cans strapped to their sides. Pilots found it easy to set entire convoys on fire.[42]

By June 20 the VIII Corps, commanded by Major General Troy Middleton, had closed on Cherbourg, the largest city in the Cotentin and a strategically vital port. Bradley demanded fighter-bomber attacks against German positions. Twenty-five Thunderbolts were lost striking targets many airmen thought were proper objectives for artillery. Still, the story had a happy ending: Cherbourg fell June 26.

At least pilots attacking fixed defenses in Cherbourg were able to see their assigned targets. Much of the Cotentin was covered with dense hedgerows known as the *bocage.* And what wasn't obscured by *bocage* was likely to be covered by swamps. This part of Normandy offered ideal terrain for a defensive battle; the Germans used it to full advantage.

Quesada had moved his tent next to Bradley's. They usually had breakfast together. Quesada urged Bradley to consider massing his armor and letting the bombers punch a hole for his tanks to go through.[43] Bradley rejected the idea. The *bocage,* he said, was filled with hidden antitank guns. The Germans would stop any armored thrust cold.

Quesada nonetheless persisted with his proposal, offering to place a flight of P-47s over every armored column from dawn till dusk if Bradley went along with his suggestion. For the present, he improved air-ground communications by putting AAF radios and pilots into tanks, to direct close support strikes.[44]

The idea of using air to smash a way through the German defenses remained in abeyance until Montgomery tried it, to break through onto the Falaise Plain. On July 7 RAF Bomber Command dropped six thousand tons of high explosive in front of the British Second Army still on the outskirts of Caen. The bombs were mainly eleven-hundred-pounders. They created huge craters and filled the streets of the city with the wreckage of stone buildings. The British were able to fight their way into Caen, but were blocked from moving beyond it by craters and rubble.[45]

While this doomed venture was under way, IX TAC was receiving some new tools: five-inch rockets and napalm. The rockets were intended for use against ground targets, such as pillboxes and tanks, but their first use in combat appears to have occurred in the air. On June 18 the 406th Fighter Group's Bill Dunn, who'd become the first American ace of the war while flying with the RAF, intercepted an Me-110 that was attacking an American ship near Cherbourg. He recalled, "The Hun pilot saw me coming flat out and turned toward me to make a head-on pass.

"I had ten rockets on board, and as I wasn't particularly fond of head-on attacks, I salvoed the whole lot at him. The rockets didn't hit him but they must have scared the bejesus out of him, for he did a steep turn to starboard. I pulled my Jug hard to port, ending up about fifty yards behind this squarehead's kite, where I let him have the full blast, all eight fifty-caliber machine guns. I had never seen an aircraft completely disintegrate in the air the way this Me-110 did. . . ."[46]

The first conventional rocket attack came on July 17, when the 406th Fighter Group used them against the marshalling yard at Nevers, on the Loire. Napalm was employed for the first time that same day against a camouflaged German position near Coutances, in the southwest Cotentin.

On July 18 the British tried carpet bombing again. The aim was to punch a hole in the German defenses for Montgomery to push seven hundred tanks through and onto the Falaise Plain. The Germans rode out the storm and wiped out half the British tanks. Monty had fallen short yet again.[47]

This operation nonetheless broke the deadlock over using American heavy bombers to aid Bradley. Spaatz had grumbled bitterly about using them "to plow up the ground" and claimed all that was preventing a breakout from Normandy was a lack of guts by American ground troops.[48] Reaching and taking the crucial crossroads town of St. Lô had cost Bradley's divisions forty thousand casualties. To move beyond it, Eisenhower suggested carpet bombing. So did Quesada. And Bradley had finally been convinced that if the British operation pinned down the Germans so they couldn't move their reserves to his sector of the front, he might be able to break out of the Cotentin. The American carpet bombing operation, code-named Cobra, was scheduled for July 19.

Cobra was designed to blow the Panzer Lehr division out of Bradley's way. He wanted saturation bombing on a rectangle three miles long and one and a half miles deep. The northern boundary of the rectangle was the straight east-west road that ran between St. Lô and Periers. He asked for a bombardment only eight hundred yards in front of his troops and conducted in the shortest time possible. The Eighth Air Force representative, Colonel John H. De Russy, recommended a minimum separation distance of three thousand yards. And even this, he said, would not preclude friendly-fire casualties. Bradley replied that he was aware of the risk of gross errors causing casualties but was prepared to accept friendly-fire losses to achieve his objective. On that basis De Russy agreed to a separation distance of fifteen hundred yards.[49]

Bradley asked for the bombers to fly parallel to the road, to minimize the risk of short bombs falling on American troops. The problem, he was told by Vandenberg, Smith and other AAF officers, was that flying fifteen hundred heavies and nearly four hundred mediums through a space only one mile wide would take several hours. It conflicted with Bradley's wish for a quick, heavy bombing, followed by a rapid ground attack to break through Panzer Lehr position's while the Germans were still reeling. Bradley agreed to the bombing being made perpendicular to the St. Lô-Periers road.[50]

Heavy rains postponed the operation until July 24. After the bombers were airborne, clouds moved into the target area. A recall message was flashed, but not before some aircraft began bombing. Short bombs fell on the 30th Infantry Division, killing or wounding 155 soldiers.[51]

Bradley was again asked if he would accept the risks of bombing perpendicular to the road. He gave his assent once more. Cobra was rescheduled for July 25.

It opened with a strike by nearly six hundred P-47 fighter-bombers. With a breeze blowing gently from the south, a strip of smoke and dust moved steadily northwards. It looked a lot like a narrow white road when viewed through a Norden bombsight.[52] Bombs rained down yet again on 30th Infantry Division positions, this time killing or wounding five hundred soldiers, including Lieutenant General Leslie J. McNair, who'd come to Europe to assume command of the ETO.

Spaatz tried to put the blame for these friendly-fire deaths on the mediums of IX Bomber Command. The Eighth's own investigation showed the 2nd Air Division was responsible.[53] The drive for air independence depended so strongly on the creed of strategic bombing that the reputation of the Mighty Eighth had to be defended. Bradley, too, was looking for a scapegoat. He accused the airmen of "duplicity," claiming they'd told him the bombing would be parallel to the road. The sad truth is Bradley lied.[54]

For all the mutual recriminations and cover-ups, Cobra worked. It was the first successful carpet bombing in history. When the VII Corps advanced, it ran into a brittle crust of German resistance, but this soon collapsed. By July 31 American troops were charging out of the Cotentin.

Opie Weyland had spent three years as one of Arnold's bright, troubleshooting colonels back at the Pentagon. He'd done well. In January 1944 he was on his way to England as a new brigadier general to command the 84th Fighter Wing. Three months later Quesada promoted him to run XIX TAC and support Patton's Third Army.

Weyland was less than delighted to learn he'd be working with Patton. In Louisiana, in North Africa, and again in Sicily, Patton had gotten along badly with nearly every air officer who crossed his path. Weyland had to find a way to win Patton's respect if they were going to forge a successful team. Before he left the 84th Fighter Wing, Weyland asked Patton to visit him and see a fighter group being briefed for a mission.

Patton was a perfectionist. At the briefing the pilots were given timings down to a tenth of a second: engine start at such an such an hour, so many minutes, so many seconds, and so many tenths. Takeoff times were just as precise; so was the rendezvous time with a combat bomb wing at twenty-five thousand feet over Berlin. Patton was incredulous. "Are you trying to pull my leg?"

It's almost certain Weyland stage-managed this briefing for theatrical effect, but he had to get Patton's attention. Weyland assured him that absolute precision was essential in air operations. If fighters traveling at 350 miles per hour were going to meet up with bombers flying at 200 miles per hour at a point five miles above the ground, without signposts or landmarks to help them, they needed split-second timing, or they'd never even see each other.[55]

On August 1, Patton's Third Army was activated. It led the charge out of the Cotentin. The only thing slowing them down, Patton's tank crews reported back, was the wreckage of German vehicles and artillery that had been knocked out by Weyland's fighter-bombers. Patton was overjoyed and sent for Weyland to come to his command post. He greeted Weyland with a full quart of bourbon. "How about a drink?" By two in the morning the bottle was empty and the two generals were pals, swearing like boys to have no secrets from one another. Thereafter they attended briefings sitting in the front row, their arms around each other's shoulders.[56]

Breaking out from the Cotentin peninsula, half of Patton's troops went west, to conquer Brittany and seize its ports. The remainder of the Third Army covered the right flank of the First Army as it pushed east. The tank columns of both armies advanced with a flight of Thunderbolts overhead from dawn to dusk.

Column cover involved both close support and armed reconnaissance: the fighter-bombers would scout the road ahead, armed with a mixture of five-hundred-pounders for fixed defenses and fragmentation bombs for trucks and personnel.

On other missions the Thunderbolts operated in twelve-plane squadrons: two flights to dive-bomb, one to provide top cover. After the assigned target had been bombed, the squadron would fly armed recon beyond the bomb line (a position identified by prominent landmarks from a few hundred yards to a mile or so ahead of the ground troops) or returned to base strafing targets of opportunity. Strafing proved surprisingly effective against tanks: if they were caught on a hard-surfaced road it was possible to ricochet fifty-caliber bullets off the asphalt and into the engine. Five-inch rockets proved too inaccurate to knock out tanks, but the sight of rocket-firing fighter-bombers could terrorize German armor crews into abandoning them.

Although it was effective, tactical air came at a high price. The Ninth's loss rate was 1.2 per 100 sorties in the summer of 1944, but its groups were flying fifty to sixty missions a month. The result was a monthly loss rate of 20–25 percent, due mainly to ground fire. It was hard to keep a Tactical Air Command at full strength when fighting was intense.[57]

With reports pouring in to Hitler's headquarters that American troops were heading both east and west, it looked to him that they were overextended and wide open to attack. He ordered a counterattack by seven panzer and panzer grenadier divisions. The blow would fall first on Mortain, a town twenty-five miles southeast of the Cotentin. With Mortain in his hands, he intended to drive on across the base of the peninsula, cut off at least six U.S. divisions and destroy them.[58]

The counterattack began early on August 7; the day's weather forecast was for fog, persisting until afternoon. German troops had come to dread the *Jabos* (from *Jagdbomber*)—the fighter-bombers. When dawn broke, the sky was mortally clear.

Instead of advancing confidently, many Germans dug in. The GAF was pledged to a maximum effort in support of this attack. Ultra revealed Hitler's plans late on August 6.[59] Next day IX TAC, the RAF and two groups from XIX TAC put nearly one thousand fighters into the air to keep the GAF at bay. The Germans flew about one hundred sorties. Not one is known to have penetrated as far as Mortain. Thirty-three enemy planes were reported shot down.

The Mortain counterattack was a colossal blunder. It petered out ignominiously after thirty-six hours. Its collapse threw the German Seventh Army and Fifth Panzer Army into full retreat toward the Seine.

During the Mortain operation Brereton was removed from command of the Ninth. He was kicked upstairs, to command the First Allied Airborne Army. It got him out of the way of Bradley, and his three stars would help prevent the British from completely taking over the FAAA.[60] The Ninth was assigned to Vandenberg, to Quesada's grief. Vandenberg had no command experience in war, but he was close to Spaatz.

As the Germans pulled out of Normandy, Bradley moved to trap them. Montgomery had finally moved beyond Caen and was heading southeast toward Falaise. Bradley turned three American divisions north. Their objective was Argentan, not far from Falaise.

The roads through the Argentan-Falaise gap were soon jammed with German troops and vehicles trying to escape. Between August 11 and August 17, IX TAC and the Second TAF strafed and bombed ceaselessly. Aircraft destroyed as many as eleven thousand enemy vehicles, creating carnage beyond anything American soldiers had ever seen or expected to see.[61]

All the same, both Bradley and Montgomery made serious errors, which allowed as many as fifty thousand Germans and ten thousand vehicles to cross the Seine.[62] Once again the lack of night reconnaissance aircraft placed limits on what air could do to block the retreat of a skilled, tenacious foe.

Two German armies had nonetheless been destroyed. American and French troops closed on Paris. The GAF had concentrated its planes on fields north and east of the city and chose to fight before quitting France. American pilots suddenly got more opportunities for dogfights than they'd come to expect. The day the city was liberated, August 25, the Ninth Air Force claimed 127 enemy planes. Weyland's 354th Group, the oldest Mustang outfit in the

ETO, claimed 38 in the air and 13 on the ground, losing four planes.[63]

By this time XIX TAC was spread out all over the map. The Brittany campaign had run into trouble at Brest, where twenty thousand German construction workers (really combat engineers) joined with several thousand paratroopers to wage one of the epic defensive battles of the war. Taking Brest would cost ten thousand American casualties. Weyland deplored having to use his fighter-bombers in what amounted to street fighting. Thunderbolts were attacking individual houses.

Anderson's IX Bomber Command was hitting the city with strikes involving hundreds of B-26s and A-20s nearly every day. On August 26 the Eighth joined it with an attack by 171 B-17s.[64] RAF Bomber Command also attacked the town. It was bombarded from the sea by large warships. Despite such pounding Brest would hold out until September 18, by which time the port was too far from the front to be used.

While the battle for Brest was coming to a head, Patton was pushing his tanks across north-central France, skirting Paris on the south and east. He had an open right flank for more than three hundred miles along the Loire. He relied on Weyland's pilots to guard that flank.

Weyland's staff worked out which railroad lines the Germans would try to use, and XIX TAC interdicted them. The Resistance harassed the German units which tried to use the roads by night. Weyland's *Jabos* clobbered them when they tried to use the roads by day.

The result was that on September 16 a German general at the head of twenty thousand troops who'd tried to march to Germany from Bordeaux gave up. The *Jabos,* said the general, made it too costly to move in daylight and the downed bridges made it impossible to cross the river. Weyland was asked to take the surrender.[65]

Mid-September found Patton thrusting into northeastern France, heading for Germany but running out of gas. Doolittle tried to keep him going by filling B-24s with gasoline. They landed at Weyland's fighter strips, tearing them to shreds. The fuel was hand pumped into Patton's tanks to keep them rolling. It helped, but it wasn't enough.

The First Army had been stopped by the German defenses along the West Wall and the Third Army had ground to a halt only thirty miles short of German soil. Had it not been for Brest, thought

Weyland, it might have been possible, just, to keep Patton's tanks rolling all the way into Germany.[66]

The Army had thirty divisions ready to ship to France during the Normandy campaign, but neither England or northern France had the port capacity to keep them supplied. Eisenhower had to capture another major port. He opted for Marseilles.

Southwestern France was defended by the German Nineteenth Army—seven infantry divisions plus the 11th Panzer Division. To defeat this force, the U.S. Seventh Army, commanded by Lieutenant General Alexander Patch, would land on the beaches of the French Riviera, take Marseilles, then drive north along the river Rhone into central France. This invasion, code-named Dragoon, would be mounted August 15.

Three weeks before the assault Mediterranean Allied Air Forces began a counterair campaign against GAF airfields in southern France and northern Italy. A bridge busting campaign dropped most of the bridges crossing the Rhone, and a mini-Transportation Plan was employed against the railroads. Hundreds of tons of weapons and supplies were dropped to French Resistance groups harassing the Germans. The GAF offered no serious opposition to any part of the air campaign.[67]

As in Overlord, troop carrier opened the invasion with an air assault. A division-size airborne force of ten thousand men had been created out of various U.S. and British paratroop and glider units. It was carried into battle by a Provisional Troop Carrier Division formed from the 50th and 53rd Troop Carrier Wings, deployed from England, and the 51st TCW, which was still in the Mediterranean. Major General Paul L. Williams arrived from his IX Troop Carrier Command headquarters to train and command the division.

On August 14 MAAF flew more than five thousand sorties against beach defenses, radar sites, airfields, railroads and enemy shipping. In the early hours of August 15 troop carrier C-47s flew the Pathfinders over the Riviera. Sea mist forced pilots to climb to two thousand feet before dropping Pathfinders. Nearly all fell to earth far from where they'd expected.[68]

At H-Hour (eight in the morning) the main drop began, ten miles inland. More than half the paratroopers were put on their drop zones, despite the fact that few Pathfinders had turned on their beacons. Troop carrier crews returned to Italy, rested for several hours, and in late afternoon flew over the invasion fleet towing several hundred gliders to reinforce the air assault.

In the two weeks following the assault, troop carrier planes flew thousands of resupply sorties. "We were dropping condoms, *Stars and Stripes,* what have you," according to Lieutenant William Taylor, a navigator in the 438th Troop Carrier Group, "so this was almost like a vacation for us. The base [at Civitacchia, north of Rome] was really grungy and we were absolutely driven crazy by fleas. . . . I was dusting my sleeping bag all the time. It was like trying to get cockroaches out of a New York apartment."[69]

By the time of Dragoon, Brigadier General Gordon P. Saville's XII TAC was the most experienced air support outfit in the AAF. It was about to reap its biggest harvest. The French divisions participating in Dragoon insisted on taking Marseilles. The Americans drove up the Rhone Valley led by an armored force that tried, on August 26–27, to trap the retreating Germans. As at the Argentan-Falaise gap, a daring effort narrowly failed.[70]

Bill Colgan, the Thunderbolt pilot (whose first mission, to Salerno, was related on page 225), had returned to the U.S. for leave after flying 115 missions in Italy. He rejoined the 79th Fighter Group on Corsica shortly before Dragoon. On August 28 he was ordered to lead an armed recon flight beyond the bomb line, now about fifty miles up the Rhone Valley. The bomb line was usually a series of features about a mile ahead of the last reported position of friendly troops. Anything moving beyond this line was considered enemy and was open to attack. As a rule, though, movement in daylight was rare.

Colgan reported: "The bomb line had never been wrong, but what we saw now made us wonder a bit about the possibility . . . the roads were full of vehicles and equipment. . . . Down there was a wide variety of vehicles, from first-rate tools of war to horse-drawn wagons. As we went north what we saw below became downright hard to believe. Now vehicles were moving north side-by-side and even three abreast for some smaller types. In time we had flown past about *thirty miles of solid traffic. . . .* [original italics] When we reached the spearhead there would surely be no horse-drawn vehicles, but instead a solid mass of tough stuff, and all the automatic weapons that could be gathered. . . . We reached the spearhead near the town of Montelimar. I gave the briefing over the radio. Red flight would attack the very lead elements and attempt to get some good fires going. . . . While knowing full well what was coming, in that last second before our next move I couldn't help thinking what a tremendous sight of war we were seeing there on the ground. . . . I rolled in on the attack and the expected reaction from below came quickly and strongly. I was partially dazed [but] I could see a huge hole in the right wing where my guns and ammo bays had been. The barrels of the two remaining inboard guns were twisted like pretzels. That round hit the wing before I ever completed the roll in. . . . I continued the attack."[71]

Colgan made a second pass, this time igniting a fuel truck. Exploding fuel and ammo at the spearhead would halt the entire column. Colgan's P-47 took a second hit, this time right in the engine. The other three planes in Red flight were shot down. He managed to nurse his burning Thunderbolt nearly one hundred miles back to base to report the halted column, which represented the Nineteenth Army in full flight. Saville threw everything he had into destroying the entire thirty-mile column. For two days it was blasted and burned. Thousands of vehicles were destroyed. As Seventh Army troops advanced, demoralized Germans threw their hands in the air, shouted *"Kamerad!"* and shuffled into captivity.

Arnold arrived a week later. Saville took him to see the charred hulks blackening the road from Montelimar to Valence from the backseat of an L-5. When the L-5 landed Arnold told Eaker, "You give Saville the DSM."[72] Colgan had to settle for a Silver Star.

By September 11 troops who'd landed in southern France linked up with Patton's patrols. Nearly all France had been freed and the skies were 10/10 Allied air.

20

WHOOSH!

Various people, including the President and Barney Giles, had tried to interest Arnold in negotiating with the Soviets for the use of Red Air Force bases to extend the reach of the AAF. Giles proposed having the Eighth fly from its bases in England, bomb targets in the Third Reich, fly on to land in the Soviet Union, refuel, bomb up, and attack other strategic targets on the way back. Not until after visiting England in September 1943 did Arnold take to the idea.

With the Eighth both performing under par and taking heavy losses, he suddenly envisaged shuttles coming to the rescue of daylight precision bombing.[1] Whatever was said for public consumption, Ploesti and the Schweinfurt-Regensburg mission were severe setbacks. Something had to be done to prevent the Combined Bomber Offensive from failing. Creating the Fifteenth Air Force was one response. Shuttle bombing to and from the Soviet Union was another.

In December Stalin personally agreed to the project at the Tehran conference. Still, the paranoia and terror of Stalin's rule hadn't been suspended. His minions consistently proved to be difficult and argumentative. They would allow in only half the twenty-two hundred people the AAF wanted to send to Red Air Force bases in the Ukraine to service American planes. They acted as if they were doing the United States a huge favor in enabling American airmen to attack what the Soviets themselves called "the Fascist Beast."

Three airfields were made available near Kiev: at Poltava, Piryatin, and Mirgorod. Not one had a hard surfaced runway. None had anything remotely resembling the facilities of an American airfield. Thousands of tons of steel mat had to be shipped to them, along with huge stocks of fuel and bombs, from which the Soviets stole gladly.[2]

By June 1944 the shuttle-bombing operation, code-named Frantic, was ready. On June 2 the Fifteenth Air Force sent 104 B-17s, escorted by 64 Mustangs, to attack a marshalling yard in Hungary. Only one plane was lost, exploding mysteriously over the target.[3] The rest of the force flew on and landed at Poltava.* Two days later it bombed GAF airfields in Poland. And on June 6 the bombers and their escorts flew back to Italy, bombing yet another GAF airfield on the way. Thanks to Overlord these events didn't attract much attention.

On June 21 the Eighth flew its first Frantic mission. A force of 114 B-17s from the 13th and 45th Combat Wings of the 3rd Air Division would bomb a synthetic oil plant fifty miles south of Berlin and fly on to Poltava. The mission would be led by Colonel Archie Old.

Escort was provided by fifty-four Mustangs from the 4th Fighter Group plus a squadron from the 352nd. At the briefing, the P-51 pilots had simply stared in disbelief at the long red ribbons stretching all the way from England to four hundred miles beyond the Soviet border. They were in for an eight-hour flight, in a seat not made with comfort in mind. Don Blakeslee would lead the fighters.

The Eighth sent a one thousand-bomber raid against Berlin as a diversion; but a target defended by two thousand flak guns was no milk run. Captain Harry Crosby, group navigator of the 100th on the flight to Poltava said, "The most impressive sight was our glimpse of Berlin. As we passed by we all vocally pitied the poor devils who drew it as their target for the day. There was the usual cloud of flak. . . . We saw a few B-24s go down as their turn came."[4]

Near Warsaw a dozen 109s attacked Old's bombers. Blakeslee and his pilots could only look on: they lacked the fuel to engage in combat. The Mustangs were there to bluff the GAF, not to mix it up.[5] Only one Fortress went down. Near the Soviet border, a Mustang was downed by flak. The plane carried marked maps and other

---

*This mission was led by Lt. Gen. Ira Eaker, CG, MAAF, flying as copilot in *Yankee Doodle II.*

documents that revealed most of the Frantic operation to German intelligence.[6]

Old, meanwhile, led his force on to Poltava. The P-51s set down at Piryatin. Guided by the captured documents, the GAF prepared to strike Poltava. That night German planes flew overhead, dropping flares to illuminate the field, followed by 110 tons of high explosive, incendiaries and antipersonnel butterfly bombs. Nearly fifty B-17s were destroyed or beyond repair.[7] This was the second-most costly air raid the AAF ever suffered, exceeded only by the debacle at Clark Field on December 8, 1941.

On June 26 Old led the surviving Fortresses and Mustangs to Italy, bombing a synthetic oil plant in Poland on the way. The German attack had wiped out Poltava's stocks of fuel and bombs. While the base was being restocked and repaired, Spaatz and Eaker tried to keep Frantic going with fighter sweeps. On July 22 the Fifteenth flew a fighter sweep over Romania with Lightnings and Mustangs. The planes landed in the Ukraine. They attacked airfields around Bucharest on the way back to Foggia. There were more sweeps in early August by the Fifteenth's P-38 groups.

On August 6 the Eighth returned to Poltava, sending seventy-six B-17s and sixty-four Mustangs to attack the Focke-Wulf plant at Gdynia, in Poland. Next day the bombers struck a synthetic oil plant. And on August 8 they headed for Italy, bombing Romanian airfields en route.

In the closing days of July the Red Army had reached the banks of the Vistula. Across the river stood occupied Warsaw. On August 1, encouraged by a message on Moscow radio, the Polish underground rose to drive the Germans out. For the next six weeks the German Army brutally suppressed the uprising. Suggestions that the AAF and the RAF drop arms, food and medical supplies to the heroic Polish resistance were evaded or brushed aside by the Soviets.[8] Stalin and his commissars were content to see the Germans kill thousands of the most patriotic and courageous people in Poland. It would make Soviet occupation easier.

The Warsaw uprising really spelled the end of Frantic. The Eighth was permitted one more shuttle bombing mission, which was flown on September 11–13. It involved an attack on an arms factory on the way to Poltava and an attack on a steel plant on the flight to Foggia. This was the most successful Frantic mission of all. One of the plants that was bombed, at Chemnitz, produced all the tank engines for German Panthers and Tigers. The bombing sparked a conflagration that ignited the oil in the machine tools and closed the plant for six months.[9]

The last Frantic mission, allowed by Stalin as the Red Army moved into Warsaw, was an air drop by 3rd Air Division on September 13. The British, with their night-bombing ability, had been dropping supplies at night, but the Eighth could operate effectively only in daylight, hence the need to secure Soviet cooperation. Nearly thirteen hundred containers were dropped on Warsaw. Even though it was day, the Poles retrieved only one in ten; the withdrawing Germans got the rest.[10]

Following the creation of the First Allied Airborne Army under Lewis Brereton, eighteen plans were drawn up for airborne operations in the space of a month. Most were discarded after Allied troops overran the planned objectives. Others were scrapped because they were aimed at helping American troops advance. Brereton's British deputy, Lieutenant General Frederick Browning, saw the airborne army as an instrument created to aid Monty, not Bradley, and threatened to resign to get his way.[11]

This in turn put pressure on Montgomery: use them or lose them. He hastily put together an ambitious plan to drop the airborne troops in Holland to enable him to cross the lower Rhine. The aim was to grab six big bridges, a dozen canal crossings and a variety of small bridges along a sixty-five-mile-corridor from Nijmegen in southern Holland to Arnhem. The U.S. 82nd and 101st Airborne divisions would seize the bridges along the corridor and keep the road open for the British tanks. A British armored division would drive north from the Belgian border, covering the sixty-five miles in two days. British and Polish airborne troops would land at Arnhem. This operation, code named Market-Garden, would be mounted on September 17, despite clear intelligence that two panzer divisions were refitting near Arnhem.[12]

British troop carrier capacity was severely limited. Williams's IX Troop Carrier Command would have to take 30,500 men into action; the RAF would take the other 4,500. In any sound plan the entire force would have been put into action within twenty-four hours, but Brereton arbitrarily ruled that out. He had no experience of airborne operations. And while Browning was known as "the father of the British airborne," he was a senior staff officer and had never made a combat jump. Brereton ruled out two lifts in one day as being too hard on troop carrier pilots. Williams could (and probably should) have told him that only one month earlier, in Dragoon, hundreds of these pilots had flown two missions in one day over similar distances.[13]

In the early hours of September 17 RAF Bomber Command struck German defenses in Holland. At dawn on this bright, sunny Sunday morning, 852 B-17s rumbled overhead, dropping 3,000 tons on 117 German flak batteries. Then came VIII Fighter Command's four Thunderbolt groups (56th, 78th, 353rd, 365th) on the most hated mission of them all—"flak-busting." This consisted of flying over camouflaged flak batteries until the gunners revealed their positions by opening up. Assuming the pilot wasn't shot down, he was then expected to dive-bomb the flak guns with 260-pound frag bombs. After which he made a second pass, strafing.

As the nearly 200 Thunderbolts roared away from flak-busting, long lines of troop carrier planes droned over the Dutch coast: 1,550 C-47s, nearly 500 gliders, escorted by more than 1,000 fighters. By noon half the airborne army was on Dutch soil. Virtually everyone had landed on or near his assigned DZ.[14]

Next day the weather over England was miserable. It was better over Holland. The reinforcement drop had to be scaled down. A supply drop by 256 B-24s from the 2nd Air Division went ahead. The 56th and 78th Fighter groups flew flak-busting missions to clear the way for the Liberators. Even so, sixteen B-24s were lost to AAA. And of the thirty-eight Thunderbolts committed by 56th Group fifteen were shot down—the worst one day loss the group ever suffered.[15]

Meanwhile more than one hundred German fighters tried to break through the escort. They were intercepted by the Mustangs of the 357th and 359th fighter groups. In a swirling, low-level dogfight over dikes and canals, the 357th shot down twenty-six enemy aircraft, for a loss of two Mustangs.[16] The 359th scored only a 2–2 draw.

Market-Garden involved too many compromises and too many risks to succeed without an abundance of good luck. The weather forced repeated postponements of reinforcement drops, while the Germans got steadily stronger. The armored drive from Nijmegen to Arnhem took five days, not two. It was the enemy who seemed to get the breaks. On September 21 the GAF managed to penetrate Allied fighter defenses, shooting down most of the thirty-five transports and bombers lost that day.

One of the planes that fell to flak was a C-47 of the 315th Troop Carrier Group, flown by Second Lieutenant Cecil H. Dawkins. He was carrying men from the Polish Parachute Brigade. As the green light went on for the paratroopers to jump, the C-47 took a hit, wounding Dawkins in the head and face. The paratroopers started jumping.

"We continued to be hit by really heavy stuff," recorded Dawkins, "and the light stuff was like flying through a rainstorm. The left engine and wing were burning, we were now at three hundred feet and I had no aileron or elevator control.

"My crew chief rushed up to the cockpit and helped me get my copilot out from behind his controls. When they ran to the rear of the plane, the nose lifted up and at about three hundred feet my crew bailed out. . . .

"Then things got tough. The plane's nose dropped again. My parachute, still hanging on the back of my seat, exploded, and then a really heavy blast went off under the cockpit. The next thing I remember was that I was on the back of a Kraut tank roaring down a blacktop road. I was mighty confused! I was stiff as a board and bleeding profusely, and just able to recognize a P-47 making a strafing run from the rear. I rolled off the tank and into a ditch. . . ."[17]

At nightfall the British started withdrawing from Arnhem. All the same, half of Holland had been liberated by American troops.

Market-Garden was the biggest operation mounted by IX Troop Carrier Command, and the costliest. Ninety eight of its planes, mainly C-47s, were shot down.

In Market-Garden VIII Fighter Command claimed 139 aerial victories, but lost fifty-eight planes, mostly P-47s shot down while flak-busting.[18] By the time the operation drew to its dreary close many of the pilots who had made this command legendary, like Don Blakeslee, were flying desks. Others, like Francis Gabreski, who'd become its highest scoring pilot with 28 aerial victories, were prisoners of war. Still others were dead. And Kepner had left to run the troubled 2nd Air Division.

Hub Zemke, however, was still flying, with more than 152 missions to his credit. In August he'd handed over the 56th to Dave Schilling, his best squadron commander, and taken over the 479th Group, a P-38 outfit with problems. Zemke retrained its pilots to fly and fight his way.

By late September the 479th was transitioning to Mustangs and the group was flying missions to help suppress the GAF's attacks on the two U.S. airborne divisions in eastern Holland. On September 26 it tangled with a force of German fighters along the Dutch-German border. In less than twenty minutes the group shot down twenty-nine enemy aircraft, for the loss of one P-38. Zemke, flying a Mustang, raised his personal tally of confirmed kills in the air to fifteen and a half. A month later he scored again. On October 30, Zemke was shot down. He spent the rest of the war behind wire. Kepner wrote Zemke's wife, "He was the best Fighter Group commander I have ever known."[19]

In two years of Eighth Air Force operations there had been nothing resembling the repeated heavy attacks on vital industrial targets that the Maxwell theorists and the authors of AWPD-1 had envisaged. Ball bearings had been hit, oil had been hit, chemicals had been hit, the electrical industry had been hit and aircraft plants had been hit—only to be allowed to recover. The need to secure air superiority had elbowed strategic bombing aside, and after that had been won, the needs of the invasion had taken priority.

In September Eisenhower's control of the strategic bombers came to an end. Spaatz and Doolittle marked the occasion with a three-day offensive against oil, September 11–13. Massive attacks by the Eighth's B-17s struck synthetic oil plants, oil storage depots and oil refineries.

The GAF had more than twenty-five hundred single-engine fighters concentrated in western Germany to meet the renewed strategic offensive. And German heavy flak batteries had proliferated during the summer like mushrooms after rain. September 11–13 brought huge air battles every day and denser flak than had ever been seen before. At the end of the three days a total of 125 heavy bombers had been shot down, along with 54 fighters.[20]

Fuel shortages had curbed Luftwaffe pilot training severely since the spring. Young men were going into combat with only about 100 hours, compared to an American pilot's 350 or more. But while the quality of German fighter pilots was going down, the quality of the planes they flew was rising alarmingly. By the fall of 1944 the GAF was receiving jet fighters.

It had also organized several *Sturm Staffeln,* squadrons equipped with the FW-190A/8, a plane designed specifically to shoot down B-17s. The 190-A/8 had an armor-plated cockpit, with bulletproof glass, and carried two 12.7mm machine guns, two 20mm cannon, and two 30mm cannon. Its pilots were trained to close on a heavy bomber from the rear and ride out the storm of fifty-caliber bullets fired from the tail turret. *Sturm Staffel* pilots were expected, if all else failed, to ram. Some did so. A few even survived the experience. Me-109s provided top cover for the less-maneuverable 190-A/8 as it went about its deadly business.[21]

On September 23 the Combined Chiefs endorsed Spaatz's strategic campaign with a directive that placed oil as the first priority. German ammunition, tank and truck plants were equal seconds. The Reich had ninety-one crude, synthetic, and oil-substitute plants in operation.[22] Knocking even half of them out would be difficult.

Moreover, for much of September the Liberators of the 2nd Air Division were occupied flying gasoline to France. The devastation of the French railroads by Transportation Plan attacks in the spring had created logistical chaos for American soldiers after the Normandy breakout.

The German army in France had been destroyed by mid-September, but there was another German army to be fought—the one defending Germany's borders. There would be numerous heavy raids that fall against that army's communications, especially the railroads. Getting across the Rhine was shaping up as another D-Day, another invasion. As in the months before June 6, strategic bombing would be split mainly between oil attacks and marshalling yards.

The biggest oil and chemical complex in Germany was centered around the towns of Merseburg and Leuna. The second biggest concentration was at Ludwigshafen. These names would soon be etched forever on the minds of the Eighth's bomber aircrews. On September 27 more than eleven hundred heavies struck Ludwigshafen and Cologne.

The 445th Bomb Group sent out thirty-eight Liberators on this mission. When the group strayed away from its escort it was mauled by a squadron of FW-190/A-8s. In the space of three minutes, twenty-six B-24s went down. Then a Mustang squadron from the 361st Fighter Group arrived like the cavalry and shot down eighteen 109s and 190s. The 445th had suffered the biggest one-mission loss by any heavy bomb group all war.[23]

Next day the Eighth dispatched one thousand bombers to attack Merseburg-Leuna. Second Lieutenant Bill Duane, a navigator in the 388th Bomb Group, kept a diary. The entry for September 28 read, "With this being our 13th mission I anticipated a hot one. . . . The bomb run was 13 miles long. About 2½ minutes before bombs away we got intense and very accurate flak. About a minute later King, the flight engineer, was hit in both legs. He fell down into the passageway. . . . I took off my flak suit, cut open five layers of clothes [and] applied a tourniquet. All this took place in some very intense and tracking flak—and me without my helmet! Interphone was shot out so I started back to the flight deck to inform the pilot. . . . Finally came the blanket and the first-aid kits. In the meantime I had given King some morphine but it was a hell of a job as it froze up and we had to experiment several times jabbing King's leg before I discovered how it worked. I wrapped King's legs in blankets and tried to keep them warm. . . . Three ships went down over the target after a collision. I hope that we won't see anything like this again."[24]

There were more than one thousand heavy flak guns defending the Merseburg-Leuna area. At least thirty heavies went down in flames that day. Hardest hit was the 303rd Bomb Group, which lost eleven planes. GAF fighter pilots were continuing their tactic of picking one group and attacking it relentlessly.

On October 7 Doolittle sent thirteen hundred bombers to hit oil, a tank factory and an aero-engine plant. The GAF put up four hundred fighters. The Eighth lost fifty-two bombers and fifteen Mustangs shot down; a dozen crippled aircraft crash-landed.

Five days later Doolittle dispatched one thousand bombers to marshalling yards and an airfield in the Bremen area. Eleven groups of fighters provided escort. The 357th Group had two squadrons keep within sight of the bombers, while the third ranged one hundred miles ahead. The squadron out front was led by Second Lieutenant Chuck Yeager. So far he had only one confirmed kill, but he boasted fantastic eyesight. He could see specks before anyone else in the group.

That hadn't saved him from being shot down over France in March. He'd been smuggled into Spain by the French underground and was allowed to return to operations only after making a personal appeal to Eisenhower. An AAF rule said no escaper could fly combat again: if he fell into German hands a second time he might be tortured to turn in those brave people who'd helped him escape. But with most of France now liberated, Ike waived the rule for Yeager.

Yeager reported, "When we were over Steinhuder Lake I spotted specks about fifty miles ahead. . . . We were at twenty-eight thousand feet and closing fast. Soon, I was able to count twenty-two individual specks. I figured they were Me-109s, just sitting up there, waiting for our bombers. . . . They didn't see us coming at them out of the sun. We closed to about a thousand yards. . . . I came in behind their tail-end charlie and was about to begin hammering him, when he suddenly broke left and ran into his wingman. They both bailed out. It was almost comic, scoring two quick victories without firing a shot . . . the big shortage in Germany was not of airplanes but of pilots, and they were probably under orders to jump for it in tight spots. . . . By now all the airplanes in the sky were spinning and diving in a wild, wide-open dogfight. I blew up a 109 from six hundred yards. . . . I turned around and I saw another angling in behind me. Man, I pulled back on my throttle so damned hard I nearly stalled, rolled up and over, came in behind and under him, kicking right rudder and simultaneously firing. I was directly underneath that guy, less than fifty feet, and I opened up that 109 as if it were a can of Spam. That made four. A moment later I waxed a guy's fanny in a steep dive; I pulled up at about a thousand feet; he went straight into the ground." Yeager was the Eighth's first "Ace in a Day."[25]

The GAF made few big attacks that month. There was no shortage of planes, but as Yeager had deduced, the Luftwaffe was running out of men, not machines. In November 1944 the GAF's front line fighter strength had risen to three thousand planes. Fortunately it couldn't maintain and fly more than half the fighters on hand.

On November 2 the Eighth sent 1,100 bombers and 800 fighters to attack Merseburg-Leuna and various rail targets. This time the GAF put up 500 fighters, mainly over the oil plants. In one of the biggest air battles of the war 40 bombers went down, along with 28 of the escorting fighters. The Eighth could easily make good a loss like this, but for the GAF fighter arm its loss of 120 fighters, including 70 pilots killed, was a disaster.[26]

Throughout November the Eighth mounted four raids a week with more than one thousand heavies against oil and transportation targets. The GAF rose in force to contest only a few of these attacks, such as the one on Merseburg-Leuna on November 21. The Eighth lost 34 bombers and fighters shot down; GAF losses were twice that. On November 26 Doolittle attacked German railroads, and the Luftwaffe put up 550 fighters. Nearly 50 bombers went down, but so did more than 100 fighters. The extent to which the Germans' lack of training left many of them fatally mismatched was demonstrated by Lieutenant Jack Daniell of the 339th Fighter Group. Daniell became an Ace in a Day flying his first combat mission.[27]

On November 27 500 heavies attacked oil and rail targets and the Germans mounted their biggest aerial defense of the war—750 fighters. German Air Force controllers had trouble handling so many planes, and directed them straight into half a dozen Mustang groups flying escort. Eleven P-51s went down, but the GAF lost nearly 100 fighters.[28] The real opposition to strategic bombing now didn't come from 109s or 190s; it came from the flak. In November the Eighth had lost only 50 heavies to fighters, despite three days when the GAF had more than 500 fighters in the air. Flak, on the other hand, had cost Doolittle nearly 200 bombers.[29]

By the end of 1944 the Luftwaffe had thirty thousand flak guns defending the Reich. Its flak batteries, whether heavy and operated by radar, or light and dependent on hand-eye coordination, commanded the absolute respect of American airmen, with the possible exception of some C-47 crews.

"We caught a lot of ground fire," according to Lieutenant William Taylor, a navigator with the 438th Troop Carrier Group, "but the Germans never learned to lead C-47s enough. It may have been the fact that we seemed to be flying more slowly than we actually were. The result of this was that 90 percent of the ground fire that we caught went into the toilet at the back of the plane."[30]

The flak-busting missions flown on the first day of Market-Garden helped ensure the success of IX Troop Carrier Command's parachute and glider drops. The second day, however, when the flak gunners were alerted and knew what to expect, cost the 56th Group dearly. As Quesada remarked, "flak-busting was like a man biting a dog."[31]

The steady flight of heavy bombers in large formations at altitudes between twenty-five and twenty-eight thousand feet also simplified the flak gunners' task, especially with the development of gun-laying radar. Doolittle's heavy bomb groups were equipped with electronic countermeasures (ECM) to jam enemy radar, but ECM was a fairly crude technology still.

To supplement it, there was "window" or "chaff." This consisted of strips of aluminum foil, like Christmas tree tinsel. Bomber crews were given bales of the stuff and told to throw out a few strips at a time, to create an electronic blizzard on enemy radar screens. Not surprisingly, window got thrown out in handfuls, or by the arm-load. During intense flak, entire bales would hurtle through bomber formations, glittering and sparkling as they came apart.[32]

Despite ECM and window, in the fall of 1944 German flak destroyed or damaged so many planes on some missions that accurate bombing was simply impossible. In three attacks on the sprawling synthetic oil plant at Leuna in October, for example, not one bomb fell on the plant, yet 119 bombers were shot down trying to hit it.[33]

Individually, flak guns were hopelessly inaccurate. The most common heavy flak weapon, the eighty-eight-millimeter Flak-36, fired more than sixteen thousand rounds for every aircraft brought down.[34] The fact that much of this ammunition was made by German slave labor may have accounted for the high proportion of duds it contained. There was even a case of eleven twenty-millimeter cannon shells penetrating the fuel tanks of a B-17 flown by the 379th Bomb Group without exploding. Inside one of the shells, taken by technical intelligence for examination, was a note in Czech that read, "This is all we can do for you now."[35]

The biggest weakness in German antiaircraft artillery was its obsolescent fuses. Hitler's scientists tried but failed to master the proximity fuse. This fuse generated a radio wave, which bounced back from the target. Once the reflected signal reached a strength that indicated close proximity, the shell would explode. British scientists met the proximity fuse challenge with a simple, elegant solution—they made the shell casing the aerial that sent and received the radio signal.[36]

Had the Germans produced proximity fuses, the Luftwaffe's flak would have been at least three times more effective. For much of the war Arnold and Spaatz worried about how German research on proximity fuses was coming along.[37]

As it was, despite the inaccuracy of individual guns, the massed firepower of Luftwaffe flak batteries took a terrible toll in lives, crippling wounds and lost aircraft. By the time the war ended, German fighters had shot down forty-three hundred AAF planes in the ETO; AAA brought down nearly fifty-four hundred.[38]

Gordon P. Saville couldn't help remembering Laurence Kuter's famous observation back at the Tactical School before the war: "While antiaircraft fire may be annoying, it should be ignored."

"Gee," thought Saville as he flew through flak and watched

planes fall in flames around him, "I sure wish Kuter was here to ignore this!"[39]

In the fall of 1944 a new threat arose to challenge the AAF for air superiority over Europe—the Me-262 jet fighter. This aircraft was no secret to Arnold and Spaatz. Long before any Allied pilot saw one, they knew what it would look like, that it would fly one hundred miles per hour faster than the Mustang, that it would burn cheap, easy-to-obtain kerosene instead of high-octane aviation fuel. British intelligence had even obtained GAF instructors' manuals, which explained how to fly one from takeoff to landing.[40]

There was a nagging fear that only a jet could counter another jet. If so, the AAF was in deep trouble. American aeronautical engineers had known since the early 1920s that a jet engine was feasible, but it seemed so fuel inefficient that it offered no major advantages over a piston engine. What they hadn't realized was that a jet engine needn't weigh very much. A small, lightweight jet engine in a small, lightweight airplane wouldn't be inefficient at all.[41] In the late 1930s Flight Lieutenant Frank Whittle convinced the RAF to let him try to build a jet engine. A German engineer named Otto Haine, meanwhile, was pressing a similar project on the GAF. When Arnold went to England in April 1941 he was shown the Gloster E28/39 jet airplane, which was about to undergo flight tests.

On his return Arnold ordered General Electric to build fifteen engines based on Whittle's design, and Bell Aircraft was told to build the airplane. On October 2, 1942, the Bell XP-59A made its official maiden flight; a Bell test pilot had already been airborne in it. The plane had been built so rapidly and in such secrecy that the normal methods of testing and improvement were skipped. As a result, the XP-59A flew no faster than a P-51.[42]

All the same, enough had been learned to create a foundation for an all-American design, the XP-80, to be produced by Lockheed. This aircraft was expected to be a match for the Me-262, but it wouldn't be ready before the spring of 1945.

The Me-262 promised to give the Germans a huge technological advantage in aerial combat. Hitler hoped to fling hundreds of Me-262s against the invasion of France, and in June Allied pilots were briefed on the possibility of running into jet fighters. They were told their best bet was to slow down, and out-turn it.[43] Although awesomely fast, the Me-262 was not highly maneuverable.

In the event, there was no jet challenge on D-Day. Junkers was wrestling with awesome technical difficulties. The tremendous heat of a jet engine called for large amounts of nickel and chrome; both were in short supply in the Third Reich. It took Junker's engineers until the summer of 1944 to get around these shortages by using steel in new ways.[44] The first Me-262 squadron became operational at the end of July, just as the Allies broke out from Normandy. It conducted some ineffective bombing from thirteen thousand feet.

The first aerial clash came on August 28 when Major Joseph Myers, a 78th Fighter Group pilot, was leading a flight of Thunderbolts on a top cover mission near Brussels. "I caught sight of what appeared to be a B-26 flying at about five hundred feet and heading in a southerly direction and going very fast. I immediately started down to investigate. When approximately five thousand feet above and very nearly directly over the aircraft, I could see it was not a B-26. It was painted slate blue in color, with a long rounded nose. . . . I closed to within two thousand feet above him. . . . At this distance I could readily see the similarity between the aircraft and the recognition plates of the Me-262. . . . I gradually started closing on the enemy and drew up to within five hundred yards astern and was about to open fire when the enemy aircraft cut his throttle and crash landed in a ploughed field. He hit the ground just as I fired. . . . It skipped over several fields and came to rest and caught fire. The pilot hopped out and started to run."[45]

By October 1944 the Me-262 was going into mass production. The Luftwaffe had an experimental unit, *Kommando Nowotny,* equipped with forty planes and eager to show what their jet fighter could do against American bombers. The four thirty-millimeter cannon in the nose, angled to converge at four hundred yards, weren't the ideal armament for dogfighting a Mustang, but they made the Me-262 a deadly peril to B-17s and B-24s. Arnold and the Air Staff were biting their nails.[46] The whole air war, which had been an emotional roller coaster ever since Pearl Harbor, was once again up for grabs.

On October 7 *Kommando Nowotny*'s Me-262s roared off their runways, as thirteen hundred heavy bombers headed for synthetic oil plants in central Germany. First Lieutenant Urban Drew of the

391st Fighter Group caught sight of two jets taxiing onto the runway at Achmer airfield.

"I waited until they took off and then I rolled over from 15,000 feet and headed for the attack with my flight behind me. I caught up with the second Me-262 when he was about 1,000 feet off the ground; I was indicating 450 miles per hour and the jet aircraft could not have been going over 200 miles per hour. I started firing from about 400 yards, 30 degrees deflection. . . . Just as I passed him I saw a sheet of flame come out near the wing root. As I glanced back I saw a gigantic explosion. . . . The other jet aircraft was about 500 yards ahead of me and had started a fast climbing left turn. I was still indicating about 400 miles per hour and had to haul back on the stick to stay with him. I started shooting from about 60 degrees deflection, 300 yards. . . . I kept horsing back on the stick and my bullets crept along the fuselage to the cockpit . . . the plane rolled over and went into a flat spin. He hit the ground on his back at about a 60-degree angle."[47]

Drew's wingman had been shot down and his gun camera had jammed, but his two victories were confirmed several weeks later by a *Kommando Nowotny* pilot, Georg Eder, who'd been shot down (for the seventeenth time!) and captured.[48]

This encounter dramatized the Achilles' heel of the German jets: they were sitting ducks when taking off or landing, and they could stay airborne for only about one hour. They also suffered from a serious design flaw: the first-model Me-262 didn't have tricycle landing gear. It was a tail-dragger. When its engines were fired up, they ignited asphalt, so they had to take off and land on concrete runways, every one of which was well known to American pilots.

Kepner, who was probably the only general to have flown the Bell P-59, had trained his VIII Fighter Command crews to counter the jet menace. He'd borrowed a couple of British jet planes and devised a box formation with Mustangs to trap Me-262s so that whichever way they turned they'd find a P-51 turning into them, guns blazing. He also trained his airmen to call "Jet!" whenever they spotted an Me-262. At that point, flights of Thunderbolts or Mustangs would head for every concrete runway within one hundred miles.[49] As the jets ran out of fuel, there was a flight of four American fighters watching every concrete runway, loitering with intent.

In mid-November all the jets were grounded, while the Germans tried to improve pilot training, install tricycle landing gear and devise new tactics to turn a brilliant aircraft into an effective weapon.

21

BLOODY SIDESHOW

The Italian campaign created serious morale problems for the ground troops, many of whom felt they'd been sent to suffer and possibly die on a forgotten front. Yet, for the AAF, Italy had a lot to offer. It brought scores of important targets—oil refineries, marshalling yards, sub pens, aircraft factories, ball-bearing plants and GAF airfields—within range of Fortresses and Liberators. That was why Spaatz had pushed hard for creation of the Fifteenth Air Force. He considered a strategic bomber force in Italy essential to winning air superiority and to his long-hoped-for campaign against Hitler's oil.

Eaker, on the other hand, assumed command of Mediterranean Allied Air Forces in January 1944 still unconvinced that it would be feasible to base a large air force in a place as remote as southern Italy. Even to Italians it was a wild and primitive land. "Christ," they said, "stopped at Eboli," a village southeast of Naples.

The challenge of creating and maintaining a huge airfield complex in this region had nonetheless been accepted by the able and dynamic head of Army Service Forces, Lieutenant General Brehon B. Somervell.[1] In the early months of 1944 Liberty ships hauled mountains of steel mat into Naples. From there they were pushed and pulled by ancient locomotives over the rocky spine of Italy to the narrow coastal plain between Foggia and Bari, where a score of fighter and bomber airfields was being wrestled from the mud.

Every week that winter, it seemed, a new group arrived, bringing Libs and Forts to crude, narrow, off-white strips with names like pizzerias back home: Guilia . . . Spinnazola . . . Lucera. . . . The group would land, climb out of its planes, stretch, gaze curiously, and be jeeped to a soggy spot on a nearby hillside. Then, as crews stood around in the revery of arrival, a truck would pull up and dump tent poles, canvas and rope at their feet.

In the days that followed, as they cursed the incessant rain and clinging mud, they gloomily contemplated something even worse—the threat to life and limb posed by the German Air Force. It currently had six hundred planes based in the Mediterranean.[3] Of these, nearly half were fighters deployed on airfields in northeastern Italy, in and around Udine. Nathan Twining opened the Fifteenth's fight for air superiority with one of the cleverest and most effective counterair operations of the war.

On January 30 he sent five groups of heavy bombers, escorted by his three Lightning groups, toward Udine. They were tracked, as expected, by German radar. In the meantime the 325th Fighter Group, flying Thunderbolts, took off, stayed low, and headed across the Adriatic skimming the waves. They arrived over Udine just as an Me-109 group was taking off to intercept the incoming force of B-17s and B-24s. The 325th tore into the 109s. They destroyed thirty-six enemy planes, in the air and on the ground, for a loss of two Thunderbolts.

As the 325th pulled away, the heavies covered the Udine airfields with nearly 30,000 fragmentation bombs. Six bombers and one fighter were drowned by flak. In the space of an hour as many as 140 GAF planes had been destroyed or damaged.[4]

It proved impossible to take immediate advantage of this stunning blow. The weather over southern Europe was appalling for most of February. The Eighth could bomb in bad weather using H2X radar, but there weren't yet enough H2X sets to equip the Fifteenth, which always took a backseat to the Eighth when it came to new equipment.

When the weather did improve briefly, in mid-February, there was a crisis at Anzio, as the Germans launched counterattacks that threatened to wipe out the beachhead. Twining's B-24s were employed in attacks on rail lines to stanch the flow of German men and matériel that sustained this offensive. Also, on February 15, the heavies were unleashed against the abbey on Monte Cassino, for reasons explained on pages 228–29.

At last came Big Week, the anticipated all-out effort against the German aviation industry. On February 22 the Fifteenth's B-17s hit the Messerschmitt facility at Regensburg, while the B-24s struck the nearby aircraft assembly plant at Obertraubling. The Eighth also attacked Regensburg, attracting most of the fighter opposition, but it had two Mustang groups in the target area to handle the GAF. The Fifteenth lacked fighters with the range to reach Regensburg. It lost fourteen B-24s and five B-17s.[5]

Next day the Eighth was grounded, but the Fifteenth struck the ball-bearing factory at Steyr, in Austria. It returned to Steyr on the 24th to bomb an aircraft components plant. These two missions cost thirty-three heavy bombers.[6]

On February 25th both the Eighth and the Fifteenth again struck Regensburg. Only 176 of Twining's heavies reached the target area, and the cost of flying into Germany unescorted this time was high. The 301st Bomb Group's Fortresses caught the worst of it.

GAF fighter attacks began near Trieste, continued as the force passed over airfields around Udine, and built to a crescendo as the group skirted Klagenfurt airfield in southern Austria. Half a dozen Ju-88s closed to one thousand yards to fire an ineffectual rocket barrage that wreathed Fortress wings in tendrils of white smoke, without scoring a hit.

Then twin-engine Me-210 fighters bore down on the bombers. "Two waves were coming in, ten in each line," noted Lieutenant John Muirhead, piloting a B-17. "One line was attacking level, heading for the lead squadron; the other line of ten was slightly higher, and were sliding over their comrades, positioning for an attack on our squadron. . . .

"The top turret and the nose opened fire. I could see the blinking wing guns of the incoming fighters, and I watched the white lines of tracers merge before me. Black bursts of twenty-millimeter shells stitched a line over our left wing. Our squadron leader began to go to pieces: large chunks of metal blew away from the lower part of the nose; the chin turret was hanging at a strange angle; the end of his right wing blew away, and the plane flipped over. It continued to turn, performing a looping barrel roll of flame before it fell from us in an almost vertical dive. The fighters broke to our right except for one flaming coffin that continued through our formation. . . .

"As the frenzy of battle raged, my terror faded and I waited for my death."[7]

Of the twenty-eight planes the 301st dispatched, five aborted and thirteen were shot down. Only ten crews completed this calvary. All told, Regensburg this day cost Twining thirty-three bombers and four fighters. Yet he considered it worth the cost: the Messerchmitt plant produced nothing for the next four months.[8]

March brought day after day of bad weather. While the Fifteenth's bombers were grounded the Luftwaffe was rebuilding its fighter force in northeastern Italy. By the middle of the month there were nearly 250 fighters at Udine and nearby airfields. On March 15 the heavies were used to flatten the town of Cassino, trying in vain to blast a path for Fifth Army.[9]

Three days later the Fifteenth tackled the GAF fighter fields again. This time 95 Lightnings crossed the Adriatic at an altitude of 75 feet, before sweeping over Udine. This maneuver pinned dozens of GAF fighters to the ground. Meanwhile, 113 Fortresses were flying along the Yugoslavian coast on what looked like a mission to southern Germany. Fighters based in Austria were scrambled to intercept them and were heading into Italian airspace. Before contact was made, however, the B-17s suddenly veered west, and appeared over the Udine fields, dropping fragmentation bombs.

The fighters from Austria landed to refuel at northern Italian bases; standard operating procedure when they flew south. While they were being gassed up a force of Liberators, escorted by Thunderbolts, swept in to cover these bases with thirty-two thousand fragmentation bombs. All told, some fifty-six GAF fighters were reported destroyed in the air or on the ground. The cost was seven heavies and four fighters.[10]

Despite this success, the German air force could still bite back. When the Fifteenth attacked the ball-bearing plant at Steyr with four hundred bombers on April 2, it lost twenty-two, mainly to fighters.

Air superiority was nonetheless almost secured and the Fifteenth was about to shift its focus away from Pointblank targets. The Red Army had reached the Romanian border. On April 2 the Combined Chiefs issued a new directive, ordering the Fifteenth to give priority to attacks on transportation targets in Romania. These would aid the advance of Stalin's troops as they thrust into the Balkans. The Fifteenth started mining the Danube, the Balkans' principal highway, and unleashed a ferocious onslaught against marshalling yards.

German plane factories and airfields would continue to be struck with heavy raids from time to time. Air superiority couldn't be maintained otherwise. Twining's bombers would also be drawn into the ground battle at critical periods. Shortly before the breakout from Anzio, four B-17s of 301st Bomb Group attacked the Avisio viaduct over which the Brenner Pass line ran between Italy and Austria. The B-17s dropped twenty-one thousand-pound Azon bombs, which were guided by radio-controlled tail fins—a medieval precision-guided munition. They scored four hits, dropping a seventy-foot section of the viaduct.[11] The Germans got it repaired in ten days, but by then the breakout was under way.

During the advance on Rome major attacks were made against harbors and marshalling yards in southern France to hamper the movement of German reserves into Italy.[12] When the German Tenth and Fourteenth armies retreated, the Fifteenth bombed towns and bridges to slow them down.

Such tactical interventions aside, however, the Fifteenth's air war, like the Eighth's, would be directed increasingly against marshalling yards and oil. Marshalling yards to satisfy the Combined Chiefs, oil to satisfy Spaatz.

In the space of six months and despite the primitive conditions in which it had to operate, the Fifteenth had become an awesome force, able to strike effectively at almost any kind of target. In May 1944 the Fifteenth reached its full size: twenty-one heavy bomb groups (two-thirds B-24s) and seven fighter groups—nearly two thousand aircraft.

Its two Spitfire groups, the 31st and 52nd, were transitioning into P-51Bs. The highly aggressive and successful 325th was also swapping its beloved Jugs for Mustangs. Twining finally had the range he needed. If anything, he needed long range escorts more than Doolittle. Nearly all the Fifteenth's major targets were on the other side of mountains, to the north and to the east. It had to fly farther on an average mission than the Eighth.

The Fifteenth was also getting replacement bombers clad in nothing but polished aluminum. Lacking several hundred pounds of paint, they flew fifteen miles an hour faster than the worn olive-drab veterans they joined The new-look Fifteenth was a collection of old pennies, new dimes.

The modest number of GAF fighters in the Med as compared to the ETO allowed the Fifteenth to bomb without having to master the complexities of the combat box and the combat bomb wing. The Fifteenth's technique was to organize "attack units" based on the bomb groups. Each group flew in what amounted to six Vs, with an extra plane slotted into the rear of each of the two rearmost Vs.[13] This reduced the number of vulnerable, "coffin corner" aircraft, like so:

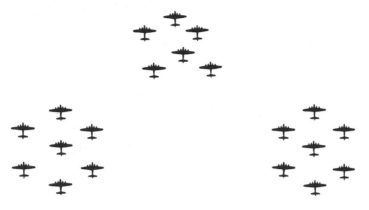

A large group might put up two "attack units," while a new one, still building up its strength, might fly only one.

As in the ETO, only the lead bombardier in a group did precision bombing; the rest were toggliers, who dropped on his signal. The result could be a tight pattern—or not. When the lead was wrong, so was everyone else.

Arnold's expectation that Italy would provide better weather than England was thwarted by incessant lows. If anything, the Fifteenth had more problems with the weather than the Eighth, yet lacked radar bombing equipment until the middle of 1944.

Typical was an April mission by the B-17 groups to attack aviation industries near Vienna. Austria was socked in, so the force headed for the secondary target, the marshalling yards at Padua. That city, too, was blanketed by cloud, but if the planes returned with bombs in their racks no one would get credit for a mission flown. "I never saw the IP," recalled John Muirhead, "and I could only vaguely surmise where the target was. . . . The bombardier was not making any drift corrections [Note: meaning he couldn't see anything either]. . . . The squadron proceeded on through the weak challenge of scattered shell bursts until the bombardier's voice came on the intercom, 'Bombs away!' I wondered what we had hit."[14]

On other missions, bombs were dropped according to the clock. An expected time of arrival (ETA) over the target was worked out to the second, and bombs were dropped on the ETA.

The arrival of H2X sets in May made it possible to bomb through the clouds, but that simply meant making area attacks, which some airmen considered "terror bombing." A mission to Munich by the Liberators shortly after several groups got H2X sets, for example, had an airfield as the primary target. It was covered by clouds. So the B-24s attacked the secondary—downtown Munich—using the new radar equipment. The city offered prominent H2X aiming points.[15]

Generally, however, the Fifteenth did less radar bombing than the Eighth, so it was able to bomb more accurately. On the other hand, because it had farther to travel, it lost many planes in the mountains. It was also flying mainly B-24s, which lacked the ruggedness of the B-17. The overall loss rate per sortie was 35 percent higher than the Eighth's.[16]

Part of the effort to assist the oncoming Soviet armies was Operation Frantic. Twining had his doubts about anything involving the Soviets. He found them dishonest, uncooperative and paranoid. On occasion his fighters were jumped over Yugoslavia by Red Air Force planes. As a rule, the Americans won the dogfights, but it was up to Twining to keep these victories from turning into international incidents.[17]

The first Frantic shuttle was flown on June 2, when 130 Fortresses escorted by the 325th Fighter Group bombed the marshalling yard at Debrecen, in Hungary. They landed in the Ukraine. On their return they attacked GAF airfields.[18]

The second Frantic mission saw 31st Group Mustangs and 82nd Group Lightnings making a sweep over Romania. From the Ukraine they attacked airfields in Poland. On their return they mounted yet another Romanian sweep. Back in Italy, they reported 129 enemy aircraft destroyed, for the loss of 10 Mustangs and 20 Lightnings.[19] The last Frantic missions for the Fifteenth were flown August 4 to 6, with P-38 attacks on railroads and airfields in Romania.

On April 5 the Fifteenth began one of the most relentless bombing campaigns of the war, to shut down Ploesti. It had been untouched since the low-level attack eight months earlier. Since then its defenses had been strengthened. As many as 700 AAA guns and 250 Luftwaffe fighters now defended Ploesti. Its very name, scrawled in yellow chalk on the blackboards used at briefings, had a totemic power that aroused fear and excitement among bomber crews.[20] It smelled, sounded and looked, like hell—a seething cauldron of sulfurous fumes, pillars of smoke, tongues of fire, violent death.

In accordance with the Combined Chiefs' new directive, Twining opened his campaign by striking the marshalling yards at Ploesti, but bombing errors were certain to scatter shorts and overs into the vast, adjacent complex of refineries.

Between April 5 and May 5 the Fifteenth attacked the marshalling yards four times, losing forty-three heavies shot down. A dozen more were written off in crash landings.

On May 18 the Fifteenth made its first direct attack on the refineries. Two hundred and six bombers reached the target area, including the Liberators of the 450th Bomb Group. Group bombardier Lieutenant Leroy Newby could hardly believe the scene before him: distinctive narrow columns of black smoke rose from shattered refineries and the sky was alive with bomb groups departing with open bomb bays, while others arrived, their course grimly set. "I gaped transfixed as I gazed at the incredible sight of Ploesti. *My God, I'm here!* . . .

"Groups of black polka-dot clouds formed a protective ring around the city, reminiscent of circled wagon trains. . . . Two miles above us were white polka-dot cloud formations. The Fifteenth was simultaneously attacking all of the refineries encircling Ploesti. The black clouds were from German Flak 37 guns. These could reach 26,230 feet and were intended for our B-24s. The white clouds were from Flak 39 guns. These were for the B-17s that flew at 32,000 feet. . . .

"The really startling sight was the nearest block of black puffs in the sky—at our altitude and off to the right . . . a barrage of flak. . . . I could see the shells coming at us as they neared our altitude. Five black spots, quickly growing larger. *Was there a piece of flak with my name on it?*"[21] Fourteen bombers were shot down over Ploesti on this mission.

A second strike, by nearly five hundred heavies on May 31, caused extensive damage, and sixteen bombers were shot down, but the third biggest refinery, the Romano Americano, owned by Standard Oil, was still virtually unscathed.

The defenders at Ploesti usually had plenty of warning of an impending attack as the bombers, overflying the mountains of Yugoslavia, came into radar view. The fighters defending Ploesti were scrambled, while on the ground two thousand smoke generators were set humming. Within thirty minutes a dense and dirty haze cloaked the refineries. Attempts to bomb through the smoke by H2X were disappointing; Ploesti lacked terrain features such as rivers and lakes that provided a good radar fix.

A daring plan was devised to dive-bomb the Romano Americano with P-38s. On June 10, forty-six Lightnings of 82nd Fighter Group, each carrying a thousand-pound bomb, took off from Vincenzo. Eight planes soon aborted. The remaining thirty-eight flew on, escorted by forty-eight Lightnings from the 1st Fighter Group. Both groups flew up the mountain valleys of Yugoslavia, then followed the Danube at low level to Bucharest, slipping under the radar coverage.

They were spotted en route and a warning was flashed to Romanian airfields. Trainers, bombers, fighters and transports were scrambled in a wild rush to save them from being destroyed on the ground. When the Lightnings reached Bucharest they got into a low-altitude brawl with dozens of planes that had just taken off. The 1st Fighter Group tore into half a dozen vulnerable, slow-moving bombers. While engaged in this gratifying task the 1st was bounced by twenty FW-190s.

Thirty-six Lightnings from the 82nd were meanwhile climbing to eight thousand feet. They went up through intense flak to gain altitude, then plunged back into it to bomb the refinery. Half a dozen dive-bombing P-38s were shot out of the sky. Once back at low level, the surviving Lightnings attacked the Ploesti marshalling yards, strafing locomotives and leaving tank cars ablaze.[22]

The 82nd lost eight planes on this mission. The 1st lost sixteen, but Lieutenant Herbert B. Hatch of the 71st Squadron returned to base triumphant, an "Ace in a Day."[23] As for the Romano Americano, it had suffered little damage.

In the last week of June the Fifteenth's heavies returned three times to strike the oil refineries. Twining lost another 40 bombers shot down or written off. On June 26 the Fifteenth struck half a dozen synthetic oil plants and refineries near Vienna with 680 heavy bombers. Thirty were shot down.[24] June had been an expensive month.

July was even costlier. Twining attacked Ploesti five times, losing nearly 100 bombers to fighters, flak, and crash landings. Between visits to Ploesti, the Fifteenth attacked marshalling yards, oil-storage depots, and airfields in France, Germany, Italy, Austria, Yugoslavia, and Romania. Aircraft losses on many of these missions ran into double figures. July would prove the most expensive month of the war for Twining's command, with 317 bombers shot down or written off. In one month the Fifteenth lost 30 percent of its bomber strength.[25]

The RAF joined in the Ploesti campaign, bringing it under night bombardment. In four attacks it dropped nearly ten thousand tons of bombs and lost thirty-eight Wellingtons.

It was August 10 before the Fifteenth returned to Ploesti, with four hundred bombers. Despite the massive devastation that repeated heavy bombing had wrought, the flak defenses remained strong. Sixteen bombers were shot down.

A week later nearly 250 bombers struck, and 15 were downed. On August 18 nearly 400 bombers attacked, but only 7 were lost.

Photo interpreters scrutinizing the strike photos saw almost nothing left worth bombing. There were thirty thousand slave laborers toiling at Ploesti, trying to make good the damage. They would produce some oil no matter what the bombers did; some fuel would be refined so long as there was oil. A total shutdown wasn't possible, but intelligence calculated that production had fallen to 10 percent of peak output.[26]

On August 19 only sixty-five bombers appeared over Ploesti, crossing and recrossing the refineries, looking for targets worth their bombs. No fighters rose to oppose them; flak was sparse and ineffectual. Not a single plane was lost. After twenty attacks by the Fifteenth, Ploesti was as good as dead.

On August 30 Red Army troops claimed its tormented, greasy carcass. That night officers and men of Fifteenth Air Force celebrated like death row inmates suddenly pardoned and set free. Glasses were drunk from and joyously shattered.[27]

Ploesti was the quintessential strategic target and Twining's campaign to put it out of business was a model of its kind: a heavy attack on average once a week until Ploesti was knocked out. The price was nearly three hundred heavy bombers and two hundred fighters shot down or wrecked in crash landings; scores of planes lost flying over the mountains to Romania; more than a thousand lives lost; and hundreds of young men left limbless, sightless, or crazy.

For Mark Clark's Fifth Army the war was one battle for mountain views after another. Soldiers always want the high ground; Italy has plenty of it. The role of Twelfth Air Force, under "Uncle Joe" Cannon, was to support Fifth Army.

Its British counterpart, the Desert Air Force, was attached to the British Eighth Army. Having insisted on an Italian campaign that by mid-1944 had achieved none of its touted objectives, however, Churchill's easily distracted attention was shifting to the even more mountainous Balkans. The Desert Air Force accordingly devoted more and more of its energies to aiding Communist partisans in Yugoslavia. Cannon would soon be left, in effect, to provide nearly all of the tactical air supporting the armies in Italy.

His XII Tactical Air Command, under Brigadier General Gordon P. Saville, was an aggressive, well-led and experienced force, with nearly one thousand aircraft on hand to support the May breakouts at Cassino and Anzio. By the time this offensive came to a halt on June 22 Rome had been liberated and the German Tenth and Fourteenth Armies were in full retreat, mainly on foot. The railroads through central Italy had been systematically wrecked and XII TAC claimed to have destroyed five thousand German vehicles and damaged another five thousand since the offensive began.[28]

The ground advance halted forty miles north of Rome while Clark reorganized Fifth Army—it was about to lose its best troops: the VI Corps, commanded by Lucian Truscott, and the French Expeditionary Corps. They were being withdrawn to prepare for the invasion of southern France, Operation Dragoon.[29] New units were being brought into the line to replace them and new boundaries were drawn between the armies.

Meanwhile, ten days of rainy weather grounded both the Twelfth and the Fifteenth. This break from both air and ground attacks allowed Kesselring to get some of the railroads running again and to resupply his hard-pressed troops. And behind him, two hundred miles north of Rome, new defenses were being constructed along the southern edge of the Po Valley. Known as the Gothic Line, these fortifications would be ready by the fall. It was up to him to fight a delaying action all summer.

The Allied advance was slowed not only by German tactics, but also by the need to spare beautiful, culturally important cities such as Siena and Florence. This kind of fighting wasn't only time-consuming, it was costly. During the advance from Rome to Florence XII Troop Carrier flew eight thousand seriously wounded men to hospitals in the rear.[30]

In mid-July XII TAC began moving most of its planes to Corsica, in anticipation of Dragoon. From Corsica it was also able to start striking transportation targets in northern Italy that had until now been the responsibility of Fifteenth Air Force. The B-26 groups of 42nd Bomb Wing and the B-25 groups of 57th Bomb Wing began a ferocious assault on twenty-one major bridges crossing the Po to cut the flow of supplies to Kesselring's forces. These bridges had so far been untouched, because Allied ground commanders had planned to use them as they drove north. That hope had died.[31]

The plan now was for mediums to knock down the bridges, after which fighter-bombers would attack repair crews and prevent rebuilding. These bridges, though, were the biggest and strongest in Italy. An army of Italian laborers, working at night and in the rain, kept half of them open.

XII TAC, moreover, couldn't give bridge-busting its undivided attention. Dragoon, scheduled for August 15, was near. Some twenty-four hundred aircraft from the Twelfth, the Fifteenth and the RAF were crammed into Corsica. Eight new airfields had been built; the six existing fields had been expanded.

The Dragoon counterair campaign opened July 24, when nearly 150 Liberators from the Fifteenth covered the largest GAF airfield in southern France, at Valence, with fragmentation bombs. Two days later XII TAC's 79th Fighter Group swept over the field at low-level and destroyed more than twenty aircraft, mainly Ju-88s.[32] On August 9 three B-26 groups attacked the large GAF airfield complex at Bergamo in northern Italy, within range of the invasion beaches. Three P-47 groups flak-busted the airfield defenses so successfully that not one Marauder was downed.[33]

Southern France was defended by the German Nineteenth Army, numbering two hundred thousand men. Its combat units consisted of seven infantry divisions and the 11th Panzer Division. The Germans knew an invasion was coming. The only question was whether it would be on the east or west side of the Rhone. Deception measures, including air attacks, persuaded them to bet on the west and deploy the 11th Panzer on that side.[34] Dragoon was scheduled to hit the beaches of the French Riviera, east of the river.

On August 4 XII TAC started knocking out the bridges over the Rhone from the Mediterranean to Lyons, one hundred miles inland. On August 10, with the invasion only five days away, XII

TAC and Fifteenth Air Force began pounding coastal gun batteries and radar installations.

On the nights of August 12 and 13 the super-secret 885th Bomb Squadron, based in Algiers, carried arms to Resistance groups to be used to harry the Germans and distract them when the invasion began. The 885th's pilots were flying heavy bombers at five hundred feet in the middle of the night, all the way up to Lyons, dropping French Resistance leaders and radio operators, along with thirty tons of arms and equipment.[35]

The Allied forces landing in southern France and driving up the Rhone would be the U.S. Seventh Army and the French First Army, under the 6th Army Group headquarters of Lieutenant General Jacob Devers. He wanted an airborne operation, and Eaker supported him. There were strong objections from Eisenhower's staff that sending most of IX Troop Carrier down from England to provide airlift would hamper the breakout from Normandy, but Devers got his airborne assault.[36] Hundreds of C-47s that might have hauled gas to Patton were parked instead in the shadow of Mount Vesuvius on the evening of August 14.

Devers had created a provisional airborne division, the First Allied Airborne Task Force, consisting of ten thousand paratroopers (80 percent of them Americans), under Major General Robert T. Frederick, legendary commander of the 1st Special Service Force, probably the finest Allied ground unit of World War II.[37]

At first light six C-47s of the Provisional Troop Carrier Division, commanded by Paul Williams, crossed the French coast dropping window and six hundred parachute dummies north of Toulon to create a diversion. Shortly after this, other C-47s brought in the Pathfinders. A coastal haze forced the planes to climb, as had happened in Normandy. Once again, the Pathfinders were widely scattered.[38]

Twelve of Twining's heavy groups and eight of Saville's medium groups began bombing beach defenses as the invasion fleet closed in. Nearly 250 mediums hit 9 coastal batteries within range of the invasion beaches. Saville's fighter-bombers struck radar installations. His A-20 groups covered GAF airfields with fragmentation bombs.[39] Before the day ended more than 4,000 sorties would be flown in support of the invasion.

At eight in the morning, the first of 396 troop carrier planes carrying the main force 400 miles from Naples flew across the Riviera. Despite the earlier failure to drop the Pathfinders accurately, most paratroopers came down on or near their assigned drop zones. An hour later the gliders passed over the invasion fleet.

Further waves of jumpers and glidermen followed during the day. By nightfall most of Frederick's troops were in France and had cut the roads leading to the invasion beaches. One parachute company, dropped in the wrong place, had captured a German corps headquarters.

The invasion met no air opposition. Not a single GAF sortie was flown against Allied troops. Caught on the wrong side of the Rhone, the Germans responded weakly and ineptly to the invasion. Over the next few days every attempt to bring 11th Panzer over to the east was thwarted by air attacks.

The French insisted on liberating Toulon and Marseilles. Lucian Truscott created an armored task force by taking the tank battalion that was attached to each of his three infantry divisions and set them racing north up the Rhone.[40]

Two weeks after the invasion, this force narrowly missed trapping the retreating 19th Army at Montelimar, but it couldn't escape the planes of XII TAC, as described earlier (see pages 317–18).[41]

Meanwhile the repeated bombing by mediums of the defenses of Toulon, the French Navy's principal Mediterranean base, speeded its surrender. And the 321st Bomb Group thwarted an attempt to block this vital port. The Germans hoped to scuttle a battleship and a cruiser at the harbor entrance. The group's B-25s swiftly sank both ships while they were still in deep water.[42]

Lyons fell to Truscott's troops September 3. Dijon fell September 11, as troops from the Seventh Army made contact with patrols from Patton's Third Army. There was now an unbroken Allied front from the English Channel to Switzerland.

Many of XII TAC's units had advanced along the Rhone. Most did not return to Italy but were joined under a new headquarters, First Tactical Air Force, with three French groups that the Twelfth had raised and trained on Sardinia. The First TAF would support Devers's 6th Army Group until the end of the war.

After Dragoon Eaker, like Marshall, saw nothing more to be gained by ground operations in Italy. He recommended sending the whole of Twelfth Air Force and the Fifth Army to France.[43] The British, however, insisted on keeping the ground war in Italy going.

By September Kesselring's Gothic Line defenses were nearly finished. They ran more or less parallel to the south bank of the wide

Po River, which flows slowly across the great Lombardy plain of northern Italy. He lacked the manpower to defend the entire plain, which stretches for 250 miles across northern Italy. He concentrated his strongest defenses on the eastern half, leaving the west seriously undermanned. The British decided to assault the Gothic Line . . . in the east. The Balkan obsession again. The Fifth and Eighth armies found themselves in September 1944 preparing for a new offensive to break through Kesselring's strongest defenses and take Bologna.[44]

The Twelfth began a new interdiction campaign along the Po while concurrently providing close support in the new offensive. Against all the odds, both armies penetrated the Gothic Line, only to bog down in torrential fall rains that hampered movement, but aided the work of Kesselring's bridge and railroad repair crews.

A new tactical air command, the XXII, was created to take the place of the departed XII TAC. It consisted of twenty-five squadrons, drawn mainly from what had formerly been XII Fighter Command, whose role had been air defense. The collapse of the GAF in the Mediterranean had left XII FC without much to do. No more than thirty German fighters were in Italy that fall. Medium bomb groups now flew without escort.[45]

After several attempts to take Bologna failed, the British started shipping entire divisions off to Greece, to restore the unpopular Greek monarchy. The interdiction campaign along the Po petered out. Nearly every bridge had sustained serious damage, but the Germans built pontoon bridges that were easy to camouflage and simple to repair. They also had a large collection of boats and ferries that crossed at night and in rain, with which commodity Italy was providing a million combatants a sodden abundance.

The Fifteenth had concentrated its efforts following the fall of Ploesti to attacks on airfields and marshalling yards in the Balkans to aid the advance of the Red Army. In November, however, the German railroad system, the Reichsbahn, became the number one target of the U.S. Strategic Air Forces, with oil at number two. The Fifteenth spent the winter of 1944 bombing Germany, when the appalling weather permitted. Losses were light, even to flak. Apart from occasional encounters with Me-262 jet fighters (discussed in the next chapter) there was no serious aerial opposition either.

On April 9 the British Eighth Army was ready to begin its final Italian offensive. The Fifteenth, its work over Germany finished, laid on a massive carpet bombing to blast a path through the defenses.

Like the Eighth, the Fifth Army had been immobilized since November. XXII TAC had flown few close support missions that winter, but mounted nearly three thousand sorties against bridges and railroads. By April 14, the day the Fifth's new offensive began, every major rail line north of the Po was cut in several places and every major bridge that remained was shattered.

Under fierce ground pressure and heavy air attack, the Gothic Line defenses crumbled. Two hundred thousand German troops retreated toward the Po. They crowded the pontoon bridges and swarmed onto the ferries. They were attacked by XXII TAC and the Desert Air Force day and night. The Germans couldn't get away with anything but the clothes they stood up in. The matériel that makes an army—artillery, tanks, trucks, and ammunition— was abandoned.[46] The end was nigh. On May 2 the Germans in Italy capitulated.

The Fifteenth Air Force's biggest campaign had been its greatest success: it was credited with destroying half the Reich's fuel. The XV Fighter Command claimed nearly 1,500 aerial victories. It lost 156 planes in dogfights and 232 to flak. The XV FC's 31st Fighter Group was the highest-scoring group in the Mediterranean Theater, with 567 confirmed kills.[47]

As for the Twelfth, its pilots claimed 2,857 enemy aircraft destroyed, but it had lost 2,667 of its own. Most had gone down attacking ground targets to help keep Fifth Army moving, as it ground the Germans down and finally out.[48]

22

A TAC ATTACK

In mid-September the Ninth Air Force moved to France. Vandenberg set up his headquarters in Chantilly. His knowledge of tactical air was doubted by contemporaries such as Gordon Saville, but he was generally considered a great improvement over Brereton. Vandenberg was not a gifted tactician or combat leader like Quesada.[1] He was essentially a high-level operator, well able to handle the political complexities of coalition warfare and interservice cooperation. He wisely allowed his TAC commanders the widest latitude. Vandenberg's main command challenge was to ensure the two thousand planes in his three TACs and Sam Anderson's 9th Bomb Division (the former IX Bomber Command) weren't wasted by being thrown at too many targets.[2]

With air superiority won, major dogfights were rare that fall. The Ninth devoted its energies to interdiction, close support and recon; missions were spiced by occasional sweeps or counterair strikes against enemy airfields to keep the Luftwaffe down. The glory days of column cover, too, were over. The war on the ground slowed to a crawl after Market-Garden.

Courtney Hodges's First Army began October with a drive to take Aachen by encircling it from the northwest and southeast. This drive was supported energetically by IX TAC, which flew six thousand sorties to help take the city, striking German pillboxes, artillery and troops.[3] Disappointingly, an attempt by the 9th Bomb Division to blast a path through enemy defenses fizzled out in the appalling fall weather.

By late October Allied armies were up against strong German defenses from the English Channel to Switzerland. The German arms industry had reached peak production in September, turning out a mountain of guns and ammunition. Hitler had two and a half million soldiers available in Germany to man the formidable West Wall defenses his engineers and slave laborers had created. To Germans, the sudden resurgence of their army's fighting power was "the miracle in the West."

As German troops and weapons moved into the West Wall the Ninth's first priority became railroads. The second priority, as of October 7, was bridges along the German border.[4] In the weeks that followed scores of bridges were attacked by the fighter-bombers.

Ideally, they would have been knocked down by Anderson's B-26s, but the miserable weather kept the 9th Bomb Division grounded much of the time. The 9th BD was probably the most accurate bombing outfit in the AAF. Anderson wouldn't allow anyone with less than fifteen missions or more than forty-five to be a lead bombardier.[5] A difficult target such as a sturdy, well-defended bridge was meat and drink to his B-26 groups. Unfortunately, the fall of 1944 brought Western Europe twice its average autumnal rainfall, keeping the mediums grounded most days.

With the capture of Aachen in mid-October the First and Ninth armies were halted forty miles from the Rhine. The First had to get past the Hurtgen Forest to reach it, and the Ninth had to get past the Roer River dams. Meanwhile Patton's Third Army was stuck outside Metz, short of supplies, and sixty miles from the Rhine.

General Hodges pushed his troops into the Hurtgen Forest to deny it to the enemy, but the Germans dug in and chewed up three of his divisions. Both IX TAC and XXIX TAC flew numerous close air support missions, but the dense, dripping forest was a defender's paradise, an attacker's hell.

As for Patton, he was under orders from Bradley to leave Metz alone. Bradley didn't think it was worth the casualties a frontal assault would cost. Patton, however, kept probing Metz's defenses, not realizing he was up against forty-three interlocking forts that were impervious to artillery and fighter-bombers. Weyland's XIX TAC pilots attacked the defenses repeatedly with five-hundred-pound bombs and drenched them with napalm, accomplishing nothing. The forts were too strong for anything but heavies, and only then if combined with a major ground offensive.

Although big dogfights had become a rarity, the GAF always

kept something back to exploit Allied mistakes or to set up an ambush, where it might fight on its own terms. On October 29, the 354th Fighter Group, Weyland's only Mustang unit, was bounced by one hundred GAF planes near Heidelberg. In the ensuing dogfight the 354th claimed twenty-eight enemy aircraft, against the loss of three Mustangs.[6]

Mainly though, complained Bill Dunn, "Despite the poor flying weather we continued to support the advance of the Army ground forces. . . . There was none of the glamour of the early war days." Dunn, with more than five hundred hours of combat behind him by this time, was a P-47 pilot in the 406th Fighter Group and was rapidly becoming disenchanted. "Close air support strikes were nothing more than flying directly into the firing barrels of hundreds of antiaircraft cannon and machine guns, with the chances about one in five you'd get hit, one in ten you'd get shot down. As the German army was gradually compressed by our forces into smaller defense pockets, so their flak was also compressed, with many more guns now defending each target area. This sort of flying, after a while, is no longer exciting fun—it's bloody tough and extremely dangerous work. . . ."[7]

By mid-November Hodges had taken enough of the Hurtgen Forest for Bradley to try pushing the First and Ninth armies twenty miles to the Roer River in a new operation, called Queen. It would open with an even bigger air attack than Cobra. Bradley proposed to use nearly five thousand aircraft this time, half of them heavy bombers.

The precautions taken to avoid friendly-fire casualties were elaborate: two huge white arrows were placed on the ground to steer the planes into the target area, a line of barrage ballons flew parallel to the front, dozens of orange Day-Glo panels were placed five hundred yards behind the forward ground positions, and red flak shells would be fired to create a mile-high line of red smoke above the most advanced troops, who would be nearly two and a half miles from the German positions being bombed. Doolittle had the Eighth mount a full-scale dress rehearsal of Queen in England.[8]

Queen began as scheduled November 16. Bad weather over France grounded nearly all the mediums and many of the fighter-bombers. The heavies dropped nine thousand tons of bombs. The Ninth's fighter-bombers, light bombers, and a handful of mediums dropped another nine thousand tons. There was only one friendly-fire casualty on the ground. But by nightfall American troops had advanced only two miles.[9] They hadn't yet reached the German defenses that Queen aircraft had pounded. It took another two weeks for Bradley's armies to batter their way through to the Roer.

Patton was pushing his Third Army troops through the rain and mud that November. Bradley had finally allowed him to mount an offensive, called Madison, but the aim was to bypass Metz, not attack it. Patton planned to advance, cross the Moselle and drive toward the Saar, forty miles distant.

Before Third Army launched any major operation, Weyland had his XIX TAC intelligence staff try to pinpoint enemy command posts and headquarters. When the new ground offensive began, on November 8, XIX TAC struck enemy command-and-control centers as hard as it could. "The Germans later complained bitterly about this," said Weyland. "They thought it was not exactly sporting."[10] The fighter-bombers' biggest success on the opening day of Madison was to destroy the headquarters of the 17th SS Panzer Division, paralyzing the division for forty-eight hours.

Meanwhile, eleven hundred heavy bombers struck Metz and the defenses surrounding it to aid Patton's drive. He was jubilant. "The day was the brightest and best we have had in two months. We are doing better than expected," he wrote in his diary. "Thank God."[11]

Madison achieved its goal of getting the Third Army to the Saar, but when Patton's troops reached the river at the end of November they found themselves smack up against the West Wall. Patton started to prepare for a new offensive.

Before he could launch it, tactical reconnaissance pilots began coming back with photos and eyewitness accounts of heavy German rail traffic west of the Rhine. Something was stirring. But what?[12]

The role of Tac R was to fly up to 120 miles behind enemy lines at altitudes of 3,000 to 6,000 feet and make a visual reconnaissance. Tac R pilots flew Mustangs equipped with strip cameras. They photographed trenches, foxholes, mortar pits, enemy artillery positions, troop movements, fixed defenses and river crossings.[13] They were also able to defend themselves: their Mustangs were fully armed.

They didn't seek combat, but if it came to them. . . . Consider a mission on July 18 by lieutenants Joe Waits and John Miefert of the

15th TAC R squadron. They were photographing a railroad bridge in Normandy when they were bounced by two Me-109s, which made a firing pass then dove away.

Miefert reported, "We were on the deck [50 feet] now and I could see the flak towers going by and cringed as we passed each one . . . the two 109s came into view. They were line abreast and Joe said, 'I'll take the one on the left and you take the right one,' and he opened fire at 200 yards. I could see hits all over the plane and it rolled over on its back and crashed. Meanwhile I have the throttle all the way back as I'm overrunning Joe and the other 109. I opened fire trying to keep the plane from the uncoordinated skid you get at high speed and no engine torque. I saw hits on the wing and turned left, right into Joe's area of fire. Joe fired a two-second burst at 150 yards. I saw strikes in the cockpit area, the canopy was blown off, the wings and engine were also hit hard, and this 109 rolled over and exploded into the ground."[14]

Patton relied heavily on Tac R during his thrust across France to let him know where his far-flung units were fighting; some were as much as five hundred miles apart. Later, in Madison, he relied on Tac R to bring him intelligence on the Moselle River crossings and the West Wall defenses. And following Madison, as Tac R reports came in of unusual activity west of the Rhine, he sensed a German attack coming. He guessed it would be aimed farther north, against Hodges's First Army. Patton had his staff make contingency plans to turn several of his divisions north on short notice. He intended to strike the Germans in the flank if his hunch proved right.[15]

In the first two weeks of December the weather was flyable roughly every other day. There was a tremendous backlog of aerial recon requests, as Allied armies prepared to mount a Christmas offensive.

When Tac R pilots returned they increasingly reported seeing what looked to them like a high level of activity on the roads and the railways. In themselves, such reports didn't mean much. But Pete Quesada and Sam Anderson were worried about the flow of reports of tracks showing armored vehicles going into the trees, but no tracks coming out. On December 15 they flew to SHAEF headquarters at Versailles to express their concern at an Allied air commanders meeting, and got the brush off.[16] Neither Ike's nor Bradley's nor Montgomery's intelligence chiefs believed the Germans were capable of mounting a major attack. On the contrary, they were putting out estimates saying the situation was like that at the end of July, on the eve of the breakout from Normandy.[17]

The German plan was to strike the weakest part of the Allied line, where it ran through the great forest of the Ardennes. This region was considered the quiet sector, where badly mauled divisions got a breather and new ones got their introduction to combat. It was held by only four divisions stretched tissue thin over a one hundred-mile front. Hitler intended to break through here, drive to the Meuse River, cross it at Liège, and push on to Antwerp. This would split the seam between the Americans and the British and could lead to the destruction of entire Allied divisions.[18] In 1940 the Germans had launched an offensive through the Ardennes that reached the outskirts of Antwerp in five days, knocked Belgium out of the war, sent the British scrambling for Dunkirk and set the French Army up for a killing blow.

The GAF had nearly fifteen hundred single-engine fighters and three hundred fighter-bombers available to support the new attack, plus five hundred twin-engine fighters and bombers. Hitler had countenanced an effort by Galland to create a fighter reserve that might be used in a Herculean one-day effort to fly twenty-five hundred sorties and bring down five hundred American bombers, in exchange for five hundred fighters. Instead, Hitler would throw Galland's fighter reserve into the Ardennes offensive.[19]

At daybreak on December 16 Frederick Anderson, Vandenberg, Quesada and an RAF air vice-marshal arrived at General Hodges's headquarters in an elegant chateau outside the town of Spa, in southeastern Belgium. The First and Ninth armies were each demanding a Cobra/Queen type bombing to kick off their Christmas offensive. This meeting was to decide which army would get the tactical benefit of the heavies. As operational maps were pinned to the wall, the telephone rang. Two hundred thousand Germans, with a thousand tanks, had just surged out of the fog and mist of the Ardennes.[20]

By nightfall, the Germans had scored only local successes. There had been no major breakthroughs. American troops gave ground grudgingly, if at all, despite being outnumbered at least three to one at every point of contact.

The heavily forested and mountainous Ardennes contained few decent east-west roads. Over the next few days the battle coalesced into a struggle for the crossroads town of St. Vith, thirty miles east of Spa. The Germans needed the town and its roads to funnel more divisions into the Ardennes. Its American defenders fought one of the best delaying actions of the war, heavily outnumbered, seriously outgunned, and hoping desperately for air support.[21]

The German attack was spearheaded by a 3,500-man battle group, with 150 tanks, that was part of the elite 1st SS Panzer Division. The battle group snaked along narrow country lanes north of St. Vith on December 17, with orders to lead the drive to Liege and Antwerp. By afternoon it had nearly reached Spa. Its advance posed a deadly threat to the rear of American defenses. Quesada asked for Tac R volunteers to locate the 1st SS Panzer spearhead despite the unflyable weather: the ceiling was about 100 feet, with drifting fog.

Two F-4 pilots of 67th Tactical Recon Group flew their Lightnings at treetop height until they found the German battle group. Then they led the P-47s of 365th and 368th Fighter Groups back to bomb, strafe and rocket the column, forcing it to grind to a halt.[22] This gave First Army's combat engineers just enough time to blow the bridges the Germans needed to keep driving west. The momentum went out of 1st SS Panzer's attack.

Forty miles southwest of St. Vith, German troops were also probing the defenses of Bastogne. This too was a major road hub, which the Germans needed to secure their southern flank against a possible attack by Patton. A race was developing between them and the 101st Airborne Division to see who could take and hold the town.

December 18 brought a slight clearing in the weather. It was enough to allow the mediums to fly. Sam Anderson's Marauders wrecked a score of bridges. On days like this, though, if the weather was good enough for the Ninth to fly, it was just as good for the GAF, and on these occasions the first task was air superiority.

By December 22 the Germans had driven a large salient, or bulge, into the Allied line, and that day the defenders of St. Vith began to fall back. The Germans would be able to feed another two hundred thousand men into the battle and reinvigorate Hitler's offensive.

Most of the time the weather had kept tactical aircraft on both sides grounded, but that afternoon Sam Anderson's meteorologist told him a Russian High was moving in—the weather would clear overnight from east to west.[23] Anderson ordered a maximum effort for the next day. He launched 625 mediums on interdiction strikes. With the heavy bombers of the Eighth joining the tactical battle, many of the mediums had to fly without escort. Anderson's 391st Bomb Group attacked a large bridge unescorted, and lost 16 planes, but fulfilled its mission.[24]

At Bastogne a ferocious ground battle had developed, with fifteen thousand Americans holding the town, and sixty thousand Germans besieging it. On December 23 Pathfinders from IX Troop Carrier jumped in to set up beacons for an airlift with gliders and C-47s to resupply the defenders.

On Christmas Eve the Eighth threw its full weight into the battle of the Bulge, launching 2,046 aircraft. It dropped 5,000 tons of bombs on German marshalling yards and airfields. Its fighter pilots and aerial gunners claimed 160 GAF planes shot down.[25]

On Christmas Day the senior 101st officer in Bastogne, Brigadier General Anthony McAuliffe, asked the Ninth for medical teams, gasoline, and ammo. IX Troop Carrier Command, which had moved most of its groups to Orléans, sent in the first glider on December 26. It carried thirteen doctors and nurses. The second glider had ammunition.

Next day the C-47s of the 440th TC Group flew over Bastogne. In one of them was 2nd Lieutenant William S. Weber, a navigator. "We would have to approach through a curtain of intense flak to reach the landing zone," he reported. "Planes were entering the flak area and actually disappearing. I went up to the cockpit and asked our pilot, 'Do we have to go through that?' He simply said 'Yes.'

"We entered the flak area . . . our plane started to stall because of the drag of the glider . . . the pilot dropped the nose to regain airspeed. Then the left engine burst into flames and the pilot yelled 'Bail out!' . . . Once I hit the ground and got out of the chute, I heard a German voice right in front of me, and I looked up into the barrel of a rifle. . . ."[26]

Of the twenty-one planes of the 440th that flew to Bastogne that day, thirteen were shot down, but most of the gliders were cut loose and came down within the defenses. The 439th Group managed to put thirty-five glider loads into Bastogne. In one day more than fifty tons of fuel and ammunition had been delivered, just as McAuliffe's artillery was down to an average of four rounds per gun.[27]

On December 26 the Germans began to fall back from the town as Patton's armor, after driving one hundred miles over ice-covered roads, thrust into it from the south. Hitler's troops never even reached the Meuse. They were turned back just as the battle at Bastogne came to a climax.

Hitler's last gasp in this failed offensive came at dawn on New Year's Day. Nearly nine hundred German fighters, what remained of Galland's fighter reserve, were hurled at seventeen Allied airfields in Holland, Belgium, and northern France. The blow fell hardest on the RAF, which had pushed a lot of its planes forward to compensate for a lack of range. It lost 160 planes destroyed outright or written off as unrepairable.

American airfields were also struck, including the one at Asch, which based the Thunderbolts of 366th Fighter Group and the Mustangs of the 352nd. The P-47s had taken off on a close support mission when fifty fighters from JG 11 appeared on the horizon at 9 A.M. The P-47s dumped their bombs and rockets and turned into the German planes (a mixture of 109s and 190s) to cover the 352nd's takeoff.

Lieutenant Colonel John C. Meyer, deputy group commanding officer and already a triple ace, reported, "As I pulled my wheels up, the Controller reported there were bandits east of the field. . . . I ran into about thirty 190s at fifteen hundred feet. There were many 109s above them. I picked out a 190 and pressed the trigger. Nothing happened. I reached down and turned on my gun switch and gave him a couple of good bursts.

"As I watched him hit the ground and explode I felt myself being hit. I broke sharply to the right, and up. A 190 was about fifty yards behind me and firing away. As I was turning with him another 51 attacked him and he broke off his attack on me. I then saw that I had several twenty-millimeter holes in each wing, and another hit in my oil tank. My left aileron control was also out. I was losing oil but my pressure and temperature were steady. I could see no reason for landing immediately so I turned toward a big dogfight. . . ." Meyer shot down three more planes before there was so much oil on his windshield he had to land.[28]

American losses at Asch and elsewhere came to four Mustangs and one Thunderbolt shot down; forty planes were destroyed on the ground. Galland's losses, however, were staggering. Roughly two hundred Luftwaffe pilots were killed or taken prisoner. Most were half-trained and inexperienced.[29]

Four days later Tac R pilots flew their first dicing missions for six months. Ground commanders wanted FEBA (forward edge of the battle) reports before they mounted the drive that would finally erase the Bulge.[30] As the Tac R pilots flew fast and low into Germany, they saw roads jammed with retreating German vehicles. Along the roads trudged long gray lines of shivering, defeated German troops.

23

THE COUNTRY
THAT WAS

By late 1944 Doolittle commanded two thousand heavy bombers, with two crews for every bomber and about 70 percent serviceability. He also had nearly twelve hundred fighters. The destructive power of the Eighth Air Force evolved a ritual which, spread by films and books, lodged in American folk memory of how modern war was waged.

It began with a group's aircrews being wakened around three in the morning for breakfast. After that, pilots, copilots, navigators, and bombardiers would go to the briefing at four o'clock. Some dark-colored drapes would be drawn, exposing operational maps on a small podium at one end of the cheerless, smoke-filled room. Long silk ribbons drew a blood-red line from the group's airfield in eastern England to the target for the day. The group commander would explain the operation. An intelligence officer would give the lowdown on expected flak and fighter opposition. The briefing would end with watches being synchronized: "Five . . . four . . . three . . . two . . . one. Hack!" Watch stems were pushed in, chairs pushed back.

If engine start had been set for 6:30 A.M., there'd be 250 men climbing aboard 25 heavies at 6:15 carrying parachutes, machine guns, flak suits, bombsights, escape kits and good-luck charms. Ten seconds before 6:30 the energizers would be started, bringing the plane's electrical system to life.

At 6:30 A.M. two yellow flares rose above the control tower. A hundred engines coughed into action, filling the countryside with a powerful throbbing that drowned out the birds. At 6:35 a yellow flare and a green flare were fired, the signal for planes to start taxiing into position for takeoff. All 21 planes the group had assigned to fly the mission moved from the long airfield perimeter track onto the runway, along with four spares to cover aborts. As watches reached 7 o'clock two green flares hissed and burned in sulfurous arcs. The first plane thundered down the runway and lifted slowly into the air.[1]

The rest of the group took off at precise thirty-second intervals. When all twenty-one heavily laden aircraft were finally in the air, it took another hour or so to form them into combat bomb wings. With more than a thousand bombers crowded into the skies of East Anglia—an area the size of Connecticut—assembly ships were needed for the planes of each group to rally on. Some fired flares to identify themselves. Others were painted in dazzling designs, with bright polka dots or lightning flashes. The most unmistakable object in the sky was probably the Day-Glo orange Liberator of the 446th Bomb Group, which had neon lights outlining its fuselage.

As it assembled above the cloud tops, this swiftly gathering host appeared clearly on German radar screens. GAF fighter control centers, or "battle opera houses," started signaling fighter and flak units to get ready.

At eight-fifteen in the morning, with the groups assembled and formed into combat wings, they set off. Even now there were group and wing commanders flying alongside in Mustangs and Thunderbolts, punching their R/Ts, barking instructions to tighten up the formation, and generally riding herd until the group was out over the North Sea.[2]

With the entire Eighth in flight, a column of as many as fourteen hundred heavy bombers stretched seventy miles, from East Anglia to the Dutch coast. Above, weaving S-patterns to keep pace with the plodding bombers, flew hundreds of Eighth Air Force fighters, while several groups ranged far ahead to keep the GAF at bay. No one could see more than a small portion of this spectacle, yet even the fragments were stunning.

Two thirds of the bombers were B-17s, mainly the G model with its distinctive chin turret. The B-17G was nine thousand pounds heavier than the B-17C of 1940. It had 300 miles more range, and three times the bomb load, carrying as many as fourteen five hundred-pound bombs.[3] Just being assigned to a B-17 made men feel part of a military elite. They loved their plane, and counted on it to bring them home. It was a wonderfully strong and dependable machine. B-17 crews had come back on two engines, with a third periodically catching fire.

The B-24, by contrast, wasn't nearly as solid, yet it needed structural ruggedness more. It flew several thousand feet lower than a B-17 with the same bomb load, and the bulbous nose turret that had been added slowed it down and made it wallow.[4]

Flying one of these missions was a unique experience for everyone who did it. For Lieutenant Bert Stiles of Denver, Colorado, his first mission as a B-17 copilot in mid-1944 was both typical and different.

"I went up to look at the bombs, and I tore the whole back end out of my flying suit crawling through the bomb bay. We were hauling ten 500s, big and blunt-nosed and ugly things. I patted one a couple of times and it felt cold and dead.

"When all the guns were in we huddled up back by the tail. It was sort of like a locker-room in high school before a ball game, only not so tense. Crone [a waist gunner] said, 'I hope the bastards come in on my side.' Sharpe [the tail gunner] said, 'I hope they all stay in the sack.' "

Once airborne, the group assembled slowly and got into formation. "We formed at seventeen thousand feet and my oxygen mask was bothering me, and my hair was soupy with sweat, and I couldn't move my shoulders in my electric suit. It was too late to do anything, though."

As Stiles's plane crossed into Germany, he was at the controls. Another B-17 began moving erratically, loosening up the entire formation. "Everyone started chopping throttles back. I overran the lead. . . . I looked up into the sun and knew right then we were meat for the Luftwaffe. I could feel them up there waiting for a chance like this. . . .

"I didn't have any idea we were near the target until I saw the lead ship's bomb-bays swing open. . . . I crouched down, waiting for the flak to start. By all the rules there was supposed to be flak around us, right in our laps. The bombs fell out of the lead ship and the bombardier yelled ours were gone. 'Wahooo!' someone yelled from the back end. 'Look at all that smoke.' Everybody was talking at once. We had the RPM jacked up, swinging off the target. Still no flak. . . . All the planes were letting down a thousand feet so we could get out of the country a little sooner. . . .

"There were quite a few airplanes in sight when we came in, but on the way out [over France] we saw thousands. Every direction up or down or sideways there were airplanes, big birds and little friends. . . . Two P-51s came jazzing by, looking for game. . . . Then I heard this guy call into the wing leader, 'I'm going down. Our oxygen's gone. Can you get us some escort.' He was breathing like a horse. 'My navigator's shot to hell. I got to go down.' There was terror in his voice. . . .

"When we hit the English coast I was flying. 'Tighten it up a little,' the pilot said. 'They said to tighten it up.' He waved me in closer. We were supposed to look sharp when we flew over some field on the coast because Doolittle and Spaatz were down there watching. . . . I don't know how we looked. I know I didn't care much. I had never been so tired."[5]

The Eighth under Doolittle was led firmly and effectively. He had the esteem of his group commanders from the start; it took him longer to become popular with bomber crews.[6] For one thing, they felt he'd left them naked when he freed the fighters to hunt down the GAF. For another, in late March 1944, with air superiority won, heavy bomber tours were increased from twenty-five to thirty missions, on orders from Arnold. Doolittle, however, took the responsibility and the scorn.[7]

A morale crisis hit the Eighth. In April 1944, fifty-two crews landed in Switzerland and Sweden; there'd been only ten foreign internments in March. Most of the fifty-two planes had suffered only slight damage; some had suffered none.[8] Dozens more crews sought sanctuary over the next few months. Once Allied armies reached the German border, the internment crisis passed. Return journeys now were mainly over liberated lands and the Eighth's loss rate was below two percent per mission. When, in September, the tour was raised to thirty-five missions crews didn't like it, but few protested.[9]

Each time the Eighth took to the air, half the men aloft were aerial gunners. They had come a long way since 1942–43 when, short of training and experience, they claimed to have shot down more than twice as many planes as the GAF possessed. Early efforts to improvise training in England had failed dismally.[10] Gunners tended to hose one small corner of the sky, or produced a W pattern to cover a larger area. Firing in protracted bursts heated gun barrels until they became distorted and the bullets dribbled out.

Aerial gunners had been taught to lead an enemy plane, the way you would a clay pigeon as it rises in the air. If you lead it properly, the target flies into the pattern of shot. Yet against a pursuit curve attack by fighters closing on a bomber from the side or rear, the right technique was to aim behind the fighter, not to lead it. As it completed the curve it would fly straight into the line of fire. When this was explained to the Ploesti groups in July 1943 by a leading RAF gunnery expert, Squadron Leader George Barlow, the gunners were simply incredulous.[11]

By early 1944 there were seven aerial gunnery schools in operation in the United States. They taught the right theories and boasted advanced teaching aids in which movie film and sound systems were linked to both fixed and flexible machine guns to provide realistic training.[12] And the most advanced method of all appeared that August. It was known as Operation Pinball and featured a new airplane, the Bell RP-63.

Bigger and faster than the P-39 but with a strong family resemblance to it, the RP-63 was painted orange and had an armor plate skin. In the propeller hub, where a thirty-seven-millimeter cannon was intended to go, a red light had been installed instead. The wings and fuselage were wired so that if struck by a bullet, the red light would flash. A frangible bullet, made of lead and plastic, was loaded into the guns aboard the obsolescent bombers that were used for aerial gunnery practice. The RP-63 would make classic pursuit curve attacks. Each bullet that hit the oncoming fighter disintegrated on impact but left a smudge on the plane's orange surface. A hit counter in the plane kept score, but if that failed a student's shooting could be judged by the number of smudges.[13]

Losses among aerial gunners were exceptionally high in 1943. Aircrew were provided with parachutes, but nearly all refused to wear them—macho pride. The chutes would pile up in the waist.[14] When the bail out bell sounded, men would grab their chutes—if they could find them.* For gunners in ball and tail turrets, chances were they wouldn't have enough time to get out, reach the waist, snap on a chute, then leave the plane. A stricken bomber was likely

---

*Archie Old's solution was to request fifteen thousand linear feet of rope: twenty feet for every crewmember in the 96th Bomb Group. This would be attached to the man at one end and his chute at the other. He could then dump his chute when he boarded the plane, but when he bailed out, the chute followed him. There was plenty of time while falling from twenty thousand feet to climb the rope and snap the parachute onto the chute harness that every aircrew member wore over his flying clothing.[15]

to go into a spin very quickly and its centrifugal force pinned men to the walls.

As the flow of volunteers dried up, men were assigned to aerial gunnery. Arnold hoped to overcome the recruitment crisis by making it glamorous again. Clark Gable was trying to get into the AAF, at the age of forty-one, and asked if he could be a captain, too. Arnold sent him to Officer Candidate School first, with an MGM cameraman. On graduation, both were commissioned and sent to aerial gunnery school. Then they went to England in mid-1943 to make a movie.[16] They flew at least three missions and returned to the United States with fifty thousand feet of film.

By the time it had been edited, the crisis had passed. The rate of bomber losses in the Eighth in early 1944 was half what it had been in October 1943, and was still falling. It was ironic, but welcome all the same, that just as aerial gunnery training became effective and as decent gun turrets finally appeared, the GAF fighter ceased to be a major threat. The biggest hazards now were the flak and the cold; the AAF seemed to be getting on top of these, too.

The prewar Air Staff had never expected to have to bomb from thirty thousand feet, so the AAF was tardy developing adequate flying clothing. In the winter of 1942 70 percent of the Eighth's casualties were frostbite cases or deaths from hypothermia.[17] George Kenney had bought the electrically heated underwear of a Luftwaffe flyer who'd crashed in the French Alps in May 1940 and put the Matériel Division on the right track. The result was the F-1 heated flying suit.[18] But as Eighth aircrew soon discovered, the wires in the F-1 broke too easily and too often. It was replaced in 1943 by the F-2, a two-piece, two-layer ensemble, with a heated inner layer and a wool "elastique" outer shell.

Not even the F-2, however, could cope with the intense coldness over northern Europe at thirty thousand feet in winter. And the gloves heated only the palm of the hand, when it was the fingers that needed the heat.[19]

In 1944 the AAF introduced the three-layer F-3 flying suit, with heat in the middle layer. The F-3 was designed to provide comfort even at − 60 degrees Fahrenheit. For the most part, the F-3 was a great success. Frostbite casualties in the winter of 1944 were only 15 percent of the Eighth's losses.

That left the flak. Three fourths of shrapnel wounds were caused by small fragments of metal traveling at relatively slow velocities:

they had been slowed down by hitting the aircraft first. In 1943 the chief surgeon of the Eighth, Colonel Malcom C. Grow, asked the Wilkinson Sword Company to help him develop body armor. Out of their efforts came flak vests, made up of overlapping tiers of small steel plates sewn into a long and sturdy canvas jacket, and groin armor, which covered a major concern.[20]

The Matériel Command meanwhile developed flak curtains, which hooked up around crew stations, or lined the floor underneath aerial gunners' feet. Wright Field also came up with the M-3 flying helmet, combining the protection of a sturdy manganese steel pot with enough room to accommodate headphones. By the winter of 1944 Doolittle's aircrews flew into battle the most heavily armored warriors since knighthood was in flower.

In the fall of 1944 the Germans rose in force to challenge only one large raid in three, but the GAF adopted a line abreast tactic that brought the combined firepower of a dozen fighters against one American bomber at a time. It was a development that had Doolittle worried. He was even more concerned by the Me-262. He feared he could lose as many as one hundred bombers to jets on a single mission.[21]

The P-51 groups learned to break up the line abreast tactic and the jets took such heavy losses when Allied fighters caught them landing or taking off that they were grounded in mid-November. The Eighth could bomb where it pleased.

Air strategy focused, as we've seen, on oil first and German transportation second. To keep Arthur Harris happy, the RAF was authorized to attack "important industrial areas," meaning German cities, with the aim of breaking morale.[22]

Back in 1940 the RAF had planned to attack oil targets instead, but when it tried to do so in 1941 it suffered heavy losses and accomplished nothing. RAF bomber crews could find synthetic oil plants by moonlight, but couldn't bomb them accurately. It was only after that failure that German homes became Bomber Command's first priority.

Spaatz had intended to attack German oil from the moment he got command of the Eighth in May 1942.[23] Unfortunately, radar and bombsights remained fairly primitive throughout the war. Synthetic fuel plants covered large areas, yet the key installations within them were small and hard to hit. Spaatz ruled out attacking them except in clear weather.

As far as Albert Speer, the mastermind behind German arms production was concerned, Allied strategic bombing had no serious impact on Germany before May 1944. Until then, nothing important had been bombed beyond repair. The bombing campaign was fitful, with long pauses between major raids. No clear goal was consistently pursued. All that changed abruptly on May 12, with the Eighth's attack on synthetic oil plants at Leuna-Merseberg.[24]

The Germans responded strongly to this new threat. Decoy plants proliferated, and these absorbed a third of the tonnage dropped in the ensuing oil campaign.[25] There were thousands of smoke generators that obscured oil targets even on perfect bombing days, making precision bombing almost impossible. The petrochemicals complex at Leuna-Merseberg had the heaviest flak defenses in the Reich, stronger even than Berlin's. There were large oil stocks on hand to cover emergencies. Even so, once the oil campaign against Ploesti and Leuna-Merseberg got rolling that summer the GAF could neither train properly for want of fuel nor rise to challenge every major raid.

In the fall, the German Army lost much of its mobility for lack of gasoline and diesel. The fifteen hundred tanks Hitler committed to the Bulge offensive couldn't go far. The Germans had to count on capturing American fuel stocks to keep their panzers moving. When American combat engineers ignited fuel drums that seemed in danger of capture, they hit the Wehrmacht where it hurt. In December 1944 German oil production crashed to 33 percent of the January level and stocks were nearly exhausted.[26]

Whenever weather permitted visual bombing, the heavies were expected to attack oil. On cloudy days they were expected to attack transportation targets. A sprawling marshalling yard or a large railroad bridge crossing a major river could be identified on H2X no matter how solid the cloud cover. And the weather was so bad from October to February that German railroads got a lot of attention. By this roundabout, backdoor way, Allied air strategy finally grasped the key to destroying the German war economy.

The German military needed oil, gasoline and diesel for its tanks, its trucks and its planes. But the war economy that produced the weapons, the vehicles and the ammunition, depended on something else—coal. Ninety percent of Germany's energy needs were provided by coal, and 90 percent of the coal was hauled by the Deutsche Reichsbahn, the German railroad. The remaining 10 percent was moved from the coal-producing areas, such as the Ruhr and Silesia, via an extensive river and canal system.

Tedder had urged transportation attacks without realizing the coal-Reichsbahn connection. No one had really figured it out, and many intelligence people, including the Eighth's Economic Objectives Unit, refused to believe it was worth attacking railroads.[27]

Nevertheless, Tedder and Zuckerman had left Italy convinced that transportation attacks worked. They argued strongly for them before D-Day, and again after the liberation of France. Tedder drew on the excellent working relationship he enjoyed with Eisenhower to put his case across.[28] He even got a concession from Harris. In October RAF Bomber Command changed its aiming points from German city centers to marshalling yards near the city centers.

The Reichsbahn came under ferocious attack from the Fortresses of 1st and 3rd Air divisions. Meanwhile the Liberators of Kepner's 2nd Air Division joined the RAF in an onslaught against the waterways. Canals were breached, leaving the coal barges high and dry. Arms production plummeted as coal piled up at pitheads, unmoved, unmoveable.

About the time Harris changed his aiming points, Hitler gave railroad repair absolute priority, even over military defenses.[29] And the failure of Operation Queen to blast a way into Germany in November seemed about to bring the Reichsbahn a reprieve, in which the million Germans and slave laborers engaged on bomb-damage repairs might get it rolling again. On December 5 Bradley secured a change in bombing priorities: first oil, and second carpet bombing to aid the ground advance.

The Bulge offensive postponed Bradley's new onslaught. Instead, the 12th Army Group found itself in a desperate defensive battle to hold the Ardennes. The Eighth and Ninth were thrown into a new interdiction campaign, whose objective was to drive the German railheads back until there was no rail traffic west of the Rhine in the region of the Ardennes.

German supply lines were stretched until they broke.[30] The 60,000 men trying to take Bastogne found themselves at the end of December clinging to a 125-mile supply line that had almost dried up. Trucks might have moved toward the front at night, and the German Army had plenty of vehicles. What it didn't have was fuel.

The Bulge offensive took the Reichsbahn to the edge of the abyss, then pushed it over. The railroads, under a Niagara of bombs day and night, couldn't cope with the Wehrmacht's demands. The signals and switching machinery in the marshalling yards were wrecked and irreplaceable; repair crews were exhausted and without essential tools. In January, rail traffic was one fourth the normal level. It was now only a matter of weeks before the Reichsbahn ground to a halt.

During the Bulge offensive, between December 16 and January 6, the Eighth and Ninth claimed more than 400 GAF fighters shot down. The RAF and the Red Air Force shot down hundreds more. The loss of as many as pilots in just three weeks still didn't end the German fighter threat. The underground Me-262 factories in southern Germany were still in production and new jet squadrons were training for combat. On January 9 Spaatz got Eisenhower to give jet factories and airfields equal priority with oil.[31]

Churchill was meanwhile pressing for cities in eastern Germany to be made high-priority targets. He hoped to swamp German civil authorities with floods of refugees. Such hordes, moreover, would swamp the roads and besiege the railroad stations, hindering German military traffic. Spaatz obliged by ordering the Eighth to strike Berlin. Not the industries of Berlin, not the marshalling yards of Berlin, but the city center—the heart of German government and an area of high population density.

Doolittle protested that such an attack would be terrorism, without any justification on military grounds.[32] The morality of heavy bombing in residential areas, where large numbers of civilians were sure to be killed and mutilated, was a long-running debate among AAF commanders. It was conducted *sotto voce,* like a family dispute you wouldn't want the neighbors to know about.[33]

Spaatz, however, wasn't prepared to discuss it. He insisted the attack go ahead. On February 3 nearly 1,000 heavy bombers struck Berlin, with the city center as their aiming point. All the 23 bombers shot down fell to flak. Some 3,000 Berliners perished; 120,000 were made homeless.

The next big city bombed was Dresden. It had never been attacked, but its arms industries, employing 50,000 workers, made it a legitimate military target. It also contained a large marshalling yard. On the night of February 13, the RAF hit Dresden with 2,700 tons of bombs; nearly 50 percent were incendiaries. What ensued, thanks in part to unusual weather conditions for a winter's night in Germany, was a fire storm. A pillar of flame and smoke rose 15,000 feet over the stricken city. At noon next day, with fires still raging, the Eighth attacked, dropping another 400 tons. And on February 15, 210 B-17s unable to bomb their primary target, an oil plant, dumped their bombs on Dresden's ruins.[34] The result of the fire storm and three heavy attacks in three days was an estimated 100,000 dead and a center of European high culture reduced to ashes.

Some months earlier Quesada had proposed creating a "Jeb Stuart Air Force" of five hundred fighter-bombers that would rove across Germany in the closing stages of the war attacking minor targets such as post offices and town halls, to bring home to every German that their country had been defeated militarily. Lovett thought it a great idea.

Spaatz turned down the Jeb Stuart idea. He preferred a different plan, called Clarion, which would underline the fact of Germany's defeat but would do so by attacking the railroad stations in hundreds of towns and villages. On February 22, nine thousand Allied fighters, fighter-bombers, light bombers, and medium bombers struck from England, France, Holland, Belgium and Italy.

For the 9th Air Division it was an unforgettable experience. When Marauder crews were briefed on the mission, navigator Carl H. Moore of the 344th Bomb Group was amazed. "We were to bomb the target by flights of six, *then peel off and strafe the target!* Shades of Ijmuiden and no Marauders returning. . . . Here we were with the war almost over and me with nearly fifty missions and points enough to be discharged and we were going out in our 'slow' Marauder to *strafe.* . . .

"Our target was deep in Germany. . . . George picked up our target—a rail junction—and dropped our bombs. I knew he had been dying to use the fifty-caliber in the nose since he started flying the Marauder. . . . The Norden bombsight was in the way of effectively using the gun. So as soon as he dropped the bombs, George unhooked the Norden and handed it to me—with the gyros in it still spinning at about 3,000 rpms. My experience of using the nose gun consisted of holding a wildly spinning bombsight while George fired away. When our ammo was gone we climbed back to our comfortable altitude of 12,000 feet."[35]

Clarion was repeated next day, but it wasn't likely to achieve much. The Reichsbahn had virtually collapsed. Ruhr coal wasn't being moved and the Silesian coal fields had been captured by the Red Army. Germany was prostrate and short of strategic targets.

Allied intelligence, however, depended on aerial recon to make accurate bomb-damage assessments, and the persistent cloud cover that imposed radar bombing most of the time simultaneously hid the results of that bombing from view.

All the same, a new interdiction campaign was launched against more than sixty large road and river bridges over the Rhine to prepare for an assault crossing of the river. Montgomery's troops had barely moved for three months while they got ready. Some of the shine was taken off Monty's crossing, scheduled for March 23–24, by Hodges's troops capturing a bridge at Remagen on March 7, and on March 22 Patton's Third Army crossed near Mainz. Monty's troops began their assault shortly before midnight the next day, March 23.

A two-division airborne assault had been written into the plan, mainly to add to the spectacle. The British 6th and the U.S. 17th Airborne Divisions would be dropped a mile and a half behind the Rhine twelve hours *after* the river assault began. At worst, the airborne troops would be dropped among alerted defenders; at best, they would arrive on their drop zones and landing zones after these had been overrun by friendly troops. Ridgway protested the pointlessness of this operation, but couldn't get it abandoned.[36]

The airlift for both divisions would be provided mainly by IX Troop Carrier Command. Operation Varsity followed the by now well-established routine: Pathfinders jumping before first light, IX TAC and XXIX TAC fighter-bombers flying more than one hundred flak-busting sorties ahead of the first serials, followed by hundreds of transports and gliders bringing nearly seventeen thousand airborne soldiers into battle.

The Varsity drop was exceptionally accurate, but marred by three misfortunes. A battalion from the 507th Parachute Infantry Regiment was dropped onto a German artillery position and shot to pieces as it hit the ground. Nineteen of the new C-46 Commandos used in the drop fell out of the sky in flames. (The older, smaller C-47s, many of which had been provided with self-sealing fuel tanks, suffered light losses.) And when 240 2nd Air Division Liberators flew over the airborne troops at 500 feet during the afternoon to drop supplies, 15 were shot down by light flak.[37]

By this time the German war economy had ground to a halt. The end was clearly in sight, as Allied troops advancing from the Rhine encircled the Ruhr. Yet, astonishingly, it was now that the Me-262 threat revived. Nearly two hundred jets were operational. The most dangerous unit was an elite formation, *Jagdverband* 44, created and led by Adolf Galland after he was fired by Hitler as commander of the German day fighter arm. JV 44 was made up mainly of pilots who'd already shot down at least twenty planes.[38]

On April 7, when Doolittle sent 1,250 heavies to attack marshalling yards and oil-storage depots in north-central Germany, they encountered more than 200 GAF fighters, including at least 50 jets. With martial music playing on the radios, a dozen German pilots attempted to ram the bombers. In this, the last really big dogfight, American pilots claimed 60 victories. Half a dozen bombers were lost to fighters or flak; another eight or nine were downed by ramming.[39]

With fewer and fewer strategic targets left, the Eighth's fighters were freer than ever to roam. Fighter groups made frequent large-scale sweeps over GAF airfields and returned with huge claims of enemy planes destroyed on the ground. The record was 747 in one day.[40]

On April 11 American troops from the Ninth Army reached the Elbe, the agreed meeting line for American and Soviet forces. The Red Army was still fifty miles from Berlin. The Ninth Army could have beaten them to it and taken the city, but Bradley felt it might cost one hundred thousand U.S. casualties. Eisenhower preferred to let the Soviets take Berlin, and the losses.[41] Under the Yalta agreement the Soviets were going to be allowed to occupy the city anyway. Taking it first wouldn't shut the Communists out.

During the long wait for the Red Army to reach the Elbe, Frederick Anderson made an inspection tour. Piloting a C-54 (followed by a C-47 carrying two jeeps, food, water, and jerry cans filled with gasoline), he took with him a photographer, an intelligence officer, and a historian, Dr. Bruce C. Hopper. The report of what Anderson's party saw of the effects of strategic bombing was called, "Jeeping the Targets in the Country That Was." It read like an elegy.

"Darmstadt, a shambles seemingly without a roof intact. . . . Frankfurt, largely roofless. Looks like Pompeii magnified. . . . Aschaffenburg. Only element intact seems to be a weary little cemetery. . . . Wurzburg. A crumpled mass of peanut shells. Schweinfurt. We read the tombstones in the church graveyard . . . the streets were choked with debris, and there is an omnipresent smell of the uncovered dead. . . . Ludwigshafen. A vast ruin of rusted iron as far as the eye can see. Frightful, fantastic spectacle. . . . Worms. Torn to shreds. . . . Hanau. A ghost town. Kassel, just miles of rust staring to the sky. . . . Weimar. Again that smell of the dead beneath the rubble. . . . Munster. Another ghost. . . ."[42]

On April 25 Doolittle launched the Eighth's last strategic attack, against the Skoda works at Pilsen, Czechoslovakia. After this mission the Eighth's heavies continued to fly, but now bomb bays were filled with canned rations. Famine had gripped northern Holland after the Germans breached the dikes to slow the Allied advance. The Eighth Air Force's last wartime missions consisted of flying over Dutch football stadiums, dropping food. After that had been accomplished, 30,000 ground crew (out of 220,000) who'd toiled to keep the Eighth flying were flown from England to Germany so they too could see the results of their labors. Like Anderson and Hopper, they were awed by what bombing had wrought.[43]

Arnold looked unlikely to survive the war. He'd suffered two heart attacks in 1943, one of which nearly killed him. He'd had another coronary in May 1944. Then, several days before Roosevelt's fourth inauguration in January 1945, Arnold nearly died at his desk from a massive heart attack. He was smuggled out of the Pentagon and the affair was hushed up, for fear that this time Marshall wouldn't waive the regulation that forced officers with heart disease to retire.[44] But Marshall, who himself suffered from a serious heart murmur, overlooked Arnold's latest coronary.

Arnold began a long convalescence in Coral Gables. He was a burned-out man. The strain of war had taken a heavy toll. To some high-ranking officers he'd become a "terrorizing and intimidating" figure. According to Major General Kenneth B. Wolfe, who'd known him for twenty-five years, Arnold wasn't impatient—"He was unreasonable."[45]

His temper tantrums defied belief. When Opie Weyland had worked for him they had gotten into an argument over sending new planes to Kenney. Arnold ranted, then picked up a full inkwell and hurled it, splattering ink all over his office wall.[46] On another occasion, when arguing with former Assistant Secretary of War Trubee Davison, he picked up the crippled Davison's cane from the desk top where Davison had placed it, and hurled it at Davison.[47]

The war had become too big and too complicated for a handful of bright young colonels on the Advisory Council to handle. Yet

Arnold still avoided operating through a staff, and the three brigadier generals who bore the imposing title of deputy chief of staff were, in the words of one of them, "errand boys."[48]

He relied increasingly on former Advisory Council members who'd been to war and returned as generals, such as Norstad, Cabell and Dean. He also engaged in extensive correspondence with George Kenney, whose quick brain he was always happy to pick.

The one management tool he liked was statistical control. He got the best statistician in the Women's Army Corps, Vi Duffie, assigned as his personal number-cruncher. Lieutenant (eventually Major) Duffie briefed him at one o'clock every afternoon on the state of the AAF. She reduced the combat readiness of the AAF worldwide to a single page, updated every twenty-four hours, showing losses, production, the number of trained crews, serviceability, tonnage dropped, etc. Arnold carried this in his wallet and recited the relevant figures whenever he needed them in a discussion with Stimson, say, or Marshall.[49]

Statistical control aside, Arnold's approach to problem solving was, said Davison, "Quite emotional. . . . Instinctive, yes."[50] Although most officers felt that Arnold was the best man by far to run the wartime Army Air Forces, there were some able young generals who felt that Andrews, had he lived, could have run it more effectively.

Yet whatever his shortcomings, real or imagined, Arnold had one indisputable advantage: he possessed a big enough personality to defend the AAF's interests in high-level conferences against imposing figures like MacArthur and King. His most likely successor, Spaatz, was too shy, too inarticulate, to have stepped into Arnold's shoes. And, of course, he had the trust of Marshall. That was an asset above price.

During the long convalescence in Coral Gables in early 1945 the AAF was run, for all intents and purposes, not by Deputy Commanding General Barney Giles, but by Robert Lovett. Marshall simply ignored Giles. Lovett sat in on Air Staff meetings and became, in effect, the chief, to Arnold's distant but intense irritation.[51]

Even so, Arnold had really had enough. Heart and mind were fixed on retirement to a small ranch in Sonoma. In the closing stages of the war all he wanted was to get his fifth star and see Germany defeated before he left. He returned to Washington at the end of March, but almost immediately fell ill again. Eaker returned from Europe to become Deputy Commanding General and Arnold went on another extended convalescence.

He traveled to France, then moved on to Italy. Arriving in Caserta, he proceeded to tell Twining that the Fifteenth Air Force was prolonging the war: a typical Arnold inspection. On the morning of May 6 he was scheduled to inspect the B-17s of the 456th Bomb Group of Fifteenth Air Force, commanded by Colonel Thomas W. "Sadie" Steed, "goat" of the West Point class of 1928.

The planes were gleaming, the aircrew standing stiffly at attention. Steed briefed Arnold before the inspection, proudly presenting photographs of the 456th's bombing, when a message arrived for Arnold. He read it, took off his reading glasses, turned to Steed and asked, "Colonel, do you have a good camera?" Steed fetched his camera. Arnold said, "Now I'm going to take some pictures of the flora and fauna." He handed the secret message to Twining. It read, "Unconditional surrender agreed, 6th of May." Steed asked, "Aren't you going to inspect my airplanes, general?"

"I've inspected my last airplane," said Arnold.[52] He never returned to his Pentagon office.

Two days later the surrender came into effect. Galland's JV 44 pilots torched their Me-262s, but more than a thousand pilots were determined to fly to the airfield nearest their homes and surrender there. The skies over Germany were crowded with the Luftwaffe's last hurrah, as grizzled old pilots and fresh-faced youths still in training climbed into every kind of plane and used the last of the GAF's fuel in a stunning aerial spectacle of defeat. They were shepherded by Tac R pilots flying their final missions, as aerial traffic cops, to ensure that yesterday's enemy got home in one piece.[53]

24

MINOR KEYS

More than 3,000,000 people served in the wartime Army Air Forces. Of these, only 190,000 were pilots. Yet from start to finish the AAF was a pilot-led, pilot-oriented, pilot-fascinated service. And within this minority were even smaller yet significant minorities. This chapter will consider three of these, because their experience excited interest out of all proportion to the number of people involved—female pilots, black pilots, and ace pilots.

Before 1940 flying was too expensive for all but a handful of civilians to contemplate. The few female pilots had rich and doting parents or rich and adoring husbands. When the Civilian Pilot Training Program—"the Putt-Putt Air Force"—was established on college campuses to create a large pool of civilian flyers, three thousand young women were enabled to get a private pilot's license.

The queen bee among female flyers was Jacqueline Cochran. This glamorous and celebrated aviator was on friendly terms with all the major players in the aviation industry, and with Arnold. A tall, striking bottle-blonde, Cochran was one of the most remarkable women of her generation. Reared in appalling poverty in Alabama, she'd become a beautician, married a multimillionaire, established a successful cosmetics business, and won a roomful of airplane-racing trophies.

Shortly before Pearl Harbor she undertook to recruit American women pilots for the RAF's Air Transport Auxiliary, which ferried planes within the British Isles. She took her recruits to England in early 1942, believing that if and when the AAF got around to establishing something similar in the United States she would be in charge of it.[1]

While she was gone another female aviator, the beautiful Nancy Harkness Love, persuaded the head of the Air Transport Command, Major General Harold L. George (one of the authors of AWPD-1) that female pilots could ease the manpower crisis besetting his Ferrying Division. Eleanor Roosevelt praised the idea in her newspaper column, making it virtually impossible for Arnold to turn it down. Moreover, Mrs. Love was well connected both by birth and by marriage. Her millionaire husband, Colonel Bob Love, was George's chief of staff and the owner of Love Field in Dallas.[2] In September 1942 the Women's Auxiliary Ferrying Service, or WAFS, began operations, at Love Field, with a small group of pilots chosen by and answering to Mrs. Love.

Jackie Cochran returned home feeling betrayed. Arnold attempted to make amends by placing her in charge of the training of all female pilots working for the AAF. Mrs. Cochran's outfit was known as the Women's Flying Training Detachment. It set up operations at the Howard Hughes Airfield outside Houston in late 1942, before moving in mid-1943 to Avenger Field in Sweetwater, Texas.

Unlike AAF aviation cadets, who never had to have left the ground before taking their first lesson, the trainee pilots Mrs. Cochran recruited had to have at least thirty-five hours in the air. She didn't want anyone who might suffer from air sickness.[3] Arnold hoped, he told her, to have as many as five thousand women pilots before the war ended. She considered this hopelessly ambitious. Not that there was any shortage of applicants: twenty-five thousand women applied for flight training. Jackie Cochran accepted only two thousand.

In August 1943 the Women's Flying Training Detachment and the WAFS were merged to create the Women's Airforce Service Pilots, or WASP. Cochran was hoping the AAF would soon turn the WASP into a Women's Flying Corps, with its own uniform, its own insignia, and its own leader—herself.[4] In such an arrangement her pilots would have military rank and entitlements. As things stood now, they were only civilian employees of the War Department. They had civil service rank, but were paid 20 percent less than men at the same grade.

Arnold had no objections to Jackie Cochran's plans, but Marshall did. He thought female pilots should be commissioned in the

Women's Army Corps. The problem with that idea was that it would put these women under the command of Colonel Oveta Culp Hobby. Jackie Cochran refused to accept that a groundling such as Hobby could be considered fit to command pilots, who were a race apart, "a different breed of cat."[5] She dropped the Women's Flying Corps idea.

The level of commitment among trainee WASPs was high, and serious discipline problems were rare. Jackie Cochran set up a board to handle infractions, such as dating instructors. Most trainees who found they couldn't put up with military discipline and military bureaucracy simply quit.[6]

Meanwhile, the twenty-three-week program at Avenger Field turned out new pilots. The course involved a lot of cross-country flying in open cockpit airplanes. Aspiring WASPs flew the standard primary, basic and advanced trainers of the AAF. There were acrobatics, which very few women had ever attempted before this program demanded it, and plenty of instrument and night flying. They had to meet AAF standards and those who didn't—roughly 50 percent—washed out.

The 1,074 who graduated could look forward to ferrying trainers and transports. A few would ferry bombers. Those hoping to ferry fighters went to pursuit school first.

The commander of the Ferrying Division, Colonel William Tunner, was critical of Avenger Field graduates. Love's pilots had a minimum of five hundred hours before they were hired; some had more than one thousand. Cochran's pilots were neophytes in comparison. Tunner retrained them. And despite the creation of the WASP he continued to consider Love to be in charge of his female ferrying pilots.

Tunner was eventually delighted with the WASPs. They delivered 12,652 planes with only three fatal accidents.[7] That was a better record than male ferrying pilots achieved. A further 34 women perished in training accidents.

Some concessions to the female anatomy were inevitable. WASPs appear to have been limited to ferrying planes where raw physical strength was not a requirement, and kept away from planes such as the B-24, which needed a fullback's legs to push on the heavy rudder pedals for seven or eight hours. They weren't expected to fly really long flights, anyway: the relief tubes in AAF aircraft were of no use to women. Still, there wasn't a plane in the inventory, including the P-59 and the B-29, that WASPs didn't fly.

Mainly, though, they took aircraft from the factory to the port of embarkation; a few took planes to the front. They test-flew repaired aircraft to ensure they were safe. They towed targets, albeit reluctantly. They also served as instructors, teaching male pilots military skills such as strafing and bombing.

Arnold and Cochran lobbied Congress hard to get the WASP made a part of the AAF. A bill was introduced into the House of Representatives and, in June 1944, failed by only nineteen votes. In December the WASP was disbanded. It wasn't until 1977 that Congress finally extended military benefits, and the Victory Medal, to former WASPs.

If blacks were ever to win equal treatment in peace they had to make equal sacrifices in war. Military service has always been one of the most powerful unifying forces in American life, along with the flag, the Fourth of July, and Thanksgiving.

The Army, however, had serious doubts about blacks. Absurd as it may seem now, there was a fundamental belief that blacks wouldn't fight. The idea that they might make fighter pilots simply seemed ridiculous.[8]

This belief had nothing to do with historical evidence. A black aviator, Eugene Jacques Bullard, had been one of the best pilots of the Lafayette Escadrille in World War I. Another black flyer, James Peck, had been credited with five aerial victories while fighting for the Republicans in the Spanish Civil War. J. C. Robinson had flown in combat against the Italian invaders of Ethiopia in 1937. Yet no black pilot had ever served in the U.S. Army or its Air Corps.

Then, in 1939, the Civilian Pilot Training Program (CPTP) began operations. Of the four hundred thousand people the CPTP accepted, some twenty-five hundred were black.[9] Meanwhile, the pressure from the black press to have black pilots in uniform became intense. In September 1940, with the election near and Arnold desperate to keep the President happy, the Air Corps decided to create a black fighter squadron.[10] It would be trained at the principal site of CPTP flight training for blacks, the Tuskegee Institute, in Tuskegee, Alabama.

When the program began in early 1941 the initial intake included Captain Benjamin O. Davis, Jr., West Point class of 1936. The son of one of the prewar Army's few black officers and first black general, Davis had accumulated so many demerits in his plebe year at the Academy he looked certain to be dismissed. The commandant, Colonel Simon Bolivar Buckner, canceled half the demerits, apparently taking the view that many were prompted by racial hostility.[11]

Certainly there was nothing about Davis that suggested anything but an able soldier who refused to let his race be a problem. Throughout his career fellow officers were consistently impressed by his military bearing, his unusual intelligence and, above all, an iron self-discipline.[12]

In his fourth year at West Point he applied, like a third of his classmates, for flight training. Davis was turned down solely because he was black. The chief of the Air Corps, Oscar Westover, thought rejecting Davis on racial grounds was an excellent idea: it would discourage other black officers from trying to become pilots.[13]

When he took up flying at Tuskegee in July 1941, Davis proved to be a competent pilot. But there were persistent, albeit unfounded, rumors that only his special status as the War Department's hand-picked commander for the proposed black fighter squadron saved him from being washed out.[14]

In August 1942, Davis took command of the squadron, although by this time he was a lieutenant colonel—the rank of a group commander. The all-black 99th Fighter Squadron was considered an experiment. It didn't move overseas until the war in North Africa drew to a close.

There, it spent a month at Fardjouana, where it was trained by combat veterans such as Philip Cochran, who'd shot down two German fighters in Tunisia and received half a dozen awards for bravery. Cochran liked the men of the 99th from the outset. "Those colored boys are fine," he reported.[15]

What would hurt them, he thought, was the fact that no one had any experience. Davis didn't know any more about combat than the most junior pilot in his command. There were too few pilots in the squadron and no adequate system of replacements for it to pull its weight. And although they'd spent a lot of time in training, about all the men of the 99th had been taught, Cochran discovered, was how to take off in their P-40s and how to land. They had no combat flying skills when they arrived in North Africa.[16]

Davis's squadron was attached to the 33rd Fighter Group, commanded by Lieutenant Colonel William S. Momyer, and made its combat debut over Pantelleria. On July 2, 1943 Lieutenant Charles Hall scored the 99th's first aerial victory, shooting down an FW-

190. Eisenhower, Spaatz and Doolittle visited the squadron to offer their congratulations. No white fighter squadron could have attracted half as much attention for one victory.

Still attached to the 33rd, the 99th moved on to southern Italy after the Salerno invasion. Davis's pilots found themselves flying three missions a day to make up for the unit's small size, yet they weren't shooting German planes down.

Momyer blamed this on a "lack of aggressive spirit," and claimed they shunned attacks on tough dive-bombing targets. He recommended the 99th be pulled out of combat and assigned to coastal patrols. The commander of XII Air Support Command, Major General Edwin House, informed Arnold the experiment had failed, because "the Negro type has not the proper reflexes needed to make a first-class fighter pilot."[17]

When these criticisms were made, in the fall of 1943, Davis had returned home to assume command of the all-black 332nd Fighter Group, in training at Selfridge Field, Michigan. He was called to testify before the War Department's committee on racial policies, chaired by Stimson's chief troubleshooter, John J. McCloy.

Davis ably defended the 99th's pilots. He acknowledged that they'd made mistakes, but that was true of all green fighter squadrons. Besides, because the 99th had deployed overseas understrength and had not received the flow of promised replacements, his men were flying considerably more missions than their white counterparts.[18]

Shortly after this the 99th was attached to the 79th Fighter Group and moved to the outskirts of Naples. On January 27, 1944, six months of drought ended. Despite having to fly obsolescent P-40s, the 99th's pilots shot down eight German aircraft over the Anzio beachhead. The next day they shot down four more. These twelve victories cost the squadron just two planes.[19]

German attempts to crush the Anzio beachhead in February failed. Shortly afterward the 79th Group turned in its P-40s for P-47Ds. The 79th was one of only two fighter-bomber groups in the Mediterranean and, as described earlier (page 225) its main task was ground support. It had considerably fewer opportunities for dogfights than other fighter outfits. This frustration apart, the 99th Squadron was happy to be part of the 79th Group. The group commander, Lieutenant Colonel Earl E. Bates, accepted it as a welcome addition. He treated it no differently than other squadrons.

There was no reason why he shouldn't. A Statistical Control Division study of the records that spring showed that the 99th's performance from July 1943 to February 1944 had been, on balance, much the same as that of other P-40 squadrons in the theater.[20]

In the meantime, the 332nd had arrived in Italy. General John Cannon, commander of the Twelfth Air Force, didn't want it. He got Eaker to offer the group to the Fifteenth. Twining wasn't enthusiastic, but a suggestion from a theater air commander is really an order.[21]

The 332nd rapidly won the acceptance of Fifteenth Air Force bomber crews. On its second mission, June 8, it was assigned to provide both penetration and withdrawal escort for the 5th Bomb Wing, which would bomb the submarine pens at Pola. The target was heavily defended by flak. B-17 pilot John Muirhead of the 301st Bomb Group was impressed. "When they joined us, precisely at the time they were supposed to, it was a spectacular rendezvous . . . suddenly the air was full of P-47s, diving and whirling through our formations. . . . [Then] they formed about five hundred feet above our planes, throttled back in a prim, decorous line. . . . Once established in their positions, the P-47s never left us. When we reached the IP, they showed no inclination to turn away from the flak rising up ahead. I couldn't believe it. . . .

"They flew through the clouds of bursting shells with deliberate aplomb, sharing the fearful passage with us as though they were performing a routine duty guarding us from any German fighters who might dare to presume we were vulnerable. It was a grand gesture, for they must have known that enemy fighters would no more enter the barrage than would our own; they would always wait for us to come out of it. . . . The insouciance of our black friends was too brazen, too brave for me to remember them in any way but as the best of shepherds."[22]

In July the 332nd transitioned into Mustangs, and was joined by the 99th Squadron, which had also recently received P-51s. Most of the 99th's pilots were dismayed at this transfer. Being part of the 79th was a step toward integration; being part of the 332nd was a step back toward segregation.

The experience the 99th brought to the group was nevertheless valuable. It became the boast of the 332nd that not one bomber it escorted was lost to enemy fighters.

In the late fall missions to Austria and southern Germany

brought sightings of Me-262s, usually at a distance. Sometimes, however, a jet would flash past, putting on a display of its unbeatable speed. In 1945 the group flew deeper and deeper into Germany. On March 31, with the jet threat revived, came the first clash. Captain Roscoe C. Brown of the 100th Squadron was breaking in a new flight leader. As the group escorted B-17s over Berlin someone called out "Bogeys!"

"It turned out they were jets," Brown wrote later. "We had seen them on photo recon missions because they'd make passes at us. I think they were trying to scare us and maybe to test themselves out. There was a lot of mystique surrounding them. The jets, however, had to slow down to shoot bombers because they were so fast. That's when we'd get them. I pulled down and came up underneath this one jet just as he was slowing down. I climbed right up his behind and got him."[23]

Black pilots had a point to make, and at moments like this they made it plain. To get there, men like Roscoe Brown had had to overcome the AAF's petty apartheid and an omnipresent institutional resentment at having blacks forced on it by political pressure. Black airmen, for their part, detested the Jim Crow regulations and customs designed to diminish them and sought to push back the frontiers of segregation. Virtually every base where black airmen were stationed in the United States was rocked by racial clashes over cafeterias and officers' clubs that presaged the postwar civil rights struggle over lunch counters and schools.

There was bloodshed, too. In May 1943 the base commander at Selfridge Field, Colonel William T. Colman, had gotten drunk at a barbeque and called for a staff car to take him home. When it appeared, he pulled his .45 and ranted, "I made it perfectly clear I didn't want a colored chauffeur!" He shot the black driver, Private Willie McRae, at point-blank range.

Colman fired a second shot in the air, screaming. "That's for the British! I wish I was there with them!"[24] Private McRae nearly died. Colman was convicted by a court-martial of nothing more serious than assault.

Arnold agreed to the creation, in January 1944, of the all-black 477th Bomb Group, which would fly B-25s. The group's training was punctuated with protests, demonstrations, and arrests. In the spring of 1945, however, it seemed almost ready to go overseas.

Arnold offered it to Kenney. Given its reputation for trouble, Kenney didn't want anything to do with the 477th. Kenney was then told he would get it anyway. In which case, Kenney informed his diary, he planned to have it bomb abandoned Japanese airbases on Formosa.[25] In the end, the 477th never went overseas. It remained in limbo, an all-black experiment that the AAF didn't want but couldn't find a way to get rid of.

The exact origins of the term "ace" are unknown. My own surmise is that it derives from French soldiers' slang. The distinctive red silk ribbon of the Légion d'Honneur, created by Napoleon in 1802, is called an *as,* or ace. Successful French fighter pilots in World War I could be sure of receiving their *as.* The French press, eager to publicize French pilots, made the term famous.[26] At first, the number of aerial victories needed for ace status varied, but by 1917 it had settled at 5—the number of figures on the ace in a deck of cards. The leading ace of World War I was a Frenchman, René Fonck, with 127 victories; Baron Manfred von Richthofen, the top German scorer, had 80.

There were other kinds of aces. An ace balloonist, for example, was someone who'd jumped five times to escape a burning balloon. A "Chinese ace" was someone who accidentally managed to destroy five planes belonging to his own air force.[27]

In World War II the term ace was in widespread use among belligerent air forces throughout the world. The AAF gave no official recognition, however, to its aces.[28] Nor was there a generally accepted method for confirming aerial victories.

It was left for U.S. Air Force historians working in the 1960s and 1970s to try to apply uniform criteria to all the wartime claims and compile an authoritative register of aerial victory credits. As a result, dozens of pilots who were at some time credited with being aces, such as Thomas Lanphier, have lost that status. Most have retained it, but often they have seen their total score reduced. Of approximately seventy thousand fighter pilots trained by the AAF only seven hundred became aces.[29]

Aerial gunners are not considered aces, even though some air forces, such as the Twelfth and Fourteenth, credited a handful of gunners with ace status. It was simply impossible to confirm whether any single aerial gunner aboard a given bomber had shot down a plane.[30] On the other hand, every member of a P-61 night fighter—the pilot, the radar operator, and the gunner—which shot down an enemy aircraft was credited with a full aerial victory credit; that is, there were three kill credits for one aircraft.

Several air forces, such as the Eighth and Fourteenth, gave credit for planes destroyed on the ground and accorded them equal status with aerial victories. Other air forces, including the Fifth and the Twelfth, rejected this policy. Although strafing an enemy airfield was far more dangerous than dogfighting some, possibly many, of the planes that were destroyed on the ground were dummies or simply out-of-commission wrecks left there to attract a low-level attack and give the light-flak crews a chance to shoot down American planes. Present U.S. Air Force policy does not put ground targets on a par with planes destroyed in the air.

In World War I victory claims had to be confirmed by ground observers who testified they had seen the plane crash. In World War II, with much aerial combat taking place over oceans or jungle, and with planes being blown up in mid-air out of sight of the ground, there had to be other criteria. Each numbered air force commander was allowed to establish his own confirmation system, but basically what was required was that so much damage had been inflicted that an enemy aircraft could not survive. The plane had to be engulfed in fire; be seen to blow up or strike the ground; have a vital part, such as the tail or a wing, shot off; or have the pilot bail out. Gun cameras substantiated 40 percent of World War II claims; the rest were confirmed by at least one eyewitness, usually another pilot.

As many as four pilots involved in shooting down an enemy aircraft could claim a share of the credit. Many aces had tallies that ended in percentages, such as Hub Zemke's final score of 17.75 or George E. Preddy's 26.83.[31]

The interwar literature on aces such as Eddie Rickenbacker, who'd downed twenty-six German planes and balloons, was enormous and, for young boys, compelling. Hundreds, possibly thousands, grew up to join the AAF and were inspired to become fighter pilots in hopes of emulating their deeds.[32] A life-threatening condition that every fighter group commander learned to recognize, called "ace fever," was likely to strike these young men. It sent more than a few haring off on their own in pursuit of enemy planes, never to be seen again.

Group commanders had to beat down ace fever to keep their pilots alive. Teamwork brought the best results. Still, fighter pilots are always seen by an adoring public as free-spirited individuals engaging in aerial duels. The ground equivalent, hand-to-hand fighting, isn't remotely glamorous and seems brutal rather than heroic.

Gordon H. Austin of the 325th Fighter Group in Italy was probably typical of group commanders in his attitude. "I didn't want any heroes. I wanted everybody to have three or four victories, and that was it."[33] All the same, his "Checkertail Clan" produced twenty-four aces.

The first AAF ace of the war was Boyd D. "Buzz" Wagner. In five days (December 12–16, 1942) he brought down five enemy planes in the Philippines.[34] The first American to shoot down a Japanese plane was George S. Welch, who'd scored four times during the attack on Pearl Harbor. Welch went on to become a triple ace and survived the war with sixteen victories to his credit.

At least twenty pilots proved lucky enough and good enough to become aces in a day. The first AAF pilot to do it was Lieutenant Colonel Neal Kearby, commander of the 348th Fighter Group, on October 11, 1943. Leading a flight of P-47s on a fighter sweep over Wewak, New Guinea, he'd just shot down a Zero when he spotted a formation of thirty-three Japanese bombers escorted by twelve Zeros. Kearby led his flight straight into the enemy. He reported shooting down seven Japanese planes, but his gun camera showed only six had definitely been destroyed. Kearby had run out of film as he went to work on number seven.[35] He got credit for six, and the Medal of Honor.

It was nearly a year before Kearby's record was equaled in the ETO. On August 6, 1944, Captain George S. Preddy, Jr., of the 352nd Fighter Group brought down six GAF fighters over France. Preddy was considered by some of his peers to be the best fighter pilot in the theater. During the Battle of the Bulge he got into a dogfight over American lines on Christmas Day, shooting down two Me-109s. While he pursued a third at low level, ground troops tried to help by shooting at the 109. They failed to lead the German plane properly and brought down Preddy instead, killing him.[36]

The highest one-day figure of the war came shortly after this unhappy incident. On January 11, 1945, the 82nd Tac R squadron's Major William A. Shomo and his wingman ran into twelve enemy fighters escorting a bomber over Luzon. Shomo shot down six fighters and the bomber. His wingman shot down three fighters. They finished by photographing the piles of smoldering wreckage. Shomo got the Medal of Honor.[37]

A handful of pilots got most of the kills. In World War I it had been estimated that 4 percent of the fighter pilots had shared 50 percent of the victories.[38] World War II seems to have been much the same.

The top pilots also tended to be concentrated in a few groups. The 56th Fighter Group, the highest-scoring outfit in the ETO, had half the theater's top ten aces: Number 1 was Francis S. Gabreski (28 victories); Number 2 was Robert S. Johnson (27 victories); Number 5 was David C. Schilling (22.5 victories); Number 9 was Walker H. Mahurin (20.75 victories); Number 10 was Hubert Zemke (17.75 victories).[39]

Half the ninety-two aces of the Fifteenth Air Force were in a single group, the 31st. Nearly half the 165 aces in the Pacific were in two groups, the 49th and the 475th. And in the CBI, the 23rd Fighter Group had 36 of the theater's 53 aces.

Some flight-training classes, too, seemed to have been exceptionally well represented. The most distinguished of all was probably the first class of enlisted pilots to graduate from Kelly Field in 1941. One in nine became an ace, compared to one in a hundred among fighter pilots as a whole.[40]

The ultimate goal for any American fighter pilot was to beat Eddie Rickenbacker's score of twenty-six. Kenney was convinced he knew who would succeed. He admired Kearby's nerve and skill, but his personal favorite was Richard Ira Bong, whose name had headed the list of the first fifty P-38 pilots he asked Arnold to send to SWPA. This blond, cherubic youth had gone to college only so he could qualify for an Air Corps commission. While a student he'd taken his first flying lessons courtesy of the Putt-Putt Air Force (the CPTP). In 1941 he'd applied to become an aviation cadet and in January 1942 he was graduated at Luke Field, Arizona, in Class 42-A. In November he arrived in New Guinea with the first Lightning squadron to reach the theater, the 39th.

On December 27, 1942, Bong got into his debut dogfight when his flight "dived on a Zeke [a Zero]. I dropped my belly tank, took pass at Zekes without firing, dived away from four Zekes which jumped my tail, taking shot at one Zeke on the way down without observed result. Reversed direction in dive and took shot at one Val [dive-bomber] near Buna, missed, turned left and went out to sea at 500 feet. Saw Val and fired long burst at range of 350 yards. Val blew up . . . Zekes on my tail, so I headed out to sea. . . . Three Vals ahead of me, so took short burst at center Val without observed result, so made shallow turn to right, found one lone Val, made pass without firing and went home. Out of ammo." Another pilot saw the Zero he'd shot at crash. Bong was credited with two kills and awarded the Silver Star.[41]

Within a month he was an ace. He was flying with another superb pilot, Captain Thomas Lynch, who'd become an ace in the dogfight that saw Bong's combat debut. By January 1944 Bong had scored twenty-one victories; Lynch had sixteen. In the space of four months Kearby had overtaken Lynch and was only one victory behind Bong.

At this point all three were taken away from their units and assigned to staff positions at V Fighter Command headquarters, under Brigadier General "Squeeze" Wurtsmith. This removed them from the obligation to do the routine missions and close support that other fighter pilots had to perform. In Kearby's case it also removed him from the burden of commanding a fighter group. Wurtsmith made it clear that he didn't want them to do any staff work. They were free to do whatever they wished.

They could now choose which missions to fly, and which to shun. They could even dream up their own missions, such as dawn patrols near enemy airfields. Lynch had recently hit a dry spell, but Kenney was looking ahead. "If Lynch once gets started," he wrote Ennis Whitehead, commander of the Fifth Air Force advanced headquarters in New Guinea, "I honestly believe he will give Bong and Kearby a little competition."[42]

Soon after this Bong and Kearby were tied at twenty-two, with Lynch at nineteen. On March 4 Kearby was shot down and killed near Wewak. Five days later, while flying with Bong, Lynch strafed a Japanese corvette. A Japanese gunner scored hits on Lynch's plane, which blew up just as Lynch bailed out. He perished with twenty victories to his name.

By April 10, Bong's score had reached twenty-five. On April 12 he racked up two more victories, both confirmed by other pilots, and reported he'd also shot down a third unseen. His gun-camera film hadn't been loaded properly, but Bong claimed he had seen the plane crash in shallow water and come to rest on a coral shelf offshore from Hollandia. When American troops took Hollandia shortly after this the wreckage was found and Bong got credit for the victory. For now, though, he had twenty-seven confirmed kills; he was the first to break Rickenbacker's record. Bong was the new American ace of aces.

He returned to the United States for several months and was acclaimed from coast to coast, but in the fall he went back to combat. His great rival now was Major Thomas B. McGuire, Jr., of the 475th Fighter Group, with whom he formed a close friendship. They lived together and often flew together.

By December 1944, with V Fighter Command operating in the Philippines, Bong's score had reached thirty-six. Kenney put him in for the Medal of Honor and MacArthur for once decorated the recipient in the field, with what Kenney considered the greatest speech he ever heard. Placing his hands on Bong's shoulders and looking him closely in the eye, MacArthur intoned slowly, "Major Richard Ira Bong, who has ruled the air from New Guinea to the Philippines, I now induct you into the society of the bravest of the brave—the wearers of the Congressional Medal of Honor of the United States."[43]

Two weeks later, with a total of forty victories to his name, Bong was on his way home. It was a record no one would break, but McGuire was fast closing in on it. On Christmas Day McGuire shot down three planes to bring his score up to thirty-four. The next day he shot down four more.

On January 7, 1945, McGuire attempted to go to the aid of his wingman, who had a Japanese fighter on his tail. McGuire made a high-speed, low-altitude turn without first dumping his 160-gallon wing tanks, and his plane spun in, blowing up on contact. McGuire was awarded a posthumous Medal of Honor.

Bong didn't survive the war either. He was killed on August 7 flying an F-80 Shooting Star from Lockheed's Burbank plant on what was supposed to be a routine acceptance flight.[44]

The last American ace of the war was Lieutenant Oscar Perdomo of the 507th Fighter Squadron. Flying his P-47 on a fighter sweep over Korea on August 13 he shot down five enemy fighters, which also made him the last Ace in a Day.[45]

In becoming an ace dozens, possibly hundreds, of pilots had fulfilled the greatest ambition of their young lives. They were now and forever part of the airmen's ultimate elite. Yet, as with all human desires, the journey could prove more interesting than the destination.

To Lieutenant Grant M. Turley of the 78th Fighter Group, nothing had seemed more thrilling than being a fighter pilot in combat. He sent his family excited descriptions of his dogfights, presenting his victories in graphic detail. Then, on February 20, 1944, he wrote to his wife in a somber key. "I am tired—had a mission today and shot down my fifth Hun. I am an 'ace,' so they say. A lot of it has been luck, maybe a little skill. I have dreamed of being an ace, but now that I have succeeded it doesn't seem important any more."[46]

25

DISORIENTING EXPERIENCES

At the age of thirty-three, Lieutenant Colonel Robert Lee Scott, Jr., feared he'd be considered too old to fly a fighter in combat. He'd written to Spaatz and others, begging for a chance to go to war.[1] One of Scott's strongest supporters was Chennault's chief of staff, Colonel Meriam C. Cooper, an able officer with a remarkable résumé. Cooper had graduated from Annapolis in 1913, become an Air Service aviator during World War I, led a Polish fighter group against the Red Army in 1920, then moved on to Hollywood, where he wrote and produced *King Kong*. But even he couldn't do much for Scott.

Someone decided that maybe Scott could go to war as a bomber pilot. He learned, hurriedly, to fly a B-17, and took it to India. Arriving there in the spring of 1942 he talked Chennault, probably with Cooper's help, into giving him a P-40. For two months, Scott flew alone over Burma, strafing, dive-bombing and dogfighting. He became known as "the one-man air force." When the Flying Tigers were disbanded he got command of their successors, the 23rd Fighter Group.

Because Brigadier General Clayton Bissell, Stilwell's air officer, had so alienated the American Volunteer Group (AVG) that only five pilots agreed to transfer to the 23rd, it was a bright-green outfit. The 23rd was also going to be heavily outnumbered by the experienced Japanese. On the other hand, Scott would get the advantage of Chennault's warning net, which had hundreds of ground observers on Chinese hilltops and mountains, calling in reports regularly: "Sound of many. . . ." "Sound of one. . . ." The observors gave the direction and estimated altitude of the Japanese planes passing overhead. The warning net was one of Chennault's few tactical advantages.

Tokyo Rose followed the demise of the AVG with interest, and boasted that Japanese pilots would destroy the 23rd Fighter Group on the day it was activated, July 4. Scott and Chennault set up an ambush. On July 2 Scott flew from Kunming to Kweilin, nearly five hundred miles to the east, with twenty-nine P-40s—all he could get airborne. Chinese workers, meanwhile, were assembling dummy P-40s at Kweilin, putting a five-gallon jerry can in each. They would explode and burn like real planes.

The next afternoon, the warning that Chennault and Scott had anticipated was flashed: forty-eight JAAF fighters were heading for Kweilin. Chennault headed for the Kweilin command cave, with his pipe and rat-chasing dachsund. Following the action over the radio, he would give the signal to spring the ambush.

Scott took off with his twenty-eight pilots. They climbed as high as they could and positioned themselves so they would be lost in the sun when the Japanese arrived. "I circled and strained my eyes," said Scott later. "Then there they were, just flashes at first, flashes of windshields in the sunlight. . . . My throat had been dry with excitement, and now my tongue seemed to stick to my teeth. . . .

"They dove for the ships they saw waiting for them, the Chinese dummies. The sky above the field was filled with circling, diving, strafing enemy fighters. When the fake P-40s were blazing, even the top cover couldn't resist. They, too, came down to strafe. . . .

"We kept circling and watching and waiting . . . Then the word we had been waiting for so eagerly came. 'Take 'em!' . . . Down we went. No verbal orders, just a flip of my rudder and a dipping of my wings. . . . I fought the temptation to open fire. . . . The Japanese formation was so perfect and so close that we couldn't miss. . . . They didn't see us until it was too late. . . . After the first dive we broke and took out after the stragglers. I followed one with my wingman all the way to Canton, two hundred miles southward, and shot him down when the pilot lowered his landing gear to land at White Cloud airport . . . we shot down thirty-four planes."[2] The Japanese had been caught by surprise while they were low on both fuel and ammo. The 23rd hadn't lost a plane or a pilot.

Despite this dazzling beginning, Chennault's China Air Task Force was a modest command with an unpromising future. He had

December 7, 1941–the Hawaiian Air Depot, under Japanese attack, blazes behind the huge, recently constructed barracks at Hickam Field.

Above: Brigadier General Claire
Chennault and Colonel Robert Lee
Scott on a visit to the primitive
advance airfield at Kweilin.

GEN. C F LE MAY

Left: Curtis LeMay was probably the
most effective commander of heavy
bombers the war produced. After
winning his second star in Europe, he
went to the Pacific to command B-29
operations.

General George Kenney waits with Major General Paul "Squeeze" Wurtsmith of V Fighter Command for MacArthur's plane to land at Clark Field.

Jimmy Doolittle takes off from the *Hornet* in a B-25 to lead the April 1942 attack on Tokyo.

A C-46 comes in to land at Kunming in 1944 after flying the Hump. In the foreground is a Flying Tigers' P-40.

A C-87 (the transport version of the B 24) overflies a Chinese airfield and a line of horse-drawn carts.

During the Battle of the Bismarck Sea, Fifth Air Force planes found, and sank, this elaborately camouflaged Japanese transport.

This B-25 of the 345th Bomb Group was hit just as it dropped a string of parafrag bombs on an oil refinery in Formosa in May 1945.

A Japanese destroyer under aerial attack by low-flying B-25s near the Bismarck Archipelago in February 1944.

Phosphorous bombs burst over a Japanese airfield in New Guinea.

A B-29 is bombed up for a mission to Japan in 1945.

August 16, 1945—the briefing room of the 500th Bomb Group on Saipan.

nothing but Scott's half-strength fighter group and the seven B-25s of the 11th Bomb Squadron. As he'd done with the AVG, Chennault courted publicity with an eagerness that annoyed Arnold, Marshall, Stilwell and Bissell, but he felt he had little choice. CATF was far away, easy to overlook, and at the end of a long, vulnerable supply line. Any air transport plane that set off from Miami for Kunming had to land at half a dozen places along the way. His cargoes were rifled at every stop.[3]

While Chennault zealously promoted his command, demanding more pilots and better planes, he was also debating the air campaign. There were two fundamental questions about air power in the China-Burma-India theater. The first: How can China be kept in the war? Chennault and Chiang Kai-shek believed it could be done by operating an airlift from northeast India into southwest China. Bissell, who took command of the Tenth Air Force in India in July 1942, opposed the airlift. So did Stilwell. They believed in building a road through the jungles and mountains of northern Burma instead. The Combined Chiefs played safe and sanctioned both a road and an airlift.

The other question was, What is the correct employment of air power in the CBI? Stilwell demanded that it be used principally to support his planned ground campaign, using Chinese divisions, in Burma. Chennault disagreed strongly. He argued that the proper use of air was to achieve air superiority and then strike strategic targets, such as the shipping that took millions of tons of ore from China to Japan each year to be turned into steel.

In late 1942 his chances of winning air superiority looked remote. Scott's fighter group was still understrength in planes and pilots, and the warning net sometimes failed. When that happened, CATF airfields got hit hard. The Japanese also supplemented their daylight strikes with night intruder missions, which at first went unchallenged.

John Alison, the diminutive fighter pilot who'd demonstrated a P-40 at Bolling to the Chinese delegation in 1941, was assigned to 23rd Fighter Group. The warning net regularly tracked bombers at night, but there didn't seem much anyone could do about it. Alison got Chennault to agree to put up to four planes over the forward airfield at Henyang, in East China, on moonlit nights. The planes would fly at different altitudes, with their lights out. Alison made the first night interception over Henyang.

"Flying a P-40 over Henyang at twelve thousand feet, I picked up the exhaust of three Jap bombers at fifteen thousand feet. I had closed to within two hundred feet when a Jap gunner in a turret position on the bomber hit my P-40 broadside. He stitched a line of holes from the prop to the tail.

"I started firing at very close range. The first bomber I hit pulled up into a steep climb, badly hit but not burning. I moved from one to the other of the remaining two bombers, and they exploded one after the other. The concussions shook my aircraft.

"I tried to get down to a friendly field just below, but as I started a landing approach my aircraft caught fire. I had to ditch quickly—and into the river I went. I emerged wet and wounded, but had two confirmed victories plus one probable."[4] The AAF didn't attempt another night bombing of Henyang for more than a year.

Chennault was an ideal commander for this kind of war. A few high-ranking AAF officers, such as Laurence Kuter, considered him one of the best combat commanders the service possessed.[5] He had the aversion to paperwork that was common among such men, especially among pilots, but in Cooper he had, said Scott, "the ideal chief of staff."[6] Bissell fixed that by ordering Cooper back to the United States in January 1943.[7] Arnold never thereafter allowed Chennault to choose his own chief of staff.

Chennault's public relations campaign and his courting of powerful allies brought the turning point in his fortunes. In October 1942 Wendell Willkie visited China. Chennault strenuously bent Willkie's ear. He followed up with a letter in which he told Willkie that with a small force of the most modern planes—105 fighters, 30 mediums, 12 heavy bombers—plus a steady flow of replacements and supplies, he would bring about "the collapse of Japan" within a year.[8] Willkie delivered this letter to Roosevelt. Meanwhile, Chiang Kai-shek was supporting Chennault's demands for an air force of his own and lobbying for the United States to create a five-hundred-plane Chinese Air Force.

Arnold visited China in February 1943 to explain why the generalissimo couldn't have five hundred planes, and to discourage him from supporting Chennault's demands for his own air force. Arnold disparaged Chennault's abilities, telling Chiang that "the officer in whom you have the greatest confidence," i.e. Chennault, didn't know how to run bomber operations.[9]

Arnold's contempt for Chennault was total. He left the CBI convinced that whatever air success there had been in the theater was due to the efforts of Clayton Bissell. He gave Chennault credit for nothing.

Chennault's campaign for his own air force nevertheless paid off. Over Arnold's objections, and by order of the President, the Fourteenth Air Force was created for him. Activated in March 1943 it would be the smallest of the sixteen numbered air forces in the AAF.

Creation of the Fourteenth Air force brought the issue of what should be done with air power in the CBI to a head. Stilwell and Chennault were recalled to Washington in April to present their arguments to the President.

Stilwell believed that a campaign to retake northern Burma could be doubly justified: First, it was necessary if the Ledo Road was going to be built, and second, getting Myitkyina back would shorten the air route between India and China and make the Hump airlift a success. Instead of arguing his case, however, Stilwell mumbled and bumbled. He was dying of stomach cancer; he may also have been overawed by Roosevelt. His arguments for a Burmese campaign fell flat.[10]

Chennault made a good case for attacking Japanese shipping on China's great rivers and coastline from bases in eastern China. Once he'd cut off the flow of raw materials, he'd move on to attacking strategic targets in Japan. Stilwell rejoined that if Chennault started to hurt the Japanese, they would advance and take his airfields away. Chiang Kai-shek solemnly assured Roosevelt that his troops would defend the airfields.[11] Given Stilwell's repeated claims that Chinese troops would be able to wrest northern Burma from the Japanese, he wasn't in a good position to argue that the Chinese couldn't defend airfields.

Roosevelt backed Chennault, giving orders that he was to get most of the tonnage being flown into China. Marshall, however, considered Chennault dishonest and disloyal to Stilwell. He personally ensured that Chennault got as little as possible.[12] Stilwell, who continued to control the distribution of all supplies flown over the Hump, used most of them to support his offensive in Burma.

Starved, the Fourteenth had to live largely by its wits. While Wright Field was trying and failing to produce wing tanks to extend fighter range, Chennault's ground crews improvised droppable eighty-gallon tanks out of bamboo, mud, cloth, lacquer and aluminum paint. These items looked and functioned like factory products.[13]

A rack was devised that would take one eighty-gallon tank—full, it weighed five hundred pounds—and one five hundred-pound bomb. This rack turned Scott's P-40s into long-range fighter-bombers.[14]

When Kuter flew into Kunming one day, Chennault met the plane holding what Kuter thought was a cane, but, "He was carrying a C-54 gasoline-tank measuring stick. He climbed up on the wing of my four-engine C-54 and started measuring the gasoline in the tanks. He ordered they be drained down to the level that he concluded was a reasonable amount to get us back. He sent the rest of the gasoline to his fighting forces."[15]

Notwithstanding its paucity of means, the Fourteenth had a full agenda. Chennault had to win air superiority over China, defend the Hump airlift, attack Japanese shipping and troop concentrations, interdict communications, and provide close support to the ground troops. There was hardly an air mission that the tiny Fourteenth wasn't tasked with, including photo recon and troop carrying.

The fight for air superiority was uphill all the way. The JAAF slipped through the air warning net a dozen times in 1943 to hit Chennault's bases, destroying and damaging hard-to-replace aircraft. The Japanese continued their night-intruder raids, bribing Chinese peasants with rice or bicycles to ignite flares on American airfields, providing bright aiming points for their bombers.[16]

At maximum strength (not reached until March 1945) the Fourteenth had only 728 combat aircraft.[17] Yet Chennault was trying to defend an area roughly the size of the United States east of the Mississippi. To simplify the command challenge, he split his air force into two wings. He would personally direct the 69th Wing, based at Kunming, which defended the Hump and supported Stilwell.

The 68th Wing, based at Kweilin, would be commanded by Clinton D. "Casey" Vincent, a former Flying Tiger, an ace, and a brigadier general at the age of twenty-nine.* Vincent's primary task

---

*Vincent, on whom Vince Casey of *Terry and the Pirates* was based, is often credited with being the youngest wartime general in the AAF. That distinction belongs to Richard C. Sanders, who became a general at the age of twenty-eight.

was to conduct the campaign against Japanese shipping, using the East China airfields.

The antishipping campaign would be carried out by a growing force of B-25s and by the 308th Bomb Group flying B-24s. Thirty C-47s were taken from the invasion of Sicily in mid-1943 and sent to India to do nothing but ferry fuel and bombs over the Hump to Kunming for the 308th. The 308th then hauled them to East China. The group made heavy strikes against major ports such as Haiphong, in northern Indochina, and against the principal Japanese Army supply base in China, at Hankow.

Chiang's hopes of getting Arnold to create a five hundred-plane Chinese Air Force had come to nothing. Chennault proposed instead to create a core of experienced officers and men around whom a modern CAF could one day be developed. This venture was the joint Chinese-American Composite Wing.[18]

Activated in October 1943, the CACW began with two fighter squadrons and a medium bomber squadron. The wing was commanded by Colonel Winslow C. Morse. Each squadron had two commanders, one American, one Chinese.

It was a brave experiment and, in time, the CACW would grow to include the 3rd Fighter Group, the 5th Fighter Group and the 1st Bomb Group. The wing produced fighter aces and good bombing results, but it was too dogged by language problems, maintenance failures, and material shortages to achieve its full potential.

The CACW's first big mission was to participate in a strike from East China against the biggest Japanese air base on Formosa, Shinchiku, on Thanksgiving Day 1943. Shinchiku had never been attacked. Vincent hit it with fourteen B-25s, escorted by the 23rd Fighter Group. The Japanese were taken completely by surprise. Fourteen Japanese planes were shot down, and as many as sixty were destroyed or damaged on the ground. Not one American or Chinese plane was lost.[19]

Counterair strikes like this complemented the antishipping campaign. The Japanese, however, were provoked by Vincent's attacks on their airfields, docks and ships into mounting an offensive to secure a road and rail corridor for fifteen hundred miles from Peking to Hanoi. This would sever East China from Chiang's capital at Chungking and shut down Chennault's forward airfields. When the monsoon season drew to a close at the end of April 1944, the Japanese offensive went into top gear.

By this time Chennault had more planes than he'd demanded in his letter to Wendell Willkie. Yet instead of launching an offensive that would bring about the collapse of Japan, the Fourteenth was fighting for its life. One by one Chennault's forward airfields were being overrun, his supply situation remained as precarious as ever, and the B-29s had arrived.

The first Superfortresses to go overseas deployed to India in April 1944, under Major General Kenneth B. Wolfe. The JCS had approved a program called Matterhorn to bomb Japan from bases in China. An airfield complex was being built around Chengtu, five hundred miles northeast of Kunming, to base the B-29s.

Wolfe's XX Bomber Command had made only one attack from India, against Bangkok, when it was hurriedly deployed to Chengtu in June 1944. Its first mission to Japan was to bomb the Yawata iron and steel works. There were hopes that this bombing might somehow slow down the Japanese drive in eastern China. The bombing of Yawata on June 15 did little damage. It proved notable only as the first attack upon Japan by B-29s. All forty-seven bombers returned from the mission, except for one that was shot down while landing in China.[20]

The Japanese drive didn't slow down. Two weeks after Yawata was bombed the Henyang airfield was overrun. Chennault's airmen had to pull out so quickly they left the runways and buildings intact.[21]

The B-29s hadn't been sent to China to aid Chennault. On the contrary, he was ordered to make defense of the Chengtu airfields his primary mission. This unwanted burden, he felt bitterly, was making it almost impossible to fight effectively in East China to defend his airfields.

The Superfortresses nonetheless represented a major AAF investment that had to be protected. The 426th Night Fighter squadron was sent to Chengtu to counter JAAF night intruder raids. The first Chinese kill by a P-61 Black Widow came in the early hours of October 30. The pilot, Captain Robert R. Scott, reported, "G.C.I. [Ground Control Interception] gave me two vectors and altitude, e/a [enemy aircraft] was 40 miles away. I flew with throttle wide open and gentle in a climb from 5,000 feet. First [radar] contact 2½ to 3 miles away. A visual was made at 11,000 feet altitude with the e/a approximately a thousand feet away. The e/a was taking gentle turns and climbing 120 miles an hour. The e/a came into my sight at 600 feet and I fired at 500 feet. Simultaneously with my fire the e/a took hard, deep diving turn to left. A dogfight took place which lasted five minutes. I don't know exactly what happened, I stalled a couple of times, we dived, climbed and turned hard in both directions. At about 4,000 feet I came into position to fire again. Still diving I got in a burst. . . . I could see the bullets hitting the starboard wing and engine. A slight yellow flame came out of the underside of the starboard engine. Small flaming fragments blew off the e/a . . . My radar observor had put me in an ideal position the first time I opened fire."[22]

Matterhorn operations were unremunerative. Wolfe was under intense pressure from Arnold to produce results, and couldn't. In September 1944 Arnold installed Curtis LeMay to run XX Bomber Command, but this made little difference. The logistical problems of operating a heavy bomber offensive from China were simply too great.[23]

Chennault tried to convince LeMay to unleash the B-29s against the huge supply dumps at Hankow. LeMay turned him down.

Stilwell returned to the United States in October. The CBI was split up and Lieutenant General Albert C. Wedemeyer, principal author of the Army's Victory Plan, became commanding general of all American forces in China.

Wedemeyer arrived with a poor opinion of Chennault. There were persistent Pentagon corridor rumors that Fourteenth Air Force planes were being used for smuggling and that Chennault himself got a cut. Wedemeyer soon discovered that while Chennault was a lousy staff officer, he was a superb combat commander.[24] He got better results from fewer resources than almost anyone in the AAF. He knew his business. Wedemeyer told LeMay to bomb Hankow. He turned down Chennault's other request, for a court-martial, which would have given him a chance to clear his name.

On December 18, some 84 B-29s dropped 511 tons of incendiaries on Hankow. They burned down half the city and virtually wiped out the supply dumps.[25]

This success was the curtain raiser on a new offensive, Operation Alpha, by Chiang's armies in the south and east. The Japanese army's land corridor from Peking to Hanoi was nearly complete, but its troops were stretched almost to the breaking point.

The Fourteenth launched an interdiction campaign against railroads and river traffic to aid Alpha. Still the enemy continued to advance. By mid-February 1945 the Japanese had overrun every Fourteenth airfield but one, at Changting. Chennault appeared to have lost his war with Japan.

Certainly he'd promised a lot more than he could deliver. That was true, though, of Spaatz and Eaker; of all those who believed in the self-defending bomber that could dispense with fighter escort; of the AWPD-1 planners who'd claimed that Germany could be brought to its knees with one hundred-pound bombs in a daylight precision bombing campaign. Chennault was a typical air power advocate of his era.

The tiny Fourteenth dropped a smaller tonnage in a year than the Eighth did in a month, yet by early 1945 it had sunk nearly a million tons of Japanese shipping.[26] The Japanese steel industry relied on China and Manchuria for coal and iron ore, but by 1945 shipments were reduced to one third the 1941 level. The Japanese had also relied heavily on steel manufactured in Manchuria. The lack of shipping meant Manchurian steel couldn't be moved to Japan to be turned into weapons and shells.[27]

With China a wasting asset, the Japanese army's offensive petered out in the spring of 1945. Under pressure from the Chinese Sixth Army, the Japanese even abandoned their recent conquests and pulled back so they could defend Manchuria, Korea, and Hong Kong. The Fourteenth moved back into East China, although it had few targets left to attack. Chennault had won after all. Yet as the war in China drew to a close, Arnold and Marshall reorganized the Fourteenth so as to force Chennault to retire.[28]

The Hump airlift had begun in April 1942 with the first military cargo flown from India to China. It consisted of thousands of gallons of high-octane gas intended to refuel Doolittle's B-25s after the Tokyo Raid.[29] It was flown to Kunming by the China National Aviation Corporation (CNAC), a subsidiary of Pan Am.

CNAC made many more flights that summer, but developed an unsavory reputation for smuggling. Arnold decided to make the Hump a military operation. For a time, though, even Air Transport Command pilots found temptation irresistible. Army medical supplies stolen in India were sold for gold in China. Parker fountain pens that cost $5 in the U.S. could each bring as much as $100 in gold from corrupt Chinese officials.[30] The golden age didn't last long. The AAF and the JAAF between them turned flying the Hump into an operation where the biggest reward a pilot could hope for was staying alive.

As the Japanese advanced into northern Burma in the summer of 1942 they captured the airfield at Myitkina (pronounced Michinaw). From here, JAAF fighters cut the direct air route between Assam, in northeast India, and Kunming, in southwest China. Hump flights were forced to fly dogleg routes farther north, through, and around the Himalayas.

The C-47 was a wonderful airplane, but it hadn't been designed to fly at twenty thousand feet in − 60-degree weather. The controls became sluggish and the engines were prone to carburetor icing. As Johnny Alison later expressed it, "Flying a P-47 in combat was not as dangerous as flying a C-47 across the Hump."[31]

In early 1943 Curtiss was told to stop producing P-40s so it could concentrate on production of the C-46 Commando for the Hump. The C-46 had more powerful engines and a capacity of four tons, nearly twice what a C-47 carried.

Yet not even the C-46 could fly over the highest Himalayan peaks. Like the C-47 it had to fly through the saddles. The Commando, moreover, had serious problems with its fuel system when it started flying the Hump. Scores simply vanished, as if swallowed by the mountains.

The weather on the five-hour, seven-hundred-mile flight from Assam to Kunming was abysmal much of the time, and changeable all the time. The Hump was a navigational horror story. When Arnold visited the CBI in February 1943 Bissell insisted on giving him his personal navigator for the journey over the Hump. The navigator spent so much of the flight boasting to his illustrious passengers of his skills that when the plane descended, the navigator had no idea where they were, except that the landscape looked like China. For several hours the commanding general of the AAF was lost. Like many who'd set off to cross the Hump, Arnold seemed to have vanished. Fortunately, his pilot managed to put down safely, nearly out of gas and more than one hundred miles from Kunming.[32]

Hump flights operated from airstrips along the Bramaputra River. Living conditions were ghastly. Hump flyers lived in tents or bamboo huts. In the summer temperatures reached 140 degrees. During the monsoons, Assam was buried in mud. Yet whatever the season, Hump flights operated around the clock. Every day was like every other day; every night was like every other night.[33]

The tour limit was 650 hours. Some pilots flew every chance they could, striving to get their tour finished in four months. Tiredness and dulled reflexes, however, could get you sent home in a box. Hump pilots flew many flights where they were on instruments from takeoff to landing, catching a brief glimpse of the ground only at the beginning and end of each flight. Instrument flying in the early 1940s called for intense concentration. Flying on instruments then was, according to one expert, "as hard as playing a good game of golf."[34]

Most flights were to Kunming, which had a single wide runway two miles long alongside a lake and ringed by six thousand-foot mountains. The runway was lined with the rusting, cannibalized carcasses of planes wiped out in accidents or bombed by the Japanese. Other flights were made to Chengtu, where up to three hundred thousand Chinese peasants were building B-29 runways by hand.[35] A typical C-46 load would be a thousand gallons of gas and three thousand pounds of bombs. Arriving in China, Hump planes spent no more than an hour on the ground.

In 1943 they departed China empty. In early 1944 they were loaded up with Chinese infantrymen, who transited through Assam on their way to fight under Stilwell in Burma. Hump flyers carried twenty-five thousand Chinese troops and Burmese guerrillas, who made his campaign possible. Having moved the men, they supplied them with airdrops of rice and salt.[36]

On May 17 Merrill's Marauders took the Myitkina airfield. It couldn't be used by Allied planes until the town fell, which didn't happen for another three months. Even so, driving the JAAF out of Myitkina made it possible to fly shorter, safer, warmer, and more southerly routes to China. Tonnage delivered simply soared. In early 1943 Hump flights delivered twelve hundred tons a month. In November 1944 they delivered twelve hundred tons a day.[37]

The Hump airlift was helped, too, by getting bigger planes, such as the C-87 (the cargo version of the B-24) and the C-54, the military version of Douglas's four-engine airliner, the DC-4. Meanwhile, the bugs had been worked out of the C-46. Its reliability made it the favorite aircraft among Hump flyers. Flying safer routes in better planes brought a spectacular fall in the accident rate, from two aircraft lost per one thousand hours flown in 1943 to two aircraft lost per ten thousand hours flown by 1945.[38]

Just as the Hump started delivering the kind of tonnage needed to make the airlift a resounding success, the Japanese army retrenched in both China and Burma and the Ledo Road, the main alternative to the Hump, was completed. Both the road and the airlift enjoyed a bittersweet, anticlimactic success.

When the Hump airlift ended in November 1945 it had carried 777,000 tons and cost the lives of 910 American airmen.[39]

The British had no appetite for a Burmese campaign, something Churchill described as being "like munching a porcupine quill by quill." Clayton Bissell had no trouble living with that judgment. During his tenure as Tenth Air Force commander, from July 1942 to August 1943, Bissell's principal military initiative was to establish a splendid war room at his New Delhi headquarters.[40]

Instead of mounting a campaign against the 250,000 troops of the Japanese Fifteenth Army, the British were content to allow a bearded, Bible-quoting brigadier named Orde Charles Wingate to plunge into Burma in February 1943, with 3,000 men. They spent several months behind enemy lines blowing up bridges and supply dumps. Wingate returned with 2,000 men; most needed prolonged medical treatment.

Churchill took the loquacious, eccentric Wingate, whose whims included wearing an alarm clock instead of a wristwatch, to the Quebec Conference in September 1943. Wingate was paraded as walking, talking proof that the British were hitting back at the Japanese in Burma.

Marshall and Arnold were fascinated by Wingate and his theories of "long-range penetration." What, they wanted to know, was his biggest problem? Getting my wounded out, Wingate replied. Bad for morale, leaving men to die in the jungle. Could the Americans help him with a few light planes to evacuate his casualties?[41]

Arnold returned home and put Philip Cochran and John Alison in charge of helping Wingate. In typical Arnold fashion he turned a request for a few light planes into a bigger, bolder idea. He wanted nothing less than "an aerial invasion of Burma."[42]

With Cochran in command and Alison as his deputy, they set about creating the 1st Air Commando Group. They recruited 540 volunteers; every man had at least two skills, such as being a qualified radio operator and a cook, or both a pilot and a trained airplane mechanic. Cochran commandeered every one of the hundred L-1 and L-5 liaison aircraft in the U.S. He also demanded and got C-47s, gliders, P-51s, B-25s, and six experimental Sikorsky YR-4 helicopters, three of which belonged to the Navy. Cochran had what amounted to a miniature air force, with 173 planes and 225 gliders.[43]

Wingate originally hoped to mount large-scale, deep penetrations in conjunction with a major British ground offensive, but there wasn't going to be one. On the other hand, Stilwell was planning a campaign using the two Chinese divisions he'd trained in India. Using Merrill's Marauders as spearheads to make breakthroughs for the Chinese, he intended to retake Myitkina.

Wingate's role was to take the 3rd Indian Division behind Japanese lines and aid Stilwell's advance by tying down large numbers of Japanese soldiers. He proposed to have the 1st Air Commando fly in two of his brigades; the third would walk in. Landing sites were chosen along the Irrawaddy River, 150 miles beyond the Burmese border. The night of March 5, 1944, the first wave of C-47s took off, towing sixty-two gliders loaded with engineer troops, baby bulldozers, scrapers and mules. The troops were expected to carve out strips so that follow-up waves of C-47s could bring in supplies. Within a week 1st Air Commando Group had taken in nearly ten thousand men and nearly fifteen hundred mules. Shortly thereafter, Wingate perished in a plane crash on a flight back to India.

Burma was probably the finest hour of the glider pilots. The success of Arnold's "aerial invasion" was really in their hands. Gliders that didn't crack up on landing were snatched back into the air by specially equipped C-47s, flown back to India, and reused.

Flight Officer Allen Hall made his second flight the night of May 9, delivering a three-ton baby bulldozer. "We were three thousand pounds over the official weight limit, and the glider responded rather sluggishly. . . . We cut off from the tow plane about midnight and headed for a rectangular landing area marked by a bonfire at each corner.

"Because of the weight of our cargo our airspeed was way up—well over one hundred miles per hour. Both the copilot and I were on the controls and when we hit the ground we tore off our landing gear and bounced about fifty feet in the air. As we hit the ground a second time, the Japanese started bracketing us with mortar fire. . . .

"The bulldozer was hooked up to a cable which was attached to the nose latch so when it lunged forward the nose raised up with my copilot and me still strapped in our seats. My copilot whacked his head hard and suffered a concussion and the sergeant who was to operate the bulldozer had his right leg ripped open. I was wounded in the left arm and elbow with shrapnel.

"British troops dug in on a nearby hillside came running to our rescue. . . . Both the copilot and the sergeant were flown out at dawn in two L-5 observation planes. . . . We were doing things in Burma with those gliders that were never taught at flying school."[44]

Wingate had assured Cochran that the airstrips could be defended: "The jungle will be our friend."[45] As it turned out, the jungle enabled the Japanese to get close enough to bring the strips under direct fire. No strip was lost, though.

With Alison handling supply and transport, Cochran ran combat operations. His twelve B-25s were the H model, which had a seventy-five-millimeter cannon in the nose. They flew as strafers, using the cannon to strike Japanese positions only fifty yards in front of British troops. Meanwhile Alison's L-5s flew in and out in a steady stream, carrying mail, newspapers and men. Each L-5, flown by a sergeant-pilot, would arrive with a healthy soldier, fly out with a wounded one. An hour later the wounded soldier would be in a general hospital in India. By the time the operation finished, in June, the entire 3rd Indian Division's seventeen thousand men had been airlifted into Burma. Thousands of casualties had been evacuated. Arnold was so impressed by what had been achieved, he created three more air commando groups.

Cochran also used his planes to fly counterair missions against JAAF airfields. They accounted for as much as 25 percent of enemy planes destroyed in Burma in 1944. When Myitkina fell in May the JAAF was a spent force in Southeast Asia. By this time the Tenth, too, had been transformed.

Bissell had been relieved in August 1943 by Brigadier General Howard Davidson, a more combative commander. Not surprisingly, he admired Chennault. "We got along like two thieves," said Davidson.[46]

His can-do spirit was the spark that ignited the Burmese ground offensive. Shortly after Davidson had gotten command of Tenth Air Force, Stilwell and his staff had demanded to know how much tonnage could the Tenth fly into Burma each month. Davidson hesitated. "Well, there's the monsoon. . . ."

Stilwell put the issue more bluntly: "Can you guarantee me four thousand tons?" "Yes," said Davidson. Stilwell slapped his ancient, battered campaign hat on his head. "Let's go."[47]

Davidson ran an effective antishipping campaign that dovetailed with Chennault's. His B-24s struck the docks at Rangoon and flew long range antishipping patrols over the Andaman Sea. His B-25s conducted an extensive mining campaign against Burmese rivers and ports. By 1944 Rangoon had virtually ceased operating. The Japanese switched their ships to Bangkok. Davidson started a mining campaign that soon shut down Bangkok.

As the antishipping campaign achieved its objectives, the Japanese relied more heavily on the railroads and rivers. The Tenth's mediums filled the rivers with mines and launched a devastating antirailroad offensive. Heavies and mediums bombed marshalling yards and locomotive works. At first, it was difficult to knock out the tracks. Bombs would strike the roadbed, bounce off and explode in the jungle. Davidson's ground crews welded eighteen-inch spikes onto the noses of one hundred-pound bombs. The spike held the bomb in the roadbed. With this technique, it was possible to put hundreds of cuts in the railroads each day.[48]

The Tenth's planes also waged a prolonged bridge-busting campaign. B-24s and P-38s brought down big railroad bridges with Azon guided bombs.

By the time Stilwell and Wingate advanced into Burma, it was evident to Imperial Headquarters in Tokyo that the country was no longer worth holding. It started to move troops out at the rate of fifteen thousand men a month.[49]

At this juncture, however, the commander of the Japanese Fifteenth Army, General Renya Mutaguchi, was stung by the activities of Stilwell and Wingate into launching an offensive to take the crucial garrison town of Imphal, on the Indian border. The British got a campaign not because they wanted one, but because it was thrust on them by Mutaguchi. First, though, Imphal had to hold out against three Japanese divisions.

Admiral Lord Louis Mountbatten, the British Southeast Asia Commander, appealed for American help. Arnold sent the 64th Troop Carrier Group, veterans of the Tunisian and Sicilian campaigns, to the Tenth. He also dispatched a new outfit, the 3rd Combat Cargo Group. Each of the four combat cargo groups had one hundred C-46s. They were expected to provide air supply under fire yet maintain close to 100 percent availability.[50] The 64th TCG and 3rd CCG kept Imphal supplied with rations, fuel, and ammunition throughout four months of siege until, at the end of July, the starving, disease-ridden Japanese called off their offensive.

By 1945 the Japanese were falling back into central Burma pursued by 350,000 Allied troops—Americans, British, Indians, Chinese. The Tenth's troop carriers and three combat cargo groups had helped save Imphal, kept Stilwell's advance on Myitkina going, and taken pipe and other supplies to construction crews on the Ledo Road. And now, as this huge Allied force moved slowly through the jungle, it was supported entirely by air: every can of C-rations consumed, every bullet fired, and every gallon of fuel burned was flown in, mainly by Davidson's airmen. Arnold's aerial invasion had been a complete, even if little-noticed, success.

26

MORALE: MAIL, MISSIONS, AND MEDALS

Arnold took a keen and constant interest in the morale of the AAF. There was a close link between men's attitudes and the effectiveness of the tactical units. Poor morale among ground crews would inevitably produce a lower standard of maintenance and reduce availability of aircraft. Flagging spirits among aircrew led to poor bombing, mediocre reconnaissance, excessive fighter losses. The popular idea that victory was somehow inevitable because the United States was a big, rich, modern country didn't carry much weight among the people who had to fight the war. It was up to them to find the will and the courage to suffer, bleed and die. There was nothing inevitable about that.

Few bomber pilots feeling their nerves fail went to their group commander and said, "I quit." Instead, they would abort, and abort, and abort, until the commander pulled them off flying duties and gave them a ground assignment. There were threats that men who refused to fly would be sent to the infantry, but this doesn't seem to have happened.[1] Why should the infantry take a man whose nerves were shattered?

It wasn't only pilots who broke. Gunners were known to jump out of airplanes in mid-flight rather than face another air battle. Bombardiers and navigators were known to jump out of planes taxiing before takeoff.[2]

The biggest depressant among bomb groups was poor bombing results. Much of the time in places like the Pacific it was impossible even to tell whether a bombing had achieved anything. But in every theater, recon photos that showed a target had been missed and would have to be struck again cast a pall of gloom that was impossible to describe. When crews were briefed for the second Schweinfurt mission, in October 1943, morale was so brittle that the standard intelligence presentation on expected fighter and flak opposition was canceled.[3]

There was no straight and obvious equation between combat losses and morale. If a new replacement got killed, he might hardly be missed. If a popular squadron commander was lost, though, the entire squadron could be plunged into grief.

The most intense grief was suffered when a man lost a close friend. For some, that was unbearable. At Thelepte in January 1943 a pilot had to bail out of a shot-up P-40 over the airfield one day and was killed on impact. His closest friend ran to a P-40, took off, climbed high above the airfield, nosed over into a whistling dive and flew straight into the ground, to join his buddy in death.[4]

During Twining's Ploesti campaign, losses in the Fifteenth Air Force drove some crews to breaking point. "One evening in the club," wrote Bill Cubbins, "one of the original 450th Bomb Group pilots was near to tears. He had flown over 40 missions and was questioning his own fitness for combat. His friends knew that he'd had a particularly rough combat tour and sympathized with him. However, I think we were all shocked when he suddenly blurted out, 'I can't take it anymore. If tomorrow's target is near Switzerland, we're going to get ourselves interned.' My second shock occurred when, after a moment's pause, all those in attendance agreed with him."[5] The group flew to Munich next day. This crew didn't come back.

Morale was low on the Hump in 1943, partly because many aircrews considered it almost suicidal to fly the route.[6] Airmen in the Aleutians were morose mainly because of the boredom and the miserable weather. Those sent to Reyjkavik called themselves "The FBI—the Forgotten Bastards of Iceland."

Morale was probably higher among the flyers than among the ground crews. Army studies showed that morale was highest among men on crew-served weapons, such as mortars and heavy machine guns. Morale among bomber crews seems to have been equally high, even though, inevitably, some crews didn't get on at all.[7]

Whether morale was high or low depended heavily on leadership. By 1945 all fighter and bomber pilots were officers, but not all officers were leaders. It did a lot for a group's morale to have the CO fly missions. Some flew too many; a few didn't fly even one. A good commander could rebuild morale after a cataclysmic disaster, such as the 322nd Bomb Group's loss of every B-26 launched on the Ijmuiden raid in July 1943. With the group CO missing in action, the former commander, Lieutenant Colonel Glenn Nye, took over and restored the unit's self-esteem and cohesion.[8]

Morale was maintained, too, by providing creature comforts that civilians took for granted but men overseas considered unbelievable luxuries. During XIX TAC's dash across France in support of Patton in the summer of 1944 the commander of the 406th Fighter Group, Colonel Anthony Grossetta, would send a P-47 back to England from time to time with a carefully washed-out 150-gallon belly tank. The jug would return with the tank filled with cold beer, well chilled after flying at fifteen thousand feet.[9] Colonel Dale Smith of the 384th Bomb Group raised enough money among his officers to buy a disused English ice cream factory. The 384th's cooks, using their unlimited supplies of powdered eggs and powdered milk, produced excellent ice cream in a variety of flavors.[10]

The biggest single material element in morale was mail. It brought needed, welcome assurances that you hadn't been forgotten; that normal life went on; that there was a world waiting for you to come back to. As Marvin Bledsoe, a P-47 pilot put it, "Mail call was the most important aspect of our day-to-day life."[11] The military mail service in World War II was, after some early hitches, excellent. In Britain and Italy AAF personnel got mail almost as regularly as people got it in the United States.

Writing letters home helped fill in the long periods of boredom that were one of the dreariest features of rear-area life. Outgoing mail was censored, giving rise to a story of the airplane mechanic who wrote to his girlfriend, "Last night we beat the officers in a game of softball." When his girlfriend received it there was an addition, in an unfamiliar hand: "Like hell they did. Captain Harry Schilling, Squadron Censor."[12]

The other great morale sustainer was mission limits. Unlike the infantry, where the only way out was by death or wounds, airmen had assigned tours. They could volunteer to extend them, and some did. It was also possible for those who'd finished a tour in Europe to ask for another tour, in the Pacific. The length of a tour varied not only from theater to theater but according to the loss rate. On the Hump, for instance, the tour was raised in late 1944 from 650 hours to 750, reflecting the dramatic decline in losses. For B-26 groups it rose from 35 missions, to 50, then to 65.

For fighter pilots, a standard tour was 100 missions. Unlike their counterparts in the GAF or the JAAF, American aces stood an excellent chance of surviving the war. The Germans and Japanese treated their flyers as warriors destined to fight until they died. One reason why air superiority was wrested rapidly from the Luftwaffe in early 1944 was the startling German loss of experience in late 1943. In a couple of months that fall, for example, 12 GAF pilots with 1,146 credited victories among them were killed in combat.[13] Experience that had taken years to acquire was lost, in effect, overnight. American pilots returned home as instructors, to teach the next crop of potential aces how to fly in combat and stay alive.

Everyday living conditions formed the framework in which morale went up or down. Conditions were best in England and worst in Southeast Asia and the Pacific. Young men, however, can adapt to almost anything. For those who liked camping, such as Lieutenant Jim Van Nada of the 318th Fighter Group, life on remote islands in the central Pacific could be agreeable. "I thought we lived pretty well on Makin, with our four-man tents under the coconut palms, our outdoor salt-water showers and our outdoor latrine in the lagoon . . . We had a well-appointed ready room with a bar, refrigerator and a piano . . . the necessities of life were furnished free. . . . We even had a squadron barber who gave free haircuts. . . . The only disadvantages I encountered were a lack of water and women. . . ."[14]

Food was a source of complaint everywhere. And if the food started out okay, then the cooks were blamed for ruining it. Three-point-two beer was part of the ration, and in England, Italy or Australia liquor was easy to obtain. In some groups officers returning from a mission got a shot of whiskey from the medical officer.

When liquor was scarce, men rediscovered the distilling pleasures of their Prohibition-era parents. In China, where whiskey cost $100 a bottle, an enterprising flight surgeon in Kunming helpfully added lemon crystal to medical alcohol, producing a kind of one hundred-proof lemonade. It was potent stuff. When the Bob Hope Show traveled to Kunming, a major (who eventually made lieutenant general) got drunk on this concoction and broke into Paulette Goddard's room in the early hours with amorous intent. The movie star fled screaming into the night while brother officers pinned the panting major to the ground.[15]

Medical officers were expected to keep a close watch on a group's morale. When a unit appeared to be getting jaded or jumpy, aircrew were likely to be given a week's "flak leave" at a luxury hotel in a peaceful spot where there were tennis courts and swimming pools, boats, bars and bicycles. The men of the Eighth and Ninth could obtain passes to London. The men of the Twelfth had Naples. The Fifteenth relaxed in Bari, a port that some men loved and others loathed. The Fifth Air Force had the distractions of Australian cities, until the war moved on from New Guinea.

Much of the recreation overseas was the do-it-yourself variety. Countless missions ended with a poker game. In North Africa, airmen learned an old Roman pastime, which consisted of catching flies, holding them under water until they passed out, putting each fly under a small pile of salt, then betting on which one would be the first to regain consciousness, struggle out of the salt and get airborne.[16]

The AAF's greatest entertainment coup was getting the services of Glenn Miller. He'd received a commission in the Army Specialist Corps in October 1942. Two months later, the Corps, a short-lived venture aimed at attracting highly qualified people into the Army, was terminated. Some astute but regrettably anonymous AAF officer noticed the name Alton G. Miller on the list of personnel in need of new assignments, and recognized it as the legal name of Glenn Miller, the musician. He put in a routine request to have Captain Alton G. Miller transferred to the AAF.[17] The Army let Miller go without realizing what it was doing.

His new assignment was to create an outstanding AAF band. Miller did what only he could do: talk some of the country's best musicians out of highly paid employment and into uniform for the sake of patriotism and great sounds.[18] Most people knew it as the "I Sustain the Wings" band, from the name of its weekly radio show; the military knew it as the 418th Army Air Forces Band. Besides generating good publicity for the service, it provided military music for military occasions, such as retreat and review.

Even so, in September 1943 *Time* accused Miller of debasing martial traditions by jazzing up the music. Miller replied that he'd merely developed a fuller, richer sound by introducing four- and five-part harmony, something that didn't exist in Sousa's day. Had it been available, he believed, Sousa would have employed it.[19]

At the end of 1943 the 418th AAF Band metamorphosed into the 2nd AAF Training Command Radio Unit! Its mission was "to glorify the unsung heroes of the Army Air Forces Training Command—the ground crew—to recruit Aviation Cadets, to recruit Air WACs, and to inform the American public of the job that the AAF Training Command is doing to hasten V-Day and provide entertainment for the morale of soldiers here and abroad."[20]

Miller's band found itself on the fast track to nowhere. Every request to take his men overseas was turned down. The band was playing mainly at Liberty Loan rallies.

In May 1944, however, Eisenhower created the Allied Expeditionary Forces Program, a new radio network that would provide entertainment for Allied troops participating in the invasion of France. Half the programming would be American; the British, Canadians, and French would provide the rest.

Eisenhower requested Miller's band be sent to England. The AEFP began broadcasting on D + 1. Miller's band arrived two weeks later, and was billed as "The American Band of the AEFP." It would soon be known as the Glenn Miller Army Air Forces Band. Much of the time it provided live music at military bases in England, but its principal mission was radio broadcasts to the troops on the Continent.

To millions of people it was the best band there would ever be; to millions more it was certainly the best white band of all time. Its sound casts a spell down the decades; a few bars of "Moonlight Serenade" or "American Patrol" and an entire era, a monumental national experience, comes flooding back, stirring, as great music must, feelings too elusive for words, too deep to forget, too marvelous to resist.

The band played on long after Glenn Miller's death in a plane crash in December 1944. Even now, the Army Personnel Records Center in St. Louis gets more requests for information about Glenn Miller than for anyone else, Elvis included.[21]

There was one thing the AAF couldn't provide, which nearly every man craved—the company of young women. There were sixty thousand WACs in the AAF, but few went overseas. Army nurses and Red Cross women were around, but they seemed to date only officers.

The Eighth and Ninth probably had it best. There were millions of single young women in Britain, and most able-bodied young British men were somewhere else. At AAF bases, girls were brought in aboard Army trucks for the usual Saturday night dance "like a load of powdered eggs."[22] Getting them to depart was less easy.

The eagerness of English women to unite with American airmen in pursuit of high morale was a serviceman's dream come true. Australia was equally good for chasing. One of the few consolations about Iceland was its surplus of females; large numbers of young Icelandic men had perished fishing in the North Atlantic. By all accounts, the women of Iceland were drop-dead gorgeous.[23]

During the AVG's six months in Kunming there had been no shortage of attractive young Chinese women from good families who were willing to sleep with the famous Flying Tigers, even though they risked being rejected by their families.[24] After that, however, as the number of Americans in Kunming rose sharply and few were glamorous figures, Chinese willingness declined. Chennault set up his own brothel, staffing it with one hundred teenage girls bought on the white slave market in Kweilin for $8 each.[25]

The sex drive of the AAF was flaunted as never before by men in uniform. Never had all the soldiers, sailors, and marines in the world advertised their libido as airmen did. It screamed brashly from a couple of feet beneath the rudder pedals of countless fighters and bombers. Curvaceous women with full breasts and long legs passed through the air at thirty thousand feet in diaphanous scraps that made Victoria's Secret models look overdressed.[26] In remote parts of the world, where generals were scarce, they flew in nothing at all. Bombs dropped from beneath angelic feet in fluffy pink mules, guns roared above lustrous bedtime eyes, and though men died, morale survived.

The most obvious official attempt to promote fighting spirit was the award of decorations. For the AAF, awards ceremonies were exercises in public relations, arranged as much to promote the service as to recognize the deeds of the recipients.[27]

Spaatz favored a liberal approach to decorations. He was also keen to make awards promptly. A medal given long after the event did nothing for a man's spirit. Spaatz was in the habit of holding brief decoration ceremonies at his quarters, between dinner and poker, for recent heroic actions.[28]

Only two awards were unique to airmen: the Distinguished Flying Cross and the Air Medal. The DFC had been created in 1926, so the fledgling Air Corps could reward its fliers. The first award went to Charles Lindbergh, in 1927, for his solo flight across the Atlantic. Lindbergh held a commission in the Air Corps reserve.

The Air Medal was much less prestigious. It was handed out with two-fisted generosity in North Africa. Aerial gunners especially were loaded down with Air Medals as reward for their claims of enemy planes shot down. The 97th Bomb Group was probably the record holder, awarding no fewer than 15,544 Air Medals and oak leaf clusters during its first two years in combat.[29]

Every one of the six hundred troop-carrier pilots who took para-troopers and glidermen to Sicily in July 1943 got an Air Medal or a cluster. Marshall believed in generosity, but he was appalled by excess.[30] Most of the airborne troops who fought in Sicily didn't get medals. The Army had no combat decoration that was awarded on a mass basis. Some AAF generals felt the service was debauching its medals by prodigality.[31]

Air force commanders established rule-of-thumb methods for awarding DFCs and Air Medals. They kept individual awards for bravery, such as the Distinguished Service Cross and the Silver Star, in their own hands. In the Eighth and Ninth, an airman got the DFC for completing a combat tour. Air Medals and clusters were given for every five missions. In the Fifth, a man got an Air Medal or cluster for every one hundred hours flown. Troop-carrier pilots in the CBI got a DFC or cluster for every three hundred hours.

Howard Davidson, commander of Tenth Air Force, awarded the Air Medal to flight nurses serving in Burma. He was exceeding his authority, but was determined to recognize the dedication of these young women who were, for all intents and purposes, serving in the front line.[32]

The only individual award that ground crew members could expect to get was the Good Conduct Medal, until late 1944, when the War Department misguidedly debased the Bronze Star by mak-ing rear-area personnel eligible for it. There was considerable bitter-ness in many commands that battle stars for campaign ribbons were awarded only to the ground crews of fighter and bomber units.

No one would admit to wanting decorations; all the same they stirred up a lot of envy and resentment. Fighter groups in North Africa were convinced that bomb groups were more favorably treated; they were probably right. Men from the Twelfth and the Fifteenth were disgusted when they saw their heavily beribboned brethren from the Eighth and Ninth.

The decoration that was sought least, yet cherished most, was the

Purple Heart.[33] George Washington had created it to reward merit (not bravery) among enlisted men in the Continental Army. Only seven awards were made before that army was disbanded. MacArthur had revived the medal during his tenure as Chief of Staff. Before 1944 it was still occasionally awarded for merit, but it was given mainly for death and wounds.

The ultimate accolade was, of course, the Medal of Honor. There were 433 awards in World War II: 218 Army, 38 AAF, 57 Navy, and 81 Marine Corps.

The first two AAF Medals of Honor were clearly intended to make Torch a public relations success. They went to a colonel and a major who were passengers in a truck. They went ashore on November 8 and were killed by machine gun fire a few hours later as they rode toward French lines to negotiate a surrender.[34] Later in the war, this might have been worth at most a Distinguished Service Cross.

Arnold, Spaatz and Eaker were all keen to find an air hero they could tout as "the Rickenbacker of the AAF." The first Medal of Honor winner in the Eighth, however, was an enlisted man, Sergeant Maynard "Snuffy" Smith, a ball turret gunner in the 306th Bomb Group.

On a mission to St. Nazaire on May 1, 1943, Smith's plane was struck by flak. Fires broke out in the tail and the radio operator's compartment. Smith scrambled out of his turret, only to see the two waist gunners and the radio operator jumping from the burning plane. Blocked by flames and with the interphone out, Smith didn't know if either pilot was still aboard, but the aircraft was still in formation. He proceeded to fight the raging fire in the radio compartment with a hand held extinguisher.

When he tackled the fire in the tail, he found the tail gunner had been wounded. As Smith tended the man's wounds, the B-17 came under attack by FW-190s. Smith spent the next hour or so firing the waist guns, fighting the fire and applying first aid. Ammunition boxes were smoldering and bullets began to explode. Smith dragged the boxes to the large hole burned in the fuselage and pushed them out. When he'd used up all the fire extinguishers available, he urinated on the fires that continued to break out.[35] The plane made it back to England and the pilot put the B-17 down safely, but it was a wreck. It never flew again.

Smith turned out to be a hero in the air, but a grade-A problem child on the ground. He was forever in trouble. Eaker sadly informed Arnold that Sergeant Smith was a great disappointment from a PR point of view.[36]

The Eighth finished the war with seventeen Medal of Honor recipients; nearly half the total for the AAF. Every one of the seventeen was assigned to a heavy bomb group or wing. There wasn't a single fighter pilot, despite the Eighth's 261 aces. Mediums were slighted, as were troop carriers and photo recon. Arnold and Spaatz were determined to keep the publicity spotlight firmly on the Mighty Eighth and the legend of strategic bombing as the airmen's greatest contribution to victory.

Fighter pilots were so admired and got so much publicity they were envied and resented by other pilots.[37] The price of fame was losing out on promotions and decorations. Not one ace became a general during the war, although men like Zemke and Blakeslee demonstrated outstanding leadership and organizational ability.

In the entire AAF, only five fighter pilots received the Medal of Honor. The Marine Corps looked after its men much better. Nine Marine Corps fighter pilots won the Medal of Honor—more than the AAF and the Navy combined. Had Arnold taken the Marine Corps approach, George Preddy would have received one for shooting down six German planes in fifteen minutes; Robert S. Johnson would have received one for tying Rickenbacker's score; Francis Gabreski would have received one for his twenty-eight aerial victories; and both Rex Barber and Thomas Lanphier would have received one for the Yamamoto mission.

Not surprisingly, most of the fighter pilots who won the Medal of Honor served in Fifth Air Force. Kenney was highly conscious of the Navy and Marine Corps approach to awards. He ensured that his pilots were treated no less generously and no one part of his command was favored at the expense of the others. Although it was barely one fourth the size of the Eighth, the Fifth Air Force had ten Medal of Honor winners. Three were fighter pilots, one was a Tac R pilot, two others were bomber personnel on a recon mission, two were B-17 pilots, one was a B-25 pilot, and one was a Navy Catalina pilot attached to Kenney's command at the time of his Medal of Honor feat.[38]

The principal criterion for AAF Medals of Honor in most air forces was life saving. More awards went to men who'd tried to land a stricken bomber with wounded crewmen aboard than for any other reason. This was the AAF equivalent of giving them to soldiers who threw themselves on hand grenades.

One way or another, the effort to create and then to sustain a high level of morale succeeded. Arnold began with a tremendous advantage: the public perception that just serving in the AAF placed a man within a fighting elite. That perception was even stronger at the end than it had been in the beginning.

27

TECHNICAL KNOCKOUT

Despite the loss of Buna in January 1943, the Japanese army was confident it would win the war in New Guinea. It had merely overextended itself in the first flush of victory and suffered minor reverses at Milne Bay and Buna. There were still more than enough planes, men and ships available to shrug off these defeats and retain the strategic initiative in the southwest Pacific.

At this point it was the Americans and Australians in eastern New Guinea who appeared overextended and ripe for the taking. There were 400 Australians at Wau, an outpost 150 miles northwest of Buna. The Australians had been there, virtually undisturbed, since early 1942, when they had arrived to carve out a 3,000-foot airstrip. The Japanese had bypassed Wau, expecting it to fall into their hands eventually, although it was regularly resupplied by Fifth Air Force.

Following the loss of Buna, the Japanese attitude toward Wau changed. They decided to send the 51st Division's 102nd Infantry Regiment from Rabaul to Lae, the port they held thirty miles north of Wau, to drive the Australians out.

MacArthur's signals intelligence service, known as Central Bureau, a joint U.S.-Australian operation based in Melbourne, monitored the buildup of the convoy taking the three thousand men of the 102nd Regiment to Lae.[1] Kenney and his hard-bitten deputy, Ennis Whitehead, who ran Fifth Air Force's advanced headquarters in New Guinea, planned to destroy the convoy. Six B-17s attacked shipping in Rabaul Harbor on January 5. Two bombers went down; one of them was flown (in his cowboy boots) by Brigadier General Ken Walker, one of the AWPD-1 authors, now the commander of V Bomber Command. He went to his death and won the Medal of Honor. Recon picked up the ten Japanese ships (five transports escorted by five destroyers) of the convoy to Lae shortly after it set sail on January 6.

Attacks by B-24s and P-38s were broken up by Japanese fighters. On January 7, however, air attacks sank one transport. On January 8, Whitehead turned his planes against Lae airfield. Seventeen Japanese planes were destroyed on the ground. The convoy steamed into the harbor a few hours later and started unloading under air attack. Another transport was beached. Only half the regiment reached Lae.[2]

Despite this setback, the Japanese continued running large convoys from Rabaul to New Guinea. A week after the Lae convoy some 10,000 men of the Japanese 20th Division were landed at Wewak, 250 miles from Lae.

The Japanese hacked a trail through the jungle and attacked the outpost at Wau. By late January they had seized the northern end of the short, narrow, airstrip that was the outpost's lifeline. Wau seemed certain to fall.

Undeterred by the hail of small-arms fire they faced, the C-47 pilots of the 374th Troop Carrier Group continued to fly in. While fighters strafed and bombed the Japanese, the C-47s touched down at the southern end of the runway just long enough for troops to jump out and rush into battle. Wau's garrison rapidly grew to thirty-two hundred men.[3] The attacking force, exhausted by sickness and combat losses, failed to break through. Either the siege would have to be abandoned or the attackers heavily reinforced. A new convoy was organized to carry the rest of the 51st Division from Rabaul to Lae.

Central Bureau gave Kenney plenty of warning of this move.[4] Kenney and Whitehead had been disappointed by the failure to stop the January convoy to Lae. The preferred AAF method for attacking moving ships was to send a large force of heavies at high altitude in tight formation to drop a pattern on each ship; whichever way it turned it was likely to be struck. Kenney had only two heavy bomb groups, the 43rd and the 90th. He would have to find another way.

Kenney had been preaching the merits of low-level attacks for twenty years, but the standard method of low-level strikes against ships was the torpedo attack. Arnold had tried to get torpedoes produced to an AAF design for antishipping strikes. Yet the Navy had a hammerlock on torpedo production and refused to let go.[5]

The Australians favored the RAF practice of "mast-head bombing"—going in just over the mast and putting a bomb on the hull from about one hundred feet. Kenney rejected that. If the ship blew up, it would probably take the plane with it.[6] His own preference was to fly even lower and skip a five hundred-pound bomb with a five-second fuse against a ship's hull, much as one might skip a stone across a pond.

The unit Kenney turned to for developing skip-bombing techniques was an old favorite. When he arrived in Australia he'd found the famous 3rd Attack Group had been renamed the 3rd Light Bombardment Group (Dive) by the Air Staff. "Look, just forget all that," said Kenney. He gave them back their old name and, by implication, their proud tradition of low-level attack.[7] The B-25s of one of the group's squadrons were modified to take a package of four fifty-caliber machine guns in the nose; four more were installed in the fuselage below the pilot's cabin. The squadron would come in low and fast using these eight guns plus the two fifty-calibers in the top turret to beat down shipboard antiaircraft defenses before the skip-bombers made their attack.[8]

These tactics were practiced on the rusting hulk of a forty-seven-hundred-ton ocean liner lying on a reef outside Port Moresby. On February 28 Whitehead ran a dress rehearsal for the attack on the next big convoy, if it turned out to be heading for Lae.[9]

The Japanese were presently combat-loading seven thousand men and large amounts of fuel, ammunition, artillery, and engineering equipment aboard six troop transports and two freighters. They would be escorted to Lae by eight destroyers and provided with air cover.

The convoy was spotted by a recon flight on March 1, the day it left Rabaul. Next morning B-17s and B-24s bombed it, sinking one transport. The convoy plowed on, crossing the Bismarck Sea at seven knots. The biggest threat would come from the mediums based at Port Moresby once the convoy got within their range.

JAAF and Imperial Navy fighters flew combat air patrols over the ships at seven thousand feet, the height at which the mediums usually attacked (too high for small-arms fire, too low for heavy flak). By nightfall on March 2, the convoy was approaching Lae. In the early hours of March 3, the Royal Australian Air Force attempted a night torpedo attack. Every torpedo missed. At dawn, the convoy was in sight of the harbor.

At ten-fifteen, 180 planes—B-17s, B-25s, A-20s, P-38s, and RAAF Beaufighters—swarmed toward Lae and fell on the ships like falcons on field mice. The convoy was struck from various directions and different altitudes. Most deadly of all were the mediums, slipping under the combat air patrols. While the Japanese fighters got into a brawl with the heavy bombers at seven thousand feet, the B-25s and A-20s were wreaking havoc with enemy ships. As one of the B-17s went down, seven men bailed out. Japanese fighters closed on the seven parachutes and machine gunned the helpless airmen.[10]

By ten-thirty all seven remaining troop transports and freighters were sinking. Kenney's losses came to one B-17, three P-38s and a B-25. At noon, as Japanese fighters landed at Lae airfield to refuel, the 8th Fighter Squadron, 49th Fighter Group swept over the field, destroying six Zeros.

In mid-afternoon, Whitehead launched a second strike to finish off the convoy. Another Japanese destroyer was sunk. Then the airmen strafed the lifeboats, the rafts, the fuel drums—anything that Japanese survivors were clinging to.[11] The final attack on the convoy was flown next morning. The only ship remaining in the area, a destroyer, was sunk. At most, one thousand Japanese soldiers reached Lae safely. Another two thousand were rescued and carried back to Rabaul; as many as four thousand perished.[12]

As exultant Allied airmen reported in, Kenney phoned MacArthur and gave him an estimate of what had been wrought. A communique from MacArthur's headquarters claimed 12 transports, 3 cruisers and 7 destroyers sunk, 59 enemy planes shot down, and 12,762 Japanese soldiers killed or drowned.[13] It was an exaggeration, as Ultra would reveal, but excessive claims were typical of aerial combat. Every combatant air force in the world claimed considerably more destruction than had actually been achieved in most encounters with the enemy. The speed of events and the adrenaline rush of combat made it inevitable.

Nothing could disguise the fact that the battle of the Bismarck Sea had destroyed the Japanese willingness to run convoys into Lae, or anywhere near it. From here on, they hunkered down and fought entirely on the defensive. In three days air power had shifted the strategic initiative in New Guinea from the Japanese to MacArthur.

Kenney went to Washington on March 4 the way every combat commander must dream of doing—with a major victory to report. He was greeted warmly by the President, who savored the details of battles fought and won. Kenney's main task at the Pentagon was to demand more planes. Arnold was away, so Kenney debated his case for more aircraft with Barney Giles, with Marshall acting as referee. Kenney won the argument. Marshall ordered that the Fifth Air Force would get 10 percent more planes than Arnold had already promised.[14] Kenney now counted on having one thousand aircraft—half of them combat planes—before the year was out. That would double his striking power.

With the direct sea route from Rabaul to Lae denied them, the Japanese brought reinforcements into New Guinea at remote spots beyond the range of Kenney's mediums. From there, they were transhipped at night down the coast on shore-hugging barges to the battlefront. Japanese air strength was rebuilt and concentrated on airfields at or near Wewak, three hundred miles northwest of Lae.

The war in New Guinea was largely a struggle for airfields: either to take existing airfields from the enemy, to deny them to him, or to create airfields from which to attack him. And as Kenney followed the buildup of Japanese planes at Wewak, he itched to get at them. In the spring of 1943, however, he could raid Wewak only at night, with high-flying B-17s that did little more than keep the Japanese awake.[15] His most advanced fighter field, at Dobadura, just south of Buna, was more than four hundred miles from Wewak. Kenney wouldn't send heavy bombers to Wewak in daylight unescorted.

His solution was to build an airfield quickly and secretly in the jungle near Marilinan, sixty miles inland from Lae. Whenever Japanese planes approached, men and equipment were hidden in the jungle and the growing airstrip was camouflaged. At the same time Kenney built another airfield, openly, at Bena Bena, fifty miles west of Marilinan. The Japanese attacked Bena Bena repeatedly. Marilinan remained undisturbed almost until the moment it became operational. On August 11 a Japanese recon plane passed over the new field, cameras clicking, revealing the nearly completed airfield.[16]

Two actions soon followed: the Japanese prepared a major attack from Wewak; and Kenney rushed the 35th Fighter Group to Marilinan. On August 15 the newly installed radar gave fifteen minutes' warning that the Japanese were coming. Nine enemy planes were shot down, for the loss of four P-39s.[17] When the Japanese returned next day they were met by P-47s of the 348th Fighter Group and P-38s of the 475th Fighter Group: both far more formidable machines than the P-39. Fifteen Japanese planes were shot down, without any American losses. The JAAF never attacked Marilinan again.

Whitehead meanwhile, had a recon flight over Wewak's four airfields. The photographs showed two entire Japanese air divisions, with more than two hundred planes, crowded undispersed on and beside the short, narrow runways. Neither air force was able to disperse its planes properly in New Guinea, but the Japanese were particularly vulnerable, because they had been slow to develop early warning radar.

In the early hours of August 17, fifty heavy bombers struck Wewak. Three were lost. Results were negligible. In midmorning, the B-25s of 3rd Attack Group and 38th Bomb Group, escorted by eighty-five P-38s, flew fast and low over Wewak.

Major Donald Hall led the Mitchells of 8th Bomb Squadron. "It was too much to ask, after the heavy bombers had made their attack in the dark, that we would catch the Japs completely off guard. Yet that is exactly what happened. . . .

"Before we were in effective range, we threw in a few shots to make them duck. We waited a few seconds, and then cut loose again. A Betty bomber blew up on the runway. From then on we held our gun switches down, raking plane after plane. The Jap airplanes were lined wing tip to wing tip the whole length of the runway. . . .

"Not an AA gun was fired. Not a plane got off the ground to intercept us. A fellow dreams of a situation like that, but never expects to see it. We let go our parachute bombs, in clusters of three, one after another. They drifted down lazily, like a cloud of snowballs. . . . Fires were blazing everywhere, and broken, twisted planes lined both sides of the runways. . . ."[18] After the bombers had done their work, the P-38s came down and strafed. Up to one hundred aircraft had been destroyed or seriously damaged. Whitehead mounted a second strike next day, destroying and damaging another twenty-eight planes. Smaller attacks continued for the rest of the month. In two weeks the JAAF had to write off nearly two hundred planes at Wewak.[19]

On September 4 the Australian 9th Division landed on the coast above Lae. There was no challenge from the JAAF to the troops or the ships that carried them. Next day, ninety-six C-47s of 54th Troop Carrier Wing dropped the American 503rd Parachute Infantry Regiment at Nadzab, twenty miles west of Lae. Whitehead had made a command reconnaissance deep into enemy territory in June and picked out Nadzab as one of the finest sites for an airfield in the whole of New Guinea. The drop was flawless. The 3rd Attack Group put down a smoke screen, mediums bombed and strafed, P-38s flew top cover, B-17s dropped fifteen tons of supplies and earth-moving equipment. It took less than three minutes for all seventeen hundred paratroopers to jump.[20] Work on building an airstrip began even before Japanese resistance was overcome. Two days later the Australian 7th Division was airlifted in.

The Japanese 51st Division was now virtually surrounded on land and cut off from reinforcement by sea. Lae fell to Allied troops on September 16, as the 51st's survivers infiltrated through the jungles, heading for Wewak.

The Japanese position in the South Pacific rested on the strong base they had built up at Rabaul, on the northeast coast of New Britain. The harbor was big enough to accommodate the entire Imperial Navy; there were three major airfields; a large town; and a garrison of one hundred thousand well-armed troops. In the spring of 1943 the Joint Chiefs approved a complex plan called Cartwheel that pooled the efforts of the forces in SWPA and those in the South Pacific under the Navy's command.

Cartwheel envisaged a huge pincer movement, with MacArthur striking northeast from New Guinea toward Rabaul, by way of New Britain and the Admiralty Islands, while South Pacific forces converged on Rabaul by ascending the Solomons. The plan called for thirteen amphibious assaults, culminating in the capture of Rabaul.

It was a target MacArthur prized highly. With the destruction of Rabaul, he believed, the way would be open for him to make a swift return to the Philippines. The alternative was to make a long, slow, arduous crawl the entire length of New Guinea.

For the present, five hundred miles from Dobodura, Rabaul was far beyond V Fighter Command's range. Kenney attacked it, with small numbers of heavy bombers, at night. When Ken Walker had tried attacking it at midday, he'd lost his life. Kenney's night technique was to have the first couple of planes to arrive drop parachute flares. Then the rest would fly in around five hundred feet and skip-bomb the shipping. Aircrews called this "Waterline Precision Bombing."[21]

Inevitably, perhaps, someone on Whitehead's staff decided to try burying Rabaul by triggering an explosion in the most active of the six volcanoes overlooking the town. B-17 pilot Carl Hustad of the 43rd flew this mission on May 22. "My plane," he wrote later, "was loaded with two 2,000-pound bombs. Fuses were set for 45 seconds to allow deep penetration of the volcano. I was not to make my run until the other bombers had cleared the area for at least 15 minutes, to avoid any losses due to the expected 'conflagration.' . . .

"We ran into a fair amount of AA fire, dropped our bombs, scooted over the rim of the crater and headed for home in a low sweep over the water north of Rabaul, waiting for the shock wave that didn't come."[22] All his bombs did was rearrange the magma.

Night missions to Rabaul were dangerous and unrewarding. There was nothing to indicate they were hurting the Japanese. Yet the loss rate per mission was 5 percent.

In June, American troops landed on two islands, Woodlark and Kiriwina, halfway between Buna and New Britain. Airfields were soon under construction. These would enable Whitehead to provide fighter escort for bombing raids to Rabaul. In July 1943, shortly after Cartwheel was set in motion, Whitehead halted the night offensive against Rabaul.[23]

Kenney intended to "make Rabaul untenable for Jap shipping and to set up an air blockade" that would isolate this enemy bastion from reinforcement.[24] The Fifth struck on October 12, with 349 aircraft. More than 100 B-25s and RAAF Beaufighters attacked first, strafing the airfields and scattering parafrag bombs. They were followed by B-24s, escorted by P-38s, which attacked the shipping in the harbor. The sweep over the airfields took the Japanese by surprise. They had radar, but it wasn't much use against low-flying planes.[25]

Weather delayed the follow-up strike until October 18. Even then, the escorting fighters had to turn back before reaching Rabaul and many of the bombers couldn't find the target. Results were unimpressive. On October 23 Whitehead mounted a high-level attack by B-24s. Twenty-four hours later the 3rd Attack Group came in low to hit the airfields; one hundred P-38s flew top cover. On the 25th, the heavies came back again.

The next big attack, on November 2, saw the mediums return. The raiders ran into Zeros flown by veteran pilots of the Imperial

Navy's First Carrier Division.[26] The Fifth lost nine B-25s and ten P-38s on this mission.

Kenney's response was to mount yet another attack, in concert with veteran U.S. Navy pilots. On November 5 the U.S. Third Fleet, commanded by Admiral William Halsey, attacked the shipping at Rabaul. As the Navy's attack drew to a close, the Fifth arrived. Most planes left on the airfields were wrecks: the flyable aircraft were fighting the Navy. So Kenney's planes bombed the town.[27] There were more raids on November 7 and 11.

In the space of a month the Japanese wrote off at least two hundred planes at Rabaul; the actual figure could be as high as five hundred.[28] The bastion had not been made untenable to shipping. Nor had it been isolated from air reinforcement. Japanese aircraft losses had been made good by bringing planes down from the Central Pacific, which seriously weakened the defenses there just as the U.S. Navy's Central Pacific offensive got rolling. The Imperial Navy pulled back from Rabaul to meet the threat farther north. With the Japanese navy's withdrawal, Rabaul ceased to be a major threat.[29]

MacArthur's original plan for isolating and ultimately taking Rabaul called for establishing an airfield and a PT boat base in southwestern New Britain.[30] In the fall of 1943 MacArthur's chief of operations, Brigadier General Stephen J. Chamberlin, was arguing for Cape Gloucester as the airfield site, despite Kenney's objections that the ground might be too swampy to take his bombers, and Kenney was urging the capture of the Arawe peninsula, fifty miles south of Cape Gloucester, as a PT boat base. MacArthur approved both operations.[31]

On December 14 the mediums made counterair attacks on the nearest large JAAF airfield to Arawe, at Gasmata. The landing went ahead next day. A small force of Japanese planes eluded the patrolling P-38s and made an ineffective attack on the beach and the assault shipping. The biggest challenge to the troops was the long wade to shore. Many divested themselves of packs and clothing. They landed armed but more or less naked.[32]

Their regimental commander, Colonel Alexander M. Miller, requested resupply by air. Whitehead's First Air Task Force at Dobodura, commanded by Brigadier General Frederick H. Smith, loaded nineteen B-17s and B-25s with the standard clothing allowance for a regiment. Smith threw in a copy of the Boy Scouts handbook to complete the consignment, and the loads were dropped next day.[33]

Large air attacks were launched from Wewak and Rabaul to break through Smith's fighter screen and maul the fleet that sustained the invaders, but none succeeded. Only one small transport was sunk. Fifth Air Force claimed two dozen enemy bombers and thirty-two fighters shot down. After December 31 Japanese attacks dwindled down to nuisance raids, usually at night.[34]

At Cape Gloucester, Whitehead bombed the Japanese defenders day and night for a week before the landing. Nearly fourteen hundred bomber sorties were flown. The area was strafed from dawn to dusk by low-flying fighters, A-20s and mediums. The 1st Marine Division's assault on Cape Gloucester was made December 26. There was little resistance from the demoralized Japanese defending the beaches.

Rabaul mounted an air attack in midafternoon on D-Day—twenty-five dive-bombers, escorted by thirty fighters. They managed to slip through the fighter screen, sink one destroyer, and damage three others before the Fifth's fighters caught up with them. Nearly fifty Japanese planes were shot down. An attempt by fifteen Japanese torpedo bombers to attack several hours later was a complete failure. Fourteen were shot down by 348th Group Thunderbolts.[35] Arawe and Cape Gloucester cost the Japanese more than one hundred aircraft and added to the neutralization of Rabaul, although the base for PT boats was never built and the swampy airfield was never used.

The next major operation that Cartwheel prescribed was a landing on Los Negros Island, in the Admiralties, northwest of New Britain. There was an objective on Los Negros that Kenney wanted badly: Momote airfield. Whitehead's recon pilots described it as the best Japanese airfield they had ever seen.[36] Although the schedule called for invading Los Negros in April, Kenney urged MacArthur to speed things up. He had photo recon missions flown at two hundred feet. They drew no enemy fire. Three B-25s flew over the Admiralties even lower—down to twenty feet. Their crews returned safely and reported seeing no sign of enemy occupation. Kenney claimed there were at most three hundred Japanese on Los Negros; MacArthur's intelligence chief said there were four thousand. MacArthur decided to gamble.

Weather disrupted the preliminary aerial bombardment of Los Negros, but the assault went ahead anyway. On February 29, one thousand men of the 1st Cavalry Division (really an infantry division, but with cavalry antecedents) landed on the southern edge of Momote airfield. By ten that morning they had overrun it. The Japanese counterattacked strongly. During the night another two thousand cavalrymen were landed. There were forty-five hundred Japanese troops in the area. Eventually the entire 1st Cavalry Division's ten thousand men were fed into the battle.[37]

The weather kept both air forces at bay during the crucial early stages, but when it did break Whitehead's bombers and troop carriers air dropped food, ammunition and blood plasma. Only a few Japanese planes appeared overhead, making brief and ineffective strafing runs before returning whence they came, pursued by P-38s.

Manus, the island adjacent to Los Negros, contained a harbor the Navy coveted. In mid-March Manus was wrested from its small Japanese garrison. With the Admiralties secured and Allied forces well-established on New Britain, SWPA's role in Cartwheel was virtually complete.

To follow the role of South Pacific forces in Cartwheel it is necessary to go back to mid-1942. SoPac, as the theater was known, was under Navy command, but in July of that year Marshall established a U.S. Army Forces headquarters in SoPac, under the command of Major General Millard Harmon, the former chief of the Air Staff. Harmon was a huge, barrel-chested figure, hence his nickname— "Tiny." He was highly able and got on well with the Navy.

Harmon's appointment came at a crucial time. The Japanese were planning to establish an airfield on Guadalcanal, at the southern end of the Solomons, five hundred miles southwest of Rabaul. Admiral King proposed to stop them, by sending the 1st Marine Division to seize Guadalcanal.[38] Arnold had the deepest doubts about this operation, code-named Watchtower. He was convinced the Navy and Marine Corps were taking on more than they could handle, and would expect the AAF and the Army to bail them out.[39] Marshall, however, strongly supported this operation.

The AAF's role in the battle for Guadalcanal was modest, but nonetheless valuable. The B-17s of 19th Bomb Group flew several missions from Australia to bomb Rabaul during the first week of Watchtower. Marines landed on August 7 and soon grabbed the unfinished airstrip. In between fighting off fierce Japanese counterattacks they tried to develop the strip, which they named Henderson Field in honor of a Marine pilot killed in the battle of Midway. A handful of Navy and Marine flyers managed to operate from it, even though Henderson was under fire from mortars and artillery.[40]

On August 26 the AAF's 67th Fighter Squadron joined them. Its P-400s (an export version of the P-39) failed as interceptors: they lacked the oxygen needed to operate above eighteen thousand feet. So they were used as bait, to lure Japanese fighters while Navy F4F Wildcats lurked high above, hidden in the sun. They were more successful, though, when they came down low and used their thirty-seven-millimeter cannon in ground attack missions to aid leather-necks engaged in close combat.[41]

Meanwhile the B-17s of the 11th Bomb Group, based in New Caledonia, three hundred miles to the south, flew antishipping patrols over the sea approaches to Guadalcanal. The group damaged half a dozen Japanese ships, including the battleship *Hiei.*

Seven weeks after the landing, Arnold visited Guadalcanal. The marines were in poor shape. The Japanese were being reinforced. The outcome of the battle was still in the balance. The Navy demanded more help from the Army and the AAF. Harmon was already moving Army troops to Guadalcanal, but Arnold got into a blazing row with senior naval commanders. He grew so insulting that he was ordered off the command ship. With Torch—another operation Arnold disapproved of—about to strip the Eighth of its planes and with Arnold considering the AAF aircraft presently in SoPac being poorly employed, he refused to provide more planes for the South Pacific beyond what the AAF had already committed.[42]

Fresh Army and Marine divisions were fed into the battle. The Navy eventually got the upper hand in the naval clashes. In January 1943, as Watchtower drew to a close, the Thirteenth Air Force was created in New Caledonia. Its commander would be Major General Nathan F. Twining, Harmon's former chief of staff. Modest, capable and well liked, Twining had spent six years in the infantry before learning to fly, in 1924. He'd been adjutant of the old 3rd Attack Group before going to Maxwell, then on to Leavenworth.

The role of the Thirteenth (which called itself "the Jungle Air Force") was to aid the advance through the Solomons as outlined in Cartwheel. Small and little publicized, it nonetheless had an early brush with fame and glory, in April 1943.

Navy cryptanalysts broke a message that revealed that Admiral Isoroku Yamamoto, the mastermind behind the attack on Pearl Harbor, planned to visit various bases in the central Solomons. The Navy urged, and Roosevelt approved, a mission to ambush Yamamoto.

The Navy admiral responsible for all air operations in the Solomons, Marc Mitscher, chose the AAF's 70th Fighter Squadron for this task. Led by Captain Thomas G. Lanphier, Jr., eight of the squadron's P-38 pilots had on March 28 made a successful fighter sweep over the central Solomons, attacking a Japanese seaplane base. Lanphier was the son of a former commander of the famous 1st Pursuit Group and was Doolittle's godson. He seemed almost destined to become an ace pilot.

On April 2 he led an antishipping attack in the central Solomons. His pilots set a Japanese freighter on fire by skipping their wing tanks against its hull, then firing tracers. Days later Lanphier's flight had strafed a destroyer until it burst into flame.

Mitscher wanted the 70th Squadron to attack and sink the subchaser that would carry Yamamoto on his visits between islands. Lanphier rejected that: we'll have a better chance of getting him, he argued, if we shoot down his plane as it comes in to land on Bougainville.[43]

The mission plan called for four planes to fly in low, with another fourteen providing top cover. It involved a round trip of nearly nine hundred miles and would take the P-38s close to the biggest airfield on Bougainville, at Kahili, where the Japanese based as many as one hundred single-engine fighters.

Shortly after dawn on Sunday, April 18, the P-38s took off. The most assistance they could count on was Yamamoto's insistence on punctuality. They would be flying over water for four hundred miles, out of sight of land most of the way, with strict radio silence. Navigation was probably the biggest weakness of the wartime AAF, and in the Pacific poor navigation cost hundreds, possibly thousands, of airmen's lives. It nearly killed Twining, who spent six days on a life raft in February 1943 surrounded by sharks when his B-17 got lost and ran out of gas; Harmon perished on a B-24 that, like many other planes, vanished over the ocean in reasonable weather.

The odds against arriving at the right spot at the right moment on an overwater flight of more than four hundred miles made the

Yamamoto mission a desperately long shot. Yet as Lanphier led his flight of four P-38s at one thousand feet, ten miles from the Bougainville coast, one of the pilots flying top cover called out, "Bogey! Ten o'clock high." There were eight specks in the distance: two twin-engine bombers, escorted by six fighters.

As the P-38s closed on the Japanese, one of the Zeros dove on Lanphier. After that, no one can say for certain what happened. Lanphier claimed that he shot down two Zeros, and then shot down the bomber carrying Yamamoto. His wingman, Rex T. Barber, later contested Lanphier's claim.

There were no gun cameras on either pilot's P-38, but on the basis of Japanese survivors' testimony and the physical evidence from the wreckage, it seems that Lanphier attacked Yamamoto's aircraft from the right, and either missed or did some slight damage. As the plane flew on, still losing altitude, Barber attacked it from the left rear, bringing it down. Neither Lanphier nor Barber saw the other's attack; they were about one minute apart.

In years to come, Lanphier would be hailed as a hero and credited in print with as many as seventeen aerial victories. At present, the Air Force credits him with four and a half kills. Barber's credit for shooting down Yamamoto's bomber, however, gives him a total of five.[44]

In mid-1943, as the advance from Guadalcanal got under way, the Thirteenth had two hundred fighters (mainly P-39s), seventy B-25s, and ninety B-17s. The primitive conditions in which it had to operate meant its availability rate rarely reached 50 percent. Yet whatever it lacked in size, it seemed determined to make up for in aggressiveness. When Arnold created the much bigger Fifteenth Air Force in Italy, he chose Twining to command it.

That summer, the Japanese were hurrying to complete a large airfield on New Georgia, at Munda Point, one hundred miles north of Guadalcanal. Almost as soon as American intelligence officers realized what was happening, plans were drawn to grab the airfield. The invasion was mounted July 2. It took three Army divisions six weeks to wrest Munda from its determined Japanese defenders.

The next major operation, in November, saw an Army division and the 3rd Marine Division land on Bougainville. They seized a beachhead big enough for a bomber runway and two fighter strips. Operations from the new airfield began in January 1944.

The Japanese counterattacked in March, hoping to capture the airfield. They were repulsed and the defensive perimeter was expanded. With the Bougainville airfield in operation, the isolation and neutralization of Rabaul was complete.

The Thirteenth would soon be redeployed. It would move to SWPA, where MacArthur was advancing toward the Philippines.

28

LUCKY NUMBERS

In March 1944 MacArthur's command was in danger of becoming a mere sideshow. The Navy was moving rapidly toward Formosa. Marshall was sympathetic to MacArthur and Kenney's arguments for advancing to Luzon instead, from SWPA, but Arnold had sided with the Navy.[1]

Fully loaded B-29s would not be able to reach Tokyo from the Philippines. The Navy, on the other hand, was going to take the Marianas. From airfields there, most of Japan would be within reach. Arnold threw his weight to the Navy's side. The main effort in the Pacific would be Nimitz's thrust westward, with SWPA operations in a supporting role.

MacArthur and Kenney found themselves badly in need of a campaign that would advance through New Guinea as rapidly as the Navy drove through the Central Pacific. Otherwise, SWPA would be left behind.

Plans were well advanced for a 250-mile leap to Hansa Bay, one of the best natural harbors in New Guinea and within range of Kenney's fighters. Three thousand men of the 32nd Division had landed at Saidor, halfway between Lae and Hansa Bay, on January 2, in an attempt to trap Japanese troops retreating from Lae. A fighter strip could be built at Saidor to cover the invasion. The Japanese, guessing what was coming, shipped an extra division to Hansa Bay to join the division already there. They proceeded to turn its palm-fringed beaches into a vast killing ground.[2]

Central Bureau's Ultra code breakers revealed the trap being set.

MacArthur studied the maps some more. Up to now, all his amphibious assaults had been covered by Kenney's planes. Hollandia, which contained a large natural harbor and three Japanese airfields, was 250 miles beyond Hansa Bay. Finally, Ultra decrypts showed that, unlike Hansa Bay, the ground defenses at Hollandia were weak and poorly organized. The Japanese counted on distance, and the impending arrival of a 100-man radar unit with the latest equipment to protect Hollandia from Fifth Air Force and invasion.

MacArthur decided to bet on Ultra and Kenney. He would bypass the Japanese at Hansa Bay and make the five hundred-mile jump to Hollandia. Halsey was prepared to provide air cover for three days from his Third Fleet carriers. Nimitz, though, was deeply troubled by this operation.

Carriers couldn't be risked against strong land-based air forces. The Japanese had rebuilt their air strength in New Guinea so it now exceeded five hundred planes. Kenney promised Nimitz that he would have the JAAF "rubbed out" by April 5, well before the invasion.[3]

The first obstacle to be demolished was Wewak, which stood almost halfway between the Fifth's new airfield at Nadzab and Hollandia. Most days there were more than one hundred aircraft at Wewak. Starting March 11 Whitehead's planes attacked Wewak relentlessly. In the course of two weeks nearly fourteen hundred bomber sorties were flown, covering its four airfields with thousands of fragmentation bombs and more than one thousand tons of high explosive. By March 25 the JAAF had pulled its remaining planes back to the safety of Hollandia.[4]

Complementing the Wewak counterair strikes, B-24s equipped with radar bombsights had attacked coastal shipping between Hollandia and Wewak by night. The night of March 17 they sank four ships, including one that carried the one hundred-man radar unit. The radar operators perished along with the equipment.[5]

That would leave Hollandia half blind, but the Japanese, contemplating the five hundred-mile distance from Kenney's fighter airfields, still felt comparatively safe. Kenney surely wouldn't risk unescorted bombers by day against a base that presently contained more than three hundred aircraft. They were right.

The Fifth, however, had recently started taking delivery of fifty P-38Js. The J model had extra tanks in the wings, giving it another one hundred miles of range. With this modification to guide them, the men of the V Air Service Command went to work developing extra wing tanks for seventy-five older model Lightnings.[6] In the meantime, Fifth Air Force made heavy raids on Hansa Bay to lull the Japanese.

On March 30, Whitehead began his Hollandia counterair offensive. The Japanese had developed a warning net along the coast of ground observers with radio telephones and binoculars. Whitehead sent a force of bombers toward Aitape, a coastal village halfway between Hollandia and Wewak that contained two small airstrips. Forty Hollandia-based fighters took off to intercept the bombers, but arrived after the bombers had attacked Aitape and were heading back toward Nadzab.

The Japanese fighters returned to Hollandia. Flying almost parallel with them, but hidden by the Owen Stanleys, was a force of sixty-five B-24s and eighty P-38s. When the Japanese planes landed to refuel, the Liberators and Lightnings swarmed over the mountains and devastated Hollandia's three airfields, deluging them with fourteen thousand fragmentation bombs.[7] Scores of aircraft were destroyed or seriously damaged; AAA positions were wiped out; large fuel dumps were set ablaze. Not one American aircraft was lost.

Next day 68 B-24s hit Hollandia. One P-38 was shot down. JAAF losses over the two days came to 199 aircraft destroyed.[8] On April 3 Whitehead launched his third counterair strike, destroying nearly every plane left at Hollandia in flyable condition. He then mounted seven devastating raids in little more than two weeks, leaving the garrison homeless, the town reduced to rubble and the beach defenses in ruins.

By April 22, the date of the scheduled assault, most of Hollandia's defenders had pulled back into the jungle to avoid the bombing. The 24th and 41st Divisions landed virtually unopposed.[9]

That same day several thousand infantryman also landed at Aitape. They soon grabbed the two fighter strips. Whitehead would use them to provide air cover at Hollandia after the Navy pulled its carriers out.

With Hollandia in his pocket, MacArthur was eager to cash in while the Japanese were still reeling from the shock of this major defeat. Kenney, too, was urging him onward: Hollandia's airfields were good enough for medium bombers, but too poorly drained to take his B-24s when the rainy season started in the fall. His eye fell on the island of Biak, 225 miles northwest of Hollandia, where the

Japanese had a large airfield, called Mokmer airdrome, and two fighter strips.

To provide air cover over Biak another island, Wakde, would have to be invaded first and its airstrip seized. On May 18 thirty-five hundred troops landed on Wakde with orders to take it quickly. It fell in forty-eight hours.

On May 29 the 41st Division attacked the beaches of Biak. The Japanese fought a tenacious battle to deny Mokmer to the Americans. As the fighting dragged on, Whitehead's aviation engineers grabbed the small, unpopulated island of Owi a few miles away. There, they carved out a narrow seven thousand-foot runway. P-40s and P-38s from Owi joined in the battle for Biak, as did B-25s from Wakde and B-24s from Hollandia.[10] Biak wasn't secured until the middle of July.

While the fighting on Biak dragged on, the Thirteenth Air Force—Kenney's other "lucky" number—was transferred to SWPA. With Rabaul neutralized and the campaign in the South Pacific petering out, there was no mission for it there. Kenney requested it be assigned to him. A new headquarters, Far Eastern Air Forces, was created under Kenney. Whitehead assumed command of the Fifth. FEAF contained two thousand combat aircraft, with another twelve hundred on the way.[11]

Kenney lacked the runways to operate so many planes within range of the battle fronts. His eye now fell on Noemfoor, a small island fifty miles west of Biak. Noemfoor possessed three airfields. On July 2 and 4 the 317th Troop Carrier Group, flying from Hollandia, dropped the 503rd Parachute Infantry Regiment on Noemfoor. With close air support from the Fifth, the paratroopers overran the four thousand Japanese defenders in little more than a week.

On July 30 the 6th Division landed at Sansapor, at the western end of New Guinea. The landing force included twenty-five hundred construction engineers, to provide new airfields for FEAF. With this operation, Kenney's leapfrogging airmen reached the end of the line in New Guinea.

They did so at a critical juncture. With both MacArthur and Nimitz moving rapidly, the question of where their forces should meet up had to be settled. They traveled to Hawaii to put their arguments to the President. If the JCS were deadlocked, Roosevelt would have to make the decision. MacArthur argued that America had a moral obligation to liberate the Philippines. The Filipinos were American subjects, suffering under a brutal occupation.

Nimitz argued that his forces and MacArthur's should converge with an invasion of Formosa. All that was needed was enough of northern Luzon to provide some airfields to cover the Formosan assault. Once Japan was conquered, the Philippines would be liberated anyway.[12]

Logistics, however, ruled out an invasion of Formosa before the defeat of Germany. MacArthur's invasion of the Philippines would go ahead, with a landing on Mindanao in October.

Ultra revealed that the Japanese were constructing a defensive triangle to block MacArthur's advance from New Guinea. The triangle was based on the island of Halamahera, in the Dutch East Indies; the Palau islands; and Mindanao. Three Japanese air armies (the equivalent of USAAF wings) and eighty thousand ground troops held the triangle. Half the troops and planes were on Halamahera, which Kenney looked certain to need if FEAF was going to support an invasion of Mindanao.

MacArthur declined to attack Halmahera and its forty thousand troops. He reached instead for the island of Morotai, ten miles from Halmahera. On September 15 the 31st Infantry Division landed on the southern coast of lightly defended Morotai and seized a beachhead. Within days two large airfields were under construction. When the wind blew from the northeast, you could almost smell the Philippines.

Kenney repeatedly pressed Arnold to let him have B-29s. Arnold just as often said no. Kenney then tried going over Arnold's head. He got MacArthur to ask Marshall for two B-29 groups. He needed them, he insisted, so that he could attack the biggest oil facility the Japanese possessed, at Balikpapan, in Borneo. Kenney intended to shut down Balikpapan, which produced four million barrels of oil per year. It was, in effect, the Empire's Ploesti. But not even MacArthur's intervention helped. The answer was still an emphatic no.[13]

Balikpapan wasn't exactly a virgin target. In August 1942 nine B-24s had flown to Borneo from Darwin and attempted to bomb it at night. This raid was too small to do serious damage, and may have done none at all. Eight of the nine B-24s managed to return to Australia landing on fuel vapors; the ninth, out of fuel, crash landed.[14]

With airfields at Morotai and Noemfoor—roughly one hundred miles from Borneo—Kenney was itching to hit Balikpapan with a heavy, daylight attack. Whitehead had his doubts, fearing losses would prove prohibitive, but Kenney insisted on going ahead.[15]

Aircrews were given strict instructions on fuel conservation. Most of the armor plate, ammunition and anything else that could be considered excess weight was stripped from the B-24s that would make the Balikpapan attacks. On September 30 the Fifth flew a diversion mission to the southern Philippines while one B-24 group from the Fifth (5th Bomb Group) and two from the Thirteenth (the 90th and 307th) headed for Borneo. The seventy-two Liberators on this mission had an eighteen-hour round trip ahead of them.

An Imperial Navy fighter group was based at Balikpapan. It rose to fight with such willingness that Zeros repeatedly flew through their own AAA to reach the American bombers. The B-24 crews were equally committed. The target was obscured by cloud on the first pass, so they did what would have been suicidal over Germany—they returned and made a second pass thirty minutes later![16] This time the cloud was more broken. Only four Liberators were shot down.

Three days later, the 90th and 307th groups returned. The 307th was intercepted by forty Zeros. Seven bombers were lost.

Before returning to Balikpapan the Thirteenth's B-24 crews practiced flying the LeMay-style combat box. Fifty 348th Fighter Group pilots volunteered to fly escort for the Liberators. They proposed to ditch their P-47s in the sea on the return leg and be rescued by Catalinas.[17] V Air Service Command had a better idea: it would make two huge wing tanks for each Thunderbolt, providing an extra 485 gallons of fuel. Flying from Morotai, the 348th's P-47s and the 35th Group's P-38s should just about make it to Borneo and back.

Two small night raids were flown to Balikpapan on October 8 and 9, to tire the defenders. On October 10 six B-24 groups attacked Balikpapan in daylight, escorted by Thunderbolts on the penetration, and P-38s on the withdrawal. More than twenty Japanese fighters were shot down. The raiders lost three bombers and a P-47.[18]

The next big attack, and the most successful, was flown on October 14. An attempt to repeat it on October 18 was foiled by the weather.

FEAF had struck Balikpapan with five large raids, put 433 tons of bombs on the refineries and the storage tanks, and inflicted some serious damage, but nothing that couldn't be repaired. The cost had been twenty-two B-24s shot down, and nine fighters.

This was a promising beginning, but Balikpapan suddenly dropped from the target list. Something much bigger was about to begin—the return to the Philippines.

In mid-September 1944 an Army division and a Marine division were preparing to invade the Palaus. This assault would deny the Japanese the use of airfields there to threaten the Navy ships which would carry MacArthur's forces to Mindanao in October, after which he planned to move north and invade Leyte in December.

While the troops were being loaded aboard the assault ships, one of Halsey's carrier task forces was making air strikes against the central Philippines. When Halsey's pilots reported that Leyte was virtually undefended, Halsey sent a message to Nimitz recommending that the invasion of the Palaus be canceled and that the troops be sent to invade Leyte instead.[19]

The JCS, meeting in Quebec, got on the radio and asked SWPA headquarters if MacArthur would be prepared to make the Leyte assault. The general was monitoring the invasion of Morotai from a Navy cruiser that was observing radio silence. Sutherland and Kenney hurriedly conferred. Leyte was far beyond the range of Kenney's fighters, and the Navy wouldn't offer air cover for more than a few days.

If Sutherland sent a negative reply, though, the Navy might demand authority to send the Marines to take Leyte. That really would freeze MacArthur's forces out. Sutherland informed the JCS that MacArthur would invade Leyte on October 20.[20]

When MacArthur was reached twenty-four hours later he endorsed Sutherland's decision. By moving the invasion of Leyte forward two months he would be short 100 landing ships; that is, he'd be lacking 450,000 tons of essential shipping. Nor did Leyte look like a good place to put airfields. When Army engineers studied the data on the terrain they urged MacArthur to find a better place to invade.[21] The soil was unstable, the land was cut with countless streams and rice paddies, and the monsoon season would begin in November. And without taking Mindanao, MacArthur would be making his first invasion without secure land-based air power. Kenney's nearest fighter airfields, on Morotai, were eight hundred miles away. Yet the choice before MacArthur was no choice at all: it was Leyte or nothing.

As promised, the invasion was mounted on October 20. Fifty thousand American troops went ashore in Leyte Gulf, on the eastern side of Leyte, against light opposition. The Japanese had twenty-one thousand men on the island, but few were near the invasion beaches. Most were dug in on high ground inland.

There were 450 Japanese planes in the Philippines, but more than half of these were on Luzon, 500 miles to the north. During the first day of the invasion, only a handful of Japanese planes attacked. One slipped through the Navy's combat air patrols and smashed into a cruiser, inflicting serious damage. More kamikaze attacks the next day hit an escort carrier and another cruiser.[22]

Kenney's chief concern was to seize the airfields at Tacloban and Dulag and get them into operation. He succeeded: both were in American hands within forty-eight hours and engineers toiled around the clock to cover them with steel mat. The Japanese, however, strafed the fields during the day and bombed them at night, slowing progress.

The Japanese Navy's response to the invasion was to send three fleets to attempt to catch the Navy ships in Leyte Gulf in a huge pincer operation. From October 24 to 27 the biggest battle in naval history, in terms of the number of ships involved, erupted in the waters of the central Philippines. The U.S. Navy won a resounding victory, but pulled its aircraft carriers out of Leyte Gulf.

On October 26 Kenney sent for P-38s of 49th Fighter Group to come up from Morotai. Next day, shortly after aviation engineers finished putting twenty-eight hundred feet of steel mat in place at Tacloban, thirty-four P-38s arrived. Japanese raids soon destroyed nearly half of them. Work on extending the runway continued.

Another twenty Lightnings, from the 475th Group, arrived October 30. They flew in from Morotai just before thirty JAAF fighters appeared. The Japanese started attacking P-38s that were slowing down to land. A huge melee ensued. Major Tommy McGuire got a kill and jubilantly touched down on the short strip: "This is the kind of place I like, where you have to shoot 'em down so you can land on your own airdrome!"[23]

The nocturnal bombing of Tacloban continued. Kenney sent for a half dozen P-61 Black Widows to come up from Morotai and defend the night.

By November, the Japanese were funneling planes and troops into the Philippines. While Ultra code breakers were absorbed in the drama of the battle of Leyte Gulf, the Japanese were shipping the elite 1st Division from Manchuria to Ormoc, a port on the western side of Leyte. This large, well-equipped division reached Ormoc November 1 and began to disembark.

Meanwhile, Kenney's planes were striking three Japanese airfields in the central Philippines, unaware of the fat, inviting and important target at anchor in Ormoc Bay. The Japanese also distracted both FEAF and Halsey by sending out radio messages referring to a nonexistent convoy. Kenney and Halsey sent dozens of planes on a fruitless search for this chimera. The real convoy, in Ormoc Bay, was discovered next day. Kenney's planes attacked it, but by then twenty-two thousand Japanese troops had landed, along with nearly all their equipment.[24]

On November 4, thirty-five Japanese planes hit Tacloban in a daylight raid that caught the defenders by surprise. There was no dispersal room and no revetments. Nearly all the forty aircraft at Tacloban were destroyed or damaged.[25]

Ultra detected another large convoy heading for Ormoc, carrying the 26th Division. On November 10 Fifth Air Force planes struck Ormoc Bay and caught an outbound convoy heading out to sea. Seven B-25s and four P-38s were shot down by AAA as they roared in to make low-level attacks.[26] Only one transport was sunk. Several hours later, however, the incoming convoy was struck by nearly 350 Navy planes. Four transports and a destroyer went down. Barely half the 26th Division's troops survived to reach the shore.[27]

Meanwhile, progress at Dulag was agonizingly slow, putting a severe brake on Fifth Air Force's ability to hit the shipping bringing in Japanese reinforcements. Since the invasion, the Japanese had sent more than three hundred planes to the Philippines. But if the enemy had plenty of planes, the quality of Japanese pilots by this stage of the war was abysmal.[28] Kenney's pilots, on the other hand, were well trained, confident and aggressively led.

In 1944 fighter pilots came to the Fifth with 350 hours of flight training. Every one had already demonstrated his skill and determination just to get into combat. The P-38 pilots sent to the Pacific in 1944 were the winners of fiercely contested mock dogfighting competitions. For every fighter pilot sent to Kenney, several others, bitterly disappointed, stayed at home.[29]

The poor quality of Japanese pilots was on display all over the sky. Shortly after the 475th Fighter Group moved into Dulag in mid-November, Lieutenant Jack Purdy got to test it for himself. He led a flight of four P-38s escorting a Navy Catalina flying boat on a search-and-rescue mission for two downed Fifth Air Force pilots. "We saw a convoy of ten to twelve ships heading southeast across the Visayan Sea toward Ormoc Bay . . . then, one of the wingmen called in that there were bogies in the area. . . .

"I estimated overall that there were twenty to thirty Japanese fighters, all between five hundred and seven thousand feet. I'm sure they had spotted us but no doubt their mission was to cover the convoy at all costs. They didn't want to go up after just four airplanes. . . .

"After we got up to twenty-two thousand feet, I looked around. . . . I wasn't going to tangle with twenty to thirty Japanese fighters—but I figured I could very safely make a pass at the top echelon." Purdy led his flight down in a swift attack, shooting down one Nakajima "Oscar." The P-38s zoomed back to high altitude. No one had taken any damage. Purdy told his pilots, "Let's do it once more."

He shot down another Oscar. "We were scoring kills, but none of the Japanese made an attempt to take any offensive action against us. We made the two passes at them with absolutely no danger at all. It was a fighter pilot's dream."[30]

The biggest challenge Kenney's airmen faced wasn't the Japanese but the mud. When the monsoon season began it dumped twenty-one inches of rain in November alone on Tacloban and Dulag. Attempts to build additional airfields elsewhere on Leyte proved futile. Kenney couldn't get even half his air power into the fight.

Despite severe shipping losses to American aircraft and submarines, Japanese ground reinforcements continued to pour into Leyte. Many arrived in small boats and barges. Although FEAF and Navy air continued sinking barges, destroyers, and transports that the Japanese couldn't replace, more than forty thousand reinforcements reached Leyte.[31] The result was a tortuous, hard-fought ground campaign.

Attempting to bring it to a close, MacArthur mounted an invasion of Ormoc. On December 7 the U.S. 77th Infantry Division steamed into Ormoc Bay to make the assault, just as a Japanese convoy appeared. Three of the fighter squadrons covering the 77th's ships were redirected to attack the Japanese vessels. Dive-bombing and strafing halted the enemy convoy. Meanwhile, 150

JAAF planes showed up and tried, but failed, to stop the American fleet from putting the 77th ashore.[32]

Even after Ormoc was taken, the ground battle dragged on. Fighting would continue on Leyte into 1945. MacArthur had planned to invade Luzon, at Lingayen Gulf, in December. This invasion date slipped back to January.

And before then the Army would have to take the island of Mindoro. Whitehead needed to build fighter strips there to provide air cover over Lingayen Gulf. On December 15 the Army invaded Mindoro.

Unlike Leyte, Mindoro was high and dry. By Christmas Day one fighter strip was in operation and another was nearing completion, but Japanese air attacks on resupply convoys made it impossible to operate more than a few planes. The Japanese were sinking oil tankers and ships carrying steel mat and aircraft ammunition.[33]

All the same, with Mindoro, Tacloban and Dulag in operation, Whitehead was able to hit targets on Luzon with repeated B-24 attacks, well escorted by P-38s. The JAAF had more than three hundred fighters at Clark and nearby airfields when the Mindoro invasion was mounted. These numbers fell sharply as Clark got the benefit of the aircraft demolition techniques perfected at Wewak and Hollandia.

The climax came on Christmas Day, when seventy Japanese fighters attempted to intercept a bombing raid. Thirty-nine were shot down in dogfights; Whitehead's losses amounted to five P-38s and no bombers.[34] This was the last big dogfight the Philippine campaign produced.

Beginning January 2 the Fifth mounted a series of counterair strikes against airfields on Luzon that left few operable planes to oppose the Lingayen Gulf invasion on January 9. The invasion fleet of six hundred ships was covered with patrols that placed at least sixty fighter planes over the fleet from dawn to dusk. Not one ship was lost to air attack.

The invasion of Luzon turned into a repetition of Leyte. The Japanese didn't offer much opposition at the water's edge, but pulled most of their 275,000 troops back into the mountains. The Fifth dropped arms and ammunition to Filipino guerrillas to harass the retreating Japanese.

In January 1945 Marshall, King, MacArthur, Eisenhower and Arnold were awarded five-star rank. One of MacArthur's first actions as a general of the Army was to recommend a fourth star for

Kenney.[35] It was a recommendation Arnold happily endorsed. Kenney became a four-star commander ahead of Spaatz.

With the Japanese digging in for a bruising ridge-by-ridge defense of the jungle-covered mountains of northern Luzon, MacArthur was convinced the ground troops would make no progress without heavy support from the air. Kenney agreed with him.[36] MacArthur pushed the commander of Sixth Army, Walter Krueger, to send two divisions south from Lingayen Gulf and head for Clark Field, sixty miles away. The huge Clark complex fell on January 25, but it would be six weeks before it could be used again.

The thrust toward Clark sparked yet another move, a race for Manila. Kenney pushed for a coup de main—dropping the 11th Airborne Division on Nichols Field, south of the city.

This was too risky for the commander of the Eighth Army, Robert Eichelberger.[37] He preferred instead to have 54th Troop Carrier Wing drop the paratroopers fifty miles southwest of Manila in an attempt to clear the enemy from southern Luzon. The Japanese force that he'd expected to find proved not to exist. It was a successful drop . . . in the wrong place. Meanwhile, the Japanese garrison of Manila was fighting a suicidal battle that destroyed the city.

Richard Sutherland, MacArthur's chief of staff, was despised by the many who knew him, respected by the few who knew him well. Now he suggested mounting one of the most difficult of all operations—a combined amphibious and airborne assault. The target was Corregidor. This seemed so dangerous that even Kenney, a man who loved daring operations, was doubtful, but MacArthur approved it.[38]

On February 16 the 54th Wing's troop carrier crews dropped two thousand men of the 503rd Parachute Infantry onto Corregidor, an island that had not one decent drop zone. The least mistake could have produced a disaster. The paratroopers were dropped onto a two-hole golf course that was 300 yards by 150 yards and a parade ground that was even smaller. Both DZs were bordered by cliffs. A thousand infantrymen came ashore in landing craft. A reinforcement drop was flown next day, taking in another one thousand paratroopers.[39] There were five thousand Japanese on Corregidor. Fifth Air Force planes drenched much of the island in napalm to burn them out.

While the Luzon campaign unfolded, Whitehead was neutralizing Japanese airfields on Formosa with repeated heavy attacks.

And Kenney, although denied B-29s, talked Arnold into letting him have the first B-32s that became operational. He used them to attack Formosa.[40]

Rabaul hadn't been forgotten. It too was being neutralized by air, by the B-24s of Thirteenth Air Force, which had moved to Morotai after the Fifth's groups moved on to Leyte and Mindoro.

The attacks on Rabaul were comprehensive. Australian troops fighting in the Dutch East Indies were troubled by Japanese patrols with K-9 teams. A field order was duly transmitted by Thirteenth Air Force for an attack on Rabaul on January 8. One paragraph read: "The First Composite Bomb Group, using nine A-20s, will bomb and strafe dog kennels in Ubulli area between 1000 and 1015. Altitude of attack—Minimum."[41]

The Thirteenth also provided attacks on coastal defenses for Eichelberger's troops as they invaded islands in the southern Philippines—Cebu, Samar, Panay, Mindanao—as the slow, grim struggle to clear Luzon continued. Once the troops were ashore, the Thirteenth provided close air support, using everything from its fighters to its B-24s.[42]

By March 1945 Japanese air didn't exist in the Philippines, except for the occasional kamikaze trying to strike a Navy ship. In April, the air war moved on, to Okinawa. Kenney started planning FEAF's next major operation—the invasion of Japan. MacArthur had scheduled the assault for September 1.

29

SUPERLATIVES

The plane on which Arnold was betting the future of the Air Force, the B-29, seemed designed to drive people crazy, if it didn't kill them first. On February 18, 1943, one of the three XB-29s was being flown by Boeing's chief test pilot, Edmund T. "Eddie" Allen. An engine caught fire, the entire left wing burst into flames and the plane crashed into a meat-packing plant in downtown Seattle.[1]

Shortly after this another XB-29 nearly flipped over and crashed when its ailerons failed. A second brush with calamity might have put the entire program on hold. To spare Arnold further stress, he wasn't told about this incident.[2]

Meanwhile, he was struggling, and failing, to secure a Triple-A Emergency rating for the program. The Navy, however, blocked him. Admiral King claimed that speeding up the B-29 would impede the war in the Pacific.[3]

To take advantage of a local labor surplus, Boeing built a new plant at Wichita, Kansas, to make the fourteen YB-29 service test models and turn out the first few hundred planes to be mass produced. B-29s would also be manufactured by Martin in Omaha, Nebraska; by Bell in Marietta, Georgia; and by Boeing in Renton, Washington.

Following Eddie Allen's death, Arnold put Major General Kenneth B. Wolfe, one of the AAF's best engineering officers, in charge of a committee to troubleshoot the B-29 to success. Wolfe moved to Kansas.

The Superfortress was an awesome beast. The B-29A had a wing span of 141 feet, a gross weight of 140,000 pounds, a maximum speed of 358 miles an hour at 25,000 feet, and a range of 4,100 miles.[4] It was powered by four huge Wright R-3350 engines, each of which had two superchargers. The plane was fully pressurized, allowing the twelve-man crew to work without heated flying suits, heavy boots, thick gloves or helmets and oxygen masks. It was crammed with state-of-the-art electrical and electronic systems. For self-defense, it carried four remotely controlled gun turrets mounting a total of twelve fifty-caliber machine guns, plus a twenty-millimeter high-velocity, long-range cannon in the tail.

Needless to say, with a plane as innovative as this one, there were many technical challenges to be overcome. The worst was the tendency of the engines to catch fire. With other combat aircraft there'd been time to work out the bugs before sending it into action. The B-29 was a major exception.[5] Arnold had to get it into the war. He had persuaded Marshall, Roosevelt and Congress to put $3 billion into this plane; more than the $2.2 billion spent on the atomic bomb; nearly twice the $1.75 billion spent on radar. It absolutely had to work.

Arnold had promised Roosevelt that he would have B-29s ready to deploy to the CBI by January 1, 1944. From bases in China, the plane would be able to strike Japan. Arnold may even have been hoping to mount that first attack on April 18, 1944—the second anniversary of the Doolittle Raid. He failed to reach the January target date, to the President's irritation. Smarting, he promised to have planes in the CBI by April 15. Now he really had to deliver. The result was an AAF legend known as "the Battle of Kansas."[6]

Of all the places to try building very heavy bombers, Kansas was not the first state a person might think of. The B-29 moved into mass production during the fall of 1943, and winter was in the air. It was soon on the ground, too, covering it with more than a foot of snow. When the planes were only about half finished, they were towed into the fields, where people in gloves and overcoats struggled to complete them in sub-zero temperatures. Arnold kept sending out troubleshooters, such as Barney Giles and Major General Benny E. Meyers, men noted for their can-do spirit. In Kansas, they merely got in each other's way. There was no central direction.[7]

When Arnold came out in January 1944 to see how things were coming along, he was shocked, probably terrified, to discover they weren't. Only sixty-seven crews had been trained, for want of training aircraft.

It wasn't possible to get out of a B-17 cockpit, climb into a B-29 and start flying. The B-29 was a hard plane to fly. The minimum prerequisite for pilots recruited to the program was a thousand hours.[8]

Although the plane was heavily armed, it was sure to attract a lot of attention from enemy fighters. Arnold asked Doolittle to pick out the best bomber pilot the Strategic Air Force possessed in the Mediterranean and send him home. Doolittle's choice fell on Paul Tibbets.

The specific assignment Tibbets was given was to improve the defense against fighter attacks. He fell in love with the plane, flying it at every opportunity. By early 1944 he was "Mr. B-29." Tibbets had one thousand hours on Superfortresses alone.[9]

Wolfe went off to the CBI to lead XX Bomber Command in Matterhorn (see pp. 398–99). Tibbets became the B-29 project officer, charged with working out some of the bugs that still dogged the plane. The Battle of Kansas raged on as snows melted and temperatures started rising toward the 105 degrees of summer days.

Everyone was clamoring for B-29s. Spaatz wanted them; so did Kenney. Kuter and Hansell, however, convinced Arnold that he should keep them under his own direct control, in order to ensure they were properly employed and not diverted to tactical missions. Another air force was created, the Twentieth. It would operate all the B-29s, and only B-29s. Hansell became chief of staff of the Twentieth and oversaw its early operations.[10]

The Twentieth had one mission: to pound Japan into the ground. Hansell proposed to create as many as four bomber commands that would hit it from an arc of bases: XX Bomber Command from China, XXI Bomber Command from the Marianas, XXII Bomber Command from Luzon and, possibly, XXIII Bomber Command from the Aleutians. On June 15 XX Bomber Command made its first attack on Japan, striking the Yawata Iron and Steel works. The invasion of the Marianas began that same day. For the next six weeks, the Army and the Marine Corps waged a grim, bitter struggle to seize the islands of Saipan, Guam and Tinian from the Japanese. Construction of B-29 runways began even before the fighting ended. Japan was fourteen hundred miles from Saipan, sixteen hundred miles from Guam.

In August 1944, Arnold rewarded Hansell for his work in establishing the Twentieth by giving him XXI Bomber Command. Norstad succeeded Hansell as the Twentieth's chief of staff.

So far there were only two B-29 wings: the 58th, which was at Chengtu, and the 73rd, commanded by Emmett J. "Rosey" O'Donnell, which went to Saipan in October. Hansell was wondering how the 73rd would even find its targets.

There was virtually no information on Japanese industries beyond the names of some of the major plants and the cities where they were located. There were no maps, no photographs, no target folders, yet Hansell had assured Marshall that his command would be ready to start striking Japan in November.

On November 1 the first of the B-29s that had been modified for photo recon reached Guam, flown by Captain Ralph Stearley. He and his crew volunteered to go to Japan at once, even though they'd made a two-day flight from Hawaii.

They set off on what proved to be one of the few clear days over Japan. They spent three hours photographing targets on Hansell's list from thirty-two thousand feet. No fighters troubled them; no Japanese flak could reach them. They returned with seven thousand high-quality photographs. When the JCS sent Hansell a target list ten days later, his staff was able to start planning the XXI Bomber Command's opening attack.[11]

Everything on the list was a candidate for daylight precision bombing. Chennault's campaign against ore carriers and LeMay's XX Bomber Command attacks on coking plants in Manchuria had knocked steel from the top of the list. Instead, pride of place went to the Japanese aviation industry. The first target struck would be the Musashino aircraft engine factory in a suburb northwest of Tokyo. O'Donnell objected to flying the mission in daylight. Given the comparatively small, undertrained force that he commanded, the 73rd Wing was likely to take heavy casualties in an unescorted, daylight attack. He felt his planes should bomb by radar and by night until escorts were available or until the B-29 had proved it didn't need escort. Hansell was one of the founding fathers of daylight precision doctrine. He insisted the mission would go ahead as planned.[12]

O'Donnell chose to lead it personally. The pilot whose seat he "usurped" was Major Robert K. Morgan, the first pilot in the Eighth to complete twenty-five missions, flying the *Memphis Belle*. Morgan had volunteered for a Pacific tour. And on November 24 he flew as O'Donnell's copilot on the first B-29 mission to Tokyo.

After crossing the Japanese coastline, the 94 bombers that had made it this far ran into jet stream winds of 150 miles per hour. Bombsights couldn't cope with so much drift. Bombs were scattered far and wide. Only forty-eight out of more than one thousand dropped, landed within the boundaries of the engine plant.[13] Two B-29s were shot down. A second mission was flown to attack the Musashino plant three days later. Once again the jet stream made accurate bombing impossible. And a third attempt on December 3 was equally frustrating.

Hansell's chief of staff, Colonel John B. Montgomery, tried in vain to persuade Hansell that they'd have to go in lower and bomb at night.[14] But under intense pressure from Arnold he mounted a small incendiary attack on Tokyo the night of November 30. The results were disappointing.[15]

Arnold had gotten fed up with the Matériel Command at Wright Field blocking his ideas by telling him they weren't feasible. He also had to overcome the repeated failures of the Ordnance Corps to provide the AAF with modern bombs. Arnold had set up his own research-and-development operation at Eglin Field, Florida, under Brigadier General Grandison Gardner, in 1942.

Eglin Field was a success story. It had developed the remotely controlled gun turrets for the B-29, for example. It had also developed napalm and the Azon guided bomb. With the B-29 moving toward deployment, Arnold ordered Gardner to consider how best to burn Tokyo to the ground.

Gardner accordingly created half a dozen blocks of plywood buildings and pitch pine houses that around the base became known as "Little Tokyo." The conventional wisdom held that the best way to torch a city was to knock down the buildings with high explosive, then ignite the debris with incendiaries. Gardner's tests showed the theory was wrong. The best way was to leave the buildings standing and to hit them with many small bombs that were filled with napalm. On impact, the napalm would splatter the walls, find its way into crevices, and get onto the furnishings and equipment inside. Once ignited, the draft that the thousands of small fires created inside the buildings would rapidly produce an enormous conflagration.[16]

Despite the disappointing incendiary attack on Tokyo, Arnold ordered a much bigger attempt be made against the city of Nagoya. Hansell protested, but Arnold wouldn't be swayed.[17] So Nagoya, which contained much of Japan's aviation industry, was attacked the night of January 3, but Hansell did it his way—from fifteen thousand feet.

This was medium altitude for a B-29, but it was still too high. The incendiary clusters broke up in mid-air and were scattered over too large an area to maximize their effects. The Nagoya raid accomplished nothing except to make Arnold more impatient with Hansell than ever. Nor did Hansell help his own cause by sending Arnold four-page single-spaced letters nearly every day, much as Eaker had done in an earlier, failed effort to appease him. Arnold hated reading anything longer than half a page.

On January 19 Hansell made his first effective attack, when sixty-two planes bombed the Kawasaki aircraft plant twelve miles west of Kobe. Without losing a single bomber, he had cut the plant's production by 90 percent; the devastation was so extensive the Japanese didn't attempt anything except temporary repairs. The plant was never again a major producer of aircraft.[18]

Norstad arrived the next day at Hansell's headquarters on Saipan. With him was the Air Corps's father figure, retired Major General James Fechet, the former chief. Fechet broke the heart-rending news to Hansell: he'd been fired.[19] LeMay had just flown in from China to take over Hansell's command.

The B-29 was undergoing much of its development in the field; the men who flew it were getting much of their training in combat; and the Twentieth Air Force was being rearranged in the heat of battle. There would be only two bomber commands, XX and XXI; both would operate from the Marianas, under LeMay.

Hansell had been fighting with one wing, the 73rd, 180 planes and operating from only one runway. LeMay took over just as Navy Seabees completed three more, with half a dozen others still to come. The buildup of B-29s was gathering speed as the advanced echelons of the 313th, 314th and 315th Bomb Wings flew in.

LeMay, scowling as ever, unleashed his merciless passion for training on his B-29 crews. Given the thick cloud that covered most of Japan most of the time, he was going to have to do a lot of bombing in which H2X radar would assist the Norden bombsights in finding their targets. One bomb wing, the 315th, commanded by Brigadier General Frank Armstrong, would bring with it the world's most advanced target radar, the AN/APQ-7 Eagle. LeMay reserved the 315th for attacks on oil refineries.

The state of radar training in B-29 groups was abysmal. Many of the operators were former aerial gunners. LeMay had a low opinion of aerial gunners at any time, but when they were put in front of radar scopes, it sank even lower. He devoted a lot of effort to raising radar training to an acceptable standard.[20]

By stripping gun turrets, ammunition, gunners and armor plate from his B-29s, he made them more maneuverable, extended their range and increased their bomb load. He also taught his crews to fly the combat box. Formation flying in B-29s was truly difficult, but he insisted on it.[21]

Whether the combat box added anything to bombing accuracy is doubtful, but it solved one looming problem. Japanese air defenses were nothing like those over Germany. By 1945 the quality of Japanese fighter pilots was poor going on wretched, even if on some missions as many as a dozen or more B-29s were shot down by fighters. Weather and navigation problems were even bigger hazards, however. Japanese flak could be a problem, but it wasn't remotely as challenging as the German variety. In January and February Japanese fighter pilots started ramming B-29s, sending a shock wave through the Twentieth. If a few hundred enemy pilots successfully rammed B-29s, daylight bombing would probably be stopped. The combat box, by uncovering the awesome firepower of the Superforts, put an end to ramming.[22]

The Japanese then resorted to something even more terrifying— the Baka (or "Fool's") Bomb. This was a two-ton bomb given wings, a tail and rocket propulsion. With a kamikaze pilot crammed into the tiny cockpit that had been welded to the bomb, it would be carried up to fifteen to twenty thousand feet by a twin-engine bomber, and cut loose. Flying into B-29 formations at six hundred miles an hour, a Baka Bomb could pulverize a Super-fortress so fast there was really no defense against it. The strain of facing Baka Bomb attacks was unendurable for some men.[23] Fortunately, the Baka's rocket motor took up scarce resources that the Japanese preferred to use elsewhere. The Baka threat appeared suddenly in the spring of 1945, and vanished almost as quickly.

The one factor working in the favor of Japanese fighters was the radar on Iwo Jima, seven hundred miles southeast of Kyushu, the southernmost of the main islands of Japan. The radar gave them two hours notice that the B-29s were on their way. On February 19 the Marines landed on Iwo Jima and began one of the bloodiest battles of the war to take this sulphorous island from its twenty-five thousand defenders. LeMay's crews looked forward to its capture not only because it would help blind the enemy, but because it would provide crippled B-29s a place to land on the way back to the Marianas, instead of having to ditch in the unforgiving sea.

During LeMay's first six weeks in command the Twentieth made few attacks on Japan. Instead, while honing its skills, it struck targets in Southeast Asia: Saigon, Kuala Lumpur, Rangoon. Arnold was still pressing for fire raids. And LeMay was ready to oblige. He had concluded from the attack on Hankow that incendiary strikes were effective only when mounted by a large force, attacking low.[24] On February 24, 105 B-29s made an all-incendiary attack on Singapore. Nearly half the dock area of Singapore was burned to the ground.[25]

Next day, 172 bombers flew to Japan to make the biggest attack yet on aviation industry plants in and around Tokyo. Most planes couldn't find the primary targets because of clouds. So they hit secondary targets. Their loads had a high proportion of incendiaries. Tokyo was covered with snow, yet one square mile of the city went up in flame. The Emperor was alarmed, but the city's fire chief assured him that incendiaries could not start uncontrollable fires.[26]

LeMay was turning the Twentieth into a force able to attack effectively with fire by night. He had crews making practice bombing runs below one thousand feet. They learned the RAF technique called "maximum compression"—planes took off at two-minute intervals, with every pilot flying the same air speed, and staggered in flight so the second plane flew two hundred feet higher than the first, the third flew two hundred feet higher still, and the fourth two hundred feet higher than that. The fifth plane flew at the same height as the first, and so on.[27]

Everything was in place for an attempt to burn the heart out of Tokyo. On March 9 he launched Mission 40. It would be an all-incendiary, low-level attack carried out by 334 B-29s of the 73rd, 313th and 314th Bomb Wings.

Pathfinder squadrons went in first and marked the aiming points by starting fires on them. A stiff breeze fanned the flames. The bomb groups flew in, at altitudes ranging from forty-nine hundred to ninety-two hundred feet.[28] It was a night and a sight that none of the aircrew would ever forget. The fires could be seen from fifty miles away. Thermal currents tossed bombers several hundred feet in the air. When bomb-bay doors opened, the acrid smell of burning flesh entered the B-29s.[29]

The Japanese had spent the past three years training the entire able-bodied adult population of Tokyo in firefighting. It made no difference. The first bomb groups to arrive created huge rings of fire around the aiming points. The following groups dropped their loads inside the raging rings. The wind, picking up to nearly thirty miles an hour, helped create a huge fire storm that made control impossible. Water in the canals boiled; glass melted as temperatures rose above five hundred degrees.

The fire would have to burn itself out. By the time it did so, sixteen square miles of Tokyo had been reduced to ashes and eighty-five thousand people were dead; a million were made homeless. It was the deadliest single attack in the long history of war.[30]

B-29s that had taken off colored silver landed black, coated with soot. Only fourteen planes had been shot down; all fell to flak. LeMay had been betting that the Japanese had no night defenses to speak of. There was nothing resembling the GAF's well-organized, well-trained night fighter force. Japanese airborne night fighter radar could pick up a target, but gave no indication of range.[31] Attempts to lock onto the H2X transmissions, which GAF night fighters did to guide them to the bombers, were foiled by electronic countermeasures. When the sun went down, Japan lay wide open to attack from above.

The night of March 11, LeMay sent 313 B-29s to attack Nagoya, the city that housed half of Japan's aviation industry. There was no fire storm this time. The city had numerous firebreaks, there was virtually no wind and the bomb pattern was too widely spread. Still, two square miles burned down.[32]

On March 13 the Twentieth hit Osaka. It was like Tokyo all over again. Lieutenant Earl Snyder, a navigator with the 73rd Bomb Wing, was incredulous as his plane approached the target. "The holocaust that met my eyes required seeing to warrant believing. There was one huge bonfire with flames licking to the altitude we were flying. . . . We would be lucky if we didn't fly through some flames! I recoiled . . . the pilot said, 'This is gonna be rough' . . . the smoke became thicker, the fumes stronger. . . . I could barely see the left inboard engine, about fifteen feet from where I was sitting. . . . The heat began to grow uncomfortable and our plane was buffeted around violently. . . .

"I looked at the pilot. The sweat was pouring off his face. . . . [He] reached over and flipped on the landing lights. Normally they would throw a good direct beam for about five hundred yards. They glowed dully in the dense smoke. I could barely see them. . . ."

The radar operator told the bombardier when to drop his bombs. Lightened of its load, the B-29 lurched upward. "Very gradually our violent shaking tapered off, the fumes grew less sickening. Very gradually we were able to see first our inboard engines, then even our outboard ones. Very gradually the red glow left us. The pilot flicked off the landing lights. . . . I went back to my desk and took a benzedrine tablet. It would be a long tiresome journey back and I needed to be awake."[33] Eight square miles of Osaka, nearly half the city, was burned to the ground.

On March 17 it was the turn of Kobe, on the other side of Osaka Bay, to be firebombed. It was the heaviest, most densely concentrated bombing with incendiaries so far. Three square miles were turned to ashes, including the naval shipyard. Two nights later Nagoya was struck again, with what remained of LeMay's incendiaries. The fire raids halted abruptly: the dumps contained only general purpose bombs.

The unusual command structure of the Twentieth gave it almost complete independence in operations, yet it depended almost totally on the Navy for logistics. It was not an arrangement that Nimitz liked; nor was it one designed to suit LeMay's undiplomatic temperament.

The Twentieth was able to keep functioning effectively only because it possessed two officers who short-circuited the Navy: Colonel Sol Rosenblatt, former Democratic party chairman for New York state, who had managed to get hold of six ships and was running a private navy that brought in some supplies outside Nimitz's control; and Brigadier General Clarence Irvine, who was responsible for maintenance, had somehow acquired C-54s and was flying in at least one planeload of vital spare parts every day.[34]

A six-week halt in firebombing ensued, while a fuming LeMay waited for the Navy to restock the bomb dumps with incendiaries. The Twentieth spent those six weeks mounting daylight attacks on the Japanese aviation, chemical and oil industries, supporting the ground battle on Okinawa and mining Japanese home waters with more than ten thousand acoustic and magnetic mines provided by the Navy.[35]

The daylight missions to Japan were escorted by Seventh Air Force P-51s. The Seventh—"the Pineapple Air Force"—had island-hopped across the Central Pacific from Hawaii in conjunction with the Navy. Its B-24s had flown some of the longest missions of the war to attack island bastions such as Truk and Rabaul.

Its VII Fighter Command had flown P-40s, then P-47s, and finally P-51s, from tenuous strips on remote atolls that few people had ever heard of to protect Navy ships and support Marine invasions.[36]

In August 1944 the Seventh had reached Saipan. During the fall and winter it flew many missions to targets in Southeast Asia. In April 1945, VII Fighter Command moved to Iwo Jima to provide escort for LeMay's B-29s. Its Mustang pilots routinely flew eight-hour missions from Iwo Jima to provide fifteen minutes of escort over the target.[37]

With the new daylight offensive against Japan, the bombers needed it. In May the Twentieth lost eighty-eight B-29s in combat, its heaviest one-month loss of the war. Losses might have proved crippling had not Iwo Jima itself provided a place where damaged B-29s could put down. Before the war ended, more than two thousand stricken B-29s would make emergency landings on Iwo Jima.

On May 14 LeMay resumed his area attacks, with a fire raid on Nagoya in midafternoon. A follow-up night attack on the 16th did so much damage that Nagoya was struck from the target list. In subsequent weeks Tokyo, Yokohama, Osaka, Kobe and Kawasaki were torched. By mid-June the six most important industrial cities of Japan were ashes.[38]

LeMay and his staff were convinced they could blast and burn Japan to its knees. Arnold, visiting the Pacific, sent LeMay back to Washington to try to convince Marshall and King there would be no need for an invasion.

But the preliminary air offensive had already begun. Kenney had moved his FEAF headquarters to Okinawa. From there, the Fifth Air Force and the VII Bomber Command were striking the defenses of Kyushu, the site of Operation Olympic, MacArthur's planned fall invasion of Japan's home islands.

Ultra provided Marshall with an awesome picture of what was happening on Kyushu. The Japanese were pouring men and materiel into Kyushu in a desperate effort to turn it into a killing ground so bloody that the United States would seek a negotiated peace. The air attacks from Okinawa were making little impact on the buildup of men, planes and artillery flooding in. Underground hangars and camouflaged runways were being built. Nearly 5,000 kamikazes were being stockpiled with enough fuel and bombs for a one-way flight. It had cost 50,000 American casualties to wrest Okinawa from 80,000 Japanese troops. Of the 780,000 men MacArthur planned to land on Kyushu in November 1945, Marshall expected roughly 275,000 would be killed or wounded.[39] While LeMay, who didn't have access to Ultra, tried to assure the JCS that the Twentieth was hitting Japan so hard the enemy would soon quit, Marshall took a nap.[40]

LeMay returned to Saipan indignant and determined. He would pull out all the stops to force the Japanese to surrender before the invasion was launched. He intended to make his crews fly 120 hours a month and doubled the tour to 100 missions.[41] Morale in the Twentieth was sky high; his crews were willing to fly their hearts out to finish the war. Nimitz's staff, on the other hand, were appalled. LeMay's plan would put a tremendous burden on the Navy.

Moreover, the Twentieth itself had a manpower crisis. It was running out of replacement crews. LeMay had appealed to Norstad back in April for more crews. While the Twentieth was declining, the Eighth was being maintained at full strength, and after Germany's surrender it started deploying to the Pacific for the invasion of Japan. The legend of the Mighty Eighth had to be kept bright.[42]

Kenney would command all the tactical air forces in the invasion, Doolittle would command the strategic air forces, and Spaatz would be over both of them. LeMay was straining every nerve, though, to make the invasion unnecessary.

He was prepared to use up every last B-29 and every last crew to win the war by November. It was a do-or-die effort. B-29 crews started trying to burn down as many as four cities a day. LeMay's demands on the Navy for bombs and fuel grew more insistent, more urgent than ever.

There was always an undercurrent between senior air and naval commanders in the Pacific. The Navy lived remarkably well, building pleasant bungalows for its admirals while their air counterparts lived in tents and huts. The Navy dined on steaks, while even AAF generals dug into canned rations. Class and comfort differences niggled airmen and strained their patience with the Navy.[43] Now, however, it was the Navy whose patience ran out. Nimitz demanded the removal of LeMay. He wanted this gruff, brusque airman off his back. If necessary, Nimitz, as theater commander, could order him out of the theater.[44]

This was a potential disaster not only for LeMay, but for the AAF. The publicity the Twentieth was generating was solid gold, helping to smooth the path to independence. LeMay, who had only recently taken command of the Twentieth, was, to his astonishment, eased out to appease the Navy, but allowed to remain in the theater. Twining succeeded him. He had gotten along well with the Navy down in the South Pacific, before going to Italy to command the Fifteenth Air Force. Twining reached Saipan in mid-July. LeMay was made Spaatz's chief of staff, a job for which he possessed neither background nor desire.

In September 1944 Paul Tibbets's assignment as the B-29 project officer ended. He was chosen to create, train and command a new outfit, the 509th Composite Group. It was an awesome responsibility for a twenty-eight-year-old lieutenant colonel. The 509th's mission was to drop the atomic bomb on Japan.

Tibbets was given carte blanche to demand whatever personnel, planes and other equipment he needed. All he had to do was invoke the secret word, "Silverplate," and two-star generals snapped to attention and gave whatever he wanted without asking.[45]

Tibbets based his group at Wendover AFB, Utah. His crews proceeded to drop large, almost round bombs, which they called "pumpkins" in tribute to the unusual shape, over the desert bombing ranges of the West. The bombs weren't as big as the nine thousand-pound atomic bomb, but had similar ballistics.

Meanwhile, Major General Cecil E. Combs, the chief of operations for Twentieth Air Force, was ordered to choose four cities that would be held off the Twentieth's target list. They would be reserved as targets for the atomic bomb. Secretary of War Henry Stimson insisted that the former capital of Japan, Kyoto, be spared. It was the cultural heart of Japanese civilization: its Paris, its Rome. The commander of the project to build the bomb, Major General Leslie Groves, repeatedly tried to get Kyoto put on the A-bomb list, but Stimson refused to budge. Combs's list read, "Hiroshima, Kokura, Nagasaki, Niigata."[46] All contained military targets.

Neither Arnold nor Spaatz thought that dropping the bomb was necessary. The decision would be made, however, not by the military, but by President Harry Truman. When the first successful atomic explosion was detonated on July 16, Truman was at Potsdam, conferring with Churchill and Stalin. The decision to drop the bomb was made during the sea voyage home, after Marshall told him an invasion would cost more than a quarter of a million American casualties. Truman, who was deeply reluctant to use this atomic bomb, ordered the first attack to go ahead.[47]

The 509th had moved to Tinian two months before. Its crews flew up to the Empire twelve times to drop pumpkins that were loaded with high explosive. By August they were ready to drop their first A-bomb. Tibbets had known too much to be allowed to fly any of the missions to Japan, but he would pilot the *Enola Gay* (named for his mother) on Special Mission 13.

With three weather planes flying an hour ahead of him to scout Hiroshima and alternative targets, Tibbets took off from Tinian at 0245 on August 6. The *Enola Gay* bore reconnaissance markings. The Japanese rarely bothered weather planes or recon aircraft.

In flight, the weaponeer, Navy Captain Thomas Parsons, armed the bulbous nine-thousand-pound "Fat Boy"—a compliment of sorts to Winston Churchill. He'd insisted on arming it in flight because B-29s regularly crashed on takeoff; four had crashed and burned on the runways at Tinian the evening of August 5. Parsons didn't want to blow Tinian off the map.[48]

Tibbets's orders were that the bomb had to be dropped visually; no radar bombing was allowed. At the same time, if something went wrong and all four potential targets were obscured, he couldn't bring the bomb back to Tinian. Nor could he descend and look for a remote place to set down: the bomb had barometric fusing.

In any event, the skies over Hiroshima were clear. The great flying challenge now was to avoid being brought down by the shockwave. Tibbets needed to put eight miles between the *Enola Gay* and the point of impact. If he maintained his present course, the bomb would explode when the plane was six miles beyond the city. Tibbets's solution, which he'd practiced and taught his pilots, was to make a diving 155 degrees turn in the opposite direction the moment the bomb was dropped. That gave him the extra two miles he needed. When the *Enola Gay* landed back at Tinian, Spaatz met the plane and pinned a DSC on Tibbets's sweat-stained coveralls.

After the Hiroshima explosion, the Japanese war cabinet voted to continue with the war, in hopes of securing better terms than an unconditional surrender would bring.[49] On August 8, the Soviet Union declared war on Japan, casting doubt on those hopes. Stalin wasn't noted for his leniency.

The second bomb was assembled and loaded aboard another 509th Superfortress. This mission would be flown by a different pilot and crew. On August 9 it set off for Kokura. The target was obscured by clouds. The crew flew on, in search of Nagasaki, running short of fuel and worrying about what they would do with the bomb if they couldn't see the target. There was no established procedure for disarming an atomic bomb. A small break appeared in the clouds over Nagasaki, as the B-29 made its third and final pass over the city.

The components of another bomb were available, but Marshall had decided that if the Japanese didn't quit now, the third bomb would be saved for the invasion.[50] The Nagasaki bomb, however, brought deadlock in the war cabinet. The three military members voted to continue the war; the three civilians voted to surrender if the monarchy was saved. Unable to agree, the cabinet for the first time in the war asked the Emperor for his opinion. He cast his ballot for peace. Some army officers attempted a coup to reverse the decision, but failed. Japan surrendered. The only campaign of the war to be fought on the Japanese home islands, the onslaught by the Twentieth Air Force, closed on this triumphant note.

30

ENVOI

Much of the time and energy of the Air Staff was devoted in the war's last eighteen months on determining how best to use the transition from war to peace to create an independent air force.[1] With the surrender of Japan, the airmen found themselves pushing at an open door. Marshall favored independence and so did his successor as chief of staff, Dwight Eisenhower.

What they couldn't have was monopoly rights. The Navy intended not only to retain its air arm, but wanted to arm it with nuclear weapons. Naval architects started work on plans for a carrier so big it could launch four-engine bombers that would reach Moscow.[2]

The United States, meanwhile, was demobilizing. Throughout 1946 hundreds of thousands of men left the military each month. By 1947 the U.S. forces that had fought the war were history. A new organization, the Department of Defense, was created to direct all the armed services. The U.S. Air Force came into existence on September 18, 1947, but for more than a year it wore Army uniforms still; it was too poor to buy new outfits of its own, in Air Force blue.[3] And the protracted, sometimes furious negotiations over the future of air power had produced compromises that left the United States with four air forces. The Army, the Navy and the Marine Corps in addition to the Air Force would all operate combat aircraft.

This was a bitter blow to Arnold. He retired to fifty acres in the Valley of the Moon, in Sonoma, California. On what he fondly called his "ranch," he had about thirty head of cattle, most donated by friends and admirers. Mrs. Arnold kept some chickens and sold the eggs. Arnold happily settled down to breeding prize cattle and making furniture for a hobby. By 1949, though, the ranch was failing and he was broke. He tried to get back onto active duty; he needed the money. He even appeared in beer advertisements, extolling the merits of Pabst Blue Ribbon. His attempt to return to duty was gently but firmly rebuffed. He died the next year. Mrs. Arnold struggled for a while on her pension, but the ranch swallowed it all. She spent her last years selling insurance to make ends meet.[4]

Spaatz wanted to retire when the war ended. Arnold insisted he succeed him and manage the fight for independence. Spaatz soldiered on until October 1, 1947. His successor was Vandenberg. Eaker, bitterly disappointed, put in for retirement. He'd expected to become first chief of staff of the U.S. Air Force, but Vandenberg had something (besides youth) that he lacked: the right uncle. Senior Air Force officers, believed anyway, that Arthur Vandenberg, the powerful, isolationist senator from Michigan, had reached an understanding with Truman that left Eaker out, the nephew in and isolation on hold.[5]

As for Kenney, he came home believing—mistakenly—that he would get command of all the combat units in the AAF. Instead, he was given the new Strategic Air Command. When it became evident that his heart really wasn't in the job, he was sent to Maxwell to run the Air University and LeMay got command of SAC.[6]

Strategic Air Command became the monument to the AAF that Arnold, Spaatz, Eaker, Doolittle and others had foreseen. The story of the air war was presented largely as a tale of heavy bombers pounding the Italians, the Germans, and finally the Japanese, into the dirt. The Army's soldiers had then marched in and taken the surrenders.

This view was strongly resisted by some of the civilians who worked on the U.S. Strategic Bombing Survey, but compromises had to be made with the Air Force and the Navy to produce a report all would accept.[7] The strategic bomber was pushed hard in various official publications, including the seven blue-bound history volumes edited by professors Wesley Frank Craven and James Lea Cate. Heavy bombers justified an independent air force, because only the AAF had employed them. These were clearly not weapons the Army could wield.

In 1949 the United States began to rearm in response to an

increasingly assertive Soviet Union, which was torn between unjustified fears and unrealistic ambitions. Stalin was not looking to unleash a war against the West, but he was more than willing to push and to prod, to test the limits of Western resolve. Without firepower, resolve between international rivals means little. For fifteen years the Strategic Air Command became the dark-blue bottom line of American defense. Its B-47s and atomic bombs, succeeded by B-52s carrying hydrogen bombs, may well have saved both Western Europe and the Soviet Union from annihilation. A grateful nation looked to the Air Force to defend it from the only enemy capable of striking the continental United States. In the 1950s the Air Force absorbed nearly half the entire defense budget, and to most people that looked like money well spent.

After 1961, however, with Polaris submarines going on station and satellite reconnaissance ripping much of the secrecy from the Soviet empire, SAC's glory days faded. It became, increasingly, a nuclear missile force. The strategic bomber's time was brief, but long enough to make the four-engine interpretation of the AAF's war pervasive if not wholly persuasive.

In Vietnam, SAC's bombers might have pounded the communist regime into submission, but they were not given the chance to do it. Since then, they have become irrelevant. The essential combat aircraft of the 1990s is the fighter-bomber. The present-day Air Force is run by what is known as "the Fighter Mafia." The long-term future of the Air Force turned out not to be in heavy bombers after all.

The story of the Air Corps between the wars is one of a small part of the military fighting to stay alive. On the one hand this consisted of publicity stunts, such as record-breaking flights. On the other it consisted of fending off the War Department General Staff's attempts to stop the Air Corps from becoming independent.

The pre-1940 Air Corps was both innovative and backward. Its demand for heavy bombers proved absolutely justified, but the airmen's aversion to schools and staff work proved a serious handicap. Wars overseas, such as the Spanish Civil War, had been studied by American air attachés, but their reports went unheeded. The lessons learned on the need for escort, the importance of close air support, and the value of airlift, were ignored. Little attention was paid to the potential of jet aircraft and radar. As a result, from Pearl Harbor to V-J Day the AAF had to improvise as it scrambled to make up for lost time and missed opportunities. The Munich Crisis airplane program had initiated a variety of fighters and bombers in time for them to become excellent front-line aircraft by 1944, but the motivating force behind them had come mainly from President Roosevelt and foreign governments.

Arnold provided firm but often erratic leadership. He was such a strong and singular figure that it is impossible to imagine anyone like him ever leading the Air Force again. Modern military bureaucracies, dominated as they are by committees and staff studies, don't allow men who are so idiosyncratic to rise to the top. For every fault, though, Arnold offered a compensating strong point, such as his belief in youth and his love of innovation and improvisation.

The AAF was as much Arnold's creation as the Army was Marshall's. Virtually all the senior commanders in the AAF before the end of 1943 were Arnold's pals, men who'd served with him on the Alaska flight or at March Field. This limited pool of talent was at times a handicap. In some instances the wrong men were thrust into important assignments, and even given second or third chances after they had clearly failed. On the other hand, some of the top leadership of the AAF was impressive. Spaatz, in his shy, inarticulate way, showed excellent judgment on nearly every important issue. Air force commanders such as Kenney, Chennault, Twining, Doolittle and LeMay were superb. Below them were gifted men like William Kepner, Sam Anderson, Gordon Saville and Ennis Whitehead. And below *them* were many splendid colonels such as Hub Zemke and Archie Old running fighter groups and bomb groups.

Even the lieutenants and the sergeants were of a high quality. Arnold had convinced Marshall that the world's best air force couldn't be created from average men. Physically, the typical airman was an inch taller and about six pounds heavier than his Army counterpart. When it came to intelligence, he scored about ten points brighter on standard tests.

The AAF was favored, too, when it came to publicity. The air war had an irresistible glamour and modernity that ground soldiers could never hope to match. An entranced public got to know the names of dozens of individual pilots, such as Colin Kelly, "Buzz" Wagner, Don Gentile and Paul Tibbets, in a way that was exceedingly rare for soldiers.

All the same, the reader who has reached this point will be aware that the tenor of this book is a skeptical one, questioning the official

Air Force view of the success of strategic bombing, criticizing the AAF's highest leadership, and casting doubt on the official history of the AAF. Yet it is only after looking closely at the problems, the failures, the mistakes, the lack of knowledge and experience, and the occasional stupidity, can anyone judge great achievements properly and appreciate them for what they are—triumphs of intelligence, imagination and moral courage.

That is as true of an organization as it is of individuals. The AAF had to rise far above its ordinary self before it could defeat well-armed, skillful and aggressive enemies. And it did so.

No one could say after V-J Day that the wartime arrangement that loosely linked air power to the Army had failed, or even performed badly. It hadn't. If anything, it had worked surprisingly well. Yet, if the airmen wanted independence—and they did—it was theirs for the asking. The AAF had won its unique two-front war.

ACKNOWLEDGMENTS

The extent of my indebtedness to Dr. Daniel R. Mortensen of the Center for Air Force History is indicated by the fact that this book is dedicated to him.

I am indebted, too, to Richard P. Hallion, Chief of Air Force history, for his encouragement. I owe a special debt to Herman Wolk, also of CAFH. Mr. Wolk has been kind enough to read parts of this manuscript and gave me unlimited access to the George C. Kenney Papers, which are in his care. I have benefited, too, from the generosity of Dr. Richard Davis and Dr. Eduard Mark, who allowed me to read their forthcoming books (on General Spaatz and on aerial interdiction, respectively), while these were still in galleys, and who discussed their findings with me. Dr. Fred Beck greatly assisted my efforts in finding suitable photographs.

The Air Force Academy library holds the Murray Green Collection, consisting of a twenty-five-year research project aimed at producing a definitive biography of Hap Arnold. That work remains to be written, but I have been guided through this mountain of research by archivist Duane Reed, a man noted for his kindness to writers and historians. Within the Green Collection is what amounts to an alternative history of the Air Corps and the AAF. I have drawn on it extensively.

I am indebted to Dr. Dick Sommers, at the U.S. Army Military History Institute at Carlisle Barracks, Pennsylvania; to Herb Pankrass at the Eisenhower Library in Abilene; to Warren Trest, at the

USAF Historical Research Agency, Maxwell AFB; and to Dr. Vincent Orange, one of the leading experts on the RAF.

I should also like to thank Dr. David MacIsaac for reading my book in manuscript. His painstaking efforts have left me seriously in his debt.

I am grateful to the late Colonel Bruce Arnold for granting me access to the Hap Arnold Oral History Collection at Columbia.

Last as always, but never least in my esteem, I thank my editor, Robert D. Loomis, for his trust, his advice and his friendship.

NOTES

This work is based mainly on primary materials located in major Air Force history collections. For brevity's sake, I have identified those that appear most frequently in these notes by their initials.

BL, CU: Butler Library, Columbia University, New York, NY. CAFH: Center for Air Force History, Bolling AFB. GCMF: George C. Marshall Foundation, Lexington, VA. MD, LC: Manuscript Division, Library of Congress. HRA: U.S. Air Force Historical Research Agency, Maxwell AFB. USAFA: U.S. Air Force Academy, Colorado Springs, CO. USAMHI: U.S. Army Military History Institute, Carlisle, PA.

Chapter 1: The Shadow of a Man

1 Geoffrey Perret, *There's a War to Be Won* (New York: 1991), 3–8; The Infantry School, *Infantry in Battle* (Washington, D.C.: 1934), 114–118. Cf. L. Wardlow Miles, *History of the 308th Infantry Regiment* (New York: 1927); Thomas Johnson and Fletcher Pratt, *The Lost Battalion* (New York: 1938).

2 George C. Kenney (Hasdorff interview), 34, (Goddard interview), 3, both CAFH. Kenney spent some time assigned to the flight that went out to find lost First Army units.

3 Steven A. Ruffin, "They Found the Lost Battalion," *Air Power History,* Fall 1989.

4 Edgar S. Gorrell, *The Measure of America's Aeronautical Effort* (Norwich, Vt.: 1940). This is an authoritative statistical account

of the Air Service's war. There is no official history of the AEF Air Service, but the gap is ably filled by Maurer Maurer, *The U.S. Air Service in World War I* 4 vols. (Washington, D.C.: 1982).

5 Burke Davis, *The Billy Mitchell Affair* (New York: 1967), 3.

6 Howard Davidson (Ahmann and Sturm interview), 114–115 CAFH.

7 Herbert A. Dargue, "How General Patrick Learned to Fly," *Army and Navy Journal* September 8, 1923. Dargue was Patrick's aide and flying instructor.

8 *Final Report of General John J. Pershing* (Washington, D.C.: 1920), 76; I. B. Holley, *Ideas and Weapons* (New Haven: 1953), 158.

9 Thomas H. Greer, *Development of Air Doctrine in the Army Air Arm 1917–1941* (Maxwell AFB: 1955), 3–4; Holley, 167n.

10 George Goddard, *Overview* (Garden City, N.Y.: 1968), 42–43, 151; William Mitchell, *Winged Defense* (New York: 1925), 155.

11 *Global Mission* ms. V, 43, MD, LC. There are several drafts of this manuscript, ghost-written by William Laidlaw. The drafts total nearly a million words. Much of the manuscript's value derives from the fact that Arnold commented extensively on it and rewrote parts by hand. Moreover, it includes entire chapters, filled with interesting material, that were dropped solely for lack of space. I have drawn on this ms., because despite some obvious risks, it is at least as reliable a source as the published work and is more detailed. The Barling cost $500,-000 to build. Its hangar cost even more, $700,000. Mitchell refused to admit the bomber had failed, insisting "it was entirely successful." *Winged Defense* 185. Also see Carl H. Tifford, Jr., "The Barling Bomber," *Aerospace Historian,* June 1979.

12 George C. Kenney (Stanley interview), 10, CAFH.

13 *Illustrated London News,* December 11, 1920.

14 Goddard, 83.

15 Maurer Maurer, *Aviation in the U.S. Army 1919–1939* (Washington, D.C.: 1987), 29–34, 115–120; Thomas DeWitt Milling (Shaughnessy interview), 96–97, BL, CU.

16 *Global* ms. V, 73–74; Beverley 22–23.

17 Memoir, "The Vital Era," unpaginated, Hugh Knerr Papers, Special Collections, USAFA.

18 Orval R. Cook (Ahmann interview), 106–107, CAFH; Philip

S. Meilinger, *Hoyt S. Vandenberg* (Bloomington, Ind.: 1989), 12.

19 Tape 10, Side 1, Box 80, Edward V. Rickenbacker Papers, MD, LC. This reference is to the untitled, unpublished autobiography in Rickenbacker's papers totaling approximately 7,000 pages. Much of it consists of transcriptions of notes dictated at various times over a period of 15 years. Also see Edward V. *Rickenbacker* (Englewood Cliffs, N.J.: 1967), 256.

20 *Global* ms. V, 134: "The thing for which he was being tried he was guilty of, and except for Billy everybody knew it."

21 Ira C. Eaker, "Major General James E. Fechet," *Air Force Magazine,* September 1978; Davidson, 475.

22 Maurer, 213. According to *Aerospace Facts and Figures,* the U.S. aircraft industry produced more than 4,000 planes in 1926–31. The bulk of these were undoubtedly for the new Air Corps.

23 Joseph J. Corn, *The Winged Gospel* (New York: 1983), offers a good account of the quasireligious rapture that enveloped aviation before World War II.

Chapter 2: Arnold Phoenix

1 Barney M. Giles (Hasdorff interview), 25, CAFH.

2 Frank P. Lahm (Shaughnessy interview), 36–39, BL, CU. Lahm was Arnold's French instructor at West Point. He heard this story from Arnold several times, over many years, and claims that Arnold never fully got over the humiliation.

3 Thomas DeWitt Milling (Shaughnessy interview), 45, BL, CU.

4 *Global Mission* ms. III, 32, Arnold Papers, MD, LC.

5 Thomas Coffey, *Hap* (New York: 1982), 84.

6 I. B. Holley, *Ideas and Weapons* (New Haven: 1951), 43–45.

7 John B. Rae, *Climb to Greatness: The American Aircraft Industry 1920–1960* (Cambridge, Mass: 1968), 1; cf. Jack R. Lincke, *Jenny Was No Lady* (New York: 1970), 98–99.

8 Diary, Arnold Papers, Box 271, MD, LC.

9 Carl A. Spaatz (Shaughnessy interview), 12–14, BL, CU.

10 Howard C. Davidson (Ahmann and Sturm interview), 191 passim, CAFH.

11 Donald Douglas (Shaughnessy interview), BL, CU.

12 *Global* ms. VI, 33–34.

13 Orval R. Cook (Green interview), 1, USAFA. Cook was outside the Riding Hall, talking to Mrs Arnold, when he first saw

Arnold, hurrying away as the graduation ceremony drew to a close.

14 Coffey, 136.

15 201 File, Arnold Papers, MD, LC. Carl A. Spaatz (Shaughnessy interview), 81, BL, CU.

16 *Global* ms. VIII, 53–58.

17 Arno H. Leuhman (Ahmann interview), 10–11, CAFH; Davidson, 382–384.

18 Benjamin Foulois, *From the Wright Brothers to the Astronauts* (New York: 1968), Chapter 14; John F. Shiner, *Foulois and the U.S. Army Air Corps 1931–1935* (Washington, D.C.: 1983), 171–192. Norman Borden, *Air Mail Emergency* (Freeport, Me.: 1968), 5–6, claims Foulois warned he needed up to six weeks to prepare, but offers no evidence to support this statement. Cf. Paul M. Tillett, *The Army Flies the Mails* (Tuscaloosa, Ala. 1955); Earle Partridge (Ahmann interview), 166–167, CAFH; William M. Crabbe, Jr., "The Army Airmail Pilots Report!" *Air Power Historian* April 1962; *The New York Times,* February 18, 1934.

19 DeWitt S. Copp, *A Few Great Captains* (Garden City, N.Y.: 1981), 238.

20 Murray Green, "The Alaskan Flight of 1934," *Aerospace Historian,* March 1977.

21 Robert T. Finney, *History of the Air Corps Tactical School 1920–1940* USAF Study 100 (Maxwell AFB: 1955) 7.

22 Ira C. Eaker, "Major General James E. Fechet," *Air Force Magazine,* September 1978; Davidson 475. Foulois was despised by some of his staff. Minton Kaye (Green interview), 80, USAFA, claimed, "Benny was dumb . . . sat with his thumb in his mouth."

23 David Mets, *Master of Airpower* (San Rafael, Calif.: 1988), 98.

24 Boyd L. Dastrup, *The U.S. Army Command and General Staff College* (Manhattan, Kans.: 1982), 70–72.

25 Geoffrey Perret, *There's a War to Be Won* (New York: 1991), 117–118.

26 Kenneth B. Wolfe (Shaughnessy interview), 35, BL, CU. Wolfe's 1937 Leavenworth classmate, Ira Eaker, claimed the horses had been on the general terrain exercise problems year after year, so he would show his proposed solution to the horse. If it appeared to nod its head, he'd hand the solution in; if the nag shook its head, he'd rewrite it.

27 Partridge 228; George H. Beverley, *A Pioneer in the Air Corps* (Manhattan, Kans.: 1982).

28 Donald Wilson (Green interview), 28–29, USAFA; Donald Wilson, "Origin of a Theory for Air Strategy," *Aerospace Historian* March 1971. Cf. Perry M. Smith, "Douhet and Mitchell: Some Reappraisals," *Air University Review* Sept.–Oct. 1967; David MacIsaac, *Strategic Bombing in World War II* (New York: 1976), 8, 171.

29 Claire L. Chennault, "The Role of Defensive Pursuit," *Coast Artillery Journal* Nov.–Dec. 1933; Jan.–Feb. 1934; March–April 1934.

30 Orval R. Cook (Ahmann and Emmons interview), 100–102, CAFH.

31 War Dept. press release Jan. 16, 1936; Peter M. Bowers, *Boeing Aircraft Since 1916* (Annapolis, MD 1989), 291; Edward Jablonski, *Flying Fortress* (Garden City, N.Y.: 1965), 4–11.

32 Henry E. Guerlac, *Radar in World War II* (Los Angeles: 1987), I, 712–715.

33 Kuter, 132.

34 Copp, 269.

35 Earle Partridge (Bartanowicz interview), 42, BL, CU.

36 Kuter, 169; Partridge, op. cit., 32–33.

37 Hugh Knerr (Goddard interview), 1, CAFH.

38 Memoir "The Vital Era," Hugh Knerr Papers, Special Collections, USAFA.

39 *Global* ms. VIII, 115.

40 The best brief treatment of this restriction is Maurer Maurer, *Aviation in the U.S. Army 1919–1939* (Washington, D.C.: 1987), 408–412. Curtis LeMay (Green interview), 8, USAFA, claimed that the restriction came about after the 49th Bomb Squadron flew over the fleet 700 miles off the East Coast while on a training flight to Bermuda.

41 Greer, 95–99.

42 Wolfe, 7; Donald Douglas (Shaughnessy interview), BL, CU.

43 Eugene Beebe (Shaughnessy interview), 26, BL, CU. Beebe was Arnold's pilot. Craig also insisted that Arnold fly only in multiengine aircraft.

Chapter 3: Critical Mass

1 James McVicker Haight, Jr., "France's First War Mission to the United States," *Air Power Historian,* January 1964; Keith

D. McFarland, *Harry H. Woodring* (Lawrence, Kans.: 1975), 183–184.

2 Mark S. Watson, *Chief of Staff: Pre-War Plans and Preparations* (Washington, D.C.: 1950), 132–136.

3 *Global Mission* ms. X, 11–13, Arnold Papers, MD, LC.

4 Laurence S. Kuter (Ahmann and Sturm interview), 122–123 CAFH; Richard Davis, *Spaatz and the Air War in Europe* (Washington, D.C.: 1993), 57–61; Jeffrey S. Underwood, *Wings of Democracy* (College Station, Tex.: 1991), 133–137. The plan that was finally adopted by Congress was one that Woodring had submitted to Arnold in October.

5 *Global* ms. X, 39–40.

6 John Morton Blum, *From the Morgenthau Diaries* (Boston: 1965), II, 66 passim.

7 Kenneth B. Wolfe (Shaughnessy interview), 19, BL, CU; Wolfe, et al. (Green interview), 1–2, USAFA. Wolfe was the Air Corps representative at the Douglas plant and selected Chemidlin to take this flight. Donald Douglas (Green interview), 16, USAFA. Cf. Wilbur H. Morrison, *Donald Douglas: A Heart with Wings* (Ames, Iowa: 1991), 104–105; Edward H. Heinemann and Rosario Ransa, *Ed Heinemann* (Annapolis, Md.: 1980), 57–59.

8 McFarland, 191–193, 210–225. Woodring's obstructionism resulted in him being one of only two Cabinet members fired by FDR.

9 "Memo for Record," March 10, 1940, Arnold Papers, MD, LC.

10 Blum, 117.

11 There is no reference to this meeting in *The Wartime Journals of Charles A. Lindbergh* (New York: 1970), but see *Global* ms. XI, 14–17. Cf. Leonard Mosley, "How the Nazis Used Lindbergh," *New York* March 3, 1976.

12 Craven and Cate, VI, 178–179; cf. Orval R. Cook (Ahmann and Emmons interview), 116 CAFH.

13 Lindbergh, *Journals,* 254.

14 Kenneth B. Wolfe (Green interview), 43–44.

15 Cook, 85–86; George Kenney (Hasdorff interview), 116, CAFH.

16 Blum, 116, 145 passim.

17 Diary, March 10, 1941, Paul D. Robinett Papers, GCMF.

Robinett worked on the General Staff and had daily contact with Arnold. Arnold's executive officer at the time, Ray Dunn, (Green interview), 33, USAFA, claims that Arnold didn't choose Knudsen. It seems almost certain that Robert Patterson, the asst secy of war responsible for procurement, insisted on recruiting Knudsen.

18 Charles A. Sorensen, *My Forty Years with Ford* (New York: 1948), 280–281.

19 John Bell Rae, *Climb to Greatness: The American Aviation Industry 1920–1960* (Cambridge, Mass.: 1968), 99, 106–107; Blum 122.

20 Lowell Thomas and Edward Jablonski *Doolittle* (New York: 1968), 140–141.

21 Bill Sweetman, *High-Speed Flight* (New York: 1984), 47–49.

22 Robert Gross (Shaughnessy interview), 14, BL, CU. Gross was president of Lockheed.

23 Cook, 133–137.

24 Walter Isaacson and Evan Thomas, *The Wise Men* (New York: 1986), 90–92.

25 Jonathan Foster Fanton, *Robert A. Lovett: The War Years* (Yale University, Ph.D., 1978), 18–20; Isaacson and Evans, 184–185.

26 Norman Beasley, *Knudsen: a Biography* (New York: 1946), 264–267; Sorenson, 274–276.

27 Robert Lacey, *Ford* (Boston: 1985), 390–395.

28 Ibid., 393.

29 Diary, Feb. 27, 1941, Stimson Papers, Sterling Memorial Library, Yale University.

30 Carl A. Spaatz (Shaughnessy interview), 12, BL, CU.

31 Davis, 75–82.

32 Douglas, (Green), 18.

33 Fanton., 36–42.

34 Letter, Hopkins to Churchill, April 4, 1941, Harry Hopkins Papers, Franklin D. Roosevelt Library, Hyde Park, NY.

35 Diary, April 19, 1941, Arnold Papers, MD, LC.

36 Elwood Quesada (Long and Stephenson interview), Section II, 22, USAMHI. Quesada was Arnold's aide, assigned for the previous six months to dealing with the British. He traveled with Arnold on this trip.

37 Henry Self (Shaughnessy interview), 32–37, 49; and Arthur

Harris (Shaughnessy interview), 31, both BL, CU; Warren F. Kimball ed. *Churchill and Roosevelt: The Complete Correspondence* (New York: 1967), I, 83.

38 John Alison (Thompson interview), 37, CAFH.

39 Laurence S. Kuter (Ahmann and Sturm interview), 122–123, CAFH.

40 Orvil Anderson (Leish interview), 26–28, BL, CU.

41 Haywood S. Hansell, Jr., *The Air Plan That Defeated Hitler* (Atlanta, Ga.: 1972), 64–65.

42 Harold George (Green interview), 21–25, USAFA; Cf. James C. Gaston, *Planning the American Air War* (Washington, D.C.: 1982), 30–31.

43 Kuter, 46.

44 Haywood S. Hansell, Jr., (Green interview), 3–9, USAFA; Hansell, *The Strategic Air War Against Germany and Japan* (Washington, D.C.: 1986), 25.

45 Thomas A. Fabyanic, *A Critique of U.S. Air War Planning 1941–1944* (St. Louis University, Ph.D., 1973) 37–39.

46 Stimson's own numbered copy of AWPD-1, in Spaatz Papers, MD, LC.

47 Haywood S. Hansell, Jr., *Air Plan,* 94.

48 Hansell, (Green), 8.

49 Hansell, *Air Plan,* 95.

Chapter 4: Spreading Wings

1 *Global Mission* ms. X, 4–5, Arnold Papers, MD, LC.

2 R. Frank Futrell, *Ideas, Concepts, Doctrine* (Maxwell AFB: 1971), I, 86; Thomas H. Greer, *The Development of Air Doctrine in the Army Air Arm 1917–1941,* USAF Study 89, (Maxwell AFB: 1955), 91–100.

3 Manuscript, "The Vital Era," unpaginated, Hugh Knerr Papers, Special Collections, USAFA.

4 DeWitt S. Copp, *A Few Great Captains* (Garden City, N.Y.: 1983), 434–435.

5 Jonathan F. Fanton, *Robert A. Lovett: The War Years* (Yale University Ph. D., 1978), 45 et seq.

6 Laurence S. Kuter (Ahmann and Sturm interview), 140, CAFH.

7 Eugene Beebe (Green interview), I, 40, USAFA.

8 Ray Dunn (Green Collection), 37, Special Collections,

USAFA, says Arnold was ordered to commission Elliott Roosevelt by Marshall. Dunn was Arnold's executive officer at the time and was given the hopeless task of calming the press furor. Also see Elliott Roosevelt's account in an interview with Murray Green, USAFA.

9 Memo, Marshall to Stimson, May 16, 1941, in Larry Bland and Sharon Ritenour, eds., *The Papers of George Catlett Marshall* (Baltimore: 1983), II, 508–510.

10 One highly placed officer on the General Staff said the airmen were "winning by degrees" in the struggle for independence. Paul D. Robinett, diary, GCMF; War Department message 888–119, from Gerow to Spaatz, Carl A. Spaatz Papers, MD, LC.

11 Dunn, 53.

12 Diary, Nov. 5 and 8, 1941, Stimson Papers, Sterling Memorial Library, Yale University; McGeorge Bundy interview with Stimson, p. 225, loc. cit.

13 Henry H. Arnold and Ira C. Eaker, *Winged Warfare* (New York: 1941), 29.

14 *Life,* October 1940.

15 John Steinbeck, *Bombs Away!* (New York: 1942), 45.

16 Reed E. Davis, *From Aviation Section, Signal Corps to U.S. Air Force* (New York: 1984), 116–117.

17 Paul K. Carlton (Thompson interview), 7–8, CAFH.

18 Howell M. Estes, Jr. (Zimmerman and Officer interview), 20, CAFH; Howard C. Davidson (Green interview), 14–17, USAFA, claimed that this was his idea, that Arnold accepted it without hesitation, and that he, Davidson, selected the nine schools.

19 Fanton, 108.

20 Arnold and Eaker, 36.

21 Lee Arbon, *They Also Flew* (Washington, D.C.: 1991), 122.

22 Jerrold E. Brown, *Where Eagles Roost: Army Airfields Before World War II* (Duke University, Ph.D., 1977); James E. Tate, *The Army and Its Air Corps* (Indiana University, Ph.D., 1976).

23 Craven and Cate, VI, 120–121.

24 Earle E. Partridge (Ahmann interview), 282–285.

25 Gilbert S. Guinn, "A Different Frontier: The AAF and the Evolution of the Sunshine Belt," *Aerospace Historian,* March 1982.

26 Martha Byrd, *Chennault: Giving Wings to the Tiger* (Tuscaloosa, Ala.: 1987), 60–61.
27 Claire Lee Chennault, *Way of a Fighter* (New York: 1949), 95. Arnold pointed out that Army regulations prohibited retired officers from commanding tactical units, but this requirement was later ignored when Chennault commanded 14th AF.
28 John Alison (Thompson interview), 56–59, CAFH; Chennault, 101–102.
29 Partridge, 224–225.
30 Gregory Boyington, *Baa, Baa, Black Sheep* (New York: 1954), 16–24.
31 Sebie Biggs Smith (self-interview), 34, BL, CU.
32 Paul Frillman (Rounds, Jr.), 162, BL, CU.
33 Charles R. Bond, Jr., *A Flying Tiger's Diary* (College Station, Tex.: 1984), 43–44.
34 Interview with Lt. Col. Robert Hays, USAF, Ret., August 22, 1991. Colonel Hayes is the leading authority on the Knight Committee.
35 Grover C. Hall, Jr., *1000 Destroyed* (Fallbrook, Calif.: 1978), 6; Charles Watry, *Washout!* (Carlsbad, Calif.: 1984), 177.
36 Philip D. Caine, *Eagles of the RAF* (Washington, D.C.: 1991), 37–40; Vern Haugland, *The Eagle Squadrons* (New York: 1978), 11–13.
37 William Dunn, *Fighter Pilot* (Lexington, KY.: 1982), 22–29.
38 John T. Godfrey, *The Look of Eagles* (New York: 1956), 14–20.
39 Haugland, 36.
40 David Burchinal (Schmidt and Straser interview), 22, CAFH.
41 Laurence S. Kuter (Ahmann and Sturm), 78, CAFH.
42 Ira Eaker (Joe B. Green interview), 7, USAFA.
43 Christopher Gabel, *The US Army GHQ Maneuvers of 1941* (Ohio State University, Ph.D., 1981), 120–126.
44 Samuel Anderson (Ahmann interview), 153, CAFH.
45 Hugh Parker (Burg interview), 65–66, Dwight D. Eisenhower Library, Abilene. Parker was an A-20 pilot in 3rd Attack Group.
46 *Global Mission* ms. XV, 15, Arnold Papers, MD, LC.
47 Philip G. Cochran (Hasdorff interview), 43, CAFH.
48 Clagett material in Murray Green Collection, Box 11 Special Collections, USAFA. Walter D. Edmonds, *They Fought with What They Had* (Boston: 1951), 21–22 refers to Clagett's fre-

quent spells in hospital, but doesn't indicate the nature of his illness.

49 This argument had been vigorously pushed by Spaatz's staff since 1939: Phillip S. Meilinger, *Hoyt S. Vandenberg* (Bloomington, Ind.: 1989), 24–25.

50 D. Clayton James, *Years of MacArthur* (Boston: 1975), I, 592; Lewis Brereton, *The Brereton Diaries* (New York: 1946).

51 Air Staff, "Data Concerning Far Eastern Situation," Dec. 1, 1941, Carl A. Spaatz Papers, Manuscript Division, Library of Congress. One Air Staff member, Colonel Orvil A. Anderson, vigorously dissented from the Spaatz-Arnold policy of sending B-17s to the Philippines in small numbers: Anderson (Shaughnessy interview), 53–55, CAFH.

52 John W. Carpenter (McCants and Thompson interview), 56, CAFH.

53 Clagett had insisted on taking a well-known drinker and renowned flyer, Lester Maitland, as his aide. Their drunken binge in China created such indignation at the State Department that Arnold had to bring Clagett home. Martin Scanlon/ Lucas V. Beau (Green interview), 31–32, USAFA. Beau had cut their orders and urged Arnold not to let Clagett take Maitland with him, confident he knew what would happen.

54 Eugene Beebe (Green interview), II, 13, USAFA.

55 William H. Bartsch, *Doomed at the Start* (College Station, Tex.: 1992), 40.

56 Albert F. Hegenberger (Hasdorff interview), 54, CAFH.

57 Gordon H. Austin (Ahmann interview), 45, CAFH.

58 Gordon W. Prange, et al. *At Dawn We Slept* (New York: 1984), 189–190.

59 DeWitt S. Copp, *Forged in Fire* (Garden City, N.Y.: 1982), 190–192.

60 Howard Davidson (Ahmann and Sturm interview), 433–434, CAFH. Davidson commanded 14th Pursuit Wing. Some HAF officers claimed that Davidson strongly protested the decision to switch over to antisabotage. Short's obsession with sabotage and refusal to take the threat of an air attack seriously was typical of Army commanders in Hawaii: see Samuel Anderson (Ahmann interview), 41–45, CAFH.

61 Confidential message #119, Arnold to Martin, 28 Nov. 1941, Arnold Papers, MD, LC.

62 Gordon H. Austin (Ahmann interview), 37, CAFH.

Chapter 5: Zero Hour

1 Gordon W. Prange, *December 7, 1941* (New York: 1986), 79–81.
2 George Raynor Thompson et al. *The Signal Corps: The Test* (Washington, D.C.: 1957), 54–55, 93–99; cf. Howard Davidson (Ahmann and Sturm interview), 430–431, CAFH.
3 Leatrice R. Arakaki, *7 December 1941: The Air Force Story* (Washington, D.C.: 1991), 71–72.
4 Harold S. Kaye, "Hickam Field, Dec. 7, 1941," *Aerospace Historian,* Dec. 1986.
5 Gordon H. Austin (Ahmann interview), 45, CAFH.
6 George S. Welch, Air Room Interview, May 19, 1942, Microfilm 142.502, HRA.
7 Francis Gabreski, with Carl Molesworth, *Gabby* (New York: 1991), 40–43; Vern Haugland, *The AAF Against Japan* (New York: 1948), 13–14.
8 John W. Lambert, *The Long Campaign: 15th Fighter Group* (Manhattan, Kans.: 1982), 24.
9 Craven and Cate, I, 195–201.
10 Prange, 347–348.
11 Carol Petillo, *Douglas MacArthur: The Philippine Years* (Bloomington, Ind.: 1981), 199–201.
12 Cecil E. Combs (Ahmann interview), 58, CAFH; John W. Carpenter (McCants and Thompson interview), 57, CAFH. Until a few weeks before the attack, Clark was commanded by Lieutenant Colonel Lester Maitland, pilot of the first successful flight to Hawaii.
13 Combs, 66.
14 Craven and Cate, I, 203–210.
15 William E. Dyess, Jr., *The Dyess Story* (New York: 1944), 30.
16 Martin Caidin, *The Ragged, Rugged Warriors* (New York: 1966), 170–172.
17 W. L. White, *Queens Die Proudly* (New York: 1943), 75, makes it sound almost quaint, but to at least one B-17 pilot it was "The asshole of Creation": Combs, 56.
18 Walter D. Edmonds, *They Fought with What They Had* (Boston: 1951), 168–172.
19 Carpenter, 83.
20 Louis Morton, *The Fall of the Philippines* Chapters X-XII (Washington, D.C.): 1953).
21 Edmonds, 220–227.
22 Letter, Francis M. Brady to Spaatz, Jan. 25, 1942, Spaatz

Papers, MD, LC. Brady was Brereton's chief of staff and his long letter is a damning indictment—e.g. "Discipline and sense of responsibility was lacking in officers even with two to three years service." The letter carries a strong endorsement from General Brett: "Frank is absolutely correct. . . . There appears an indifferent attitude on the part of the average pilot."

23 Lauris Norstad (Ahmann interview), 502, CAFH; George Kenney (Stanley interview), 21, CAFH.

24 Diary, September 19, 1942, Arnold Papers, MD, LC; Orval R. Cook (Ahmann interview), 235–237, CAFH.

25 Francis C. Gideon (Cleary interview), 12–13, CAFH.

26 Marvin L. McNickle (Ahmann interview), 18–19, CAFH.

27 Dale O. Smith, *Screaming Eagle* (New York: 1987), 9–33.

28 Paul D. Tibbets, *The Paul Tibbets Story* (New York: 1977), 66–67.

29 Robert Lee Scott, *God Is My Co-pilot* (New York: 1944), 54.

30 Michael Gannon, *Operation Drumbeat* (New York: 1990), 182–183, 349–353.

31 Henry E. Guerlac, *Radar in World War II* (Los Angeles: 1987), I, 712–715; Thompson, 93–101.

32 Craven and Cate, I, 514–553.

33 Charles Barton, *Howard Hughes and His Flying Boat* (Fallbrook, Calif.: 1982), 53–68.

Chapter 6: Bombing Range

1 E.g. Laurence S. Kuter (Ahmann and Sturm interview), 125, CAFH: "Bombers could do anything; anything at all."

2 Lauris Norstad (Ahmann interview), 460–461.

3 Stuart Leslie, *Boss Kettering* (New York: 1983), 296–299; *Global Mission* ms. XVII, 5–11, Arnold Papers, MD, LC.

4 Archie J. Old (Ahmann interview), 75–77, CAFH. On 3rd Attack Group's training methods, see George W. Mundy (Cleary interview), 6–9 and Earle Partridge (Ahmann and Sturm interview), 49–51, 70–71, CAFH.

5 John F. Whiteley, *Early Army Aviation* (Manhattan, Kans.: 1975), 79.

6 George C. Kenney (Hasdorff interview), 72–73, CAFH.

7 Ed Heinemann (Mortensen interview), 11–14, 21–25, CAFH. Heinemann was the principal designer of the A-20. Also see Gordon Swanborough and Peter M. Bowers, *U.S. Military Aircraft Since 1909* (Washington, D.C.: 1989), 277–281; Ray

Wagner, *American Combat Planes* (Garden City, N.Y.: 1968), 70–74; James C. Fahey, *U.S. Army Aircraft 1908–1946* (New York: 1946), 20.

8   John Alison (Thompson interview), 162, OAFH.

9   Diary, April 16, 1941, Arnold Papers, MD, LC.

10   Robert Frank Futrell, *Command of Observation Aviation* (Maxwell AFB: 1956), 8–9; also see Thomas Greer *Development of Air Doctrine in the Army Air Arm* (Maxwell AFB: 1955), 87–88, 122–123.

11   David R. Mets, *Master of Air Power* (San Rafael, Calif.: 1988), 110.

12   Arno H. Luehmann (Ahmann interview), 26–28.

13   William Hess, *A-20 Havoc at War* (New York: 1980), 23–31.

14   Craven and Cate, I, 658–659.

15   George C. Kenney (Hasdorff interview), 35.

16   John Leland Atwood (Rae interview), 3–8, Honnold Library, Claremont Colleges, Claremont, CA.

17   Benjamin S. Kelsey, *The Dragon's Teeth* (Washington, D.C.: 1982), 82.

18   Charles Mendenhall, *The Deadly Duo* (Osceola, Wis.: 1981), 24–26.

19   Swanborough and Bowers, 458–461; Wagner, 129–132; Fahey, 22.

20   George C. Kenney, *The Saga of Pappy Gunn* (New York: 1960), 54–57.

21   Ernest R. McDowell, *B-25 Mitchell at War* (Carrolton, Tex.: 1979).

22   Roger A. Freeman ed. *B-26 Marauder at War* (New York: 1978), 8–9.

23   Mendenhall, 28–36.

24   Lawrence Loftin, *Quest for Performance* (Washington, D.C.: 1985), 125–126.

25   Swanborough and Bowers, 437–443; Wagner, 132–135.

26   Samuel Anderson (Ahmann interview), 150–152, CAFH.

27   William E. Lee (Burg interview), 266–273, Dwight D. Eisenhower Library, Abilene, Kans.; Arno H. Luehmann (Ahmann interview), 29–30, CAFH.

28   Carroll V. Glines, *The Doolittle Raid* (New York: 1988), 18–19.

29   Jacqueline Cochran (Leach interview), 42–43, BL, CU. Cf. Orval R. Cook—"The trouble was all with the people who

maintained and who flew it." (Ahmann and Emmons interview), 151, CAFH.

30 Howard Davidson (Ahmann and Sturm interview), 184, CAFH.

31 Craven and Cate, VI, 200.

32 John W. Carpenter III (McCants and Thompson interview), 48, CAFH; Mathew K. Diechelmann (Dick, Jr.), 75, CAFH; Lauris Norstad (Ahmann interview), 495, CAFH.

33 Peter M. Bowers, *Boeing Aircraft Since 1916* (Annapolis, MD: 1989), 292–293; Cf. Craven and Cate, VI, 204–207.

34 DeWitt S. Copp, *Forged in Fire* (Garden City, N.Y. 1982), 20–22; Edward Jablonski, *Flying Fortress* (Garden City, N.Y.: 1965), 22–25. Brett's attitude was unjustified and potentially foolhardy. For a cogent account of the precarious finances of the aviation industry 1938–1941, see John Bell Rae, *Climb to Greatness* (Cambridge, Mass.: 1968), 121–122, 126, 153–156.

35 *Global Mission* ms. XVII, 13–17, Arnold Papers, MD, LC.

36 Paul W. Tibbets, *The Tibbets Story* (New York: 1979), 84. He was copilot of the lead aircraft. The conclusion Brigadier General Ira Eaker, commanding VIII Bomber Command and present as an observor, drew was that "the German fighters are going to attack very gingerly" because they were much impressed by the B-17's armament. Letter, Eaker to Spaatz, August 18, 1942, Eaker Papers, MD, LC. Cf. Craven and Cate, I, 661–665.

37 Orval R. Cook (Ahmann interview), 123–124, CAFH.

38 Martin Bowman, *B-24 Liberator* (New York: 1980), 6–8; *B-24 Liberator at War,* 4–5; Loftin, 121.

39 Allen G. Blue, *B-24 Liberator* (New York 1977), 11–12. Robert F. Dorr, "B-24 Liberator: The Mostest," *Air Power History,* Spring 1990, and William Carigan, "B-24, Liberator: A Man's Airplane," *Aerospace Historian,* March 1988, offer wartime pilots' assessments of flying this controversial aircraft in combat.

40 Wagner, 118–119, 127–128.

41 Clarence Irvine (Green interview), 3, USAFA; Craven and Cate, VI, 356.

42 *B-24 Liberator at War,* 11.

43 Greer, 95–99.

44 Craven and Cate, VI, 202–204, 208–211, 243–246.

45 Swanborough and Bowers, 187–188; Fahey, 23.

Chapter 7: Lofty Pursuits

1 Kimbrough Brown, et al., *U.S. Army and Air Force Fighters* (Aero 1961), 54–56; Gordon Swanborough and Peter M. Bowers, *U. S. Military Aircraft Since 1909* (Washington, D.C.: 1989), 547–548; Ray Wagner, *American Combat Planes* (Garden City, N.Y.: 1968), 196–198.

2 Swanborough and Bowers, 225–229.

3 Jacqueline Cochran (Leish interview), 22, BL, CU.

4 Maurer Maurer, *Aviation in the U.S. Army 1919–1939* (Washington, D.C.: 1987), 365–366; Brown, et al., 52–53; Wagner, 203–204.

5 Orval R. Cook (Emmons interview), 273, CAFH.

6 William E. Kepner (Green interview), 24, USAFA. Kepner was rebuked by Arnold's exec, fighter pilot Ira Eaker, but was sure the order came from Arnold.

7 Thomas H. Greer, *The Development of Air Doctrine in the Army Air Arm* (Maxwell AFB: 1955), 84; Robert T. Finney, *History of the Air Corps Tactical School 1920–1940* (Maxwell AFB: 1955), 38–39.

8 Orvil A. Anderson (Leish interview), 26, BL, CU; Cf. Greer, 117–120, on the lowly status of fighters.

9 Howard Davidson (Ahmann interview), 429–432, CAFH.

10 William Emerson, "Operation, POINTBLANK: A Tale of Bombers and Fighters," in Harry R. Borowski, ed., *Harmon Memorial Lectures* (Washington, D.C.: 1989), 450.

11 Bill Sweetman, *High Speed Flight* (New York: 1984), 49–55. Herschel Smith, *History of the Aircraft Piston Engine,* rev. ed. (Manhattan, Kans.: 1986), 127–128.

12 Cook, 89–91; Peter M. Bowers, *Boeing Aircraft Since 1916* (Annapolis: 1989), 293–294; Lawrence Loftin, *Quest for Performance* (Washington, D.C.: 1985), 94–95; Wagner, 116.

13 Benjamin S. Kelsey, *The Dragon's Teeth* (Washington, D.C.: 1981), 113–117; Warren M. Bodie, *The Lockheed P-38 Lightning* (Hiawassee, Ga.: 1991), 11–37; Joe Christy and Jeffrey P. Ethell, *P-38 Lightning at War* (New York: 1978), 3–16; Loftin 132–133; Swanborough and Bowers, 358–365; Wagner, 213–218.

14 Benjamin S. Kelsey (Green interview), 5, USAFA.

15 John F. Whiteley, *Early Army Aviation* (Manhattan, Kans.: 1975), 114.

16 Clarence L. Johnson, *Kelly: More Than My Share of It All*

(Washington, D.C.: 1985), 78–79; Robert Gross (Shaughnessy interview), 12–14, BL, CU. Gross was president of Lockheed.

17 Kelsey, op. cit.

18 Arthur Harris (Shaughnessy interview), 17–18, BL, CU; claims to have talked Arnold into keeping the P-38 alive.

19 Brown, et al. 71–72.

20 Ernest R. McDowell, *P-39 Airacobra in Action* (Carrolton, Tex.: 1980), 3–4; Ivan Hickman, *Operation PINBALL* (Osceola, Wis.: 1990), 64–65; Craven and Cate, VI, 212–214.

21 Typical is the comment of William Dunn, *Fighter Pilot* (Louisville, Ky.: 1983), 114: "I felt sorry for the poor SOBs who had to fly it. If you got into a flat spin or a tumble with the damned thing—and it was easily done if you weren't careful—there was nothing to do but bail out." Even pilots who found it fun to fly acknowledged it had terrible defects. See Marvin McNickle (Ahmann interview), 19–20, CAFH; Chuck Yeager, *Yeager* (New York: 1985), 14–15.

22 Donald J. Norton, *Larry: A Biography of Lawrence D. Bell* (Chicago 1981), 92–94.

23 Smith, 87.

24 McDowell, 10.

25 Craven and Cate, IV, 41–42, 262–263.

26 Joe Christy and Jeffrey Ethell, *P-40 Hawks at War* (New York: 1980), 8–12; Brown, 55.

27 Kenneth B. Wolfe (Green interview), 9, USAFA.

28 Kelsey, 9.

29 Wagner, 209–210; Swanborough and Bowers, 231–234.

30 John Alison (Thompson interview), 67–68, CAFH.

31 Lord Tedder, *With Prejudice* (London: 1956), 186.

32 Robert Lee Scott, *God Is My Co-pilot* (New York: 1943), 260.

33 Hugh J. Knerr (Green interview), 11–12, USAFA; Whiteley, 89–90; Thomas Coffey, *Hap* (New York: 1981), 252–253.

34 Swanborough and Bowers, 522.

35 Alexander Kartveli (Leish interview), BL, CU.

36 Wagner, 224–225; Brown, et al., 60–61; Robert F. Dorr, "P-47 Thunderbolt," *Air Power History* Fall 1990.

37 William N. Hess, *P-47 Thunderbolt at War* (Garden City, N.Y.: 1977), 13.

38 Kartveli, 19.

39 Roger A. Freeman, with Hubert Zemke, *Zemke's Wolf Pack* (New York: 1988), 51–54.

40   Henry Self (Pringle interview), 9–10, BL, CU.
41   John L. Attwood (Rae interview), 9, Honnold Library, Clare-
     ment Colleges, Claremont, CA.
42   Ray Wagner, *Mustang Designer* (New York: 1991), 51.
43   Unpublished article on the P-51, by a member of the NAA
     design team, on file at CAFH.
44   Robert Gruenhagen, *Mustang* (New York: 1976), 41–42; Wil-
     liam Newby Grant, *P-51 Mustang* (Englewood Cliffs, N.J.:
     1983), 15.
45   Swanborough and Bowers, 468; Wagner, 230–231.
46   Whiteley, 152.

Chapter 8: On Target

1   Irving B. Holley, Jr., *Development of Aircraft Gun Turrets in
    the AAF, 1917–1944* (Maxwell AFB 1947), 48.
2   Ibid., 55.
3   Arthur Harris (Shaughnessy), 56, BL, CU.
4   Kenneth B. Wolfe (Green), 11, USAFA, describes Arnold's
    belated recognition of the problem. Cf. Holley 92–95.
5   *Harmon Memorial Lectures,* 429.
6   Edward Jablonski and Lowell Thomas, *Doolittle* (New York:
    1973), 163.
7   Charles Mendenhall, *The Deadly Duo* (Osceola, WI: 1981), 34.
8   Charles Watry, *Aerial Gunners: The Unknown Aces of World
    War II* (Carlsbad, Ca; 1986), 24.
9   John Steinbeck, *Bombs Away!* (New York: 1942), 76–91.
10 Kenneth B. Wolfe (Leish), 14–16, BL, CU; George C. Kenney
    (Stanley), 17, CAFH. Wolfe says Arnold was willing to accept
    Ordnance's insistence on putting only .30-caliber guns into
    fighters. Kenney claims he got cyclic rate of fire in the .50
    machine gun up to 1,200 rpm.
11 Harold J. Conway, "Ordnance with the Air Forces," *Army
    Ordnance,* Sept.–Oct., 1943.
12 Ordnance File, Section 5.19, Murray Green Collection,
    USAFA.
13 Harry C. Thomson and Peter C. Roots, *Ordnance Department:
    Planning Munitions for War* (Washington, D.C.: 1957), 452.
14 Harry C. Thomson and Lida Mayo, *Ordnance Department:
    Procurement and Supply* (Washington, D.C.: 1960), 136;
    Thomson and Root, 463–464.

15 Diary, April 16, 1941, Arnold Papers, MD, LC.

16 Memo for Record, Dec. 31, 1941, Arnold Papers, MD, LC. There were also hopes of turning 15-inch naval shells into bombs: Twining Diary, December 19, 1941, Spaatz Papers, MD, LC.

17 Arnold or somebody on his staff wrote an article that presented a picture of a harmonious relationship between Ordnance and the AAF. See, H.H. Arnold, "Wings, Bombs, and Bullets," *Army Ordnance,* Sept.–Oct. 1943.

18 *Global Mission* ms. VIII, 99–100, Arnold Papers, MD, LC.

19 Barney M. Giles (Hasdorff interview), 14–15, CAFH.

20 Air Technical Service Command, *Case History of the Norden Bombsight and the C-1 Automatic Pilot* (Wright Field: 1945). 2–3.

21 Whiteley, 42–43.

22 Air Technical Service Command, *Case History of the S-1 Bombsight and the A-5 Automatic Pilot* (Wright Field 1945), 1–5.

23 Sebie Biggs Smith (self-interview), 21, BL, CU.

24 Andre Brissaud, *Canaris* (New York: 1974), 46–47.

25 William Dunn, *Fighter Pilot* (Louisville, Ky.: 1983), 114–115.

26 Arthur T. Harris (Shaughnessy interview), 39, BL, CU.

27 Arnold was defensive about the lack of armor in U.S. aircraft, and blamed it on the British and French who, he says, "withheld such information as they had" on the need for it in combat. *Global* ms. X, 19–20.

28 Armor Plate file, Microfilm 142.053A-15, Frames 1661–1719, HRA.

Chapter 9: Happenings

1 A. C. Peterson (Shaugnessy interview), 9, 30, BL, CU.

2 *Global Mission* ms. XVIII, 4–6, Arnold Papers, MD, LC.

3 Laurence S. Kuter, "How Hap Arnold Built the AAF," *Air Force* (September 1973).

4 Earle E. Partridge (Ahmann interview), 324–326, CAFH.

5 Elwood Quesada (Long/Stephenson interview), Section II, 23–24, USAMHI.

6 Forrest C. Pogue *George C. Marshall: Ordeal and Hope* (New York 1966), 189–190, 289–301; Frederick S. Haydon, "War Department Reorganization," *Military Affairs* Spring 1952.

7   Laurence S. Kuter (Ahmann and Sturm interview), 219–223, CAFH; Saturday Evening Post, *These Are the Generals* (New York: 1944), 136–147.

8   Lauris Norstad (Ahmann interview), 471, CAFH; Howard Davidson (Ahmann and Sturm interview), 422, CAFH, contends that Arnold only gave the impression of making decisions off the top of his head.

9   Fred M. Dean (Emmons interview), 60–61, CAFH.

10 Eugene Beebe (Green interview), 29, USAFA. Beebe, Arnold's pilot, took notes at these sessions.

11 Norstad, 185.

12 Ray Dunn (Green interview), 11–12, USAFA.

13 Frederick H. Smith, Jr. (Green interview), 7–8, USAFA.

14 Laurence S. Kuter, "The General vs The Establishment," *Aerospace Historian,* XXII (Winter 1974).

15 Earle E. Partridge (Ahmann and Sturm interview), 265, CAFH; cf. Partridge (Bartonowicz), 42, BL, CU; Kuter, 230; Norstad, 485.

16 Eugene Beebe (Shaughnessy interview), 31, BL, CU; and (Green interview), 36–37.

17 Charles R. Bond, Jr., *A Flying Tiger's Diary* (College Station, Tex.: 1984), 217.

18 Hugh J. Knerr (Green interview), 11, USAFA.

19 Diary, March 10, 1941, Paul Robinett Papers, GCMF. Lovett wasn't alone in thinking the Air Staff was a pretty inept bunch; see Norstad, 474.

20 Robert T. Patterson (Pringle interview), Box 18, Murray Green Collection, USAFA.

21 *Global Mission* ms. XII, 3, MD, LC.

22 Kuter, 219.

23 Jonathan Foster Fanton, *Robert Lovett: The War Years* (Yale Ph.D. 1977), 33.

24 Ibid., 74–76.

25 John E. Brigante, *The Feasibility Dispute* (Washington D.C.: 1950), 30–32; Irving B. Holley, Jr., *Buying Aircraft* (Washington, D.C.: 1964), 237–244. Cf. Geoffrey Perret *There's a War to Be Won* (New York: 1991), 76–77.

26 Margaret Case Harriman and John Bainbridge, "The 13th Labor of Hercules," *New Yorker,* Nov. 6, 1943.

27 Dunn, 31. He was Arnold's executive officer and chose these officers.

28 Jacob Smart (Green interview), 5, USAFA; (Hasdorff interview), 45–47, CAFH. Smart served on the Advisory Council for nearly a year.

29 Memo, Marshall to Arnold, July 28, 1942, Arnold Papers, MD, LC. Marshall, in conversation with Forrest Pogue, referred scathingly to "That high school staff he [Arnold] had." *Marshall Tapes* GCMF, Lexington, VA.

30 Kuter.

31 William Kepner (Hicks and Philips), USAMHI.

32 John R. Dean (Green interview), USAFA.

33 Robert Lovett (Green interview), loc. cit.

34 A. C. Peterson (Shaughnessy interview), 12, BL, CU.

Chapter 10: Bloody But Unbowed

1 Allison Ind, *Bataan: The Judgment Seat* (New York: 1944), 167–168.

2 Ibid. 251–255; John Goodman, *Bataan: Our Last Ditch* (New York: 1991), 247–248.

3 William E. Dyess, Jr., *The Dyess Story* (New York: 1944).

4 D. Clayton James, *The Years of MacArthur* (Boston: 1975), 98–100.

5 Frederick H. Smith, Jr. (Hasdorff interview), 38, CAFH.

6 Louis Morton, *The Fall of the Philippines* (Washington, D.C.: 1953), 360.

7 John W. Carpenter (McCants/Thompson interview), 69, CAFH.

8 Craven and Cate, I, 418.

9 Cecil E. Combs (Ahmann interview), 57, CAFH.

10 George C. Kenney, *The Saga of Pappy Gunn* (New York: 1959) 37–38.

11 Walter Edmonds, *They Fought with What They Had* (Boston: 1950), 442.

12 Combs, 75. He commanded 19th Bomb Group.

13 Carpenter, 91–93.

14 John Davies, Air Room Interview, Nov. 23, 1942, Microfilm 142.052, HRA. He commanded 27th Bomb Group.

15 Eugene Eubank, Air Room Interview, July 2, 1942, Microfilm 142.052, HRA. Eubank commanded 7th BG.

16 Combs, 118–119. Orvil A. Anderson, the Air Staff officer responsible for sending the money, says there was $25 million: Anderson (Shaughnessy), 55, CAFH. However, Stephen Am-

brose, *Eisenhower: The Soldier* (New York: 1984), put it at $10 million.

17 Edmonds, 352–360.
18 *Global Mission* ms. XVIII, 11, Arnold Papers, MD, LC.
19 Lowell Thomas and Edward Jablonski, *Doolittle* (New York: 1968), 158. Orvil Anderson, the Air Staff officer for the Pacific, was already working on three plans for a raid on Japan. A carrier strike was his third choice, the one he thought least likely to succeed. Anderson, op. cit.
20 See above, p. 148.
21 Hughes Memoir, Chapter VIII, p. 12, Richard Hughes Papers, Lyndon B. Johnson Presidential Library, Austin, Tex.
22 *Global,* XVIII, 17.
23 Carroll V. Glines, *The Doolittle Raid* (New York: 1988), 61.
24 Craven and Cate, I, 441.
25 Claire Chennault, *Way of a Fighter* (New York: 1949), 168; Giles, 74.
26 Paul Frillman (Rounds interview), 238, 248, BL, CU; Charles Bond, *A Flying Tiger's Diary* (College Station, Tex.: 1986), 58, 64–65; Martha Byrd *Channault: Giving Wings to the Tiger* (Tuscaloosa, Ala.: 124–132).
27 Chennault, 129–130.
28 Duane Schultz, *The Maverick War* (New York: 1987), 165–166.
29 Daniel Ford, *Flying Tigers* (Washington, D.C.: 1991), 275; Bond, 118.
30 Bond, 116. Craven and Cate, I, 489–490, pointedly declines to accept any of the claims made by the AVG, as the relevant footnote makes clear.
31 Ford, 275.
32 Ford, 119–120. Disney had been asked to design an insignia for the AVG. The result was a Bengal tiger with wasplike wings. Hence the name Flying Tigers. It was *Time,* however, that made it world famous.
33 Byrd, 137–138; Jack Samson, *Chennault* (New York: 1986), 105.
34 Diary, Feb. 6, 1943, Arnold Papers, MD, LC.
35 Chennault, 155–156; Frillman, 206–208; Bond, 140–142.
36 Ford, 369–370. Part of the legend is that the AVG had the toughest confirmation system in the world—no debris, no bonus. Considering that 70 percent of claims were for aircraft

reportedly shot down over Burma, Thailand, or Vietnam, neither the Chinese nor the AVG could track down the debris. No more than 25 percent of claims were corroborated by physical evidence.

Chapter 11: Taking the Scenic Route

1 Craven and Cate, I, 411.
2 Richard Carmichael, Air Room Interview, 19th Bomb Group, Dec. 14, 1942, Microfilm 142.052, HRA. He commanded the group.
3 Craven and Cate, I, 412.
4 Donald Hough and Elliott Arnold, *Big Distance* (New York: 1945), 43–44.
5 William Hess, *Pacific Sweep* (Garden City, N.Y.: 1977), 45–47; Craven and Cate, IV, 476.
6 Hess, 37.
7 Eric Hammel, *Aces Against Japan* (New York: 1992), 40–42.
8 Francis C. Gideon, Jr. (Cleary interview), 26, CAFH.
9 William D. Hassett, *Off the Record with FDR* (New Brunswick, N.J.: 1958), 88.
10 Ronnie Dugger, *The Politician* (New York: 1964), 245–249, 444. Cf. Martin Caidin and Edward Hymoff, *The Mission* (Philadelphia: 1964), 131 passim.
11 Frederick H. Smith, Jr. (Hasdorff interview), 41–42, CAFH.
12 George C. Kenney (Green interview), 7, USAFA.
13 Samuel Anderson (Ahmann interview), 186–187, CAFH.
14 Thomas Darcy (Green interview), 10, USAFA. Darcy was Andrews's aide and was with him in Washington when he berated Arnold for having tried to send him to SWPA. MacArthur told Kenney, however, that he had rejected Andrews, for want of combat experience: George C. Kenney (Hasdorff interview), 107–108, CAFH.
15 Lowell Thomas and Edward Jablonski, *Doolittle* (Garden City, N.Y.: 1976), 205.
16 Kenney (Green interview), USAFA.
17 Diary, July 12, 1942, Kenney Papers, CAFH.
18 Carl Bong and Mike Connor, *Dick Bong: Ace of Aces* (Mesa, Ariz.: 1983), 15. Kenney (Stanley interview), 24–25, CAFH maintained that Bong had flown under the Golden Gate Bridge, but was evidently confusing him with Lt. John "Jump" O'Neill, Bong's friend in the 49th Pursuit Squadron, who'd

flown under the bridge. Both pilots appeared before Kenney at the same time and both were grounded for six weeks.

19 Diary, July 29, 1942, Kenney Papers, CAFH. Kenney's book, *General Kenney Reports* (New York: 1949), is based on the diary, but sometimes there are significant differences in emphasis, detail, and tone between the diary entries and the published account.

20 "Comments of General Brett re. Personnel, etc." Aug. 2, 1942, Kenney Papers, CAFH.

21 Kenney (Stanley interview), 26.

22 Carmichael 2; Samuel Anderson, 180–181.

23 Kenney, 29.

24 Diary, July 30, 1942, Kenney Papers, CAFH.

25 Kenney (Hasdorff), 50.

26 D. M. Horner, *Crisis in Command: Australian Generalship and the Japanese Threat 1941–1943* (Canberra: 1978), 135–144.

27 Steve Birdsall, *Flying Buccaneers* (Garden City, N.Y.: 1977), 20–22; Craven and Cate, IV, 496–497.

28 Smith, 62.

29 R. Dan Richardson, "The First Military Airlift: Wings Over the Strait of Gibraltar," *Aerospace Historian,* June 1987.

30 *General Kenney Reports,* 99. Kenney doesn't mention that when the Japanese closed on Kokoda in early August the then AAF commander in New Guinea, Brigadier General Martin "Mike" Scanlon, had airlifted several hundred Australian infantrymen to Kokoda from Port Moresby: Martin Scanlon (Green interview), 5, USAFA; AAF Historical Study No. 17, *Air Action in the Papuan Campaign July 1942–January 1943* (Washington, D.C.: 1944), 19, 26.

31 Hough and Arnold, 53.

32 Samuel Milner, *Victory in Papua* (Washington, D.C.: 1957), 99–100.

33 Joe Gray Taylor, "The American Experience in the Southwest Pacific," in *Close Air Support,* ed. Benjamin Franklin Cooling, (Washington, D.C.: 1990), 306.

34 Craven and Cate, IV, 121.

35 Ibid., 120–121.

Chapter 12: The Lamplighters

1 Lord Tedder, *With Prejudice* (London: 1966), 158–161.

2   Dennis Richards, *Portal of Hungerford* (London: 1977), 230–231, 237.

3   Tedder, 169; Vincent Orange, *Coningham* (London: 1989), 79.

4   Earle F. Partridge (Ahmann interview), 127, CAFH.

5   Lewis Brereton, *The Brereton Diaries* (New York: 1946), 156.

6   Cecil E. Combs (Ahmann interview), 59, CAFH.

7   James Dugan and Carroll Stewart, *Ploesti* (New York: 1964), 12–14; Craven and Cate, I, 341.

8   Craven and Cate, II, 27. Cf. Roderic Owen, *Tedder* (London 1958), 167, on Tedder's plan for integrating American pilots into RAF units.

9   Brereton, 159.

10 Matthew Cooper, *The German Air Force 1933–1945* (London: 1984), pp. 210–211.

11 Cornelius Vanderbilt Whitney, Air Room Interview, April 6, 1943, Microfilm 142.052, HRA. Whitney served on Brereton's staff at MEAF and 9th Air Force. On the significant role played by 15,000 American airmen in the battle of El Alamein, see his book, *Lone and Level Sands* (New York: 1946), 73–77.

12 Craven and Cate, II, 41–47; Maurice Matloff and Edwin M. Snell, *Strategic Planning for Coalition Warfare 1941–1942* (Washington, D.C.: 1953), 236 passim.

13 C.B.A. Behrens, *Merchant Shipping and the Demands of War* (London: 1955), 332–338. As Professor Behrens makes clear repeatedly in this official history, the British never devised an effective method of keeping track of shipping. Their shipping companies operated more or less as they pleased.

14 James Doolittle, with Carroll V. Glines, *I Could Never Be So Lucky Again* (New York: 1991), 298–300.

15 Philip Meilinger, *Hoyt S. Vandenberg* (Bloomington, Ind.: 1989).

16 Vandenberg was known as AB—for "Area Bird"—from walking so many tours: Earle Partridge (Bartanowicz interview), 36, BL, CU. His coolness under pressure is attested to by George Goddard, *Overview* (Garden City, N.Y.: 1980), 389.

17 Craven and Cate, II, 59–60.

18 F. H. Hinsley, *British Intelligence in the Second World War* (London: 1988), III, part 1, p. 465.

19 Fred M. Dean (Emmons interview), 20, CAFH, Dean com-

manded a squadron in the 31st Group, flying Spitfires from Gibraltar to Oran on November 8.

20 Albert Kesselring, *A Soldier's Story* (London: 1954), 163; British Air Ministry, *The Rise and Fall of the German Air Force* (London: 1948), 145.

21 John C. Warren, *Airborne Missions in the Mediterranean* (Maxwell AFB: 1955), 5–16.

22 Edson D. Raff, *We Jump to Fight* (New York: 1944), 59–63. Raff commanded the airborne battalion.

23 Lauris Norstad (Ahmann interview), 511, CAFH.

24 George F. Howe, *Northwest Africa: Seizing the Initiative in the West* (Washington, D.C.: 1957), 149–153, 164–168; William Momyer (Mortenson interview), 12, CAFH.

25 Letter, Doolittle to Arnold, November 19, 1942, Arnold Papers, MD, LC.

26 Hinsley, 486.

27 Craven and Cate, II, 79.

28 Warren, 17–18.

29 Alfred D. Chandler, ed., *The Papers of Dwight D. Eisenhower* (Baltimore: 1970), II, 779.

30 I.S.O. Playfair and C.J.C. Molony, *The Mediterranean and the Middle East* (London: 1966), IV, 174; Hinsley, II, 499; Craven and Cate, II, 85.

31 Paul Tibbets, *The Tibbets Story* (New York: 1985), 119–120.

32 Daniel R. Mortensen, Untitled, Unpublished study of tactical air in North Africa, Chapter VI, p. 19, on file at the Center for Air Force History.

33 Philip Cochran (Hasdorff interview), 56–60, CAFH. Cochran took the first group of replacement pilots into Thelepte. David Ludlum (Mortensen interview), 13, CAFH. Ludlum was the weatherman at Thelepte. Christopher Shores, et al. *Fighters Over Tunisia* (London: 1975), describes conditions at all the fighter airfields and provides a valuable day-by-day chronicle of fighter operations on both sides.

Chapter 13: Reversals of Fortune

1 Williamson Murray, *Strategy for Defeat: The Luftwaffe 1939–1945* (Maxwell AFB: 1983), 182–189.

2 Lord Tedder, *With Prejudice* (London: 1966), 314.

3 Quesada, II, 30.

4 Lowell Thomas and Edward Jablonski, *Doolittle* (Garden

City, N.Y.: 1968), 219; Earle E. Partridge (Ahmann interview), 404, CAFH; Vicki Goldberg, *Margaret Bourke-White* (New York: 1986). 262–264.

5 George C. Marshall (Larson, et al. interview), page 6, USAMHI.

6 Dwight D. Eisenhower, *Crusade in Europe* (Garden City, N.Y.: 1948), 126, 140.

7 Daniel Mortensen, Unpublished study on tactical air in North Africa, Chapter IX, p. 90, CAFH.

8 Ibid., Chapter VII.

9 Richard Davis, *Spaatz and the Air War in Europe* (Washington, D.C.: 1993); Report, Rickenbacker to Arnold, Box 91, Edward V. Rickenbacker Papers, MD, LC.

10 Elliott Roosevelt, Air Room Interview, July 27, 1943. Microfilm 142.052, HRA; Elliott Roosevelt (Green interview), 17, USAFA.

11 Philip Cochran (Hasdorff interview), 61–64; John Bainbridge "Flip Corkin," *Life* Aug. 9, 1943; William W. Momyer (Mortensen interview), 15–16, CAFH.

12 Philip Cochran, Air Room Interview, June 3, 1943, Microfilm 142.052, HRA.

13 George F. Howe, *Northwest Africa: Seizing the Initiative in the West* (Washington, D.C.: 1957), 388 passim.

14 Frederick M. Dean (Emmons interview), 26–27, CAFH; Ludlum 13–14. Dean commanded 31st FG.

15 Martin Blumenson, *Kasserine Pass* (New York: 1966), 214–216; Howe 438–458.

16 Craven and Cate, II, 159–160.

17 Vincent Orange, *Coningham* (London: 1989), 144–145, 149–151.

18 David Syrett, "The Tunisian Campaign," in *Close Air Support,* Benjamin Franklin Cooling, ed., (Washington, D.C.: 1991), 176–177.

19 Tedder, 410–411; Martin Blumenson, *The Patton Papers* (Boston: 1975), II, 203–209.

20 Howard E. Engler, Air Room Interview, May 27, 1943, Microfilm 142.052, HRA. Engler was Doolittle's A-3 and provides an excellent account of NASAF.

21 Paul Tibbets, *The Tibbets Story* (New York: 1987), 119.

22 Partridge. 384–385.

23 Friedrich Ruge, *Der Seekrieg: The German Navy's Story,*

1945 (Annapolis: 1957), 330. Ruge commanded the German Navy in the Mediterranean. Cf. Hinsley, II, 607–608.

24 Howe, 365–366.

25 Eduard Mark, *Aerial Interdiction* (Washington, D.C.: 1993), 35–36.

26 Marc Antonio Bragadin, *The Italian Navy in WW II* (Annapolis: 1957), 241–243.

27 Mark, 45–46; Bragadin, Table 2, p. 357, shows how the amount shipped each month fell dramatically, so that although a higher percentage made a safe passage in April the amount involved was much less than that arriving safely in March.

28 Laurence S. Kuter (Ahmann/Sturm interview), 308–309; Craven and Cate, II, 189–190; Shores, 306–322.

29 Army Air Forces, *Statistical Digest* (Washington, D.C.: 1945), 52, 256.

Chapter 14: Mediterranean Cockpit

1 Albert N. Garland and Howard McGaw Smyth, *Sicily and the Surrender of Italy* (Washington, D.C.: 1965), 69; Albert Chandler ed. *The Papers of Dwight D. Eisenhower* (Baltimore: 1970), II, 1230.

2 Richard Davis, *Spaatz and the Air War in Europe* (Washington, D.C.: 1993).

3 Lord Zuckerman, *From Apes to Warlords* (New York: 1978), 187.

4 Earle E. Partridge (Ahmann interview), 377–378, CAFH.

5 Chandler, II, 1231.

6 Garland and Smyth, 72.

7 Craven and Cate, II, 423–430.

8 Lord Tedder, *With Prejudice* (London: 1966), 426.

9 James H. Doolittle, with Carrol V. Glines, *I Could Never Be So Lucky Again* (New York: 1991), 356.

10 Donald Douglas (Green interview), 32–33, USAFA; Robert Gross (Shaughnessy interview), 16–17, BL, CU.

11 Nathan Twining diary, Dec. 19, 1941, Carl A. Spaatz Papers, MD, LC.

12 Ray A. Dunn (Green interview), 8–9, USAFA. Cf. James A. Huston, *Out of the Blue* (Purdue 1972), 68.

13 Rickenbacker, 16.

14 Milton Dank, *The Glider Gang* (Philadelphia: 1977), 51

passim; Gerard Devlin, *Silent Wings* (New York: 1985), 49–59; John H. Lowden, *Silent Wings at War* (Washington, D.C.: 1992).

15   John H. Warren, *Airborne Missions in the Mediterranean* (Maxwell AFB: 1956); Huston, 116–117.

16   Drew Pearson, *The Washington Post,* April 29, 1944.

17   Davis, 376–377; Dunn, 44; Patrick Timberlake (Green interview), 19, USAFA.

18   S.W.C. Pack, *Operation Husky* (New York: 1977); Garland and Smyth, 58–61, 88–91; Harry C. Butcher, *My Three Years with Eisenhower* (New York: 1946), 293.

19   Chester Wilmot *The Struggle for Europe* (London: 1952), 174. Cf. Arthur Coningham (Pogue interview), USAMHI, in which Coningham is bitterly critical of Montgomery.

20   Richard Davis, *Spaatz and the Air War in Europe* (Washington, D.C.: 1993), 361–365; Samuel Anderson (Ahmann interview), 112–116, CAFH; Laurence S. Kuter (Ahmann and Sturm interview), 58, 312, 328, CAFH.

21   Craven and Cate, II, 445; S. E. Morison, *Sicily-Salerno-Anzio* (Boston: 1954), 142–143.

22   F. H. Hinsley, *British Intelligence in the Second World War* (Cambridge, England: 1987), III, Part 1, 59–60.

23   Matthew Cooper, *The German Air Force, 1939–1945* (London: 1983), 289.

24   Johannes Steinhoff, *Messerschmitts Over Sicily* (Baltimore: 1987) 56, 189. Steinhoff commanded a GAF fighter group on Sicily.

25   British Air Ministry, *The Rise and Fall of the German Air Force* (London: 1947), 258–259.

26   Warren, 32–37.

27   Devlin, 98–100.

28   Siegfried Westphal, *The German Army in the West* (London: 1951), 144; Frido von Senger and Etterlin, *Neither Fear Nor Hope* (London: 1963), 130–132.

29   Elliott Roosevelt, Air Room Interview, July 27, 1943, Microfilm 142.052, HRA. This probably came about because of demands and criticisms from Lucian K. Truscott, Jr., commanding 3rd Infantry Division: See Truscott, *Command Missions* (New York: 1954), 200.

30   Craven and Cate, II, 452.

31 Kit C. Carter and Robert Mueller, *Combat Chronology 1941–1945* (Washington, D.C.: 1973), 156. This is a companion volume to Craven and Cate.
32 Timberlake 18. He was Tedder's Chief of Plans during Husky.
33 Memo, Matthew B. Ridgway, "Reported Loss of Transport Planes and Personnel Due to Friendly Fire," August 2, 1943, Arnold Papers, MD, LC; Garland and Smyth, 175–182.
34 Ray A. Dunn (Green interview), 42–43, USAFA; Dunn, 201 File, Modern Military Records Branch, National Archives; *The Washington Post* April 29, 1944. Giles's treatment of Dunn appears vindictive, as if he was jealous of the man he had, in effect, replaced. The source of the leak was a colonel in Operations, Commitments and Requirements: Howard Craig (Green interview), 20, USAFA. Craig headed OC&R.
35 Warren, 47–50.
36 Doolittle, 358–359; Lewis Brereton, *The Brereton Diaries* (New York: 1946), 194–195; Craven and Cate, II, 464–465.
37 James Dugan and Carroll Stewart, *Ploesti* (New York: 1964), 47–49.
38 *Patton Papers,* II, 254; Omar Bradley and Clay Blair, *A General's Life* (New York: 1983), 178; Davis, 415–416.
39 Carlo D'Este, *Bitter Victory* (New York: 1987), 464–465.
40 Mark, 45.
41 Ibid., 50; Vincent Orange, *Coningham* (London: 1989), 167–168.
42 Garland, 416.
43 Davis, 425–431.
44 Cooper, 304; Adolf Galland, "The Birth, Life and Death of the German Day Fighter Arm," 38, Spaatz Papers, MD, LC. The GAF lost more than 1,000 planes, mainly fighters, and several hundred experienced pilots, in the Sicilian air campaign, which extended far beyond Sicilian airfields.
45 Jacob E. Smart (Green interview), 9–15, USAFA, and (McCants and Hasdorff interview), 70–84, CAFH. In his published diary Brereton claimed that attacking Ploesti at low level was his idea, but I believe the truth is what Smart told Green: It was "a bad idea that I dreamed up." Cf. Memoir, Chapter IV, 12, 42–43, Richard Hughes Papers, Lyndon B. Johnson Presidential Library, Austin, Tex.
46 Gordon P. Saville (Green interview), USAFA. The plan and relevant field orders are reproduced in AC/AS Intelligence-

Historical Division, *AAFRH-3: The Ploesti Mission,* 151–156, HRA.

47 Dugan and Stewart, 75–76.

48 Leon W. Johnson (Green interview), 11. Johnson commanded the 44th Bomb Group and won the Medal of Honor at Ploesti.

49 Dugan and Stewart, 147–148.

50 Norman H. Whalen, "Ploesti: Group Navigator's View," *Aerospace Historian,* March 1976.

51 Philip Ardrey, *Bomber Pilot* (Lexington, Ky.: 1978), 103–105.

52 Arthur Gordon, "Three Years Over Europe," *Air Force Magazine,* September 1945. This was an official AAF publication and Major Gordon's article was a summary of major operations. Gordon puts the loss at 73 B-24s. Craven and Cate, II, 483, put it at 54, on the basis of Brereton's reports. However, there were persistent doubts about the publicly announced figures for losses in this raid. And since December 7, 1941, Brereton had shown a disconcerting willingness to be economical with the truth. On crew losses, see Dugan and Stewart, 222.

53 Leon Wolfe, *Low-Level Mission* (New York: 1961), 182–183.

Chapter 15: Nearly, Nearly

1 Maurice Matloff, *Strategic Planning for Coalition Warfare 1943–1945* (Washington, D.C.: 1959), 130–133, 155–156.

2 Craven and Cate, II, 493, 496–497.

3 Eduard Mark, *Aerial Interdiction* (Washington, D.C.: 1993), Chapter 3; Lord Zuckerman, *From Apes to Warlords* (New York: 1978) 197–198.

4 Craven and Cate, II, 495.

5 Ibid., 525–526; Samuel E. Morison, *Sicily-Salerno-Anzio* (Boston: 1954).

6 Mark, Chapter 3, 9–10. Adding to the fuel crisis was the action of a panicky German supply officer who reacted to news of the invasion by blowing up the German Army's fuel storage facility at Naples: Martin Blumenson, *Salerno to Cassino* (Washington, D.C.: 1969), 98.

7 John G. Warren, *Airborne Missions in the Mediterranean* (Maxwell AFB: 1955), 66–69; Clay Blair, *Ridgway's Paratroopers* (New York: 1985), 148–155.

8 Craven and Cate, II, 529–530.

9 William Ludlum (Mortensen interview), 55, CAFH.

10 Gordon P. Saville (Green interview), 83, USAFA.

11 Alan F. Wilt, "Sicily and Italy," in *Close Air Support,* Benjamin Franklin Cooling, ed., (Washington, D.C.: 1991), 220.

12 Elliott Roosevelt (Green interview), 18, USAFA; Barney Giles (Green interview), 64, USAFA; Mark, Chapter 4.

13 Bill Colgan, *Fighter-Bomber Pilot* (Blue Ridge Summit, Penn.: 1985), 41–42.

14 Ibid., 63–65.

15 Dominick Graham and Shelford Bidwell, *Tug of War* (London: 1986), 421–424; David Hapgood and David Richardson, *Monte Cassino* (New York: 1984), 144 passim; James Parton, *Air Force Spoken Here* (Bethesda, Md.: 1986), 361–364; Craven and Cate, III, 362–364; Saville, 46.

16 Craven and Cate, III, 356.

17 Blumenson, 428–431.

18 Lucian K. Truscott, Jr., *Command Missions* (New York: 1953), 353–355.

19 Diary, Nov. 19, 1943, John P. Lucas Papers, USAMHI; Walter T. Kerwin (Doehle interview), USAMHI. Kerwin was a brigade artillery officer at Anzio who surveyed the effects, and counted the duds, of incoming artillery fire.

20 Mark, 131.

21 Richard Davis, *Spaatz and the Air War in Europe* (Washington, D.C.: 1993), 455–456.

22 Craven and Cate, II, 725–726.

23 Idwal Edwards (Green interview), 21, USAFA.

24 Nathan Twining (Green interview), 30, USAFA.

25 John Muirhead, *Those Who Fall* (New York: 1986), 5.

26 Matthew Cooper, *The German Air Force 1939–1945* (London: 1981), 307; David Irving, *The Rise and Fall of the Luftwaffe* (Boston: 1973), 239.

27 Letter, Arnold to Eaker (no date, but around March 1, 1944), Vol. 1 Eaker-Arnold Correspondence, Eaker Papers, Box 22, MD, LC; Craven and Cate, III, 365.

28 Saville, 34–35.

29 Parton, 372–375.

30 "German records do not support D'Aurelio's statement": Mark, 145, fn. 8.

31 Report, Zuckerman to Tedder, Dec. 28, 1943, "Air Attacks on Rail and Road Communications," Microfilm 519.425-1, HRA. For a critical view, see Henry D. Lytton, "Bombing

Policy in the Rome and Pre-Normandy Invasion Aerial Campaigns of World War II," *Military Affairs,* April 1983.

32 Craven and Cate, III, 373–374.

33 Ibid., 367–368.

34 Colgan, 72–73.

35 Mark, Chapter 5, p. 17, fn. 91. The standard account has long been F. W. Sallagar, *Operation STRANGLE* (Santa Monica: 1972), which offers a different and less nuanced perspective on this operation.

36 Craven and Cate, III, 384–391.

37 Mark, Chapter 6, page 10, fn. 32.

38 Ernest F. Fisher, Jr., *Cassino to the Alps* (Washington, D.C.: 1977); Georges Boule *Le CEF en Italie: Les Campagnes de Printemps et d'Eté* (Paris: 1973), 60–78; Mark Clark, *Calculated Risk* (New York: 1951).

39 Leroy Newby, *Target Ploesti* (San Rafael, Calif.: 1983), 82–84.

40 Mark, Chapter 6.

41 Diary, May 25, 1944, Don Carleton Papers, Hoover Institution, Stanford University. Carleton was Truscott's chief of staff. Cf. Truscott, 375–376; Fisher, 165–166.

Chapter 16: The Price of Progress

1 Diary, May 16, 1942, Spaatz Papers, MD, LC; Richard Davis, *Spaatz and the Air War in Europe* (Washington, D.C.: 1993), 116–117.

2 Ira C. Eaker (Joe B. Green interview), 14, USAFA.

3 Diary, May 28, 1942, Arnold Papers, MD, LC; Cf. John F. Whiteley, *Early Army Aviation* (Manhattan, Kans.: 1975), 143.

4 David E. Omissi, *Air Power and Colonial Control 1919–1939* (Manchester, England: 1991), 154; Denis Richards, *Portal of Hungerford* (London: 1977), 108–110.

5 Charles Webster and Noble Frankland, *The Strategic Bombing Offensive Against Germany* (London: 1961), I, 172–180.

6 Arthur Harris (Shaughnessy interview), 75–76, BL, CU.

7 Paul Tibbets, *The Tibbets Story* (New York: 1977), 97.

8 F. H. Hinsley, et al., *British Intelligence in the Second World War* (Cambridge, England: 1986), II, 269.

9 Eaker (Green interview), 9–10, USAFA. Eaker claims to have threatened to resign if ordered to join Harris's night bombing campaign and to make a public issue of it, and that Arnold

reacted with delight at this threat. Neither Churchill nor Portal would have wanted a story like this to break in the U.S. press. Also see, *Global Mission* ms. XXII 31–32, Arnold Papers, MD, LC, and Spaatz (Shaughnessy interview), 67, BL, CU.

10 Spaatz protested to Arnold against Andrews's appointment to the ETO: Diary, Feb. 23, 1943, Spaatz Papers, MD, LC. He could hardly bear the thought of Andrews, rather than himself, directing the Combined Bomber Offensive.

11 Craven and Cate, II, 305–307; Haywood S. Hansell, *The Air Plan that Defeated Hitler* (Atlanta: 1972), 157–158.

12 Jonathan Foster Fanton, *Robert A. Lovett: The War Years* (Yale University, Ph.D.: 1977), 162.

13 Hansell, 167.

14 Tibbets, 9–21.

15 Beirne Lay, Jr., and Sy Bartlett, *Twelve O'Clock High* (New York: 1948), Chapters 2 and 3.

16 Letter, Spaatz to Arnold, Aug. 24, 1942, Spaatz Papers, MD, LC.

17 Davis, 166.

18 Tibbets (Green interview), 34–35, USAFA.

19 Kuter (Ahmann/Sturm interview), 279, CAFH.

20 Eaker (Green interview), 17, USAFA.

21 Robert W. Burns (McCants, Jr.), 49, CAFH. Burns commanded a B-17 squadron.

22 Archie J. Old (Ahmann interview), 170–171; John Comer, *Combat Crew* (New York: 1989), 110.

23 Kuter, 263.

24 Report, Edward V. Rickenbacker to Henry L. Stimson, Oct. 13, 1942, Rickenbacker Papers, MD, LC.

25 Carl A. Spaatz (Shaughnessy interview), 67.

26 Craven and Cate, II, 222.

27 Stephen MacFarland and Wesley P. Newton, *To Command the Sky* (Washington, D.C.: 1991), 93.

28 William R. Emerson, "Operation Pointblank," in Harry Borowski, ed., *Harmon Memorial Lectures* (Washington, D.C.: 1989), 445.

29 Eighth Air Force, *The First 1100 Bombers Dispatched by the VIII Bomber Command* (Dec. 9, 1942), 18–22, 27.

30 Tibbets, 97. The 44th Bomb Group was for a long time the only B-24 group in the Eighth. It became known as "the hard-luck group."

31 Williamson Murray, *Luftwaffe: Strategy for Defeat* (Baltimore: 1985), 174.

32 Hansell, 114; Kit C. Carter and Robert Mueller, *Combat Chronology* (Washington, D.C.: 1991), 786–787.

33 Craven and Cate, II, 323–325, 327.

34 Tibbets (Green interview), 36–37, USAFA.

35 Carter and Mueller, 107–108; Craven and Cate, II, 326, 343–344.

36 Craven and Cate, II, 330–334.

37 Craven and Cate, II, 340.

38 Charles Francis, *Flak Bait* (New York: 1948), 113 passim; Roger A. Freeman, *B-26 Marauder at War* (New York: 1978), 52–68.

39 Hinsley, II, 517; Webster and Frankland, I, 490; II, 56.

40 Lawrence Boylan, *The Development of the Long Range Escort Fighter* USAF Study #136 (Maxwell AFB: 1955), 87; Arthur Gordon, "Three Years Over Europe," *Air Force,* September 1945.

41 Archie Old (Ahmann interview), 152, CAFH.

42 Letter, Eaker to Myers, August 12, 1943, Eaker Papers, MD, LC. Eaker informed Major General Benny Meyers that Masefield "has done some combat missions with our units and has written several articles which have been a great help. . . . Masefield has proven a great friend to us here. . . ."

43 MacFarland and Newton, 152–153; Memoir, Chapter IV, 17–18, Richard Hughes Papers, LBJ Presidential Library, Austin, Tex.

44 MacKinley Kantor, *Mission with LeMay* (Garden City, N.Y.: 1965), 232–245; Craven and Cate, II, 331–345; Burns, 47.

45 Old.

46 Kuter (Ahmann and Sturm), 410; Cecil E. Combs (Ahmann interview), 61, CAFH.

47 Hunter Harris (Ahmann interview), 88–89, CAFH; Old, 198–199; Russell A. Strong, *First Over Germany* (Kalamazoo: 1982), 14–15.

48 Hansell, 118–119.

49 Letter, Arnold to Eisenhower, June 22, 1942, Arnold Papers, MD, LC. Spaatz, however, proved to be flexible on this question. See Diary, October 22, 1942, Spaatz Papers.

50 Fred M. Dean (Emmons interview), 14–17 and Marvin McNickle (Ahmann interview), 21–25, CAFH.

51 Edward J. Sims, *Fighter Tactics and Strategy, 1914–1970* (New York: 1960), 93.

52 John Alison (Thompson interview), 222–223.

53 Robert S. Johnson, *Thunderbolt!* (New York: 1958), 120–121.

54 Hunter, 46; Philip D. Caine, *Eagles of the RAF* (Washington, D.C.: 1991) 285.

55 MacFarland and Newton, 106.

56 Dictations, Reel 27, Side 1, pp. 9–10, Rickenbacker Papers, MD, LC; Davis, 96–97.

57 Francis Gabreski, with Carl Molesworth, *Gabby* (New York: 1991), Chapter Three; Hubert Zemke, and Roger A. Freeman, *Zemke's Wolf Pack* (New York: 1991), 63.

58 Boylan, 91–92.

59 William E. Kepner (Green interview), 23–24, USAFA.

60 There is an undated letter in the Eaker Papers from Arnold to the ETO commander, Lieutenant General Jacob Devers, to be forwarded to Eaker. It says sweeps "accomplish nothing except to burn up gasoline." This roundabout procedure seems intended to put pressure on Hunter while keeping Arnold's criticisms out of the documentary record. Eaker evidently informed Hunter of its contents and hinted a cable was being considered that would put these criticisms into the record. Hunter's reply, dated July 20, begins "If such a cablegram should be received, I recommend my immediate relief from command of the VIII Fighter Command." Eaker Papers, Box 18, MD, LC.

Chapter 17: Pointblank

1 David Irving, *The Rise and Fall of the Luftwaffe* (Boston: 1973), 150.

2 Craven and Cate, II, 364–367.

3 Roger A. Freeman, *The Mighty Eighth* (New York: 1989), 63.

4 Grover C. Hall, *1000 Destroyed* (Montgomery, Ala.: 1946), 20.

5 Lynn Farnol, et al., *To the Limit of Their Endurance* (England: 1943), Spaatz Papers, MD, LC; Roger A. Freeman, *The Mighty Eighth War Diary* (New York: 1981), 83.

6 Hughes, memoir, Chapter IV, 31–33.

7 Craven and Cate, II, 483.

8 Hubert Zemke, with Roger Freeman, *Zemke's Wolf Pack* (New York: 1990), 109.

9   Dale O. Smith, *Screaming Eagle* (Chapel Hill, N.C.: 1987) page 141.

10   Martin Middlebrook, *The Schweinfurt-Regensburg Mission* (London: 1983), 80; Archie J. Old (Ahmann interview), 200–202, CAFH.

11   John Comer, *Combat Crew* (New York: 1989), 52.

12   Middlebrook, 197.

13   Irving, 248.

14   Zemke, 110–112.

15   Donald L. Caldwell, *JG 26* (New York: 1991), 190–191.

16   Williamson Murray, *Luftwaffe* (Annapolis: 1983), 176.

17   Curtis E. LeMay, with McKinlay Kantor, *Mission with LeMay* (New York: 1965), 290–291, 296.

18   Freeman, *Mighty Eighth War Diary,* 89–90, has 60 destroyed and four written off. LeMay admitted to leaving "about 20" in North Africa: Thomas Coffey, *Decision Over Schweinfurt* (New York: 1977), 234. Considering that he entered the Continent with 139 B-17s, had 24 shot down, and took off from North Africa with 60, the true figure must be 50+ aircraft abandoned.

19   Jacob E. Smart (Green interview), 16, USAFA. The word Smart uses to describe Arnold is "distracted," which suggests considerable mental distress.

20   Barney Giles (Green interview), 37–38, USAFA.

21   U.S. Strategic Bombing Survey, *Europe: Overall Report* (Washington, D.C.: 1945), Chart 14, p. 28; Albert Speer, *Inside the Third Reich* (New York: 1970), 285, puts the loss at a temporary fall of 17 percent of total output. Cf. USSBS *Anti-Friction Bearing Industry* (Washington, D.C.: 1946).

22   Charles Webster and Noble Frankland, *The Strategic Bombing Offensive* (London: 1961), II, 158–160, 283–284.

23   Richard Suchenwirth, *Command and Leadership in the GAF,* USAF Study #174 (Maxwell AFB: 1969), 284–290. Milch claimed that Hitler berated Jeschonnek into killing himself (Irving 235 and Murray 176, 198). Suchenwirth makes a more convincing case to the contrary; that Hitler was unusually sympathetic toward him.

24   William E. Kepner (Green interview), 26–28, USAFA; Kepner (Hicks and Philips interview), unpaginated, Quesada Papers, USAMHI; Bernard Boylan, *Development of the Long Range*

Escort Fighter, USAF Study #136 (Maxwell AFB: 1955), 132–133; Also see Barney M. Giles (Porretto interview), 1–3, and (Hasdorff interview), 63–65, both CAFH.

25 Report, Kepner to Eaker, Aug. 31, 1943, Spaatz Papers, MD, LC. For Hunter's reaction to his relief, see Frank O'D. Hunter (Green interview), 11–12, USAFA.

26 Letter, Kepner to Murray Green, March 16, 1970, Murray Green Collection, USAFA.

27 Robert S. Johnson, *Thunderbolt!* (New York: 1956), 146.

28 Francis Gabreski, with Carl Molesworth, *Gabby* (New York: 1991), 111–112.

29 Hubert Zemke, with Roger A. Freeman, *Zemke's Wolf Pack* (New York: 1988), 114–115.

30 Diary, September 3, 1943, Arnold Papers, MD, LC.

31 Craven and Cate, II, 693; Freeman, *Mighty Eighth,* 73.

32 Charles Messenger, *Bomber Harris* (London: 1983), 132.

33 R. V. Jones, *Most Secret War* (London: 1974), 319, 392.

34 Adolf Galland, "The Birth, Life and Death of the German Day Fighter Arm," 37, Spaatz Papers, MD, LC; Irving 243–244. GAF pilots managed to fly three sorties on several occasions in 1943, but never in 1944. Even second missions weren't flown unless there were 25 planes ready to go up.

35 Craven and Cate, II, 695.

36 Comer, 140.

37 Ian Hawkins, *The Munster Raid* (London: 1987), 85.

38 Earle Partridge (Sturm and Ahmann), 400–401, CAFH.

39 Hawkins, 188.

40 Zemke, 123; Johnson, 215–217.

41 Martin W. Bowman, *Castles in the Air* (Wellingborough, England: 1984), 96. Hughes didn't get a commendation; his group commander wouldn't excuse the fact that he'd broken formation.

42 Freeman, *Mighty Eighth War Diary,* 126.

43 Speer, 286.

44 Samuel Anderson (Ahmann interview), 252–253, CAFH; Clarence Irvine (Green interview), 22, USAFA. Cf. Devon Francis, *Flak Bait* (New York: 1948). Anderson's reward was a star and command of the B-26s; the 3rd Bomb Wing commander, Francis Brady was fired. Irvine, too, got a star, and command of a B-24 wing in Fifteenth Air Force. There was also a problem in that the 386th Bomb Group was commanded by the alcoholic

Lester Maitland. After disgracing himself in China (see Chapter 4, fn. 52), he got a second chance by promising Arnold never to drink again. When Arnold visited England in August-September 1943 Maitland was clearly drunk. The solution to this problem was to throw Maitland out of the AAF. He became an Episcopalian priest.

45 Freeman, *The Mighty Eighth,* 60–62.

46 Ira C. Eaker (Green interview), I, 29, USAFA.

47 Copp, 403.

48 Barney M. Giles (Hasdorff), 23.

49 Idwal Edwards (Green interview), 23, 49 loc. cit. Edwards was Eaker's chief of staff after June 1943.

50 A. C. Peterson (Shaughnessy interview), 25–27, BL, CU.

51 Memo, Kuter to Arnold, October 26, 1943, Kuter Papers, Special Collections, USAFA.

52 Leon Johnson (Green interview), 14, USAFA.

53 Richard Davis, *Spaatz and the Air War in Europe* (Washington, D.C.: 1993), 288.

54 Bernard Boylan, *Development of the Long Range Escort Fighter,* USAF Study #136 (Maxwell AFB: 1955).

55 Kit C. Carter and Robert Mueller, *Combat Chronology* 215–223 (Washington, D.C.: 1991), 215–233.

56 Diary, Dec. 8, 1943; *Global Mission* ms. XXII, 34, both in Arnold Papers, MD, LC.

57 Letter, Arnold to Spaatz (undated but evidently February 1944), Microfilm A1657A, Frames 1082–1085, HRA. Hansell aptly called it "an attempt to gain stature through size" (Green interview), 17, USAFA. All this subtlety was lost on Eisenhower, who looked at USSTAF from a military perspective and, as he told Marshall, couldn't figure it out: Albert D. Chandler, *The Papers of Dwight D. Eisenhower* (Baltimore: 1970), III, 1611–1612.

58 Letter, Eaker to Fechet, Dec. 22, 1943, Eaker Papers, MD, LC. According to Clarence Irvine, there was a bitter three or four hour argument between Arnold and Eaker over this. It was so intense and involved so much anguish that Irvine couldn't bear to listen to it.

59 Craven and Cate, III, 8.

60 Kepner letter to Murray Green, op. cit.; Partridge 238–239. Partridge, who was present, gives a somewhat different account. There are at least four Doolittle versions to choose

from. The most recent is Jimmy Doolittle, with Carroll V. Glines, *I Could Never Be So Lucky Again* (New York: 1991), 380.

Chapter 18: *Jägerschreck*

1 Forrest C. Pogue, *George C. Marshall: Organizer of Victory* (New York: 1973), 321–325.

2 Lewis Brereton, *The Brereton Diaries* (New York: 1947). Brereton's life-style didn't endear him to the theater commander, Jacob Devers, who was irked to discover that Brereton "carried a woman around with him all the time." Devers (Green interview), 23, USAFA.

3 Arthur Harris (Shaughnessy interview), 79, BL, CU. LeMay (Green interview) 15, USAFA, called Leigh-Mallory "a bump on a log." For a recent, more flattering view, see the biography of Leigh-Mallory: Bill Newton-Dunn, *Big Wing* (London: 1992).

4 Lynn D. Farnol, et al. "To the Limit of Their Endurance," Spaatz Papers, MD, LC.

5 VIII Fighter Command, *"Achtung Indianer!"* (England, 1944), Microfilm 168.6005, Frame 54, HRA; Bernard Boylan, *Development of the Long Range Escort Fighter,* USAF Study #136 (Maxwell AFB: 1956). It wasn't only extra tankage that gave the P-51 a bomber's range. It was a gas miser, while the P-47 guzzled fuel at a rate of two gallons a minute, rising to three a minute in combat.

6 William E. Kepner (Hicks and Philips interview), unpaginated, Quesada Papers, USAMHI.

7 Craven and Cate, III, 22–24.

8 War Department, *The U.S. Army Medal of Honor* (Washington, D.C.: 1948), 286; Martin W. Bowman, *Castles in the Air* (Wellingborough, England: 1984), 111.

9 Craven and Cate, III, 95.

10 Kit C. Carter and Robert Mueller, *Combat Chronology* revised edition (Washington, D.C.: 1991), 268. For some reason this mission does not appear in Craven and Cate. Carter and Mueller were USAF historians working from official records.

11 Eighth Air Force, *Tactical Developments August 1942–May 1945,* Microfilm, 520.04–11, HRA. Kepner states clearly that in his view it was the Thunderbolt that broke the back of GAF

fighter defenses. The Mustang did not create air superiority over Germany so much as it inherited and maintained it.

12 Memoir, Chapter IV, 40, Richard D'Oyly Hughes papers, LBJ Presidential Library, Austin, Tex.

13 Craven and Cate, III, 33–35; *Combat Chronology*, 276.

14 Hughes, 41.

15 Bowman, 116.

16 Craven and Cate, III, 45; Roger A. Freeman, *Mighty Eighth War Diary* (New York: 1981), 172–190. In February the Eighth saw 299 heavy bombers shot down or written off due to damage: 20 percent of its strength. *AAF Statistical Digest*, 255, however, puts the loss at 271 heavy bombers.

17 Irving, 272; Albert Speer, *Inside the Third Reich* (New York: 1970), 332.

18 U.S. Strategic Bombing Survey, *Overall Report* (Washington, D.C.: 1946), 16–25; British Air Ministry *The Rise and Fall of the German Air Force 1933–1945* (London: 1948), 309.

19 Hubert Zemke, with Roger A. Freeman, *Zemke's Wolf Pack* (New York: 1988), 148.

20 Williamson Murray, *Luftwaffe* (Annapolis: 1985), 229.

21 Jimmy Doolittle with Carroll V. Glines, *I Could Never Be So Lucky Again* (New York: 1991), 397.

22 Roger A. Freeman, *The Mighty Eighth* (New York: 1989), 122.

23 Ian L. Hawkins, *Courage, Honor, Victory* (Bellevue, Wash.: 1987), 163.

24 Ibid., 167.

25 Craven and Cate, III, 50; Jerry Scutts, *Lion in the Sky: U.S. Eighth Air Force Fighter Operations 1942–1945* (Wellingborough, England: 1987), 53.

26 Richard Davis, *Spaatz and the Air War in Europe* (Washington, D.C.: 1993), 374; *Combat Chronology*, 287.

27 Bowman, 122–123.

28 Freeman, *The Mighty Eighth*, 123, puts it at 23. Craven and Cate, III, 51, puts escorts lost at 11.

29 Freeman, *War Diary*, 195.

30 Zemke, *Zemke's Wolf Pack*, 153.

31 *Combat Chronology*, 289; Donald L. Caldwell, *JG 26* (New York: 1991), 229. This mission does not appear in Craven and Cate.

32 Adolf Galland, "The Birth, Life and Death of the German Day Fighter Arm," 35, Spaatz Papers, MD, LC.
33 Farnol, 59.
34 Scutts, 57–58.
35 *Combat Chronology,* 312; Freeman, *Mighty Eighth,* 133. These April 1–13 Pointblank missions do not appear in Craven and Cate, presumably because Pointblank had formally ended.
36 *AAF Statistical Digest,* 255.
37 *Combat Chronology,* 314; Bowman, 130.
38 Freeman, *War Diary,* 217.
39 Caldwell, 233.
40 The Eighth lost or wrote off due to battle damage 420 heavy bombers in April 1944; its highest monthly loss of the war. Nearly 100 more were destroyed in accidents. See *AAF Statistical Digest.*
41 Diary, April 20, 1944, Spaatz Papers, MD, LC.
42 Caldwell, 236; Galland, 36. On the general decline in pilot quality, cf. U.S. Strategic Bombing Survey, *The Defeat of the German Air Force* (Washington, D.C.: 1946), 3.
43 Farnol, 69.
44 Murray, Table LIV, 228.
45 F. H. Hinsley, et al., *British Intelligence in the Second World War* (Cambridge, England: 1988), III, Part 2, p. 104 et seq.

Chapter 19: Liberation Skies
 1 Lord Zuckerman, *From Apes to Warlords* (New York: 1978), 232; Charles P. Kindleberger, "World War II Bombing Strategy," *Encounter* Nov. 1978; Lord Zuckerman, "Bombs and Illusions in World War II," *Encounter* June 1979; Walt Whitman Rostow, *Pre-Invasion Bombing Strategy* (Austin, Tex.: 1981), 12 passim.
 2 Memo, "Conference Held at AEAF Headquarters, Feb. 15, 1944," Spaatz Papers, MD, LC.
 3 Carl A. Spaatz (Hopper interview), 15–16, Spaatz Papers, MD, LC.
 4 Charles Messenger, *Bomber Harris* (London: 1980), 157–161.
 5 Winston S. Churchill, *The Second World War* (Boston: 1953), 466–468; Lord Tedder, *With Prejudice* (London: 1966), 529–531.
 6 Samuel Anderson (Ahmann interview), 244; Memoir, Chapter

IV, 47, Richard Hughes Papers, LBJ Presidential Library, Austin, Tex.

7 Rostow, 116–118; Frederick E. Smith (Hasdorff and Parrish), 86–87.

8 Anthony Cave Brown, *Bodyguard of Lies* (New York: 1975), 522.

9 Eduard Mark, *Aerial Interdiction* (Washington, D.C.: 1993), Chapter 7.

10 Eighth Air Force, *Tactical Development, August 1942–May 1945*, Microfilm 520.04-11, HRC.

11 Craven and Cate, III, 103n.

12 Ibid., III, 176–177.

13 Adolf Galland, *The First and the Last* (New York: 1954), 210.

14 Carter and Mueller, *Combat Chronology,* 357.

15 Martin Caidin, *Fork-Tailed Devil* (New York: 1971), 135.

16 Craven and Cate, III, 155.

17 *Tactical Development,* 13-A.

18 Kenneth B. Wolfe (Green interview), 50; and Hugh Knerr (Green interview), 42, both USAFA.

19 St. Clair Street (Green), 29, USAFA.

20 Robert Frank Futrell, *The Command of Observation Aviation,* USAF Study #24 (Maxwell AFB: 1956), 6, 10, 22.

21 Elliott Roosevelt (Green interview), 17; Barney M. Giles (Green interview), 64, both USAFA.

22 George W. Goddard, *Overview* (Garden City, N.Y.: 1969), 282–284.

23 Roosevelt, 18.

24 Samuel Anderson, (Ahmann interview), 378.

25 Thomas G. Ivie, *Aerial Reconnaissance: The 10th Photo Group* (Carrolton, Tex.: 1980), 175–176.

26 Gordon Harrison, *Cross-Channel Attack* (Washington, D.C.: 1951), 278–300; Clay Blair, *Ridgway's Paratroopers* (New York: 1985), 213–235.

27 Smith, 89–91.

28 Samuel Anderson (Ahmann interview), 256; Craven and Cate, III, 191–192; Devon Francis, *Flak Bait* (New York: 1948), 250–251.

29 Carl H. Moore, *Flying the B-26 Marauder Over Europe* (Blue Ridge Summit, Pa.: 1985), 89–90.

30 Otto P. Weyland (Green interview), 17, USAFA.

31 William E. Kepner (Hicks interview), n.p., USAMHI.
32 British Air Ministry, *The Rise and Fall of the German Air Force* (London: 1947), 328–329; Adolf Galland, "The Birth, Life and Death of the German Day Fighter Arm," 51, Spaatz Papers, MD, LC.
33 Hubert Zemke, with Roger A. Freeman, *Zemke's Wolf Pack* (New York: 1988), 177–178.
34 Diary, June 12, 1944, Spaatz Papers, MD, LC; Craven and Cate, 188–194.
35 Chester Wilmot, *The Struggle for Europe* (New York: 1963), 273–280.
36 Vincent Orange, *Coningham* (London: 1989), 160, 170, 177–178.
37 Mark, Chapter 7.
38 Chester Hansen Papers: Hansen Diary—Bradley Commentaries 30A/S-21, S-8, Archives, USAMHI.
39 British Air Ministry, 330–332; Galland, "Birth, Life and Death . . ." 51; *The First and the Last,* 214–215.
40 Anderson, 255.
41 Kepner (Hicks interview).
42 Anthony V. Grossetta (Leish interview), 21, BL, CU. He commanded the 406th Fighter Group.
43 Diary, June 18, 1944, Chester Hansen Papers, USAMHI.
44 Quesada (Burg interview), 178–179.
45 L. F. Ellis, *Victory in the West* (London: 1962), I, 316.
46 William Dunn, *Fighter Pilot* (Lexington, Ky.: 1983), 140.
47 Carlo D'Este, *Decision in Normandy* (New York: 1984), 370 passim.
48 Diary, June 15, 17, 1944, Spaatz Papers, MD, LC.
49 Report, "Investigation of Operation COBRA," 1, Spaatz Papers, MD, LC.
50 Diary, July 23, 1944, Vandenberg Papers, MD, LC.
51 Martin Blumenson, *Breakout and Pursuit* (Washington, D.C.: 1961), 232–235.
52 Quesada (Burg), 187–188; Craven and Cate, III, 230–233.
53 "Investigation of Operation COBRA," 2. Also see "Special Report on Operations, July 24 and 25, 1944," Spaatz Papers, MD, LC. Anderson, 283–284, said he had a near mutiny on his hands after Spaatz identified the 409th Bomb Group (M) as being responsible for McNair's death. However, Spaatz's

Diary, July 27, 1944, refers only to heavy bombers dropping their ordnance short.

54 Omar Bradley, *A Soldier's Story* (New York: 1951), 345; Omar Bradley and Clay Blair, *A General's Life* (New York: 1985), 1983. He even attempted to create a documentary record to cover his tracks: see Hansen Diary, Memorandum for Record, July 25, 1944, Archives, USAMHI. Doubt has recently been cast on whether this memo was produced at the time, or was written some weeks later: Davis, Chapter 13, fn. 60.

55 Otto P. Weyland (Leish interview), 7–8, BL, CU; Weyland (Green interview), 13, USAFA.

56 Grossetta, 30.

57 Robert L. George, *Ninth Air Force April–Nov. 1944* USAF Study 36 (Maxwell AFB: 1945), 129–131, 166–167.

58 Milton Shulman, *Defeat in the West* (London: 1947) 145–147.

59 F. H. Hinsley, *British Intelligence in the Second World War* III, Part 2, 236–245; Donald L. Cantwell, *JG 26* (New York: 1991), 262.

60 Albert D. Chandler, *Papers of Dwight D. Eisenhower* (Baltimore: 1970) III, 1947, 2001–2, 2008, 2013.

61 Blumenson, 553–558; Ellis, 448; George, 169–171; Richard P. Hallion, *Strike from the Sky* (Washington, D.C.: 1989), 219–222.

62 D'Este, 438–439; Bradley and Blair, 304.

63 XIX TAC, "Twelve Thousand Fighter-Bomber Sorties," Sept. 30, 1944, Spaatz Papers, MD, LC.

64 Craven and Cate, III, 262–264.

65 AAF Evaluation Board, *Tactics and Techniques Developed by the U.S. TACs in the ETO* (Washington, D.C.: 1945).

66 David Spires, Unpublished, untitled study of XIX TAC, 136, on file at CAFH.

67 Craven and Cate, III, 420–427.

68 John A. Warren, *Airborne Operations in the Mediterranean* USAF Study 74 (Maxwell AFB: 1955), 93–102; Jacob A. Devers (Green interview), 17–18, USAFA; cf. Robert H. Adleman and George Walton, *The Champagne Campaign* (New York: 1966).

69 William Taylor, in Stuart Leuchner and Oliver Jensen eds., *High Honor* (Washington, D.C.: 1990), 344.

70 Jeffrey C. Clarke, *From the Riviera to the Rhine* (Washington,

D.C.: 1993); Lucian K. Truscott, *Command Missions* (New York: 1954).
71 Bill Colgan, *Fighter-Bomber Pilot* (Blue Ridge Summit, Pa.: 1985), 108–110.
72 Gordon P. Saville (Green interview), 40, USAFA.

Chapter 20: Whoosh!
1 Laurence S. Kuter Papers: Folders 8–11, Box 2, Special Collections, USAFA; Thomas A. Julian, *Operation FRANTIC* (Syracuse University, Ph.D. dissertation, 1967), 97–104; Daniel P. Bolger, *Reluctant Allies* (Chicago University, Ph.D. dissertation, 1986), Chapter 2.
2 Letter, Green to Knerr, September 21, 1971, Knerr Papers, USAFA.
3 Craven and Cate, III, 312.
4 Martin W. Bowman, *Castles in the Air* (Wellingborough, England: 1984), 152.
5 James A. Goodson, *Tumult in the Clouds* (New York: 1983), 85–86. Goodson was flying this mission, in a P-51.
6 Archie J. Old, "Report on Shuttle Mission to Russia," July 6, 1944, Microfilm 522.01-1, HRA; Bolger, 184.
7 Archie Old (Ahmann interview), 277–279, CAFH; Glenn B. Infield, *The Poltava Affair* (New York: 1973), 131–134, Ian L. Hawkins, *Courage*Honor*Victory* (Bellevue, Wa.: 1987), 220. Craven and Cate, III, 314 says 15 Mustangs were destroyed. All the Mustangs were at Piryatin and, as Old's official report makes clear, none were destroyed. The fighters destroyed at Poltava were Red Air Force Yaks.
8 Winston S. Churchill, *The Second World War* (Boston: 1953), VI, 132–149; Bolger, 263–265; Julian, 282–287.
9 U.S. Strategic Bombing Survey, 2nd ed., *Ordnance Industry Report; Munitions Division* (Washington, D.C.: 1947), 15.
10 Craven and Cate, III, 317; Neil Orpen, *Airlift to Warsaw* (Norman, Okla.: 1984), 158–160.
11 Diary, Sept. 2–3, 1944, Floyd Parks Papers, Archives, USAMHI. Parks was Brereton's chief of staff.
12 F. H. Hinsley, et al., *British Intelligence in the Second World War* (Cambridge, England: 1989), III, Pt. 2, 383–384.
13 Clay Blair, *Ridgway's Paratroopers* (New York: 1985), 344.
14 John G. Warren, *Airborne Operations in the ETO* Study 97 (Maxwell AFB: 1956), Chapter 2.

15 Albert H. Davis, et al., *The 56th Fighter Group in World War II* (Washington, D.C.: 1948), 79–81.

16 Roger A. Freeman, *Mighty Eighth War Diary* (New York: 1981), 349.

17 John H. Lowden, *Silent Wings at War* (Washington, D.C.: 1992), 104–105.

18 Craven and Cate, III, 610.

19 Hubert Zemke, with Roger A. Freeman, *Zemke's Wolf Pack* (New York: 1988), 209.

20 Kit C. Carter and Robert Mueller, *Combat Chronology* rev. ed. (Washington, D.C.: 1991), 448–450.

21 John M. Gray, "Sturm Staffel Flieger," *Friends Journal,* USAF Museum, Spring 1992. This contains an interview with Oscar Boesch, one of the first men to fly the FW-190/A-8 in combat.

22 Craven and Cate, III, 640.

23 Freeman, *Mighty Eighth War Diary,* 354–355.

24 Roger A. Freeman, *The Mighty Eighth* (New York: 1970), 177; cf. *Combat Chronology,* 461.

25 Chuck Yeager, with Leo Janos, *Yeager* (New York: 1985), 56–57.

26 Williamson Murray, *Luftwaffe* (Annapolis: 1983), 276.

27 Jerry Scutts, *Lion in the Sky* (Wellingborough, England: 1987), 120.

28 *Combat Chronology,* 507.

29 AAF, *Statistical Digest: World War II* (Washington, D.C.: 1945), 255.

30 William H. Taylor, in Stuart Leuchner and Oliver Jensen, eds., *High Honor* (Washington, D.C.: 1989), 342.

31 Elwood Quesada, "The Effects of Anti-Aircraft Artillery on IX TAC Operations," *Coast Guard Artillery Journal* Sept.–Oct. 1946.

32 Leroy Newby, *Target Ploesti* (San Rafael, Calif.: 1983), 87–88; John Comer, *Combat Crew* (New York: 1988).

33 U.S. Strategic Bombing Survey, *European War,* Report #115, (Washington, D.C.: 1947), 7–21.

34 Murray, 182, 191.

35 Elmer Bendiner, *The Fall of Fortresses* (New York: 1980), 138–139.

36 Guy Hartcup, *The Challenge of War* (London: 1969), 170–181.

37 Letter, Arnold to Kenney, Oct. 8, 1943, Kenney Papers,

CAFH; Letter, Spaatz to Arnold, Oct. 4, 1944, Spaatz Papers.
MD, LC; Earle E. Partridge (Green interview), 15–16,
USAFA.

38 AAF, *Statistical Digest: World War II,* 255–256.

39 Gordon P. Saville (Green interview), 56, USAFA.

40 AC/AS Intelligence, *Command Informational Intelligence Series,* 44–103 to 44–107: "GAF Fighter Aircraft," Spaatz Papers, MD, LC.

41 Grandison Gardner (Shaughnessy interview), 35, BL, CU.

42 Donald J. Norton, *Larry: A Biography of Lawrence D. Bell* (Chicago: 1981), 117–125; Raymond Wagner, *American Combat Planes* (Garden City, N.Y.: 1968), 244–245; John Rae Bell, *Climb to Greatness* (Cambridge, Mass.: 1968), 164–167.

43 Edward Sims, *Fighter Tactics and Strategy 1914–1970* (New York: 1975), 201. When this idea was put to Arnold, he ordered the Air Staff to think again: Memo to CAS, from Major General H. A. Craig, May 18, 1944, "Defense Against Enemy Jet Propelled Aircraft," Spaatz Papers, MD, LC.

44 David Irving, *The Rise and Fall of the Luftwaffe* (New York: 1973), 220, 284–287; British Air Ministry, 313.

45 Jeffrey Ethell and Alfred Price, *The German Jets in Combat* (New York: 1980), 24–25.

46 Orvall R. Cook (Emmons and Ahmann interview), 266, CAFH.

47 Ethell and Price, 31.

48 Laddie Lucas, *Out of the Blue* (London: 1985), 263.

49 William H. Kepner (Green interview), 50–51, USAFA; Partridge, 424; Quesada (Long and Stephenson), USAMHI.

Chapter 21: Bloody Sideshow

1 Richard Davis, *Spaatz and the Air War in Europe* (Washington, D.C.: 1993), 461–462.

2 Leroy Newby, *Target Ploesti* (San Rafael, Calif.: 1987), 9–10.

3 British Air Ministry, *The Rise and Fall of the German Air Force* (London: 1948), 264–265.

4 Craven and Cate, III, 351; U.S. Strategic Bombing Survey, *The Defeat of the German Air Force* (Washington, D.C.: 1947), 8; William R. Cubbins, *War of the Cottontails* (Chapel Hill: 1989), 12.

5 Craven and Cate, III, 41–42; Kit C. Carter and Robert

Mueller, *Combat Chronology* rev. ed. (Washington, D.C.: 1991), 277.

6 Kenn C. Rust, *The Fifteenth Air Force Story* (Temple City, Calif.: 1976), 14.

7 John Muirhead, *Those Who Fall* (New York: 1988), 54–55.

8 Nathan Twining (Green interview), 32–33, USAFA.

9 Letter, Arnold to Eaker (no date, but approximately March 1, 1944), vol. 1, Eaker-Arnold correspondence, Eaker Papers, MD, LC.

10 Rust, 16–17.

11 Muirhead, 163–167.

12 Craven and Cate, III, 390–391.

13 Cubbins, 21–22.

14 Muirhead, 118.

15 Cubbins, 69.

16 Kenneth P. Werrell, "Friendly Rivals: the Eighth and Fifteenth Air Forces in World War II," *Air Power Historian,* Summer 1991.

17 Twining, 30–31.

18 Daniel Bolger, *Reluctant Allies* (Chicago University, Ph.D., 1986), 107–122; Thomas A. Julian, *Operation Frantic* (Syracuse University, Ph.D., 1967), Chapter V; Cf. Glenn B. Infield, *The Poltava Affair* (New York: 1973).

19 Rust, 31–32.

20 Muirhead, 132–133,

21 Newby, 60 passim.

22 Craven and Cate, III, 283; Leon Wolfe, *Low-Level Mission* (New York: 1961), 215–216; Cubbins, 180–181.

23 Rust, 27; *Aerial Victory Credits* (Maxwell AFB: 1989).

24 *Combat Chronology* (Washington, D.C.: 1973), 382.

25 Craven and Cate, III, 303.

26 Twining (Momsher interview), 20, CAFH.

27 William Carigan, *Ad Lib: Flying the B-24 Liberator* (Manhattan, Kans.: 1988), 77.

28 Craven and Cate, III, 298; Twining (Momsher), 13.

29 Ernest F. Fisher, Jr., *Cassino to the Alps* (Washington, D.C.: 1977), 236 passim.

30 Mark Clark, *Calculated Risk* (New York: 1950), 378.

31 Craven and Cate, III, 403–405.

32 Bill Colgan, *Fighter-Bomber Pilot* (Blue Ridge Summit, Pa.: 1985), 94–96.
33 Craven and Cate, III, 423.
34 F. H. Hinsley, et al., *British Intelligence in the Second World War* (Cambridge, England, 1986), III, Part 2, 274.
35 Monro McCloskey, *Secret Air Missions* (New York: 1966), 74–89. He commanded the 885th Bomb Squadron.
36 Jacob Devers (Green interview), 17–18; Frederick H. Smith (Green interview), 13, USAFA.
37 Burhans ms. in Robert T. Frederick Papers, Hoover Institution, Stanford, Calif. This manuscript, with Frederick's comments and corrections attached, is the most authoritative account of 1st Special Service Force.
38 James A. Huston, *Out of the Blue* (West Lafayette, Ind.: 1972), 188–190; John T. Warren, *Airborne Operations in the Mediterranean* (Maxwell AFB: 1956).
39 Army Air Forces, *The AAF in the Invasion of Southern France* (Washington, D.C.: 1945).
40 Saville, 38–39, claims to have been the originator of this idea, first selling it to the theater commander, General Sir Henry Maitland Wilson, who then imposed it on Devers and Patch. Lucian Truscott, *Command Missions* (New York: 1954), 403–405, tells a different story.
41 Jeffrey C. Clarke, *From the Riviera to the Rhine* (Washington, D.C.: 1993).
42 Kenn C. Rust, *The Twelfth Air Force Story* (Temple City, Calif.: 1975), 38–39.
43 Craven and Cate, III, 440.
44 Fisher, 302–309.
45 Craven and Cate, III, 470.
46 Fisher, 492, 496.
47 Rust, *Fifteenth Air Force,* 44.
48 Rust, *Twelfth Air Force,* 44.

Chapter 22: A TAC Attack

1 Gordon Saville (Green interview) 64, USAFA; Memoir, Chapter IV, Richard Hughes Papers, Lyndon B. Johnson Presidential Library, Austin, Tex. Hughes considered Quesada "a genius . . . who had gradually worked out all the technical details necessary for the successful support of ground troops by tactical air power."

2 Philip Meilinger, *Hoyt S. Vandenberg* (Bloomington, Ind.: 1987), 48 passim; Devon E. Francis, *Flak Bait* (New York: 1948), xv.

3 Craven and Cate, III, 615; Elwood Quesada (Long/Stephenson interview), USAMHI.

4 Kit C. Carter and Robert Mueller, rev. ed., *Combat Chronology* (Washington, D.C.: 1991), 468–469, 475; Craven and Cate, III, 617–618.

5 Samuel Anderson (Ahmann), 285–286.

6 David Spires, Unpublished, untitled study of XIX TAC, 185, on file at CAFH.

7 William Dunn, *Fighter Pilot* (Lexington, Ky.: 1983), 157.

8 Charles B. MacDonald, *The Siegfried Line Campaign* (Washington, D.C.: 1963), 404–406; Richard Davis, *Spaatz and the Air War in Europe* (Washington, D.C.: 1993).

9 Craven and Cate, III, 631–633. According to Quesada, the advance was also slowed by the heavies' obliteration of a main road the soldiers had counted on using. Bradley's engineers "couldn't even find it." Quesada (Leish interview), 53, BL, CU.

10 Otto P. Weyland (Leish interview), 20–21.

11 Martin Blumenson, ed., *The Patton Papers* (Boston: 1975), II, 571.

12 Craven and Cate, III, 677–680.

13 Roy M. Stanley, *World War II Photo Intelligence* (New York: 1981), 185 passim.

14 Thomas G. Ivie, *Aerial Reconnaissance: The 10th Photo Group* (Carrolton, Tex.: 1980), 50.

15 Oscar Koch, *G-2: Intelligence for Patton* (Philadelphia: 1971), 79–87. Koch was Patton's G-2.

16 Anderson, 318–319. Ironically, Vandenberg was afraid that the intelligence failure in the Battle of the Bulge would be blamed on Tac R; Hughes, 59.

17 Benjamin A. Dickson, "Estimate No. 37," and *G-2 Journal: Algiers to the Elbe,* Special Collections, West Point; Hugh M. Cole, *The Ardennes: The Battle of the Bulge* (Washington, D.C.: 1965), 56–62.

18 Charles B. MacDonald, *A Time for Trumpets* (New York: 1984), 19–38; Craven and Cate, III, 390.

19 Adolf Galland, "The Birth, Life and Death of the German Day Fighter Arm," 43, Spaatz Papers, MD, LC.

20 Cole, 80 passim.
21 Bruce C. Clarke, "The Battle of St. Vith," Special Collections, West Point; Clarke (Kish interview), USAMHI. Clarke was one of the principal figures in this battle.
22 Kenn C. Rust, *The Ninth Air Force Story* (Temple City, Calif.: 1978), 30–31; Craven and Cate, III, 687.
23 Anderson, 268–269.
24 Craven and Cate, III, 690.
25 Roger A. Freeman, *The Mighty Eighth War Diary* (New York: 1981), 398–404.
26 John H. Lowden, *Silent Wings at War* (Washington, D.C.: 1991), 124.
27 Harry O. Kinnard (Crouch interview), USAMHI. Kinnard was the 101st's chief of staff.
28 Norman Frank, *Battle of the Airfields* (London: 1984), 150.
29 Craven and Cate, III, 665 gives lower figures. However, I have relied on Frank, 187–188, who has made a careful study of this subject. Cf. British Air Ministry, *Rise and Fall of the German Air Force* (London: 1948), 380; Donald L. Caldwell, *JG 26* (New York: 1991), 340–341.
30 Stanley, 62.

Chapter 23: The Country That Was

1 Dale O. Smith, *Screaming Eagle* (Chapel Hill, N.C.: 1988), 68–69.
2 Philip Ardery, *Bomber Pilot* (Lexington, Ky.: 1978), 196; Archie Old, Jr. (Ahmann interview), 242. Earle E. Partridge, commanding 3rd Bomb Division, would fly up and down the column in a P-51, photographing his groups and combat bomb wings, to encourage his pilots to fly better formations: Partridge (Ahmann interview), 416, CAFH.
3 Ibid., 431–432. Most carried a maximum of 12 × 500-lb. bombs, but Partridge claims he found a way to get 14 500-pounders into the 3rd Bomb Division's B-17s.
4 Allen G. Blue, *B-24 Liberator* (New York: 1977), 63, 144; William Carigan, "B-24 Liberator: A Man's Airplane," *Aerospace Historian,* Spring 1988.
5 Bert Stiles, *Serenade to the Big Bird* (London: 1947), 15–21.
6 Leon Johnson (Green interview), 14, USAFA. Johnson had won the Medal of Honor leading the 389th Bomb Group over Ploesti. "There wasn't anything we could do," said Johnson,

"that Jimmy couldn't do better." Cf. Jimmy Doolittle, with Carrol V. Glines, *I Could Never Be So Lucky Again* (New York: 1991).

7 Letter, Arnold to Doolittle, March 4, 1944, Arnold Papers, MD, LC.

8 Richard Davis, *Spaatz and the Air War in Europe* (Washington, D.C.: 1993), 378.

9 Lowell Thomas and Edward Jablonski, *Doolittle* (New York: 1968), 266.

10 Haywood S. Hansell, Jr., *The Air Plan That Defeated Hitler* (Atlanta: 1972), 122.

11 James Dugan and Carroll Stewart, *Ploesti* (New York: 1965), 55–57; cf. Russell A. Strong, *First Over Germany* (Winston-Salem, N.C.: 1982), 20.

12 Charles A. Watry and Duane L. Hall, *Aerial Gunners: The Unknown Aces of World War II* (Carlsbad, Calif.: 1983), 24–37.

13 Ivan Hickman, *Operation Pinball The USAAF's Secret Aerial Gunnery Program* (Osceola, Wis.: 1990); Donald R. Norton, *Larry: A Biography of Larry D. Bell* (Chicago: 1981), 115. For the recollections of an RP-63 pilot see Robert D. Thirkield, "Pinball Remembered," *Friends Journal,* USAF Museum, Spring 1991.

14 George K. Bernhard, Jr., "Close Encounter of a B-17 Gunner," *Aerospace Historian* June 1982.

15 Old, 304–312.

16 Lyn Tornabene, *Long Live the King* (New York: 1976), 284–293; Watry, 136–137. Cf. Letter, Donald L. Wilson to Murray Green, September 7, 1970, Murray Green Collection, USAFA.

17 C. Glen Sweeting, *Combat Flying Clothing*(Washington, D.C.: 1984), 38 passim.

18 George C. Kenney (Hasdorff interview), 44; Kenney (Stanley interview), 16–17, both CAFH.

19 John Comer, *Combat Crew* (New York: 1988), 131.

20 C. Glen Sweeting, *Combat Flying Equipment* (Washington, D.C.: 1989), 124 passim.

21 Doolittle, 417.

22 Charles Webster and Noble Frankland, *The Strategic Bombing Offensive* (London: 1961), IV, 178–179.

23 Diary, May 14, 1942, Spaatz Papers, MD, LC.

24 Combined Intelligence Objectives Sub-Committee, "The Inter-

rogation of Albert Speer," July 18, 1945, 4, Spaatz Papers, MD, LC.

25 U.S. Strategic Bombing Survey, *German Oil Industry: Ministerial Report, Team 78* (Washington, D.C.: 1947), 54.

26 Webster and Frankland, IV, 516, Appendix 49.

27 Allen C. Mierzejewski, *The Collapse of the German War Economy: Allied Air Power and the German Railway* (Chapel Hill, N.C.: 1990), 78, 83.

28 Lord Tedder, *With Prejudice* (London: 1966), 610 passim; Cf. Lord Zuckerman, *From Apes to Warlords* (New York: 1978).

29 Mierzejewski, 107.

30 Speer, interrogation, 14.

31 Diary, Jan. 8 and 9, 1945, Spaatz Papers, MD, LC.

32 Davis, 555.

33 Ronald Schaffer, *Wings of Judgment* (New York: 1985), xii.

34 Craven and Cate, III, 731–732.

35 Carl H. Moore, *Flying the B-26 Marauder Over Europe* (Blue Ridge Summit, Pa.: 1980), 104–105.

36 Diary, Feb. 15–19, 1945, Floyd Parks Papers, USAMHI; Cf. Matthew Ridgway (Blair interview), USAMHI.

37 John C. Warren, *Airborne Operations In World War II, European Theater,* USAF Study 97 (Maxwell AFB: 1956), 177–195.

38 Adolf Galland, *The First and the Last* (New York: 1954), 273–279; Jeffrey Ethel and Alfred Price, *The German Jets in Combat* (New York: 1980), 43–45.

39 Kit C. Carter and Robert Mueller, *Combat Chronology* (Washington, D.C.: 1991), 620; Matthew Cooper, *The German Air Force, 1939–1945* (London: 1981), 373; Doolittle, 436.

40 *Combat Chronology,* 629.

41 Stephen Ambrose, *Eisenhower and Berlin, 1945* (New York: 1967), 89.

42 "Jeeping the Targets in the Country That Was," Spaatz Papers, MD, LC. It seems likely that this account was written by Dr. Hopper.

43 Old, 281–282.

44 Frederick Smith, Jr. (Green interview), 11; Eugene Beebe (Green interview), 52, both USAFA.

45 Arthur H. Vanaman (Green interview), 15, USAFA; Kenneth B. Wolfe (Shaughnessy interview), 13, BL, CU.

46 Otto P. Weyland (Green interview), 4, USAFA.

47 Lloyd P. Hopwood (Green interview), USAFA.

48 Smith, 7.
49 Vi Duffie (Green interview), 2–3, USAFA.
50 Trubee Davison (Green interview), 6.
51 Letter, Lovett to Spaatz, April 22, 1945, Spaatz Papers, MD, LC; Robert Lovett (Green interview), and Barney M. Giles (Green interview), both USAFA.
52 Nathan Twining (Green interview), 23–25, USAFA.
53 Thomas G. Ivie, *Aerial Reconnaissance: The 10th Photo Recon Group* (Carrolton, Tex.: 1980), 168–169.

Chapter 24: Minor Keys

1 Jackie Cochran, in *High Honor,* Stewart Leuthner and Oliver Jensen, eds. (Washington, D.C.: 1990), 197.
2 Marianne Verges, *On Silver Wings* (New York: 1991), 37–38.
3 Jackie Cochran (Shaughnessy interview), 45, BL, CU.
4 Richard Carmichael (Green interview), 17–18. Carmichael, who'd commanded the 19th Bomb Group in the Philippines and Java, had the misfortune to be assigned to help Mrs. Cochran get what she wanted. All he gained from this experience was the wrath of Mrs. Hobby. He later got command of a B-29 group, was shot down over Japan, but survived the war.
5 Cochran, *High Honor,* 207.
6 Cochran (Green interview) 11, USAFA; J. Merton England and Joseph Rieter, *Women Pilots with the AAF 1941–1945* USAF Study 55 (Maxwell AFB: 1946); Sally Van Wanganen, Nemhouser Kiel, *Those Wonderful Women in Their Flying Machines* (New York: 1979). Cf. D'Ann Campbell "Servicewomen of World War II," *Armed Forces and Society,* Winter 1990.
7 William H. Tunner, *Over the Hump* (Washington, D.C.: 1985), 39.
8 Alan M. Osur, *Blacks in the Army Air Forces in World War II* (Washington, D.C.: 1977), 2–6.
9 Patricia Stickland, *The Putt-Putt Air Force: The Story of the CPTP* (Washington, D.C.: 1971), 40–43.
10 Richard M. Dalfiume, *Desegregation of the U.S. Armed Forces* (Columbia, Mo.: 1969), 28–29.
11 Stanley Sandler, *Segregated Skies* (Washington, D.C.: 1991), 25.
12 Benjamin Castle (Shaughnessy interview), 18, BL, CU; William Lee (Burg interview), Eisenhower Presidential Library,

Abeline, Kans. Cf. Diary, May 19, 1943, Spaatz Papers, MD, LC.

13 Sandler, 26.

14 C. Alfred Anderson (Hasdorff interview), 26, asserted that Davis was "a good pilot." Anderson was his instructor in primary. But see J. Alfred Phelps, *Chappie* (San Rafael, Calif.: 1991), 41.

15 Philip Cochran, Air Room Interview, June 3, 1943, Microfilm 142.052, HRA.

16 Philip Cochran (Hasdorff interview), 120–125, CAFH.

17 Letter, Edwin House to Joseph Cannon, Sept. 16, 1943, Spaatz Papers, MD, LC.

18 Benjamin O. Davis, Jr., *American* (Washington, D.C.: 1990) 104–105; Ulysses S. Lee, *The Employment of Negro Troops* (Washington, D.C.: 1966), 458–460; Osur, 50.

19 Charles E. Francis, *The Tuskegee Airmen* (Boston: 1955), 49–52.

20 Report, Statistical Control Division, "Operations of the 99th Fighter Squadron," March 30, 1944, Microfilm 135.65-496, HRA.

21 Nathan M. Twining (Green interview), 27–28, USAFA.

22 John Muirhead, *Those Who Fall* (New York: 1988), 177–178. Cf. Leroy Newby, *Target Ploesti* (San Rafael, Calif.: 1983), 109.

23 Roscoe C. Brown, in *High Honor,* 244–245.

24 Phelps, 50–51.

25 Diary, July 12, 1945, Kenney Papers, CAFH.

26 Charles Christienne and Pierre Lissarague, *A History of French Military Aviation* (Washington, D.C.: 1984), 165.

27 Lowell Thomas and Edward Jablonski, *Doolittle* (New York: 1973), 44.

28 USAF, "Official USAF Policy Concerning the Term 'Ace,' " (Maxwell AFB: 1975).

29 Wesley P. Newton, *A Preliminary List of U.S. Air Force Aces, 1917–1953* USAF Study 73 (Maxwell AFB: 1962), identifies 693 individuals as aces.

30 Charles Watry, *Aerial Gunners: The Unknown Aces of World War II* (Carlsbad, Calif.: 1986), is the only comprehensive work on the claims made by aerial gunners in the AAF.

31 All the figures for aerial victories given in this book are based

on Daniel L. Haulman and William C. Stanck, eds., *Aerial Victory Credits* USAF Study #85 (Maxwell AFB: 1988).

32 Raymond Tolliver and Trevor Constable, *Fighter Aces of the USA* (Fallbrook, Calif.: 1979), 74.

33 Gordon H. Austin (Ahmann interview), 69, CAFH.

34 Wiliam H. Bartsch, *Doomed at the Start* (Washington, D.C.: 1992), 157–158.

35 George C. Kenney, *Dick Bong: Ace of Aces* (New York: 1960), 35–36.

36 Tolliver and Constable, 102

37 Steve Birdsall, *Flying Buccaneers* (Garden City, N.Y.: 1977), 252–253.

38 Christienne and Lissarague, 166.

39 Roger A. Freeman, *The Mighty Eighth* (New York: 1989), 272–276.

39 Lee Arbon, *They Also Flew: The Sergeant-Pilot Legacy* (Washington, D.C.: 1992), 133.

40 Carl Bong and Mike O'Connor, *Ace of Aces* (Mesa, Ariz.: 1984), 22.

41 Letter from Kenney to Whitehead, Feb. 11, 1944, Kenney Papers, CAFH.

42 It's interesting that after the war Kenney adamantly insisted that he'd told Lynch and Kearby *not* to be competitive with Bong. Kenny: *Dick Bong*, 45–46.

43 Ibid., 86.

44 Bong and O'Connor, 110–112.

45 Mary Scott, "The Last Ace of World War II," *Air Power History,* Fall 1989.

46 Tolliver and Constable, 133.

Chapter 25: Disorienting Experiences

1 Letter, Scott to Spaatz, March 8, 1942, Spaatz Papers, MD, LC.

2 Robert Lee Scott, Jr., in Joe Foss and Matthew Brennan, eds., *Top Guns* (New York: 1991), 64–66.

3 Cecil A. Combs (Ahmann interview), 107.

4 Raymond Tolliver and Trevor Constable, *Fighter Aces of the USA* (Fallbrook, Calif.: 1979), 73; cf. John Alison (Thompson interview), 254–262.

5 Howard A. Davidson (Ahmann interview), 367.

6 Robert Lee Scott, Jr., *God is My Co-Pilot* (New York: 1944), 221.

7 Martha Hoyt Byrd, *Chennault: Giving Wings to the Tiger* (Tuscaloosa: 1988), 169–171. Kenney, a ruthless judge of men, thought so highly of Cooper that after Bissell fired him, he got Cooper assigned to his staff: Diary, Jan. 28, 1943, Kenney Papers, CAFH.

8 Claire Chennault, *Way of a Fighter* (New York: 1949), 212–216.

9 Diary, Feb. 7, 1943, Arnold Papers, MD, LC.

10 Charles Romanus and Riley Sunderland, *Stilwell's Mission to China* (Washington, D.C.: 1958), 317; Theodore H. White, ed., *The Stilwell Papers* (New York: 1948), 167–168; Chennault 220–224; Henry L. Stimson and MacGeorge Bundy, *On Active Service in Peace and War* (New York: 1948), 534–535.

11 Barbara W. Tuchman, *Stilwell and the American Experience in China* (New York: 1972), 469–470.

12 Laurence S. Kuter (Ahmann interview), 364, CAFH.

13 *Global Mission,* ms., XXIII, 8–9, Arnold Papers, MD, LC.

14 Edward V. Rickenbacker, autobiography, Tape 29, Side 1, page 21, Rickenbacker Papers, MD, LC.

15 Kuter, 363.

16 Barney M. Giles (Green interview), 61, USAFA

17 Craven and Cate, V, 257

18 Carl Molesworth, *Wing to Wing: Air Combat in China 1943–1945* (New York: 1990), 10 passim; Malcolm Rosholt, *Flight in the China Air Space* (Rosholt, Wis.: 1984), 166–173.

19 Clinton D. Vincent and Glenn McClure, *Fire and Fall Back* (San Antonio, Tex.: 1975), 132; Rosholt, 163–165.

20 Craven and Cate, V, 98–100.

21 Donald S. Lopez, *Into the Teeth of the Tiger* (New York: 1986), 145.

22 Kenn C. Rust, *The Fourteenth Air Force Story* (Temple City, Calif.: 1977), 30.

23 Curtis LeMay, with MacKinley Kanter, *Mission with LeMay* (Garden City, N.Y.: 1965), 332–333.

24 Keith Eiler, ed., *Wedemeyer on War and Peace* (Stanford, Calif.: 1987), 104; Byrd, 265.

25 Thomas M. Coffey, *Iron Eagle* (New York: 1986), 127–128; Wilbur H. Morrison, *Point of No Return* (New York: 1979), 140–141.

26 U.S. Strategic Bombing Survey, *The War Against Japanese Transportation* (Washington, D.C.: 1947), 100, 122; Rust 31.

27 U.S. Strategic Bombing Survey, *Coal and Metals in Japan's War Economy* (Washington, D.C.: 1947), 62–63, 78–86.

28 Chennault, 349–350; Craven and Cate, V, 257.

29 William H. Tunner, *Over the Hump* (Washington, D.C.: 1985), 60.

30 Rickenbacker, autobiography, Tape 29, Side 1, p. 20, Edward V. Rickenbacker Papers, MD, LC.

31 Alison, 315.

32 Jacob Smart (Green interview), 24–25, USAFA. Smart was aboard this flight.

33 Bliss K. Thorne, *The Hump* (Philadelphia: 1965), 64.

34 John F. Whitely, *Early Army Aviation* (Manhattan, Kans.: 1975), 99.

35 Kuter, 349–350; Rickenbacker, 21.

36 Craven and Cate, V, 257.

37 Raymond D. Callaway (Taber interview), 18–19, CAFH; Scott, 109.

38 Tunner, 116.

39 Thorne, 166.

40 Howard A. Davidson (Ahmann interview), 539, CAFH.

41 Christopher Sykes, *Orde Wingate* (London: 1958), 538–542; Forrest C. Pogue, *George C. Marshall: Organizer of Victory* (New York: 1973), 257.

42 Alison, 345–347; cf. H. H. Arnold, "The Aerial Invasion of Burma," *National Geographic,* August 1944.

43 Philip G. Cochran (Hasdorff interview), 220–225; Kenn C. Rust, *The Tenth Air Force Story* (Temple City, Calif.: 1980), 21. Cf. Luigi Rosseto, "The First Air Commandos," *Aerospace Historian,* March 1982.

44 John H. Lowden, *Silent Wings at War* (Washington, D.C.: 1991), 62–63.

45 Cochran (Hasdorff), 194.

46 Davidson, 33.

47 Ibid., 540.

48 Rust, 31.

49 Charles Romanus and Riley Sunderland, *Time Runs Out in CBI* (Washington, D.C.: 1959), 100.

50 John G. Martin, *It Began at Imphal: The Combat Cargo Story* (Manhattan, Kans.: 1988), 3.

Chapter 26: Morale: Mail, Missions, and Medals

1 Cecil F. Combs (Ahmann interview), 171; Jacob E. Smart (Hasdorff and McCants interview), 25, CAFH.
2 Leroy Newby, *Target Ploesti* (San Rafael, Calif.: 1983), 118; Samuel Anderson (Ahmann interview), 394, CAFH.
3 Martin Caidin, *Black Thursday* (New York: 1960).
4 Philip G. Cochran (Hasdorff interview), 106–107, CAFH.
5 William R. Cubbins, *The War of the Cottontails* (Chapel Hill, N.C.: 1989), 68.
6 Rickenbacker considered their fears about flying the Hump absurd. He thought the Hump was no more difficult to fly than Chicago to Boston in winter: Rickenbacker autobiography, Tape 21, Side 2, page 23, Rickenbacker Papers, MD, LC.
7 Russell A. Strong, *First Over Germany* (Kalamazoo, Mich.: 1982), 16–17; William A. Carigan, "B-24 Liberator," *Aerospace Historian,* March 1988.
8 Charles Francis, *Flak Bait* (Boston: 1946), 125–128.
9 William R. Dunn, *Fighter Pilot* (Lexington, Ky.: 1983), 143.
10 Dale O. Smith, *Screaming Eagle* (Chapel Hill, N.C.: 1988), 82–83.
11 Marvin Bledsoe, *Thunderbolt* (New York: 1982), 135.
12 James Dugan and Carrol Stuart, *Ploesti* (New York: 1965), 52–53.
13 Stephen McFarland and Wesley P. Newton, *To Command the Sky* (Washington, D.C.: 1991), Table 2, p. 136.
14 John W. Lambert, *The Pineapple Air Force* (St. Paul: 1991), 63.
15 Raymond D. Callaway (Taber interview), 51–52, CAFH.
16 Leon Wolfe, *Low Level Mission* (New York: 1967), 102–103.
17 Edward F. Polic, *The Glenn Miller AAF Band* (Metuchen, N.J.: 1989), I, 4–9.
18 George T. Simon, *Glenn Miller and His Orchestra* (New York: 1974), 324–330. Simon was one of the musicians Miller recruited.
19 *Time,* September 6, 1943.
20 Polic, I, 31.
21 *Kansas City Star,* October 18, 1990.
22 Elmer Bendiner, *The Fall of Fortresses* (New York: 1981), 117.
23 Rickenbacker autobiography, Tape 34, Side 1, pp. 8–9, Rickenbacker Papers, MD, LC.
24 Paul Frillman (Rounds interview), 251 passim, BL, CU.
25 Rickenbacker, Tape 29, Side 1, pp. 15–20.

26 Jeffrey C. Ethell, *The History of Aircraft Nose Art* (Osceola, Wis.: 1991), offers hundreds of examples.

27 Paul Tibbets, *The Tibbets Story* (New York: 1978), 96.

28 Lord Zuckerman, *From Apes to Warlords* (New York: 1978), 192–193.

29 Martin R. Goldman, *Morale in the AAF in World War II* USAF Study 23 (Maxwell AFB: 1953), 51.

30 Letter, Arnold to Eaker, Sept. 6, 1943, Arnold Papers, MD, LC.

31 Idwal Edwards (Green interview), 39, USAFA.

32 Howard A. Davidson (Ahmann interview), 546; cf. Davidson (Green interview), 30, USAFA.

33 Robert S. Johnson, *Thunderbolt!* (New York: 1957), 203.

34 War Department, *The Medal of Honor of the U.S. Army* (Washington, D.C.: 1948), 272. Also see Philip S. Gage, Jr., "Fliers and Medals of Honor," *Aerospace Historian,* Dec. 1983.

35 Roger A. Freeman, *The Mighty Eighth* (New York: 1989), 30–31.

36 Letter, Eaker to Arnold, July 20, 1943, Eaker Papers, MD, LC.

37 Paul Tibbets (Green interview), 28–29, USAFA.

38 Diary, Oct. 11, 1943, Kenney Papers, CAFH; *General Kenney Reports* (Washington, D.C.: 1988), 59–60, 216, 259–262, 311, 357–358, 489, 504, 510–511.

Chapter 27: Technical Knockout

1 Diary, Jan. 3 and 4, 1943, Kenney Papers, CAFH. Kenney refers to "Ultra dope" in his diary, but not in his book, where he calls it "special intelligence."

2 John Miller, Jr., *Cartwheel: The Reduction of Rabaul* (Washington, D.C.: 1959), 38, says three fourths; Edward Drea, *MacArthur's Ultra* (Lawrence, Kans.: 1992), 66, says one third. I have split the difference.

3 Craven and Cate, IV, 137; Frederick H. Smith (Hasdorff and Parrish interview), 69, CAFH; Steve Birdsall, *Flying Buccaneers* (Garden City, N.Y.: 1977), 46–47.

4 Letter, Kenney to Whitehead, Feb. 25, 1943, Kenney Papers, CAFH.

5 Howard A. Davidson (Ahmann interview), 27–28, CAFH.

6 George C. Kenney (Hasdorff interview), 17, CAFH.

7   George C. Kenney (Stanley interview), 35, CAFH.

8   George C. Kenney, *The Saga of Pappy Gunn* (New York: 1959), 54–59; Francis C. Gideon (Cleary interview), 36, CAFH

9   Diary, Feb. 26, 1943, Kenney Papers, CAFH; Lex McAuley, *The Battle of the Bismarck Sea* (New York: 1991), 20–22.

10 Birdsall, 57.

11 Martin Caidin, *The Ragged, Rugged Warriors* (New York: 1960), 24.

12 U.S. Strategic Bombing Survey (Pacific), *Interrogation of Japanese Officers* (Washington, D.C.: 1946), 498; Drea, 71.

13 Craven and Cate, IV, 147–150; Paul P. Rogers, *The Bitter Years: MacArthur and Sutherland, 1942–1945* (New York: 1990) 50–51. Arnold was in England when the Air Staff challenged the Bismarck Sea claims. On his return, he wrote to Kenney, apologizing for any embarrassment caused and assuring him that had he not been out of the country this issue would never have been raised. Letter, Arnold to Kenney, Oct. 11, 1943, Kenney Papers, CAFH.

14 Barney M. Giles (Green interview), 44, USAFA. Marshall was much impressed by Kenney, informing Roosevelt shortly after this that the only theater where air power was being employed properly was SWPA. Everywhere else, he said, the AAF suffered "constant embarrassment." Memo, Marshall to Roosevelt, March 22, 1943, FDR Library. Hyde Park.

15 *General Kenney Reports,* 253, 269–272; Donald Hough and Elliott Arnold, *Big Distance* (New York: 1945), 83–84.

16 Drea, 83. He says that senior officers of the Japanese Fourth Air Army were "incredulous" and "dumbfounded" when they saw the August 11 photos of Marilinan.

17 Craven and Cate, IV, 177.

18 Birdsall, 90–91.

19 Arnold's statisticians put the figure at 175 enemy aircraft destroyed: Craven and Cate, IV, 180.

20 Craven and Cate, IV, 184–186; James A. Huston, *Out of the Blue* (West Lafayette, Ind.: 1972), 220.

21 Kenney (Hasdorff interview), 80.

22 Lex McAuley, *Into the Dragon's Jaws* (Melbourne: 1990), 18.

23 Letter, Whitehead to Kenney, July 18, 1943, Kenney Papers, CAFH.

24 Letter, Kenney to Arnold, October 10, 1943, Kenney Papers, CAFH.

25 U.S. Strategic Bombing Survey *Interrogations,* 209; Birdsall, 113–118; Craven and Cate, IV, 319–320.

26 Drea, 89.

27 *General Kenney Reports.*

28 Allied airmen claimed 560 Japanese planes destroyed and 150 probables. Japanese records admit losses only one third the size of Allied claims, yet these records are themselves open to question. Drea, 89–90, accepts the Japanese figures; McAuley, 97, does not.

29 U.S. Strategic Bombing Survey, *The Fifth Air Force in the War Against Japan* (Washington, D.C.: 1946), 59.

30 Grace Pearson Hays, *The History of the JCS in World War II: The War Against Japan* (Annapolis, Md.: 1982), 142–144.

31 Miller, 273–274; *General Kenney Reports,* 327.

32 Craven and Cate, IV, 336; Miller, 284–285.

33 Smith, 72.

34 *General Kenney Reports,* 331–332.

35 Craven and Cate, IV, 340–341.

36 Letter, Whitehead to Kenney, Feb. 11, 1944, Kenney Papers, CAFH.

37 Miller, 36.

38 John Miller, Jr., *Guadalcanal: The First Offensive* (Washington, D.C.: 1949), 9–16.

39 Thomas C. Coffey, *Hap* (New York: 1983), 284.

40 Richard Frank, *Guadalcanal* (New York: 1990), 267, 315; Frank E. Hough, et al., *Pearl Harbor to Guadalcanal* (Washington, D.C.: 1958), 275 passim.

41 Thomas G. Miller, Jr., *The Cactus Air Force* (New York: 1969), 79; Martin Caidin, *The Ragged, Rugged Warriors* (New York: 1960), 310.

42 Nathan Twining (Green interview), pages 9–10 USAFA; Twining (Marmor interview), 8, CAFH; Diary, Sept. 16–29, 1942, Arnold Papers, MD, LC. There are comments hostile to the Navy and Marine Corps on nearly every page of Arnold's diary. Their vitriolic tone is only hinted at in his ghosted autobiography.

43 Thomas G. Lanphier, Jr., in, Stuart Leuchner and Oliver Jensen, eds., *High Honor* (Washington, D.C.: 1989), 217.

44 R. Cargill Hall, *Lightning Over Bougainville* (Washington, D.C.: 1992), 155–156; Daniel L. Haulman and William C. Stanck, eds., *Aerial Victory Credits* (Maxwell AFB: 1988), 82,

276. Cf. Carroll V. Glines, *Attack on Yamamoto* (New York: 1990).

Chapter 28: Lucky Numbers

1 Diary, March 12 and 28, 1944, Kenney Papers, CAFH; Grace Pearson Hayes, *The History of the JCS in World War II* (Annapolis: 1982), 496.

2 Robert Ross Smith, *The Approach to the Philippines* (Washington, D.C.: 1953), 97–98.

3 George C. Kenney, *General Kenney Reports* (New York: 1949), 377.

4 Craven and Cate, V, 588–589.

5 Edward Drea, *MacArthur's Ultra* (Lawrence, Kans.: 1992), 107.

6 *General Kenney Reports,* 374.

7 Drea, 111–112.

8 Craven and Cate, V, 594.

9 Smith, 53–57, 99–100.

10 Donald Hough and Elliott Arnold, *Big Distance* (New York: 1945), 141.

11 *General Kenney Reports,* 420–421.

12 Robert W. Coakley and Richard M. Leighton, *Global Logistics and Strategy 1943–1945* (Washington D.C.: 1968), 468–470, 571; D. Clayton James, *The Years of MacArthur* (Boston: 1975), II, 541–542.

13 Cable, Kenney to Arnold, Sept. 8, 1944, Kenney Papers.

14 Craven and Cate, IV, 169–170.

15 Diary, Sept. 17, 1944, Kenney Papers, CAFH.

16 Hough and Arnold, 161–162.

17 Craven and Cate, V, 319.

18 Birdsall, 218–219.

19 Hayes, 620–621; E. B. Potter, *Nimitz* (New York: 1974), 323.

20 Diary, Sept. 16, 1944, Kenney Papers; Francis C. Gideon (Clearly interview), 45–46, CAFH. The fear of the Navy as the strongest factor behind this decision is spelled out in the diary, but is not even hinted at in *General Kenney Reports,* 432, nor in Douglas MacArthur, *Reminiscences* (New York: 1965), 211–212.

21 M. Hamlin Cannon, *Leyte: The Return to the Philippines* (Washington, D.C.: 1954), 35–36.

22 Samuel E. Morison, *Leyte* (Boston: 1970), 148–149.

23 *General Kenney Reports,* 472.

24 Drea, 167–169.

25 Hough and Arnold, 246–247.

26 Diary, Nov. 10, 1944, Kenney Papers, CAFH; Birdsall, 230–232.

27 Drea, 174–175.

28 Diary, Sept. 26, 1944, Kenney Papers.

29 Perry J. Dahl (Meilinger, et al.), 7, CAFH.

30 Eric Hammel, *Aces Against Japan* (New York: 1992), 228–229. One of the pilots being searched for was Dahl, who'd been shot down, left by the Japanese for dead, and rescued by Filipino guerrillas.

31 Cannon, 102.

32 Hough and Arnold 195.

33 Craven and Cate, V, 397–398; Birdsall, 242–243; Karl C. Dod, *The Corps of Engineers in the War Against Japan* (Washington, D.C.: 1974), 586–587.

34 Craven and Cate, V, 406–407; Birdsall, 245–247.

35 Cable, MacArthur to Kenney, Jan. 18, 1944, Kenney Papers, CAFH.

36 Diary, Feb. 18, 1945, Kenney Papers, CAFH.

37 Diary, Jan. 23 25, 1945, Kenney Papers, CAFH.

38 Diary, Feb. 7, 1945, Kenney Papers, CAFH.

39 Robert Ross Smith, *Triumph in the Philippines* (Washington, D.C.: 1963), 348–350; James A. Huston, *Out of the Blue* (Purdue: 1972), 225–227.

40 Diary, March 20, 1945, Kenney Papers, CAFH.

41 Diary, Jan. 8, 1945, Kenney Papers, CAFH.

42 For a graphic firsthand account of Thirteenth Air Force operations in 1945, by a B-24 pilot, see John Boeman, *Morotai* (New York: 1981).

Chapter 29: Superlatives

1 Wilbur H. Morrison, *Point of No Return* (New York: 1979), 33.

2 Kenneth B. Wolfe (Green interview), 17, 19, USAFA.

3 Thomas Coffey, *Hap* (New York: 1982), 326.

4 Peter M. Bowers, *Boeing Aircraft Since 1916* (Annapolis, Md.: 1989), 318–322; Ray Wagner, *American Combat Planes* (Garden City, N.Y.: 1968), 134–136; Gordon Swanborough and Peter M. Bowers, *U.S. Military Aircraft Since 1909* (Washing-

ton, D.C.: 1989), 113–119; Charles Watry, *Aerial Gunners* (Carlsbad, Calif.: 1987), 191.

5 Orval A. Cook (Ahmann interview), 254–255; Guy M. Townsend (Hasdorff interview), both CAFH; Haywood S. Hansell (Green interview), 33, USAFA.

6 Cook, 21.

7 Clarence Irvine (Green interview), 4, USAFA; Paul W. Tibbets, Jr. (Green interview), 32, USAFA; Morrison, 62.

8 Earle E. Partridge (Ahmann interview), 459; Townsend, 51.

9 Tibbets, 2–3, 31.

10 Haywood S. Hansell, Jr., *The Strategic Air War Against Germany and Japan* (Washington, D.C.: 1986), 157–159.

11 Ibid., 179; Craven and Cate, V, 555.

12 Cecil F. Combs (Ahmann interview), 169; David Anderton *B-29 Superfortress at War* (New York: 1978), 73; Morrison, 182–184.

13 David A. Burchinal (Schmidt and Straser interview), 59–60, USAMHI; Craven and Cate, V, 559.

14 Clarence E. Irvine (Green interview), 11, USAFA.

15 Craven and Cate, V, 561; Combs, 92–93; Lee Kennett, *A History of Strategic Bombing* (New York: 1982), 169.

16 Grandison Gardner (Shaughnessy interview), 23–24, BL, CU; Louis F. Fieser, *The Scientific Method* (New York: 1964), 13 passim; John W. Mountcastle, *Trial by Fire: U.S. Incendiary Weapons* (Duke University, Ph.D., 1979), Chapter V describes development of incendiaries used in the ETO; Chapter VII deals with those used against Japan.

17 Haywood S. Hansell (Green interview), 43, USAFA; Mountcastle, 212–214.

18 Craven and Cate, V, 565–566.

19 Lauris Norstad (Ahmann), 542–546. He maintains, "I looked him in the eye. Poss, you will be relieved. . . ." Hansell is not clear on this incident in his book, but in his interview with Green, 38, in response to a direct question he says flatly, "General Fechet told me."

20 Curtis LeMay (Green interview), 2, 10, USAFA. One reason he took aerial gunners out of B-29s was so they wouldn't shoot each other's planes down.

21 Tibbets, 39–40.

22 Burchinal, 62–63.

23 Robert Ramer, in Stuart Leuchner and Oliver Jensen, eds., *High Honor* (Washington, D.C.: 1990), 186.
24 LeMay, 18–19.
25 Kit C. Carter and Robert Mueller, *Combat Chronology* (Washington, D.C.: 1991), 581.
26 Harold Bond, *Fire and the Air War* (Boston: 1946), 141; *Combat Chronology,* 582; Craven and Cate, 611–612.
27 Guy M. Townsend (Hasdorff interview), 39; George W. Mundy (Cleary interview), 69, both CAFH.
28 U.S. Strategic Bombing Survey, *Effects of Incendiary Bombing Attacks on Japan* (Washington, D.C.: 1947), 90–102; Craven and Cate, V, 616–617.
29 Ramer, 192.
30 Curtis LeMay and Bill Yenne, *Superfortress* (New York: 1988), 1233–125; Craven and Cate, V, 617; Morrison, 222–224.
31 See Townsend, 70, for a description of being stalked by Japanese night fighters.
32 Craven and Cate, V, 618–619.
33 Earl F. Snyder, *General Leemy's Circus* (New York: 1966), 116–119.
34 LeMay (Green), 13–14; Hansell, *Strategic* 162–163, 227; LeMay and Yenne, 97.
35 Craven and Cate, V, 666–673; Combs, 46; Ellis A. Johnson and David A. Katcher, *Mines Against Japan* (Silver Spring, Md.: 1973), 21–38.
36 John W. Lambert, *The Pineapple Air Force* (St. Paul, Minn.: 1990); Clive Howard and Joe Whitney, *One Damned Island After Another* (Washington: 1979).
37 Combs, 23.
38 Craven and Cate, V, 643; Combs, 46.
39 Edward J. Drea, *MacArthur's Ultra* (Lawrence, Kans.: 1992), 209–210, 222.
40 LeMay and Yenne, 143.
41 Burchinal, 73.
42 Fritz Sallagar (Green interview), 67.
43 Laurence S. Kuter (Ahmann interview), 413–414; Combs, 6.
44 Nathan Twining (Green interview), 9–10; Hansell, *Strategic,* 254.
45 Tibbets (Green), 9, 23.
46 Letter, Combs to Green, March 1, 1974, Murray Green Collec-

tion, USAFA; Combs (Ahmann), 94–95; Leslie R. Groves (Green interview), 31, USAFA; Henry L. Stimson and McGeorge Bundy, *On Active Service in Peace and War* (New York: 1948), 617–632.

47 Truman's account of his decision to drop the bomb appears between pages 712–713 in volume V of Craven and Cate; cf. Vincent C. Jones, *Manhattan: The Army and the Atomic Bomb* (Washington, D.C.: 1985), 533–534.

48 Paul W. Tibbets, Jr., *The Tibbets Story* (New York: 1977), 199.

49 Tibbets (Green), 22, USAFA.

50 Marc Galliccio, "After Nagasaki" *Prologue* Winter 1991; George C. Marshall (Pogue interview), GCMF, Lexington, Va; Geoffrey Perret, *There's a War to Be Won* (New York: 1991), 530.

Chapter 30: Envoi

1 Perry McC. Smith, *The Air Force Plans for Peace* (Baltimore: 1970); George H. Watson, *The Secretaries of the Air Force* (Washington, D.C.: 1990), I, Chapter 1.

2 E. B. Potter, *Admiral Arleigh Burke* (New York: 1990), 324–330; Jack Raymond, *Power at the Pentagon* (New York: 1964), 198–201.

3 Orval R. Cook (Emmons and Ahmann interview), 303, CAFH; Lee Arbon, *They Also Flew: The Sergeant Pilot Legacy* (Washington, D.C.: 1991), 183.

4 Howard Davidson (Green interview), 40–46, USAFA; Lauris Norstad (Ahmann interview), 253.

5 Idwal Edwards (Green interview), 25, 49; Barney M. Giles (Porretto interview), 21, CAFH.

6 Arno H. Luehman (Ahmann interview), 55; Frederick H. Smith (Hasdorff and Parris interview), 131–142; Earle E. Partridge (Sturm and Ahmann interview), 486, all CAFH.

7 Paul H. Nitze, *From Hiroshima to Glasnost* (New York: 1989), 25–45; John Kenneth Galbraith, *A Life in Our Times* (New York: 1981), 91 passim; David MacIsaac, *Strategic Bombing in World War II* (New York: 1976) is the essential account of the USSBS.

INDEX

A-17, 89
A-20, 90–91
A-24, 170
A-36, 119, 235
Aachen, 350–351
aces, 285, 327–329, 342, 384–390, 417
  see also individual entries
ABDA Command, 147, 160–161
Admiralty Islands, 428–429
Advisory Council, 137–138, 142, 214, 373
aerial gunnery, 249, 269, 363–365, 384,
  453
  gun turrets, 35, 121–125, 274
  training, 124, 363–364
Airacuda, 105–106
airborne operations
  in North Africa, 183–185
  in Sicily, 203, 207, 209–210
  in Italy, 222
  on D-Day, 302–303
  Dragoon, 316–317, 323, 346–347
  Market-Garden, 322–325, 329
  Varsity, 371
  in New Guinea, 425, 437
  in the Philippines, 445
Air Commandos, *see* Groups, 1st Air
  Commando
Air Corps: creation of, 13
  and air mail, 23
  expansion programs, 14, 34–36, 42–43,
  48, 57
  GHQ Air Force, 29, 54, 56
  Tactical School, 9, 24 passim, 50, 87,
  106, 325, 330
aircraft: *see specific type*
Air Divisions, 273n

Air Force Combat Command, 56, 240
Air Forces
  First, 85
  First Tactical, 347
  Second, 302
  Fourth, 167
  Fifth, 385, 415, 417, 419–429, 435–446,
  457
  Seventh, 456
  Eighth, 181–182, 188, 214, 245–262,
  264–269, 272–279, 286–295, 299, 310,
  319, 328, 335, 352, 360–373, 385, 415,
  458; organization of, 240; cooperation
  with RAF, 241–243
  Ninth, 101, 179, 210–211, 215–221, 283,
  285–286, 292, 299, 300–301, 306–307,
  312–313, 350–359, 368–370, 415
  Tenth, 175, 177, 400–407
  Twelfth, 181–188, 229, 231, 344–349,
  384–385, 415
  Thirteenth, 430–433, 437, 439, 446
  Fourteenth, 384–385, 391–400
  Fifteenth, 229–232, 282, 287, 319–321,
  334–340, 343–349, 409, 415
  Twentieth, 450–461
Air Medal, 414–415
Air Service, 5, 24
Air Staff, 49, 55, 69, 90, 127, 137, 142,
  181, 236, 240, 365
Air Transport Command, 377
  see also Hump airlift
Air War Plans Division, 49
Aitape, 436
Alabama, USS, 10
Alaska, 23, 31
Alexander, Sir Harold, 178, 200, 228

Aleutian Islands, 110
Algeria, 180
Algiers, 181, 184, 186
Allen, Edmund T., 447
Alison, John, 48, 63, 393–394, 401, 403, 405
Allied Expeditionary Air Forces, 283, 294, 299, 306
Allison engines, 40, 44, 105, 107, 111, 112, 114
American Expeditionary Forces, 3–5
American Volunteer Group: see Flying Tigers
Anderson, Frederick L., 254, 262 passim, 284, 287–288, 299, 354, 372
Anderson, Sir Kenneth, 185, 187
Anderson, Samuel E., 165–166, 279–280, 283, 304, 350–351, 354, 356, 465
Andrews, Frank M., 32, 67, 73, 139, 166, 179, 280
   commands GHQ Air Force, 29–30, 53, 125, 127–128
   and Marshall, 54, 56, 244
anti-aircraft artillery (AAA), 4, 28, 49, 453
   German, 4, 196, 210, 212–213, 216, 226, 246, 248, 279–280, 289, 292, 300, 325, 327, 329–31, 340–341, 365–367
   flak-busting, 323
antisubmarine warfare (ASW)
   in the Atlantic, 84–86, 91, 93, 247
Antwerp, 355
Anzio, 227–229, 233, 237–239, 335, 338, 344, 381
Arawe, 427–428
Arcadia Conference, 141–142, 150
Ardrey, Philip, 217
Argentan-Falaise gap, 314
Argument, see Big Week
Armies
   First, 3, 307, 315, 350–355
   First Allied Airborne, 322–323
   Third, 312–313, 315, 351, 353–354, 371
   Fifth, 219 passim, 337, 343–344, 347, 349
   Seventh, 203, 204, 211, 316–317, 346–347
   Eighth, 445
   Ninth, 355, 372
armor plate, 131–132
Armstrong, Frank A., 245, 253, 254, 452
Army Air Forces: creation of, 55–56
Army Ground Forces, 67, 136
Army Groups
   6th, 346–347
   12th, 368
Army Industrial College, 20, 37
Army-Navy Joint Board, 10, 54
Army Service Forces, 136, 140, 231
Arnhem, 322–323

Arnim, Jürgen von, 189
Arnold, Henry H., 61–69, 75, 95, 175, 214, 232–233, 256, 269–270, 280, 330, 339, 417, 434, 446, 465
   in World War I, 15, 18, 88
   early career, 16–30
   and Mitchell, 12, 13, 17, 20
   and Spaatz, 19, 45, 240, 249
   and Roosevelt, 31–32, 35, 133
   becomes Chief of Air Corps, 31–32, 53
   and aid to the Allies, 33–36, 46–47
   and aviation industry, 15, 39–42, 133, 140–141
   and Lovett, 44–45
   and training, 59–60, 134
   and Chennault, 62–63, 393, 394, 400
   visit to England in 1941, 46–47, 67, 90, 187, 331
   and MacArthur, 70, 71, 166
   and Pearl Harbor, 73, 83
   and the Navy, 85, 141–143, 421
   and the B-29, 102–103, 339, 438, 444–449, 451
   and long-range escorts, 106, 116, 249, 260, 261, 270–272, 281
   and new fighters, 109–110, 114, 116
   working methods described, 136–139, 374
   and Marshall, 142–144, 373, 465
   in JCS, 141–143
   and Doolittle, 150, 152
   and Kenney, 167
   opposes Torch, 179, 180
   and troop carriers, 201–202, 209
   and Twining, 232, 375
   and Eaker, 240, 243–244, 269, 279–282
   and Impact, 246
   visit to England in 1943, 272–273, 280–281
   and photo recon, 302
   and German jets, 331
   and aerial gunnery, 365
   health of, 373
   and VE-Day, 375
   and Jacqueline Cochran, 376–379
   and blacks, 379, 383–384
   and morale, 408, 418
   and decorations, 416
   and Guadalcanal, 429, 430
   gets fifth star, 444
   retirement of, 462–463
Asch, Belgium, 358
Atkinson, J. Hamp, 188
Atomic bomb, 448, 459–461
Augsburg, 295
Austin, Gordon H., 73, 386
Avalanche, 221–223
AWPD-1, 49–51, 107, 264, 325
Azon: see bombs, guided

B-10, 23, 27, 122
B-15, 101–102
B-17, 27–28, 31, 48, 70, 96–98, 100–101,
    108, 122, 123, 161, 213, 248, 249, 278,
    361–362
    modifications, 264, 267, 274
B-18, 27–28, 48, 85, 122
B-19, 101–102
B-24, 39, 99–101, 123, 129, 250
B-25, 39, 92–95, 124
B-26, 93–96, 124, 205
B-29, 37, 41, 102–103, 447–449
B-32, 102–103
Baka bomb, 453
Bali, 149
Balikpapan, 438
Barber, Rex T., 417, 431–432
Bari, 222, 334, 412
Barling bomber, 8, 21
Bastogne, 356–357, 368
Bataan, 81–83, 145–147
Bates, Earl E., 381
battles
    Bismarck Sea, 421
    Britain, 40, 46, 149
    Bulge, 351, 354–359, 367–369
    Coral Sea, 163
    El Alamein, 179
    Leyte Gulf, 441
    Sidi-bou-Zid, 192
Baumler, Alex, 63
Beaverbrook, Lord, 47
Bell Aircraft Company, 105, 110–112,
    331–332, 364, 447
Bell, Lawrence D., 110–112
Bena Bena, 423
Berlin, 289–292, 367, 369
Biak, 436–437
Big Week, 287–289, 335
Bishop, William, 65
Bissell, Clayton L., 106–107, 157, 158, 391,
    393–395, 403
Bizerta, 182, 195, 198, 205
blacks, 192, 379–384
Blakeslee, Donald J. M., 259, 271, 286,
    320, 324
Bleckley, Erwin, 4–5
Bledsoe, Marvin, 410
Boeing Aircraft Corporation, 27–28, 97,
    112
bombs, 125–127, 269
    atomic, 448, 459–461
    guided, 338, 406, 451
    incendiary, 451
    napalm, 309–310, 451
    parachute fragmentation, 89, 196, 205
bombsights, 28, 128–131, 248, 256
Bond, Charles, Jr., 65
Bone, Algeria, 185

Bong, Richard I., 168, 387
Borneo, 148, 438
Bourke-White, Margaret, 188
Boyington, Gregory, 64
Bradley, Omar N., 198, 283, 307, 309–311,
    314, 351–353
Brady, Francis M., 82, 251
Bremen, 251, 253, 274
Brereton, Lewis H., 24, 350
    commands FEAF, 71, 73, 78 passim,
    145
    commands Ninth Air Force, 101,
    175–179, 215, 218, 283, 307
    commands Allied Airborne Army, 314,
    322–323
Brest, 315–316
Brett, George H., 39, 97, 112, 161 passim,
    175
Broadhurst, Harry V., 212
Brooke, Sir Alan, 179–180
Brown, Roscoe C., 383
Browning, Sir Frederick A. M., 322
Brunswick, 286, 288, 292, 294
Buna, 163 passim
Burma, 64–65, 153, 393

C-46, 371, 401
C-47, 131, 202, 371, 401
C-54, 402
C-87, 402
Caen, France, 300, 306
Cairo Conference, 283
Cannon, John K., 189, 224, 236, 344, 382
Cape Gloucester, 327–428
Carentan, France, 307
Cartwheel, 425, 429, 430
Casablanca, 180, 184
Casablanca Conference, 189, 199,
    243–244
Cassino, 228–229, 233, 237, 335, 337, 344
Cate, James Lea, 463
CG-4A Waco glider, 202
Chamberlin, Stephen J., 427
Charles, William, 289–290
Chattanooga Choo-Choo, 299
Chemidlin, Paul, 35, 90
Chemnitz, 321–322
Chenango, USS, 184
Chennault, Claire L., 26, 62, 106–107,
    152–153, 162, 414, 450, 465
    commands AVG (Flying Tigers), 64,
    115, 154–159
    commands Fourteenth Air Force,
    391–400
Chiang-kai Shek, 48, 62, 393–395
Chiang Mai, 155 passim
China, 48, 153, 393 passim, 411, 448
China Air Task Force (CATF), 392–393
Chinese-American Composite Wing, 397

Churchill, Winston S., 46, 141, 175–176, 179–180, 215, 242–244, 298, 344, 403, 460
Civilian Air Patrol, 58
Civilian Conservation Corps, 22
Civilian Pilot Training Program, 376, 379, 387
Clagett, Henry B., 69–71
Clarion, 370
Clark Field, 444, 445
Clark, Mark W., 219 passim, 236, 238–239, 344
close air support, 69
  in the Pacific, 174
  in Sicily, 208, 211
  in North Africa, 190–195, 203
  in Italy, 220, 222, 224, 229–230, 317
  in the ETO, 317, 351
Cobra, 310–312
Cochran, Jacqueline, 95, 376–379
Cochran, Philip, 191–192, 380, 403, 405
Colgan, Bill, 225–227, 317–318
Colman, William T., 383
Cologne, 326
Combined Bomber Offensive, 244, 319
Combined Chiefs of Staff, 142–143, 212, 214, 241, 262, 282, 326, 337–338, 340
Comer, John, 267, 274
Command and General Staff School, 20, 24–25, 28
Commands (numbered)
  I Bomber, 85
  I Troop Carrier, 202
  V Air Service, 435, 439
  VII Bomber, 457
  VII Fighter, 457
  VIII Air Support, 240, 252
  VIII Bomber, 240–256, 263, 269, 279, 282, 289, 308
  VIII Fighter, 256–261, 270–272, 282, 284, 299, 305, 308, 323, 324, 333
  IX Bomber, 215, 283, 304–305, 315, 350 passim
  IX Fighter, 283, 286, 305, 307
  IX TAC, 307, 309, 313–314
  IX Troop Carrier, 304, 316, 322, 324, 329, 346, 357, 371
  XII Air Support, 190–195, 203, 224, 233, 235, 238
  XII Bomber Command, 196
  XII Fighter Command, 348
  XII TAC, 317, 344–347
  XII Troop Carrier, 344
  XIX TAC, 307–308, 314–315, 351, 353
  XX Bomber Command, 398, 449
  XXI Bomber Command, 449
  XXII TAC, 348–349
compressibility, 109–110, 117–118

Compton, Keith K., 215
Coningham, Sir Arthur, 176, 189, 193–195, 204, 208, 211, 213, 223–234, 283, 306
Conklin, Joseph, 305
Consolidated Aircraft Corporation, 39, 99–102, 123
Convair, 101
Cook, Orval, 38, 39
Coolidge, Calvin, 11, 13
Cooper, Meriam C., 391, 394
Corps
  II, 189–190, 192–195, 198
  VI, 219–222, 237, 344
  VIII, 309
Corregidor, 81, 145–147
Corsica, 345
Craig, Malin, 22, 31–32, 34, 53, 54, 167
Craven, Wesley Frank, 463
Crissy, M. S., 125
Crosby, Harry, 320
Crossbow, 285, 294–295, 300, 308
cross-Channel invasion: see Overlord
Cubbins, William, 409
Cunningham, Sir Andrew, 205, 212
Curtiss Aircraft Company, 105, 113–115, 118, 141
Czechoslovakia, 33

D-Day: see Overlord
DB-7, 35, 89–90
DC-2, 92
DH-4, 4, 18
Daniels, Josephus, 9
Danniell, Jack, 329
Darwin, Australia, 80, 150, 161–162
Davidson, Howard C., 405–406, 415
Davis, Benjamin O., 379–380
Davis, Reed E., 58–59
Davison, F. Trubee, 21, 373, 374
Dawkins, Cecil H., 324
Dean, Fred M., 142, 374
Del Monte field, 79, 145
Deutsche Reichsbahn, 367–371
Devers, Jacob L., 280–346
Diadem, 235–238
Dieppe, 25
Divisions (U.S. Army and Marine)
  1st Cavalry, 429
  1st Infantry, 192, 206, 208, 211
  1st Marine, 169, 428
  2nd Armored, 68
  3rd Infantry, 206
  3rd Marine, 432
  4th Infantry, 304
  5th Infantry, 69
  6th Infantry, 437
  11th Airborne, 445
  17th Airborne, 371
  24th Infantry, 436

31st Infantry, 438
32nd Infantry, 171–174, 434
41st Infantry, 436
42nd Infantry, 6
45th Infantry, 206, 221
77th Infantry, 443–444
82nd Airborne, 201–202, 207–208, 222, 302–303
101st Airborne, 202, 302–303, 356–357
Distinguished Flying Cross (DFC), 415
Dobodura, 173, 423
Doolittle, James H., 40–41, 95, 124, 150–153, 224, 231, 245, 381, 463
   and Tokyo Raid, 93, 166, 177
   commands Twelfth Air Force, 181, 186 passim
   commands Strategic Air Force, 201, 210, 220, 223
   commands Eighth Air Force, 282, 284, 286–290, 294, 297, 315, 325, 328, 329, 352, 360, 363, 366, 369
   in the Pacific, 449, 458
Douglas Aircraft Corporation, 35, 89–90, 92, 98, 101–102
Douglas, Donald W., 20, 32, 41, 83, 201
Douglas, Sir Sholto, 67, 243, 284
Douhet, Giulio, 26
Dragoon, 316–317, 323, 344–347
Dresden, 369–370
Drum, Hugh A., 134
Duane, Bill, 326
Duffie, Vi, 374
Dulag, 441, 442
Duncan, Glenn, 293
Dunn, Ray A., 201–203, 209
Dunn, William, 66, 310
Dyess, William E., 82, 146

Eagle Squadrons, 66–67, 257
Eaker, Ira C., 68, 87, 374–375, 463
   commands VIII Bomber Command, 240–241, 243–248
   commands Eighth Air Force, 215, 220, 248–262, 269, 271, 273, 280–282, 284, 416
   commands Mediterranean Allied Air Forces, 224, 228, 231, 282, 284, 318, 320n, 321, 334, 347, 382
   and long range escorts, 260–261, 271
Echols, Oliver, 39, 41
Edwards AFB, California, 23
Edwards, Idwal, 231
Eglin Field, Florida, 451
Egypt, 175
Eichelberger, Robert L., 445
Eisenhower, Dwight D., 68, 137, 149n, 179, 215, 381, 413, 462
   in North Africa, 181, 184 passim
   and Pantelleria, 199, 201

and Sicily, 203, 206, 213
and D-Day, 301, 303
as Supreme Commander, 283, 294, 298, 308, 310, 316, 325, 327, 369
and Transportation vs. Oil, 297–298
gets fifth star, 444
Ent, Uzal G., 215, 217
Enterprise, USS. 77, 93, 151–152

F-4, 110, 302
F-6, 303
Far Eastern Air Forces, 71, 73, 81, 437, 439, 445–446
Fechet, James E., 13–14, 21, 282, 452
Ferrying Division, 47, 377–378
Field Manual 31-35, 190
Field Manual 100-20, 204, 208
First Air Task Force, 427
flak: see anti-aircraft artillery
Fleet, Reuben, 99
flight clothing, 365
Flying Fortress: see B-17
Flying Tigers, 63–65, 115, 153–159, 44
   see also Groups, 23rd Fighter
Foggia, 210, 214, 220–222, 231, 334
Ford, Henry, 33, 43, 101
Formosa, 78, 80, 438, 445
Fort Benning, Georgia, 67, 167
Fort Worth, Texas, 39
Foulois, Benjamin D., 14, 16, 21, 23, 29, 127
France, 33, 69
Frankfurt, 273, 274, 289
Frantic, 319–322
Fredendall, Lloyd, 190, 195
Frederick, Robert T., 346
Friedrichshafen, 292
Frillman, Paul, 63–64
Frost, Edwin, 267
FW-190, 186, 281–282, 325

Gabreski, Francis, 76, 260, 271–272, 295, 324, 387
Galland, Adolph, 250, 355, 372
Galland, "Wutz," 268–269
Gardner, Grandison, 451
Gela, Sicily, 208–209
General Electric Company, 108
General Headquarters Air Force: see Air Corps, GHQ Air Force
General Motors, 38, 100
Gentile, Donald, 295, 465
George, Harold H., 69, 71, 81, 145–146
George, Harold L., 49–50, 69, 107, 377
German Air Force (GAF, Luftwaffe), 33, 41, 130
   in North Africa, 176, 179, 182, 185–186, 189 passim, 243
   and Pantelleria, 200

German Air Force (*cont'd*)
  in Sicily, 205
  in Italy, 220, 227–228, 335, 337–338, 348
  in battle for France, 300–301, 305, 308, 314, 316
  defense of the Reich, 251, 273, 287–288, 294–295, 300, 325, 329, 355, 358, 362, 372
  tactics of, 250, 253, 275–277, 293, 327, 351–352, 411
  and aircraft production, 252, 262–263, 288–289, 328
  and jet fighters, 288, 331–333
Gerow, Leonard, 49
Gibraltar, 182
Giles, Barney M., 127, 203, 209, 249, 261, 270, 319, 374, 423, 448
Giller, William, 301
glider pilots, 202–203
gliders: *see* CG-4A
Goddard, George W., 301–302
Goddard, Paulette, 411
Godfrey, John T., 66, 295
Goering, Herman, 205, 250, 262, 274, 295
Goettler, Harold, 4–5
Gona, 174
Gothic Line, 344, 347–349
Greece, 348
Grossetta, Anthony, 410
Groups, 193n
  1st Air Commando, 403–404
  1st Bomb, 397
  1st Fighter, 182, 240, 341
  1st Pursuit, 7, 84, 256
  2nd Bomb, 7, 47, 49, 96, 127
  3rd Attack, 7, 69, 88–89, 91–92, 121, 245, 421, 424–426
  3rd Combat Cargo, 406
  3rd Fighter, 397
  4th Fighter, 257–259, 263, 265, 275, 286, 291, 295, 320
  5th Bomb, 439
  5th Fighter, 397
  7th Bomb, 21, 79, 100, 149
  8th Fighter, 106, 113, 162–163, 260
  10th Photo Recon, 303, 306
  11th Bomb, 72, 430
  12th Bomb, 177, 178
  14th Fighter, 182, 186, 192
  15th Fighter, 77, 260
  17th Bomb, 93, 151, 182
  17th Pursuit, 21
  19th Bomb, 70, 78, 100, 127, 148, 429
  20th Fighter, 281
  22nd Bomb, 83, 96, 163, 165–166
  23rd Demonstration and Test, 256
  23rd Fighter, 387, 391–393, 397
  24th Pursuit, 148
  27th Bomb, 71

  31st Fighter, 182, 184, 192, 208, 240, 256, 338, 340, 349, 387
  33rd Fighter, 183, 184, 187, 191, 192, 208, 380–381
  35th Fighter, 163–164, 169, 423–424, 439
  38th Bomb, 424
  39th Fighter, 163
  43rd Bomb, 420, 425
  44th Bomb, 215, 247, 281
  47th Bomb, 182
  49th Fighter, 161–162, 387, 422, 441
  52nd Fighter, 182, 338
  55th Fighter, 281, 300–301
  56th Fighter, 117, 257–260, 265, 268, 271, 276, 277, 288, 292, 293, 295, 306, 323, 387
  57th Fighter, 177, 179
  60th Troop Carrier, 183–185, 241
  62nd Troop Carrier, 184–185
  64th Troop Carrier, 184–185, 406
  67th Tactical Recon, 303, 356
  68th Observation, 182
  78th Fighter, 257–258, 295, 323, 332, 389
  79th Fighter, 60, 178, 208, 225–227, 318, 345, 381–382
  81st Fighter, 182
  82nd Fighter, 60, 340, 342
  90th Bomb, 420, 439
  91st Bomb, 253, 267, 277
  92nd Bomb, 247, 288
  93rd Bomb, 215
  94th Bomb, 251
  95th Bomb, 251, 275, 276, 278, 289, 291
  96th Bomb, 251, 253–254, 266, 276–278, 364n
  97th Bomb, 98–99, 182, 188, 221, 241, 245, 246, 415
  98th Bomb, 177, 178, 215, 216
  99th Bomb, 221
  100th Bomb, 275, 278, 289, 291, 320
  301st Bomb, 182, 247, 336, 338, 340, 382
  303rd Bomb, 285, 327
  305th Bomb, 247, 254, 273
  306th Bomb, 247, 254, 416
  308th Bomb, 397
  310th Bomb, 182
  315th Troop Carrier, 324
  316th Troop Carrier, 178, 210
  317th Troop Carrier, 427
  318th Fighter, 410
  319th Bomb, 182
  320th Bomb, 182
  321st Bomb, 182, 347
  322nd Bomb, 251–252, 280, 410
  323rd Bomb, 280
  325th Fighter, 192, 335, 386

332nd Fighter, 381–382
344th Bomb, 305, 370
348th Fighter, 386, 424, 428, 439
350th Fighter, 182
351st Bomb, 251, 285
352nd Fighter, 271, 306, 320, 358, 386
353rd Fighter, 265–266, 277, 293, 295, 323
354th Fighter, 285, 314–315
355th Fighter, 271, 275, 293
357th Fighter, 291, 323, 327
359th Fighter, 293, 323
361st Fighter, 293, 326
365th Fighter, 299, 323, 355
366th Fighter, 358
368th Fighter, 355
374th Troop Carrier, 420
376th Bomb, 178, 215
379th Bomb, 330
381st Bomb, 247, 267, 274
384th Bomb, 410
386th Bomb, 280
387th Bomb, 280
388th Bomb, 326
389th Bomb, 215, 217
390th Bomb, 275–276, 278, 291
391st Fighter, 333, 357
406th Fighter, 310, 410
438th Troop Carrier, 317, 329
439th Troop Carrier, 357
440th Troop Carrier, 357
445th Bomb, 326
446th Bomb, 361
450th Bomb, 341, 409
452nd Bomb, 291
456th Bomb, 375
460th Bomb, 237–238
475th Fighter, 387, 389, 424, 441, 443
477th Bomb. 383–384
479th Fighter, 324–325
482nd Bomb, 273
Groves, Leslie R., 459
Grow, Malcolm C., 366
Guadalcanal, 113, 169, 170, 243, 429–430
gunsights, 131
gun turrets: see Aerial Gunnery
Gunn, Paul "Pappy," 148

H2S and H2X: see radar
Hall, Allen, 404
Hall, Charles, 380–381
Hall, Donald, 424
Halsey, William, 151, 427, 440, 442
Halverson, Harry A., 100–101, 177
Hamburg, 263
Hamilton Field, California, 60
Hankow, 397, 399, 454
Hansa Bay, 434–436

Hansell, Haywood S., Jr., 50, 244, 250, 449–452
Harding, Edwin F., 172–173
Harding, Warren G., 11
Harmon, Millard F., Jr., 106, 113, 429, 431
Harris, Sir Arthur, 131, 241 passim, 297–298, 366, 368
Harvard University, 140n
Hatch, Herbert, 342
Hawaiian Air Force, 71–73, 75–77
Hegenberger, Albert F., 72
Hengyang, 393, 398
Hickam, Horace M., 88–89
Hickam Field, Hawaii, 60, 75–76
Hiroshima, 459, 460
Hitchcock, Tommy, 120
Hitler, Adolph, 33, 84, 195, 197, 223, 228, 230–231, 262, 270, 279, 288, 307, 368
  and Mortain counterattack, 313–314
  and jet fighters, 288, 331
  and Bulge, 351, 355
Hobby, Oveta, 378
Hodges, Courtney, 350, 351
Hollandia, 435–436
Hoover, J. Edgar, 65
Hopkins, Harry, 34, 36, 44, 46
Hornet, USS, 150, 152
Hough, Cass, 261, 272
House, Edwin, 381
Howard, James, 285, 289
Hughes, Howard, 86, 109
Hughes, Lloyd D., 217
Hughes, Richard D'Oyly, 151, 215, 264, 269, 287, 289
Hughes, Robert L., 278–279
Huie, William Bradford, 56
Hump airlift, 158, 393, 395, 400–403, 409
Hunter, Frank O'D., 21, 46, 240, 256–261, 270, 271
Hurtgen Forest, 351–352
Husky, 199, 201, 203 passim
Hustad, Carl, 426

Iceland, 110, 409, 414
Ijmuiden, Holland, 251, 279, 410
Impact, 246
Imphal, 406
Indiana, USS, 8
Iraq, 177, 241
Irvine, Clarence S., 100, 279–280, 456
Italy, 219, 236, 334 passim, 410
Iwo Jima, 453

Java, 148, 149, 161
Jeschonnek, Hans, 262, 270
jet aircraft, 37, 325, 331–333, 366, 371–372
Joint Chiefs of Staff, 141–143, 214, 440

Johnson, Clarence "Kelly," 109–110
Johnson, Leon, 281
Johnson, Louis, 34
Johnson, Lyndon B., 165–166
Johnson, Robert S., 387
Jones, Jack, 163

Kaiser, Henry J., 86
Kanarkowski, Philip, 289
Kane, John R., 216–217
Kartveli, Alexander, 116–117
Kassel, 263
Kaye, Minton, 302
Kasserine Pass, 190, 193
Kearby, Neel, 386, 387
Kelly, Colin, 80, 465
Kelsey, Ben, 40, 109–110, 119
Kenney, George C., 8, 26, 30 passim. 46,
    53, 89, 299, 463, 465
  commands Production Division, 37–38,
    125, 167, 365
  and Arnold, 167, 374
  commands Fifth Air Force, 166–170,
    383–384, 388, 389, 417, 419–423,
    425–429, 434–435, 437–442
  and MacArthur, 168, 170, 438, 445–446
  and B-29, 449
Kepner, William E., 68, 106, 260, 261,
    270–271, 282, 284, 293, 294, 300, 305,
    324–325, 333, 465
Kesselring, Albert, 183, 197, 223, 228, 231,
    235, 344
Kettering, Charles, 18, 88
Kiel, 253, 259, 263, 284
Kilner Board, 37, 102
Kindleberger, James H., 43, 92, 118, 150
King, Ernest J., 84, 180, 429, 444, 447, 457
Knerr, Hugh J., 23, 24, 29, 53–54, 56, 88,
    139
Knight, Clayton, 65
Knox, Frank, 63
Knudsen, William, 38, 43, 88, 112
Kobe, Japan, 152
Kokoda, 170
Krueger, Walter, 68
Kunming, 154, 392, 402
Kuter, Laurence S., 28, 49–51, 87, 135,
    166, 247–248, 281, 330, 394, 396, 449
Kweilin, 392
Kyushu, 453, 458

LB-30, 149
Lae, 160, 162, 165, 170, 419–420, 425
Lafayette Escadrille, 66, 379
Lampert, Florian, 10, 12, 13
Lang, Herman, 130
Langley Field, Virginia, 9, 24
Lanphier, Thomas G., 417, 431–432
Latham, John L., 266

Leahy, William D., 141, 143
Ledo Road, 393, 402, 407
Legaspi, 80
Leigh-Mallory, Trafford, 283
LeMay, Curtis E., 463
  in the ETO, 247, 254–255, 262, 264–265,
    279
  in China, 399, 450
  in the Pacific, 452–460
Lend-Lease, 45, 62, 91, 153
Leuna, 326, 330, 367
Lexington, USS, 164
Leyte, 440–444
Liberator: see B-24
Liberty engine, 18
Life, 188
Lightning: see P-38
Lindbergh, Charles A., 36–37, 414
Lingayen Gulf, 80, 447
Lockheed Aircraft Company, 98, 107–109
Long Beach, California, 22
Longfellow, Newton, 246–248, 251–252,
    254
long-range escorts, 106, 116, 249, 258,
    260–261, 263, 270–272, 276, 284, 395,
    436, 439
Los Angeles, 83
"Lost Battalion," 3–5
Love, Nancy Harkness, 377, 378
Lovett, Robert A., 41–42, 46, 55–57,
    59–60, 75, 130, 140–141, 261, 302, 370
  and Arnold, 44–45, 139, 374
Lucas, John P., 227–228
Luce, Clare Boothe, 156
Luce, Henry, 156
Ludwigshafen, 284, 326
Luftwaffe: see German Air Force
Luke, Frank, 5n
Luzon, 446–447
Lynch, Thomas, 388

MacArthur, Douglas, 24, 29, 389, 416, 432
  in the Philippines, 70, 73, 78–79, 81, 83,
    145–146
  in Australia, 146, 165–166, 168
  and New Guinea campaign, 164,
    169–174, 422, 427, 434–438
  and Leyte campaign, 437, 440–443
  and Luzon campaign, 444–446
  gets fifth star, 444
  plans invasion of Japan, 457–458
Mackay Trophy, 17, 24
Mackensen, Eberhardt von, 223
McAuliffe, Anthony C., 357
McCloy, John J., 381
McGuire Thomas B., 389–390, 441
McNair, Leslie J., 90, 135, 204, 311
McNamara, Robert S., 140n
McNarney, Joseph T., 21, 135, 138

McRae, Willie, 383
Magruder, Peyton M., 124
Magwe, Burma, 154
Mahoney, Grant, 80
Mahurin, Walker, 269, 387
Maitland, Lester J., 71, 79
Malta, 195–196
Maneuvers
    Carolina, 68
    Louisiana, 68–69
Manila, 445
Marauder: see B-26
March Field, California, 21
Marianas, 449
Marienbad, 274
Marilinan, New Guinea, 423
Marshall, George C., 34, 44, 67–68, 75,
    135, 138, 141, 166, 167, 172, 189, 241,
    373, 423, 429, 447, 457
    demands dive-bombers, 48–49
    and AWPD-1, 52
    and Andrews, 54, 56, 67
    and air independence, 55, 57, 204, 462
    and Chennault, 63, 393, 400
    and plane production, 140
    and Arnold, 142–144, 204, 465
    and MacArthur, 146
    and Tokyo Raid, 150
    opposes Torch, 179–180
    and Pantelleria, 199
    and Italy, 347
    and WASPs, 377–378
    and decorations, 415
    gets fifth star, 444
    and atomic bomb, 461
Marseilles, 316, 447
Martin, Frederick L., 71–72
Martin, Glenn L., 93, 141
Masefield, Peter, 253–254
Massachusetts Institute of Technology, 40,
    60
Matériel Command, 37, 39, 41, 112, 201,
    203, 365, 451
    and bombers, 93, 102
    and fighters, 106, 116, 117, 119
    and armament, 122, 127, 129, 132
    and range extension, 259, 395
Matterhorn, 398, 399
Maxwell Field, 50, 66
Mayer, Egon, 250, 289
Me-262, 288, 331–333, 348, 371–372, 383
Medal of Honor, 5, 153, 217–218, 281,
    285, 386, 388, 416, 420
Mediterranean Air Command, 189, 195,
    224
Mediterranean Allied Air Forces, 224–225,
    233, 282, 316–317
Memphis Belle, 253, 450
Menoher, Charles T., 6

Merrill's Marauders, 402, 404
Merseburg, 326, 327, 328
Messina, 203, 211
Metz, 351
Meyer, John C., 358
Meyers, Benny, 448
Middle East Air Force, 175–179
Middleton, Troy, 309
Miefert, John, 353–354
Milch, Erhard, 262, 270, 288
Miller, Glenn, 412
Miller, Henry L., 151
Milling, Thomas DeWitt, 9, 16, 24, 26
Milne Bay, 164, 171, 174
Mindoro, 444
Mingaladon, Burma, 154–155
Mitchell, William, 3 passim, 17, 18, 53, 93,
    157
    and bombing tests, 8–10
    court-martial of, 11–13, 177
    influence of, 26, 29
Mitscher, Marc, 431
Molotov, Vyacheslav, 180
Momyer, William W., 184, 192, 380
Montgomery, Sir Bernard
    in North Africa, 178, 193, 194
    in Sicily, 204, 205, 212
    in Italy, 220
    in France, 306, 309–310, 314
    and Market-Garden, 322
    and Varsity, 371
Montgomery, John B., 451
Moore, Carl H., 305, 370
Morale, 363, 408–418, 458
Morgan, Robert K., 450
Morgenthau, Henry J., Jr., 35 passim, 45
Morocco, 180
Morotai, 438, 440
Morse, Winslow C., 397
Mortain, 314–315
Morrow, Dwight W., 11
Mountbatten, Lord Louis, 406
Muirhead, John, 232, 336, 339, 382
Munda, 432
Munich, 340
Munster, 274–275
Mussolini, Benito, 195, 210
Myers, Joseph, 332
Myitkyina, 158, 395, 400, 402

Nadzab, 425, 435
Nagasaki, 460–461
Nagoya, Japan, 152, 451
Nagumo, Chuichi, 77
napalm: see Bombs
Neutrality Act, 33, 65
Newby, Leroy, 237, 341
Nichols Field, P.I., 71, 145
Nielson Field, P.I., 82, 145

Nimitz, Chester, 435, 438, 456
Noemfoor, 437
Norden, Carl L., 128
Norstad, Lauris, 87, 136, 142, 181, 199,
    214, 374, 458
North American Aviation, 43, 92, 118,
    143n
Northwest African Air Forces, 189
    Coastal Air Force, 189, 196
    Photo Recon Wing, 189, 208
    Strategic Air Force, 189, 196, 199–201,
        209, 220, 222, 233, 236–237
    Tactical Air Force, 189, 193, 199–210,
        213, 233–234, 236
    Troop Carrier Command, 203
Nye, Glenn, 410

Obertraubling, 336
Observation, 7, 90
O'Donnell, Emmett, 70, 450
Okinawa, 446, 456
Old, Archie J., 88, 253–254, 265, 276,
    320–321, 341n, 465
Olds, Robert, 27, 47
Omaha Beach, 304, 307
Oran, 180, 181, 183
Ordnance Corps, 125–127, 269, 451
Ormoc, 442
Osaka, 455
Oschersleben, 263, 288, 295
Ostfriesland, 10, 94
Overlord, 297, 303–306, 308

P-35, 105, 116
P-36, 33, 105
P-38, 107–110, 133, 281–282
    modifications, 301, 435
P-39, 111–113, 163, 430
P-40, 62–63, 113–115, 156, 159, 177–178,
    235
P-44, 116
P-47, 116–117, 133, 235, 258, 259, 263,
    268, 271
    modifications, 286–287
P-51, 118–120, 133, 289
P-59, 331, 333
P-61, 441
P-400, 163, 430
Packard Motor Car Company, 43
Palau Islands, 440
Palermo, 203
Pantelleria, 199–201, 380
Pan American Airways, 47
Paris, 254, 281
Parmalee, Philip O., 125
Parson, Thomas, 460
Partridge, Earle E., 27
Patch, Alexander, 316
Patterson, Robert, 42, 201, 202

Patton, George S., Jr., 180, 195, 203, 211,
    212, 312, 315, 353, 371
    and Bulge, 354, 356–357
Patrick, Mason M., 6, 11, 120
Pearl Harbor, 75–77
Pearson, Drew, 209
Peenemünde, 270, 285
Perceful, Paul, 276
Perdomo, Oscar, 389
Perrin, Elmer D., 95
Pershing, John J., 3, 6, 7, 42
Peterson, Chesley C., 65, 67, 257
Philadelphia, USS, 222
Photo reconnaissance, 110, 251, 301–302,
    343, 371, 428
    in North Africa, 189, 191
    in Italy and Sicily, 212, 225
    in the ETO, 303
    in the Pacific, 174
Pinball, 364
Ploesti, 101, 177, 214–218, 231, 264, 319,
    363, 367, 409
Pointblank, 262 passim, 286, 294, 295,
    298
Portal, Sir Charles, 47, 134n, 141, 150,
    241, 256, 259
Port Lyautey, 180, 184
Port Moresby, 162 passim
Preddy, George E., Jr., 385, 386
proximity fuse, 330
Purple Heart, 416
Purdy, Jack, 443

Quebec Conference, 403, 440
Quesada, Elwood R., 29, 134–135, 283,
    286, 307 passim, 329, 350, 354, 356,
    370

RP-63, 364
Rabaul, 160, 163, 169, 171, 420 passim,
    446, 456
Radar, 34, 37, 74–75, 85–86, 191, 273, 304,
    329, 366, 448, 453
    H2X, 273n, 292, 335, 339–340, 367, 452,
        455
Raff, Edson D., 183
Randolph Field, 21, 59, 60
Rangoon, 153 passim
Red Air Force, 113, 369
Regensburg, 264–266, 269, 287, 288, 319,
    336
Remagen, 371
Republic Aviation, 116
Rickenbacker, Edward V., 5n, 12–13, 201,
    248, 259, 385, 388
Rome, 210, 214
Rommel, Erwin, 175, 178–179, 189,
    192–194, 299
Roosevelt, Eleanor, 377

Roosevelt, Elliott, 55–56, 189, 212, 302
Roosevelt, Franklin D., 22, 33, 35, 55–56,
    62, 81, 146, 150, 214, 243–244, 394,
    423, 430
  sets production goals, 34, 45, 140
  and Arnold, 31–32, 133, 143
  and strategy, 179–180, 243, 298, 319,
    395, 437–438
Rose, Bill, 288
Rosenblatt, Sol, 456
Royal Air Force, 40, 98, 162, 215, 309,
    343, 345, 358, 366, 369
  seeks U.S. planes, 35–36, 48, 90–91, 97,
    110, 119, 126, 142
  relations with USAAF, 45–46, 51,
    240–243, 251
  Eagle Squadrons, 67, 257
  in North Africa, 115, 175 passim, 193,
    196, 211
  in Sicily, 204
  fighter sweeps, 243, 259, 283–284
  radar, 74–75, 85–86
  2nd TAF, 282, 286, 306–307, 314
  night bombing by, 242, 263, 270, 288
  and Dresden, 369–370
Royal Australian Air Force, 161, 170,
    421
Royal Navy, 176, 204, 221
Russy, John H. de, 311

St. Nazaire, 247, 250
Saville, Gordon P., 215, 224, 233, 317,
    318, 330–331, 350, 465
Schilling, David C., 324, 387
Schlatter, David, 61
Schmued, Edgar, 118
Schweinfurt, 264–267, 269, 276–278, 288,
    295, 319
Scott, Robert Lee, Jr., 115, 391–392, 394
Scott, Robert R., 398
Self, Sir Henry, 118
Seversky, Alexander de, 9, 41, 104–105,
    115–116, 128
Shahan, Elza K., 110
Shell Oil Company, 40
Shenandoah, USS (dirigible), 11
Shingle, 227
Shomo, William A., 286
Short, Walter G., 72–73
Shutting, Carl, 248
Sicily, 184, 186, 194 passim
Sidi-bou-Zid, 191
Signal Corps, 74–75, 125, 138
Singapore, 148, 149
Slayton, Samuel, 277
Smart, Jacob E., 214
Smith, Frederic H., 298, 304, 311, 427
Smith, Homer, 65
Smith, Maynard "Snuffy," 416

Smith, Walter Bedell, 413
Snyder, Earl, 455
Somervell, Brehon B., 136, 189, 231, 334
Sorenson, Charles, 43
Spaatz, Carl A., 12, 25, 37, 46, 60, 69, 85,
    87, 91, 95, 97, 179, 318, 370, 381, 391,
    417, 445, 449, 463
  and Arnold, 19, 45, 240, 249
  as Chief of Air Staff, 56, 181
  and War Department reorganization,
    135
  in North Africa, 188–190
  and Pantelleria, 199
  and Sicily, 205, 213–214
  advocates Fifteenth Air Force, 231, 334
  commands Eighth Air Force, 240–241,
    366
  commands U.S. Strategic Air Forces,
    282, 284, 287, 294, 297
  and Crossbow, 295
  and Transportation Plan, 297–298, 301
  and oil targets, 298, 300, 325, 326, 334
    338, 340–343, 348, 349, 366–367
  and Cobra, 310–311
  and Frantic, 319, 321
  and German jets, 331
  and Berlin, 369
  and Clarion, 370
  and decorations, 414, 416
  in the Pacific, 458, 459, 460
Spanish Civil War, 62, 172n, 464
Speer, Albert, 270, 279, 367
Sperry Gyroscope Company, 128–129
Squadrons
  8th Photo Recon, 164
  9th Bomb, 177, 178
  11th Bomb, 393
  12th Aero, 177
  13th Aero, 19, 71
  15th Bomb, 91, 182
  15th Tac R, 306, 354
  17th Pursuit, 148
  20th Bomb, 84
  33rd Pursuit, 150
  45th Pursuit, 76
  47th Pursuit, 73, 76–77
  49th Bomb, 70
  50th Aero, 4–5
  67th Fighter, 430
  70th Fighter, 431
  71st Fighter, 342
  82nd Tac R, 386
  99th Fighter, 192, 380
  100th Fighter, 383
  155th Night Photo, 303
  422nd Bomb, 273
  426th Night Fighter, 398
  507th Fighter, 389
  885th Bomb, 346

Squier, George O., 17
Stalin, Josef, 180, 319, 321, 322
Statistical Control Division, 139–140, 374
Stearly, Ralph, 450
Steed, Thomas W., 375
Steinbeck, John, 58
Stiles, Bert, 362
Stilwell, Joseph W., 157–158, 391, 393, 395–396, 399, 405
Stimson, Henry L., 42, 44, 51, 55–57, 140, 179, 248, 459
Strangle, 234–236
Strategic Air Command, 463, 464
Street, St. Clair, 302
Stuttgart, 288
Superchargers, 107–108, 114
Supreme Headquarters, Allied Expeditionary Force (SHAEF), 294
Sutherland, Richard K., 79, 167, 169, 173, 440, 445
Sweden, 262, 363
Sweeny, Charles, 66
Switzerland, 264, 292, 363

Tacloban, 441
Taylor, Kenneth, 76, 77
Taylor, William, 317, 329
Taylor, William, E. G., 67
Tedder, Sir Arthur
    in North Africa, 175–176, 178–179, 188–189, 195, 198
    and Sicily, 205, 210, 213, 215
    and Italy, 220–221, 224, 368
    in the ETO, 295, 297, 368
Thailand, 155
Thelepte, 187, 190, 409
Thornton, Charles B., 139–140
Thunderbolt: see P-47
Tibbets, Paul, 245–247, 449, 459–461
Time, 156, 412
Torch, 175 passim, 203
Tokyo, 93, 152, 166, 177, 400, 451–458
Transportation Plan, 297–298, 301, 326
Truman, Harry S, 459, 463
Truscott, Lucian K., 184, 229, 344, 347
Tulsa, Oklahoma, 39
Tunis, 182, 185, 195, 198, 205
Tunisia, 180
Tunner, William H., 378
Turley, Grant M., 389
Tuskegee Institute, 379
Twelve O'Clock High, 245
Twining, Nathan F., 88, 465
    commands Fifteenth Air Force, 232, 253, 335, 336, 341, 382
    commands Thirteenth Air Force, 430–431
    commands Twentieth Air Force, 459

Udine, Italy, 335, 337
Ultra intelligence, 176, 194, 197–198, 205, 236, 295, 301, 314
    in the Pacific, 419–420, 422, 435, 442, 458
U.S. Navy, 8 passim, 22, 28, 30, 34, 51, 74, 140, 146, 302, 421, 448
    and U-boats, 84–85, 127, 129–130
    and Tokyo Raid, 150–152
    and Sicily/Italy, 200, 208, 222, 229
    on D-Day, 304
    in Solomons, 431
    and Leyte, 440
U.S. Strategic Bombing Survey, 463
U.S. Strategic Air Forces: see Spaatz
Utah Beach, 304, 307

V-1, 270, 285
    see also Crossbow
Valmontone, 237, 239
Van Nada, Jim, 411
Vandenberg, Hoyt S., 181–182, 302, 311
    commands Ninth Air Force, 314, 350, 354
    becomes USAF Chief of Staff, 463
Vegesack, 251, 259, 274
venereal disease, 302
Vernon, 299
Victory Program, 51, 399
Vietinghoff, Heinrich von, 221
Vincent, Clinton D., 396

Wagner, Boyd D., 386
Wainwright, Jonathan, 81, 147
Waits, Joe, 353
Wakde Island, 437
Walker, Kenneth, 27, 50–51, 420
War Department
    reorganization of, 135
    War Plans Division, 49, 236
    Operations Division, 165
War Production Board, 140
Warnemünde, 263
Warsaw, 321–322
Watson, Edwin P., 32
Wau, 419–420
Wavell, Sir Archibald, 147
Weber, William S., 357
Wedemeyer, Albert C., 399
Weeks, John W., 6
Welsh, A. L. "Al," 17
Welch, George, 76–77, 386
Westphal, Siegfried, 231
Westover, Oscar, 23, 30, 31, 380
Wewak, 420, 423, 435
Weyland, Otto P., 307, 312, 315–316, 352, 373
Whalen, Norman M., 216

Wheeler Field, Hawaii, 72, 75–77
Whitehead, Ennis C., 170, 388, 419–421, 436 passim
Whittlesey, Charles, 3
Wiener-Neustadt, 232, 264
Wilhelmshaven, 250, 252, 259, 281
Williams, Paul L., 184, 185, 190, 203, 316, 323, 346
Williams, Robert, 262
Willis, Allan R., 291
Willkie, Wendell, 56, 395
Willow Run, 43, 101
Wilson, Donald, 26
Wilson, Woodrow, 17
Wingate, Orde, 403–404
Winged Defense (book), 11
Wings, 30n, 193n
  1st Bomb, 247, 250, 262–263, 266–267
  2nd Bomb, 246
  3rd Bomb, 266
  4th Bomb, 181, 253, 254, 262 passim
  5th Bomb, 382
  14th Pursuit, 72
  18th Bomb, 75
  42nd Bomb, 222, 224, 237, 345
  50th Troop Carrier, 304
  51st Troop Carrier, 184, 186, 203, 207, 209–210, 222
  52nd Troop Carrier, 203, 207, 209, 222, 345
  53rd Troop Carrier, 304
  54th Troop Carrier, 425, 445
  57th Bomb, 222, 224, 237
  58th Bomb, 450
  68th Composite, 396
  69th Composite, 396

73rd Bomb, 450, 452, 454
84th Fighter, 312
313th Bomb, 452, 454
314th Bomb, 452, 454
315th Bomb, 452
325th Photo Recon, 302–303
Wolfe, Kenneth B., 37, 138, 372, 398, 399, 448
Women's Airforce Service Pilots, 96, 377–379
Women's Army Corps, 378, 413
Women's Auxiliary Ferrying Service, 377–378
Women's Flying Training Detachment, 377
Woodring, Harry H., 34–36, 42, 97
Woods, Robert, 111
Wright Field, 21, 28, 30, 37, 41, 96, 111, 122
  also see Matériel Command
Wright, Orville, 16
Wright, Wilbur, 16
Wurtsmith, Paul B., 161–162, 170, 388

XB-19, 123
XP-37, 105, 107, 113
XP-40, 113
XP-46, 114, 118
YB-40, 259, 263, 274
Yamamoto, Isoroku, 431–432
Yeager, Chuck, 327–328
Yokohama, 152, 457
Yorktown, USS, 164

Zemke, Hubert, 48, 117, 257–258, 268, 276, 306, 324–325, 385, 387, 457
Zuckerman, Sir Solly, 199–200, 210, 220, 224, 233, 297, 298, 368

GEOFFREY PERRET was born into an Anglo-American theatrical family and reared as a transatlantic commuter. He served in the U.S. Army from 1958 to 1961, and attended the University of Southern California, where he was elected Phi Beta Kappa, Harvard, and the University of California at Berkeley. *Winged Victory* is Mr. Perret's seventh book.

ABOUT THE TYPE

This book was set in Times Roman, designed by Stanley Morison specifically for *The Times* of London. The typeface was introduced in the newspaper in 1932. Times Roman has had its greatest success in the United States as a book and commercial typeface, rather than one used in newspapers.

9/02 (14) 7/00
12/05 (16) 7/04
3/07 (17) 11/06
12/11 (20)